P9-EKJ-947

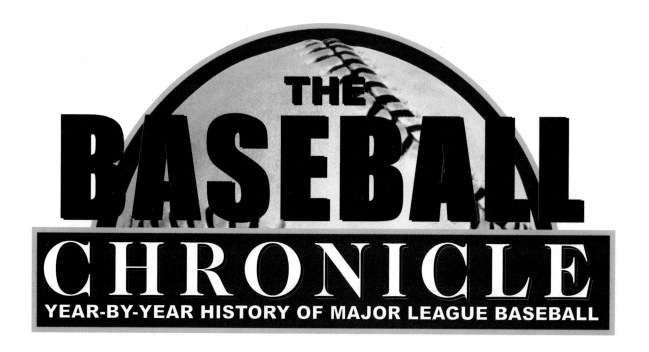

THE BASEBALL CHRONICLE
YEAR-BY-YEAR HISTORY OF MAJOR LEAGUE BASEBALL

DISCARD

Contributing Writers

David Nemec

Stuart Shea

Stephen Hanks

Dick Johnson

David Raskin

Thomas W. Gilbert

Andy Cohen

Joe Glickman

Danny Green

pil Publications International, Ltd.

David Nemec is a baseball historian and novelist. He is the author of *Great Baseball Feats, Facts & Firsts* and the coauthor of *The Ultimate Baseball Book*. He has written numerous baseball history, quiz, and memorabilia books as well as the franchise histories for major league team yearbooks.

Stuart Shea is a baseball writer, researcher, and editor. He contributed to *Baseball Legends of All Time* and several editions of the *Baseball Almanac*. In addition, he coauthored *The USA Today Baseball Weekly Insider* for Total Sports Publishing and contributes to ESPN.com.

Stephen Hanks has served as vice-president and editor of Phenom Publishing, Inc., a New York-based sports magazine publishing company. Mr. Hanks has also written about baseball for many national publications, including *Esquire, SPORT, Inside Sports*, and *The Village Voice*.

Dick Johnson serves as associate director and curator of The Sports Museum in Boston, where he has mounted exhibits on the history of Fenway Park and the Boston Braves, among others. He has also been book review editor of *Diehard*, the Red Sox monthly, and serves as an active member of the Society for American Baseball Research (SABR). He coauthored *Ted Williams, A Portrait in Words and Pictures*.

David Raskin is a sports writer whose work has appeared in *The New York Times, SPORT, Sports, Inc.*, and *Yankees Magazine*.

Thomas W. Gilbert is a writer and artist. He has been a member of the Society for American Baseball Research (SABR) and has served as contributing baseball writer for Phenom Publishing, Inc.

Andy Cohen is a freelance writer who has written about baseball for *The Village Voice* and for Phenom Publishing's baseball magazines.

Joe Glickman is a Brooklyn-based freelance writer who has written baseball articles for Phenom Publishing, Inc., and contributed to *The Village Voice* and many New York-area publications.

Danny Green is a freelance writer who has written about New York City and sports for *The Village Voice*.

Copyright © 2005 Publications International, Ltd. All rights reserved. This book may not be reproduced or quoted in whole or in part by any means whatsoever without written permission from:

Louis Weber, CEO
Publications International, Ltd.
7373 North Cicero Avenue
Lincolnwood, Illinois 60712

Permission is never granted for commercial purposes.

Manufactured in China.

8 7 6 5 4 3 2 1

ISBN: 1-4127-1210-6

Library of Congress Control Number: 2004118180

Photo credits:
Front cover: **AP/Wide World Photos** (top center), Robert Borea (bottom left), Brian Kersey (top left), Charles Krupa (bottom center), Ben Margot (bottom right); **PhotoFile** (top right).

Back cover: **National Baseball Library & Archive, Cooperstown, NY** (right center); **PhotoFile** (left, left center & right).

AP/Wide World Photos: 58, 137, 138, 168, 174, 185, 186, 192, 195, 198, 199, 201, 204, 211, 213, 215, 228, 229, 231, 233, 235, 237, 238, 241, 243, 250, 251, 255, 256, 264, 271, 274, 285, 288, 289, 310, 316, 321, 323, 324, 327, 330, 331, 334, 342, 345, 355, 366, 374, 375, 377, 382, 383, 394, 401, 407, 415, 419, 569, 570, 572, 574, 575, 578, 579, 580, 582, 585, 588, 589, 590, 591, 592, 594, 597, 598, 599, 606, 629, 652, 654, 655, 657, 658, 659, 660, 662, 663, 665, 666, 667, 668, 669, 670, 671, 674; Elise Amendola: 673; Al behrman: 679; Mary Butkus: 623; Eric Draper: 617, 623; Timothy Fitzgerald: 612; Dave Hammond: 614; Charles Krupa: 678; Ben Margot: 676, 677; Tom Olmscheid: 613; Amy Sancetta: 678; Elaine Thompson: 621; **Archive Photos/Reuters:** Tami Chappell: 639; Gary Hershorn: 634; Peter Morgan: 635; Mike Segar: 639, 647; Joe Skipper: 646; Ray Stubblebine: 637, 639, 647; Susumu Takahashi: 642; **Dan Arnold:** 573, 603; **Corbis:** 186, 205, 210, 217, 227, 229, 233, 267, 271, 282, 289, 291, 297, 300, 310, 322, 327, 332, 335, 342, 343, 350, 353, 359, 366, 367, 369, 385, 389, 390, 391, 396, 398, 402, 409, 410, 414, 418, 420, 430, 431, 439, 443, 452, 455, 457, 459, 463, 465, 467, 473, 475, 478, 479, 484, 486, 487, 489, 495, 497, 499, 502, 503, 505, 509, 511, 518, 519, 527, 533, 534, 537, 547, 550, 559, 564, 574, 577, 590, 591, 593, 596, 599, 649, 651, 652, 653, 654, 660, 666, 667, 669; **Tom DiPace:** 633, 634, 635, 636, 641, 642, 646, 647, 649, 650, 651, 658, 659, 661, 662; **Focus On Sports:** 358, 586, 587, 588, 594, 595, 596, 597, 598, 599; Michael Ponzini: 587; Ron Vesely: 589; Jerry Wachter: 588, 595; **Getty Images:** 548, 558, 561, 566, 567, 582, 586, 589, 613; Brian Bahr: 629, 645; Al Bello: 614, 615, 620, 622, 628, 670, 674; Robert Beck: 563; Glenn Cratty: 578, 606; Jonathan Daniel: 573, 579, 580, 598, 614, 618, 620, 622, 623, 637, 645; Tim DeFrisco: 556; Tomasso DeRosa: 618, 619; Stephen Dunn: 571, 573, 578, 580, 584, 604, 605, 622, 676, 679; Kathleen Economou: 628; Jon Ferrey: 635; Greg Fiume: 644; Otto Greule: 553, 556, 559, 562, 581, 582, 584, 586, 594, 607, 610, 612, 618, 619, 629, 630, 636, 677; Jim Gund: 582, 583, 592; Elsa Hasch: 620, 621, 631, 675; Tom Hauck: 642, 643; Bill Hickey: 571; Jeff Hixon: 579; Harry How: 619, 621, 644, 645; Jed Jacobson: 626, 653, 655, 679; Mitchell Jaspan: 584; Daniel Jonathan: 618; Dave Kaup: 677; Jonathan Kirn: 626; Vincent Laforet: 627, 631; Streeter Lecka: 678; Ken Levine: 573; Andy Lyons: 630; Lonnie Major: 572; MLB Photos: 675, 676; Gary Newkirk: 572; J. Patronite: 581; Doug Pensinger: 603, 615, 625; J. Rettaliatta: 570; David Seelig: 627, 628; Ezra Shaw: 644; Allen Steele: 558; Rick Stewart: 576, 583, 591, 601, 607; Matthew Stockman: 626, 627, 630; Damian Strohmeyer: 555, 604; John Swart: 565, 570; Todd Warshaw: 611; Rick Yeatts: 606; **National Baseball Library & Archive, Cooperstown, NY:** 6, 9, 10, 11, 13-15, 17-19, 21-23, 26-27, 29-31, 33-35, 37-39, 41-43, 45-47, 49-51, 53-55, 57-59, 61-63, 65-67, 69-71, 73-75, 77-79, 81-83, 85-87, 89-91, 93-95, 97-99, 101-103, 105-109, 112-115, 117-121, 123-127, 129-133, 135-139, 141-145, 147-151, 154-157, 160-163, 165-169, 172-173, 175, 177-181, 183-184, 186-187, 189-191, 193, 196-197, 202-205, 207-211, 214-217, 219-223, 225-229, 232, 234-235, 238-241, 244-247, 249-253, 256, 258-259, 261, 263, 265, 268-271, 273, 275-277, 279-281, 283, 286-289, 292-295, 298-299, 301, 303-307, 311-313, 315, 317, 319, 322-323, 325-327, 330, 332-335, 338-343, 346-349, 351, 354-359, 362-365, 371, 373-375, 379, 381-383, 386-387, 391, 393-397, 399, 402-407, 411-413, 415, 417, 419-423, 425-431, 433-439, 444-447, 450-455, 458-462, 466-471, 474, 476-477, 479, 481-487, 490-495, 498-501, 503, 506-508, 510, 513-519, 521, 523-527, 530-531, 534-535, 538, 540-542, 546; **PhotoFile:** 7, 25, 95, 102, 111, 112, 120, 130, 131, 136, 143, 149, 153, 159, 160, 162, 166, 167, 169, 171-174, 181, 184, 185, 187, 190-193, 197, 203-205, 214-215, 223, 232-234, 238-241, 246, 253, 256-257, 259, 262-264, 274-277, 280-282, 286-288, 292-295, 298-300, 304-307, 309, 310, 313, 316-318, 323-325, 329, 331, 333, 335, 338-343, 346-351, 354-357, 359, 361-365, 370-373, 378-382, 387-391, 394-396, 398-399, 403-405, 410-415, 418-421, 426-427, 434-435, 437, 442-445, 449-454, 458, 460-462, 466, 468-469, 471, 474-476, 478, 482-486, 490-495, 498-503, 506-507, 509-511, 514-517, 519, 522-523, 524-526, 529-535, 538-543, 546-549, 551, 554, 555, 557, 562, 563, 564, 565, 566; Patrick Quinn: 11; **Sports Illustrated:** Heinz Kluetmeier: 575; Richard Mackson: 575; Ronald C. Modra: 590; Damian Strohmeyer: 596; **Sports Photo Masters:** Jonathan Koplitz: 611; Mitchell B. Reibel: 611, 612; **SportsChrome USA:** 602, 604, 605; Jonathan Kirn: 638; Rich Kane: 610; Rob Tringali Jr.: 7, 602, 603, 605, 609, 610, 611, 613, 636, 637, 646; Michael Zito: 643; **Transcendental Graphics:** 8, 10; B. Sloute: 9.

THE CONTENTS BASEBALL CHRONICLE

SHATFORD LIBRARY

MAR 2006

1570 E. Colorado Blvd.
Pasadena, CA 91106

CONTENTS

CONTENTS

"Baseball is continuous, like nothing else among American things, an endless game of repeated summers, joining the long generations of all the fathers and all the sons." —Donald Hall, poet

That's what impressed us most about the game, as we compiled *The Baseball Chronicle.* Throughout the years, baseball has remained so consistently strong, so rich in tradition, so true to its colors. Sure, the uniforms may be a little snappier and the players may earn a few more bucks. But when you come right down to it, baseball 1901 style remains the same today.

New York Giants

Roy Campanella

It's still three outs per inning, nine innings per game. Take ball four and you walk to first base, hit it over the fence and you trot all the way around. Even the teams are the same. The Pirates still play in Pittsburgh and the Cubbies still suit up in Chicago. And though Walter O'Malley may have moved his troops from Brooklyn to Los Angeles, we still call them the Dodgers.

This uniformity, this consistency is one of baseball's greatest traits. Throughout the years, the game has stood tall and proud, holding strong through the toughest of times.

Baseball rode through the dead-ball years and the Black Sox scandal. It survived the Great Depression, World War I, and World War II. Players struck for 50 days in 1981 and then demanded multi-million dollar salaries, but the game bounced back better than ever. Attendance continues to reach record levels. Nothing can shake this grand old game.

In *The Baseball Chronicle,* we pay tribute to baseball's rich tradition. Through stories, stats, and photos, we capture the game's great moments, year by year, from 1900 up to today.

Each year in *The Baseball Chronicle* includes a season overview, which recounts the year's biggest stories: the pennant races, the World Series, the MVPs, and the rising stars—as well as the season's hottest controversies. For example, a big story in 1942 centered around the

Ted Kluszewski

American League MVP voting. Boston's Ted Williams led the league in batting, home runs, RBI, runs, walks, runs produced, total bases, slugging average, and on-base percentage, but did *not* win the MVP Award. Instead it went to New York's Joe Gordon, who led the league in strikeouts, errors at his position, and double plays grounded into!

Mickey Mantle

Each in year in *The Baseball Chronicle* also contains a timeline that lists the season's highlights, lowlights, stats, and trivia. Overall, the book's timelines list approximately 5,000 pieces of information. Here are just three examples:

1902: *Nig Clarke of the Texas League's Corsicana goes 8-for-8 with eight homers.*

1921: *Specs Toporcer of the Cards is the first infielder in ML history to wear glasses.*

1968: *On May 8, Catfish Hunter of A's pitches a perfect game vs. Twins, and collects three hits and four RBI in his own cause.*

Don Newcombe

The Baseball Chronicle contains more than 1,400 photographs. All the greats are pictured, of course, but you'll also see some of the game's lesser-known characters. For example, you'll catch a glimpse of Bert Shepard, a one-legged hurler who pitched in 1945, as well as Bobo Holloman, who threw a no-hitter in his first major league start before disappearing into obscurity.

The photo captions are packed with fascinating anecdotes and little-known facts—as well as engaging quotes. Said Waite Hoyt of his famous Yankee teammate: "Every major leaguer and his wife should teach their children to pray, 'God bless Mommy, God bless Daddy, and God bless Babe Ruth.'"

Mark McGwire

As you stroll through *The Baseball Chronicle,* you'll see names and faces come and go, from Wee Willie Keeler to Joe DiMaggio to Mark McGwire. But when you reach the end, we feel you'll come to the same conclusion we did: Baseball, America's favorite pastime in 1900, is the same grand game that it's always been.

America's Game Takes Root In 1800s

By the time the National League of Professional Base Ball Clubs began play in 1876, baseball was already the national game. Spreading from its initial urban settings to farms, small towns, and even Civil War battlefields, baseball captured the hearts and minds of the developing American nation like no other leisure activity.

By the 1840s, the 70-year-old United States of America was already feeling its oats as a world power, and it wanted to put itself head and shoulders above other nations. This self-consciousness spread not only to politics, military matters, and culture, but also to sports and recreation. Like the Ancient Greeks, Americans of the 19th century saw physical activity as key to a budding nation's survival.

When well-to-do young urban men began to search for ways to enjoy their free time, they came upon the idea of playing a good game of ball. Using rules drawn from such English games as cricket and rounders, "town ball" evolved. The new game was a gentlemanly amusement played before or even during the afternoon tea rituals enjoyed by the upper class of the day. The sport gradually became known as baseball, with the alternative spellings of "base ball" and "base-ball."

As more affluent young men played the game, more attention came to baseball, and the game began to expand even more widely in popularity. Kids in the cities and the country began playing, changing rules of the games they knew to mirror those of the chic amusement of baseball.

As the game grew in popularity in the nation's great cities, its derivations from the English games were downplayed by patriotic writers such as Henry Chadwick, who as a well-known newspaperman did much to aid in the spread of baseball's fame. Chadwick's efforts to codify the rules of the young game, and his endless championing of baseball in the press, were paramount in the development of baseball into the National Game.

Baseball was painted as a uniquely American creation, free of influence from all other games and all other cultures. Chadwick would write in 1876: "What cricket is to an Englishman, baseball has become to an American."

A visionary man named Alexander Cartwright, often called the Father of Baseball, did as much as anyone to build the game's sense of structure and organization. His club, the New York Knickerbockers, began play in 1842. Other clubs, such as the Excelsiors and the New York Nine, sprang up to join the Knickerbockers in competition. By the 1860s, the desire to win, rather than just to play a gentlemanly game of ball, led to the hiring of ringers and professional players.

Many baseball devotees, especially those in the upper classes, bemoaned the rise of "professional" barnstorming clubs, feeling that baseball could never recover once clubs began paying for players. However, most fans (or, as they were called back then, "bugs" or "cranks") found that they liked watching the game played by the best athletes at the highest level—a condition only permitted by a professional setting.

Such barnstorming clubs as the Cincinnati Red Stockings toured the nation, beating up on local teams but bringing fans

New York Nine vs. New York Knickerbockers

from miles around, spreading the pleasures of baseball to the hinterlands. Given the appeal of traveling baseball clubs, it was only a short time before a formal league would appear. The first organized professional circuit was the National Association, which set sail in 1871.

The NA's five-year history was rife with gambling scandals, bankruptcies, vanishing franchises, and other misadventures. The league was not run well, and schedules were often ignored. The Boston Red Stockings featured pitcher Al Spalding and brothers Harry and George Wright, who were so good that many other teams simply couldn't compete, and the league eventually fell apart in 1875.

In February 1876, Chicago businessman William Hulbert and several other wealthy businessmen met in New York City to found the National League of Professional Base Ball Clubs. This aggregation was dedicated to putting the highest quality baseball product available on the field,

1869 Cincinnati Red Stockings

which meant charging regular admission for games and paying players a steady salary. Teams would not be allowed in the league if they couldn't remain fiscally viable. Hulbert was the league's first president, and he vowed to entertain fans with the best possible product.

The National League remains in operation to this day, and it is the oldest professional sports league in the country. Several cities with charter NL franchises still have clubs, such as St. Louis, Cincinnati, Philadelphia, and New York, but only the Chicago Cubs have been in operation without interruption since 1876.

In 19th-century baseball, runs were often hard to come by. The balls weren't as hard as they are today, and the bats weren't as smooth. Strategy—bunting, stealing bases, "trick" plays and pitches, and often downright cheating—were the order of the day. The biggest stars were contact hitters such as Cap Anson, "Orator" Jim O'Rourke, Dan Brouthers, and Buck Ewing; home runs were eschewed as showy and as poor strategy.

Pitchers, who didn't have to exert themselves on every pitch, could throw complete game after complete game. Cy Young, Pud Galvin, and Mickey Welch were three of the top pitchers of the period. Often in the early days of the game, a club would go an entire 100-game season with just a couple pitchers taking on the entire load.

Baseball prided itself as the nation's game, boasting the best athletes and strategic minds to be had in sports. Very early on, baseball was seen as a combination of brawn and brain, with the biggest stars not only being the most physically gifted but also the wisest in "baseball sense."

Of course, some of the athletes who could have played at the best levels—those with dark skin—weren't allowed to take the field. Many well-known white players, such as Anson, didn't want to perform on the same diamonds as blacks. Therefore, African-American players were not welcome in organized baseball almost from the very start.

The last African-American to play major league baseball until

Alexander Cartwright

1894 Baltimore Orioles

Jackie Robinson did in 1947 was Moses Fleetwood Walker, who appeared in 42 games as a catcher for the 1884 Toledo club in the American Association. (His brother Welday also briefly played with Toledo that season.) The last African-American in organized ball until Robinson was Bert Jones, who played in the Kansas State League as late as 1898.

Baseball reflected America's 19th-century social structure. As separatist Jim Crow laws were slowly instituted across the union, baseball took on the character of its "separate but equal" nation—which often was far from equal. Negro baseball leagues began to spring up late in the 19th century, producing such stars as Bud Fowler and George Stovey, players who were just as great as the celebrated white stars of the era. Historians of the mid- to late 20th century would eventually help restore these great players, and the others who toiled in the Negro leagues through the 1950s, to their deserved stature.

The other controversies in 19th-century baseball involved "blue laws," which were designed to protect the "moral character" of a town's citizens. Many cities did not allow ball to be played on Sundays, while some governmental and temperance groups wished to remove the temptation of "demon rum" and other alcohol from the stadium. The National League sold itself as a clean and proper form of entertainment in the 1870s and early 1880s, as rules governing gambling, sales of liquor, umpiring, and sportsmanship were instituted.

Into this cultural landscape stepped the American Association, often referred to as the "Beer and Whiskey League" because its owners knew that plenty of fans liked to go to the park and enjoy a few drinks along with their baseball. The AA even played Sunday games, and it cut its ticket prices to just 25 cents while NL clubs' admissions were 50 cents. The upstart league entered the picture in 1882. Two years later, a *third* major league, the Union Association, began play.

With baseball riding high, newspapers and books carrying the facts, figures, and stories of players and teams did big business. The sports media grew in earnest in the 1880s—far before ESPN and the Internet but just as important in spreading the word about the nation's new sporting heroes.

While the Union Association couldn't last more than one season, the American Association held on until 1891, finally expiring after another third league emerged.

This final third-league challenge came from John Montgomery Ward, a star pitcher with Providence in the early days of the National League. As a former player and a student of economics, Ward was acutely aware of the tenuous position held by players of the time. With no union, no leverage in contract negotiations, and no say in how their careers were handled, players were regarded as chattel and paid poorly despite their public stature.

Ward, and several like-minded colleagues, began the Players League in 1890. The new

Buck Ewing

Mickey Welch

league was meant to instill a sense of fairness between owners and players, but competition proved too much for too few dollars. The financial ruin suffered by all three leagues (the Players League, the National League, and the American Association) during 1890 left all sides weak. The National League was the strongest of the three bodies, and by 1891 it had pushed out the other two leagues to become the only remaining major.

By this time, minor leagues dotted the nation, bringing professional ball to all outposts. These leagues were not like today's minor leagues, most of which feature clubs affiliated with major league organizations. Therefore, residents of Omaha, Spokane, Atlanta, or Amarillo could wholeheartedly root for *their* teams to win and not have to worry about losing their players to the "big club." These old minor leagues were extremely competitive, often featuring players just as good as those in the majors.

The National League remained the only major league from 1892 to 1900. However,

trouble loomed on the horizon for the "senior circuit." The dominance of John McGraw's Baltimore Orioles club—a hard-as-nails bunch of street toughs who played aggressive and often dirty baseball, bullying umpires and beating up opponents—turned off many fans. By 1899, the 12-team National League was struggling, and following that season four clubs dropped out.

Into this crisis stepped a businessman named Byron "Ban" Johnson, who in 1899 declared that his heretofore "minor" Western League would henceforth be called the American League and would be a major league by 1901. This act would radically change baseball history. The AL offered cleaner, better-run baseball, with on-field authority going to umpires rather than bullying players. The deep-pocketed AL owners had the financial ability to compete with NL owners for contracts, and they raided existing teams for star players.

Johnson and his owner cohorts secured such star players as

Ban Johnson

John Montgomery Ward

Young, Nap Lajoie, Willie Keeler, and Sam Crawford for AL clubs. The American League competed with the NL only in Chicago, Philadelphia, and Boston. It instead concentrated on bringing the game to such major league-caliber cities as Detroit, Cleveland, and Washington. The new circuit was an immediate success.

Of the AL's eight franchises in 1901, all are still in operation today, including four clubs—the Boston Red Sox, Chicago White Sox, Cleveland Indians, and Detroit Tigers—in their original cities. The NL's eight franchises extant in 1901 are also still in operation.

The contraction of the National League, and the growth of the American League into a major league, set up a 16-club structure that lasted until expansion in 1961. By 1903, the NL acknowledged the AL's status as a major league, and two years later the leagues' champions were playing in an annual World Series. Aside from a brief 1914-15 challenge by the Federal League, the two-loop major league structure continues unabated.

THE AL SETS UP SHOP, RAIDS NL ROSTERS

In 1901, for the first time in a decade, there were two major leagues. Two years were to pass before they learned to coexist peacefully. In the meantime, it was all-out war—over ticket sales, over player contracts, and over the hearts and minds of the fans.

The American League opened for business in Milwaukee, Cleveland, Washington, Baltimore, Detroit, Philadelphia, Boston, and Chicago, the latter three franchises located on prime National League turf. Fortunately for the upstarts, the National League was bitterly divided into two factions, one led by New York's Andrew Freedman and another by Chicagoan Al Spalding. In 1901, they couldn't even get together to elect a president, much less mount an effective defense against the new league.

Refusing to respect NL contracts, Ban Johnson and the AL owners ruthlessly raided NL rosters. More than 100 players, dissatisfied with the low salaries and dictatorial policies of 1890s NL management, gladly jumped at the chance to change leagues. Among the biggest names were John McGraw, Cy Young, Clark Griffith, Hugh Duffy, and Jimmy Collins. Stars such as these lent legitimacy to the AL, and fans came out in droves to see ex-Cardinal Cy Young win 33 games for Boston with a 1.63 ERA, as well as ex-Cub Clark Griffith, who crossed town to go 24-7 for the Chicago White Sox.

But the brightest star of all was second baseman Napoleon Lajoie of Connie Mack's Philadelphia Athletics. A good player but no superstar in five seasons with the Phillies, Lajoie led the AL in nearly every offensive category in 1901, including the Triple Crown stats. He batted .426 (the highest mark in the 20th century), drove in 125 runs, and hit 14 home runs; he slugged .643. Though he was playing under essentially expansion conditions and without the foul-strike rule (which was not implemented by the AL until 1903), his batting average was still 86 points higher than runner-up Mike Donlin's .340. Lajoie's 145 runs scored are among the most in history, but were surpassed only once between 1900 and 1920.

The A's won their attendance war with the Phillies, but in spite of Lajoie's heroics, finished 9 games back of a running White Sox club that stole 280 bases, led the league in runs and ERA, and finished 83-53, 4 games ahead of Boston.

For the first time in the National League, foul balls were counted as strikes (before the count reached two strikes), and offense suffered across the board. Total runs dropped by almost 800. The league batting average fell from .279 to .267. Even stolen bases were affected, as at-bats were shortened and strikeout totals skyrocketed.

A relatively intact Pittsburgh Pirates team won that city's first-ever pennant in 20 years of major league status, compiling a 90-49 record on the strength of pitchers Jack Chesbro, who finished 21-10; Deacon Phillippe, who went 22-12; and three-time 20-game winner Jesse Tannehill, who won the ERA title at 2.18. The Pirates' attack consisted of outfield duo Ginger Beaumont and Fred Clarke, both of whom scored well over 100 runs and batted over .320, and of course Honus Wagner. Wagner stole a league-high 49 bases, batted .353, and drove in 126 runs.

Brooklyn's Jimmy Sheckard slugged .534 to lead the league, hammering 19 triples and 11 homers. In New York, 20-year-old rookie Christy Mathewson went 20-17 with a 2.41 ERA, the first of his 13 20-win seasons. Another future star, Wahoo Sam Crawford, played his first full season and hit .330 with a league-leading 16 home runs. And 32-year-old Jesse Burkett, an 1890s legend who twice hit .400, won his final batting title at .376 for fourth-place St. Louis.

1901

- The first game in AL history is played on April 24—Chicago 6, Cleveland 2—at Chicago Cricket Club.

- Pittsburgh wins its first major league pennant.

- Chicago takes the first American League pennant.

- St. Louis' Jesse Burkett leads the NL in batting (.376), runs (142), and hits (226).

- Philly's Nap Lajoie sets 20th-century record when he hits .426 to lead AL; he also wins the Triple Crown.

- The Phillies finish second in NL after losing Lajoie to AL raiders.

- Brooklyn's Wild Bill Donovan leads the NL in wins (25) and walks (152).

- Boston's Cy Young leads the AL with 33 wins.

- Connie Mack manages the fledgling Philadelphia A's and will be their only manager until 1951.

Nap Lajoie topped the American League in 1901 in every major batting department except triples and led the circuit's second basemen in fielding average and total chances per game. Incidentally, try to imagine a uniform with a pocket big enough to hold a contemporary player's glove.

- Baltimore, behind fiery manager John McGraw, finishes only fifth despite leading the AL in batting.

- Noodles Hahn sets a modern record for most pitching wins for a last-place team, by winning 22 for the Reds.

- Hahn has 41 complete games, a record for a 20th-century lefty.

- In his first full season, Christy Mathewson wins 20 games for the Giants and hurls a no-hitter vs. St. Louis on July 15.

- On May 9, Cleveland's Earl Moore throws no-hitter for nine innings, but loses 4-2 to the White Sox in ten innings.

- Sam Crawford of the last-place Reds leads the NL with 16 homers.

- Roscoe Miller of the Tigers sets a rookie record when he pitches 35 complete games.

- The Phillies' keystone combo of Bill Hallman and Monte Cross hit .184 and .197, respectively.

Honus Wagner

Wagner Makes Mark

If there had been a Most Valuable Player Award in 1901, Honus Wagner almost certainly would have swept up the honor in the National League, as he topped the circuit with 126 RBI and 49 swipes. Yet at age 27, he still didn't have a position, dividing his time between the outfield and shortstop and third base.

Noodles Hahn

Hahn Fans Over 200

From 1899 to 1904, the left arm of Noodles Hahn had no equal. He won 121 games and struck out 878 batters during that period for poor Cincinnati teams, 22 of those victories and a National League-best 239 of those Ks coming in 1901. Hahn was already on the wane by age 25, when he slipped to just 98 strikeouts.

Cy Young

Cross Yields Weak Year

After hitting only .197 in 1901, Monte Cross jumped from the Phillies to the crosstown A's in 1902 and grew a mustache, but neither move improved his hitting. Playing in 153 games for the Athletics in 1904, he batted .189 and collected just 95 hits. As a fielder, however, Cross was among the better shortstops of his era.

Monte Cross

Young Comes of Age

Cy Young was coming off his poorest season since his 1890 rookie year when he jumped to the fledgling American League in 1901. Despite his circuit-best 33 wins that season, most observers thought it was the last gasp of a once-great pitcher, 34 years of age at the time. It turned out, instead, to be a mid-point season in Young's career.

1901

- Trailing 13-4 in the ninth inning of their first game in the AL, the Tigers rally to beat Milwaukee 14-13.

- On April 28, for fourth straight day, Detroit beats Milwaukee in its final at-bat.

- Hahn fans 16 Boston Braves on May 22, a post-1893 record.

- The White Sox collect 23 hits in a game off Cleveland's Bock Baker—all singles.

- Giants smack record 31 hits on June 9, six of them by Kip Selbach.

- Philadelphia's Chick Fraser hits an AL record 31 batters.

- On May 23, Lajoie is the first player to be intentionally walked with the bases full.

- Irv Waldron leads the AL in at-bats (598) and hits .311 in his lone ML season.

- Miller pitches an AL rookie record 332 innings.

Pittsburgh Pirates

Pirates Take NL

This photograph of Pittsburgh's first flag-winner was actually taken prior to the 1902 season—which explains why Wid Conroy, who was not with the ballclub in 1901, is pictured. All the others were returning vets, including George Merritt, who was 3–0 in three starts as a rookie in 1901 but never started another game in the majors.

Jesse Burkett

McGraw, 28, Washed Up

Although new manager John McGraw hit .349 with the Baltimore club in 1901, injuries and suspensions held him to only 73 games; just 28 years old at the time, he was, for all intents and purposes, finished as a productive player. Never again would he total more than 42 hits in a season. In 1902, he jumped from the Orioles to become the manager of the Giants. He would become the most famous skipper of all time.

John McGraw

Burkett Is a Hit

Jesse Burkett is probably the least known great hitter. A member of the Cleveland Spiders in the 1890s, Burkett had 2,249 hits at the conclusion of the 1901 season, topping the National League with 226 hits that year. He would have finished with a .362 career batting average if he'd quit then and there instead of defecting to the American League, where he was but an average hitter during his remaining four years of play.

- Willie Keeler collects at least 200 hits for the eighth straight year, an NL record.
- Roy Thomas of the Phils leads the NL in walks (100), but compiles only eight extra-base hits.
- The modern infield-fly rule is adopted.

- The Tigers commit an AL record 12 errors in a game on May 1.
- Harley Parker of Cincinnati gives up 21 runs in a game on June 21.
- The A's and Senators play five straight doubleheaders against each other in August.

- Honus Wagner leads the NL in steals (49) and RBI (126).
- Deaf-mute Dummy Taylor of New York leads NL in starts with 43 and losses with 27.
- On August 10, A's pitcher Lew Wiltse collects four extra-base hits in one game.

MCGRAW AND JOHNSON DROP THE GLOVES

The war between the leagues was fought hard and ruthlessly during the 1902 season, with the main battles taking place in Baltimore, Philadelphia, and St. Louis.

John McGraw's American League career was over almost before it started, as the old National League firebrand and king of the umpire-baiters clashed repeatedly with Ban Johnson over rowdy behavior on the field. In 1901, Johnson had infuriated McGraw by suspending him for verbal abuse of an umpire. By early '02, McGraw was beginning to feel like a marked man.

In April, McGraw was treated with a little of his own medicine by umpire Jack Sheridan, who watched as Boston's Big Bill Dinneen hit McGraw five times with pitches. Each time, Sheridan refused to award him first base on the grounds that McGraw had gotten hit intentionally. Finally, Sheridan added insult to literal injury by ejecting McGraw from the game. The league backed its umpire and suspended McGraw for five more days.

McGraw got even with Johnson later in the season. McGraw enlisted two NL owners to secretly buy up a controlling interest in the Orioles' stock and then release virtually the entire lineup—including Joe Kelley, Roger Bresnahan, and Joe McGinnity—to the New York Giants and the Cincinnati Reds. Shortly afterward, McGraw was named the Giants' manager. An irate Johnson took control of the Baltimore franchise and, a year later, moved it into New York to compete with McGraw's Giants. The franchise was renamed the "Highlanders" and, later, the "Yankees."

In Philadelphia, the battleground moved from the boardroom to the courts, as the Phillies obtained a ruling from a Pennsylvania judge that Athletics star Napoleon Lajoie be returned to his former NL club. A's manager Connie Mack undid the National League's strategy by transferring him to Cleveland. Lajoie remained with the Cleveland team, which was christened the "Naps" in his honor, for a dozen years and continued to be an important AL drawing card. However, he had to avoid the jurisdiction of the Pennsylvania courts by skipping Cleveland's away series in Philadelphia for the remainder of the 1902 season.

Spurred by successes in Chicago, Philadelphia, and Boston, the AL moved its Milwaukee franchise into another NL market, St. Louis. The new team promptly raided the St. Louis Cardinals' roster for most of its stars, including Jesse Burkett, Bobby Wallace, and Jack Powell. Another blow to the National League was the defection of slugger Big Ed Delahanty from Philadelphia to Washington, where he won the AL batting title at .376 and led in slugging average at .590.

In the almost anticlimactic pennant races, hard-hitting Philadelphia won in the American League with an 83-53 record, mainly on the strength of Lave Cross's 108 RBI; Topsy Hartsel's league-leading 47 stolen bases, 87 walks, and 109 runs scored; and Socks Seybold's 16 home runs.

In the National League, Pittsburgh repeated and won a then-NL-record 103 games against 36 losses. The Pirates made a clean sweep of virtually every major offensive and defensive category. Ginger Beaumont won the batting title at .357; Jack Chesbro led in wins with 28 and winning percentage at .824; Honus Wagner led in runs with 105, RBI with 91, doubles with 30, stolen bases with 42, and slugging average at .463; and Tommy Leach led the league in triples with 22 and homers with six. Chicago's Jack Taylor turned in a 1.33 ERA, and in an historic iron-man season, Boston's Vic Willis started 46 games (the sixthmost in the 20th century), completed 45 (second-best), and threw 410 innings, the fifth-best ever.

1902

- Pirates win the NL flag again—by a record 27 1/2 games.

- Pittsburgh's Jack Chesbro leads the NL in wins (28) and win pct. (.824).

- Pittsburgh's Tommy Leach leads the NL with six homers, fewest by a leader in 20th century.

- The A's win their first AL flag.

- John McGraw jumps the AL in midseason to manage the Giants, but can't keep them out of last place.

- Washington's Ed Delahanty wins AL batting title (.376) after winning NL title in 1899.

- Philly's Socks Seybold leads the AL with 16 homers, tying Sam Crawford's 20th-century record.

- Pittsburgh and Brooklyn lead the NL with 19 homers; every AL team but Chicago has more.

- Pirate Ginger Beaumont leads the NL in batting (.357) and hits (193).

The National League Champion Pirates won 103 of 139 games in 1902. Some of the notables pictured here are owner Barney Dreyfuss (the blade with the mustache), catcher Chief Zimmer *(back row, far left)*, Honus Wagner *(to the right of Dreyfuss)*, and Fred Clarke *(to the left of Dreyfuss)*.

- Cy Young again leads the AL in wins with 32.

- Last in the AL in 1901, Milwaukee moves to St. Louis—the AL's first franchise shift.

- Jack Taylor of second-division Cubs leads the NL in ERA (1.33) and posts a dazzling 23-11 record.

- George Davis of the White Sox has a .951 FA, a new record for shortstops.

- After an erratic showing in the NL, Philly's Rube Waddell goes 24-7 and leads AL in Ks (210).

- Harry Pulliam is named NL president.

- The *Chicago Daily News* coins the nickname "Cubs" for the Chicago NL team.

- Nig Clarke of the Texas League's Corsicana goes 8-for-8 with eight homers.

- In his AL debut, Danny Murphy of the A's goes 6-for-6 vs. Cy Young.

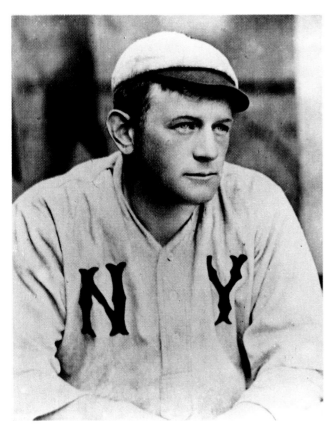

Jack Chesbro

Chesbro Tops in Wins

Jack Chesbro was one of the last National League stars to jump to the upstart AL, joining New York in 1903. Prior to bailing out, in 1902, Chesbro topped the senior circuit with 28 wins and set a record with 41 consecutive scoreless innings. Had he remained with the Pirates, who were much deeper in pitching than the New Yorkers, he would never have won 41 games in a season as he did in 1904. His arm, however, would almost certainly have been the better for it.

Roy Thomas

Thomas High in OBP

The mystery surrounding Roy Thomas that may never be satisfactorily answered centers on the frequency with which opposing pitchers walked him: The league's leader in bases on balls seven out of 13 years, Thomas totaled 1,042 walks. His on-base percentage in 1902 (best in the National League) topped his slugging percentage by nearly 100 points.

Vic Willis

Willis Lugs Heavy Load

A look at Vic Willis, who in 1902 not only set the modern National League record for complete games (45) but also led the circuit in saves (three). The 1902 season was the last year that his Boston Braves finished in the first division until they copped their "Miracle" pennant in 1914.

Rube Waddell

Waddell Tops AL in Ks

Rube Waddell, the American League's strikeout leader in 1902 (210), began the season with Los Angeles in the Pacific Coast League. After winning 12 games there, he was acquired by the pennant-winning A's and netted another 24 victories, second in the AL only to Cy Young's 32 triumphs.

1902

- Chesbro sets a record with 41 consecutive scoreless innings in NL.

- Cubs Joe Tinker, Johnny Evers, and Frank Chance first play together in a game on Sept. 15.

- Chicago's Nixey Callahan no-hits the Tigers on Sept. 20.

- The Pirates are 56-15 at home, the best home record ever in NL.

- Boston's Vic Willis has an NL record 45 complete games.

- Pete Childs of the Phils has a .266 SA, the lowest ever by a player with more than 400 at-bats.

- Cardinals Jack and Mike O'Neill form the NL's first brother battery.

- White Sox George Davis becomes the first switch-hitter to collect 2,000 hits.

- Sam Mertes of the White Sox plays all nine positions during the season.

Tinker Makes His Debut

After starring for Portland in the Pacific Northwest League the previous year, Joe Tinker took over the Cubs' shortstop post in 1902 to lead the National League in both assists and errors. One of the immortal trio (Johnny Evers and Frank Chance were the other two), he gave the Bruins the most service—11 full seasons as a regular before he joined the Reds in 1913.

Joe Tinker

George Davis

Davis Hits a Record

Many historians believe that George Davis is unequivocally the best player not in the Hall of Fame. After reaching the 2,000-hit mark in 1902—a record for switch-hitters—Davis went on to collect over 600 more (Pete Rose surpassed his 2,660-career hit record in 1976). Davis excelled at every phase of the game and still holds the marks for both the most triples (27, in 1893) and the most RBI (134, in 1897) in a season by a switch-hitter. Like Rose, Davis was extremely versatile defensively. Rose began as a second baseman before moving to the outfield and then to third; Davis started as an outfielder before moving to third and then to short.

Seybold Socks 16 Home Runs

A late-season trial with the 1899 Cubs was Socks Seybold's only taste of major league competition prior to the formation of the American League. Past 30 years of age at the time, he gave the A's eight solid seasons—none of them better than 1902, when he garnered 97 RBI and tagged 16 home runs, a figure that stood as the loop record until Babe Ruth arrived.

Socks Seybold

- Cleveland makes an AL record six errors in an inning on June 2.
- Cleveland's Piano Legs Hickman leads the AL in hits (193) and total bases (289).
- Cleveland rookie Addie Joss tops the AL in shutouts with five.

- Detroit's Ed Siever tops the AL in ERA (1.91) and is first ERA leader to post a below-.500 win pct.
- Honus Wagner leads the NL in runs (105), doubles (30), SA (.463), and steals (42).
- Braves have two 27-game winners, Willis and Togie Pittinger.

- Phillie Ham Iburg sets a modern NL record for losses in a season (18) by a pitcher in his lone ML season.
- Baltimore's Jimmy Williams again tops the AL in triples (21).
- Red Donahue and Jack Powell lead the second-place Browns with 22 wins apiece.

After a disastrous 1902 season in which it had been out-drawn by the AL by more than a half-million fans, the National League agreed to peace. Ban Johnson rejected the NL's offer to form another 12-team league, and the modern two-major league format was born.

Other points of the new National Agreement included the AL's adoption of the foul-strike rule and the NL's acceptance of an AL franchise in New York. The Agreement also set up a new National Commission consisting of league presidents Harry Pulliam and Johnson, as well as Johnson ally Garry Herrmann. This arrangement guaranteed Johnson's paramount influence; he would remain the de facto lord of baseball until the gambling scandals of the late teens brought about the modern sole baseball commissionership.

Johnson gave pitcher/manager Clark Griffith the job of building a successful AL club in New York City. Partially owned by Tammany Hall figure Joseph Gordon, the club was first called the "Highlanders," as a play both on the well-known British regiment, Gordon's Highlanders, and the team's hastily constructed park at 168th and Broadway, the highest point in Manhattan. Later, newspapermen thumbed their noses at a team nickname with British associations and began calling the team the "Yankees."

BOSTON (AL) TAKES FIRST WORLD SERIES

Both pennant races were laughers. Boston led the American League in runs scored and fewest runs allowed behind slugger Buck Freeman, who hit 13 home runs and drove in 104; fan favorite and runs scored leader Patsy Dougherty; and pitchers Cy Young (28-9), Long Tom Hughes (20-7), and Bill Dinneen (21-13). They finished 14½ games ahead of a Philadelphia team that featured improved pitching—thanks to Eddie Plank, Rube Waddell, and rookie Chief Bender—but an attack weakened by off-years from Harry Davis and Lave Cross. Nap Lajoie's one-man show in Cleveland, including a league-high .344 batting average and a .518 slugging average, could push his team no higher than third place, 15 games out.

Nineteenth century great (and legendary drinker) Ed Delahanty was killed one night in 1903 when he was kicked off a train for disorderly behavior and then pursued it on foot over a bridge above Niagara Falls. He fell in and drowned. Delahanty had a lifetime .346 batting average, behind only Rogers Hornsby among righthanded hitters.

In Honus Wagner's first year as regular shortstop—he had been playing first, third, short, and the outfield—Pittsburgh won its third-straight pennant with a 91-49 record. The Flying Dutchman won another batting title at .355, and he and teammates Ginger Beaumont, Fred Clarke, and Tommy Leach monopolized the leader board in most other hitting categories.

Second-place New York had the NL's top pitching staff in Iron Man McGinnity (31-20) and Christy Mathewson (30-13), but John McGraw's club never got close enough to make a race of it. McGinnity lived up to his nickname by totaling 48 starts (fourth-most in modern history), 44 complete games (third-most), and 434 innings (the third-highest total).

Late in the 1903 season, the owners of the two first-place clubs agreed amongst themselves to play a best-of-nine, postseason world championship series. AL Boston came back to win 5-3 after being down 3-1 to the heavily favored Pirates. The star of the series was Pittsburgh's Deacon Phillippe, a great control pitcher who pitched an incredible five complete games, going 3-2 with a 2.86 ERA. The recent war between the leagues and the drama of underdog versus dynasty made the series a big success and led to the formal World Series, which started in 1905 and has continued until today.

1903

- The Baltimore team is transferred to New York, the last franchise move until 1953.

- Boston wins the AL flag.

- The Pirates win their third straight NL pennant.

- Boston wins first modern World Series.

- Deacon Phillippe wins three Series games for the losing Pirates.

- Honus Wagner wins his second NL batting crown at .355.

- Nap Lajoie leads the AL in BA (.344) and SA (.518).

- Rube Waddell fans 302, a post-1893 record.

- Giants post two 30-game winners—Joe McGinnity (31) and Christy Mathewson (30).

- Foul balls are counted as strikes by both leagues for the first time.

- Pirate Ginger Beaumont leads NL in hits (209) and total bases (272).

The Pittsburgh Pirates won their third consecutive National League pennant in 1903, only to lose their first World Series. Although they were 21-strong when this team photo was taken, only 14 members took part in the World Series. One who did was Kitty Bransfield *(middle row, center)*. Two years later, Bransfield was traded to the Phils, a deal that cost the Pirates several more pennants as his departure left a hole at first base that went unfilled for nearly a decade.

- Washington's Ed Delahanty falls from a railway trestle to his death.

- Boston's Buck Freeman leads AL in homers (13), total bases (281), and RBI (104).

- First moving picture of game is made, featuring Cleveland's Lajoie and Harry Bay.

- Cleveland shortstop John Gochnauer makes a 20th-century record 98 errors and hits .185.

- When part of the Phillies' park, Baker Bowl, collapses, 12 fans are killed.

- Pirate utility man Wagner is installed at shortstop and plays there the rest of his career.

- White Sox tie AL record with 12 errors on May 6; in the same game, the Tigers make six errors.

- Gambler Frank Ferrell and Bill Devery, reputedly a crooked cop, become owners of New York AL team.

- Pirates blank foes for a record 57 consecutive innings.

Huntington Grounds

Huntington Hosts First World Series

A photograph of Huntington Grounds, the home of the 1903 Boston Pilgrims and the site of the first modern World Series game. The eight-game Series spanned nearly two weeks. The players on both sides combined for 553 at-bats.

Honus Wagner

Phillippe Goes 25-9

Deacon Phillippe became the Pirates' pitching ace in 1903, in part by default when both Jack Chesbro and Jesse Tannehill, who won 48 games between them for the 1902 club, defected to the American League. Phillippe ended his 25–9 season in 1903 with a trio of World Series wins. Control was his bread-and-butter, as Phillippe is the only starting pitcher in history to issue less than one walk for every game in which he appeared.

Deacon Phillippe

Wagner High in BA

Wid Conroy's defection to New York in the American League forced the Pirates to put Honus Wagner (pictured) at shortstop in 1903 and leave him there until his retirement 14 years later (Wagner won his second NL batting title with a .355 average that year). Even so, Wagner continued to play every other position except pitcher and catcher upon occasion; serving as a pitcher earlier in his career, he registered a perfect 0.00 ERA in eight innings.

1903

- McGinnity pitches and wins two doubleheaders in an eight-day period and three in a month.

- Cubs get Three Finger Brown and Jack O'Neill from Cards for Jack Taylor and Larry McLean.

- The Phils' Chick Fraser no-hits the Cubs on Sept. 18.

- Cincinnati shortstop Tommy Corcoran makes a record 14 assists in a game on August 7.

- Jack Doscher becomes the first son of an ex-major leaguer to play in the majors.

- The pitcher's mound is restricted in height to no more than 15 inches.

- Pittsburgh's Sam Leever leads the NL in ERA (2.06) and shutouts (seven).

- Mathewson tops the NL in strikeouts with 267.

- The Giants' jump from the cellar to second in 1903 is one of the biggest gains by a team in the century.

Joe McGinnity

McGinnity: Indestructible

Most posed photographs of Joe McGinnity, for some reason, show him with his arm cocked and ready to deliver an overhand pitch rather than one of the sidearm slings that were his trademark. McGinnity made the world indelibly aware of his nickname "Iron Man" in 1903, winning three doubleheaders and working a National League-record 434 innings. McGinnity led the majors that year with 31 triumphs.

Bill Dinneen, Deacon Phillippe

Dinneen, Deacon Go Head-On

Featured on the front cover of the scorecard that was sold at the eighth and final game of the 1903 World Series were the contest's two preannounced starters, Bill Dinneen of Boston *(left)* and Deacon Phillippe of Pittsburgh. They won a combined six of the eight games.

Three Finger Wins Nine

Mordecai Brown spent most of 1903, his rookie season, with St. Louis, where he went 9–13; he was playing for the Cubs at the start of the 1904 season. Brown lost most of his index finger in a childhood accident. Asked if his curve was aided by the truncated digit, he said that to be certain, he would have had to throw with a normal hand—something he had never done. To this day, the Cubs have never won a World Series in which he didn't appear.

Mordecai Brown

- Bill Keister hits .320 and leads the Phils in homers and RBI, but is cut by the team after the season.

- McGinnity pitches an NL record 434 innings.

- Boston ties the AL record with 112 triples.

- Togie Pittinger of Boston NL surrenders a post-1901 record 196 runs.

- Pirates commit an NL record six errors in one inning on August 20.

- The Cubs' Frank Chance steals 67 bases, a record for first basemen.

- Pat Moran of Boston NL makes 214 assists, a record for catchers.

- The Tigers' newly appointed player/manager Win Mercer commits suicide in the preseason.

- Waddell pitches a four-hitter vs. New York on August 1—Kid Elberfeld collects all four hits.

AL fans enjoyed the first of many Boston-New York pennant races in 1904, thanks mainly to Yankees pitcher Jack Chesbro's record 41 wins, 51 starts, and 48 complete games. After a season-long dogfight, the race came down to a last-day doubleheader between the two teams in New York. Boston's half-game lead meant that New York needed to sweep.

In the opening game, Chesbro dueled Bill Dinneen until the ninth, when a Boston rally threatened to break a 2-2 deadlock. With catcher Lou Criger on third, two out, and two strikes on good-hit shortstop Freddy Parent, Chesbro launched a spitball past catcher Red Kleinow's head. Criger scored, and Boston held off New York in the bottom of the inning to win 3-2 and clinch the flag.

Chesbro died in 1931, about a decade too soon to see the world remember him as the winningest pitcher in 20th-century history, instead of one of the all-time pennant-race goats.

Fourth-place Cleveland featured the league's best offense in 1904. Nap Lajoie banged out 49 doubles and batted .376 to win another batting title; he also led the AL in both on-base average at .405 and slugging average at .552. Teammate Elmer Flick scored 97 runs, cracked 17 triples, and collected 260 total bases.

CHESBRO WINS 41, BUT LOSES THE BIG ONE

Cleveland pitcher Addie Joss took the ERA title at 1.59, the first of his five sub-2.00 ERA seasons.

Philadelphia flamethrower Rube Waddell struck out 349 AL batters at a very modern-looking rate of 8.2 per nine innings. Waddell struck out 110 more batters than Chesbro, the AL runner-up in Ks. Waddell's strikeout total is the fifth-best ever—and every other season on the Top Ten list came in the strikeout-happy post-World War II era.

John McGraw won his first NL pennant in grand style; his Giants won a then-record 106 games and lost only 47. A typical McGraw team, the pitching was ably handled by workhorses McGinnity and Mathewson, who won 68 games between them; but New York's NL-leading offense was a complete team effort. Lacking a dominant star, the Giants lineup was made up of beautifully complementary parts, including George Browne, who led the league in runs with 99; Bill Dahlen, who led in RBI with 80;

and Sam Mertes, who was second in doubles with 28. As a team, the Giants led the league in runs, hits, doubles, home runs, walks, batting average, and stolen bases. McGinnity won the National League's ERA title at 1.61, the finest ERA mark of his Hall of Fame career.

The Pirates were let down by poor pitching and finished fourth; Honus Wagner won his third batting title and stole a league-leading 53 bases. Frank Selee's second-place Chicago club won 93 games with rising young stars like Frank Chance, Johnny Evers, and Joe Tinker. The Cubs would be heard from soon.

Fans who anticipated another exciting interleague, postseason series were disappointed. Late in the year, John McGraw and New York owner John Brush issued a press release that called the AL a "minor league" and stated that the Giants "desired no greater glory than to win the pennant in the National League" and would therefore refuse to meet the AL pennant winner—McGraw had struck one more spiteful blow against his old enemy, Ban Johnson. After the season, however, owners from both leagues sat down to make sure that this would never happen again. They drafted a set of guidelines that established a formal World Series under rules that remain more or less intact today.

1904

- No World Series is played, since the NL pennant-winning Giants call the AL a "minor league" and refuse to play.
- Giant John McGraw wins his first pennant as manager.
- The 154-game schedule is adopted.

- Jack Chesbro's wild pitch gives Boston the AL flag on the last day of the season.
- Chesbro wins a record 41 games, and sets a 20th-century record with 48 CGs.
- Joe McGinnity wins 35 and Christy Mathewson 33 for Giants to set a modern teammates tandem record.

- Honus Wagner leads NL in BA (.349), SA (.520), total bases (255), and steals (53).
- Nap Lajoie leads AL in BA (.376), SA (.552), hits (211), total bases (305), and doubles (49).
- Rube Waddell fans 349, a record for 154-game season.

The nickname "Happy" seems as if it were given to Jack Chesbro as an irony. Although he won a major league-record 41 games in 1904, his career took a downhill turn that year—his wild pitch handed the American League flag to Boston on the final day of the season—only to accelerate with each passing year. By 1910, he was pitching for Whitinsville, a semipro Mill League team, in a comeback attempt that failed to materialize.

- Cy Young pitches first perfect game in 20th century on May 5, 3-0 over A's and Waddell.

- Harry Davis of A's leads AL in homers (ten) for first of four straight seasons.

- Washington sets new 20th-century record for losses with 113.

- On June 11, Cub Bob Wicker throws no-hitter vs. New York for nine innings; loses no-hitter in tenth, but wins game.

- Boston AL uses just five pitchers all season.

- John Lush of Phils is youngest regular in NL history (18).

- Giants players, fomented by ump-baiter McGraw, beat an ump unconscious after a spring game.

- Cards pitcher Jack Taylor is accused of dumping games, but nothing comes of the charge.

- Giants clinch the NL flag in a record 137 games.

Wagner Stars at SS

Never before and never again would two middle infielders dominate every phase of the game as did Honus Wagner (pictured) and Nap Lajoie in the early 1900s. The only two major batting departments in which Wagner failed to lead the NL at least once were home runs and bases on balls. In 1904, he led the NL with a .349 batting average, a .520 slugging average, and 53 steals.

Honus Wagner

Bill Dinneen

Dinneen is Divine

Like Jack Chesbro, Bill Dinneen fell on hard times after the 1904 campaign, a year in which he went 23–14 in 336 innings without being relieved (a season record in the American League). A 20-game winner in each of his first three seasons with the Boston Americans, Dinneen won only 47 more games in his five remaining years in the majors and just once, in 1908, was a better than .500 pitcher.

Joe McGinnity

McGinnity Hits Zenith

Joe McGinnity *averaged* more than 27 victories a year in his first eight major league seasons—no other pitcher since 1893 has won as many games as quickly at the commencement of his career. In 1903, McGinnity also became this century's only 30-game winner to lose 20 games in the same season. He came back in 1904, reaching the peak of his career with 35 wins, best in the National League.

1904

- Young allows only 29 walks in 380 innings.

- The dead-ball era begins in earnest—Cleveland is the only AL team to average four runs a game.

- Giant Hooks Wiltse wins his first 12 major league decisions before suffering his first loss.

- Herman Long retires as the only ML player to make 1,000 or more career errors.

- Frank Huelsman plays for a record four AL teams in the same year.

- Ginger Beaumont sets an NL record when he leads the loop in hits for the third straight year.

- Boston's Bill Dinneen pitches an AL season record 337 innings without being relieved.

- Jesse Tannehill of Boston no-hits the White Sox on August 17.

- Brooklyn's Harry Lumley tops the NL in triples (18) and homers (nine).

McGraw Wins NL Flag

No baseball immortal aged more rapidly than John McGraw (born in 1873), who captured his first pennant in 1904 as manager of the New York Giants. Photos of him in the early 1900s show a man who seemed too young to have already played ten years in the majors; by the end of the decade, he looked to be deep into middle age.

John McGraw

Harry Davis

Lajoie Still Going Strong

Nap Lajoie topped the American League in 1904 with a .376 batting average, a .552 slugging average, 211 hits, 305 total bases, and 49 doubles. Only once in his 21-year career did he play on a team that came close to winning a pennant—in 1908, when the Cleveland club he piloted finished just a half-game behind Detroit. It was his greatest disappointment, in part because he played poorly in the season-ending series with St. Louis that could have brought Cleveland the flag.

Nap Lajoie

Davis Kicks In

Like many of the A's stars in the early part of the century, Harry Davis was a slow starter. Following a good season with Pittsburgh in 1897, he went into a tailspin and spent most of the rest of the 1890s in the minors before joining the Mackmen in 1901. By 1904, he was the American League's top first sacker (and its leader in home runs with ten).

- The Giants lead the NL in BA (.262), FA (.956), runs (744), homers (31), steals (283), and ERA (2.17).

- Chesbro pitches a 20th-century record 455 innings (since broken).

- Mathewson tops the NL in strikeouts (212) and is the only NLer to fan more than 200.

- Cleveland leads the AL in runs (647) and BA (.260), but finishes only fourth.

- Young's ten shutouts top the majors.

- The NL has 366 more stolen bases than the AL and scores 441 more runs.

- Kid Nichols wins 21 games for lowly Cardinals after being out of game for two seasons.

- Chesbro and Jack Powell set AL teammates tandem record with 64 wins between them.

- At age 52, Jim O'Rourke catches a full game for the Giants.

DEAD-BALL BASEBALL IN FULL SWING

The 1905 season was one of the deadest of the dead-ball years, especially in the American League, where only three men—Harry Bay, Wee Willie Keeler, and Elmer Flick—batted over .300. Flick won the AL batting title by hitting only .308, the lowest average to lead either league until Carl Yastrzemski's .301 in 1968. The entire AL batted only .241. The league's top run-scoring team, Philadelphia, scored only 623 runs and batted .255.

On the pitching side, every team had ERAs under 3.00. Rube Waddell won the ERA title at 1.48, beating out Doc White at 1.77, Cy Young at 1.82, Andy Coakley at 1.84, and Nick Altrock at 1.88. Of the all-time Top 20 pitchers in lifetime ERA, 15 pitched in 1905.

Three of the Top 20—Waddell, Chief Bender, and Eddie Plank—pitched for the Philadelphia Athletics, who fought a long pitcher's duel of a pennant race with Chicago to win the AL flag by a slim 2 games. Waddell, the league's win leader with 27, pitched 44 straight scoreless innings down the stretch in September.

The White Sox pitching was actually a shade better, compiling a staff ERA of 1.99, thanks to Altrock; Frank Owen, who went 21-13 with a 2.10 ERA; Frank Smith, who won 19 and had an ERA of 2.13; and Doc White. Chicago's fifth starter was spitballing sophomore Ed Walsh, who was to retire in 1917 with the lowest career ERA in history: 1.82.

The Athletics' edge over Chicago was a versatile offense of Harry Davis, who led the AL in runs scored with 92, RBI with 83, and doubles with 47; Lave Cross, who knocked in 77 runs; and run-scoring machine Topsy Hartsel, who drew an AL-high 121 bases on balls. Outfielder Danny Hoffman played only 119 games before hurting his hand and missing the rest of the season, but still led all AL hitters with 46 stolen bases.

Elmer Flick led the American League in triples with 18 and slugging average at .462, but Cleveland faded to fifth after Nap Lajoie's season was ruined by blood poisoning. In Detroit, several young stars pulled the Tigers out of the second division and into third place. George Mullin and Ed Killian each won more than 20 games, and 25-year-old Sam Crawford was fourth in hitting at .297 and second in doubles with 38. Eighteen-year-old Ty Cobb was called up in late August, played 41 games, and batted .240—the first and last time he would hit below .300 in his 24-year career.

The National League race was over on April 23, when McGraw's defending champions took over first place for good; the Giants won 105 games to finish 9 games ahead of Pittsburgh and 13 ahead of Chicago. Led by Ed Reulbach, the Cubs boasted the NL's best pitching—with four of the top five on the ERA list. But New York's combination of Mathewson, McGinnity, and Red Ames on the mound and .356-hitting Mike Donlin at the plate proved unbeatable.

Fifth-place Cincinnati's Cy Seymour won the batting title at .377; he also led in RBI with 121, hits with 219, doubles with 40, and triples with 21. Vic Willis lost a 20th-century-high 29 games on a 3.21 ERA for seventh-place Boston.

Not surprisingly, the 1905 World Series was the best-pitched Series ever. All five games were shutouts and the loser, Philadelphia, had an ERA of 1.47. It was also one of the most one-sided Series. Behind Christy Mathewson's three shutouts and 15 baserunners allowed in 27 innings, New York took the Series by a composite score of 15-3. The Giants' ERA for the Series was a perfect 0.00.

1905

- A's win their first pennant.
- Giants repeat as NL champs.
- Giants win World Series four games to one, with every game a shutout.
- Christy Mathewson hurls three shutout Series wins.
- Ty Cobb debuts with the Tigers.

- New York's Roger Bresnahan experiments with first "batting helmet" after being beaned.
- Cincinnati's Cy Seymour misses NL Triple Crown by a margin of one home run.
- Cleveland's Elmer Flick leads AL with .308 BA.

- Braves have record four 20-game losers, as Vic Willis loses a 20th-century record 29 games.
- A's lead AL with 623 runs, fewest ever by a loop leader.
- St. Louis rookie George Stone leads AL in hits (187) and total bases (259).

Christy Mathewson won 30 or more games for the third consecutive season in 1905. In addition to his 31 victories, he topped the National League in ERA (1.27) and shutouts (eight) that year. It seemed impossible for him to continue to pitch at that level, yet he did. In the eight years between 1903 and 1910, he won 229 games and lost but 83 for a .734 winning percentage.

- Rube Waddell again leads AL in Ks (287).

- Mathewson becomes first in century to pitch two no-hitters, blanking Chicago on June 13.

- White Sox post new AL record 1.99 ERA and give up just 451 runs.

- Cubs post new NL record 2.04 ERA and allow just 442 runs.

- Waddell leads AL in wins (27), ERA (1.48), and win pct. (.730).

- Nap Lajoie becomes Cleveland's player/manager; team is now known as "Naps" in his honor.

- Mathewson leads NL in wins (31), ERA (1.27), and shutouts (eight).

- Cy Young typifies the plight of dead-ball hurlers when he posts an 18-19 record despite a 1.82 ERA.

- On April 26, Jack McCarthy of the Cubs makes a record three double plays by an outfielder.

A's Win AL

The Philadelphia A's won 92 games and lost 56 in their quest for the 1905 American League Championship. Easy to spot in the back row are Chief Bender *(far left)* (who posted an 18–11 year with a 2.83 ERA and 142 strikeouts), Rube Waddell *(fourth from the left)* (27–10, 1.48 ERA, 287 Ks), and Eddie Plank *(to the right of Waddell)* (24–12, 2.26 ERA, 210 Ks).

Philadelphia A's

Nap Lajoie

Lajoie Bolsters Naps

One sportswriter had the audacity to suggest that Cleveland was not renamed "the Naps" in honor of Nap Lajoie, its stellar player/manager, but because the club played much of its games as if it were napping. In any case, the 1905 season was a disaster in the Forest City. The team finished below .500 and Lajoie, who was hitting .329, nearly died of blood poisoning after being spiked. Nap was back the next season, though, leading the league in hits.

Mike Donlin

Donlin Takes Center Stage

Turkey Mike Donlin was the only man in history to be a runner-up for a batting title in both the AL and NL. Never a batting champ himself, he nonetheless had the highest career average of any outfielder whose peak years came in the first decade of the 20th century. He placed first in the NL in 1905 in runs (124), came in second in hits (216), and ranked third in batting average (.356). Married to Mabel Hite, an actress who died young of cancer, Donlin himself was drawn away from the game by the stage.

1905

- The Red Sox use only 18 players all year—an ML record low.

- John McGraw is suspended for 15 days and fined $150 by the NL for abusing umpires.

- Waddell beats Young in a 20-inning game on July 4.

- Weldon Henley of the A's no-hits the Browns on July 22.

- Frank Smith of the White Sox no-hits Detroit on Sept. 6.

- Irv Young of the Braves sets modern ML rookie records with 41 starts, 41 complete games, and 378 innings.

- Bill Dinneen of Boston no-hits the White Sox on Sept. 27.

- Cincinnati's Fred Odwell, NL home run leader with nine, never hits another homer in the majors.

- Cub Frank Chance is hit by pitches a record five times in a Decoration Day doubleheader.

Willis, Braves Fall Apart

In the years between 1902 and 1905, Vic Willis lost 91 games; that he managed to win 69 during that four-year span is even more of a marvel. With Willis hurling for a 12–29 record in 1905, Boston finished 54^1/$_2$ games out of first place in the NL. One year later, minus Willis, the club ended up 66^1/$_2$ games in arrears.

Elmer Flick

Flick Snags BA Title

Elmer Flick averaged 17 triples a year during the ten full seasons he played in the majors. Although he won his only batting title in 1905 with a .308 average, the campaign was not his highwater mark in a single offensive department. Owing to illness and injuries, Flick was pretty well washed up as a player when he was 31 years old. He lived until 1971, dying at age 94.

Vic Willis

Rube Waddell

Waddell Sits Out Series

Rube Waddell, far and away the finest pitcher in the American League in 1905 with 27 wins, a 1.48 ERA, and 287 strikeouts—all circuit-bests that year—lost his sole chance to participate in a World Series when he was injured on the eve of the that season's finale in a bit of horseplay with teammate Andy Coakley.

Five Balls Peg Chance

Along with being an able manager, Frank Chance was quite possibly the best all-around first baseman of his time. His fiery nature led to numerous beanings, which shortened his career. Although Chance hit .316 in 1905, he is remembered more for being hit by pitches a record five times during a doubleheader. Joe Tinker once said of his teammate, "Chance and [John] McGraw were born to battle on baseball fields."

Frank Chance

- Jim Dunleavy of Oakland in the Pacific Coast League plays in an organized baseball record 227 games.

- Noodles Hahn, who won 100 games before he was 25, is felled by arm trouble at 26.

- Flick leads the AL in slugging with a .462 mark.

- The Browns' Harry Howell averages 4.68 assists per game—an all-time record for pitchers.

- Seymour collects 325 total bases, the most in the National League during the dead-ball era.

- Brooklyn rookie Harry McIntire loses 25 games.

- On August 24, the Cubs beat the Phils 2-1 in 20 innings.

- The Giants boast three 20-game winners: Mathewson (31), Red Ames (22), and Joe McGinnity (21).

- Dave Fultz leaves the majors after stealing 44 bases—the most ever by a player in his final ML season.

THREE FINGER LEADS CUBS TO 116 WINS

The year 1906 saw the first one-city World Series. Over the next 83 years, there would be 14 more—13 played in New York. But the '06 Series was the first, last, and only all-Chicago affair.

In early June, player/manager Frank Chance's Cubs kicked off the greatest NL dynasty of the 1900s by building a big lead over John McGraw's Giants and then coasting to a major league-record 116 wins against only 36 losses.

First baseman Chance led an offense that outscored the nearest team by 80 runs; he tied Honus Wagner for the league lead in both runs with 103 and on-base average at .406. Chance anchored the NL's tightest-fielding infield, made up of .327 hitter and RBI leader Harry Steinfeldt and the immortal double-play combination of Joe Tinker and Johnny Evers. Up-and-coming star Frank "Wildfire" Schulte led the Cubs outfielders with 13 triples and four home runs, and Jimmy Sheckard banged out 27 doubles. Chicago pitchers allowed only 381 runs, 89 fewer than the nearest team, and turned in a 1.76 ERA.

Four of the five Cubs starters—Three Finger Brown, Ed Reulbach, Jack Pfiester, and Orvie Overall—had ERAs below 2.00, and Brown's ERA of 1.04 is the second-lowest in history.

The Cubs finished a mere 20 games ahead of the Giants, who won 96 games. The entire second division—Brooklyn, Cincinnati, St. Louis, and Boston—came in 50 or more games off the pace. Among the few offensive categories not dominated by Cubs were batting average, led by Wagner at .339, and slugging average, led by Brooklyn's Harry Lumley at .477.

Chicago's American League counterpart had a more difficult summer, as the White Sox wallowed in fourth place behind Philadelphia, New York, and Cleveland. Then in early August, the Sox reeled off an AL-record 19 straight victories to secure the pennant. Unlike their crosstown rivals, the White Sox did not monopolize the offensive leader board, but their attack—which produced 570 runs, third-most in the league—hardly deserved its nickname, the "Hitless Wonders."

Chicago had no sluggers to compare with St. Louis' George Stone, the league leader in batting at .358 and slugging at .501, nor with Cleveland's Elmer Flick, who knocked 33 doubles and a league-high 22 triples. But slugging was not the name of the game in the dead-ball era. Fielder Jones' Sox scratched out their runs by drawing walks (outfielders Jones and Ed Hahn were two and three in the AL in free passes) and working a running game (both second baseman Frank Isbell and first baseman Jiggs Donahue were in the Top Five in stolen bases). Chicago's only big RBI man was shortstop George Davis, who drove in 80 runs, third in the league behind Lajoie and Philadelphia slugger Harry Davis.

It was only in pitching where the White Sox could compete with the Cubs. But even with ace Doc White (who won the ERA title at 1.52) and Ed Walsh (the author of a league-leading ten shutouts), the American Leaguers went into the World Series as distinct underdogs.

Played in snowy October weather in Chicago, games one through four were understandably low-scoring. Nick Altrock beat the Cubs 2-1 in the opener, played in the Cubs' West Side Park, and Walsh won game three 3-0. But going into the fifth game, the Series was tied 2-2. Then suddenly, the Hitless Wonders' bats caught fire, defeating Reulbach 8-6 and banging around both Brown and Overall to win the deciding game 8-3. The White Sox narrowly outhit their opponents, .198 to .196, but more than halved the mighty Cubs' ERA, 1.50 to 3.40.

1906

- Cubs cop NL flag, win record 116 games, and post record .763 win pct.
- White Sox win AL flag despite .230 team BA.
- White Sox win AL record 19 straight games.
- Sox win World Series in huge upset.

- On Oct. 10, Cub Ed Reulbach pitches the first one-hitter in Series history.
- St. Louis' George Stone leads AL in BA (.358), SA (.501), and total bases (291).
- Honus Wagner tops NL in BA (.339) and total bases (237).

- New York's Al Orth leads AL in wins (27) and CGs (36).
- Rube Waddell drops to 196 Ks, but still leads AL.
- Cubs break own record when they post 1.76 ERA and allow just 381 runs.

The 1906 Cubs could actually have won as many as 118 games had they been
allowed to play two contests that were postponed. Ed Reulbach and Johnny Kling
(back row, far right) are now recognized as one of the great batteries in history.
Reulbach went 19–4 that year, with a 1.65 ERA and 94 Ks; Kling batted .312 with
15 doubles, eight triples, and a pair of home runs.

- Braves finish last, a record 66¹/₂ games out of first, and again have four 20-game losers.

- Joe McGinnity leads NL in wins (27).

- Cub Three Finger Brown leads NL with 1.04 ERA, lowest ever by pitcher with more than 250 innings.

- On August 1, Harry McIntire of Brooklyn throws no-hitter for ten innings, but loses no-hitter in 11th.

- Boston AL finishes last two years after winning pennant.

- Jack Taylor's record streak of 118 consecutive complete games ends on August 9.

- Ty Cobb leaves Tigers to testify for his mother, who's on trial for shooting and killing his father.

- John McGraw gets into a savage fight with Phils rookie infielder Paul Sentell.

- St. Louis' Jake Beckley is hired as an NL umpire while out with an injury.

Jake Beckley

Beckley Hired as Ump

Jake Beckley remains a rather shadowy figure—although he played 20 years in the majors and made 2,930 hits—and this photograph only heightens the enigmatic tinge he possessed. He is shown wearing a St. Louis uniform despite the fact that he played for Pittsburgh the year the photo was taken (1888). In 1906, he was hired as an umpire for the National League.

Three Finger Brown

Brown Starts His Run

Beginning in 1906, Three Finger Brown won 20 or more games for the Cubs for six consecutive years. He went 26–6 that year to post the highest winning percentage of his career (.813), and his nine shutouts and 1.04 ERA led the National League that season. When he showed signs of slipping in 1912, the team rewarded him by trying to send him to the minors. Brown got a bit of revenge, though, when he helped the Chicago Whales win the Federal League pennant in 1915 while the Cubs finished below .500.

McIntire Loses No-No

Harry McIntire's luck in 1906 typified that of most Brooklyn pitchers in the early years of the century: Not only was he defeated despite throwing a no-hitter, he also was a 20-game loser for the second season in a row. In 1908, another Brooklyn pitcher, Jim Pastorius, had a 2.44 ERA yet finished with a 4–20 record as the Brooks scored just 375 runs in 154 games.

Harry McIntire

1906

- Harry "Rube" Vickers pitches an OB record 526 innings with Seattle in the Pacific Coast League.

- On July 18, Washington's Cy Falkenberg becomes the first AL pitcher to hit a grandslam.

- The Pirates shut out Boston a record ten times during the season.

- On April 12, Johnny Bates becomes the first player in the century to homer in his first ML at-bat.

- The Cubs go 60-15 on the road, the best road record in ML history.

- Johnny Lush of the Phils no-hits Brooklyn on May 1.

- Mal Eason of Brooklyn no-hits St. Louis on July 20.

- Giant Mike Donlin marries actress Mabel Hite and they form a successful vaudeville team.

- Cobb hits .320 in first full season, misses a lot of games due to injury.

World Series

Chance Meets Fate

Frank Chance holds both the season and career records for the most stolen bases by a first baseman—57 swipes in 1906, 401 thefts total. Given the added challenge of managing, he seemed only to improve as a player—at least initially. The 1906 campaign, however, turned out to be the last in which he was able to perform to full capacity.

Frank Chance

Walsh Defeats Pfeister

The match: Game three of the 1906 World Series. The place: West Side Park, then the home ground of the Cubs. On the mound for the Cubs is Jack Pfeister, a 3–0 loser that day to Ed Walsh of the White Sox, who threw a two-hitter to give the Sox a 2–1 lead in the Series. Walsh shut out the Cubs.

- Center fielder Chick Stahl is named Boston AL manager after Jimmy Collins is fired.

- Chicago's Doc White tops the AL in ERA (1.52).

- Brooklyn's Tim Jordan leads the NL in homers with 12.

- Philadelphia's Harry Davis leads the AL in homers (12) and RBI (96).

- Spike Shannon collects 151 hits but just 162 total bases.

- On May 15, the Giants' Hooks Wiltse becomes the first pitcher since 1893 to fan seven batters in a row in one game.

- In September, the A's go 48 straight innings without scoring a run.

- Christy Mathewson's brother Henry walks an NL record 14 batters in his only ML start.

- Phillie Roy Thomas leads NL in walks with 107—26 more than anyone else.

When former Orioles short-stop Hughie Jennings took over from Bill Armour as manager of the Detroit Tigers, the first thing he did was insert the young Ty Cobb into the everyday lineup. This move helped the Tigers climb 21 games in the standings, from sixth place in 1906 to first in 1907.

With Cobb batting behind him in the cleanup slot, Sam Crawford hit .323 and slugged .460 (both second in the league to Cobb), scored an AL-high 102 runs, and banged out 34 doubles and 17 triples. All summer long, Cobb drove in Crawford and lead-off man Davy Jones—who was second in runs scored at 101—and the Detroit offense tallied 694 runs, 89 more than the also-ran Yankees' second-place total. Cobb himself drove in 119 runs, collected 212 hits, 283 total bases, and 49 stolen bases, all league-leading figures. He also led in batting at .350 and slugging at .468.

The resurgent A's had a deep staff, led by Eddie Plank (24-16, 2.20 ERA) and 22-year-young Jimmy Dygert (20-9, 2.34 ERA), along with Rube Waddell, Chief Bender, and Jack Coombs. Philadelphia made it a close race, but with 10 players over age 30 the A's ran out of gas at the end of the season. The defending cham-

'YEAR OF COBB' IS WON BY THE CUBS

pion White Sox posted almost the same numbers as in 1906, scoring the third-most runs in the league and allowing the fewest. But in the Year of Cobb, they could finish no higher than third. Washington finished in the cellar, but the Senators debuted a young fastball pitcher named Walter Johnson, who went 5-9 with a 1.86 ERA and 5.5 strikeouts per game.

The NL race could be summed up in one word: Chicago. Frank Chance's juggernaut fell off to a 107-45 record, 17 games in front of a Pittsburgh team that featured the NL's best offense; a resurgent Honus Wagner won his fifth batting title at .350 and also led the league in doubles (38), stolen bases (61), on-base average (.403), and slugging (.513). With no hitters over .300, the Chicago attack slipped by more than a hundred runs, but the Cubs pitching continued its utter domination of NL hitters. Led by Jack Pfiester's league-leading 1.15 ERA (the fifth-lowest

in history) and Carl Lundgren's 1.17 ERA (the eighth-best ever), Chicago pitchers occupied four of the top five spots on the ERA leader board. Each member of the five-man staff compiled ERAs under 2.00 and the team allowed 390 runs, only nine more than in their 1906 tour de force.

The Phillies rode to third place in the National League as outfielder Sherry Magee led the NL with 85 RBI and hurler Tully Sparks had a 22-8 record with a 2.00 ERA. New York slipped to fourth—as age and years of over-use finally started to take its toll on Iron Man Joe McGinnity. He had an 18-18 record with an unusually high 3.16 ERA.

The World Series was a mismatch, with Detroit managing only a first-game 3-3 tie out of the five games played. For the remainder of the Series, the Tigers were held to three runs—never more than one run in a single game—as each of four Cubs starters went 1-0 and the staff posted a composite ERA of 0.75. Cobb and Crawford batted only .200 and .238 and managed only two extra-base hits between them. But the biggest surprise of the Series was that Cobb was shut out on the basepaths by Chicago catcher Johnny Kling. Led by Jimmy Slagle's six stolen bases, the Cubs outstole the Tigers 16-6.

1907

- Cubs repeat as NL champs.
- Tigers win their first AL flag.
- Cubs first to sweep a World Series (though one game is a tie).
- Cubs limit Tigers to six runs in five-game Series.

- Cubs are so pitcher-rich that 18-game winner Carl Lundgren (1.17 ERA) isn't even needed in the Series.
- Chicago's Harry Steinfeldt leads all Series hitters with a .471 BA.
- Ty Cobb wins first batting crown (.350) and first steals crown (49).

- Honus Wagner easily tops NL in BA (.350), SA (.513), total bases (264), and steals (61).
- Christy Mathewson leads NL in wins (24) and Ks (178).
- Cards rookie Stoney McGlynn leads NL in innings (352), CGs (33), and losses (25).

Ty Cobb, who racked up an American League-leading .350 average and 119 RBI in 1907, was far from being the only player in his day who deliberately tried to cut the legs out from under infielders when he slid. Many infielders in turn blocked the basepaths as if they were guarding something made of gold—which, to a degree, they were. Runs were scarce in 1907, and would grow even scarcer in the years ahead.

- Jack Pfiester tops NL in ERA (1.15), as Cubs have four of loop's top five in ERA.

- Cleveland's Addie Joss ties for lead in wins (27) and is third in ERA (1.83).

- Chicago's Ed Walsh hurls 422 innings, leads AL in CGs (37) and ERA (1.60).

- Rube Waddell wins his seventh, and last, AL K crown (232).

- Chick Stahl, Boston AL player/manager, commits suicide during spring training.

- Al Spalding creates a commission to unearth the origins of baseball.

- Walter Johnson debuts with Washington.

- Cy Young, now 40, wins 22 games and posts a 1.99 ERA.

- Philly's Harry Davis wins the last of his four consecutive AL homer crowns, as he cracks eight.

Tigers Seize AL Flag

The first Motor City crew to capture an American League pennant, the 1907 Tigers, looked like a surly bunch, and most were. Ty Cobb *(middle row, third from the left)* was the batting king at .350. Sam Crawford *(back row, third from the left)* hit .323. Holding the dog is manager Hugh Jennings.

Detroit Tigers

Nick Maddox

Maddox Stirs Up Hopes

Nick Maddox won five late-season games in 1907, his no-hitter against Brooklyn on September 20 among the victories, and seemed to deliver on his promise when he knocked off 20 victories for the Pirates the following year. By 1911, however, he was back in the minors for good.

Spalding Rewrites History

The commission of Al Spalding concluded that Abner Doubleday invented baseball. The decision was, for the most part, based on the vague testimony of one witness to what was purported to have been the first game. Although many baseball people knew better, the Hall of Fame was nevertheless put in Cooperstown, New York, a town Doubleday may never have visited, let alone made the site of a new sport.

Al Spalding

1907

- The Pirates top the NL with a .254 BA, the lowest ever by an NL leader.

- Catching for New York AL, Branch Rickey allows a record 13 stolen bases to Washington on June 28.

- After owning the Braves since 1877, Arthur Soden sells them to the Dovey brothers.

- Big Jeff Pfeffer of Boston NL no-hits Cincinnati on May 8.

- Nick Maddox of Pirates no-hits Brooklyn on Sept. 20.

- On August 11, Ed Karger of the Cards pitches a seven-inning perfect game.

- The Boston AL team is first called the "Red Sox."

- A rule is put in that *any* appearance by a player in a game counts as a game played.

- Jim Price of the *New York Press* revives the practice of recording RBI.

Donovan Goes 25-4

Historians are still trying to piece together how Bill Donovan (pictured) was able to post a 25–4 record for the 1907 Tigers on a 2.19 ERA, while teammate George Mullin, whose ERA was only four-tenths of a run higher, managed to become the only hurler in this century to lose 20 games for a pennant-winning team.

Bill Donovan

Ed Walsh

Walsh Goes All Out

Ed Walsh is reputedly the player Ring Lardner used as his model to construct Jack Keefe, the cocky bumpkin protagonist in *You Know Me, Al*. Walsh was described by one writer as the only man who "could strut while standing still." He worked 866 innings in 1907 and 1908, a full career for some modern-day pitchers. He led the American League with 37 complete games and a 1.60 ERA in 1907.

Honus Wagner

Wagner Hits NL-High .350

An examination of the failure of the Pirates to win a pennant since 1903 reveals that, outside of Honus Wagner, Pittsburgh didn't have much in its arsenal in 1907. Wagner outhit the entire National League by 107 points and his team by 96 points to post a .350 average that season. At that, the Pirates had the top club batting average in the league.

- Claude Ritchey tops NL second basemen in FA for record sixth consecutive year.

- Traded to the Braves, Ginger Beaumont returns to the NL top spot in hits (187).

- Cobb's 119 RBI top ML by 27, as AL runner-up Socks Seybold has 92.

- Wild Bill Donovan of Detroit leads the AL in win pct. (.862).

- Cleveland refuses a trade offered by the Tigers—Elmer Flick for Cobb even up.

- Cincinnati manager Ned Hanlon is fired after a sixth-place finish and never again manages in majors.

- Braves outfielder Cozy Dolan dies of typhoid fever.

- George Mullin loses 20 games for Detroit, even though the Tigers lose just 58 all year.

- Jake Beckley becomes the first to play 20 years in the ML without ever playing on a pennant winner.

The 1908 season was the biggest year for pitching in a decade of pitchers' years. Both leagues batted .239, both record lows. Only one of the 16 major league pitching staffs, the Yankees', had an ERA over 3.00. Seven pitchers threw no-hitters and seven of the all-time 50 lowest season ERAs came in 1908. Individual milestones included Ed Walsh's 40 wins (the second-greatest total in history) and 464 innings pitched (the most ever); Christy Mathewson's 37 wins; Addie Joss's 1.16 ERA (seventh-lowest in history); and Cy Young's 1.26 ERA (the tenth-best).

This wealth of pitching produced two of the closest, most exciting, and most controversial pennant races of all time. A three-team NL race between Chicago, Pittsburgh, and New York hinged on the still-talked-about Fred Merkle blunder, which occurred in a September 23 game between the Giants and the Cubs.

The score was tied 1-1 and the sun was setting over the Polo Grounds in New York. Fred Merkle, a rookie substitute, was standing on first and Moose McCormick occupied third with two outs in the bottom of the ninth, when Giants shortstop Al Bridwell singled to center. Thinking the game was won, and with a crowd of happy fans swarming the infield, Merkle bypassed second base and made for the New York clubhouse. But Chicago

MERKLE'S MUFF COSTS GIANTS THE PENNANT

second baseman Johnny Evers got the attention of the umpire who, after seeing Evers tag second base with a ball (there was some dispute over whether it was actually the game ball), declared Merkle forced out at second, nullifying the winning run.

This ignited a storm of protests, counter-protests, and league hearings. Finally, NL president Harry Pulliam ruled that the game would be replayed after the season if it proved to have a bearing on the pennant race. Unfortunately for the Giants, it did. New York and Chicago finished in a tie, which was broken when Chicago's Three Finger Brown defeated Mathewson 4-2 in the make-up game. The Cubs finished with a 99-55 record, 1 game up on the Giants and Pirates, both at 98-56.

While the 1908 Cubs exhibited their usual combination of great pitching and team defense, the Giants were carried by Christy Mathewson, who led the league in wins, games, complete games,

strikeouts, and ERA. He threw a league-high 11 shutouts and recorded five saves, pitching in a dozen games out of the bullpen between starts. Once again, Pittsburgh was the Honus Wagner Show, as Wagner won his usual batting title at .354 and led in on-base average at .410 and slugging average at .542. He also made a clean sweep of six other key offensive categories: hits, RBI, doubles, triples, total bases, and stolen bases.

In the AL, a four-team race came down to the wire, with Detroit (90-63) finally slipping past Cleveland (90-64) by .004 percentage points, the smallest margin of victory in AL or NL history. Chicago finished 1½ back and St. Louis faded late to end up 6½ behind.

As in 1907, Ty Cobb and Sam Crawford led the AL in nearly everything. Cobb won the batting title at .324 and was No. 1 in hits, doubles, triples, total bases, RBI, and slugging. Crawford led in home runs and was second in runs, RBI, hits, total bases, batting, and slugging.

For the second straight year, Cobb's team was humiliated in the World Series, this time 4-1. Cubs batters hit .293 off Tigers pitching, while Brown's 0.00 ERA in 11 innings paced the Chicago staff to a 2.60 ERA. Cobb's personal performance improved, as he batted .368 with four RBI and a pair of stolen bases.

1908

- Fred Merkle commits his famous boner, costing Giants crucial win in pennant stretch.

- Cubs win pennant by 1 game when they beat Giants in makeup of Merkle game.

- White Sox Ed Walsh wins 40 games, hurls 42 CGs and 464 innings.

- Tigers win AL flag by a half-game, the smallest margin of victory in AL or NL history.

- Cubs win the World Series—their last postseason triumph.

- Hooks Wiltse of Giants throws no-hitter on Independence Day, blanking Philadelphia.

- In July, Giants stun baseball world by paying $11,000 for minor leaguer Rube Marquard.

- George Baird of Chicago invents electric scoreboard.

- Cleveland's Addie Joss pitches a perfect game over Chicago on Oct. 2, the first ever in a pennant race.

Fred Merkle is erroneously believed by many to have been a raw rookie in 1908; actually, he was with the New York ballclub much of the 1907 season. Green or not, however, he alone should not bear the guilt for his boner. All the Giants, from John McGraw on down, should have alerted him to tag second in the event of a hit, as the Cubs had tried to capitalize on this same kind of lapse in a prior game.

- Joss is second in AL in wins (24) and has top ERA (1.16).

- Cobb leads the AL in doubles (36) and triples (20).

- Sam Crawford of Detroit becomes only player ever to be a league home run leader in both NL and AL, as he leads AL with seven.

- Ty Cobb wins second bat crown (.324) and also leads in SA (.475) and total bases (276).

- Teammates Cobb and Crawford finish one-two in AL in RBI (109-80), total bases (276-270), and SA (.475-.457).

- Honus Wagner again tops NL in BA (.354), hits (201), and steals (53).

- Wagner leads NL in doubles (39), triples (19), SA (.542), and total bases (308).

- The Cardinals score a record-low 371 runs and finish last.

- On Sept. 26, Ed Reulbach of Cubs notches two shutouts in one day.

Rucker Picks Up Slack

Nap Rucker's offensive support in 1908 included a trio of outfielders who hit .243, .216, and .195—and had just 74 RBI combined. Rucker, nevertheless, won 17 games. In 1916, when Brooklyn finally assembled enough hitters to go with its always-excellent pitchers and won the pennant, he was nearly through.

Ty Cobb

Cobb Takes AL BA Title

Ty Cobb won the American League batting crown in 1908 with a .324 average, a low figure even for that time. Sam Crawford was second with a .311 mark and Matty McIntyre came in three places behind him at .295 to make it a trio of Tigers that finished among the top five. Detroit's .264 team batting average led the league. The other seven clubs hit a combined .236, which suddenly gives Cobb's circuit-topping figure quite a different look. Cobb's .324 average would be his lowest mark in the next 20 years. In 1928, his final season, he batted .323.

Hooks Wiltse

Wiltse an Odd Man Out

Hooks Wiltse was a very good pitcher—he went 23–14 in 1908 with a 2.24 ERA and 118 strikeouts—who happened to be on a team that, during his peak years, had a couple of great hurlers. The upside was that he got to play on five pennant-winning clubs. The downside was that with people like Christy Mathewson and Joe McGinnity around, he was always the odd man out whenever there was a big game to be pitched.

Nap Rucker

Roger Bresnahan

Bresnahan Catches 139

During most of his career, Roger Bresnahan at times played other positions besides catcher; he was capable of playing them all, in fact. In 1908, though, he was stationed only behind the plate—for 139 games, no less—and it left its mark on him. He never again was a full-time player.

1908

- Christy Mathewson leads NL in wins (37) and ERA (1.43).
- White Sox finish third, just 1¹/₂ games out, despite hitting .224 and having just three homers.
- Cubs DP combo Joe Tinker, Johnny Evers, and Frank Chance are immortalized in a poem.
- Giant Roger Bresnahan, wearing shinguards and a padded mask, catches a record 139 games.
- The NL as a whole has a record-low .239 BA and .306 SA.
- The song "Take Me Out to the Ball Game" is first introduced to the public.
- Reulbach beats Brooklyn a record nine times.
- In the AL, Walsh beats *both* New York and Boston a record nine times.
- Cy Young throws a no-hitter vs. New York on June 30.
- Cleveland's Dusty Rhoads no-hits Boston on Sept. 18.

Reulbach Wins a Pair

What makes Ed Reulbach's doubleheader win against Brooklyn on September 26, 1908, all the more extraordinary is that never during his career was he considered a workhorse. He seems in retrospect merely to have been a good pitcher—at times, a very good hurler—who on one particular day, with a pennant in the offing, was able to rise to greatness.

Ed Reulbach

Crawford Leads in HRs

Not only did Sam Crawford top the American League in home runs in 1908, he also set a new club record for the Tigers. He totaled seven four-baggers that year. Ty Cobb swatted nine circuit clouts the following season to set a new team mark that endured until 1920, when Bobby Veach banged 11.

Sam Crawford

Christy Mathewson

Mathewson Still a Winner

The 1908 season was the last in which Christy Mathewson won 30 or more games. His 37 victories were one short of the number the Giants needed to claim the National League flag, as he was beaten by the Cubs on the last day of the season. His circuit-topping numbers included 34 complete games, 11 shutouts, five saves, 391 innings, 259 strikeouts, and a 1.43 ERA.

- Frank Smith of the White Sox no-hits the A's on Sept. 20.

- Nap Rucker of Brooklyn no-hits Boston on Sept. 5 and fans 14 hitters.

- Bill Donovan pitches a two-hitter on the season's last day to beat the White Sox and give Detroit the flag.

- Walter Johnson pitches three shutouts in a four-day period vs. New York.

- Walsh's 464 innings set a 20th-century record, breaking Jack Chesbro's old mark.

- The A's finish sixth with only 68 wins—but 23 of them are by shutouts.

- White Sox Billy Sullivan's .228 SA is the lowest in AL history by a player with at least 400 at-bats.

- The Giants' Fred Tenney hits just .256 but leads the NL in runs (101).

- Interim manager Kid Elberfeld goes 27-71 for New York AL; team finishes 51-103.

The 1909 Cubs won 104 games. They had done worse before and won the pennant, but this time Honus Wagner and the resurgent Pirates finally put it all together and went 110-42 to take the NL pennant by 6½ games.

Wagner led the Pittsburgh offense on its way to a league-best 699 runs scored, winning another batting title at .339 and stroking 39 doubles and 100 RBI. Fred Clarke led the league in walks with 80. The NL leader board in runs scored was crowded with Pirates, from Tommy Leach with 126 to Clarke with 97 to Bobby Byrne and Wagner, both with 92.

A much improved Pittsburgh pitching staff included Howie Camnitz, who went 25-6 to tie for the NL lead in winning percentage at .806, and 22-game winner Vic Willis. The Pirates led from May 5 until the final day of the season.

Chicago's pitching continued to be its strongest points. Three Finger Brown had a 27-9, 1.31 ERA season; Orvall Overall was 20-11 with a 1.42 ERA; and Ed Reulbach won 19 games and had a 1.78 ERA. No Cub, however, notched more than 60 RBI. The New York Giants won 92 games and finished third. Christy Mathewson took the ERA title at 1.15, the fifth-best ERA ever. Larry Doyle's league-leading 172 hits and .302 average paced the Giants' offense.

The AL race was a two-team affair between Detroit, the de-

POWERFUL PIRATES PUT IT ALL TOGETHER

fending champion and winner for the past two seasons, and Connie Mack's rising Philadelphia dynasty. The A's infield featured third baseman Frank "Home Run" Baker (age 23), second baseman Eddie Collins (22), and shortstop Jack Barry (22)—three of the four men who would make up Philadelphia's famed "$100,000 Infield" of the 1910s. Mack's pitching staff was anchored by Harry Krause, whose 1.39 ERA nosed out White Sox Ed Walsh's 1.41 for the ERA title. Baker and outfielder Danny Murphy combined for 33 triples and supplied the power for a late-season charge that carried the A's briefly into the lead over Detroit.

Ty Cobb turned in his best performance to date and dominated the AL at least as much as Wagner did the NL. Cobb led the league in batting at .377 and slugging at .517; he was also first in runs with 116, RBI with 107, stolen bases with 76, and on-base average at .431. The Tigers had two of the AL's three 20-game winners in Mullin and Ed Willett.

The BoSox had notable performances by several youngsters: Tris Speaker (age 21) hit .309 and

had 77 RBI; Harry Hooper (age 21) batted .282 in part-time work; Larry Gardner (age 23) had a .432 slugging average; and Smokey Joe Wood (age 19) won 13 games, losing only five, and had a 1.97 ERA. Boston finished third, 9½ games back. Cleveland shortstop Neal Ball made history in a July 19 game against Boston when he turned the 20th century's first unassisted triple play. Interestingly, six of history's eight unassisted triple plays came in the 1920s.

In 1909, the first two modern steel-and-concrete ballparks, Shibe Park in Philadelphia and Forbes Field in Pittsburgh, opened their doors. Another first was the seven-game World Series, which was won by Pittsburgh. While the fans who came to see a Cobb/Wagner match-up were disappointed—Wagner had a decent Series, hitting .333, but Cobb flopped completely, batting .231—the Series was an exciting nip-and-tuck contest in which the teams alternated victories.

The hero of the 1909 Series was 27-year-old rookie Babe Adams, who had gone 12-3 during the season with a 1.11 ERA in limited spot-starting duty. Adams's junk held the great Cobb to a single hit in 11 at-bats as he won games one, five, and seven to finish 3-0 with a 1.33 ERA for the Series. This would be the last World Series for Detroit until 1935 and the last ever for Cobb and Wagner.

1909

- Tigers win third straight flag.
- Pirates win their last NL flag under Fred Clarke.
- Pirates win most exciting World Series to date in seven games.
- In World Series, Honus Wagner hits .333; Ty Cobb hits .231.

- Pittsburgh rookie Babe Adams wins three Series games.
- Wagner leads NL in BA (.339), SA (.489), total bases (242), and RBI (100).
- Cobb wins the Triple Crown in AL, batting .377 with nine homers and 107 RBI.

- Cobb also leads AL in SA (.517), total bases (296), hits (216), runs (116), and steals (76).
- Cubs win 104 games, most ever by a runner-up team.
- Detroit's George Mullin leads the AL in wins (29) and win pct. (.784).

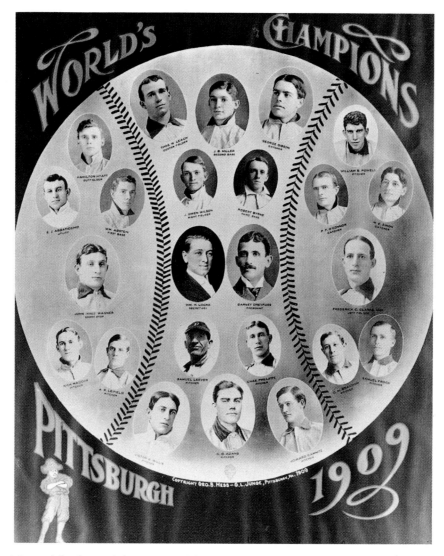

Many of the faces of the 1909 World Champion Pirates are unfamiliar to all but the most ruthless of baseball mavens now. They were famous that year, though: They placed first in the National League with 699 runs scored, 1,332 hits, 218 doubles, 92 triples, and a collective .260 batting average. They came in second in home runs (with 25, just one short of the lead) and team ERA (2.07).

- Chicago's Frank Smith tops AL in CGs (37), Ks (177), and innings (365).

- Harry Krause of A's sets AL rookie record for lowest ERA (1.39).

- Forbes Field and Shibe Park open—first all-concrete-and-steel stadiums.

- On July 9, Cleveland shortstop Neal Ball performs first unassisted triple play in majors.

- Three Finger Brown leads NL in wins (27), CGs (32), innings (343), and saves (seven).

- Christy Mathewson posts 1.15 ERA to top NL.

- Mathewson and Pirate Howie Camnitz have 25-6 records to tie for NL lead in win pct.

- Red Ames of Giants pitches Opening Day no-hitter for nine innings, but loses to Brooklyn 3-0 in 13 innings.

- Cleveland's Tris Speaker tops AL in putouts, assists, and DPs.

Krause Turns in 1.39 ERA

Harry Krause won precisely half of his 36 victories in the majors as a rookie with the 1909 A's, leading the American League with his 1.39 ERA that year. He won his first ten starts, six of which were shutouts. By 1912, he was in the minors, where he stayed until 1929 without ever getting a second chance up top. A native San Franciscan, Krause pitched for over a decade with the Oakland Oaks in the Pacific Coast League. He won well over 200 games in the PCL, and over 300 games in his professional career.

Camnitz Posts Best Season

Howie Camnitz had a career year in 1909—a 25–6 record, a league-leading .806 winning percentage, a 1.62 ERA, and 133 strikeouts—and the Pirates needed all of it to hold off the charging Cubs. In the 1909 World Series, the Kentucky native was knocked out early in his lone start and saddled with the loss. Camnitz would post two more 20-win seasons before going a miserable 9–20 in 1913. He ended his career in 1915 with the Pittsburgh Rebels of the Federal League.

Harry Krause

Howie Camnitz

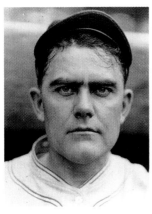

Babe Adams

Adams Stars in Series

Unknown to Tiger hitters prior to the 1909 World Series, Babe Adams would become unforgettable to them over those nine days. Adams is the only pitcher to win three games in a Series after serving during the regular season as only a second-line hurler.

Ball Turns Triple Play

There is still some doubt as to whether or not Neal Ball's unassisted triple play in 1909 was really the first in major league history. In any event, it was his main claim to fame in a mediocre seven-year career. Ball, oddly enough, was deemed in his day to be a decent hitter for a shortstop, yet not much of a fielder.

Neal Ball

1909

- Brooklyn catcher Bill Bergen hits .139 in 112 games, the lowest average in history by a regular.
- Detroit and Washington play an 18-inning scoreless tie on July 16, Ed Killian going the route for Detroit.
- Washington scores an AL record-low 380 runs.

- The Cubs beat Boston an NL record 21 times during the season.
- The Phils are rained out of games a record ten straight days.
- Walter Johnson loses an AL record ten games in which his team is shut out—five of them to Chicago.

- Cub Jimmy Sheckard collects an NL record 46 sacrifice hits.
- On August 23, catcher Bergen throws out seven would-be base thieves.
- The Cardinals commit a record 17 errors in a doubleheader on July 3.

Forbes Field

Forbes Field Opens Doors

A photograph of Forbes Field, as it looked on June 30, 1909, the afternoon it opened. The standing-room crowd in the outfield cut the size of the playing field somewhat on this day, but it was still gigantic: The plate-to-foulpole distances were the longest in the NL.

Mullin Has Career Year

George Mullin holds many Tiger pitching records, among them the most losses in a season (23 in 1904). Although his 1909 campaign was the best by far (29–8, .784, 2.22 ERA), he had several other good years as well. Mullin closed his career in the Federal League.

George Mullin

Ty Cobb

Cobb Wows 'Em Again

No one came close to matching Ty Cobb's stats in any of the three Triple Crown categories in 1909: a .377 average, nine home runs, 107 RBI. One irony is that even as Cobb first demonstrated his hitting greatness, he was playing on his last pennant-winning team.

- Wagner gets a raise to $10,000—his top yearly salary as a player.

- Cobb is indicted for the felonious assault of a Cleveland night watchman.

- Sam Crawford is again the AL runner-up to Cobb in RBI (107-97) and total bases (296-266).

- Cy Young returns to Cleveland where he began his career in 1890—wins 19 games and is the club leader.

- Cincinnati's Bob Bescher wins his first of four straight NL stolen base crowns, as he pilfers 54.

- Washington loses 29 games in which it's shut out—an AL record low.

- On June 19 vs. New York, Walter Johnson walks seven and throws four wild pitches, but wins 7-4.

- Frank Baker of the A's hits 19 triples—an AL rookie record.

- Red Dooin sets a 20th-century NL record for catchers when he commits 40 errors.

DEAD-BALL DAYS DRAG ON; A'S OUTPITCH CUBS

The new decade brought another season of dead-ball baseball. With few home runs, baseball for most of the 1910s was low-scoring and dominated by pitching, defense, and the running game. The National League compiled ERAs under 3.00 in six seasons; the AL, seven.

Once again, the greatest stars were pitchers, and a new generation came along to replace Christy Mathewson, Cy Young, and Three Finger Brown. Like those of their predecessors, the names of Walter Johnson and Pete (Grover Cleveland) Alexander still dot the pitching record books.

The 1910 season also saw the beginning of two new trends that would ultimately contribute to the rise of modern, home run baseball in the '20s: the widespread building of enclosed, steel-and-concrete ballparks and the invention of the livelier cork-centered baseball.

Two of the parks built in the 1910s are still in use today. The most influential was Comiskey Park, which was considered the finest baseball facility in the world when it opened in 1910 with a then-staggering capacity of 48,600. Washington's Griffith Park and Cleveland's League Park also debuted that year. The cork-centered ball was invented by Philadelphia's Ben Shibe and, after a successful experiment with its use in the 1910 World Series, was adopted by both leagues for the following season.

Already being referred to as "the dean of managers"—he had

only 41 more years to go as manager of the A's—Connie Mack brought his team in at 102-48, 14 1/2 games ahead of second-place New York. Complementing Philadelphia's veteran pitching staff of 31-game winner Jack Coombs (who posted a 1.30 ERA and 13 shutouts), 23-5 Chief Bender, Cy Morgan, and Eddie Plank was a still-maturing lineup that included Eddie Collins, Jack Barry, and Frank Baker—all under 25 years of age. One of the greatest second basemen in history, Collins led the league in stolen bases with 81 and his team in RBI with 81; he hit .322.

The A's ran away with the AL flag after beating back a midsummer challenge from Ty Cobb's Tigers, whose league-leading offense carried a poor pitching staff to an 86-68 record. Cobb himself led the league in runs with 106, on-base average at .456, and slugging at .551. His only rival as a hitter was Cleveland's Nap Lajoie, who led Cobb 51-35 in doubles,

304-279 in total bases, and .384 to .383 to take the batting title.

The Cobb/Lajoie rivalry heated up when the Chalmers Motor Co. offered a car to the winner of the 1910 AL batting title, a promotion that inspired the modern MVP Award. Anybody who complains that the criteria for today's MVP Award are vague should look up the 1910 batting race. The race ended in scandal when the St. Louis Browns allegedly lay back and let Lajoie beat out seven bunts on the last day of the season in order to rob Cobb of the batting title and his Chalmers "30" roadster. The Browns manager was fired and the Chalmers Award was allowed to continue in an altered form: one car was to be given to the "most important and useful" player in each league, as determined by a committee of sports writers. A player could only win one Chalmers Award in his career.

Frank Chance's Chicago club went 104-50 to win its fourth NL pennant in five years. Outfielder Solly Hofman led the club in hitting at .325 and RBI with 86, and Wildfire Schulte tied for the league lead in home runs with ten. Rookie pitcher King Cole went 20-4 with a league-low 1.80 ERA, and Three Finger Brown went 25-14 with the NL's second-best ERA at 1.86.

However, Chicago's pitching evaporated during the World Series, as the A's batted .316 and Bender and Coombs shut down the Cubs' bats to bring Philadelphia an easy 4-1 Series victory.

1910

- Cubs return to top in NL.
- Philadelphia breaks Tigers' three-year reign in AL.
- A's win World Series in five games.
- Jack Coombs of A's wins three Series games.
- A's set AL mark with 1.79 staff ERA.

- Sherry Magee tops NL in BA (.331), SA (.507), RBI (123), and total bases (263).
- Christy Mathewson leads NL in wins (27) for last time.
- Cub King Cole goes 20-4, leads NL in win pct. (.833), and sets NL rookie record for win pct.

- Ed Walsh tops AL in ERA at 1.26.
- Walsh nonetheless loses 20 games, as Sox hit record-low .211 as a team.
- Coombs leads the AL with 31 wins.
- Walter Johnson becomes first Washington AL pitcher to win 20 in a season, as he cops 25.

Although he was the leading pitcher in the majors in 1910 with 31 wins and 13 shutouts, Jack Coombs was never one to be removed late in a close game for a pinch hitter. Rather, he himself was frequently employed to pinch swing, and also did duty in the outfield on occasion.

- William Taft starts custom of president throwing out first ball at Washington home opener.
- Comiskey Park, one of the longest-lasting ballparks, opens.
- Johnson leads AL in Ks (313) for the first of 12 times.

- Ty Cobb and Nap Lajoie vie for AL batting title that is still cloaked in controversy as to who won.
- In an effort to produce more scoring, both leagues introduce a new "jack-rabbit" ball during the season.
- Two amateur teams play the first-ever night game at Comiskey Park.

- Player salaries range from $900 to around $12,000.
- On June 28, Cub Joe Tinker is the first player to steal home twice in the same game.
- Earle Mack of the A's is the first son to play in the ML for his father (Connie Mack).

Joe Tinker

Joss Hurls Final Shutout

Addie Joss's no-hitter on April 20, 1910, was his last career shutout and one of only five games he won that season. Less than a year after tossing his hitless gem, he was dead of tubercular meningitis. Cleveland players threatened mutiny until American League officials canceled their game the day of his funeral so they could attend it en masse.

Tinker Super at Swiping

Although Frank Chance may have been the base thief of the immortal trio, Joe Tinker (pictured) and Johnny Evers were not far behind. Tinker, it turns out, was the most enduringly consistent of the three. He stole bases in double digits in all 13 seasons that he was a full-time player. In 1910, Tinker and Chance each had 16 swipes, Evers had 28.

Young Sets Dual Record

Cy Young won his 500th game in 1910, almost precisely 20 years after he won his first. In the 19 seasons between the two marks, he averaged 25.68 victories per year. He also lost his 300th game during the 1910 campaign, a record that seems equally secure.

Cy Young

Addie Joss

Comiskey Builds Park

The 1990 season marked the 81st and last year that the original Comiskey Park, named after White Sox owner Charles Comiskey, was still in use. No other pro team had ever called the same facility home for so long. Comiskey built his park on what had been a city dump. Now, that land is a parking lot next to the second Comiskey Park.

Charles Comiskey

1910

- Cleveland hosts its first game at new League Park on April 21.

- Portland of the Pacific Coast League holds opponents scoreless for an OB record 88 consecutive innings.

- Coombs throws an AL record 13 shutouts.

- The White Sox compile an ML record-low .261 SA.

- Sox SA leader Patsy Dougherty's .300 slugging average is 84 points below Lajoie's BA.

- Tom Hughes of New York no-hits Cleveland for nine innings on August 30, loses 5-0 in 11 innings.

- Coombs and Walsh lock up in a 16-inning scoreless tie on August 4.

- Cy Young wins No. 500 on July 19.

- Addie Joss no-hits the White Sox 1-0 on April 20 for the second time in 18 months.

- Lajoie leads the AL with 227 hits, 33 more than Cobb.

A's Take World Title

The 1910 Philadelphia A's may have been the best team in the American League during the dead-ball era. They were so superior that Connie Mack *(center)* had no need to use Hall of Fame hurler Eddie Plank *(to the left of Mack)* in the World Series. The A's, in fact, employed just 12 players, a record-low, in beating the Cubs in the fall classic.

Philadelphia A's

Ed Walsh

Walsh Stumbles Under Load

Ed Walsh posted a 1.26 ERA in 1910, yet finished the season with an 18–20 record—thanks to his White Sox teammates who had a collective batting average of .211 (they weren't the greatest fielding outfit, either).

Ty Robbed of BA Title

Ty Cobb died believing he was the American League batting champ in 1910 with a .383 average, and many historians still feel he was the rightful owner of the crown. However, Nap Lajoie (a .384 average) is not the only performer to cop a hitting or home run or RBI title on the last day of the season under circumstances that arouse suspicion, nor is the incident even the most egregious instance of a title being thrown the way of a more favored player. Despite his .383 average, Cobb had a rather disappointing year in 1910. He didn't lead the league in hits, steals, or RBI, three departments he had gotten used to winning. Nevertheless, he did top the AL in runs (106) and slugging (.554).

Ty Cobb

- Detroit's Sam Crawford tops the AL in triples (19), RBI (120), and runs produced (198).

- New York's Russ Ford goes 26-6, setting AL rookie record for highest winning pct. (.813).

- Ford's 26 wins and eight shutouts are also rookie records.

- Lajoie collects eight hits on the last day of the season against the Browns, and seven are bunt singles.

- Browns third basemen ordered to play Lajoie deep so he can bunt and beat Cobb out of the batting title.

- Steve Evans of the Cards is hit by 31 pitches.

- A record 46 minor leagues begin the 1910 season.

- On Sept. 17, Detroit pitcher Ed Summers hits two homers in one game.

- On Sept. 30, the Browns' Ray Jansen plays in his only ML game and goes 4-for-5.

HOME RUN'S HOMERS THUMP THE GIANTS

Both leagues used the lively, cork-centered ball throughout the 1911 season, bringing if not the end of the dead-ball era, then at least a holiday from it. Pitchers were put on the defensive as major league runs scored totals and batting averages shot up: the NL batted .260; the AL, .273. Two teams in the AL, Philadelphia and Detroit, batted over .290.

The New York Giants won the pennant, thanks to the league's best offense. Catcher Chief Meyers hit .332 and second baseman Larry Doyle slugged 25 triples (tied for fifth-best all-time) and scored 102 runs; John McGraw's team racked up 756 runs. All this run production didn't inhibit the Giants on the basepaths. Outfielder Josh Devore stole 61 bases, second in the league to Cincinnati's Bob Bescher with 81, and was followed on the leader board by teammates Fred Snodgrass at 51 and Fred Merkle at 49.

As a team, New York swiped a modern record 347 bases, 58 more than runner-up Cincinnati. The Giants also had the NL's best pitching staff, anchored by Christy Mathewson (who won 26 games and was the only NL pitcher with an ERA below 2.00 at 1.99) and Rube Marquard (who in his first full year in the rotation went 24-7).

The loss of Johnny Evers due to a nervous breakdown in May probably cost the Cubs the pen-

nant, as they came in 7$^1/_2$ games off the pace. Chicago's Wildfire Schulte won the NL Chalmers Award after tying with Pittsburgh's Chief Wilson for the lead in the league in RBI (107) and topping the circuit in home runs (21). Honus Wagner, age 37, won his final batting title at .334 for third-place Pittsburgh. Philadelphia, in fourth place, was buoyed by rookie sensation Pete Alexander. At 24 years of age, Alexander went 28-13 (with seven shutouts and a 2.57 ERA) to lead the NL in wins.

In the AL, Connie Mack's powerhouse repeated, but not without being given a run for its money by good-hit, no-pitch Detroit. Second to last in team ERA, the Tigers held first place for much of the first half of the season on the strength of the one-two punch of Ty Cobb and Sam Crawford, who were first and second in the AL in RBI with 127 and 115. Crawford batted .378 and slugged .526, both third-best.

Cobb led in runs with 147, hits with 248, doubles with 47, triples with 24, and stolen bases with 83 and won the Chalmers Award. Cobb and Cleveland's Joe Jackson batted .420 and .408 to become the only men to break the .400 barrier between 1901 and 1920. The A's scored an AL-high 861 runs and batted a league-topping .296; their big gun was third baseman Frank "Home Run" Baker, who led the league in homers with 11 and drove in 115 runs.

The death of pitching legend Addie Joss from meningitis provoked an outpouring of grief all over the baseball world. A 160-97 lifetime pitcher over nine seasons with perennial contender Cleveland, the popular Joss left a 1.89 career ERA, the second-lowest in history.

With the Giants hitters held to a puny .175 batting average in the World Series, Mathewson, Marquard, and the rest of the New York staff managed a pair of one-run victories in games one and five. They pitched just well enough to lose 3-1, 3-2, and 4-2 in games two, three, and four. The deciding blows were two game-winning home runs by Baker, one off each of the Giants aces, in games two and three. Baker collected two more hits in Chief Bender's 13-2, four-hit win in game six. For the Series, Baker batted .375 and led all hitters in runs with seven, RBI with five, and home runs with two.

1911

- The A's repeat as AL champs.
- The Giants take their first NL flag since 1905.
- The A's win the World Series in six games.
- Philly's Baker receives the nickname "Home Run" when he hits two crucial homers in Series.

- Christy Mathewson wins game one of the World Series, loses game two in 11 innings on two unearned runs.
- Cub Wildfire Schulte wins the first Chalmers Award (MVP) in the NL.
- Ty Cobb receives the first AL Chalmers Award.

- Cobb hits .420 (20th-century record for outfielders) to win AL bat crown.
- Cobb leads in SA (.621), hits (248), runs (147), doubles (47), triples (24), and total bases (367).
- Cobb hits in 40 straight games, a new AL record.

The first third baseman to be selected for the Hall of Fame solely for his achievements as a player, Home Run Baker's credentials now seem to be a trifle slim. For a four-year run (1911 to '14), though, there may never have been a more productive hot corner man in history. He posted a .334 average, a league-leading 11 home runs, and 115 RBI in 1911.

- Cleveland rookie Vean Gregg wins 23 games and tops AL in ERA (1.80).

- Honus Wagner wins the NL bat crown (.334) by a single point.

- Schulte hits 21 homers, a new 20th-century record, and ties for the NL RBI lead with 107.

- Phils rookie Pete Alexander leads the NL with 28 wins; sets the 20th-century ML rookie record.

- Alexander fans 227, a new rookie record (since broken).

- The Polo Grounds—the Giants' home—is ravaged by fire and has to be rebuilt.

- The Giants' 347 steals set a 20th-century ML record for a team.

- The Braves post a home record of 19-54, the worst in the 20th century by an NL team.

- Cobb's 367 total bases are the most by anyone during the dead-ball era.

Joe Jackson

Jackson Has .408 BA

According to the rule for what constituted a rookie, Joe Jackson was not a yearling when he hit .408 in 1911, his first full season; by today's rule, however, he was. In any case, he still holds the record for the highest single-season batting average for the Naps, and he has both Cleveland and White Sox records for the highest career average.

A's Wear World Crown

Many teams in the early part of the century hired cripples, dwarfs, or zany illiterates to serve as mascots, believing they would bring good luck, and the 1911 World Champion Philadelphia A's were no exception. Hunchback Louis Van Zeldt *(front row, center)* was with the team for several years and collected quite a few World Series checks.

Turner Tops at 3B, SS

Prone to injuries and somewhat lacking in range, Terry Turner was not regarded as being in the same class as Honus Wagner, Nap Lajoie, Lee Tannehill, Bill Dahlen, and the other great fielding shortstops and second basemen of his day. But he was, without a doubt, one of the most versatile glovemen and, arguably, the steadiest. For 17 years, he gave solid and sometimes brilliant service at whatever station he was put. In 1911, he held the season's fielding average records at both third base and shortstop.

Terry Turner

Philadelphia A's

1911

- Cleveland's Joe Jackson hits .408 to set an ML rookie BA record.
- Both leagues adopt the dual-umpire system for every game.
- Helen Britton becomes the first woman to own a major league team when she takes control of the Cardinals.
- Jimmy Walsh of the Phils plays all nine positions during the season.
- At this juncture, Cleveland's Terry Turner holds the season FA records at *both* third and short.
- On Sept. 22, Cy Young beats Pittsburgh 1-0 for his 511th and last career win.
- Cliff Curtis of the Braves ends his all-time record skein of 23 consecutive losses.
- Cincinnati's Bob Bescher's 81 steals set an NL record for a 154-game season.
- Three Finger Brown's 13 saves set a new relief record.

Cobb Wins Chalmers

Several of Ty Cobb's playing colleagues share in his proud moment as he receives the brand-new Chalmers automobile awarded him for being the American League's Most Valuable Player in 1911. Cobb (pictured behind the wheel of the car on the right) led the majors that year in runs (147), hits (248), doubles (47), total bases (367), RBI (127), and batting and slugging averages (.420 and .621). Interestingly, and perhaps significantly, the players are all members of the Philadelphia A's.

Ty Cobb

Bob Bescher

Bescher Sets Swipes Mark

Not many men who were 6'1" and weighed 200 pounds were used as leadoff batters in 1911; fewer still were deft at collecting walks; and only one could also steal bases by the bundle. Bob Bescher set a National League record in 1911 with his 81 thefts, a mark that stood until 1962. The following year, he established a modern Reds club record for runs (120) that lasted until 1956.

Walter Johnson

Johnson Does It All

The first pitcher to win 20 games with a Washington American League team the previous year, Walter Johnson revealed additional evidence in 1911 that indicated he would soon mature into a most extraordinary performer. That year, not only did he once again win 25 games for the lowly Nats, his hitting improved to .234, whereupon he began to function as a pinch hitter.

- Joe Wood of the Red Sox no-hits St. Louis on July 29.
- Ed Walsh of Chicago no-hits the Red Sox on August 27.
- Rube Marquard tops the NL in strikeouts with 237 and win pct. at .774.

- Mathewson posts 27 wins and leads the NL in ERA at 1.99.
- The A's hit an AL record (since broken) .296 as a team.
- On May 13 vs. the Cards, the Giants score ten runs before recording their first out of the game.

- The Giants' Larry Doyle leads the majors with 25 triples.
- The AL batting average jumps 30 points over 1910 with the introduction of a livelier ball.
- Walter Johnson wins 25 games for seventh-place Washington and leads the AL in CGs (36).

BoSox Top Giants In Year Of The Triple

Three new ballparks opened in 1912—Fenway, Navin Field (now Tiger Stadium), and Cincinnati's Redland Field (later Crosley Field)—and, coincidentally or not, the major leagues reached the offensive peak of the decade. The NL hit .272, the AL hit .265, and all batting stats were up—especially triples. Three of the all-time Top Ten triples seasons came in 1912: Ty Cobb's 23 (which tied for tenth), Joe Jackson's 26 (which tied for second), and Pittsburgh outfielder Owen Wilson's major league-record 36.

Third baseman Heinie Zimmerman of the third-place Cubs was the league's best hitter. Although he led in doubles with 41, home runs with 14, batting at .372, and slugging at .571, he lost out in the Chalmers voting to New York's Larry Doyle. Doyle's .330 average, Red Murray's 20 triples and 92 RBI, and Fred Merkle's 11 home runs paced a hard-hitting, hard-running Giants team that stole a league-high 319 bases and scored 823 runs, No. 1 in the NL.

The 103-48 Giants also led the league in team ERA at 2.58. Christy Mathewson went 23-12 and, again, New York had the only NL pitcher to break the 2.00 ERA mark as 23-year-old spitball specialist Jeff Tesreau took the ERA title at 1.96. Rube Marquard won a league-high 26 games, 19 of them coming in a consecutive-win streak that lasted from April 11 to July 3; this tied the 19th-century record set by

another Giant, Tim Keefe, in 1888.

The Boston Red Sox rolled over their competition in the AL, compiling, in the process, the decade's highest winning percentage (.691), going 105-47. That put them 14 games up on a Washington Senators team that was lifted single-handedly out of the second division by Walter Johnson, who went 33-12 with a league-leading 1.39 ERA.

Johnson and Boston's Smokey Joe Wood—who was second in the loop with a 1.91 ERA, a 34-5 record and ten shutouts—engaged in a personal battle over the AL record for consecutive pitching victories. In early September, Wood had 13 straight victories and was threatening Johnson's record of 16, set early that same season when he met Johnson face-to-face in a dramatic showdown. Wood came out on top in a tight pitcher's duel, 1-0, then went on to tie the record before finally losing to Detroit on September 20.

AL Chalmers Award-winner Tris Speaker hit a league-leading 53 doubles and ten home runs for Boston while batting .383; the Red Sox center fielder also put together a 30-game hitting streak.

Cobb's suspension in May for attacking a heckler in the stands in New York contributed to one of the most bizarre events in major league history. Angry that their best player had been suspended indefinitely (he hit .410—his second consecutive year over .400), the Tigers refused to take the field in a game against Philadelphia, forcing management to recruit amateur ballplayers, former major leaguers, and even some fans from the stands to avoid a forfeit. Seminarian and pitcher Allan Travers set an all-time record for runs allowed in the 24-2 loss. One of the replacement players, a supporter by the name of Ed Irvin, tripled twice in three times up for a lifetime .667 batting average. Cobb was reinstated by the next Tigers game.

The 1912 World Series was a thrilling, eight-game contest that featured a variety of drama. There was a tie, called by darkness. There was great defense, including the bare-handed catch of a Doyle home run by Red Sox outfielder Harry Hooper. And there was a critical dropped fly ball in the tenth inning of game eight by New York center fielder Fred Snodgrass; it came to be known as the "$30,000 Muff" (the dollar amount referring to the winner's share). Boston won the Series four games to three.

1912

- The Red Sox win AL flag.
- The Giants repeat in the NL.
- The Sox win the most exciting World Series to date in seven games (plus one tie).
- Fred Snodgrass is the goat of the Series, as he muffs a fly ball in the tenth inning of the finale.

- Buck Herzog of the Giants gets 12 hits in the World Series, a new record.
- Joe Wood of the Red Sox wins three Series games.
- New York's Christy Mathewson allows only four earned runs in 28.2 innings in Series, but goes 0-2.

- The Giants' Larry Doyle wins the NL Chalmers Award.
- Tris Speaker of the Red Sox is the AL Chalmers winner.
- Rube Marquard wins an ML record 19 straight games for the Giants.
- Walter Johnson wins an AL record 16 straight games.

Whereas the Senators needed every one of Walter Johnson's 32 wins to finish second in 1912, the Red Sox could have used Smokey Joe Wood sparingly during the last six weeks of the season and still won the flag handily. Instead, because he was a drawing card, they ended up wringing out his arm as he collected 34 wins, 35 complete games, and ten shutouts, all league-highs that year. He was never again able to turn out a full season's work from the mound.

- Wood begins a record-tying skein of 16 straight wins even while Johnson's 16-straight streak is still going.

- Twice in an 11-day period, Eddie Collins steals six bases in a game.

- Cub Heinie Zimmerman tops the NL in BA (.372), hits (207), homers (14), and doubles (41).

- Ty Cobb leads the AL in BA (.410) with his second consecutive .400-plus average.

- Wood's 34 wins top the AL.

- Home Run Baker leads the AL in RBI with 130 and ties for the homer crown with ten.

- Johnson's 1.39 ERA is the best in the majors by a wide margin.

- Chief Wilson of the Pirates cracks an all-time record 36 triples.

- Ted Easterly collects 13 pinch hits, a new record.

- The Boston NL team is first called the "Braves."

Wagner Gets Older, Better

Umpire Al Schacht (the "Clown Prince of Baseball") and minor league catcher Ike Danning watch retired great Honus Wagner bang out a single in a benefit exhibition game. At 38 years of age, Wagner was still a top player in the National League in 1912, tallying a .324 average, seven home runs, and a league-high 102 RBI.

Rube Marquard

Speaker Best in AL

Had he played in the National League, Tris Speaker would probably have won four or five batting titles. Because he was in the same circuit with Ty Cobb, Babe Ruth, and George Sisler, however, he is remembered more now for his glove than his stickwork. The American League Chalmers Award winner in 1912, Speaker posted a .383 average and 90 RBI. His career stats prove he was great through and through.

Honus Wagner

Tris Speaker

Marquard on a Roll

According to the current rule for determining the winning pitcher in a game, Rube Marquard would have had 20 straight victories in 1912—all before he suffered his first loss of the season. Once the record skein ended, however, he was only 7–11 the rest of the way.

1912

- New York features the first brother battery—Homer and Tommy Thompson.
- Earl Hamilton of the Browns no-hits Detroit on August 30.
- Jeff Tesreau of the Giants no-hits the Phils on Sept. 6.

- George Mullin celebrates his birthday by hurling a no-hitter for Detroit over St. Louis on July 4.
- Cobb is suspended for going into the stands in New York on May 15 to fight with heckler Claude Lueker.
- On May 18, the Tigers respond to Cobb's suspension by going on strike.

- The Tigers are forced to use local amateurs in a game at Philadelphia; A's win 24-2.
- The Red Sox win an AL record 105 games (since broken).
- Joe Jackson hits an AL record 26 triples.

Doyle Comes Out a Winner

The awarding of MVP honors to Larry Doyle in 1912 was the first instance of a popular player on a pennant-winning team being selected over a more deserving candidate (he had a .330 average and 90 RBI that season). There were at least three contenders in the National League that year: Pittsburgh's Honus Wagner, Chicago's Heinie Zimmerman, and Boston's Bill Sweeney. Wagner finished second in the balloting, Sweeney and Zimmerman tied for sixth.

Larry Doyle

Tesreau is NL ERA Champ

Jeff Tesreau shot off the mark as if he were headed for Cooperstown. After debuting with a 17–7 season and a National League-best 1.96 ERA in 1912, Tesreau went on to win 101 games in his first five seasons, consistently ranking among the ERA leaders. He netted just 17 more victories before the Giants dropped him. Control was his gravest problem, and he never quite solved it. Tesreau ended his seven-year career with a 119-72 record and a 2.43 ERA.

Jeff Tesreau

Ty, Tris Tear Up AL

Cleveland's Tris Speaker *(right)* joins hands with Ty Cobb as the "Georgia Peach" is feted by Tiger fans near the tail end of both their careers. The two finest outfielders in baseball in 1912—Speaker turned in a .383 average, a league-high ten home runs, and 90 RBI while Cobb racked up a whopping .410 average and 83 RBI—were nearly barred from the game 14 years later when they were accused by pitcher Dutch Leonard of rigging a 1919 contest between Detroit and Cleveland.

Ty Cobb, Tris Speaker

- Speaker cracks 53 doubles, a new loop record.

- Honus Wagner leads the NL in RBI (102) and runs produced (186).

- Marquard and Larry Cheney, a Cubs rookie, tie for the NL lead in wins with 26.

- Johnson wins 33 and also leads the majors in strikeouts with 303.

- Navin Field (now Tiger Stadium) opens on April 20.

- Phils owner Horace Fogel is barred from the majors for accusing the Giants and Cards of conspiring to throw the pennant.

- For the second year in a row, Ed Walsh is the runner-up for the Chalmers Award.

- Walsh wins 27, tops the AL in innings (393), and sets a new AL record with ten saves.

- Fenway Park opens on April 20, the Red Sox beating New York 7-6.

BIG TRAIN WINS 36, BUT A'S WIN IT ALL

Somehow—possibly by increased use of the spitball and other trick pitches—major league pitchers began to regain their mastery over hitters in 1913. Although the cork-centered baseball introduced in 1911 was still around, runs scored dropped by more than 1,000 and the days of the sub-2.00 individual ERA returned. One new stadium, Brooklyn's Ebbets Field, opened.

For the second year in a row, the New York Giants won in excess of 100 games and ended the pennant race before the weather got hot. John McGraw's team featured a typical combination of an overachieving, starless lineup and two or three of the best five pitchers in the league. In this case, they were the 25-11 Christy Mathewson (who won the NL ERA title at 2.06), the 23-10 Rube Marquard, and the 22-13 Jeff Tesreau (who finished third in ERA at 2.17).

Just about the only Giant hitter to show up on an offensive leader board was outfielder George Burns, who hit 37 doubles. Yet Fred Merkle, Chief Meyers, Larry Doyle, and the rest of the New York attack scored 684 runs, third-most in the league.

Gavvy Cravath, the pre-Babe Ruth home run sensation, turned in the year's best offensive season for second-place Philadelphia. He led the league in RBI with 128, homers with 19, and slugging average at .568; his .341 batting average was second-best. The Chalmers Award went to Brook-

lyn's Jake Daubert, the batting champion at .350.

Pitching also figured in the Phillies' rise to second. Tom Seaton led the NL with 27 wins while notching a 2.60 ERA. Grover Cleveland "Pete" Alexander went 22-8 with a 2.79 ERA.

With great hitting years from Eddie Collins (who led the league in runs with 125), Frank "Home Run" Baker (who batted .337 and drove in 116 runs), and Stuffy McInnis (who hit .324), Philadelphia won its third AL pennant in four years. It finished with a 96-57 record, 6 1/2 games ahead of Washington—or, to be more accurate, Walter Johnson. "The Big Train" had his finest season in 1913, winning 36 and losing only seven and leading the league in wins, ERA, strikeouts, fewest hits per game, and almost everything else. He threw 11 of his career 110 shutouts and pitched a record 55 2/3 consecutive scoreless innings; his 1.14 ERA is the fifth-best single-season performance in history. The Senators played .837 ball with their ace on the mound, .486 without him. Johnson became the first and only pitcher to

receive the Chalmers Award.

The low-powered Senator offense scored almost 200 fewer runs than did the White Elephants. Washington first baseman Chick Gandil hit .318 and drove home 72 runs, and outfielder Clyde Milan led the AL with 74 stolen bases; they were the starts of an attack that finished fifth in the league.

Once again, Ty Cobb and Joe Jackson came in first and second in batting at .390 and .373. Jackson led the league in doubles with 39 and Sam Crawford of the Tigers banged out a league-high 23 triples. None of these feats made much difference for Cleveland or Detroit, who finished a combined 39 1/2 games back. An up-and-coming White Sox staff—Reb Russell (ERA 1.90), Eddie Cicotte (second in the AL at 1.58), and Jim Scott (also at 1.90)—compiled the league's top ERA of 2.33.

As they had in 1911, Philadelphia defeated the Giants in the World Series. Connie Mack's staff of Chief Bender, Bullet Joe Bush, and Eddie Plank had an easy time of it against a New York lineup depleted by injuries to Merkle, Fred Snodgrass, and Meyers. The Giants' pitching fell apart: Marquard had an ERA of 7.00, Al Demaree had a 4.50 mark, and Tesreau a 6.48. The lone exception was Mathewson, who pitched two complete games, including New York's only victory, and allowed two earned runs in 19 innings.

1913

- The A's return to the top in the AL.
- New York again triumphs in the NL.
- In the World Series, the Giants hit just .201 and lose in five games.
- Christy Mathewson's shutout win in game two is the lone New York bright spot.

- Home Run Baker hits a two-run homer in game one, leads all Series players in hits (nine) and RBI (seven).
- Brooklyn's Jake Daubert is voted the winner of the NL Chalmers Award.
- Walter Johnson takes the Chalmers Award in the AL.

- Johnson hurls a record (since broken) 55.2 consecutive scoreless innings.
- Mathewson hurls an NL record 68 consecutive innings without giving up a walk.
- Burt Shotton of the Browns scores an ML record 19.9 percent of his team's runs.

If ever there was a more bizarre team photograph than this shot of the 1913 World Champion Philadelphia A's, it has yet to be found. Notables include Connie Mack (in suit) and Eddie Collins *(front row, second from the right)*, who posted a .345 average and a circuit-high 125 runs scored.

- Daubert takes the NL bat crown (.350) but leads in no other department.

- Philly's Gavvy Cravath, the MVP runner-up, is considered by most historians to be the true MVP.

- Ty Cobb again tops the AL in BA with a .390 mark.

- Cravath tops the NL in hits (179), homers (19), total bases (298), SA (.568), and RBI (128).

- Johnson leads the majors with 36 wins, and also leads in CGs (29), innings (346), and strikeouts (243).

- Tom Seaton of the Phils tops the NL with 27 wins.

- The Federal League begins rumblings that it will become a third major league by next season.

- Johnson's ERA is a microscopic 1.14, easily the best in the majors.

- New manager George Stallings lifts Braves to fifth place, their highest finish since 1902.

Eddie Cicotte

Home Run Baker

Gavvy Cravath

Baker Dips in Average

An erratic fielder early in his career, Home Run Baker was rated one of the soundest third basemen in either league by 1913. The first player in American League history to be a back-to-back leader in both home runs (12) and RBI (117), Baker hit .337 in 1913 to fall slightly short of his .347 mark of 1912 (an AL-record for third basemen until 1980).

Cicotte on the Rise

Eddie Cicotte was emerging as one of the American League's top pitchers—he placed second in the circuit in 1913 with a 1.58 ERA—when he got caught up in the Black Sox scandal of 1919. After years of being a .500 hurler, he hit .600 in 1913—his best season by far prior to 1916, the year he finally began reaching his potential.

Cravath Makes a Comeback

Gavvy Cravath, who had previously flopped with three American League teams, was given a last chance at age 31 by the Phils after topping the American Association in batting and home runs in 1911. Over the next eight seasons, he was the game's leading slugger, winning six National League home run crowns. In 1913, he was the MVP runner-up, topping the NL with 179 hits, 19 home runs, 128 RBI, 298 total bases, and a .568 slugging average. Cravath clubbed 19 homers in 1914 and 24 in 1915—a freakish total for this era.

1913

- Mathewson tops the majors in fewest walks per game—an incredible 0.62.
- Idled by arm trouble, Joe Wood tumbles to just 11 wins for the Red Sox.
- Honus Wagner likewise has his last .300 season, as he hits .300 on the nose.
- Nap Lajoie hits .335, his last .300 season.
- Mathewson, Marquard, and Jeff Tesreau all win 20-plus games for the Giants.
- Three members of the Athletics' $100,000 infield hit .326 or better (Jack Barry does not).
- Frank Chance is hired to manage the Highlanders.
- Doc Miller of the Phils collects 20 pinch hits, a new record.
- Washington rookie Mel Acosta, age 17, becomes the youngest player to get a pinch hit in AL history.

Daubert Bats .350

The Mickey Vernon of his day, Jake Daubert was a contender for the National League hitting title only twice in his 15-year career apart from the 1916 season—in 1913 (when he posted a .350 average) and in 1914 (when he had a .329 mark). He won both times. As a fielder, Daubert was quite a bit better than Vernon.

Chief Bender

Seaton in Tip Top Form

Tom Seaton, photographed in the uniform of the Federal League Brooklyn Tip Tops, had a dazzling assortment of offspeed pitches, yet no great ability to control them. One of the few pitchers during the dead-ball era who walked nearly as many batters as he fanned, he nevertheless won 83 games over a four-year period, 27 of which came in 1913.

Jake Daubert

Bender a Chief in Relief

Chief Bender, the American League-leader in saves in 1913 with 13, left the Athletics after the 1914 season to join the Federal League; he took with him a 193–103 career record. He then wrapped up his last three years as a pro with a 19–25 record. There is no doubt that Bender was a fine pitcher; there is, however, some speculation as to what his stint in the majors would have been like had he joined a team other than the A's, who could afford to nurse his somewhat fragile arm as they had so many other good hurlers.

Tom Seaton

- Phils Cravath, Fred Luderus, and Sherry Magee finish one-two-four in the NL in homers.

- Ed Cicotte, Reb Russell, and Jim Scott of the White Sox finish two-three-four in ERA in the AL.

- Philly's Chief Bender saves an AL record 13 games.

- Three-year vet Vean Gregg of Cleveland wins 20 games for the third straight year.

- Joe Tinker is sent to the Reds by the Cubs and becomes Cincinnati's manager.

- Baker leads the AL in homers (12) and RBI (117).

- Detroit adds big-hitter Bobby Veach to its outfield of Cobb and Sam Crawford.

- Branch Rickey is named the Browns' new manager.

- Ebbets Field opens on April 9, Brooklyn losing 1-0 to the Phils.

MIRACLE BRAVES PULL RABBIT OUT OF THE HAT

The 1914 year belonged to the "Miracle Braves," baseball's all-time comeback kids, who rose from last place in July to a pennant in the fall. Starting the season with a 4-18 record and temporarily without injured star shortstop Rabbit Maranville, master motivator and pioneer of platooning George Stallings saw his team come together to form a running, clutch-hitting unit by midsummer.

The Braves won eight straight in early July, part of a 34-10 stretch that put them in fourth place; nine consecutive wins later, they closed to within 7 games of front-running New York. On August 10 and in second, they headed into a three-game, make-or-break series with the Giants. The Braves swept, roared into the lead in early September, and sprinted to a 94-59 record, 10½ games up on New York.

With just one .300 hitter (outfielder Joe Connolly), Boston finished in fourth place in batting with a mediocre .251 team average; in addition, the Braves had only the NL's fourth-best team ERA at 2.74. Their performance was based on patient hitting and great defense: They posted a league-leading 502 bases on balls. Chalmers winner Johnny Evers was the team leader with a .390 on-base average (he also headed up all second basemen in fielding); runner-up Maranville led in double plays while setting an NL record for putouts and the still-unbroken major league-record for

total chances at shortstop (he also contributed a team-high 78 RBI).

The Giants, who occupied first place for almost five months, left the door open for the Braves with their inability to pull away from the pack. The great Christy Mathewson finally got old, winning more than 20 games for the last time and turning in an ERA of 3.00 for the first time in 14 full seasons. The New York hitters, led by George Burns with a league-high 100 runs and 62 stolen bases, couldn't pick up the slack. Philadelphia's Gavvy Cravath repeated his 19-home run performance of 1913, and a young Brooklyn outfielder named Casey Stengel hit .316 and led the NL in on-base average at .404.

In 1914, a group of wealthy industrialists—including bakery magnate Robert Ward and, later, oilman Harry Sinclair—mistakenly chose a slump period in attendance to launch a third major league. The well-heeled Federal League lured such big names as Three Finger Brown, Jack Quinn, and the ever-mercenary Hal

Chase, and caused an increase in salaries in the other leagues.

Benny Kauff was the Ty Cobb of the new league, as he spearheaded all hitters in runs with 120, doubles with 44, and batting at .370 for pennant-winning Indianapolis. A legacy of the league is Wrigley Field, originally named for restauranteur Charles Weeghman, who built it for his Chicago Whales.

In the American League, Cobb won the batting title at .368 and Connie Mack's dynasty won its fourth pennant in five years, going 99-53, 8½ games ahead of Boston. The Red Sox had the league's best ERA at 2.35 despite the loss of Smokey Joe Wood, who was limited to 18 games by an arm injury that would end his pitching career by 1916. Back in the majors as a regular outfielder by 1918, Wood retired after the 1922 season with a lifetime .283 batting average. Boston's Ernie Shore had a 10-4 record with an ERA of 1.99 and Dutch Leonard went 19-5 with the lowest-ever season ERA, 0.96. Making his major league debut, 19-year-old lefty Babe Ruth went 2-1 in four appearances.

The underdog Braves swept the World Series in four games from Philadelphia. Mack, fed up in part with what Federal League competition had done to his payroll, auctioned off his stars one-by-one to the highest bidder. As a result, the Athletics finished last every season for the next seven years.

1914

- The Federal League debuts as a third major league.
- Joe Tinker is one of many former AL and NL stars who jump to the FL because it offers more money.
- Baltimore beats Buffalo on April 13 in the first FL game.

- Indianapolis wins the FL by 1½ games over the Chicago Whales, who are managed by Tinker.
- Indy's Benny Kauff tops the FL in BA (.370) and steals (75), and becomes known as the Ty Cobb of the FL.
- The A's win their fourth AL flag in five years.

- The Braves, in last place on July 4, win their first NL flag of the century.
- The Braves sweep the heavily favored A's in the World Series.
- Catcher Hank Gowdy of Boston hits .545 to lead all Series hitters.
- Boston co-aces Dick Rudolph and Bill James each win two Series games.

The 1914 World Champion Boston Braves live up to their reputation of being a rough-hewn, not overly gifted, but above all, fun-loving bunch. Rabbit Maranville *(front row, fourth from the right)* seems to be taking a siesta after a season in which he batted .246, nailed four home runs, and drove in 78 runs. Chalmers Award-winner Johnny Evers *(front row, far right)*, who looks ancient, was actually only 31 at the time; he turned in a .279 average, one home run, and 40 RBI that year.

- The Braves play their World Series home games in Fenway Park because it seats more than their home park.
- Johnny Evers, traded to the Braves by the Cubs for Bill Sweeney, wins the NL Chalmers Award.
- Eddie Collins is an easy Chalmers winner in the AL.
- Brooklyn's Jake Daubert is a repeat NL batting champ (.329).
- Cobb wins the AL bat title at .368.
- Sam Crawford ties the AL record for most triples in a season (26).
- Jake Ruppert and Til Huston buy the New York AL team.
- On June 9, Honus Wagner becomes the first player in ML history to collect 3,000 hits.
- Pete Alexander leads the NL in CGs (32), innings (355), strikeouts (214), and wins (27).
- Nap Lajoie collects his 3,000th hit.

Sherry Magee

Magee Posts Banner Year

A victim of bad timing, Sherry Magee starred for the Phils in 1914, the year the Braves won the pennant. He racked up 171 hits, 103 RBI, a .509 slugging average, and 277 total bases that year, all tops in the National League. Traded to the Braves in 1915, he helplessly watched the Phils cop their first flag. Finally in 1919, his last season, Magee got some of it back, managing to hook on with the World Champion Cincinnati Reds as they took their first league championship.

Benny Kauff

Kauff Displays Skill in FL

Benny Kauff was just one of several good ballplayers buried in the minor leagues who might have stayed there if the Federal League had not given them a chance to showcase their talents. In 1913, he still was only in Class-B at age 23, playing for Hartford in the Eastern Association. He led the circuit with a .345 batting average. In 1914, Kauff led the Federal League with a .370 average and 75 steals.

James, Rudolph Win 53 Games

Braves skipper George Stallings sits between his two mound aces of the 1914 season, 26-game winner Bill James *(left)* and 27-game winner Dick Rudolph. Both hurlers each won a pair of World Series games that year. The rest of Stallings's hurlers went 41-42 on the year and only one, Lefty Tyler, was a significant factor. During the early part of the century, there were quite a few managers, Stallings and Connie Mack among them, who preferred wearing street clothes to a baseball uniform while they worked.

Bill James, George Stallings, Dick Rudolph

1914

- Red Sox Babe Ruth makes his major league debut on July 1, pitches seven innings to beat Cleveland.

- Jim Scott of Chicago no-hits Washington on May 14, loses 1-0 in ten innings.

- Joe Benz of Chicago no-hits Cleveland on May 31.

- George Davis of the Braves no-hits the Phils on Sept. 9.

- The New York AL team becomes known universally as the "Yankees."

- Roger Peckinpaugh, age 23, is named Yankees manager, the youngest skipper ever.

- Cardinal Miller Huggins is caught stealing 36 times, an NL record.

- New York's Fritz Maisel leads the AL with 74 steals, setting an ML record for third basemen.

- A rule is put in giving a runner three bases if a fielder stops a ball with a thrown glove or cap.

Deal Tags Out Murphy

Charlie Deal of the Braves tags out Eddie Murphy of Philadelphia at third base while Rabbit Maranville backs up the play in the 1914 World Series. The A's coach incomprehensibly seems to have signaled Murphy to come into the bag standing up.

World Series

Jake Ruppert

Ruppert Buys Yanks

Jake Ruppert was one of the two well-heeled young sportsmen (Captain Tillinghast L'Hommedieu Huston the other) who were encouraged by John McGraw to buy the New York Yankees from original owners Frank Farrell and Big Bill Devery in 1914. The $460,000 sum was astonishingly meager even for its time.

Joe Tinker

Tinker's Forte Is Managing

Although nearing the end of his career as a player, Joe Tinker did such a good job as the skipper of the Federal League's Chicago Whales in 1914 (1¹/₂ games out of first) and 1915 (first place) that he got a crack at the Cubs' managerial post in 1916. After one year, however, his contract was not renewed. The 1914 Whales featured Claude Hendrix, the loop's best pitcher (a league-leading 29 wins, 49 games, 34 complete games, and a 1.69 ERA), and Dutch Zwilling, its top slugger (a .313 batting average, a .480 slugging average, a league-high 15 home runs, and 95 RBI).

- Red Sox Dutch Leonard posts a 20th-century record-low 0.96 ERA.

- Sherry Magee leads the NL in hits (171), RBI (103), SA (.509), and total bases (277).

- Collins, never a power hitter, tops the AL in runs produced (205) by a substantial margin.

- Weeghman Park, now known as Wrigley Field, opens on April 23 as home of the FL Chicago Whales.

- Rube Waddell dies at age 37.

- In addition to his bat crown, Cobb leads the American League in slugging average (.513).

- Tris Speaker tops the junior circuit in hits (193), total bases (287), and doubles (46).

- Brooklyn boasts four of the top five leaders in batting average.

- Cleveland, which lost ace pitcher Cy Falkenberg to the FL, falls to the basement in the AL.

The 1915 season brought major league fans another Boston-Philadelphia World Series. This time, it was the Boston Red Sox against a surprising Philadelphia Phillies team that jumped from sixth to first in one year.

Boston's strong-armed and deep pitching staff dominated the Phillies' batters in the Series, holding slugger Gavvy Cravath to two hits and the entire lineup to a mere .182 batting average. The slick-fielding outfield duo of Harry Hooper (who hit .350) and Duffy Lewis (who drove in a team-high five runs) provided the punch for the Red Sox as Philadelphia fell, four games to one.

Kicking off the season with an 8-0 spurt, the Phillies fended off an early-season charge from a Chicago team that featured three of the NL's top four sluggers in Cy Williams, Wildfire Schulte, and Vic Saier. They combined for 36 home runs. Playing in brand-new Braves Field, Boston put on another late-season drive, but worked no miracles to come in with a record of 83-69, 7 games back.

Philadelphia had the NL's best offense thanks to career years from outfielder Cravath and first baseman Fred Luderus. Cravath set a new 20th-century major league-record for home runs with 24. He also led in runs with 89, RBI with 115, and bases on balls with 86; Luderus was second in the NL in hitting at .315 and second in doubles with 36.

Rookie shortstop Dave "Beauty" Bancroft captained the

PHILS FALL TO BOSOX; FEDERAL LEAGUE FOLDS

Phillies' defense and chipped in 85 runs and 77 bases on balls at the plate. Pete Alexander's 31-10 record and league-low 1.22 ERA led the league's best pitching staff, rounded out by 21-game winner Erskine Mayer, Al Demaree, and Eppa Rixey, to a team ERA of 2.17. Pittsburgh's Max Carey led the league in stolen bases with 36, the second of his ten stolen base crowns. The last-place Giants' pitching continued to disintegrate; their only bright spot was Larry Doyle, who won a batting title at .320 and led the league in hits with 189 and doubles with 40.

The AL pennant race was a battle between Boston's arms and Detroit's bats, narrowly decided in favor of the Red Sox by 2½ games. Five Boston starters reached double figures in wins, including righties Rube Foster (19-8) and Ernie Shore (19-8) and lefties Babe Ruth (18-8) and Dutch Leonard (15-7). Pitching out of the bullpen and in great pain, Smokey Joe Wood led the AL in winning percentage at .750 and ERA at 1.49, just ahead of

27-game winner Walter Johnson at 1.55. Shore was third in ERA at 1.64.

The Tigers nearly overcame a mediocre pitching staff spearheaded by Harry Coveleski and Hooks Dauss to score an AL-high 778 runs. Bobby Veach and Sam Crawford tied for the RBI lead with 112. And as Veach swatted 40 doubles and Crawford 19 triples, Ty Cobb won another batting title at .369. Cobb combined 118 walks, a league-high 208 hits, and a new 20th-century record 96 stolen bases (broken in 1962 by Maury Wills) to score 144 runs, the best in the circuit.

Chicago won an exciting Federal League race in which 16 games separated the first- and seventh-place clubs. But with the baseball establishment sweating out an antitrust suit filed by the Federal League and the Fed backers nervous over their investments, the time came in 1915 for compromise and a return to the two-league system. In a complicated settlement, some Federal League backers were bought out while others, such as Chicago's Charles Weeghman and St. Louis' Phil Ball, were allowed to purchase the existing major league franchises in their cities. A number of FL player contracts were auctioned off: The Giants paid $35,000 for Benny Kauff and the Yankees bought Lee Magee for $22,500, both of whom turned out to be disappointments. On an up note, the Federal League also produced the talented outfielder Edd Roush and manager Bill McKechnie.

1915

- The Phils win their first NL pennant since their inception in 1883.

- Boston wins the World Series in five games; Pete Alexander's victory in the opener is all that averts a sweep.

- In game five, Boston's Harry Hooper hits two short home runs into temporary right field seats.

- Rube Foster, with two CG wins for Boston, is the Series hero.

- Chicago wins the FL flag by one percentage point over St. Louis and just four points over Pittsburgh.

- Ty Cobb leads the AL in BA (.369) and total bases (274), plus runs (144) and hits (208).

- Cobb steals 96 bases, the ML record for a 154-game season.

- As per usual, Walter Johnson tops the AL in wins (27), CGs (35), and Ks (203).

- Joe Wood's arm recovers enough to allow him to lead the AL in win pct. (.750) and ERA (1.49).

1915

Gavvy Cravath hit a 20th-century record 24 home runs in 1915. At the plate in 1919, he rapped .341 and topped the National League with 12 homers in just 214 at-bats; he had, however, slowed to a point where he was a severe liability in the field. Born about 55 years too soon, he might have played well into his 40s had there been a designated hitter rule in his day.

- In his first full season, Boston's Babe Ruth wins 18 games and hits .315 with four home runs.

- Alexander tops NL pitchers in wins (31), ERA (1.22), strikeouts (241), and shutouts (12).

- Gavvy Cravath hits 24 homers, a new 20th-century ML record.

- Cravath also heads the NL in RBI (115), SA (.510), total bases (266), runs (89), and walks (86).

- Home Run Baker holds out all season, is sold prior to the 1916 campaign to the Yankees for $35,000.

- The Yankees first wear pinstripes.

- Ruth hits his first major league homer on May 5 off Jack Warhop of the Yankees.

- Cleveland is first known as the "Indians."

- Cleveland trades Joe Jackson to Chicago for Braggo Roth and cash.

Philadelphia Phillies

Phillies Earn NL Pennant

Taking the National League by 7 games, the Philadelphia Phillies of 1915 went 90-62—just one triumph shy of their 1916 club record, the best of any Phillies team until 1976. Although Eppa Rixey (the 6' 5" - giant in the back row) and Pete Alexander *(back row, fourth from the left)* won 55 games between them in 1916, the Phils dropped to second. The team was hurt by the demise of Erskine Mayer, who fell from 21 wins in 1915 to 7 wins in 1916.

Joe Jackson

Tribe Sells Jackson

Only the A's kept the Indians from a second consecutive cellar finish in 1915. The team was so desperate for cash to keep afloat that all it took was a reported $31,500 and three players—only one of whom, Braggo Roth, ever helped the Cleveland club much—for White Sox owner Charlie Comiskey to obtain Joe Jackson (pictured). Jackson turned in a .272 average and 36 RBI in 158 at-bats in Chicago in 1915. Jackson brought Commy's team two pennants (in 1917 and 1919) and everlasting infamy.

1915

- Rube Marquard of the Giants no-hits Brooklyn on April 15.

- Jimmy Lavender of Chicago no-hits the Giants on August 31.

- The A's fall to last place with a 43-109 record, down an all-time record 56 games from their 99-53 mark in 1914.

- Prior to the 1915 season, the White Sox buy Eddie Collins from the A's for $50,000.

- The Cards lead the NL with 590 runs, the fewest ever by a loop leader.

- Braves Field opens on August 18 replacing South End Grounds, in existence as an ML park since 1876.

- In a switch from 1914, the Red Sox play their World Series home games in new Braves Field.

- George Sisler debuts for the Browns—as a pitcher—and beats Johnson 2-1.

- The Tigers have the top three men in RBI in the AL.

Plank Sets Record for Wins

Eddie Plank won his 300th game in 1915, sporting the uniform of the Federal League St. Louis Terriers. Though 40 years old, Plank toyed with Federal League hitters, going 21-11 with a 2.08 ERA. He finished his career in 1917 with the St. Louis Browns after notching 326 victories. Plank's record for the most career wins by a southpaw endured until Warren Spahn of Milwaukee hurled the last victory of the 1962 season.

Eddie Plank

Sisler Starts in St. Louis

George Sisler spent most of his career with the Browns. His debut season in 1915 produced a .285 average, three home runs, and 29 RBI in 274 at-bats. By rights, however, he probably should have played for the Pirates, who came within a hair of having him declared their property in 1915. He would have plugged the first base hole that had existed in Pittsburgh since 1905.

Jimmy Lavender

Lavender Has Day in the Sun

Jimmy Lavender is one of a host of pitchers who have tossed no-hit games in the midst of otherwise nondescript careers. Lavender's no-hitter came on August 31, 1915, in a game with the Giants. As a rookie, Lavender showed considerable promise, winning 16 games in 1912 while working 252 innings. He never matched either figure again after that year, lasting only six seasons in the majors.

George Sisler

- The Tigers, the last team to wear collars on their uniforms, finally abandon them.
- Eddie Plank becomes the first southpaw to win 300 games.
- The Chalmers Award is discontinued prior to the season, ending MVP selections until the 1920s.

- The Federal League folds on Dec. 22.
- Brooklyn's Benny Kauff is again the FL bat champ (.342) and also leads in SA (.509) and steals (55).
- Giant Larry Doyle tops the NL with a .320 BA, the lowest prior to 1988 to lead the senior loop.

- On April 24, Ruth is pinch-hit for for the last time, as Hack Cady bats for him.
- In his big league debut, Bruno Haas of the A's walks an AL record 16 Yankees and loses 15-7.
- The Giants finish last despite a 69-83 record.

BoSox Too Much For Brooklyn And Wheat

In 1916, Brooklyn won its first pennant since the days of Ned Hanlon in 1900. Fan favorite Zach Wheat batted .312 with 32 doubles and 13 triples and led the NL in slugging average at .461. Wheat, Jake Daubert (whose .316 batting mark was second in the league to Hal Chase's .339), and outfielder Hy Myers (who slugged 14 triples), combined to give Brooklyn the league's second-best offense; only the Giants scored more runs, 597 to 585. Carried by Pete Alexander's 33 wins and a league-low 1.55 ERA, second-place Philadelphia finished 2¹/₂ games off the pace; Boston came in 4 games back.

The NL's strangest team was undoubtedly John McGraw's chameleon-like Giants. They opened the season with eight straight home losses, followed with a 17-game winning streak on the road, then slumped. Trying to rebuild in midseason, McGraw put young outfielder Dave Robertson into the lineup, released catcher Chief Meyers, traded Fred Merkle to Brooklyn, and swapped Larry Doyle to Chicago for legendary hothead Heinie Zimmerman. McGraw sent the great Christy Mathewson to Cincinnati to take over for player/manager Buck Herzog, and in return acquired Herzog and Red Killefer. Federal League star Benny Kauff became an every-day outfielder.

The result of all this shuffling was that the Giants went on an all-time record 26-game winning streak—this time, all at home—but played badly enough before and after the streak that they came in fourth, with an 86-66 record. Hall of Famer Rogers Hornsby played his first full season with St. Louis, batting .313. In Chicago, dead-ball great Three Finger Brown recorded his 239th career win against only 130 losses; his lifetime ERA over 14 seasons was 2.06, the third-lowest in history.

Boston overcame the sale of Tris Speaker to Cleveland after a salary dispute to repeat, finishing 2 games ahead of Chicago with a 91-63 record in the American League. This year was almost the same story as 1915 for the Red Sox: Their sixth-best offense was carried by an awesome pitching staff that included emerging ace Babe Ruth, who won 23 games and the ERA title at 1.75. Dutch Leonard, Rube Foster, and underhand power pitcher Carl Mays were also part of a Sox staff that led the AL in shutouts with 24. Boston was bested in team ERA only by a Chicago staff of Eddie Cicotte (ERA runner-up at 1.78),

Red Farber (who had an ERA of 2.02), Reb Russell, and young Lefty Williams.

Ty Cobb's Tigers finished third, 4 games out, as Cobb led the AL in stolen bases with 68 and runs with 113; for the first time in the past ten years, however, Cobb lost the batting title. He was beaten out by Speaker, who outhit him .386 to .371 and led the league in hits with 211, doubles with 41, on-base average at .470, and slugging average at .502. Joe Jackson, traded before the season from Cleveland to the White Sox, was third in the loop in hitting at .341 and first in triples at 21.

The 1916 World Series was a reprise of 1915, as Boston's 1.47 ERA pitching proved too strong for the National League lineup (Brooklyn logged a .200 batting average; Boston posted a .238 average against Brooklyn's 3.04 ERA). In Ernie Shore's 6-5 game one victory over Rube Marquard, Mays executed the last out in relief in the ninth to halt Brooklyn, which had racked up five runs and had one more on base. Boston finally pulled out a 2-1 win in game two—after Ruth and Sherry Smith went at it for 14 innings—on a Del Gainor pinch single that brought in Mike McNally. Jeff Pfeffer stepped in for Jack Coombs in the seventh inning of game three—and retired eight men—for Brooklyn's sole triumph, a 4-3 game. Boston claimed the remaining games, winning by scores of 6-2 and 4-1.

1916

- Brooklyn becomes the third NL team in succession to cop its first flag since 1901.

- The Red Sox repeat as AL champs.

- The Sox win Series in five games.

- Game two is the Series highlight, the Sox winning 2-1 in a Series record 14 innings.

- In game two, Boston's Babe Ruth gives up a first-inning run and then hurls 13 scoreless innings.

- Boston's Larry Gardner has just three hits in the Series, but leads all hitters with two homers and six RBI.

- Tris Speaker beats out Ty Cobb in BA, .386-.371.

- Cincinnati's Hal Chase is the surprise bat crown winner in the NL (.339) and also leads in hits (184).

- Pete Alexander hurls an incredible 16 shutouts, an all-time ML record.

- Alexander wins 33 games and tops the NL in CGs (38) and strikeouts (167).

1916

It is worth speculating what kind of baseball career Babe Ruth would have carved out had he been a rotten hitter. Chances are, he would still be in the Hall of Fame. Even after conceding that he pitched for the Red Sox, an excellent team that gave him strong support, his mound stats suggest that he might have been the best southpaw in American League history. He gave up a first-inning run, then pitched 13 scoreless frames in game two of the 1916 World Series.

- Walter Johnson again leads the AL in wins (25), CGs (36), and Ks (228).

- Ruth wins 23 games and cops the AL ERA title with a 1.75 figure.

- Speaker is traded to Cleveland for Sam Jones, Fred Thomas, and $55,000.

- The Cardinals pirate manager Branch Rickey from the crosstown Browns to run their front office.

- Joe Jackson tops the majors in triples (21) and total bases (293).

- Ex-big leaguer John Dodge, now in the Southern Association, is killed by a pitch thrown by Shotgun Rogers.

- Prior to the season, the Chicago FL club sells ten players to the Cubs.

- Giants trade Christy Mathewson, Edd Roush, and Bill McKechnie to Reds for Buck Herzog and Red Killefer.

- Mathewson replaces Herzog as the Reds manager.

Roush Makes Good in NL

Although many players who first came to maturity in the Federal League later left their marks in either the National or American League, Edd Roush was the Feds' top graduate by a wide margin. He became the property of the Giants after the FL folded (hitting .188 in 69 at-bats), only to be dealt to the Reds before the end of the 1916 season, a year in which he hit .287 in 272 at-bats. It was the trade John McGraw lived to regret more than any other, and he strove for the next 11 years to reacquire Roush before he finally succeeded.

Edd Roush

Wally Schang

Schang Homers from Both Sides

Wally Schang just might be the best catcher not in the Hall of Fame. Schang played on six pennant-winners, hit .287 in World Series action and .284 career-wise, and, on August 8, 1916, was the first switch-hitter to homer from both sides of the plate in the same game. The only thing his career seems to lack is the recognition clearly due to him. Schang caught for 19 major league seasons.

Dutch Leonard

Leonard Wins Series Finale

An exceptional pitcher early in his career, Dutch Leonard turned into only an average hurler when the lively ball era began. Leonard posted a 0.96 ERA in 1914 (some sources say 1.01)—still a modern season record—and had several other seasons in which he was nearly as effective. In 1915, he went 15-7 and won a World Series game. In 1916, he notched 18 victories and bested the Dodgers 6–2 in game four of the World Series.

1916

- On August 8, switch-hitter Wally Schang homers from both sides of the plate in the same game.

- Ruth has nine shutouts, an AL southpaw record.

- Tom Hughes of the Braves no-hits Pittsburgh on June 16.

- Rube Foster of the Red Sox no-hits New York on June 21.

- Joe Bush of the A's no-hits Cleveland on August 26.

- Dutch Leonard of the Red Sox no-hits the Browns on August 30.

- Sam Crawford collects his career record 312th and last triple.

- For one game only, the Indians wear numbers on their sleeves—first team this century to do so.

- Cubs owner Charlie Weeghman adopts the policy of allowing fans to keep balls hit into the stands.

- On August 13, Ruth beats Johnson 1-0 in 13 innings.

Speaker Deal Pays Off

Cleveland's acquisition of Tris Speaker in 1916 was the most sensational trade in history up to that point. It served to make the otherwise lackluster Indians instantly respectable. After the 1915 season, when the Red Sox let him go, Speaker played like a man whose cage had been opened. He came out roaring in 1916, posting a .386 average to beat Ty Cobb by .015 in the race for the batting title. Speaker also led the AL in hits (211), doubles (41), and slugging (.502).

Zach Wheat

Zach Whacks NL Pitching

Like the collars the Tigers sported until 1915, the sartorial flair exemplified by the Brooklyn club's checked home uniform of the 1910s was soon to become extinct in the majors. Zach Wheat, however, would remain with the Dodgers until 1926, setting many team career and season records along the way. In 1916, he posted a .312 batting average (fifth in the league), a circuit-best .461 slugging average, 177 hits (third in the loop), and nine home runs (tied for third). Zach's brother, Mack Wheat, batted just .207 in seven major league seasons.

Pete Alexander

Tris Speaker

Alexander Posts 16 Shutouts

Pete Alexander blanked every National League opponent he faced at least once in 1916—a major league record 16 shutouts. Amazingly, the majority of his shutouts were pitched in his home park, the Baker Bowl—an Eden for the circuit's hitters even during the dead-ball era.

- Pittsburgh's Bill Hinchman, back in the majors after six years in the minors, leads NL in triples (16).

- Speaker tops the AL in SA (.502), OBP (.470), and ties for top in doubles (41).

- The Giants win 26 consecutive games but finish only fourth.

- Washington finishes seventh with a .497 winning pct., by far the highest ever for a seventh-place team.

- In a specially arranged matchup, Cincy's Mathewson beats Chicago's Three Finger Brown 10-8.

- The A's lose 117 games, the modern ML record for a 154-game season.

- Del Pratt of St. Louis leads the AL in games played (158) for the fourth consecutive season.

- Charlie Pick of the A's becomes the last ML regular until 1978 to field below .900.

- Brooklyn's Zach Wheat leads the NL in SA (.461) and total bases (262).

Only two years removed from the NL cellar, John McGraw's retooled New York Giants developed into an easy pennant-winner over Philadelphia in 1917. Had it not been for another stellar performance by Pete Alexander, the Phillies would have finished much further out than second place, 10 games behind. The Philly attack had faded, due in part to slumps by Fred Luderus and Dode Paskert and in part to newcomers Johnny Evers (who hit .224 and retired following the season) and Wildfire Schulte (who hit .214 and reached the end of the line a year later).

Alexander led the NL in wins with 30, complete games with 34, shutouts with eight, strikeouts with 200, and innings pitched with 388. His 1.83 ERA was second only to the 1.44 mark turned in by Giants spot-starter Fred Anderson.

McGraw's new-look offense—first baseman Walter Holke, Heinie Zimmerman (who led the league in RBI with 102), George Burns (the runs scored leader with 103), and Dave Robertson (who knocked an NL-high 12 home runs)—produced a league-best 635 runs. New York also led the NL in fewest runs allowed with 457. Lefty Ferdie Schupp won 21 games against seven losses to lead the NL in winning percentage at .750; Schupp was one of four New York starters to win more than 15 games. Three Giants pitchers made the top five in ERA leaders:

ChiSox Clobber The Bungling Giants

Anderson at 1.44, Pol Perritt at 1.88, and Schupp at 1.95.

Ex-Federal Leaguer Edd Roush won the batting title for Cincinnati at .341. He beat out third-place St. Louis' Rogers Hornsby, who batted .327 and led the league in triples with 17 and slugging average at .484.

In Cincinnati, 24-win man Fred Toney hooked up with Chicago's Hippo Vaughn for major league history's only double no-hit game: With one out in the tenth, Reds shortstop Larry Kopf singled for the first hit and moved to third base on a fly ball misplayed by center fielder Cy Williams; he scored the winning run on an infield dribbler by Olympic legend Jim Thorpe, who spent six years in the big leagues as the world's fastest .250 hitter.

In Pittsburgh, Honus Wagner retired with a .327 lifetime batting average over a 21-year career that coincided almost exactly with the dead-ball era. He joined a crowd of legends who retired in 1917, including Ed Walsh (whose 1.82 career ERA is still the best

ever), Ed Reulbach, Jim Scott, and Eddie Plank.

The AL pennant-winner was Chicago, which went 100-54 with a lineup that put Chick Gandil at first, Eddie Collins at second, Swede Risberg at short, Buck Weaver at third, Ray Schalk behind the plate, and Happy Felsch and Joe Jackson in the outfield. Felsch hit .308, fifth in the league, and Jackson hit .301 with 17 triples. Although Boston once again led the league in pitching thanks to Carl Mays (second in the AL in ERA at 1.74), Babe Ruth (second in wins with 24), and Ernie Shore, the Red Sox hitting was no match for the probing White Sox attack.

Ty Cobb staged something of a comeback, winning the batting title at .383 (30 points better than George Sisler of St. Louis), as well as leading in stolen bases with 55, hits with 225, doubles with 44, and triples with 23.

Chicago won the World Series four games to two as the Giants suffered one of their patented postseason collapses in the fourth inning of game six. First, Zimmerman's throwing error put Collins on second; then, Robertson dropped Jackson's harmless fly to right. With runners on first and third, pitcher Rube Benton fielded Felsch's comebacker and caught Collins too far off third. He threw to Zimmerman, who pathetically chased Collins toward home plate, which both first baseman Holke and catcher Bill Rariden had neglected to cover.

1917

- Chicago claims its first AL flag since 1906.
- The Giants return to the top in the NL by a ten-game margin.
- The White Sox win the World Series in six games.
- Red Faber wins three games in the Series for the Sox.

- Dave Robertson of the Giants collects 11 hits in the Series, hitting .500.
- In game six of Series, New York's Heinie Zimmerman botches a run-down, allowing Eddie Collins to score.
- Edd Roush of Cincinnati takes his first NL bat crown (.341).

- Cardinal Rogers Hornsby tops the NL in total bases (253), triples (17), and SA (.484).
- Pete Alexander wins 30 for the third consecutive year.
- Ty Cobb reclaims the AL bat crown with a .383 BA, tops in the majors.

Although most of the rest of the 1917 World Champion Chicago White Sox look incensed, Eddie Collins *(back row, far left)* seems to be trying to conceal his happiness. Collins's suppressed jubilation may have come from his performance that year (.289 average, 18 doubles, 12 triples, and 67 RBI) and from the fact that his salary was more than three times higher than the majority of the Sox regulars, Joe Jackson *(front row, far right)* among them. (Jackson had a .301 average, 20 doubles, 17 triples, five home runs, and 75 RBI that season.)

- Cobb leads in hits (225), total bases (336), doubles (44), triples (23), OBP (.444), and SA (.571).

- Eddie Cicotte tops AL in wins (28).

- Cincinnati's Fred Toney and Chicago's Hippo Vaughn pitch double no-hit games on May 2, though Vaughn loses his in the tenth.

- On May 2, Toney beats Vaughn 1-0 in ten innings to break up a double no-hit game.

- Cleveland's Ray Chapman sets a major league record with 67 sacrifice hits.

- In August, the Pirates play a record four consecutive extra-inning games.

- George Mogridge of the Yankees no-hits Boston on April 24.

- Ernie Koob of St. Louis no-hits the White Sox on May 5.

- On May 6, Bob Groom of St. Louis again no-hits the Sox.

Jim Thorpe

Lefty Hippo Wins 23

Chicago's Hippo Vaughn (pictured) (23–13, a 2.01 ERA, 195 strikeouts, and five shutouts in 1917) and Pittsburgh's Wilbur Cooper (17–11, a 2.36 ERA, 99 Ks, and seven shutouts that year) were the two top southpaws in the National League during the late 1910s. Originally with the Yankees, Vaughn won 142 games for the Cubs over a seven-year span before his skills deserted him in 1921.

Hippo Vaughn

Thorpe So-So at Baseball

The reason Jim Thorpe never did much in baseball, allegedly, was because he could not hit breaking-ball pitchers. In 1917, for example, he spent 77 games in Cincinnati, hitting .247 with four home runs and 36 RBI before heading to New York for 26 games, a .193 average, and four RBI. He must have gotten a hold of at least a few such pitches during his coda season in 1919, however, when he batted .327. There is no record of the type of pitch Hippo Vaughn threw when Thorpe broke up the greatest no-hit duel in history on May 2, 1917.

Max Carey

Carey Leads Pitiful Pirates

The Pirates were so bad in 1917 that the 51 RBI collected by Max Carey topped the club that season. With that kind of support, future Hall of Famer Burleigh Grimes could manage just a 3–16 record that year.

Ernie Shore

Shore Runs Out of Steam

It has still not been decided whether or not Ernie Shore's gem in relief of Babe Ruth, in which he retired the succeeding 27 batters, qualifies as a perfect game. Ruth walked the first Senator of the game, was ejected for arguing the call, and Shore pitched nine perfect innings in relief. In any case, 1917 was Shore's last productive season. He finished as a teammate of Ruth's with the 1920 Yankees.

1917

- Three weeks before two Brownies no-hit his team, Cicotte no-hits the Browns on April 14.

- On June 23, Boston's Babe Ruth walks the first Senator of the game, argues the call, and is ejected.

- On June 23, Ernie Shore relieves Ruth and retires the next 27 batters.

- Donie Bush of Detroit tops the majors in runs with 112.

- Bobby Veach of Detroit wins the AL RBI crown with 103.

- Sore-armed Reb Russell of Chicago leads the AL in win pct. (.750).

- Max Carey once again heads the NL in thefts (46).

- Zimmerman leads the NL in RBI (102) and runs produced (158).

- The Pirates hire Hugo Bedzek, a college football coach, as their manager.

- Ferdie Schupp of New York tops the NL in win pct. (.750).

Hornsby Tops in SA, Triples

Rogers Hornsby in 1917 was a lean, hungry young Texan of seemingly unlimited hitting ability who had not yet found an infield position to call home. After being stationed mostly at third as a rookie in 1916, he played short all of 1917, posting a league-high .484 slugging average, 17 triples, and 253 total bases.

Rogers Hornsby

Dave Robertson

Robertson Vies for NL Dinger Title

In 1916 and 1917, with nearly a third of his extra-base hits being four-baggers, Dave Robertson tied for the National League home run crown both years with the identical sum of 12. World War I then carved nearly two full seasons out of his career, leaving him with only one more year as a full-time player.

Edd Roush

Roush Wins NL Bat Title

The last surviving Federal League participant as well as the last living player of the 1919 World Series, Edd Roush died in 1988 at the age of 94. In 1917, he took the National League batting crown with a .341 average. Something of an iconoclast and very much his own man, Roush was a frequent holdout when he was not offered what he felt was his worth.

- Giant Dave Robertson and Gavvy Cravath tie for the NL home run crown with 12.

- Wally Pipp repeats as the AL homer king (nine).

- Christy Mathewson, in his only full year as manager, brings the Reds home fourth.

- The Pirates finish last for the first time this century.

- The Pirates move Honus Wagner to first base where he hits .265; Wagner retires after the season.

- Walter Johnson slips to 23 wins, leads the AL in only Ks (188).

- Cobb hits safely in 35 consecutive games.

- Tigers have three men in the top four in RBI, including Veach (103), Cobb (102), and Harry Heilmann (86).

- On June 17, the Braves' Hank Gowdy becomes the first ML player to enlist in the service for World War I.

America actively entered World War I in 1918. It was a development that not only affected the outcome of both pennant races, but also made the home run revolution of the 1920s possible by indirectly causing Babe Ruth's conversion into an outfielder.

War had formally been declared in April of 1917, but players did not begin to join the armed services in significant numbers until Provost Marshall General Crowder issued his "work or fight" order in June of 1918. Unlike in World War II, baseball made no attempt to claim essential employment status on the grounds of aiding public morale, and the government ordered the season cut off on Labor Day, September 2. Personnel losses due to the enlistment or drafting of major leaguers were the biggest factor in both pennant races.

In the American League, the defending champion White Sox lost Red Faber, Swede Risberg, Joe Jackson, Happy Felsch, and Lefty Williams; they dropped to sixth place, 17 games out. A depleted Cleveland Indians team finished second, only 2½ games behind, thanks to big hitting seasons from Tris Speaker and shortstop Ray Chapman; they scored the most runs in the league with 504. The winner was a completely overhauled Boston Red Sox team that was run by executive Ed Barrow after manager Jack Barry was drafted.

WWI Raids Rosters, Cuts Season Short

Barrow filled the holes in his lineup by acquiring Stuffy McInnis, Wally Schang, and Bullet Joe Bush from the last-place Athletics and altered the course of history by playing staff ace Ruth in the outfield, mostly against righties, between starts. The Babe went 13-7 with a 2.22 ERA on the mound, but batted .300 with 11 triples, 11 home runs, and 66 RBI (third-best in the AL) in his 317 times at bat. He tied Philadelphia's Tilly Walker (who batted 414 times) for the league-lead in homers, the first of his 12 career home run titles. After he swatted a record 29 round-trippers the following year, Ruth's career as a pitcher was over. The 31-year-old Ty Cobb won the 1918 batting title at .382, as well as leading in triples with 14. Walter Johnson won 23 games, most in the league, and the ERA title at 1.27.

For the defending NL champion New York Giants, the war cost them outfielder Benny Kauff and pitchers Rube Benton and Jeff Tesreau; McGraw's team finished second, 10½ games behind Chicago. The relatively intact Cubs turned the pennant race into a cakewalk on the strength of

Fred Merkle's .297 batting average and 65 RBI, outfielder Max Flack's ten triples and 74 runs, and Hippo Vaughn's league-leading 22 wins and 1.74 ERA.

Brooklyn's Zach Wheat won the batting title at .335, nosing out the Reds' Edd Roush at .333. The third-place Reds suspended first baseman Hal Chase 74 games into the season for what was euphemistically termed "indifferent play"—in other words, fixing ball games for gamblers. The enigmatic Chase, whose enormous personal charm masked what one teammate called his "corkscrew mind," was given one more chance by the Giants.

The World Series set the stage for a player's strike. Rumors that the players would not be paid their prize money (a $2,000 share for each winner, a $1,400 share for each loser) had spread. After approaching the National Commission and receiving no support, the players planned to boycott the rest of the event (the Series stood at three games to one, Red Sox). With almost 25,000 fans in attendance at game four, Boston Mayor Fitzgerald made a public appeal to the patriotism of the players, who ultimately gave in; the owners, however, somehow escaped adhering to the players' compromise proposal that all proceeds from the Series be donated to a war charity.

The Red Sox won the World Championship four games to two.

1918

- The Red Sox vault back to the top in the AL.

- The Cubs are an easy NL winner.

- Owing to World War I, the season is ended on Labor Day, Sept. 2.

- The Red Sox triumph in a six-game World Series that begins on Sept. 5 and ends on Sept. 11.

- Babe Ruth extends his Series scoreless streak to 29.2 innings.

- The players strike prior to game five for higher World Series shares, but then back off.

- George Whiteman, a career minor leaguer, is the Series hero, though he'll never play in the majors again.

- Ty Cobb leads the AL and the majors at .382.

- Walter Johnson tops the majors in wins (23) and Ks (162).

- Johnson pitches 300 or more innings for a record ninth consecutive year.

- Ruth, still a part-time pitcher, ties for the AL homer lead with 11.

Stuffy McInnis was small for a first baseman and had almost no power, hitting a meager 20 home runs in 7,822 career at-bats. That he lasted as long as he did is partly a tribute to his remarkable consistency—between 1911 and 1924 he never hit below .272 or above .327—which was further reflected in the fact that he almost never made an error or struck out. He hit .272 in 1918, with 11 doubles, five triples, and 56 RBI.

- Detroit's Bobby Veach collects 78 RBI, most in the majors.

- Chicago's Hippo Vaughn leads the NL with 22 wins.

- The majority of the minor leagues shut down in midseason due to the war.

- Cubs rookie Charlie Hollocher leads the NL in hits with 161.

- Many players are drafted or else enlist in war, including Cincy manager Christy Mathewson.

- While in the service, Mathewson is accidentally gassed and subsequently contracts TB.

- Philadelphia's Scott Perry tops the AL in innings with 332, an AL rookie record.

- Perry wins 20 games for the last-place A's, who play just 130 games.

- On August 30, the Giants beat the Dodgers 1-0 in a game that lasts only 57 minutes.

Charlie Hollocher

Vaughn All Alone at 22

Because the curtain closed the 1918 regular season on Labor Day, reducing the number of games played by some teams to as few as 124, Hippo Vaughn of the Cubs was the lone National League hurler to win in excess of 20 games (22 victories). Two other Cubs, Lefty Tyler and Claude Hendrix, won 19 contests that year, giving the Bruins three of the NL's top five winners.

Hippo Vaughn

Benny Kauff

Kauff Departs Early

The leading hitter on the second-place Giants in 1918, Benny Kauff played just 67 games before his season was ended by a military call-up, turning in a .315 average, two home runs, and 39 RBI. Almost every team suffered at least one key loss that year to Uncle Sam; no club, however, was hit harder than the defending champion White Sox, who lost Joe Jackson, Swede Risberg, Red Faber, Lefty Williams, Eddie Collins, and Happy Felsch (among others) and fell to sixth place.

Hollocher Leads NL in Hits

The scouting report on Charlie Hollocher when he joined the Cubs in 1918 was that he was a fine-fielding shortstop, not much of a hitter, and pretty shaky upstairs. The scouts were wrong on the second count, dead accurate otherwise. He posted a .316 average and a National League-high 161 hits in 509 at-bats that year, nailing 23 doubles, six triples, a pair of home runs, and 38 RBI. In 1922, his last full season, he hit .340, led all National League shortstops in fielding, and fanned just five times. He took a gun to himself 18 years later with fatal results.

1918

- On August 1 vs. Pittsburgh, Brave Art Nehf pitches 20 scoreless innings before losing 2-0 in 21 innings.

- Dutch Leonard of Boston no-hits Detroit on June 3.

- Tris Speaker makes an ML season record two unassisted double plays by an outfielder.

- Carl Mays gives up only one run in winning both ends of a doubleheader on August 30.

- The Cards, under Jack Hendricks, fall to the NL cellar.

- Brooklyn's Zach Wheat becomes the last to win an NL bat crown (.335) without hitting a home run.

- Cincinnati's Heinie Groh tops the NL in runs (86) and doubles (28).

- Cincinnati's Sherry Magee leads the NL in RBI (76).

- Chicago's Hippo Vaughn tops the NL in ERA (1.74) and Ks (148).

- Cleveland's Ray Chapman tops the AL in runs (84) and walks (84).

Art Nehf

Nehf Hurls 20 Scoreless Innings

Art Nehf was an excellent pitcher who fell just a shade short of stardom. He posted a 2.69 ERA in 284 innings in 1918, hurling 20 scoreless innings against Pittsburgh on August 1 only to lose 2–0 in 21 frames. His last major league appearance came with the Cubs in the catastrophic seventh inning of game four of the 1929 World Series, when the Philadelphia A's tallied ten runs. Nehf had pitched in four Series with the Giants prior to that performance, becoming the New York ballclub's lone hurler to win 20 games during the run when the Giants copped a National League-record four consecutive flags.

Zach Wheat

Wheat Takes NL Bat Title

Two years after he topped the National League in total bases, Zach Wheat in 1918 became the last player to lead the senior loop in batting (.335) without hitting a single home run. To deepen the mystery, he collected just 18 extra-base hits and scored only 39 runs that season. Come 1920 and the arrival of the lively ball era, he jumped to 48 extra-base hits and 89 tallies.

Tesreau Calls It Quits After the War

Jeff Tesreau was one of the few players who did not return to the majors upon completing his part in the war effort (he closed his career with a 4–4 record in 1918, striking out 31 batters and posting a 2.31 ERA). Indeed, most major leaguers came through the experience virtually unscathed. Of the handful who perished, perhaps the most promising was Ralph Sharman, a young outfielder with the 1917 A's who died in the influenza epidemic.

Jeff Tesreau

- George Burns of the A's leads the AL in hits (178) and total bases (236).

- George Sisler wins the AL stolen base crown with 45.

- Twenty-game winner Claude Hendrix of Chicago is the NL's win pct. leader (.741).

- Tilly Walker of the A's ties Ruth for the AL homer crown (11).

- Dave Shean of Boston becomes the first 40-year-old regular to play in a World Series.

- Though the schedule is shortened, Jake Daubert sues the Dodgers for his full-season salary—and wins.

- Daubert leads the senior loop in triples (15), as the NL offensive crowns are again distributed among many players.

- Max Carey tops the NL in steals (58) and walks (62).

- In 126 games, the Red Sox get 105 complete games from their pitchers.

With the end of World War I in 1919, both baseball and the nation as a whole returned to business as usual. For some ballplayers, "business as usual" unfortunately meant plotting with gamblers to fix games. Gambling-related scandals had been a part of baseball going back to the mid-19th century, but in 1919 the national pastime suffered the ultimate corruption—the intentional throwing of the World Series by eight members of the Chicago White Sox.

In a season limited to 140 games by a baseball establishment still worried about its patriotic image, Cincinnati compiled a 96-44 record to run away with the NL pennant by 9 games over second-place New York.

The Giants had the league's best offense, scoring 605 runs on the strength of good years from George Burns (who led the league in stolen bases with 40, runs with 86, and walks with 82), Benny Kauff, and budding superstar Ross Youngs. A hustling right fielder who would finish with a .322 lifetime batting average in a ten-year career tragically cut short by death from Bright's disease at age 30, the popular Youngs led all NL hitters in doubles with 31. At .311, he was third in batting behind Rogers Hornsby's .318 and Edd Roush's .321.

The Reds had a two-prong attack. They had Roush, Heinie

BLACK SOX FIX SERIES, REDS WIN FREEBIE

Groh, Jake Daubert, and little leadoff hitter Morrie Rath; and they had a staff that allowed the fewest runs in the league and included 20-game winners Slim Sallee and Hod Eller, as well as Dutch Ruether, who recorded the third-lowest ERA in the league at 1.81. Although the Cubs' Pete Alexander and Hippo Vaughn were one and two in ERA at 1.72 and 1.79, their team scored the fewest runs in the NL and came in third, 21 games out.

In the AL race, an illusory powerhouse in Chicago had an unexpectedly difficult time shaking Cleveland and New York—or perhaps the cabal later responsible for the Series fix was dumping games for money down the stretch—before finally finishing at 88-52, 3½ up on Cleveland. The White Sox offense was powered by the .351-hitting Joe Jackson (who drove in 96 runs), Eddie Collins (who stole an AL-high 33 bases), and Happy Felsch. Their pitching staff allowed the second-fewest runs in the league thanks to 29-game winner Eddie Cicotte and 23-game winner Lefty

Williams, who, with a combined 604 innings pitched, carried most of the load.

Walter Johnson of the seventh-place Senators led in ERA at 1.49; Cicotte was second at 1.82. Detroit's Ty Cobb won the batting title at .384, but from the direction of Boston came the first distant rumblings of the coming home run explosion from Babe Ruth. In 432 at-bats, Ruth hit 29 home runs—19 more than runners-up Tilly Walker, George Sisler, and Frank Baker—and led the AL in runs with 103 and RBI with 114. His .657 slugging average set a 20th-century record that would stand until Ruth himself broke it the following year—by almost 200 points.

The Reds won the crooked best-of-nine World Series five games to three. The most dramatic moments—seen in retrospect, as the scandal didn't break until the following year—came in games three and six, when pitcher Dickie Kerr overcame the best efforts of his eight dishonest teammates to win 3-0 and 5-4.

The best-known player in on the fix, Jackson, always maintained afterward that he was innocent. He pointed to his Series-high .375 batting average and six RBI, although he never explained why he accepted money from the conspirators beforehand with free knowledge of their plans.

1919

- White Sox win AL flag.
- The Reds take their first NL flag.
- The World Series is extended to a best-of-nine affair for extra revenue, and the Reds triumph in eight.
- Suspicions are raised that the White Sox may have thrown the Series.

- Joe Jackson, one of the Sox under suspicion, leads all Series players with 12 hits and a .375 BA.
- White Sox Lefty Williams sets a Series record when he loses three games in three starts.
- Williams wins 23 games in the regular season.

- Hod Eller of the Reds is the pitching star of the Series with two CG wins.
- The season is abbreviated to 140 games because of the war.
- Cincinnati's Edd Roush wins his second NL bat crown in three years (.321).

In 1919, for the third consecutive year, Heinie Groh and his famous "bottle" bat
finished fourth in the National League in batting (he had a .310 average). Groh also
had the third-best slugging average with a .431 mark that year. A knee injury in 1925
short-circuited his career while he was still at his peak (especially as a fielder).

- Ty Cobb wins his final AL bat crown (.384).

- Babe Ruth hits an ML record 29 homers.

- Ruth also tops the AL in runs (103), RBI (114), SA (.657), OBP (.456), and total bases (284).

- On Sept. 28, the Giants beat the Phils 6-1 in a record 51 minutes.

- Eddie Cicotte of the White Sox tops the majors in wins with 29, finishing 29-7 with a 1.82 ERA.

- Cicotte tops the majors with 30 CGs and ties for the AL lead in innings with 307.

- Pete Alexander returns to the game with Cubs and tops the NL in ERA (1.72).

- Giants release Hal Chase, Heinie Zimmerman, and Jean Dubuc and they never play in majors again.

- The A's finish last for the fifth straight year.

Lefty Williams

Williams Blows Series

Lefty Williams joined the White Sox in 1916 after fashioning a 33–12 record for Salt Lake City in the Pacific Coast League the previous year. He went 23–11 with a 2.64 ERA and 125 strikeouts in 1919, then set a World Series record by losing three games in as many starts. He had assumed the place of Babe Ruth as the top southpaw in the American League when he was implicated in the Black Sox scandal.

George Burns

George Burns Up Bases

Both the National League and the American League had a standout player named George Burns in 1919. The two have remarkably similar career stats. George J. Burns of the Giants (pictured), however, was the better of the two at coaxing walks, stealing bases, and scoring runs. He racked up 82 bases-on-balls, 40 swipes, and 86 runs, all tops in the NL in 1919. He was, in fact, the best in the NL in all three departments for almost a full decade.

Eller Wins 20 for Reds

Hod Eller appeared to have a prosperous career ahead of him when he first won 20 games in 1919 and a pair of contests in the World Series, yet less than two years later he was out of the majors. Slim Sallee, the Reds' other 20-game winner in 1919, was also gone after 1921.

Hod Eller

1919

- On July 7, Giant catcher Mike Gonzalez allows eight stolen bases in an inning.

- Ruth becomes the first to hit four grandslams in a season.

- Ruth becomes the first to hit a homer during the season in every AL park.

- Doc Johnston of Cleveland sets a new AL record when he collects nine consecutive hits.

- Ed Konetchy of Brooklyn sets a 20th-century NL record with ten consecutive hits.

- Ray Caldwell of Cleveland no-hits New York on Sept. 10.

- Walter Johnson pitches a record fifth Opening Day shutout, 1-0 over the A's in 13 innings.

- Eller no-hits the Cards on May 11.

- Joe Oeschger of the Phils and Burleigh Grimes of Brooklyn battle to a 9-9, 20-inning tie on April 30.

Chicago White Sox

Tris Speaker

Tris Sparks Tribe to 2nd

Tris Speaker was the second great Cleveland player to be appointed player/manager. Unlike his predecessor, Nap Lajoie, Speaker enjoyed almost instant success. Under him, the Indians put on a stretch drive that nearly overhauled the White Sox in 1919. Yet Speaker himself slumped, hitting just .296 that year, a result of being saddled with the additional responsibility of managing.

Sox Take AL Flag

Is it pure coincidence that Eddie Collins *(front row, far left)*, the American League stolen base king that year with 33 swipes, sits somewhat at a distance from his teammates in this photo of the 1919 Chicago White Sox? Other notables: manager Kid Gleason *(back row, far left)*, Joe Jackson *(back row, second from the right)*, and Buck Weaver *(middle row, far right)*. Jackson tallied 12 hits and hit .375 in the World Series, but was kicked out of baseball anyway. In the 1989 movie *Field of Dreams*, Jackson came back from the dead to collect a few more at-bats.

Ty Cobb

Cobb Earns Last BA Title

In 1919, Ty Cobb picked up his last batting crown with a .384 average. In 1920, nearing 34 years of age, he seemed to have lost something when he hit just .334, his lowest average in 12 years. Cobb rebounded from the lapse to hit .389 in 1921 and .401 the year after.

- Joe Wilhoit of Wichita in the Western League hits in an OB record 69 consecutive games.

- Giant George Burns tops the NL in runs (86), walks (82), and steals (40).

- Gavvy Cravath leads the NL in homers (12) despite having only 214 at-bats.

- Cards new manager Rogers Hornsby is the NL runner-up in BA (.318).

- Chicago's Hippo Vaughn leads the NL in innings (307) and Ks (141).

- Tris Speaker leads the AL in total chances by an outfielder for a record eighth straight season.

- The last-place Phils are so short of pitching that Lee Meadows is the staff leader with just eight wins.

- The Pirates' keystone combo of George Cutshaw and Zeb Terry both top the NL in FA at their positions.

- Al Sothoron is the Browns' first 20-game winner since 1903.

In 1920, Babe Ruth played his first season as a New York Yankee. Showing the way for a new generation of upper-cutting power hitters, the Bambino posted slugging numbers the game had never seen.

.Besides hitting a Cobbian .376, Ruth swatted 54 home runs, which not only surpassed his own record of 29 but also each of the other seven AL teams. The nearest individual hitter, St. Louis' George Sisler, hit 19. Ruth led the league in slugging at .847, the highest mark recorded in either league until 2001. AL pitchers were no fools—they walked Ruth 148 times—but he still led the league in RBI with 137 and runs scored with 158.

Where Ruth led, others soon followed, as offense in almost every category rose steadily throughout the 1920s. Runs in the AL increased by about 1,000 in 1921. The NL followed the same pattern, although at a slower pace.

Sisler, who in 1920 actually collected 11 more total bases than Ruth at 399, batted .407, the seventh-best average of all time. Sisler also banged out 257 hits— still a record. In the National League, Cardinals second baseman Rogers Hornsby batted a league-leading .370, and led in doubles with 44, total bases with 329, and RBI with 94.

The baseball rule-makers assisted the new home run style of baseball by changing two rules.

RUTH BATS .376 AND BLASTS 54 HOMERS

The first was the outlawing of trick pitches such as the shine ball, the emery ball, and especially the spitball. That this had an enormous (and underrated) effect on major league pitching can be seen from the subsequent careers of 17 spitball pitchers, who were allowed, under a "grandfather clause," to continue to throw the pitch legally. While ERAs in both leagues shot up in 1920, the composite ERA of the 17 spitballers remained virtually unchanged.

The second change was the new practice of keeping clean baseballs in play throughout the game. This made for a more lively ball that traveled much farther in the air; thus, more home runs. Baseball's justification for the change was the fatal beaning of Cleveland shortstop Ray Chapman by Yankee pitcher Carl Mays, which many blamed on Chapman's inability to see a worn, discolored ball as it sped toward his skull.

Chapman's death greatly affected the AL pennant race, as New York faded to third, 1 game behind second-place Chicago. Cleveland won the flag thanks to Jim Bagby (31 wins) and rookie shortstop Joe Sewell, who sparked the Indians with a .329 batting average in August and September. The White Sox' chances were ruined when, after months of rumor, the team suspended the eight players suspected of throwing the 1919 World Series in the critical, final days of the season.

In the Series, the Indians met NL champion Brooklyn, which was led by spitballer Burleigh Grimes's 23 wins and 2.22 ERA. Cleveland won the Series five games to two. On the Indians' side, the games were marked by several World Series firsts, including Elmer Smith's grandslam, pitcher Bagby's homer, and Bill Wambsganss's unassisted triple play.

Besides the passing of the dead-ball era, 1920 also saw the establishment of the sole baseball commissionership under Judge Kenesaw Mountain Landis. This replaced the old three-man commission, which had been dominated by AL president Ban Johnson since its inception in 1903. One of Landis's first official acts was to ban for life the eight members of the "Black Sox," whose trial for fraud had resulted in a fishy acquittal that was rumored to have been engineered by powerful White Sox owner Charles Comiskey.

1920

- In January, the Red Sox sell Babe Ruth to the Yankees for $125,000.
- Cleveland wins its first major league pennant.
- Brooklyn triumphs for the second time in five years in the NL.
- Cleveland wins the World Series five games to two.

- In game five of Series, Cleveland second baseman Bill Wambsganss makes an unassisted triple play.
- Stan Coveleski wins three games for Cleveland in the Series.
- Doc Johnston (Cleveland) and brother Jimmy (Brooklyn) oppose each other in the Series.

- Cleveland shortstop Ray Chapman is beaned by NY pitcher Carl Mays August 16 and dies the next day.
- Ruth hits an ML record 54 homers.
- Ruth scores 158 runs, also a new ML record.
- Ruth sets an ML record with an .847 slugging average.

In 1919, Babe Ruth led all American League outfielders in fielding. In 1920, he had the lowest fielding average of any regular AL outfielder. It was virtually the only department in which he did not show a dramatic improvement. Ruth even topped the Yankees in stolen bases in 1920 with 14.

- Ruth produces 241 runs, also a new record.

- St. Louis' George Sisler wins the AL bat title with a .407 average.

- Rogers Hornsby cops his first NL bat title (.370).

- Jim Bagby of Cleveland is the last AL righty until 1968 to win 30 games.

- Late in the season, eight members of the White Sox are suspended for allegedly dumping the 1919 World Series.

- Judge Kenesaw Mountain Landis is named the first commissioner of baseball, a post he'll serve for the next 24 years.

- The eight White Sox are found innocent of rigging the Series by a Chicago jury.

- Landis permanently bars all eight suspended White Sox from organized baseball.

- Sisler sets an all-time major league record with 257 hits.

Ray Chapman

Chapman Killed

Ray Chapman hugged the plate so closely when he batted that his head was usually in the strike zone. Carl Mays, to his dying day, insisted that the pitch that killed Chapman would have been called a strike had he managed to duck out of the way. Chapman had a .303 average in 1920, with 27 doubles and 49 RBI.

Indians Mourn Ray

The 1920 World Champion Cleveland Indians wore black arm bands in memory of Ray Chapman *(inset)*, killed by a beaning. Joe Sewell *(front row, far right)* was Chapman's replacement. Jack Graney *(middle row, second from the left)* was a longtime Cleveland broadcaster.

Eddie Cicotte

Cicotte Proves Dependable

Eddie Cicotte was one of the four 20-game winners on the 1920 White Sox. The quartet had a composite 87-46 record, while the rest of the Sox staff was 9-12. Manager Kid Gleason went with just six pitchers for most of the year, using Roy Wilkinson and George Payne primarily in relief. Late in the season, Cicotte was banned for his part in the Black Sox scandal. Eddie was truly sorry for dumping the Series. His words dripped with irony when he said, "I'd give a million dollars to undo what I've done."

Cleveland Indians

1920

- The spitball and all other similar pitches are abolished.
- Detroit's Sammy Hale collects 17 pinch hits, an AL rookie record.
- Walter Johnson wins his 300th game.
- Johnson no-hits Boston on July 1.

- Cleveland's Larry Gardner is thrown out 20 times in 23 steal attempts.
- On Oct. 2, Pittsburgh and Cincinnati play the last ML tripleheader.
- Tris Speaker sets a new ML record with 11 consecutive base hits.
- Rube Foster organizes the Negro National League.

- On May 1, Ruth hits his first homer as a Yankee.
- On May 1, Leon Cadore of Brooklyn and Joe Oeschger of Boston both pitch all 26 innings of a 1-1 tie.
- Hornsby tops the NL in doubles (44), total bases (329), and SA (.559), and ties for the RBI crown (94).

Foster Forms NNL

The "Father of Black Baseball," Rube Foster created the Negro National League, the first organized black major league, in 1920. Although Foster was a pitcher in the early part of the century, by 1920 he functioned mainly as league administrator and manager of the Chicago American Giants, victors of the first three NNL pennants.

Rube Foster

Sisler Leads AL in Hitting

George Sisler was one of the greatest hitters in the game, though he seldom walked. He drew just 46 free passes as opposed to 257 hits in 1920. Strong in all other respects, Sisler also came close that year to becoming the first player to total 20 or more doubles, triples, and home runs in the same season.

Judge Kenesaw Mountain Landis

George Sisler

Landis Takes Charge

In his early years as commissioner, Judge Kenesaw Mountain Landis was like a kid at his first carnival, immediately trying all the wild rides. Landis was both feared and loathed by players, several of whom he banished for infractions that in retrospect seem ridiculously trivial. Landis later became known as a player's commissioner who was feared and loathed by many owners.

Bagby Leads AL in Wins

After netting an American League-high 31 victories in 1920, Jim Bagby (pictured) was good for only 21 more wins in his career. Ray Caldwell, a 20-game winner that year, collected just six more victories. And Duster Mails, a late-season sensation, was back in the minors two years later.

Jim Bagby

- Philly's Cy Williams tops the NL with 15 homers, 39 fewer than Ruth.

- Pete Alexander heads the NL in wins (27), ERA (1.91), CGs (33), innings (363), and Ks (173).

- Joe Jackson's 20 triples top the AL; Jackson is also high in almost every other hitting department.

- The White Sox have a record four 20-game winners, including Ed Cicotte and Lefty Williams.

- White Sox Jackson, Cicotte, and Williams are among the Eight Men Out.

- Owing to Ruth, the Yankees hit 115 homers, shattering the ML record.

- Phillies batters walk just 283 times, an ML record.

- The Giants' Benny Kauff is banned during the season after he's tried for being part of a stolen car ring; he's found not guilty.

- Phillie Gene Paulette is banned for allegedly betting on games in 1919.

BABE CRACKS 59 HRS IN BEST SEASON EVER

The home run revolution rolled on in both leagues in 1921, as the majors' homer production increased by about 50 percent over 1920. Babe Ruth, of course, led the way, as he cracked a record-setting 59 home runs for the first great team of the Yankees dynasty.

This may have been Ruth's finest season ever. He set all-time major league records for runs with 177 and total bases with 457. He also boasted an .846 slugging average—just one percentage point below his 1920 mark. Moreover, Ruth batted .378 in 1921, walked 144 times, and knocked in 171 runs.

Teammate Bob Meusel batted .318, drove in 135 runs (third-best in the AL), and hit 24 home runs (tied for second in the AL with St. Louis' Ken Williams). Besides receiving the best support in the league, the New York pitching staff was first in team ERA at 3.79 and strikeouts with 481. Staff workhorse Carl Mays went 27-9 and led the AL in wins, games, and innings pitched. Righthander Waite Hoyt (age 21) went 19-13 with a 3.10 ERA, fourth-best in the league behind Mays's 3.04.

Tris Speaker's Indians finished second, 4½ games back behind New York, as Speaker hit .362 and led all hitters with 52 doubles. Sixth-place Detroit fea-

tured a strong hitting duo of young Harry Heilmann (who won the batting title at .394) and old Ty Cobb, who was second in hitting at .389, fifth in runs with 124, and third in slugging at .596.

John McGraw won his seventh NL pennant by 4 games over Pittsburgh behind strong performances from George Kelly, the NL home run leader with 23; Frankie Frisch, who was first in stolen bases with 49 and second in runs with 121; and Ross Youngs, who was third in RBI with 102. The Giants fended off a season-long challenge from a strong-armed Pirates team that compiled the league's lowest ERA at 3.16, thanks to Babe Adams (runner-up in ERA at 2.64) and Whitey Glazner (third in ERA at 2.77).

Rogers Hornsby, of third-place St. Louis, dominated the NL hitters even more completely than Ruth did the AL's. Hornsby took the batting title with a .397

average, and also led the NL in runs, hits, doubles, triples, total bases, RBI, on-base average, and slugging.

Interestingly, a year after baseball's limited prohibition of the spitball, pitching categories in both leagues were dominated by the 17 legal spitball pitchers. In the AL, Chicago's Red Faber led in ERA at 2.47 and won 25 games; St. Louis' Urban Shocker led in wins with 27. In the NL, Cardinal Bill Doak won the ERA title at 2.58 and led in winning percentage at .714; Brooklyn's Burleigh Grimes spat his way to a league-leading 22 wins.

The first-ever "Subway Series" demonstrated that the New York Giants' bad postseason luck had changed, as the NL champs overcame a 2-0 deficit to win in eight games. The Giants were helped by a Ruth injury that kept him out of action for games seven and eight, which were won by the Giants 2-1 and 1-0.

Pitching decided the Series, as Giants Jesse Barnes and Phil Douglas went 4-1 with a combined ERA under 2.00. Waite Hoyt was the only pitching bright spot for the Yankees, compiling a 2-1 record with an ERA of 0.00 (Hoyt lost game eight 1-0 on an unearned run). Ruth's then-Manhattan Bombers were outhit .269 to .207, and matched in team home runs—two apiece.

1921

- The Yankees win their first AL pennant, leaving only the Senators and Browns winless.

- The Giants grab their first NL flag since 1917.

- In the last best-of-nine World Series and the first "Subway Series," the Giants beat the Yanks in eight.

- Yank Waite Hoyt has two wins and a perfect 0.00 ERA in three starts, but loses Series finale 1-0.

- First-inning error by Yankees shortstop Roger Peckinpaugh leads to only run in game eight of Series.

- Irish Meusel is the Series' top batsman with ten hits and seven RBI.

- Babe Ruth clubs 59 homers to shatter his own year-old record.

- Ruth produces an all-time record 457 total bases.

- Ruth scores an all-time record 177 runs.

- Ruth sets a new major league RBI record with 171.

Along with all his massive offensive accomplishments in 1921—an .846 slugging average, 177 runs scored, 59 home runs, 171 RBI, and 144 walks, highs in both leagues that year—Babe Ruth found time to pitch and win two games. During the 15 years Ruth played for the Yankees, he appeared on the mound five times, usually as a lark in a late-season starting assignment after the pennant was clinched. Ruth tailored a perfect 5–0 record in pinstripes.

- The A's finish last in the AL for an all-time record seventh straight year.

- Ruth hits his 137th career homer, breaking Roger Connor's record mark of 136.

- Yank Carl Mays leads AL in win pct. (.750) and ties for the lead in wins (27) and saves (seven).

- Detroit's Harry Heilmann hits .394 to win his first AL bat title.

- Heilmann also tops the AL in hits with 237.

- Rogers Hornsby, now installed at second for the Cards, cops his second NL bat crown at .397.

- The introduction of a livelier ball results in the Tigers hitting .316.

- Red Faber's AL leading 2.47 ERA is the only ERA figure below 3.00 in that circuit.

- On August 25, Harold Arlin of radio station KDKA in Pittsburgh does the first broadcast of a baseball game.

World Series

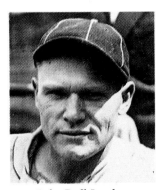

Baby Doll Jacobson

Baby Doll Bats .352

Despite a belated start—he didn't stick in the majors until he was nearly 27 years of age—Baby Doll Jacobson totaled 1,714 hits and posted a .311 career average over 11 years. In 1921, he racked up a .352 average, 211 hits, five home runs, and 90 RBI. He spent more than nine seasons as a Brownie.

Harry Heilmann

Polo Hosts NY Affair

All the games of the first "Subway" World Series were played in the Polo Grounds, the home park of both the Giants and the Yankees. The Giants, donned in white caps, were the home team on this day. Yankee first baseman Wally Pipp is photographed coming off the bag.

Heilmann Rises to .394

Most great hitters display their superiority almost from the first day they don a major league uniform. Harry Heilmann was the exception. After his first six seasons, his career batting average was .291. In his next season, 1921, he led the American League with a whopping .394 average.

1921

- Hornsby tops the NL in hits (235), RBI (126), runs (131), doubles (44), and total bases (378).

- Hornsby leads in runs produced (236), OBP (.458), and SA (.639), and ties in triples (18).

- Faber and Dickie Kerr win 44 of the White Sox's 62 victories.

- The White Sox, the game's most powerful team just two years earlier, sink to seventh place.

- Chewing gum magnate William Wrigley buys the Cubs.

- The AL as a whole hits a record .292.

- On April 28, Cleveland pitcher George Uhle collects six RBI in a game.

- The game's moguls rule that 17 pitchers can continue to use the spitball for the rest of their careers.

- Specs Toporcer of the Cards is the first infielder to wear glasses.

Jack Tobin

Tobin Nets 236 Hits

Jack Tobin was another Federal League alumnus who subsequently had a substantial career in the majors. In 1921, Tobin corralled 236 hits and scored 132 runs for a Browns team that may have had the best lineup in the American League. Only Urban Shocker, however, kept the Browns from having the worst pitching staff in the majors (he won 27).

Stan Coveleski

Coveleski Still Going Strong

Stan Coveleski was one of the few fortunate pitchers permitted to throw spitballs until they retired. The 1921 season was the fourth in a row in which Coveleski won 22 or more games for the Indians (he had a 23–13 record that year). His three complete-game victories in the 1920 World Series were the high point of his career.

Toporcer Wears Specs

In 1921, George Toporcer broke a barrier that was nearly as strong as the color line that existed until 1947. Toporcer became the first bespectacled player other than a pitcher to perform in the majors. A light hitter whose glovework also left something to be desired, Toporcer was never more than a utility man; he hit .264 and had a pair of RBI in 53 at-bats in 1921. He did, however, pave the way for other bespectacled players.

George Toporcer

- Red Sox Stuffy McInnis's .999 FA is a new ML record for first basemen.

- Browns Jack Tobin, George Sisler, and Baby Doll Jacobson all collect more than 200 hits.

- Burleigh Grimes leads the NL in CGs (30) and Ks (136), and ties for the lead in wins (22).

- Al Sothoron pitches the entire season (179 innings) without surrendering a home run.

- Eppa Rixey of the Reds gives up just one home run in 301 innings.

- The Reds pitching staff registers a record-low 308 strikeouts.

- The Reds' Ivy Wingo leads NL catchers in errors for the seventh time.

- The Giants' George Kelly tops the NL in homers with 23.

- Walter Johnson leads the majors in Ks with just 143.

The trend toward runs and homers continued in 1922, particularly in the National League. Philadelphia and St. Louis became the first NL teams in this century to crack more than 100 home runs during the season; the Phillies hammered 116, St. Louis hit 107. The NL batted .292 to the AL's .285 and saw its overall ERA rise to a bloated 4.10.

Only one NL pitcher, Shufflin' Phil Douglas of the Giants, recorded an ERA under 3.00. Once again, spitballers led each league in ERA—Douglas at 2.62 and White Sox Red Faber at 2.81 (though Douglas's ERA crown is disputed).

In both leagues, a host of sluggers crowded Babe Ruth for the limelight. In the AL, the St. Louis Browns' George Sisler won the batting title at .420—the third-best batting average of the century—and also led the league in runs with 134, hits with 246, triples with 18, and even stolen bases with 51.

The modern MVP Award was established in the AL in 1922 as successor to the defunct Chalmers Award, last given in 1914. Sisler won handily over Philadelphia knuckleballer Eddie Rommel, who went 27-13 to lead the AL in wins. Sisler's teammate Ken Williams led the AL in home runs with 39, two more than runner-up Tilly Walker of the Athletics. Williams also led the league in runs batted in with 155 and total bases with 367.

GIANTS TAKE THEIR SECOND SUBWAY SERIES

In the NL, Rogers Hornsby completed his adjustment to the home run era by producing the National League's first undisputed 20th-century Triple Crown (some historians say Heinie Zimmerman won the Triple Crown in 1912). Hornsby put together one of the greatest seasons in National League history, hitting .401 with 42 home runs and 152 RBI. He also banged out 250 hits and 46 doubles, slugged .722, and scored 141 runs. To top it off, Hornsby led NL second basemen in putouts, double plays, and fielding average.

Ruth's season was ruined by a preseason run-in with new commissioner Kenesaw Mountain Landis. The two battled over the Babe's post-World Series barnstorming trip, which Landis had ruled illegal. Angry at being openly defied by the Yankees slugger, Landis suspended Ruth (and teammate Bob Meusel, who also made the trip) for the first month of the 1922 season. A pouting Ruth batted only .315 with 35 home runs in 110 games.

As a result of the partial loss of their two best hitters, the Yankees were outscored 867-758 by a

Browns team that nipped at their heels all season and even took over the lead for a while in midsummer. Besides Sisler and Williams, St. Louis fielded Baby Doll Jacobson, who hit .317 with 16 triples, as well as the American League's best pitching staff, led by 24-game winner Urban Shocker.

Nevertheless, the Yankees edged the Browns by 1 game to repeat as pennant-winners. A big factor was the addition of several more former Red Sox, including 26-game winner Joe Bush, pitcher Sad Sam Jones, and shortstop Everett Scott. The Yankees' Wally Pipp batted .329 with 32 doubles and ten triples, and Whitey Witt scored 90 runs and led the AL in walks with 89.

The 1921 NL pennant-winners also repeated in 1922, as the Giants finished 7 games ahead of a Cincinnati team led by pitchers Eppa Rixey, who topped the NL in wins with 25, and Pete Donohue, who was third in ERA at 3.12.

In a rematch of the 1921 Subway Series—this time under a best-of-seven format—Ruth and the Yankees were thrashed again, managing only a game two 3-3 tie out of five games. Giants pitchers Jesse Barnes, Art Nehf, Hugh McQuillan, and Jack Scott completely shut down the Yankees, who scored only 11 runs in the five games. Irish Meusel knocked in seven runs for the Giants, while Ruth batted just .118 with no homers.

1922

- The Yankees take their second AL flag in a row.
- The Giants take their second straight NL pennant.
- The second Subway Series comes a cropper as the Giants win in a four-game sweep (plus one tie).

- Giant Irish Meusel is again the slugging star in the Series with a homer and seven RBI.
- Babe Ruth hits .118 in his second World Series.
- Suspended part of the season for an illegal barnstorming tour the previous fall, Ruth drops to 35 homers.

- The AL gives out a league MVP Award for the first time; George Sisler wins handily.
- Ken Williams of the Browns becomes the new AL homer king (39).
- Williams also leads in RBI (155), total bases (367), and runs produced (244).

The camera catches a Giants rally in the 1922 World Series. John McGraw's men scored 18 runs in five games, hardly an offensive onslaught. The Yankees managed only 11 runs, just one of them driven in by Babe Ruth. The Giants hit .309 as a team, yet Bob Meusel was the lone Yankee to bat .300.

- Sisler leads the AL with a .420 BA, a record for first basemen in this century.

- Spearheaded by Sisler, the Browns finish second in the AL, 1 game out.

- Rogers Hornsby sets new NL records with 42 homers, 152 RBI, and .722 slugging average.

- Hornsby's .401 BA makes him the first NLer since 1901 to top the .400 mark.

- Eddie Rommel of the seventh-place A's leads the AL with 27 wins.

- Sisler hits in 41 straight games, a new AL record.

- Ray Grimes of the Cubs drives in at least one run in 17 straight games.

- White Sox fork over $125,000 to San Francisco of the Pacific Coast League for Willie Kamm.

- George Uhle becomes the first pitcher since 1901 to both win 20 games and have an ERA over 4.00.

Charles Comiskey

Comiskey's Sox Flop

Charles Comiskey's uncharacteristic extravagance proved too little too late. In 1922, Comiskey's White Sox finished fifth, 17 games out. A year later, even their expensive new purchase, Willie Kamm, could not keep them from tumbling to seventh. In 1924, the Pale Hose landed in the basement for the first time in club history.

Giants Take NL Flag

A shot of the ballclub that would be John McGraw's last World Championship team. By 1922, Frankie Frisch *(second row, far right)* had already emerged as the club leader. Hugh Jennings *(to the right of McGraw, who is in the center)* and Casey Stengel *(beside Jennings)* would make the Hall of Fame primarily for their managerial contributions.

Ken Williams

Williams Tops AL in HRs

Ken Williams interrupted Babe Ruth's unchallenged reign as the American League slugging king in 1922, topping the league with 39 home runs (Ruth hit 35 dingers). On his home turf, Sportsman's Park, Williams was virtually unstoppable that year; on the road, he, as the rest of the Browns, had problems.

New York Giants

1922

- Detroit's Harry Heilmann hits 21 homers, and ten of them come in Shibe Park against the A's.

- On April 22, Williams becomes the first player since 1900 to hit three homers in a game.

- The Browns are the first team in ML history to have four 100-RBI men.

- Hornsby hits in 33 straight games.

- In late August, the Cubs beat the Phils 26-23 in the highest-scoring game in ML history.

- The Supreme Court rules baseball is a sport, not a business, and thus not subject to anti-trust laws.

- Pittsburgh's Max Carey sets a stolen base pct. record of .962 when he's successful in 51 of 53 attempts.

- White Sox Ray Schalk leads AL catchers in FA a record eighth time.

- Jesse Barnes of New York no-hits the Phils on May 7.

Carey Pilfers 51

Max Carey was an ace basestealer in the 20 seasons of his major league career, though records are not available as to the number of times he was caught swiping. On what evidence there is, however, Carey was not only a prolific basestealer but an efficient one as well. In 1922, he stole 51 bases in 53 attempts.

Irish Meusel

Irish: .331 BA, 132 RBI

Of the members of the Giants and Yankees dynasties of the 1920s who played at least ten seasons and had career batting averages above .300, all but two are in the Hall of Fame. Oddly, the two were siblings: Irish and Bob Meusel. Irish (pictured in uniform) hit .331 with 132 RBI in 1922. Standing behind him is brother Bob.

Max Carey

So-So Uhle Wins 22

George Uhle's 22 wins and 4.08 ERA for Cleveland in 1922 were just one important measure of how different the game had suddenly become. Uhle became the first pitcher since 1897 to reach 20 wins while posting an ERA over 4.00.

George Uhle

- On April 30, White Sox Charlie Robertson tosses a perfect game vs. Detroit—baseball's last until 1956.

- Carey steals a record (since broken) 31 consecutive bases.

- Chicago's Red Faber tops the AL in ERA (2.81), CGs (31), and innings (352).

- Led in wins by Art Nehf with 19, the Giants are the first NL team to win a pennant without a 20-game winner.

- The Reds' Eppa Rixey tops the NL with 25 wins and 313 innings pitched.

- Cards catcher Pickles Dillhoefer dies of typhoid fever.

- Cards outfielder Austin McHenry, a .350 hitter in 1921, dies of a brain tumor.

- Dodger Dazzy Vance's 134 Ks are the fewest ever by an NL leader.

- Pittsburgh's Rabbit Maranville goes a single-season record 672 at-bats without hitting a home run.

SWEET REVENGE: YANKS TOPPLE HATED GIANTS

In 1923, the Giants-Yankees rivalry extended beyond the white lines of the baseball diamond. John McGraw's venerable NL club evicted the upstart Yankees from their newly renovated home park, the Polo Grounds, which the two teams had shared since 1913. The Yankees responded by building Yankee Stadium, a monumental state-of-the-art facility a short distance across the Harlem River in the Bronx. As luck would have it, both teams won their third straight pennants to meet again in October.

The Yankees had an easy time of it during the season, winning the AL flag by 16 games over the offensive-minded Detroit Tigers. Detroit featured Harry Heilmann, the batting champ at .403; Ty Cobb, who hit .340 and scored 103 runs; and first baseman Lu Blue, who drew 96 walks to score 100 runs on only a .284 batting average.

A half-game behind Detroit were the Cleveland Indians, the league's top scorers with 888 runs. They were paced by 35-year-old Tris Speaker, who posted 130 RBI (tied for league-best with Babe Ruth), 133 runs, and a .380 batting average (good for third place behind Ruth's .393). Cleveland spitballer Stan Coveleski took the ERA title at 2.76, and teammate George Uhle led in wins with 26 and innings pitched with 358. The St. Louis Browns

fell from second place to fifth that season after an eye injury benched their ace, Gorgeous George Sisler.

Ruth regained his status as the AL's best hitter by leading in runs with 151, home runs with 41, slugging at .764, and on-base average at .545. He also drew 170 walks, the most by any batter until 2001. Ruth won the MVP Award over Chicago's Eddie Collins.

But contrary to their all-slugging image, the real strength of this Yankee team was pitching. Herb Pennock, another Red Sox refugee, went 19-6 for New York to lead the AL in winning percentage. Waite Hoyt was second in ERA at 3.01, and Sad Sam Jones led New York in victories with 21. The Yankees' 3.66 team ERA led all AL staffs.

It was the other New York team that led its league in runs scored, with 854, but the Giants' attack was more of a team effort. Ross Youngs batted .336 with a league-high 121 runs scored; Frankie Frisch was fifth in hitting

at .348, scored 116 runs, and drove in 111; and Irish Meusel led the NL in RBI with 125.

Once again, New York beat out a strong-armed Cincinnati Reds team that compiled an ERA of 3.21, thanks largely to a career year from Dolf Luque, one of the first Cubans to star in the major leagues. He led the NL in wins with 27, shutouts with six, winning percentage at .771, and ERA at an incredible 1.93. In a year when two NL teams batted in the .290s, opponents hit only .235 off Luque.

Rogers Hornsby won the batting title at .384, beating out teammate Jim Bottomley at .371, but his heroics had no bearing on the pennant race. The Cardinals finished at 79-74, 16 games out. Cy Williams's league-leading 41 home runs mattered even less, as his Phillies lost 104 games and came in last.

Colorful Giants outfielder Casey Stengel hit Yankee Stadium's first-ever World Series homer, an inside-the-parker that gave Rosy Ryan a 5-4 victory over the Yankees' Joe Bush. Stengel also cracked a game-winning homer in game three. But the Yankees finally broke the Giants' spell to win games four, five, and six, taking the Series four games to two. Ruth batted .368 with three home runs, and his team batted .293. Bob Meusel knocked in eight runs in the Series while Joe Dugan drove in five.

1923

- The Yankees cop their third straight AL flag.
- The Giants follow suit in the NL.
- The Yankees get World Series revenge, beating the Giants in six games.
- Babe Ruth bounces back to hit .368 with three homers in Series.
- Aaron Ward of the Yankees leads all Series hitters with a .417 BA.
- Ruth is selected the AL's MVP.
- Rogers Hornsby takes his fourth consecutive NL bat crown (.384).
- Hornsby tops the NL in OBP (.459) and SA (.627).
- Harry Heilmann begins his odd knack for copping the AL bat crown every other year as he hits .403.
- Ruth regains the AL homer crown by belting 41.
- The Phils' Cy Williams hits 41 homers to top the NL.

The scene depicted here could have occurred in every game of the 1923 World Series but one. Only in the third contest did the Yankees fail to have a multiple-run inning. On that day, they lost 1–0 to the Giants on a homer by Casey Stengel. Stengel also won game one with an inside-the-park blow.

- Tris Speaker sets a new modern record for doubles with 59.

- Yankee Stadium opens on April 18; New York wins 4-1 over Boston on a three-run homer by Ruth.

- Ruth reaches base an all-time season record 379 times.

- Radio station WEAF in New York becomes the first station to broadcast a World Series.

- The Yankees collect an AL record 30 hits vs. Boston on Sept. 28.

- On July 7 vs. Boston, Cleveland scores 13 runs in the sixth inning after two men are out.

- Pittsburgh's Charlie Grimm sets an NL record by hitting in 23 consecutive games to begin the season.

- New York's Jack Bentley hits .427, an NL record for pitchers.

- George Uhle of Cleveland bangs out 52 hits, a season record for pitchers.

Bentley: 13-8, .427 BA

Playing for Baltimore in 1920, Jack Bentley led the International League in ERA and RBI. The following year, he topped the IL in batting and homers and was 12–1 as a pitcher. It seemed for a while that he could also do double duty in the majors. In 1923, he went 13–8 for the Giants and hit .427. By 1926, however, his arm was out of gas.

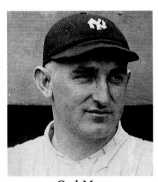

Carl Mays

Mays Beats A's 23 Times

The A's never got another crack at Carl Mays after he beat them for a record 23rd straight time on August 24, 1923. The Yankees released him that fall after exiling him to the bullpen for most of the season (he went 5–2 with a 6.22 ERA). Mays proved he wasn't yet washed-up by winning 20 games for the Reds in 1924.

Jack Bentley

Babe Ruth

Babe's Bat Bounces Back

Babe Ruth's dismal performance in the 1922 World Series nearly cost manager Miller Huggins his job. After Ruth's big 1923 Series, however—a 368 average, three home runs, and three RBI—his teammates shared the sentiments of Waite Hoyt, who once said, "Every major leaguer and his wife should teach their children to pray: 'God bless Mommy, God bless Daddy, and God bless Babe Ruth.'"

Blue Nets Walks, Runs

Almost every player was enamored with hitting home runs by the mid-1920s. One notable exception was Lu Blue, a nimble switch-hitting first baseman who tagged more than six homers in a season just once, yet scored more than 100 runs in a year six times (in 1923, he tallied a .284 average, one home run, and 100 runs). Blue was gifted at collecting walks (96 in 1923). His total of 127 walks in 1931 was the White Sox season record for 60 years.

Lu Blue

1923

- The Yankees become the first team in history to average less than one error per game.
- On August 24, Yankee Carl Mays beats the A's for a record 23rd consecutive time.
- Sam Jones of New York no-hits the A's on Sept. 4.

- Howard Ehmke of Boston no-hits the A's on Sept. 7.
- Ehmke loses another no-hitter in his next start on a questionable decision by the official scorer.
- George Burns, Red Sox first baseman, performs an unassisted triple play on Sept. 14.

- Ernie Padgett, Braves shortstop, performs an unassisted triple play on Oct. 6.
- Yankee Everett Scott leads AL shortstops in FA for a record eighth consecutive year.
- Ruth collects a record 170 walks.

Yankee Stadium

Cy Williams

Williams Hits 41 HRs

Cy Williams led the National League in home runs four times, the last when he was approaching 40 years of age. He was crowned the home run champion in 1923 with 41 four-baggers. Nearly age 28 before he won a regular job in the majors, Williams went on to surpass 250 round-trippers—only the second NL player to do so (Rogers Hornsby was the first).

Charlie Grimm

Yankee Stadium Opens Doors

Here is how it looked to anyone in the vicinity of East 161st Street in the Bronx on April 18, 1923, the day that Yankee Stadium opened. The entire structure took just 284 days to complete.

Grimm Bats Career-Best

Owing in part to his 23-game hitting streak at the start of the season, Charlie Grimm hit a career-high .345 in 1923. Grimm was one of the first to accumulate 1,000 RBI without ever netting 100 in a season.

- Ty Cobb scores his 1,741st run, moving him ahead of Honus Wagner on the all-time list.
- Lou Gehrig debuts with the Yankees, batting .423 in 26 at-bats.
- Paul Strand of Salt Lake City in the PCL collects an OB record 325 hits in a season.

- Pete Schneider of Vernon in the PCL hits five homers and a double in one game.
- Giant Frankie Frisch leads the NL in hits (223), total bases (311), and runs produced (215).
- Ruth is the AL runner-up in batting with a .393 BA, his personal best.

- Ruth's .545 OBP sets an ML record that will stand until 1941.
- George Sisler, the AL's leading hitter in 1922, is idled all season after sinus surgery and never really recovers his batting eye.
- Dolf Luque of Cincinnati leads ML with 27 wins and a 1.93 ERA.

The big news in 1924 was not what happened, but what didn't happen. The New York Giants won again—their fourth flag in four years—but that was becoming routine. The Yankees, however, dropped to second place, 2 games behind the underdog Washington Senators, who had finished 23¹/₂ games out only a year earlier.

You couldn't blame it on Babe Ruth; he won his only career batting title at .378 and led in homers (46), runs (143), walks (142), on-base average (.513), and slugging (.739). The rest of the offense wasn't bad, either. Wally Pipp legged out a league-leading 19 triples, third baseman Jumping Joe Dugan scored 105 runs, and Bob Meusel hit .325 and drove in 120 runs.

It was the Yankees' pitching that faltered a bit, compiling an ERA of 3.86, second in the league. Joe Bush's 17-16 record and Bob Shawkey's 4.11 ERA offset good efforts from 21-game winner Herb Pennock, Waite Hoyt, and Sad Sam Jones.

But the deciding factor in the 1924 AL race was the pitching of Walter Johnson, who after 19 years finally played on a team that provided him decent offensive support. The 36-year-old dead-ball veteran led the AL in strikeouts with 158, wins with 23, shutouts with six, and ERA at 2.72. He was voted AL MVP.

SENATORS SLAY GIANTS IN CLASSIC SERIES

Rounding out the rest of Washington's staff, which led the AL in ERA at 3.34, was lefty Tom Zachary, who went 15-9 with a 2.75 ERA; George Mogridge, who finished 16-11; and early relief ace Firpo Marberry, who recorded 15 saves. The Senators' offense included Hall of Fame outfielder Goose Goslin, who hit .344 with a league-leading 129 RBI; Sam Rice, who hit .334 and scored 106 runs; and first baseman Joe Judge, who batted .324.

The NL race also featured a surprise contender in Brooklyn, which rose from sixth place in 1923 to win 92 games in 1924. Brooklyn was sparked by hitting stars Jack Fournier, who was second in the NL in RBI with 116 and first in home runs with 27; and Zach Wheat, who hit .375, second only to Rogers Hornsby's .424. Brooklyn also featured the pitching duo of spitballer Burleigh Grimes and Dazzy Vance, who combined for 50 wins, 60 complete games, and 620 innings. Vance, who led the league with a

2.16 ERA, won the NL's first MVP Award.

While Hornsby—with a league-leading 121 runs, 227 hits, 373 total bases, and 89 walks—was turning in a fine year for sixth-place St. Louis, it was the New York Giants who led the NL in runs scored. The Giants were driven by George Kelly, who batted .324 and drove in an NL-high 136 runs, as well as Frankie Frisch and Ross Youngs. McGraw's team survived tough challenges from Brooklyn, 1¹/₂ games back at 92-62, and Pittsburgh, which came in 3 games off the pace at 90-63.

The Giants and Senators played an exciting, seven-game Series that was one of the closest in history. Four of the games were decided by one run and two went into extra innings.

New York won game one on a Youngs single in the 12th. Washington won game two on a Roger Peckinpaugh double in the ninth. The two teams split the next four games, thus setting up a game-seven showdown.

The finale went 12 innings, with Washington the winner. The game was decided by two bad-hop hits over third baseman Freddy Lindstrom's head, and comical misplays by New York catcher Hank Gowdy and shortstop Travis Jackson. Walter Johnson got the win in relief, his first career World Series victory.

1924

- The Giants win their NL record fourth straight flag.
- Washington wins its first American League flag.
- The Senators win one of the most exciting World Series in history in seven games.

- Washington wins game seven of Series on a bad-hop single by Earl McNeely in the 12th inning.
- Walter Johnson loses his two Series starts, but wins game seven in relief.
- Washington's Goose Goslin is the Series' hitting star with a .344 BA, three homers, and seven RBI.

- John McGraw wins his NL record tenth and last pennant.
- Johnson wins the AL MVP Award.
- The NL joins the AL in giving a league MVP award; the first NL winner is Brooklyn's Dazzy Vance.
- Rogers Hornsby leads the NL with a .424 BA, a post-1901 NL record.

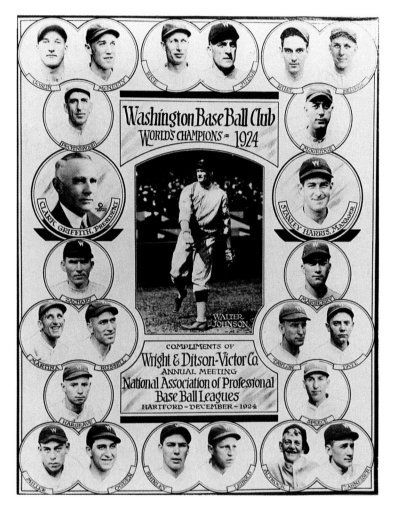

The nation's capital fielded a team in the original major league, the 1871 National Association, and at least one in virtually every season after that, yet had to wait 53 years for its first pennant-winner. Not in the picture are Wid Matthews and Doc Prothro, two subs who figured prominently in the pennant drive in 1924 yet were no longer with the Senators by Series time.

- Babe Ruth tops the AL in homers (46) and BA (.378).

- Ruth fails to win the Triple Crown when he finishes second in RBI to Goslin (129-121).

- Johnson's 23 wins and 158 strikeouts pace the AL.

- Vance leads the majors in wins with 28 and also in Ks with 262—a very high figure for this era.

- Washington's Firpo Marberry (15 saves) becomes the first relief specialist in ML history.

- Jim Bottomley of the Cards collects an ML record 12 RBI in a Sept. 16 game vs. Brooklyn.

- Giant Heinie Groh's .983 fielding percentage sets a new ML record for third basemen.

- The Giants' Jimmy O'Connell becomes the last major leaguer to be banned for life while still active.

- O'Connell banned for life for offering an oral bribe to a Phils player on the last weekend of the season.

Jimmy O'Connell

O'Connell Banned for Life

Jimmy O'Connell was the last major league player to be barred for either accepting or offering a bribe. His two-year career ended at the conclusion of the 1924 season. He contended that he solicited Phils shortstop Heinie Sand at the behest of several other Giants players, all of whom were exonerated by Kenesaw Mountain Landis. It was widely believed that O'Connell, a substitute, was only a convenient fall guy. Nevertheless, O'Connell was cut short of a promising career. In 1924, at the tender age of 23, he batted .317. In just 104 at-bats, he scored 24 times. Two years earlier, the Giants had paid $75,000 for O'Connell's services.

Rogers Hornsby

Hornsby Takes NL Bat Title

Hitting was the obsession of Rogers Hornsby, and for the five-year period between 1921 and 1925 his dedication paid off in a .402 composite batting average. His mark would have been even higher were it not for an illness in 1923 that held him to just 107 games and reduced his average to a "mere" .384. He came back in 1924 to take the batting crown with a .424 average, a post-1901 record in the National League.

Goslin Tops AL in RBI

Although Goose Goslin spearheaded the American League in 1924 with 129 RBI, he whacked just a dozen home runs. Not until 1952 would the AL again have an RBI leader who failed to finish among the loop's top five home run hitters (Al Rosen). In subsequent years, even though he played in mammoth Griffith Stadium, Goslin became one of the AL's more prolific sluggers, often finishing among the leaders in four-baggers.

Goose Goslin

1924

- Max Carey leads NL outfielders in chances accepted a loop record ninth time.
- On August 2, Joe Hauser of the A's sets a new AL record with 14 total bases in a game.
- Sam Rice of Washington hits in 31 consecutive games.

- Freddy Lindstrom of the Giants, age 18, becomes the youngest World Series participant.
- Johnson's AL strikeout crown is his record 12th.
- Lyman Lamb of Tulsa in the Western League hits an OB record 100 doubles.

- Jesse Haines of St. Louis no-hits the Braves on July 17.
- Hornsby tops the NL in runs (121), hits (227), doubles (43), total bases (373), and SA (.696).
- Brooklyn's Jack Fournier leads the NL in homers (27) and is second to Hornsby in walks (89-83).

Bottomley: 12 RBI in One Day

One of the eyewitnesses to the record-shattering 12-RBI performance of Jim Bottomley (pictured) on September 16, 1924, was Dodger manager Wilbert Robinson, who held the one-game RBI record of 11. Bottomley started his onslaught against Dodger rookie Rube Ehrhardt, who had debuted with five straight wins before encountering Sunny Jim's hot bat.

Jim Bottomley

Max Carey

Carey Brilliant in Field

Although it is safe to venture that Max Carey was the game's top base thief during the late 1910s and early 1920s, it is not so easy, in retrospect, to gauge his fielding prowess. On the evidence that is currently available, he would seem to have been one of the best, perhaps nearly the equal of Tris Speaker. In 1924, he led National League outfielders in chances accepted for the ninth time.

Travis Jackson

Jackson's a Series Bomb

Travis Jackson hit just .074 and made three errors in the 1924 World Series, the first in which he appeared as the regular shortstop for the Giants. In the 12th inning of the finale, he bobbled an easy grounder by Walter Johnson that ought to have been Washington's third out, opening the door for Earl McNeely's pebble-struck hit that won it. Jackson, a Hall of Fame shortstop, was an absolute bomb in World Series play. Along with his critical errors, he batted .074 in the '24 Series. In the 1933 fall classic, he batted .222. And in the 1936 Series, Jackson hit a mere .190. In 19 career World Series games, he posted a .149 batting mark and a .164 slugging average.

- WMAQ broadcasts the home games of both the Cubs and the White Sox in Chicago.

- Ruth tops the majors in runs (143), walks (142), OBP (.513), SA (.739), and total bases (391).

- Pittsburgh rookie shortstop Glenn Wright knocks in 111 runs, tops NL shortstops in assists and DPs.

- World Champ Washington hits the fewest homers in the majors—22.

- Pirates rookie Kiki Cuyler hits .354 and is fourth in BA and SA (.539).

- Cleveland's George Burns goes 6-for-6 on June 19.

- Cuyler goes 6-for-6 on August 9.

- Giant Frankie Frisch goes 6-for-7 on Sept. 10.

- Vance's 2.16 ERA is .53 runs better than any other pitcher's in the ML.

- The Giants win their third straight pennant without a 20-game winner.

- Reds manager Pat Moran dies in spring training of Bright's disease.

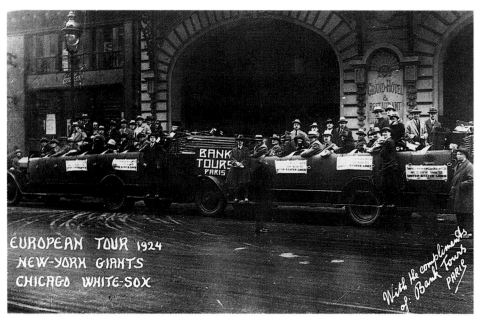

European Tour

Giants, Sox Depart for Europe

The Giants and the White Sox embarked on a tour of Europe after the 1924 season to display the American pastime to an audience which, for the most part, had never before seen baseball played. The players and their spouses who made the trip are shown here in front of the Grand Hotel in Paris. Baseball couldn't have sent two more diverse teams to Europe. The Giants won the National League pennant in '24, while the Sox finished in the AL basement.

Senators Best Giants

A shot of a pickoff attempt by the Giants in the 1924 World Series that failed. John McGraw's last appearance in a fall classic made him the only manager ever to lose two deciding Series games in overtime. As in the 1912 loss to the Red Sox, the Giants lost on a misplayed pop foul that gave a Senators batter a second chance. McGraw won only three of the nine World Series in which he managed. He lost more Series games (28) than any manager in history.

World Series

1924

- Tony Boeckel becomes the first MLer to be killed in an auto accident.

- Jake Daubert dies at 40 after a routine operation.

- The Cubs swap Vic Aldridge, George Grantham, and Al Niehaus to Pittsburgh for Rabbit Maranville, Charlie Grimm, and Wilbur Cooper.

- The Cubs are caught stealing an NL record 149 times.

- George Grantham tops the NL in batter Ks with 63, the fewest ever by a leader.

- Stuffy McInnis fans just six times, an NL record for fewest by a first baseman.

- Edd Roush of the Reds leads the majors with 21 triples.

- The Giants' George Kelly leads the NL in RBI (136) and runs produced (206).

- Brooklyn's Burleigh Grimes leads the NL in innings (311) and is second in wins (22).

Griffith Hosts Series

A look at Washington's Griffith Stadium, the American League site of the 1924 World Series. Despite its enormous dimensions—the distance to the left-field foul pole was 350 feet—the park seated just 27,410 attendees.

Griffith Stadium

Jesse Haines

Haines Posts Dismal Year

The Cardinals paid the Kansas City team of the American Association about $10,000 for Jesse Haines after he won 21 games for the club in 1919; in 1924, Haines no-hit the Braves on July 17 yet posted an 8–19 record for the season. Not until World War II would the Cards purchase another minor leaguer, as their farm system supplied them with all the talent they needed for a quarter of a century.

Hank Gowdy

Gowdy Stumbles into Notoriety

A standout defensive receiver and a solid hitter, Hank Gowdy was 35 years old in 1924 and had not been a regular backstopper for a number of years. Because Frank Snyder was ailing, Gowdy had to do yeoman duty in the World Series that year. He was catching his seventh game in as many days when his foot got tangled in his own mask on Muddy Ruel's pop foul. Gowdy's goof, along with an error by Travis Jackson and two bad-hop hits past Freddy Lindstrom, allowed Washington to win the decisive game 4-3 in 12 innings.

- Carey leads the majors with 49 steals.
- Wally Pipp, in his last full season as Yankees first baseman, leads the AL in triples (19).
- Rice tops the AL with 216 hits.
- Sloppy Thurston wins 20 games for the last-place White Sox and tops the AL in CGs (28).

- Johnson's 2.72 ERA narrowly edges teammate Tom Zachary's 2.75 mark for the AL crown.
- Johnson leads the majors in shutouts with six.
- A's rookie Al Simmons hits .308 and knocks in 102 runs.

- The Giants top the majors with a .300 team BA.
- Joe Shaute wins 20 games for Cleveland, but the Indians sag to sixth place.
- Brooklyn's Zack Wheat finishes second in NL in BA (.375), hits (212), doubles (41), and total bases (311).

The New York Yankees found out just how dependent they were on the 30-year-old Babe Ruth in 1925. In spring training, their overweight and worn-down right fielder suffered an intestinal abscess brought on by too much eating and drinking. Stomach surgery and a suspension levied by manager Miller Huggins for insubordination limited Ruth's season to 98 games, and the Yankees collapsed to seventh place with a 69-85 record.

The good news for New York was that Huggins seized the opportunity to rebuild his aging team, replacing outfielder Whitey Witt with young Earle Combs, catcher Wally Schang with Benny Bengough, and first baseman Wally Pipp with rookie Lou Gehrig to form the foundation of the famous "Murderer's Row." Ironically, Gehrig started his famous consecutive-game streak on June 1, less than a month after Everett Scott's then-record 1,307-game streak ended. Scott had played shortstop every game from June 20, 1916 to May 5, 1925.

Washington, though, repeated in 1925, going 96-55 to finish 8 1/2 games ahead of a rebuilding Philadelphia A's team, which featured young slugger Al Simmons and rookies Mickey Cochrane and Lefty Grove. The Senators were a running team; Sam Rice and Goose Goslin were tied for second in stolen bases with 26 apiece, and Goslin hit a

RUTH'S EATING HABITS WEIGH DOWN YANKS

league-leading 20 triples. Rice and Goslin also scored a combined 227 runs and drove in 200. AL MVP shortstop Roger Peckinpaugh batted .294 and formed, with 28-year-old player/manager Bucky Harris, the team's double-play combo.

Key Washington acquisitions shored up the bench and the pitching staff, including first baseman/outfielder Joe Harris, who hit .323 with 12 homers in 100 games; Dutch Ruether, who went 18-7 after being released by Brooklyn; and ex-Indian Stan Coveleski, who matched Walter Johnson in victories with 20 and led the AL in ERA at 2.84.

Johnson, now age 37, slipped slightly to 20-7 with a 3.07 ERA. Rookie Grove surpassed him in strikeouts 116-108 to take the AL crown. Relief ace Firpo Marberry led the AL in games with 55 and saves with 15. Yankee Bob Meusel led the league in home runs with 33, and Detroit's Harry Heilmann barely beat out Tris Speaker for the batting title on the final day of the season, .393 to .389, with an exciting September charge.

In the NL, the Cincinnati Reds dominated nearly every pitching category and compiled a league-low 3.38 team ERA, an amazing accomplishment for the 1920s' biggest run-scoring year. Eppa Rixey and Pete Donohue each won 21 games, and Rixey, Donohue, and Dolf Luque combined for 879 innings pitched. The trio was also one, two, and three in ERA at 2.63 for Luque, 2.89 for Rixey, and 3.08 for Donohue.

The Cardinals boasted the NL's top hitter in Rogers Hornsby, who batted .403 and won a second Triple Crown. St. Louis, though, finished 18 games out of the money.

It was the Pittsburgh bats that made the big noise in 1925, as the Pirates won their first pennant since 1909 and became the first NL team to score 900 runs. Pittsburgh was led by Kiki Cuyler's league-topping 144 runs and 26 triples, Max Carey's NL-high 46 stolen bases, and third baseman Pie Traynor's 39 doubles and .320 batting average.

The Pirates won a seven-game World Series that was almost the reverse of 1924. Johnson won games one and four, only to lose the deciding contest 9-7; and Peckinpaugh was a defensive disaster with eight total errors at short. One of the few Senators highlights was Rice's diving circus catch of Earl Smith's game three drive into the right field stands.

1925

- The Pirates break the Giants' string and win the NL flag.

- Washington cops its second straight AL flag.

- Babe Ruth's famous "stomachache" idles him for much of the season, holds him to .290 BA and 25 homers.

- Minus Ruth's big bat, the Yankees fall to seventh place.

- The Pirates triumph in another exciting seven-game World Series, rallying from a three-games-to-one deficit.

- Joe Harris of the Senators leads all Series hitters with a .440 BA, three homers, and six RBI.

- Senator Roger Peckinpaugh's eight Series errors are a record and make him the goat.

- Rogers Hornsby is selected the NL MVP.

- Peckinpaugh wins the AL MVP Award, which is given only for regular-season performance.

Those privy to the true nature of Babe Ruth's mysterious malady could be forgiven for wondering if his mediocre performance in 1925—a .290 average, 25 home runs, 66 RBI—was an indication that "the Sultan of Swat" was nearly washed up. After all, he was past age 30 and he seemed disinclined to improve his training methods. By the middle of the 1926 season, however, all doubts of his ability to rebound were dispelled.

- Bob Meusel, Ruth's New York teammate, leads the AL in homers (33) and RBI (138).

- Harry Heilmann continues his penchant for taking the AL bat crown every other year, as he hits .393.

- Hornsby wins his sixth straight NL bat crown (.403).

- Hornsby wins the Triple Crown, leading in BA, homers (39), and RBI (143).

- Dazzy Vance leads the majors with 22 wins and 221 Ks.

- Joe Sewell of Cleveland fans just four times, the fewest in a full season by a regular player.

- Hornsby's .756 SA sets an all-time NL record.

- George Burns steals home for the 27th time, an NL career record.

- Sam Rice collects an AL record 182 singles.

- Walter Johnson hits .433, a record for pitchers with 75-plus at-bats.

Washington Senators

Senators Take Flag

A look at the 1925 American League Champion Washington Senators. Bobby Veach *(back row, far right)* joined the club just in the nick of time to participate in his only World Series. First baseman Joe Judge *(middle row, third from the left)* and outfielder Sam Rice *(middle row, far right)* were Senator teammates for 18 seasons.

Dazzy Vance

Heilmann Tops AL in BA

Led by Harry Heilmann (pictured), all three regular Tigers outfielders in 1925 finished among the top five hitters in the American League. Heilmann paced the loop with a .393 mark; Ty Cobb was fourth at .378; and Al Wingo fifth at .370 (Wingo is the only player in history to hit .370 or better in his lone year as a regular).

Harry Heilmann

Vance Shuts Batters Down

With only four pitchers in the majors able to achieve as many as 100 strikeouts in 1925, Dazzy Vance (pictured) of the Dodgers collected 221 Ks, 81 more than runner-up Dolf Luque of the Reds. Vance posted the second-best winning percentage in the National League even though he toiled for a team that finished just a half-game out of the cellar.

1925

- Tony Lazzeri of Salt Lake City in the PCL hits 60 homers, an OB record.

- Pete Donohue of the Reds loses to the Phils after beating them 20 straight times.

- On July 3, Brooklyn's Milt Stock bangs out four hits for a record fourth day in a row.

- George Sisler hits in 34 straight games to begin the season, an AL record.

- Eddie Collins gets his 3,000th hit.

- Max Carey tops the NL in steals for a record tenth time.

- On June 20, Carey becomes the first switch-hitter to hit for the cycle.

- Tris Speaker collects his 3,000th hit.

- Philly's Al Simmons collects 253 hits, an AL record for outfielders.

- Simmons leads the American League in total bases (392), runs produced (227), and hits.

- On May 5 in St. Louis, Ty Cobb goes 6-for-6 with three homers.

1925

Cuyler Outdoes Himself

A good, never spectacular hitter in the minors, Kiki Cuyler seemed to catch National League hurlers off guard when he hit .354 as a rookie in 1924. When he exceeded all of his first-year stats in his sophomore season by averaging .357, nailing 18 home runs, and totaling 102 RBI, even greater things were expected of him. But though he was a solid player for more than a decade, he never again scaled the heights he reached in 1925. Cuyler paced the National League in '25 with 144 runs scored and 26 three-base hits.

Kiki Cuyler

Bob Meusel

Meusel Nets 138 RBI

Bob Meusel had one of the most remarkable seasons in history in 1925: He played for a seventh-place team, hit .290 (two points below the American League average), and yet paced the loop with 33 home runs and 138 RBI (70 more than any other Yankee player produced that season).

Pie Traynor

Traynor Hits .320 at Third

Some 50 years ago, Pie Traynor was voted the best third baseman of the first half-century; in the time since, his reputation has suffered considerably. No matter how true it may be that his glovework was overrated, the fact remains that his .320 career batting average (also his average in 1925) is among the best ever for a hot-corner player.

- Yankee Everett Scott's streak of 1,307 consecutive games played ends.
- Yankee Lou Gehrig bats for Pee Wee Wanninger on June 1 and starts a skein of 2,130 consecutive games.
- Vance no-hits the Phils on Sept. 13.
- Pittsburgh's Glenn Wright performs an unassisted triple play on May 7.
- Wright becomes the first player in ML history to collect at least 100 RBI in each of his first two seasons.
- Pirate Kiki Cuyler hits 26 triples, the most by any player between 1915 and the present.
- Cuyler's 144 runs top the majors.
- Hornsby leads the majors in SA (.756), runs produced (237), and OBP (.489).
- The A's finish second in the AL, their best finish since 1914.
- Rookie Lefty Grove, purchased by Connie Mack from the International League, tops the AL with 116 Ks.

Sam Rice

Donohue's Skein Ends

During the years between 1922 and 1926, Pete Donohue racked up 96 victories, more than any pitcher in the National League. His record string of 20 straight wins over the Phils was broken on August 19, 1925, when Cy Williams hit an opposite-field single in the ninth inning to pin a 5–4 loss on Donohue. In '25, he went 21-14 with a 3.08 ERA and led the National League in complete games (27) and innings pitched (301). Besides his record skein against the Phillies, Donohue had another claim to fame: He was credited with perfecting the changeup. His change couldn't have fooled too many hitters, though; he fanned a mere 571 batters in his 12-year career.

Pete Donohue

Rice Hits a BA High

In almost every aspect, Sam Rice had his best season in 1925, posting a career-high .350 average. The season culminated with his extraordinary catch of Earl Smith's bid for a home run in the World Series—if indeed he really held onto the ball when he tumbled into the stands. Opinions were divided among witnesses.

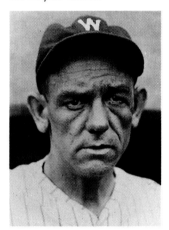

Joe Harris

Harris Revs Up in Series

A utility man for most of the regular 1925 season, Joe Harris (pictured) replaced Earl McNeely, the previous year's Series hero, in the opener of that year's fall classic and remained in the lineup when his bat came up hot. He rapped .440 and slugged three home runs in the seven games.

1925

- Grove's strikeout mark is the lowest ever to lead a league.

- Cincinnati's Dolf Luque posts the best ERA in the majors (2.63).

- Christy Mathewson dies at 45.

- The Cubs suffer their first cellar finish in their 53 years of existence.

- The Reds' Elmer Smith ties Speaker's career record for outfielders when he makes his fourth unassisted DP.

- A's rookie Mickey Cochrane becomes the first catcher to hit three home runs in a game.

- Cochrane catches a rookie record 133 games.

- Joe Harris of the Senators is the first player to homer in his first World Series at-bat.

- The Browns' Elam Vangilder wins 11 games in relief, a new record.

- On June 15, the A's trail the Indians 15-4 in the bottom of the eighth, then beat the Tribe 17-15.

Sewell Fans Four Times

Joe Sewell's batwork alone made him one of the top shortstops of his era; in 1925, he fanned just four times to post the fewest strikeouts by a regular player in a full season. When his glove is figured into the equation, Sewell emerges as one of the best infielders ever. Despite his small size (he stood just 5'6 1/2") he had good power, great range, and an excellent arm. He also hit .312 in his career, including a .336 average in '25. In fact, Sewell had 98 RBI that year despite hitting only one home run. Sewell got his start with Cleveland in 1920. Just two weeks after shortstop Ray Chapman suffered his fatal beaning, the Tribe brought in rookie Sewell to replace him.

Joe Sewell

Combs Back in Action

Idled by a broken leg most of his rookie season in 1924, Earle Combs claimed the Yankees' job at center field the following year (he tallied a .342 average, three home runs, and 61 RBI in 1925). For the next four decades, almost without interruption, the Bronx Bombers would have a future Hall of Famer patrolling the middle pasture in Yankee Stadium.

Earle Combs

Roger Peckinpaugh

Peckinpaugh Named AL MVP

No winner of the Most Valuable Player Award ever had a more miserable World Series or a shorter time left to him in the majors than Roger Peckinpaugh. In game seven of the 1925 Series, his dropped pop fly in the seventh inning and wild throw in the eighth stuck Walter Johnson with four unearned runs in his 9–7 loss to the Pirates; the following year, Peckinpaugh lost his job to rookie Buddy Myer.

- The Baltimore Orioles of the International League win their OB record seventh straight pennant.

- Cincinnati's Sparky Adams has a .983 FA, a new record for second basemen.

- The Cards' Jim Bottomley tops the NL in hits (227) and doubles (44).

- Detroit's Al Wingo, in his only season with enough at-bats to qualify for a BA title, hits .370 and finishes fifth.

- Stan Coveleski, now with Washington, tops the AL in ERA (2.84) and win pct. (.800).

- Johnny Mostil of the White Sox tops the AL in runs (135) and steals (43).

- The Pirates and A's both hit .307 to top the majors in BA.

- Speaker, at age 37, hits .389 and tops the AL in OBP (.479).

- Major league hitters hit a combined .292—the highest composite ML average since 1986.

AGED ALEXANDER ENJOYS ONE LAST HURRAH

Under new manager Rogers Hornsby, who had replaced Branch Rickey 38 games into the 1925 season, the Cardinals brought St. Louis its first pennant in a half-century of National League competition. It was the first St. Louis championship of any kind since the American Association St. Louis Browns had won in 1888.

Perhaps distracted by his off-field duties, Hornsby slipped to a .317 batting mark with 11 home runs, 96 runs, and 93 RBI. His team, though, scored a league-leading 817 runs. First baseman Sunny Jim Bottomley led the NL in doubles with 40 and RBI with 120, third baseman Les Bell drove in 100 runs and hit .325, and MVP catcher Bob O'Farrell hit .293 with 30 doubles.

Hornsby put together a durable starting rotation of Flint Rhem, who tied for the league lead in wins with 20; Bill Sherdel, who finished 16-12; and veteran Jesse Haines, who went 13-4 with a 3.25 ERA. Cardinals pitchers combined for an NL-high 90 complete games. The bullpen was held up by 39-year-old ex-Cub Pete Alexander, who went 9-7 in a relief/spot-starting role.

Cincinnati came in second by 2 games on the strength of good years from former Yankee Wally Pipp and .323-hitting Eddie Roush, as well as pitchers Pete Donohue (who won 20 games) and Carl Mays (who went 19-12 with a 3.14 ERA). Somehow, Pittsburgh managed only a third-place finish in spite of rookie Paul Waner's NL-high 22 triples and .336 batting average, Cuyler's league-leading 113 runs, and two 20-win performers—ace Ray Kremer and Lee Meadows.

In the American League, the Yankees returned to the top with a 91-63 record, 3 games better than Cleveland, but had to survive late-season scares from the Indians, A's, and Senators, who nearly overcame New York's 10-game lead in August.

Washington's Walter Johnson finally showed his age, going 15-16 in his last full year as a starting pitcher, and the rest of the staff collapsed around him to allow 761 runs, fourth-most in the AL. Washington's Sam Rice and Goose Goslin turned in excellent years, batting .337 and .354, and scoring 203 runs with 58 doubles and 29 triples between them.

For New York, shortstop Mark Koenig solidified the defense, and the big three of Murderer's Row—Babe Ruth, Lou Gehrig, and Earle Combs—all had big years. Ruth hit .372 (second to Detroit's Heinie Manush at .378), scored a league-leading 139 runs, and drove in an AL-high 146; he also led in walks with 144, home runs at 47, on-base average at .516, and slugging average at .737. A blossoming Gehrig led all AL hitters in triples with 20, banged out 47 doubles, and scored 135 runs. Combs hit .299 with 12 triples and 113 runs.

Philadelphia had the AL's best pitching staff, including ERA winner Lefty Grove at 2.51; 12-4 junkballer Howard Ehmke; Rube Walberg; and Eddie Rommel, who was fourth in ERA at 3.08. And Cleveland's veteran first baseman George Burns won the MVP Award, hitting 64 doubles (second-most in history) along with 114 RBI and a .358 batting average.

In spite of Ruth's four-home run performance, the World Series went the full seven games and was decided when wily old Pete Alexander, who had already beaten the Yankees with complete-game efforts in games two and six, came out of the bullpen to protect Jesse Haines's 3-2 lead in the seventh. Alexander struck out rookie second baseman Tony Lazzeri with the bases loaded and two out, and shut down New York until he walked Ruth with two down in the ninth. A frustrated Ruth, who was walked 11 times by St. Louis pitching, tried to steal second, but was gunned down by O'Farrell to end the game and the Series.

1926

- The Cards win the first pennant by a St. Louis NL or AL team.

- The Yankees leap from seventh place to their fourth AL flag of the decade.

- Down three games to two, the Cards win the two final games in New York and take the World Series.

- Pete Alexander's stellar relief work stifles the Yankees in the final game of the Series.

- Cards shortstop Tommy Thevenow is the Series' leading hitter with a .417 BA, a homer, and four RBI.

- Babe Ruth hits a Series single-game record three homers in game four and a record four homers overall.

- Cards catcher Bob O'Farrell wins the NL MVP Award.

- George Burns of Cleveland takes the AL MVP prize.

- Burns sets a new ML record with 64 doubles and hits .358.

- Ruth tops the AL in homers with 47, 28 more than anyone else.

After finishing last the previous year for the first time in their history, the Cubs returned to the first division in 1926. Heavily responsible for the club's resurgence were two outfielders with glaring defensive weaknesses who were retrieved from the minors: Hack Wilson (pictured) claimed the home run title in the National League that season with 21; Riggs Stephenson, the Cubs' leading hitter that year, collected a .338 average, three home runs, and 44 RBI.

- Ruth leads in runs (139), total bases (365), SA (.737), OBP (.516), RBI (146), walks (144), and runs produced (238).

- Pirate Paul Waner breaks Rogers Hornsby's stranglehold on the NL bat title, winning with a .336 average.

- Cleveland's George Uhle leads the majors with 27 wins.

- Uhle tops the AL in innings (318) and CGs (32).

- Philly's Lefty Grove wins his first AL ERA crown (2.51) and again tops the loop in Ks (194).

- Firpo Marberry has 22 saves for Washington, a new ML record.

- Detroit's Heinie Manush takes the AL bat crown (.378).

- Hack Wilson of the Cubs wins his first NL home run crown (21).

- St. Louis' Jim Bottomley tops the NL in RBI (120), doubles (40), and total bases (305).

George Burns

Burns Cops AL MVP

Due to the fact that in the 1920s Most Valuable Player Awards could not be given to previous winners, it made a certain amount of sense to honor a member of the second-place Indians in 1926. It seems, however, that the wrong Indian was chosen. Although "Tioga George" Burns (pictured) had a fine season (a .358 average, 114 RBI, and a league-leading 216 hits and 64 doubles), George Uhle turned in a better performance (27 wins, a 2.83 ERA, and 159 strikeouts).

Carl Mays

Mays Takes Reds to Second

The 1926 season was the last year as a productive starter for Carl Mays (pictured). Mays and Pete Donohue had a large hand in the Reds' second-place finish that year, just 2 games back of the Cardinals. Mays went 19–12 with a 3.14 ERA and a league-leading 24 complete games; Donohue went 20–14 with a 3.37 ERA in a league-high 286 innings, topping the circuit in wins and shutouts (five). The following year, Mays and Donohue won only nine games between them and the Reds fell into the second division, where they would remain until 1938. After '26, Mays won just 14 more games in his career and was out of baseball by 1929.

Grove Tops AL in Ks, ERA

After winning 26 games for the Baltimore team of the International League in 1924, Lefty Grove was sold to the A's for close to $100,000, a record at the time. He had a rocky sophomore season in 1926, turning in a .500 pitching performance despite heading the American League in both strikeouts (194) and ERA (2.51). When his control improved sharply the following season, he never again had a losing record.

Lefty Grove

1926

- In his first full season as the Cards' player/manager, Rogers Hornsby slumps to .317.

- On Dec. 20, the Cards deal Hornsby to the Giants for Frankie Frisch and Jimmy Ring.

- The Red Sox finish last in the AL and lose a club record 107 games.

- On Sept. 26, the Browns and Yankees play the shortest game in AL history—55 minutes.

- On Sept. 26, Browns and Yankees play the shortest doubleheader in ML history—two hours and seven minutes.

- Giant Mel Ott, age 17, becomes the youngest NL player to get a pinch hit.

- Wilson's 69 walks, which top the NL, are the fewest ever to lead a league.

- On August 28, Dutch Levsen of Cleveland becomes the last pitcher to win two CGs in one day.

- Ted Lyons of Chicago no-hits the Red Sox on August 21 in one hour and seven minutes.

Lyons Bested by Only Uhle

Ted Lyons was most likely the American League's second-best pitcher in 1926, behind George Uhle of the Indians. As with most of the top hurlers during the 1920s and early 1930s—Lefty Grove especially—Lyons was used as both a starter and a reliever. Seventeen of his 260 career wins came in relief roles. Lyon's big moment in 1926 came on August 21, when he no-hit the Red Sox. Lyons made short work of the Bostonians, dusting them off in a mere one hour and seven minutes.

Heinie Manush

Ted Lyons

Manush Hits Career-High

Unable to gain a regular job in the Tigers' outfield the year before, Heinie Manush got his chance in 1926 when age and injuries reduced Ty Cobb to a part-time player and Al Wingo proved to be a flash in the pan. Manush's batting title that year (.378) was the high point in a career that was most notable for a .330 average but only a .377 on-base percentage.

Paul Waner

Young Waner Hits .336

According to the modern rule for determining batting leaders, Paul Waner and his .336 average would have seized the National League hitting crown in 1926 to become the first rookie since Pete Browning did so in 1882. Instead, he had to wait until the following year to bag his first official batting title. In 1927, Waner hit .380, the best mark of his career.

- On August 15, Dodger Babe Herman doubles into a double play as three Dodgers wind up on third base.

- Reading of the International League posts a .194 win pct. (31-129).

- Yankee Tony Lazzeri hits 18 homers, both a new AL rookie record and a new record for AL second basemen.

- Accused of betting on and perhaps conspiring to dump a game in 1919, Ty Cobb and Tris Speaker are released by Detroit and Cleveland, respectively.

- Marberry pitches in 64 games, a new 20th-century ML record.

- Player/manager Eddie Collins hits .344 for the White Sox.

- Paul Waner has a 6-for-6 day on August 26.

- Held by injuries to only 233 at-bats, Cobb hits .339 in his last year with the Tigers.

- In his final year as a big league manager, Speaker boosts the Indians to second place and bats .304.

New York Yankees

Yankees Win AL Flag

A shot of the 1926 New York Yankees. Lou Gehrig and Babe Ruth justly occupy positions of prominence *(back row, sixth and fourth from the right)*. As was often the case with rookies, Tony Lazzeri got stuck in the rear *(left side)*, where only his head is visible. Lazzeri was second in the American League that year in RBI with 114 and third in home runs with 18.

Babe Herman

Other Babe Debuts in NL

Babe Herman was so promising a rookie in 1926 that he bumped Jack Fournier, the National League's former home run leader, off the Dodgers' first-base post. As a frosh, Herman topped the Bums in hitting (158), home runs (11), and RBI (81); he also had the poorest fielding average of any NL first baseman. When he had even more trouble at the initial hassock in 1927, he was moved to the outfield, where his errors were fewer albeit more egregious.

World Series

Ruth Can't Save Yankees in Series

Babe Ruth lays into a pitch in the 1926 World Series. The Babe had another Ruthian year in '26, leading the league in home runs (47), RBI (146), runs (139), walks (144), and slugging average (.737), among other categories. Ruth clubbed four homers in the seven-game Series, but it wasn't enough. The Cardinals won game seven 3–2.

1926

- Max Bishop of the A's sets a new FA record for second basemen (.987).
- Washington's Sam Rice and Cleveland's George Burns tie for the AL lead in hits (216).
- William Wrigley hires Joe McCarthy to manage the Cubs.

- In their first year under McCarthy, the Cubs lead the NL in FA and ERA and rise to fourth.
- Lou Gehrig's 20 triples top the AL and are the most ever by an AL first baseman.
- Chicago's Johnny Mostil, second in the AL MVP vote, tops the loop in steals (35) and outfield putouts.

- Four hurlers tie for the NL lead in wins with 20.
- Pittsburgh's Remy Kremer wins 20, leads the NL in ERA (2.61) and win pct. (.769).
- Pete Donohue of the Reds wins 20, tops the NL in innings (286) and shutouts (five).

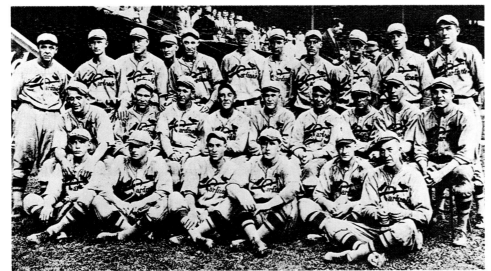

St. Louis Cardinals

Cards Take Championship

A look at the 1926 World Champion St. Louis Cardinals: The bespectacled George Toporcer *(back row)*, player/manager Rogers Hornsby *(middle row, center)*, and Series hero Pete Alexander *(front row, far right)*, who registered two wins, a 1.33 ERA, and 17 strikeouts in 20¹/₃ innings.

Tommy Thevenow

Cards Celebrate Victory

The 1920s were golden years for baseball, and nowhere did they glisten as brightly as in New York. By the 1926 World Series, residents of the Big Apple had become accustomed to being part of mob scenes on an almost annual basis; in contrast, fans in St. Louis were taking part in their premier victory celebration since 1888, the first ever for a National or American League team. In time, the Cardinals would celebrate nine World Championships, more than any major league team other than the Yankees.

Victory Celebration

Thevenow Comes Alive

Tommy Thevenow hit four home runs in the minors before taking possession of the Cardinals' shortstop post in 1926. After swatting two round-trippers during the regular season and an inside-the-park four-bagger in the '26 World Series, he played 12 more years in the majors without ever hitting another circuit-clout.

- Dazzy Vance leads the NL in Ks with just 140.

- Cleveland's Joe Sewell again leads the AL in fewest batter Ks with seven.

- Ruth and Gehrig fan 148 times between them, and the Yankees hitters top the majors in strikeouts with 580.

- George Sisler hits .290, down .130 points from 1922.

- Willie Kamm of the White Sox tops all ML third basemen in FA and assists for the second year in a row.

- The A's have the top ERA in the majors (3.00) and yield the fewest homers (38).

- Boston's Glass-Arm Eddie Brown leads the NL in hits (201).

- Paul Waner's 22 triples top the ML.

- Pirate Kiki Cuyler leads the NL in steals (35).

- Reds second baseman Hughie Critz, a fielding whiz who hits .270, is NL MVP runner-up.

Meusel Nets 103 RBI

In 1927, Bob Meusel finished seventh in the American League in RBI with 103 (a distant third on his team). The Yankees were so deep offensively and so much stronger than the other clubs in the league that they outscored their opposition by nearly 400 runs.

Bob Meusel

Yanks Get a Deal on Moore

Wilcy Moore did not start his professional career until he was age 25. After four undistinguished years in the minors, he won 30 games in the South Atlantic Association in 1926. Purchased by Yankees general manager Ed Barrow for about $4,500, he proceeded to stand American League hitters on their heads in 1927, collecting a combined 32 wins and saves.

Charlie Root

Root Leads Majors in Wins

Charlie Root joined the Cubs in 1926 and remained with them through 1941, winning a club-record 201 games. In 1927, Root topped both leagues with 26 wins and 309 innings pitched. His four shutouts tied for second while his 145 strikeouts were 39 Ks behind the lead in the National League. When Root began to falter as a starter in the middle 1930s, he moved to the bullpen, where he twice led the NL in relief victories. He and catcher Gabby Hartnett were battery mates a record 15 years.

Wilcy Moore

1927

- After the season, the Pirates trade Cuyler to the Cubs for Adams and Pete Scott.

- The Giants trade George Kelly to the Reds for Edd Roush.

- Released by the Dodgers, for whom he played his whole career, Zach Wheat signs with the A's.

- Fired as White Sox player/manager, Eddie Collins signs with the A's.

- The A's have a record seven future Hall of Famers on their active roster in 1927.

- The A's fan just 326 times, an AL record-low for a season by a team.

- Giants star Ross Youngs dies of Bright's disease at age 30.

- Lloyd Waner scores 133 runs and has just 27 RBI for a differential of 106—the largest in ML history.

- Cobb gets five hits in a game for a career record 13th time.

Ted Lyons

Shocker: Out in Style

Urban Shocker may have been the best pitcher in the American League during the 1920s. With his health failing, he was used sparingly by the Yankees in 1927; nevertheless, he won 18 games in just 200 innings. He made one relief appearance the following year, was too weakened to continue, and died before the season ended.

Earle Combs

Combs Leads Pack in Outfield

Although Earle Combs led all American League outfielders in putouts in 1927 and again in 1928, his arm was not the strongest; consequently, he was sometimes stationed in left field. Offensively, he was the perfect table-setter for Babe Ruth and Lou Gehrig and customarily ranked among the leaders in both runs (137 in 1927) and hits (231 that year, best in the loop).

Urban Shocker

Lyons Collects 22 Victories

After Ted Lyons (pictured) retired, Ken Smith wrote: "For 21 years, Lyons pitched as though the White Sox were in pursuit of the pennant. It was a game of make-believe." During his long sojourn with the Sox, the club never once finished as high as second place. In 1927, Lyons tied for first place in the American League with 22 wins in 308 innings pitched.

- On June 19, Phillie Jack Scott (age 35) becomes the oldest pitcher to hurl two CGs in one day.
- Scott leads the NL in losses (21) and ties for the lead in games (48).
- Frankie Frisch sets a record for second basemen with 1,059 chances accepted.

- Frisch also sets a record for assists by a second baseman (641).
- The Yankees' .489 SA establishes an ML record.
- Pittsburgh's Remy Kremer cops the NL ERA crown (2.47).
- Dazzy Vance, as usual, tops the NL in Ks (184).

- Jesse Haines wins 24 games for the Cards and leads the majors in shutouts with six.
- New York's Earle Combs tops the AL in hits (231) and triples (23).
- Chicago's Hack Wilson and Philly's Cy Williams tie for the NL homer crown with 30—half of Ruth's total.

The Yankees declined from being stratospheric to merely awesome in 1928, and were surprised to find themselves with a good fight on their hands. The Bronx Bombers started strong and finished with a 101-53 record, but Connie Mack's resurgent Athletics put together a 25-8 stretch in July and caught the New York ballclub in September.

The 1928 A's were a talented mixture of youth and age, including the up-and-coming Al Simmons (who hit .351 with 107 RBI), Jimmie Foxx, and MVP catcher Mickey Cochrane, as well as dead-ball veterans Ty Cobb (who hit .323), Tris Speaker, and Eddie Collins. The Philadelphia lineup was rounded out by outfielder Bing Miller, who was fifth in batting at .329, and Max Bishop, who drew 97 walks and scored 104 runs.

Mack's league-leading pitching staff was anchored by 28-year-old Lefty Grove, who was first in the AL in wins with 24 and Ks with 183; 17-12 Rube Walberg; 13-5 Eddie Rommel; and old men Jack Quinn, who went 18-7 at the age of 44, and Howard Ehmke.

The A's and Yanks met for a September 9 doubleheader showdown at Yankee Stadium, which was attended by a record crowd of 85,264. The Yankees swept, 3-0 and 7-3, and clinched the AL flag less than two weeks later. Phila-

YANKS ROLL ON, OUSTING THE A'S AND CARDS

delphia finished with a 98-55 record, 2$^1/_2$ games out.

The Yankees pitching staff came down to earth in 1928, as only George Pipgras and Waite Hoyt won more than 20 games, and only Herb Pennock made the ERA leader board. But the hitters once again led the league in runs, with 894, and home runs, with 133—44 more than the nearest team. Babe Ruth and Lou Gehrig were first and second in home runs with 54 and 27, runs with 163 and 139, and slugging at .709 and .648. They tied for the league lead in RBI with 142.

Washington's Goose Goslin won his only career batting title at .379, just beating out St. Louis' Heinie Manush, who hit .378 with 47 doubles, 20 triples, and 108 RBI.

The NL race was another dogfight, as the 95-59 Cardinals outlasted an intrepid New York Giants team that won 25 games in September but came up 2

games short at 93-61. St. Louis slugger Jim Bottomley led the NL in triples with 20 and tied the Cubs' Hack Wilson for the home run lead with 31. The St. Louis lineup was fortified by young outfielders Chick Hafey, who hit .337 and belted 46 doubles and 27 homers, and Taylor Douthit, who drew 84 walks and scored 111 runs.

The Giants matched the Cardinals exactly with 807 runs on the strength of Bill Terry's .326 average and 101 RBI, Fred Lindstrom's .358 mark and 39 doubles, and 19-year-old Mel Ott's .322 average and team-leading 18 home runs.

Playing for Boston, his third team in three seasons, the irascible Rogers Hornsby led the league in hitting at .387, on-base average at .498, and slugging at .632. Pittsburgh's Burleigh Grimes and New York's Larry Benton tied for the lead in wins with 25, and Brooklyn's Dazzy Vance took the ERA title at 2.09.

The Yankees dominated the 1928 World Series to an even greater degree than the year before, as they again swept 4-0. New York hitters scored 27 runs, 17 more than their pitchers allowed, and out-homered the Cardinals nine to one. To make their revenge for 1926 complete, the Yanks defeated Pete Alexander 9-3 in his only start. He recorded an ugly Series ERA of 19.80.

1928

- The Yankees edge the A's by 2 $^1/_2$ games to take their third straight AL flag.

- The Cards, managed by Bill McKechnie who piloted the 1925 Pirates, return to the top in the NL.

- The Yankees sweep the most one-sided World Series to date.

- Waite Hoyt is the Series' top pitcher, winning two CGs.

- Babe Ruth hits .625 in the Series to set an all-time Series BA record.

- Lou Gehrig hits .545 in Series and has a 1.727 SA, an all-time World Series record.

- Between them, Ruth and Gehrig hit seven homers and knock in 13 runs in Series.

- Jimmy Bottomley of the Cards is named NL MVP.

- Philly's Mickey Cochrane wins the AL MVP by two votes over St. Louis' Heinie Manush.

Known as the "Brooklyn Schoolboy" early in his career, Waite Hoyt was signed by John McGraw when he was just age 16. He went on to become the best pitcher in the 1928 World Series, winning a pair of games, posting a 1.50 ERA, and striking out 14 batters in 18 innings. With the Yankees dynasty crumbling in 1930, Hoyt said, "The trouble with this club is there are too many guys on it who aren't Yankees." A few days later, Hoyt himself was no longer a Yankee.

- Rogers Hornsby, playing now for the Braves, tops the NL in batting (.387).

- Washington's Goose Goslin wins the AL bat crown (.379) by one point over Manush.

- Ruth tops the majors in homers (54), runs (163), walks (135), and SA (.709).

- Ruth and Gehrig tie for the ML lead in RBI with 142.

- Gehrig leads the majors in runs produced (254) and is third in the AL in hitting (.374).

- Manush tops the AL in hits (241) and doubles (47).

- Cub Hack Wilson again ties for the NL homer crown (31), this time with Bottomley.

- Dazzy Vance's 2.09 ERA is the best in the majors.

- Vance wins 22 games, ties for the NL lead in shutouts (four), and leads the majors in Ks (200).

Taylor Douthit

Douthit a Hit in Field

In 1928, Taylor Douthit set all-time season records for the most putouts and most total chances by an outfielder. He also set the 20th-century record for the most total chances per game. Douthit lost his job to Pepper Martin.

Hornsby Hits .387

In 1928, his sole year with the Braves, Rogers Hornsby became the first Brave in this century to win a hitting crown (.387). He also set 20th-century season records for the franchise for both the highest batting and slugging averages (.632).

Rogers Hornsby

Jim Bottomley

Bottomley Reaches Prime

At his peak in 1928 (in which he led the National League with 20 triples and 136 RBI and tied for the loop-high with 31 home runs), Jim Bottomley suffered the same fate as virtually every Cardinals star in the 1920s and '30s. Almost as soon as he turned age 30, his days as a regular were numbered. Even though Bottomley nearly led the circuit in batting in 1931, Cardinals general manager Branch Rickey wanted him platooned with rookie Ripper Collins.

1928

- Giant Larry Benton ties for most wins in ML (25) and leads the NL in win pct. (.735).

- Hornsby, in his only season with the Braves, hits .387, a franchise record.

- Ty Cobb retires; still holds career ML records for BA (.366) and runs scored (2,245).

- Cobb retires with ML records in hits (4,190), stolen bases (892), and RBI (1,933) (all since broken).

- Tris Speaker retires; still holds ML career records for doubles (793), as well as DPs by an outfielder (139).

- Speaker retires holding record for assists by an outfielder (448) and putouts by an outfielder (6,787).

- Eddie Collins plays the last of his career record 2,651 games at second base.

- Giant Freddy Lindstrom's 231 hits set an NL record for third basemen and top the senior loop.

- Yankee Tom Zachary posts a 12-0 record.

Herb Pennock

Pennock Tops AL in Shutouts

Herb Pennock went 17–6 in 1928, leading the American League with five shutouts. He also posted a 2.56 ERA, the best of his 22-year career. With his 240–162 lifetime record, Pennock approached Hall of Fame credentials. Voters, however, were not fooled. With the powerful Yankees, Pennock went 162–90; with mere mortal teams, he was a mediocre 78–72.

Ruth No. 1 Once Again

In 1928, Babe Ruth (pictured) and Lou Gehrig once again finished one-two in the American League in every major slugging department except total bases, where Heinie Manush of the Browns snuck into second place just ahead of Gehrig. Between them, the Yankees' dynamite duo hammered seven home runs in the World Series and hit .593.

Babe Ruth

Hack Wilson

Wilson Bangs 31 Homers

Cubs slugger Hack Wilson was 5' 6", weighed 190 pounds, and wore a size 18 collar and a size $5^1/2$ shoe. Chicago sportswriter Warren Brown described him as "a high-ball hitter on the field and off it." His postgame escapades notwithstanding, Wilson paced the National League in home runs four times between 1926 and 1930. In 1928, he tied for the lead (31 round-trippers) with Cardinal Jimmy Bottomley.

- On July 10 vs. Cleveland, Washington's Milt Gaston pitches a 14-hit shutout.

- The Giants win 25 games in September to nearly overtake the Cards at the wire.

- Bob Meusel sets an ML career record when he hits for the cycle the third time.

- Ruth leads the majors in runs a record eighth time.

- The last-place Phils have a 5.52 staff ERA, the worst in modern history to this point.

- Taylor Douthit of the Cards handles 566 chances, an all-time record for an outfielder.

- In January, the Giants trade Hornsby to the Braves for Shanty Hogan and Jimmy Welsh.

- In November, the Braves send Hornsby to the Cubs for five players and $200,000.

- In May, Washington sells George Sisler to the Braves for $7,500.

1928

Mickey Cochrane

Cochrane Named MVP

By 1928, Mickey Cochrane (shown here making an acrobatic tag at home) had clearly established himself as the American League's premier receiver, taking the Most Valuable Player Award by two votes over Heinie Manush. Beginning the following year, he would have competition from Yankees rookie Bill Dickey, who hit .324 and led AL backstoppers in assists.

Ruth Renews Contract

With Yankees owner Jake Ruppert at his side, Babe Ruth signs a new contract with the Bombers. In 1930, Ruth earned an $80,000 salary, the highest in baseball. When informed that he was making $5,000 per year more than President Herbert Hoover, Ruth reportedly quipped, "I had a better year than he did." Ruth clubbed 54 homers in 1928, and 49 in 1930.

Babe Ruth

Goose Goslin

Goslin Wins AL Bat Title

Goose Goslin became the first Senator since 1902 to win a batting title (.379). He copped the honor on the last day of the 1928 season in a tight three-way race with Heinie Manush and Lou Gehrig. Goslin's 17 homers that year represented nearly half the Senators' total, as the club fell below .500 in its last season under player/manager Bucky Harris.

1928

- Washington obtains Buddy Myer from the Red Sox for five players.
- Urban Shocker dies at 38 of heart disease.
- The Braves finish with a .327 win pct. (50-103), the poorest ever by a seventh-place team playing a 154-game schedule.

- Del Bissonette hits 25 homers, a Dodgers rookie record.
- Cochrane hits 12 triples, a record for AL catchers.
- Washington's Sammy West has a .996 FA, a new ML record for outfielders.
- Myer leads the AL in steals with 30.

- Kiki Cuyler, now with the Cubs, leads the NL in thefts with 37.
- Lefty Grove and Yankee George Pipgras tie for the AL lead in wins with 24.
- Washington's Garland Braxton is the AL ERA king (2.52).
- Paul Waner leads NL in runs (142).

Yankees Are World Champions

A look at the 1928 World Champion New York Yankees. Miller Huggins (wearing a club jacket) had piloted six pennant-winners by 1928—more than any other manager at the time except for Connie Mack and John McGraw. Rookie Leo Durocher *(middle row, second from the left)* would serve as a manager against the Yankees in a World Series just 13 years later.

New York Yankees

World Series

The Babe Brings it Home

Babe Ruth is greeted at home plate after hitting one of his record three home runs in game four of the 1928 World Series. In the two Series games that Sportsman's Park hosted that year, seven home runs were hit—all of them by the visiting Yankees, who won both clashes by identical 7-3 scores. For the Series, Ruth set a fall classic record by batting .625 (10-for-16); this mark would stand until 1990, when Cincinnati's Billy Hatcher hit .750 (9-for-12). Ruth also scored nine runs in the four-game affair.

- Joe Sewell continues to be the hardest player to fan, as he Ks seven times.
- Ruth tops the AL in strikeouts (87) for the fifth and last time.
- The Browns finish a surprising third, as they have two 20-game winners—Al Crowder (21) and Sam Gray (20).

- Crowder tops the AL in win pct. (.808), becoming the only Brownie ever to do so.
- Red Ruffing of the Red Sox leads the league in losses with 25.
- The Red Sox finish last for the fourth straight year.

- The Pirates' .309 BA is the best in the majors by 13 points.
- The sixth-place Dodgers, thanks largely to Vance, have the best ERA in the majors (3.25).
- Chick Hafey, the first bespectacled outfielder in ML history, hits 27 homers for the Cards.

MACK MANAGES TO RESURRECT THE A'S

Connie Mack brought his Philadelphia A's back to first place in 1929 after a 15-year pennant drought. After finishing dead last seven years in a row, the ballclub rose to seventh in 1922, sixth in 1923, fifth in 1924, third in 1925 and '26, and the runner-up position both in 1927 and '28.

Mack built his team on young sluggers Al Simmons, who was second in hitting at .365 and first in RBI with 157, and Jimmie Foxx, who hit .354 and scored a team-high 123 runs. Simmons and Foxx were third and fourth in the AL in home runs with totals of 34 and 33, behind Babe Ruth at 46 and Lou Gehrig at 35.

From the minor leagues, Mack had purchased Foxx, second baseman Max Bishop, backup infielder Jimmy Dykes, and the heart of his pitching staff: 29-year-old Lefty Grove, who won the ERA title at 2.81, and righty George Earnshaw, who went 24-8 to lead the AL in wins. The A's staff of Grove, Earnshaw, 12-2 Eddie Rommel, hard-throwing Rube Walberg, and aged reliever Jack Quinn recorded the AL's best team ERA at 3.44. They were the only staff under 4.00.

The AL race was over early, as Mack's 104-46 White Elephants beat out second-place New York by 18 games. Ruth and Gehrig had their usual great years, but Bob Meusel slumped to .261 with only ten home runs. New York got little offensive contribution from Leo Durocher at short and Gene Robertson at third, and the team's ERA was a fat 4.17. The Yankees' season ended tragically, as beloved manager Miller Huggins died suddenly on September 25.

The Chicago Cubs, 98-54, finished first in the NL for the first time since 1918; Pittsburgh was 10½ games back in second. The Cubs boasted the most fearsome righthanded-hitting attack in history, as left fielder Riggs Stephenson batted .362, center fielder Hack Wilson hit .345, and right fielder Kiki Cuyler hit .360. This trio combined for 71 homers, 337 runs, and 271 RBI.

The infield featured a double-play combination of shortstop Woody English (who scored 131 runs) and nomadic MVP Rogers Hornsby (who hit .380, clubbed 39 homers, drove in 149 runs, and scored 156). Pat Malone led the Cubs and the NL in wins with 22, Charlie Root added 19, and Guy Bush won 18.

Playing in tiny Baker Bowl, the fifth-place Phillies produced some truly unusual numbers. MVP runner-up Lefty O'Doul led the NL in hitting at .398, swatted 32 homers, and knocked out 254 hits (still an NL record). Chuck Klein led in home runs with 43 and batted .356. However, Philadelphia pitchers undid their work by allowing an incredible 1,032 runs.

Ty Cobb and Tris Speaker retired before the 1929 season. Cobb holds the all-time career batting average record at .366. When he retired, he was also the all-time major league career leader in games, at-bats, runs, hits, and stolen bases. Speaker quit with a .344 average, eighth-best in history, and still holds the career mark for doubles with 793.

The 1929 World Series opened with one of the gutsiest gambles in Series history, when Connie Mack sent seldom-used Howard Ehmke to face the Cubs' righthanded wrecking crew in game one. The gamble paid off handsomely, as Ehmke's slow stuff struck out a then-record 13 on the way to a 3-1 win. Righties George Earnshaw and Eddie Rommel also got wins as Philadelphia won the Series four games to one.

A great moment came in game four, when the A's overcame an 8-0 deficit with a wacky ten-run seventh that included two balls lost in the sun by Hack Wilson. This is still the biggest inning in World Series history.

1929

- The Cubs breeze to the NL pennant by 10½ games.
- The A's have an even easier time in the AL, romping home 18 games ahead of the Yankees.
- The A's win the World Series in five games.

- In game four, the A's score ten runs in the seventh and win 10-8.
- Mule Haas of the A's, with two big homers, is the Series' hitting star.
- Howard Ehmke fans a Series record 13 Cubs in game one.
- Cub Hack Wilson leads all hitters in the Series with a .471 BA.

- Rogers Hornsby of the Cubs wins the NL MVP (the AL discontinues the award after the 1928 season).
- Lefty O'Doul of the Phils, the NL bat champ with a .398 mark, is the MVP runner-up.
- O'Doul's average is an NL record for outfielders.

1929

Signed by the Baltimore Orioles of the International League when he was pitching for Swarthmore, George Earnshaw waited five years to report. At the age of 27 and still in the minors, Earnshaw was ready to quit the game before the Orioles finally sold him to the A's. In his first four full seasons under Connie Mack, he won 86 games. In 1929, he led the majors with 24 victories.

- Chuck Klein of the Phils wins the NL homer crown (43) in his first full season.

- Babe Ruth tops the majors with 46 homers and a .697 SA.

- George Earnshaw of the A's leads the majors with 24 wins.

- Wilson's 159 RBI are the most in the majors.

- Lefty Grove's 2.81 ERA is the only one in the majors below 3.00.

- Grove's 170 Ks are the most in the majors.

- Yankees manager Miller Huggins dies near the end of the season.

- Joe McCarthy of the Cubs wins the first of what will be a record number of ML pennants.

- Giant Mel Ott, age 20, becomes the youngest player ever to hit 40 homers in a season; he hits 42.

- Hornsby's .380 BA sets a Cubs team record—the fourth such record he's set in the decade.

Rogers Hornsby

Hornsby Scores 156

Not even in the tumultuous 1880s did any great player change teams more often than Rogers Hornsby. In 1929, he was playing with his fourth different club in four years. If his play suffered from the constant change, it was certainly never manifest in his year-end stats. His first year with the Cubs was his best overall since 1925, as he posted a .380 average and a league-leading 156 runs scored in 1929.

Howard Ehmke

Ehmke Has Last Hurrah

Howard Ehmke's stunning victory in the opening game of the 1929 World Series was his last triumph in the majors. Six years earlier, then with the Red Sox, he was prevented only by a controversial scorer's decision from becoming the first pitcher to throw two consecutive no-hit games.

Charlie Gehringer

Gehringer Best at Second

Owing to his Sphinx-like demeanor, Charlie Gehringer had attracted no particular notice anywhere except for Detroit before 1929. His performance that year (131 runs scored, 215 hits, 45 doubles, and 19 triples—all highs in the American League) made him the loop's top second baseman, a label he retained for the next decade. In a 14-year span, Gehringer's average dropped below .300 only once.

1929

- Braves owner Emil Fuchs manages his own team for the full season—the last owner to do so.

- The Braves finish with the worst record in the majors (56-98).

- Carl Hubbell of the Giants no-hits Pittsburgh on May 8.

- Ike Boone of the Mission Reds in the PCL collects 553 total bases.

- O'Doul's 254 hits are an ML record for outfielders.

- Johnny Frederick of Brooklyn sets an all-time rookie record with 52 doubles.

- O'Doul reaches base an NL record 334 times.

- The 1929 Phils are the only team in history to have four 200-hit men.

- Dale Alexander of Detroit collects 215 hits, an AL rookie record for 154-game season.

Huggins Dies

Tormented by his failure to motivate the complacent Yankees, exhausted almost beyond endurance, Miller Huggins entered the hospital on September 20 after an ugly blemish under his left eye refused to disappear. Five days later, he was dead of blood poisoning. Several of the pallbearers at his funeral were players whom he managed.

Carl Hubbell

Funeral of Miller Huggins

Hubbell Arrives in NY

In 1928, after six seasons in the minors, Carl Hubbell had advanced no higher than the Texas League. He then drew the attention of Dick Kinsella, a Giants scout who was an Illinois delegate to the Democratic national convention that summer at Houston. Within days, Hubbell was in New York where he stayed until 1943. In 1929, he went 18–11 with a 3.69 ERA.

Mule Haas

Haas: Two Series HRs

Mule Haas is best known today for his two key homers (one apiece in games four and five) in the 1929 World Series. However, he himself considered his finest achievement to be the three spectacular running catches he made to squelch potential Cleveland uprisings in the Indians' 18-inning, 18–17 loss to the A's in 1932.

- Philly's Al Simmons leads the AL in total bases (373), RBI (157), and runs produced (237).
- Detroit's Charlie Gehringer tops the AL in runs (131), triples (19), and steals (27), and ties in hits (215).
- Lew Fonseca of Cleveland leads the AL in BA (.369).

- Jimmie Foxx leads AL in OBP (.463).
- Chicago's Pat Malone leads the NL with 166 strikeouts.
- Firpo Marberry returns to form and tops the majors with 11 saves.
- The Indians and Yankees become the first teams to put numbers on their uniforms and keep them on.

- On July 5, the Giants become the first ML team to use a public address system.
- New York's Bill Walker leads the NL in ERA at 3.08, the highest mark ever to lead the senior loop.
- Lloyd Waner goes 6-for-8 in a 14-inning game on June 15.

Shibe Park

Bishop Ties Up Game Five

Max Bishop of the A's scores ahead of teammate Mule Haas following Haas's two-run homer in the bottom of the ninth to tie the final game of the 1929 World Series at 2–2. Minutes later, Bing Miller doubled home Al Simmons from second base to give the A's their first championship since 1913.

World Series

SRO at Shibe Park

The scene here was once a common one in many cities whenever the home team had a sellout crowd. Pictured is a row of rooftops across the street from Shibe Park in Philadelphia just prior to a 1929 World Series game. Unable to get into the stadium, hundreds were willing to pay $5 a throw to sit in the hastily built stands.

Cubs Snare NL Flag

A look at the 1929 Chicago Cubs, Joe McCarthy's first pennant-winning team. Seated to the right of the club's female secretary is Bill Veeck, Sr., team president and father of the famous Indians and White Sox owner. To the secretary's left is Cubs owner William Wrigley, followed by Joe McCarthy, Rogers Hornsby, Kiki Cuyler, and Hack Wilson, Hall of Famers all.

Chicago Cubs

1929

- Hank DeBerry of the Dodgers goes 6-for-7 in a 14-inning game on June 23.

- The Phillies finish fifth, their best showing since 1917.

- Pat Malone of the Cubs wins 22 games and is the NL's only 20-game winner.

- Burleigh Grimes wins his first ten starts, a Pirates club record.

- Bill Terry hits .372 for the Giants, breaking Hornsby's club record.

- White Sox Art "The Great" Shires, a prizefighter in the off-season, beats up manager Lena Blackburne three times during the season.

- Phils catcher Walt Lerian is killed when he's struck by an out-of-control truck.

- After hitting .344 for Detroit, Harry Heilmann is released after the season on waivers to Cincinnati.

- Hornsby's ML-leading 156 runs are a 20th-century record for a second baseman.

A's Take World Title

A's players congratulate Bing Miller *(far right, with back to camera)* after his hit won the decisive game five of the 1929 World Series. The A's had been trailing the Cubs 2–0 in the ninth, but Mule Haas cracked a two-run homer in the bottom of the frame to tie the score. Al Simmons then doubled, Jimmie Foxx walked, and Miller doubled Simmons home, thus winning the game and the Series. For the Cubs, this was just another in a series of World Series hardships. In ten fall classic appearances, the Cubbies have lost eight times. Their only wins came in 1907 and 1908; since then they've lost seven straight World Series. They haven't played in the tournament since 1945.

World Series

Philadelphia A's

A's Win in AL

A shot of the 1929 World Champion Philadelphia A's. Bing Miller *(back row, far left)* hit .335 on the year. Mickey Cochrane and Jimmy Dykes *(front row, second and fourth from the left)* flank Walter French, a substitute outfielder who also played pro football, as did many players in the 1920s and '30s.

- On April 16, Cleveland's Earl Averill becomes the first AL player to homer in his first at-bat.

- On April 29, Brooklyn pitcher Clise Dudley homers in his first at-bat.

- On May 24, Ted Lyons of Chicago beats Detroit 6-5 in 21 innings.

- Ivy Wingo retires with the most career errors by a catcher (234).

- Jimmy Austin retires with the most career errors by a third baseman (359).

- Russ Miller of the Phils sets an NL season record for most losses without a win, as he goes 0-12.

- Cleveland rookie Wes Ferrell wins 21 games, second in the AL to Earnshaw.

- Cincinnati radio announcer Harry Hartman becomes the first announcer to say, "Going, going, gone."

- Rough Carrigan resigns as Red Sox manager after leading the club to three straight cellar finishes.

Baseball had been riding a roller coaster of offense that started in 1920, when Babe Ruth fired the first 54 shots in the home run revolution, and continued throughout the 1920s, as home runs and run-scoring increased almost every year. The home run trend peaked in 1930; in 1931, the baseball was deadened, assuring a long life for many of the hundreds of hitting records set the year before.

Whether viewed from a hitting or a pitching perspective, the 1930 season was equally wild. The New York Yankees and the St. Louis Cardinals each scored more than 1,000 runs, and the Philadelphia Phillies allowed 1,199. Seventy-one individual hitters, nine whole teams—and the National League—batted over .300; the league set a record for total home runs with 892. On the pitching side, only one NL hurler, Brooklyn's Dazzy Vance, had an ERA lower than 3.87. The NL ERA, swelled by the Phillies' 6.71 team mark, was 4.97.

In the most telling commentary on baseball's lack of balance, the Cardinals sent outfielder Showboat Fisher to the minor leagues at a time when he was hitting .374 in 254 at-bats. Perhaps fittingly, no MVP honors were awarded in either league.

Myriad individual hitting records were set in 1930. Hack Wilson's 56 home runs established an NL record. The Giants' Bill Terry batted .401, the last NL

HACK KNOCKS IN 190; RUNS ARE UP ALL OVER

.400 batting mark and the second-to-last in the majors; Terry's 254 hits tied Lefty O'Doul's 1929 performance for the NL record. Wilson drove in the most runs ever, 190, to outdo Lou Gehrig's 174 (sixth-best in history), Chuck Klein's 170 (eighth-best), and Al Simmons's 165 (13th-best). Klein banged out 59 doubles (to tie with Tris Speaker for seventh on the all-time list) and scored 158 runs (to tie with Babe Ruth for the fifth-most ever); Kiki Cuyler's 155 runs are ninth-best and Simmons and Woody English are tied for tenth place, all-time, with 152 runs.

In spite of the heroics of Wilson, Cuyler, and English, the Cubs came up 2 games short in the NL pennant race. St. Louis took the flag with a team that featured an eerie consistency on both sides of the ledger: The Cards led the league in runs with a lineup in which all eight hitters batted over .300—only Chick Hafey made the top four in a major hitting category, ranking

fourth in slugging average—and a staff of five pitchers with between 12 and 15 wins.

An oddity of the race was that last-place Philadelphia outhit the pennant-winners, .315 to .314, on the strength of twin .380-plus-hitters O'Doul and Klein, who hit 96 doubles and 62 homers between them.

The slugging A's won their second straight AL pennant, as Jimmie Foxx and Simmons combined for 321 RBI and 73 homers and catcher Mickey Cochrane batted .357. With 128, little Max Bishop was second in walks to the Babe and scored 117 runs.

The Athletics pitching staff consisted of three starters with ERAs well over 4.00 and Lefty Grove, who put up numbers that would look impressive in any year, much less the most disastrous year for pitchers in this century. The 28-5 Grove led the league in wins, winning percentage, games, strikeouts, and saves; in a year when the overall AL ERA rose by nearly half a run to 4.65, Grove lowered his ERA over the previous year by 0.27 to 2.54, lowered his walks total by 21, and upped his strikeouts by 39.

Grove finally got his first World Series start in 1930 and combined with George Earnshaw to dispatch the Cards in six games. The A's were held to a .197 batting average, but still outscored St. Louis 21-12, as Grove and Earnshaw went a combined 4-1 with a 1.02 ERA.

1930

- The A's win their second consecutive AL flag.
- The Cards come home first in the NL, 2 games ahead of the Cubs.
- The A's again win the World Series, this time in six games.
- George Earnshaw and Lefty Grove both win two Series games for A's.

- In a hitter's year, neither Philadelphia nor St. Louis hit above .200 in the World Series.
- On Oct. 2, Cardinal George Watkins becomes the first NL player to homer in his first Series at-bat.
- Hack Wilson drives in an ML record 190 runs.

- Wilson sets an NL record with 56 home runs.
- Dodger Dazzy Vance's 2.61 ERA is 1.15 runs better than the next-lowest ERA in the NL.
- Grove's 2.54 ERA is 0.76 runs better than the next-lowest ERA in the AL.

Hack Wilson poses beside four of the wagon models named after him to boost sales following his record-shattering 1930 season (56 homers, 190 RBI). Wilson spent much of the year dodging lemons thrown by Cubs fans who were still angered by the fly ball he lost in the sun in the 1929 World Series.

- Grove leads the majors in wins (28), win pct. (.848), Ks (209), and, amazingly, saves (nine).

- Grove is the only AL pitcher to fan more than 200 since 1916.

- Al Simmons tops the AL in batting (.381), runs (152), and runs produced (281).

- Giant Bill Terry leads the NL with a .401 BA, the last .400 average in the league.

- After a long holdout, Babe Ruth signs for $80,000—an ML record salary at this juncture.

- Adam Comorosky of the Pirates leads the majors with 23 triples.

- Philly's Chuck Klein sets NL records for runs (158), total bases (445), and runs produced (288).

- Klein tops the NL in doubles (59) and runs produced (288).

- Klein hits .386 with 40 homers, 170 RBI, and 250 hits.

Chuck Klein, Bill Terry

Klein, Terry Burn Up NL

Chuck Klein *(left)* scored 158 runs in 1930, a record in the National League, to become the circuit's top all-around hitter that year. Bill Terry led the league with a .401 batting average, the last .400 mark in the loop.

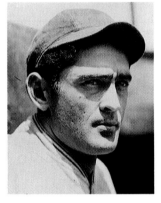

Guy Bush

Bush Gives Up 155 Runs

Apart from the 1930 season, the year in which he surrendered 155 runs (a 20th-century National League record), Guy Bush usually had a respectable ERA and a bundle of wins. Arriving in the majors in 1925 from the Mississippi back country, he became Pete Alexander's protege and learned enough to net 176 victories. Bush is best remembered for surrendering Babe Ruth's final home run.

Malone Posts 20 Wins

Pat Malone's frequent tantrums on the diamond and highly publicized escapades off it slowed his progress to the majors and shortened his stay after he arrived. But for a brief while, he was the best righthanded pitcher in the National League. In 1930 with the Cubs, he tied for the league-lead in victories with 20 and paced the league in complete games with 22. With the Yankees in 1936, he paced the American League in saves and relief wins.

Pat Malone

1930

- Klein registers a 20th-century NL record 44 assists by an outfielder.

- Dodger Babe Herman's .393 BA is the highest in this century by an NL runner-up.

- Phillies pitchers give up a record 1,199 runs and have a record-high 6.71 ERA.

- Opponents hit .342 off Phillie pitching.

- Les Sweetland's 7.71 ERA for the Phils is the worst ever by an ERA qualifier.

- Phillie Claude Willoughby posts a 7.59 ERA.

- The NL as a whole has a 20th-century record .303 BA and .448 SA.

- The AL posts a loop record .421 SA.

- The Cards score an NL record 1,004 runs.

- All eight Cardinal regulars hit .300 or better.

Joe Cronin

Cronin Fails to Rate

Joe Cronin of the Senators had a seemingly monster year in 1930. He hit .346 with 203 hits, 41 doubles, 127 runs, and 126 RBI. Being a run-frenzy year, though, Cronin didn't even make the leader board in any offensive category that season. His RBI total fell 64 short of Hack Wilson's mark. Still, Cronin's numbers that year are some of the best ever by a shortstop.

Lefty Grove

Grove Triumphs in 30

Including his World Series output that year, Lefty Grove won 30 games and lost just six in 1930 (a half-dozen of his wins came in relief). Grove also rang up nine saves, as he toed the rubber in 53 contests. Heywood Broun once wrote: "When danger beckoned thickest, it was always Grove who stood towering on the mound."

Rice Sets Records

The only ostensible sign that Sam Rice might have slowed down in 1930, when he turned 40 years old, was that his number of stolen bases diminished from 16 the previous year to 13 that season. In every other respect, he more than held his own, setting four major league records and five American League records for players past their 40th birthdays.

Sam Rice

- Cincinnati's Hod Ford is the only NL regular to hit below .250.

- The Cubs slug an ML record .481.

- The Giants hit an ML record .319.

- The Senators have a staff ERA of 3.96 and are the only ML team with an ERA below 4.00.

- Cub Gabby Hartnett's .630 SA sets a 20th-century record for catchers.

- Cub Pat Malone and Pirate Remy Kremer tie for the NL lead in wins with 20.

- Harry Heilmann becomes the first player to homer in every major league park in use during his career.

- Ruth becomes the first documented player to fan 1,000 times.

- On May 6, Gene Rye of Waco in the Texas League hits three home runs in one inning.

- At age 46, Jack Quinn of the A's becomes the oldest player to homer in an ML game.

Cuyler Totals 134 RBI

Kiki Cuyler (pictured) and Hack Wilson set a National League record for teammates in 1930 when they totaled 324 RBI between them. Although Gabby Hartnett chipped in another 122 ribbies, the Cubs still were outscored by the Cardinals, largely because Rogers Hornsby missed most of the season with a foot injury.

Al Simmons

Simmons Cops AL Bat Title

The last righthanded hitter to win back-to-back batting crowns in the American League (.381 in 1930, .390 in 1931), Al Simmons was traded by Connie Mack after the 1932 season. He returned twice more to the A's before retiring as an active player in 1944.

Kiki Cuyler

A's Repeat as Champs

A shot of the 1930 Philadelphia A's, Connie Mack's last World Championship team. Jack Quinn *(back row, second from the right)* is the oldest player to hit a home run in an American League game. Kid Gleason *(front row, far right)* and Eddie Collins *(beside Gleason)* were coaches on the 1930 A's.

Philadelphia A's

1930

- Guy Bush of the Cubs gives up a post-1901 NL record 155 earned runs by a pitcher.

- Watkins sets an ML rookie record when he hits .373.

- Watkins's .621 SA is also a rookie record.

- Brave Wally Berger sets all-time NL rookie records with 38 homers and 119 RBI.

- Senator Sam Rice's 207 hits, 121 runs, and 271 total bases all set records for a player past his 40th birthday.

- Red Barber begins his broadcast career with WRUF in Gainesville, Florida.

- Lou Gehrig tops the AL in total bases (419) and RBI (174).

- Cleveland's Johnny Hodapp leads the AL with 225 hits and 51 doubles.

- Ruth leads the AL with 49 homers.

- Cub Kiki Cuyler tops the majors with 37 steals; AL leader Marty McManus of Detroit has just 23.

World Series

Foxx Excels in Series

In the six-game 1930 World Series, the A's hit only .197 as a team. Jimmie Foxx (pictured batting) and Al Simmons, however, both registered healthy postseason stats (Foxx hit .333, Simmons hit .364). In game one, the A's garnered only five hits, one a home run by Simmons, but made every hit count for a run. Foxx homered in the game-five shutout while Simmons again homered in game six. In the sixth game, the A's scored seven runs on just seven hits.

Cards Win NL Pennant

Victory parades for winning teams seemed to grow in significance during the Great Depression. Here, St. Louis denizens fete the Cardinals on September 27, 1930, the day after the Birds clinched the National League flag they ultimately won by a 2-game margin over the Cubs. During the season, the Cardinals scored a whopping 1,004 runs and batted .314. This was clearly a team effort: All eight Cardinals starters batted over .300. Moreover, reserve Showboat Fisher hit .374 in 254 at-bats, Gus Mancuso hit .366 in 227 at-bats, and Ray Blades hit .396 in 101 at-bats.

Victory Parade

- Jimmie Foxx goes 6-for-7 on May 30.
- On Jan. 10, Art Shires knocks out Braves catcher Al Spohrer in a boxing match at Boston Garden.
- On July 25, the A's perform two triple plays in a game against Cleveland.

- The 1930 Pirates are the last NL team to hit 100 triples in a season as they bang out 119.
- Earle Combs tops the AL with 22 triples.
- Wild Bill Hallahan of the Cards leads the NL in Ks with 177.

- Cubs pitcher Hal Carlson dies of an intestinal hemorrhage.
- The average player's salary in 1930 is around $7,000
- In June, Washington trades Goose Goslin to the Browns for Al Crowder and Heinie Manush.

An A's Dynasty Is Not In The Cards

The 1931 year brought the passing of the two fathers of the American League, Ban Johnson and Charles Comiskey. Once best friends, the two hadn't spoken for years due to several bitter disagreements dating back to Johnson's tenure as AL president. Both died unhappy, with Johnson enduring a forced retirement from the league he had founded, courtesy of Commissioner Kenesaw Mountain Landis, and Comiskey forever broken-hearted after the Black Sox Scandal of 1919.

With the introduction of a less lively baseball, the major leagues returned to somewhat of a balance between offense and defense. Still, 1931 was no pitchers' year by modern standards; although total major league home runs fell by almost 500, the National League batted .277, the AL rapped .278, and the Yankees and Indians batted over .290.

In yet another AL runaway, Connie Mack's Philadelphia dynasty proved too much for New York and Washington (the only two AL clubs within 30 games of the A's), and it finished 13½ games out in front at 107-45.

Al Simmons led the AL in hitting at .390 and was fourth in RBI with 128; Jimmie Foxx, age 23, batted .291 with 30 home runs (fourth in the league behind the 36-year-old Babe Ruth and the 28-year-old Lou Gehrig, who tied for the major-league lead at 46, and 29-year-old Earl

Averill with 32) and drove in 120.

The real strength of the A's, however, was pitching. George Earnshaw won 21 games while Rube Walberg took 20 and the staff compiled the AL's lowest ERA at 3.47. Again the league's best pitcher, Lefty Grove went 31-4 to spearhead the league in wins (by a margin of nine), strikeouts with 175, complete games with 27, shutouts with four, and ERA at 2.06 (more than half a run better than runner-up Lefty Gomez of New York). Grove was voted AL MVP over Gehrig.

The A's were a team of streaks; Grove won 16 straight to tie the record shared by Walter Johnson and Smokey Joe Wood, and the team put together win streaks of 17 and 13 games.

Under new manager Joe McCarthy, the Yankees returned to hitting form, scoring a league-high 1,067 runs on a .297 team batting average; Gehrig led the AL in runs with 163 and RBI with an all-time AL-record 184, and Ruth had the greatest season ever by a player his age with 149

runs, 163 RBI, 46 homers, and a .373 batting average. The starting pitching after the 21-9 Gomez unfortunately was far from pennant-caliber.

In the NL, 101-53 St. Louis repeated, thanks to an MVP year from second baseman Frankie Frisch (who scored 96 runs and led the league in stolen bases with 28) and 27-year-old Pepper Martin (who hit .300). Hard-hitting Chick Hafey won the batting title by a fraction over Bill Terry, .3489 to .3486, and led the team in homers with 16.

One of the heroes of 1930, Hack Wilson slumped to a .261 batting average with only 13 homers; another, Chuck Klein, proved that it was always a hitter's year in the Baker Bowl by hitting .337 with 121 runs, 121 RBI, and 31 home runs, all first in the NL.

A pair of Giants, Bill Walker and Carl Hubbell, led the league in ERA at 2.26 and 2.65, but New York could only manage an 87-65 record and finished in second place, 13 games out.

Once again, Earnshaw and Grove pitched superbly in the World Series, compiling ERAs of 1.88 and 2.42 in a combined 50 innings, and the A's outscored their opponents. The underdog Cardinals prevailed, however, thanks to Martin's inspired base-running, .500 Series average, and great catch that preserved Burleigh Grimes's 4-2 Series-clinching victory in game seven.

1931

- The Athletics roar to their third consecutive flag with a franchise record .704 win pct.

- The Cards repeat in the NL.

- Cards take the World Series in seven games.

- Burleigh Grimes and Bill Hallahan both win two games for the Cards.

- Cardinal Pepper Martin is the Series' offensive star, hitting .500 and swiping five bases.

- The Baseball Writers Association of America appoints two committees, one in each league, to elect the MVPs.

- Lefty Grove is selected as the first BBWAA winner in the AL.

- Frankie Frisch of the Cards wins the MVP Award in the NL.

- The ball is dejuiced in 1931, and hitting stats, especially in the NL, tumble accordingly.

- Chuck Klein tops the NL in homers with 31 and RBI with 121.

Pepper Martin launches one of his patented headfirst slides into third base. Four of the top five base thieves in the National League in 1931 were Cardinals. Frankie Frisch led with 28 pilfers, Martin tied Sparky Adams for third place with 16, and George Watkins brought up the rear with 15 swipes.

- Klein leads in total bases (347) and slugging (.584).
- Cardinal Chick Hafey wins the batting title at .349, a tad better than Giant Bill Terry who also hits .349.
- Hafey is the first batting crown winner to wear glasses.

- No NL pitcher wins 20 games—the first time the NL or AL hasn't had 20-game winner.
- The AL's Grove becomes the last southpaw to win 30 games in a season, as he cops 31.
- Grove's .886 win pct. is the best in history by a 30-game winner.

- Lou Gehrig has an ML record 301 runs produced.
- Gehrig sets an AL record with 184 RBI.
- Gehrig also tops the AL in hits (211), runs (163), and total bases (410).
- Babe Ruth wins his last home run crown by tying with Gehrig (46).

Bobby Burke

Burke Hurls a No-No

Standing more than 6' and weighing barely 150 pounds, Bobby Burke was short on stamina. In ten seasons, he accumulated less than 1,000 innings and figured in only 84 decisions. He had a burst of power in 1931, however, no-hitting Boston on August 8.

Ruth, Gehrig Total 347 RBI

Between them, Babe Ruth (pictured) and Lou Gehrig tagged 92 homers in 1931 and netted 347 RBI, the most ever by a pair of teammates. With shortstop Lyn Lary and left fielder Ben Chapman kicking in over 100 RBI each, the Yankees averaged more than seven runs a game.

Frankie Frisch

Frisch Averages .311

Frankie Frisch was a great all-around athlete who jumped directly from the college campus to the Giants' regular lineup in 1919. While at Fordham University, he captained teams in three sports—football, baseball, and basketball—and was even chosen at halfback on Walter Camp's All-America team. He hit .311 in 1931, with four home runs and 82 RBI.

Babe Ruth

1931

- Ruth leads the league in OBP (.495), SA (.700), and walks (128).

- Grove tops the majors in Ks (175), win pct. (.886), and ERA (2.06), and ties in CGs (27).

- Bill Walker of the Giants wins his second NL ERA title (2.26).

- The Yankees have a record six men who score 100 or more runs.

- Joe McCarthy, fired the previous year by the Cubs, becomes manager of the Yankees.

- The Yankees score an ML record 1,067 runs.

- Cleveland's Wes Ferrell hits a season record nine home runs while serving as a pitcher.

- Ferrell ties Grove for the AL lead in CGs (27) and is second in wins (22).

- The AL rules that all teams must have numbers on their uniforms.

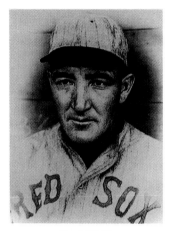

Earl Webb

Webb Clubs 67 Doubles

Before joining pro ball, Earl Webb lived in the Tennessee mountains, where he drove a mule in a coal mine to earn $1.40 a day. Between long stints in the minors, he played 649 games in the big show, collecting 155 career doubles—67 of them in 1931, a major league record.

Grove Good As Gold

Thanks in part to his glittering 31–4 season in 1931, Lefty Grove finished his 17-year career with 300 wins and 141 losses. Adding in his minor league stats, Grove totaled 411 victories and only 190 defeats for a .684 winning percentage, the best record in the history of organized baseball.

Philadelphia A's

Lefty Grove

A's Take AL Flag

The 1931 Philadelphia A's were the last pennant-winner for Connie Mack (seated in the center of the trio wearing suits). Philadelphia was solid everywhere except at the shortstop position, which was shared by Dib Williams and a fading Joe Boley. Lefty Grove *(behind Mack)* had another banner year: 31 wins, 27 complete games, four shutouts, and a 2.06 ERA—all top statistics in the American League that year. George Earnshaw *(to Grove's right)* posted 21 victories and 23 complete games. Jimmie Foxx *(middle row, far right)* posted a .291 average, 30 home runs, and 120 RBI.

- On July 17, the White Sox beat the Browns 10-8 in 12 innings; no strikeouts are thrown in the game.

- The sacrifice fly rule is abolished.

- Balls bouncing over or going through a fence, heretofore considered home runs, are now ruled doubles.

- Earl Webb of the Red Sox hits an ML record 67 doubles.

- Grove wins an AL record 16 straight games during the season.

- Bobby Burke of Washington no-hits Boston on August 8.

- Ferrell no-hits St. Louis on April 29.

- Gehrig hits a record three grandslams in a four-day period.

- Brooklyn's Babe Herman hits for the cycle twice during the season— the first MLer to do so.

- On August 5 vs. Washington, Detroit's Tommy Bridges loses a perfect game with two out in ninth.

Pepper Martin

Martin Takes Charge

Pepper Martin (batting) was the hero of the 1931 World Series with a .500 average in 24 at-bats, and Mickey Cochrane (behind the plate), his victim. Pitcher George Earnshaw was so enraged by Martin's basestealing (five swipes) that he wanted Connie Mack to replace Cochrane with rookie receiver Joe Palmisano.

Babe Herman

Hallahan Leads in Ks

Bill Hallahan didn't get a single MVP vote in 1931, despite topping the National League in strikeouts with 159 and tying for the lead in wins with 19. Unquestionably the best pitcher in the World Series that year, he relinquished just one run in two complete-game victories and saved the deciding seventh contest. Wild Bill lived up to his nickname. He led the league in both strikeouts and walks in both 1930 and 1931. He averaged about four walks a game in his mediocre 12-year career.

Bill Hallahan

Herman: .313 BA, 97 RBI

The story that Babe Herman once tripled into a triple play is apocryphal—he doubled into a double play. When Herman returned to the Dodgers in 1945, eight years after he last played in the majors, he tripped over first base on his first hit and fell to the ground. In 1931, he collected a .313 average, 18 home runs, and 97 RBI.

1931

- Terry tops the NL in runs (121), runs produced (224), and triples (20).

- Philly's Buzz Arlett, perhaps the greatest minor league star in history, hits .313 in his only ML season.

- Brooklyn's Wally Gilbert goes 6-for-7 on May 30.

- The Cards' Jim Bottomley goes 6-for-6 on August 5.

- Cincinnati's Tony Cuccinello goes 6-for-6 on August 13.

- In May, Cleveland trades Lew Fonseca to the White Sox for Willie Kamm.

- The Red Sox ship Red Ruffing to the Yankees for Cedric Durst and cash.

- Giant Shanty Hogan's .996 FA is a new record for catchers.

- Roy Johnson of Detroit heads the AL in triples with 19.

- New York's Ben Chapman steals 61 bases, the most in the AL since 1920.

- Frankie Frisch tops the NL with just 28 steals.

Cards Win NL Pennant

Although he made the picture, Dizzy Dean pitched only in batting practice for the Cards in 1931. Outstanding pitching, hitting, and baserunning were not all that this team had going for it. Second baseman Frankie Frisch and shortstop Charlie Gelbert were the best keystone combo in the National League.

St. Louis Cardinals

Burleigh Grimes

Grimes Has 17–9 Season

Burleigh Grimes looks deferent as he shakes hands with commissioner Kenesaw Mountain Landis. On the mound, however, Grimes "always looked like a man about to commit assault and battery when he threw the ball," according to John Kiernan. Grimes went 17–9 in 1931, racking up a 3.65 ERA and 67 strikeouts.

Chick Hafey

Hafey Smacks .349

Chick Hafey was yet another Cardinals star who came out on the losing end after clashing with Branch Rickey. Hafey wanted more money after tying for the National League-lead in 1931 with a .349 average, and got it—from the Reds, to whom he was traded when he held out. He was so dangerous a pull-hitter that Fred Lindstrom said, "It sure will be difficult for third basemen to get insurance while that guy is in the league."

- Jack Quinn, at age 48, sets a new NL save record with 15 for Brooklyn.

- By finishing sixth, the Red Sox escape the cellar for the first time since 1924.

- The last-place White Sox feature the AL's top loss leader in Pat Caraway, who drops 24.

- The A's have three of the five 20-game winners in the majors: Grove, George Earnshaw (21), and Rube Walberg (20).

- Hallahan ties for the lead league with 19 wins and tops the loop in Ks with 159.

- Lloyd Waner has the most hits in the NL (214).

- New York's Mel Ott heads the NL in walks with just 80.

- The Reds finish last for the first time since 1901.

- The Giants lead the NL in ERA (3.30) and tie for the lead in BA (.289) and FA (.974).

The New York Yankees came back in 1932 to go 107-47 and reclaim the AL pennant after a three-year exile. The year was the end of an era; the next Yankee pennant would not come until 1936, with Joe DiMaggio, Red Rolfe, George Selkirk, and Monte Pearson replacing Babe Ruth, Earle Combs, George Pipgras, and Herb Pennock.

In his last great year, the 37-year-old Ruth hit .341 with 120 runs, 137 RBI, and a league-leading 130 walks. Under manager Joe McCarthy and for the first time in the six seasons since his famous "bellyache" in 1925, the Babe did not lead the AL in home runs. Philadelphia's Jimmie Foxx won the Triple Crown with 58 homers, 169 RBI, and a .364 batting average. (Lou Gehrig was second in hitting at .349, tied for second in RBI with 151, and fourth in home runs with 34.)

Combs, the greatest leadoff man of the 1920s, also had his last big season, batting .321 and scoring 143 runs (third-most in the AL). Ben Chapman stole a league-high 38 bases and banged out 41 doubles, 15 triples, and ten homers. Lefty Gomez and Red Ruffing won a combined 42 games (Ruffing was runner-up to Lefty Grove in ERA at 3.09); 26-year-old Johnny Allen went 17-4 to lead the junior circuit in winning percentage.

Defending champion Philadelphia scored plenty of runs, as the one-two punch of Foxx and Al Simmons outproduced Ruth

RUTH CALLS HR SHOT; YANKS BACK ON TOP

and Gehrig, only to be let down by their second-line pitching. Grove won another ERA title at 2.84 and posted a 25-10 record, while George Earnshaw and Rube Walberg (Connie Mack's only other reliable starters) slipped to ERAs of 4.78 and 4.73.

Chicago manager Rogers Hornsby, with his team in first place, got himself fired on August 2 over a tiff with management. Charlie Grimm took over the reins, guiding the Cubs to the pennant by 4 games over Pittsburgh. The once-fearsome home run attack of the Cubs disappeared along with Hornsby and Hack Wilson, who was shipped off to Brooklyn before the season; the offensive load was carried by rookie second baseman Billy Herman, who scored a team-high 102 runs, and veterans Kiki Cuyler and Riggs Stephenson, who hit .324 with 49 doubles (third in the NL behind Paul Waner with 62 and league MVP Chuck Klein with 50).

Cubs pitching, however, led

the NL with a 3.44 team ERA on the strength of Lon Warneke, the NL wins leader with 22 (against only six losses) and the ERA titlist at 2.37, 19-11 Guy Bush, 15-10 Charlie Root, and 15-17 Pat Malone.

Brooklyn's Lefty O'Doul won the batting crown at .368. The Giants' Mel Ott and Philadelphia's Klein tied for home run honors with 38. First baseman Don Hurst led in RBI with 143; Klein, the outfielder, had 137.

The World Series featured one of the best-known episodes in Ruth legend—the supposed "called shot" off Root. There was, as lore has it, bad blood between the two teams over the Cubs' alleged bad treatment of their former manager and then-Yankee skipper McCarthy, and the fact that the Cubs had voted only a half-share in the Series money for ex-Yankee shortstop Mark Koenig. New York was leading the Series 2-0 when Ruth came to bat.

With the score tied four-all in the fifth inning of game three, he took strike one from Root. As the Cubs players heckled Ruth—and the fans hurled insults and fruit—the Babe held up his hand, a gesture he repeated after strike two. He drove the next pitch deep into the center field stands; New York went on to win the game 7-5 and sweep the Series.

It will never be known for certain, but on-deck hitter Gehrig insisted that Ruth had meant to call his home run and point out where it would go.

1932

- The Yankees win their first flag under Joe McCarthy.

- The Cubs triumph in the NL after Charlie Grimm replaces Rogers Hornsby as manager.

- The Yankees sweep the third World Series in a row in which they've appeared.

- In game three in Series, Babe Ruth hits two home runs.

- According to some, Ruth "calls" his last Series homer, pointing toward where it eventually lands.

- Overshadowed by Ruth, Lou Gehrig leads all Series hitters with a .529 BA, three homers, and eight RBI.

- Philly's Jimmie Foxx is selected AL MVP.

- Philly's Chuck Klein is the NL MVP.

- Foxx wins the Triple Crown in the AL (though some sources give the bat title to Boston's Dale Alexander).

- Foxx's 58 homers are the most at this juncture by anyone other than Ruth.

Lefty Gomez had a personality and sense of humor as multifaceted as his pitching talent. Beginning his ascent in 1932, he went 24–7 with a 4.21 ERA. Gomez coined the expression, "I'd rather be lucky than good," and was the first to concede that he owed much of his success to the pinstriped uniform he wore. Released by the Yankees after the 1942 season, he started one game for the Senators in 1943, was bombed, and promptly retired.

- Al Crowder of Washington tops the majors with 26 wins.
- John McGraw steps down as Giants manager after 40 games and turns the reins over to player Bill Terry.
- The Red Sox again tumble into the cellar and set a new club record for losses with 111.

- St. Louis rookie Dizzy Dean tops the NL with 191 Ks.
- Lon Warneke of the Cubs is the NL's top winner with 22.
- Warneke leads the NL in ERA (2.37) and win pct. (.786).
- Lefty Grove leads the AL in ERA (2.84).

- Grove "slips" to 25 wins and posts his most losses (ten) since 1927.
- Red Ruffing leads the AL in Ks (190).
- Brooklyn's Lefty O'Doul wins his second NL bat crown in four years.
- Paul Waner sets an NL record (since broken) with 62 doubles.

Ferrell Wins 23

Wes Ferrell may have won 20 games for the Indians in each of his first four seasons (he also took 23 games in 1932), yet manager Roger Peckinpaugh thought he had a bad attitude. Hence, he gave the coveted starting assignment on July 31, 1932, to Mel Harder, as the Tribe played its inaugural game in Cleveland Municipal Stadium.

Mel Ott

Ott Smacks 38 Homers

Mel Ott neither played a single day in the minors nor for any team other than the Giants. When he joined the club as a 17-year-old in 1926, John McGraw said, "No minor league manager is going to have a chance to ruin him." Ott nailed 38 home runs in 1932, tied for first in the National League. He tallied 511 career round-trippers, the most by any NL player prior to expansion.

McCarthy Propels Yanks to Top

In 1926, Joe McCarthy's first year at the helm of the Yankees, New York finished 13 1/2 games behind the A's. In 1932, the Yankees nearly reversed the record, topping the A's by 13 games.

Joe McCarthy

Wes Ferrell

Cubs Take NL Pennant

A shot of the 1932 Chicago Cubs. Coach Charlie O'Leary *(front row, fourth from the left)* appeared in a game as a pinch hitter for the Browns in 1934, his first major league action in 21 years, and delivered a single at age 52.

Chicago Cubs

1932

- New York's Mel Ott wins his first NL homer crown (38).

- After the 1932 season, the A's sell Al Simmons, Jimmy Dykes, and Mule Haas to the White Sox for $100,000.

- Giant Sam Leslie sets a new ML record with 22 pinch hits.

- On June 27, Goose Goslin becomes the first to hit three homers in a game three times in his career.

- Ray Hayworth of the Tigers becomes the first catcher to work 100 consecutive errorless games.

- Brooklyn's Johnny Frederick hits a record six pinch-hit home runs during the season.

- On June 3, Gehrig becomes the first player in the 20th century to hit four home runs in a game.

- Twice during the season, Buzz Arlett hits four homers in a game for Baltimore of the International League.

- Philly's Don Hurst tops the NL in RBI with 143, a record for NL first basemen.

Paul Waner

Johnny Burnett

Burnett Racks Up Nine Hits

On July 10, 1932, Johnny Burnett of the Indians banged out nine hits in an extra-inning game against the A's. The game went into extra frames when Cleveland first baseman Eddie Morgan fumbled Jimmy Dykes's two-out dribbler in the ninth inning. The botched play allowed the tying Philadelphia run to score and send the game into overtime.

Dykes Heads for Chicago

Jimmy Dykes

Jimmy Dykes may have welcomed his trade from the contending A's to the seventh-place White Sox after the 1932 season, a year in which he hit .265 and collected seven home runs and 90 RBI. In Philadelphia, Dykes became the target of the notorious Kessler brothers, who hounded him so relentlessly from their seats behind third base that the A's considered barring them from Shibe Park.

Waner Tops NL in Doubles

Paul Waner ranks ninth in career doubles, tenth in triples, and 11th in hits, yet just 26th in runs. The reason for the disparity is partly explained by his ranking 24th in games played; more to the point, however, is the fact that the Pirates were not a high-scoring team in his prime and never had a real slugger. In 1932, Waner hit .341 with a National League-high 62 doubles.

- On July 10, Ed Rommel of the A's gives up a record 29 hits and 14 runs in relief.

- Rommel pitches an AL relief record 17 innings in July 29 game.

- On July 29, Johnny Burnett of Cleveland bangs out an ML record nine hits.

- Doc Cramer of the A's goes 6-for-6 on June 20.

- Klein ties Ott for the homer crown (38), and leads the NL in runs produced (251).

- Klein leads the NL with 420 total bases and becomes the only player to collect 420 total bases twice in his career.

- Klein becomes the last ML player to lead the league in SA (.646) and steals (20) in the same season.

- Klein's 20 thefts are the fewest to this juncture to lead an ML.

- Four-year vet Wes Ferrell of Cleveland wins 20-plus games for the fourth straight year.

Bill Terry

Terry Takes Over Reins

When Bill Terry replaced John McGraw as the Giants manager in 1932, the club was six games under .500. The Giants finished ten games below .500 that year, despite outscoring their opponents by 49 runs. In contrast, the Pirates finished second, 18 games over .500, while giving up ten more runs than they scored.

Yankees Win World Title

A look at the 1932 World Champion New York Yankees. Apart from Babe Ruth *(middle row, center)* and Lou Gehrig *(two to the right of Ruth)*, Herb Pennock *(front row, far left)* was the only member on the club's first World Championship squad in 1923.

Al Crowder

Crowder Tops AL in Wins

Al Crowder was nicknamed "General" by admirers in memory of General Enoch Crowder, a World War I hero. In 1928, he became the only Browns hurler ever to top the American League in win percentage; that same year, he shut out the World Champion Yankees in two consecutive starts against them. In 1932, he led the circuit with 26 wins. Crowder's control in 1932 was impeccable. He pitched 327 innings without hitting a batter and without throwing a wild pitch. He did, however, walk a fair amount of batters (77).

New York Yankees

1932

- Yankees rookie Johnny Allen tops the AL in win pct. (.810).

- The Phils finish fourth, their only first-division finish between 1918 and 1950.

- Red Sox pitcher Ed Morris is slain during spring training.

- Detroit trades Roy Johnson and Alexander to Boston for Earl Webb.

- Cardinals trade their holdout star, Chick Hafey, to the Reds for Harvey Hendrick and Benny Frey.

- Brooklyn trades Ernie Lombardi, Babe Herman, and Wally Gilbert to the Reds for Joe Stripp, Clyde Sukeforth, and Tony Cuccinello.

- Pirate Earl Grace's .998 FA is a new ML record for catchers.

- Max Bishop of the A's sets an ML record for FA by a second baseman (.988).

- The Yankees go 62-15 at home.

- Yankee Joe Sewell strikes out just three times in 503 at-bats.

Goose Goslin

Goslin Tallies 104 RBI

Goose Goslin (pictured) and Senators owner Clark Griffith had what seemed at times to be a father-son relationship. Piqued when Goslin had a bad season in 1929, Griffith swapped him to the Browns, only to regret it almost immediately. Griffith worked for three years to get him back in time to play on Washington's last flag-winner. Goslin hit .299 with 17 home runs and 104 RBI for St. Louis in 1932.

Lefty O'Doul

McGraw Bids Farewell

John McGraw won his last pennant in 1924, and by the time he stepped down as the Giants manager in 1932 (leaving the team at 17–23), much of the aura that surrounded him had dimmed. He had become, said Bill Terry, "the type of fellow who would call all your pitches until you got in a spot, then he'd leave you on your own." Nevertheless, McGraw's career managerial record was astounding. In 33 years, he won 4,879 games—second only to Connie Mack. Little Napoleon guided his team to ten pennants.

John McGraw

O'Doul Wins NL Bat Title

Three years after he won his second National League batting crown (.368 in 1932), Lefty O'Doul returned to the Pacific Coast League as the player/manager of the San Francisco Seals. O'Doul had a ploy he used to touch off a rally: Pacing the third-base coach's box and waving a white handkerchief.

- Washington becomes the last ML team to hit 100 triples in a season, as it bangs out an even 100.

- Herman of the Reds leads the NL with 19 triples.

- Cincinnati's Red Lucas leads the majors with 28 complete games.

- Yankee Ben Chapman repeats as the AL stolen base champ (38).

- Lefty Gomez leads the Yanks with 24 wins.

- Monte Weaver (22 wins) teams with Crowder (26 wins) to give Washington the top tandem in the majors.

- Firpo Marberry tops the majors with 13 saves.

- Hired by Cleveland, Jack Graney is the first former major leaguer to become a radio play-by-play announcer.

- Crowder pitches 327 innings without either hitting a batter or throwing a wild pitch.

HUBBELL-LED GIANTS HUMBLE THE SENATORS

For the first time in three decades, the National League season opened without John McGraw in uniform. The fiery Giants manager had resigned 40 games into the 1932 campaign in favor of first baseman Bill Terry, who then rallied the last-place Giants to a sixth-place finish.

Terry continued his good work in 1933, building a new Giants pennant-winner around screwballer Carl Hubbell, Mel Ott, and imports Gus Mancuso (a catcher traded from St. Louis), leadoff man Jo-Jo Moore (up from the minors), and spark plug Blondy Ryan. Ott's 23 homers were third-best in the league, as were his 103 RBI. Terry himself was third in batting at .322.

The strong suit of the 91-61 Giants was pitching, as the MVP Hubbell and supporting cast members Hal Schumacher and Freddie Fitzsimmons compiled the NL's best team ERA of 2.71. Hubbell went 23-12 to lead the league in wins. His ERA of 1.66 was the lowest NL ERA since Pete Alexander's 1.55 in 1916.

Although Paul Waner scored the second-most runs and triples and the fourth-most doubles in the league, the Pirates came in five back at 87-67. Wally Berger carried Boston as far as fourth place on his 27 home runs and 106 RBI, both league second-bests.

Philadelphia's Chuck Klein won the Triple Crown, adding 120 RBI to his league-leading batting average of .368 and 28 home runs. Although Klein also spearheaded the circuit in hits (223) and doubles (44), and teammate Spud Davis had the second-best league batting average (.349), the Phillies couldn't rise above seventh.

While the fifth-place St. Louis club finished 9½ games out, the Branch Rickey-inspired farm system was busy producing the building blocks of the famous "Gas House Gang" teams. Ripper Collins, who hit .310, and Joe "Ducky" Medwick, who had 40 doubles and 18 homers, were called up to replace Jim Bottomley and Chick Hafey; they joined veterans Pepper Martin, Frankie Frisch, and Leo Durocher to lead the NL in runs with 687.

Baseball bid McGraw a classy adieu by naming him manager of the NL entry in the first All-Star Game, held in Comiskey Park, July 6. Connie Mack's AL squad won 4-2 on Babe Ruth's homer.

Shortstop Joe Cronin managed a Washington team to the pennant by 7 games over a fading New York club in the American League. The Senators' attack consisted of Cronin (who led the league in doubles with 45), Heinie Manush (who was second in hitting at .336 and first in triples with 17), first baseman Joe Kuhel (who had 107 RBI), and veteran Goose Goslin (who banged out 55 extra-base hits). Led by General Crowder at 24-15, Washington's pitchers allowed the fewest runs in the league (665); Earl Whitehill was third in wins with 22 and Monte Weaver was fifth in ERA at 3.26.

Ruth "slid" to 97 runs, 34 homers, and a .301 batting average in his second-to-last Yankee season, as New York used Ruth's momentum to lead the AL in runs with 927 and in homers with 144; Lou Gehrig was third in hitting at .334 and in homers with 32, second in RBI with 139, and first in runs with 138. Lefty Gomez helped on the pitching end with his league-high 163 strikeouts.

Philadelphia's decline continued unchecked; MVP and Triple Crown-winner Jimmie Foxx (.356 average, 48 home runs, 163 RBI) and Lefty Grove (24-8) kept the third-place A's out of the second division virtually by themselves.

New York dominated the World Series, as Hubbell's 2-0 record and perfect 0.00 ERA led the way to a 4-1 Giants victory. Terry's team outpitched the Senators, 1.53 to 2.74, and outscored them 16-11 in the affair.

1933

- The Senators win the last pennant by a Washington-based ML team.
- The Giants, piloted by Bill Terry, win their first NL flag since 1924.
- The Giants win the World Series in five games.
- Carl Hubbell is the Series star: two CG wins and no earned runs.

- Mel Ott hits .389 with two homers to lead all Series batters.
- Hubbell wins the NL MVP vote.
- Jimmie Foxx wins the AL MVP.
- Chuck Klein wins the Triple Crown in the NL, batting .368 with 28 homers and 120 RBI.

- Klein leads the NL in hits (223), doubles (44), total bases (365), and runs produced (193).
- Foxx takes the Triple Crown in the AL, batting .356 with 48 homers and 163 RBI.
- This is the only time both leagues have a Triple Crown winner in the same season.

In 1933, Carl Hubbell notched more shutouts than the entire pitching staffs of seven of the eight American League teams. His ten whitewashes were the most by any pitcher in either league between 1917 and 1942. In addition, the Giants got seven shutouts from Hal Schumacher that year, second in the majors only to Hubbell.

- Foxx leads the AL in SA (.703) and total bases (403).

- Lefty Grove and Washington's Al Crowder tie for the ML lead in wins with 24.

- Grove tops the majors with a win pct. of .750.

- On August 3', the Yankees are blanked by Grove—the first time in 309 games that they're shut out.

- Mel Harder of Cleveland tops the AL in ERA with a 2.95 mark.

- Klein sets a 20th-century NL record when he collects 200 hits for the fifth consecutive year.

- In November, the financially strapped Phillies send Klein to the Cubs for three second-line players and $65,000.

- In the first All-Star Game, the AL beats the NL 4-2 at Comiskey Park.

- Total attendance in the majors falls to 6.3 million.

Senators Win AL Flag

A look at the 1933 Washington Senators. Seated to the left of owner Clark Griffith is his son-in-law, player/manager Joe Cronin. Alex McColl *(back row, fifth from the right)*, a 39-year-old rookie pitcher, hurled two perfect innings in the World Series that year.

Washington Senators

Jimmie Foxx

Foxx is AL MVP

Jimmie Foxx earned the second of two Most Valuable Player Awards in 1933, although he was just age 25. Yet he still had not established himself as the American League's premier first baseman and never would. It was in no way Foxx's fault, as he had to compete first with Lou Gehrig and then with Hank Greenberg.

Rick Ferrell

Ferrell Catches All-Star Game

Rick Ferrell started for the American League behind the bat in the first All-Star Game in 1933. He caught all nine innings while Mickey Cochrane and Bill Dickey sat on the bench. The following year, he began a string of five straight seasons in which he and his brother Wes formed the best sibling battery in AL history. On July 19, 1933, the two became the first brothers on opposing teams to hit home runs in the same game. To cap off his highlight-filled year, Ferrell tallied 77 RBI, the most in his career.

1933

- NL pitchers have a collective ERA that's nearly a full run below the AL's (3.34-4.28).

- Lou Gehrig surpasses Everett Scott's record streak of 1,307 consecutive games played.

- Nick Altrock, age 57, pinch-hits in a game for Washington.

- On May 16, Washington's Cecil Travis collects a modern record five hits in his ML debut.

- On July 19, Dizzy Dean fans 17 Cubs, a modern ML record (since broken).

- Dean again tops the NL in Ks (199).

- Washington's Heinie Manush has a 33-game hitting streak.

- On July 19, Wes and Rick Ferrell become the first pair of brothers on opposing teams to homer in the same game.

- Hubbell's 1.66 ERA is the lowest ever by an NL lefty for over 300 innings.

1933

General Crowder

AL All-Star Team

Pepper Martin

Crowder Mounts Wins

General Crowder is one of the few pitchers to lead the American League two years in a row in both wins and most hits allowed (26 wins, 319 hits in 1932; 24 wins, 311 hits in 1933). Like Pete Alexander, another pitcher who twice performed the feat, Crowder's strength was pinpoint control. Although he gave up his share of walks, most came in an effort to get one of the many great sluggers in the AL during the 1930s to bite on a bad pitch.

AL Wins First All-Star Game

A look at the 1933 American League All-Star team. The gem of the first midsummer classic was the oldest player on the field, Babe Ruth *(back row, fourth from the left)*. At the age of 38, Ruth lined a two-run round-tripper in the third inning. He then took away an extra-base hit in the eighth with a running catch of Chick Hafey's line drive.

Martin Scores Big

When asked what the Cardinals looked for, a scout on the staff replied, "Hard guys. I don't care whether they can field or not. I want strong-armed, strong-legged guys who can hit and run and throw. Guys like—well, like Pepper Martin." Martin tallied 122 runs scored in 1933, tops in the NL.

- Hubbell's ERA is the best in the majors since the advent of the lively ball era.
- Hubbell's ten shutouts are the most in the majors since 1916.
- Hubbell also paces the NL in wins with 23.

- Hubbell hurls an 18-inning shutout vs. the Cards on August 2.
- Tom Yawkey buys the moribund Boston Red Sox.
- The bank takes over the bankrupt Reds—Powel Crosley buys the club.
- Cardinal Pepper Martin tops the NL in runs (122) and steals (26).

- Babe Ruth leads the AL for the last time in a major offensive department—walks with 114.
- Gehrig tops the AL in runs (138) and runs produced (245).
- Ruth hits the first homer in All-Star competition—a two-run shot.

Judge Bolts

Joe Judge (pictured) missed a chance to join Sam Rice, Ossie Bluege, and Goose Goslin (the only members of the 1924 World Champion Senators still with the team when they won their flag in 1933), when he was sent to the Dodgers after the 1932 season. In 1933, he hit .214 in Brooklyn and .296 in Boston.

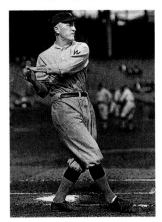

Joe Judge

Giants Win World Crown

A shot of the 1933 World Champion New York Giants. Bill Terry's squad was so deep in outfielders that Lefty O'Doul got into only one World Series game. Another backup gardener was Homer Peel *(back row, second from the left),* the holder of the best career average in the Texas League (a .325 mark).

Bill Terry

Terry's Team Well-Armed

Although the Giants under Bill Terry (pictured) had neither the best hitting nor the best fielding team in the National League in 1933, they did have, by far, the best pitching staff. Spearheaded by Carl Hubbell (23 victories, a 1.66 ERA), the Giants had a composite 2.71 ERA—0.13 runs per game better than Lefty Grove's American League-leading ERA.

New York Giants

1933

- Cincinnati's Red Lucas paces the majors in fewest walks per game—an incredible .74.

- Washington's Joe Judge and Sam Rice are broken up after 18 years as road roommates, as Judge is traded.

- Brownie Sammy West goes 6-for-6 in an 11-inning game on April 13.

- Mickey Cochrane becomes the only catcher ever to lead the majors in OBP (.459).

- On April 25, Russ Van Atta of the Yankees debuts with four hits—a record for pitchers.

- Lloyd Waner's eight Ks are fewest ever by an ML regular outfielder.

- Brownie Ski Melillo's .991 FA is a new ML record for second basemen.

- Indian Willie Kamm's .984 FA is a new ML record for third basemen.

- Phils infielder Mickey Finn dies of an ulcer.

- The average ML player's salary is now down to $6,000.

1933

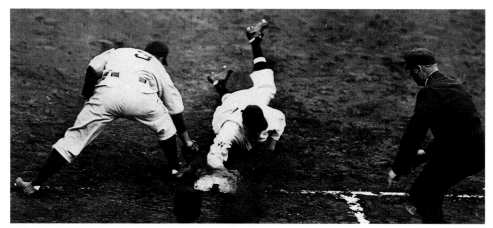

World Series

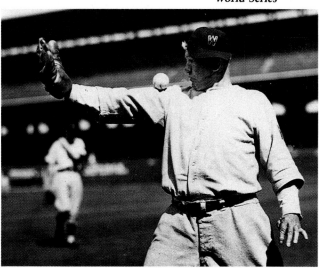

Nick Altrock

Altrock Pinch Hits at Age 57

Forgotten by 1934 was the fact that Nick Altrock had once been much more than a clown and a coach who would take an occasional swing to perk up the Washington crowd (as he had done in 1933, when, at 57 years of age, he pinch hit in a game for the Senators). For three straight years beginning in 1904, Altrock won 20 or more games for the White Sox and was among the best lefties in the game.

Chuck Klein

Mel Ott

Giants Take Series 4–1

Giants first baseman Bill Terry just misses nailing a Senator baserunner on a pickoff play in the 1933 World Series. Attendance for the four games following the opening contest was down; as a result, the Giants took home the smallest winning shares since 1920.

Klein King in Philadelphia

All of Chuck Klein's hitting stats declined so precipitously when he was traded to the Cubs—.368 average, 223 hits, 28 home runs, and 120 RBI (all league-highs) in 1933 and .301 average, 131 hits, 20 home runs, and 80 RBI in 1934—that his great years with the Phils are often attributed to his having played with a weak team in a bandbox park. The fact, however, is that in his two full years with the Cubs, injuries severely cut his playing time.

Ott One of Few to Walk

In 1933, National League hurlers gave up 1,386 fewer walks than American League pitchers. Mel Ott (pictured) and Gus Suhr were the only two NL hitters to get more than 70 free passes.

- The Cards swap Sparky Adams, Paul Derringer, and Allyn Stout to Cincinnati for three players.

- The A's send Cochrane to Detroit for John Pasek and $100,000.

- The A's send Grove, Rube Walberg, and Max Bishop to the Red Sox for two players and $125,000.

- The A's finish third in 1933, the last time they'll finish that high under Connie Mack.

- Player/manager Joe Cronin is second in the AL MVP vote—the highest finish ever by a Washington player.

- Cronin leads the AL in doubles (45), as well as FA by a shortstop.

- Ott tops the NL in walks with 75.

- Arky Vaughan of Pittsburgh leads the majors with 19 triples.

- Ben Chapman again wins the AL theft crown (27).

- The Yankees top the AL in runs with 927—240 more than the NL-leading Cards score.

DIZZY WINS 30 AND CARDS TAME THE TIGERS

Bill Terry's New York Giants had another good season in 1934, scoring 760 runs, second-best in the league, and allowing only 583, the fewest of any NL staff. Young Mel Ott hit .326 with 119 runs scored (second only to Paul Waner's 122) and drove in a league-leading 135; Ott also drew 85 walks and tied with Ripper Collins for the home run title at 35. New York's other big gun, player/manager Terry, was second in the NL in hitting at .354 (behind Waner at .362) and scored 109 runs; leadoff man Jo-Jo Moore batted .331 and crossed the plate 106 times. Hal Schumacher won 23 games; Carl Hubbell won 21 contests and took the NL ERA title at 2.30.

It was, however, the rough and tumble St. Louis Cardinals, nicknamed the "Gashouse Gang" after the street gangs of one of Manhattan's worst neighborhoods, that won the pennant by 2 games in an exciting race. New York had led for 127 straight days, when, on September 28, ace Dizzy Dean defeated the Reds 4-0 to bring the Cardinals even with New York. The next day, Dizzy's younger brother Paul won 6-1, while the Giants lost to Brooklyn. The day after that, the elder Dean shut out Cincinnati again, 9-0, to give St. Louis a lead it never relinquished.

Dizzy had been ridiculed for his preseason promise that the Dean brothers would win 45 games. By season's end, they had

exceeded that total by four, and the 30-7 Dizzy was voted NL MVP. The other principal Gashousers were second baseman/manager Frankie Frisch, who hit .305; Collins, who batted .333 and drove in 128 runs; Leo Durocher, the league's top-fielding shortstop; Pepper Martin, the league's stolen base leader (23); and Ducky Medwick, who hit .319 with 18 triples.

Hard-hitting Detroit batted .300—the only major league team to do so—on its way to a 101-53 record, 7 games better than a New York Yankees team that finished second in runs scored. The 39-year-old Babe Ruth gave only a .288, 22-homer season performance; Lou Gehrig carried most of the weight, winning the Triple Crown with a .363 average, 165 RBI, and 49 homers. The New York pitchers rebounded to post a league-low 3.76 team ERA courtesy of titlist Lefty Gomez (who went 26-5 with a 2.33 ERA), 19-game winner Red Ruf-

fing, and 14-game winner Johnny Murphy.

The Tigers lineup featured an awesome five 100-run men (including Charlie Gehringer, the league leader with 134), and four 100-RBI men (led by first baseman Hank Greenberg with 139). MVP Mickey Cochrane, purchased from Philadelphia, hit .320 and was credited with turning around the Tiger pitching staff, which finished second in team ERA at 4.06.

Schoolboy Rowe (24-8) and Tommy Bridges (22-11) were Detroit's big winners. Jimmie Foxx drew an AL-high 111 walks and hit 44 homers for fifth-place Philadelphia, and Connie Mack sold 34-year-old Lefty Grove to the Boston Red Sox for $125,000. The defending champion Senators fell to seventh-place, 34 out.

The Dean duo was the deciding factor in the close-fought, seven-game 1934 World Series. The brothers each recorded ERAs under 2.00 and won two games.

The Series ended on a bizarre note, when, in the midst of a St. Louis rout, the Detroit crowd interrupted the game to shower left fielder Medwick with garbage to protest his sixth-inning hard slide into Tiger third baseman Marv Owen. Commissioner Kenesaw Mountain Landis ruled that the Cardinal outfielder leave the game for his own safety.

The departure made no difference to the Tigers, who went on to lose by a score of 11-0.

1934

- The Tigers cop their first AL flag since 1909.

- The Cards take the NL flag by 2 games over the Giants with a club that's known as the "Gashouse Gang."

- The Cards take the World Series in seven games under manager Frankie Frisch.

- In game seven of Series, Ducky Medwick's hard slide into Tiger third baseman Marv Owen triggers a near riot among Detroit fans.

- The Dean brothers, Dizzy and Paul, win two games each in the World Series.

- Dizzy Dean is selected the NL MVP.

- Detroit player/manager Mickey Cochrane is the AL MVP.

- Lou Gehrig wins the Triple Crown in the AL, batting .363 with 49 homers and 165 RBI.

- Paul Waner tops the NL in batting at .362.

Said J. Roy Stockton of the Dean brothers, "Dizzy *(right)* talked. Paul listened. Dizzy wisecracked. Paul laughed. Dizzy was a great comedian. Paul was his best audience. Each was the other's hero." The duo won all four of the Cardinal victories in the 1934 Series.

- Dizzy Dean becomes the last NL hurler to win 30 games, as he wins 30 games exactly.

- The Dean brothers win a sibling record 49 games for the Cards.

- Yankee Lefty Gomez leads the AL in wins (26), win pct. (.839), Ks (158), and ERA (2.33), and ties in shutouts (six).

- Carl Hubbell's 2.30 ERA is the best in the majors.

- In the All-Star Game, Hubbell fans Babe Ruth, Gehrig, Jimmie Foxx, Al Simmons, and Joe Cronin consecutively.

- The AL wins the All-Star Game 9-7.

- Ruth hits his 700th career homer.

- Yankees obtain Joe DiMaggio from the PCL San Francisco Seals for $25,000 and four players.

- Clark Griffith of the Senators sends his son-in-law, Cronin, to the Red Sox for Lyn Lary and $250,000.

- Gehrig ties an AL record by leading the loop in RBI for a fifth time.

Pepper Martin

Martin Has .289 Average

Pepper Martin tallied a .289 average in 1934 with five home runs and 49 RBI. At the beginning of the season, his roommate was Vallie Eaves, a pitcher of Indian descent who failed to stick with the Cardinals. Martin, however, never kept any of his roommates long. His normal attire was jeans and a workshirt open at the throat.

Paul Waner

Hubbell Ks the Best

After witnessing the incredible strikeout string established by Carl Hubbell (pictured) in the 1934 All-Star Game—Babe Ruth, Lou Gehrig, Jimmie Foxx, Al Simmons, and Joe Cronin all fanned in order in the first two frames—Frankie Frisch said, "I could play second base 15 more years behind that guy. He doesn't need any help." Heywood Broun wrote that with Hubbell pitching "first base itself is a Marathon route." On the year, Hubbell won 21 games and posted a league-leading 2.30 ERA. In his spare time, he toiled in the bullpen—where he led the league in saves with eight.

Carl Hubbell

Waner Takes NL Bat Title

Even with bat leader Paul Waner (pictured) hitting .362, the Pirates could finish no better than fifth place in 1934. When the team, predicted by many to take it all, got off to a 27–24 start, popular George Gibson was replaced at the helm by Pie Traynor. Under Traynor, the Pirates played sub-.500 ball and finished with a 74–76 record. Pitching was their main problem. They posted a 4.20 team ERA.

1934

- The World Champion Cardinals draw only 350,000 fans in home attendance.

- Hal Trosky of Cleveland collects 374 total bases, a rookie record.

- On Sept. 21, the Deans take turns shutting out the Dodgers in a twinbill.

- A few members of the Reds fly to a game in Chicago, the first ML teammates to travel together by air.

- The Yankees release two future Hall of Famers, Herb Pennock and Joe Sewell, on the same day.

- On May 1, Burleigh Grimes wins the last game in ML history by a pitcher legally allowed to throw a spitball.

- Detroit's Schoolboy Rowe wins an AL record 16 straight games.

- Goose Goslin has a 30-game hitting streak.

- Bobo Newsom of St. Louis no-hits Boston for nine innings on Sept. 18, loses 2-1 in ten innings.

Earl Averill

"Rock" Averill Solid Again

Earl Averill's year of fame came in 1936, when he hit .378 with a league-leading 232 hits. "Rock" had plenty of other excellent seasons as well. In 1934, he hit .313 with 31 homers and 113 RBI. In fact, his only off year in his first ten seasons came in 1935, when he hit .288—largely because he burned his hand testing Fourth of July fireworks.

Charlie Gehringer

Gehringer Hits .356

Known as "The Mechanical Man," Charlie Gehringer was second in the American League in 1934 with a .356 batting average. Satchel Paige deemed Gehringer the best white hitter he ever faced. What he lacked in flamboyance, Gehringer more than made up for in consistency. As teammate Doc Cramer said, "You wind him up on opening day and forget about him."

The Babe Takes a Break

Admirers surround Babe Ruth during a postseason tour of Japan. Wherever Ruth went, Jimmy Cannon said, "He was a parade all by himself, a burst of dazzle and jingle. Santa Claus drinking his whiskey straight...Ruth made the music that his joyous years danced to in a continuous party." The 1934 year would be the Bambino's last full season. During the campaign, he hit .288 with 22 homers, 84 RBI, and 103 walks in a mere 125 games—not bad numbers for an out-of-shape 39-year-old.

Babe Ruth

- Paul Dean no-hits the Dodgers on Sept. 21.

- Waner tops the NL in runs (122) and hits (217).

- New York's Mel Ott leads the NL in homers (35), RBI (135), and runs produced (219).

- Cardinal Ripper Collins tops the NL in total bases (369) and SA (.615) and ties in homers (35).

- Dizzy Dean leads the NL in win pct. (.811), shutouts (seven), and Ks (195).

- Tiger Charlie Gehringer leads the AL in hits (214), runs (134), and runs produced (250).

- Teammate Hank Greenberg tops the AL with 63 doubles.

- The Yankees' Myril Hoag goes 6-for-6 on June 6.

- This is the last season that both pennant-winning teams are piloted by player/managers.

Detroit Tigers

Tigers Grab AL Flag

A shot of the 1934 Detroit Tigers. Mickey Cochrane *(front row, third from the right)* and Goose Goslin *(front row, far right)* were the only two players in the American League to be on five pennant-winning teams between 1921 and 1939 without ever playing for the Yankees. In 1934, Cochrane had a .320 batting average, two home runs, and 76 RBI; Goslin had a .305 average, 13 home runs, and 100 RBI.

Babe Ruth

The Bambino Nails No. 700

Babe Ruth crosses the plate on July 13, 1934, after hitting his 700th career home run against Detroit at Navin Field. The sports pages the following day deemed it "a record likely never to be surpassed in baseball." Lou Gehrig was second at the time with 314 homers and Rogers Hornsby third with 301.

Hal Trosky

Trosky Brings Respect to Tribe

The Indians had a team batting average of .261 and just 50 home runs in 1933. Rookie slugging star Hal Trosky helped pump up the stats to a .287 average and an even 100 four-baggers in 1934. What aided the Indians hitters even more, however, was moving most of the Tribe's home games from gigantic Cleveland Stadium to tiny League Park, the American League's version of the Baker Bowl.

1934

- John McGraw dies.
- The Reds finish last in the NL for the fourth straight year.
- On April 28, Goslin grounds into a record four double plays.
- Detroit's four regular infielders miss a combined total of one game during the season.

- Asked to assess the Dodgers' chances prior to the season, Giants manager Bill Terry says, "Is Brooklyn still in the league?"
- The Dodgers beat the Giants the last two games of the season to give the Cards the flag.
- Washington's Jack Russell is the first reliever selected to an All-Star Game.

- Firpo Marberry is the first pitcher to post 100 career saves.
- Cleveland deals Wes Ferrell and Dick Porter to the Red Sox for Bob Weiland, Bob Seeds, and cash.
- On June 30 against Washington, Gehrig hits three triples by the fifth inning, but the game is rained out and the feat isn't counted.

Cochrane Wins AL MVP

In 1934, Mickey Cochrane became the first player who had studied under Connie Mack for at least one full season to manage a pennant-winning club. In the American League MVP balloting that year, Cochrane (.320, a pair of home runs, 76 RBI) narrowly edged teammate Charlie Gehringer for the title.

Mickey Cochrane

Cards Take World Title

A look at the 1934 World Champion St. Louis Cardinals. Dubbed "The Gashouse Gang" by New York sportswriter Frank Graham, the Cardinals' gritty, aggressive brand of ball came to symbolize the game during the 1930s—at least in the National League. The American League had the Yankees, an altogether different breed of team.

World Series

Cards, Tigers Go Neck-and-Neck

The stretch by Cardinals first sacker Ripper Collins gets the call on a close play in a 1934 World Series game. The Tigers returned home to Navin Field on October 8 with a 3–2 lead in games, only to lose a 4–3 squeaker to Paul Dean. The following day, they suffered an 11–0 blowout at the hands of Paul's brother Dizzy.

St. Louis Cardinals

- Milt Gaston leaves the majors with a .372 win pct. (97-164), the worst ever by a pitcher with more than 250 decisions.

- Kiki Cuyler and Phillie Ethan Allen tie for the NL lead in doubles (42).

- Medwick leads the majors in triples with 18.

- Red Sox Billy Werber leads the majors in steals with 40.

- Rowe (24 wins) and Tommy Bridges team to win 46 games for Detroit.

- Rookie Curt Davis wins 19 for the seventh-place Phils and tops the NL in games pitched (51).

- The last-place Reds have two 20-game losers: Paul Derringer (21) and Si Johnson (22).

- Foxx leads both leagues with 111 walks.

- The Tigers lead the AL in BA (.300) and FA (.974).

GREENBERG POWERS TIGERS TO WORLD TITLE

Both defending pennant-winners were leading comfortably late in the 1935 season, when the surprising Chicago Cubs put on a 21-game winning streak that propelled them into first place; they finished at 100-54, 4 games ahead of the Cardinals and 8½ up on New York.

Chicago led the NL in runs scored and fewest runs allowed. Billy Herman topped the league in hits with 227, scored 113 runs, and batted .341 (tied for third-best in the league behind Pirates shortstop Arky Vaughan at .385 and St. Louis' Ducky Medwick at .353). The infield corners were held down by 18-year-old Phil Cavarretta (a .275 average) and 25-year-old Stan Hack (a .311 average). Outfielder Augie Galan drew 87 walks, stole a league-best 22 bases, led in runs scored with 133, and batted .314 with 41 doubles. Catcher Gabby Hartnett, the NL's MVP, hit .344.

Chicago's deep, balanced pitching staff included Larry French and Bill Lee, who tied for fourth in ERA at 2.96, 20-game winner Lon Warneke, and Charlie Root. Lefty Roy Henshaw and righty Tex Carleton made six pitchers in double figures in wins.

The Dean brothers went a combined 47-24 with Dizzy leading all NL pitchers in wins, innings, complete games, and strikeouts. Cy Blanton and Bill Swift were one and two in ERA at 2.59 and 2.69 for also-ran Pittsburgh.

The career of baseball's greatest player, Babe Ruth, came to a close in 1935. Ruth was released by New York and moved to the Boston Braves, a team that finished with the worst record (38-115) since the Philadelphia A's went 36-117 in 1916. He retired 28 games into the season, batting .181 with six homers; in one final display of the old Ruthian form, the Babe hit career homers number 712, 713, and 714 in a game against Pittsburgh on May 25.

He retired with a .342 lifetime average, tenth on the all-time list. He led the league in runs eight times, home runs 12 times, RBI six times, and bases on balls 11 times. He had a career on-base average of .474 and a .690 slugging mark—figures that would lead any league most years.

Detroit took the AL pennant with a 93-58 record, 3 games better than the Yankees at 89-60. MVP Hank Greenberg was the Tigers' big banger, hitting .328 with 121 runs, 46 doubles, 16 triples, and 36 home runs (tied for the league lead with Jimmie Foxx); he drove in 170 runs, 51 more than runner-up Lou Gehrig.

Charlie Gehringer was fifth in hitting at .330 and scored 123 runs, second only to Gehrig. Outfielder Pete Fox batted .321 and scored 116 runs.

As a team, Detroit scored 919 runs, 101 more than the second-place team. Tommy Bridges, Schoolboy Rowe, and Eldon Auker all recorded ERAs below 4.00 and, together with 36-year-old General Crowder, gave the Tigers four pitchers with between 16 and 21 wins.

In Boston, Lefty Grove made a comeback to finish 20-12 with the AL's lowest ERA, 2.70; teammate Wes Ferrell led the AL with 25 wins. Washington's Buddy Myer took the batting crown at .349, one point ahead of Cleveland's Joe Vosmik, who led the league in hits with 216, doubles with 47, and triples with 20.

The Tigers began the 1935 World Series down 1-0. When Greenberg left game two with a season-ending injury, things looked bleak. Bridges, Rowe, and Crowder won games two, three, and four, however; and, after losing to Warneke 3-1 in game five, Detroit clinched the Series on Bridges's second win, 4-3.

In the top of the ninth of the final game, with the score tied three-all, Hack led off with a triple, but stayed put as shortstop Bill Jurges, pitcher French, and Galan failed to drive him in. When the Tigers won the game in the bottom of the inning, Cubs skipper Charlie Grimm was widely second-guessed for having let the pitcher bat.

1935

- The Tigers repeat in the AL.
- Chicago takes the NL flag.
- Detroit wins its first World Championship in six games.
- The Tigers' Pete Fox leads all Series batters with ten hits and a .385 BA.

- Tommy Bridges wins two CG victories for Detroit in Series, including the finale.
- Lon Warneke wins the Cubs' only two victories in Series and gives up just one run.
- Cubs catcher Gabby Hartnett is the NL MVP.

- Hank Greenberg wins the AL MVP Award.
- Boston pitcher Wes Ferrell rebounds from a sore arm to top the AL in wins with 25.
- Ferrell leads the AL in CGs (31) and innings (322).

It is a mistake to remember Hank Greenberg as the slow-footed slugger who returned from World War II. During his prime, Greenberg could steal a base if needed, was always among the leaders in runs scored, and also frequently ranked high on the triples list. In 1935, he ripped 46 doubles (second in the American League), 16 three-baggers (third in the loop), and 36 home runs (tied for first place in the circuit).

- Ferrell ties the ML record for pitchers by banging out 52 hits.
- Bridges leads the AL in Ks (163) and wins (21).
- Lefty Grove, now with Boston, leads the AL in ERA (2.70).
- Dizzy Dean again paces the NL in wins (28).

- Dean leads the NL in CGs (29), Ks (182), and innings (324).
- Arky Vaughan tops the NL at .385.
- Vaughan tops the NL in OBP (.491), SA (.607), and walks (97).
- Washington's Buddy Myer wins the AL bat crown by a single point over Cleveland's Joe Vosmik (.349-.348).

- Released by the Yankees, Babe Ruth signs a three-year contract with the Braves.
- On May 25, Ruth hits three homers vs. Pittsburgh at Forbes Field, then retires a few days later.
- Ruth retires with a .690 career SA and 2,056 walks—still ML records.

Lefty Gomez

The Babe Bows Out

Though Babe Ruth was 40 years of age in 1935 and woefully out of shape, he could still hit, especially when he had to think about nothing else. But baseball then required that half the game be played in the field, and there was simply no place Ruth could be stationed without hurting himself and the team. In his last game, he injured his knee and had to leave in the first inning.

Babe Ruth

Gomez, Yankees Fall Short

Had Lefty Gomez finished with a won-lost record of 15–12 rather than 12–15, the Yankees would have won the 1935 American League flag by one percentage point. As it was, the Yankees still conceivably could have won had they and the Tigers both made up all of their contests that were postponed and played a full 154-game schedule.

Dean Brothers Do It Again

Dizzy Dean (pictured) and brother Paul won 47 games between them for the 1935 Cardinals, nearly equaling their sibling record of 49 victories set the previous year. However, they each lost to the Cubs on consecutive days in late September to scotch the last chance for the Cards to catch the red-hot Bruins.

Dizzy Dean

1935

- Ruth retires with ML records in homers (714), RBI (2,209), OBP (.474), and extra-base hits (1,356) (all since broken).

- On May 24, Reds beat Phils at Crosley Field in first ML night game.

- Tigers owner Frank Navin dies shortly after seeing his club win its first World Series.

- The Braves go 38-115, totaling the most losses ever by an NL team in a 154-game schedule.

- The Braves have the worst road record in modern ML history—13-65.

- The Braves' Ben Cantwell, the NL win pct. leader two years earlier, goes 4-25.

- Cantwell is the last pitcher in ML history to lose 25 games.

- Greenberg's 170 RBI top the majors by 40 and the AL by 51.

- The Cubs win 21 straight games, setting a record for most consecutive wins without a tie.

Wes Ferrell

Ferrell Wins 25, Hits .347

A lame arm mixed with a hot temper caused Wes Ferrell to be shipped to the Red Sox by the Indians. Ferrell came back to have his finest all-around season in 1935. He led American League pitchers in wins with 25, complete games with 31, and innings pitched with 322. Ferrell batted .347.

Buddy Myer

Myer Wins AL Bat Title

Buddy Myer won the 1935 American League batting title (.349) by going 4-for-5 on the season's final day, while Cleveland's Joe Vosmik was protecting what seemed a safe lead by sitting out the first game of a doubleheader. Alarmed when he learned of Myer's outburst, Vosmik played the second game but went 1-for-4 and lost the crown by a point.

Phil Cavarretta

Cavarretta Racks Up Records

Phil Cavarretta set six season batting records for teenage players in 1935. He never played a day in the minors but probably should have. His lack of development reduced him to a bench-warmer by the late 1930s. During World War II, he became a regular again.

- Vern Kennedy of the White Sox no-hits Cleveland on August 31.
- The AL wins the All-Star Game 4-1.
- Lefty Gomez becomes the first pitcher to win two All-Star Games.
- William Wrigley of the Cubs is the first owner to allow all of his team's games to be broadcast.

- On July 5, Al and Tony Cuccinello become the first brothers on opposing teams to homer in the same NL game.
- On July 10, Cub Babe Herman hits the first homer in a night game.
- The Tigers' $6,544.76 World Series share is the highest prior to 1948.

- Wally Berger of the cellar-dwelling Braves leads the NL in homers (34) and RBI (130).
- Ducky Medwick leads the NL in total bases (365) and runs produced (235).
- Chicago's Augie Galan tops the NL in runs (133) and steals (22).

1935

Lots of Light, Little Action

Only three runs were tallied in the first night game in major league history, played on May 25, 1935, in Crosley Field, as scores remained scarce in contests played under the lights throughout the 1930s.

First Night Game

Gabby Hartnett

Gehrig: Only 119 RBI

Although Lou Gehrig didn't win the Triple Crown in 1935, as he did in '34, he still had reason to smile. The Iron Horse led the league in runs (125), walks (132), and on-base percentage (.466). He also knocked in 119 runs but, amazingly, it was his lowest output between 1927 and 1937 (during that 11-year stretch, Gehrig averaged 153 RBI per year).

Lou Gehrig

Gabby Shines at Plate

The most multitalented catcher of his era, Gabby Hartnett (pictured) had more power than Mickey Cochrane and was clearly superior to Bill Dickey defensively. In 1935, Hartnett was third in the National League in batting average (.344) while leading all of the loop's backstops in assists and fielding average.

1935

- Galan is the first player to play an entire 154-game season without grounding into a double play.
- Lou Gehrig paces the AL in runs (125) and walks (132).
- Jimmie Foxx leads the AL in SA (.636) and ties Greenberg for the AL homer crown (36).

- After selling most of their top talent, the A's finish last in 1935.
- After the '35 season, the A's sell Foxx and Johnny Marcum to the Red Sox for $150,000.
- Vosmik leads the AL in hits (216), doubles (47), and triples (20).

- Greenberg leads in total bases (389) and runs produced (255).
- Cub Phil Cavarretta, age 19, compiles 82 RBI and plays in the World Series.
- Len Koenecke of the Dodgers is killed by the pilot in a fight on a private plane.

THE BASEBALL CHRONICLE

Pete Fox

Navin Dies After Series

Frank Navin became president of the Tigers in 1911, two years after Detroit had won three straight pennants, and was convinced that with Ty Cobb on the team there would be many more flags. Unluckily for Navin, the Tigers didn't win again until 1934, and his park (built in 1912) was seldom filled. Navin died in 1935, after seeing the ballclub win its first World Series.

Frank Navin

Fox Tops Series Hitters

Pete Fox was known by some followers of the game as "Single X," not only to distinguish him from Jimmie Foxx ("Double XX") but also because he was primarily a singles hitter. In the 1935 World Series, Fox went the extra mile, spearheading all batters with a .385 average and ten hits.

Tigers Go All the Way

A look at the 1935 World Champion Detroit Tigers. The World Series triumph rendered the Browns the only American League team that was still in search of its first championship. Hank Greenberg *(front row, second from the right)* and Tommy Bridges *(middle row, fourth from the left)* were the lone members of the 1935 club still in Bengal livery when Detroit copped its second title in 1945.

Detroit Tigers

- On Sept. 29, Pirate Pep Young becomes the first nonpitcher since 1893 to whiff five times in a game.

- Cleveland sends Monte Pearson and Steve Sundra to the Yankees for Johnny Allen.

- Cardinals catcher Bill DeLancey is felled by TB.

- Herman tops the NL in doubles with 57, a record for NL second basemen.

- Cincinnati's Ival Goodman tops the NL in triples with 18.

- Bill Lee of the Cubs wins 20 games and tops the NL in win pct. (.769).

- Pirates Cy Blanton (2.59) and Bill Swift (2.69) finish one-two in ERA.

- Boston's Billy Werber wins his second straight steals crown (29).

- Detroit leads the majors in both batting (.290) and fielding (.978).

- The Cubs' middle infielders, Herman and Billy Jurges, both lead the NL at their respective positions in all major fielding departments.

The 1936 season was the first without Babe Ruth since 1913. The 1936 season was also the year that the Yankees discovered another legend: Joe DiMaggio. DiMaggio ushered in a new Yankee dynasty that rivaled, and possibly even surpassed, the great "Murderer's Row" clubs of the late 1920s.

The 21-year-old DiMaggio had been purchased from the Pacific Coast League San Francisco Seals, his hometown team, for $25,000; the Yankees got a bargain when a knee injury lowered the price from $70,000. Breaking into the New York lineup with a triple and two singles against St. Louis on May 3, DiMaggio went on to bat .323 with 132 runs, 44 doubles, 29 homers, 125 RBI, and a league-leading 15 triples.

DiMaggio's Yankees went 102-51 to take the AL flag by 19½ games, thanks to MVP Lou Gehrig (who hit .354 and racked up a league-leading 167 runs, 130 walks, and 49 home runs), shortstop Frankie Crosetti (who drew 90 walks and scored 137 runs), catcher Bill Dickey (who hit .362 with 22 homers in only 423 at-bats), and George Selkirk (who drove in 107 runs).

Second-place Detroit had its early-season hopes dashed by Mickey Cochrane's breakdown from exhaustion, which came 33 games into the season, and Hank Greenberg's broken wrist, which came after he had opened the month of April with 16 RBI in just 12 games. Tommy Bridges

YANKS DEBUT JOLTIN' JOE, BEAT GIANTS

took over to win a circuit-topping 23 games. The bright spot in Cleveland's fifth-place finish was Hal Trosky's league-leading 162 RBI and Earl Averill's second-best .378 average. Luke Appling of third-place Chicago was the leagues's best hitter at .388.

The 1936 pennant marked the beginning of a record streak of four consecutive World Championships for the Yankees. From 1936 through 1939, DiMaggio led New York to totals of 102, 102, 99, and 106 victories, and a 16-3 record—including nine wins in a row—against their World Series opponents.

Another historic debut came on July 7, when 17-year-old Cleveland pitcher Bob Feller struck out eight Cardinals in three innings in an exhibition game; in his first official game on August 23, the fireballing righty created a national sensation by beating the Browns 4-1 on six hits and 15 strikeouts, just one shy of Rube Waddell's AL record set back in 1908.

The 1936 year was a strong hitting season in the AL, whose pitchers recorded an overall ERA

of 5.04. (Boston's Lefty Grove had the league's best ERA at 2.81). In both leagues, 1936 was the year of the double, with five of the all-time top 21 doubles seasons. Ducky Medwick of St. Louis tied George Burns's 1926 total for second-place on the all-time list with 64. Charlie Gehringer of the Tigers hit 60 (sixth-best ever), Billy Herman of the Cubs had 57 (tenth-best), Detroit's Gee Walker hit 55 (15th-best), and Pittsburgh's Paul Waner had 53 (good for 21st all-time).

In a seesaw NL race, New York overtook Chicago and St. Louis for the flag with a 15-game team win streak and a personal 16-game streak from 26-6 MVP pitcher Carl Hubbell. Hubbell led the NL in ERA at 2.31 and wins; pacing the Giants' attack were Jo-Jo Moore, who scored 110 runs, and Mel Ott, who had 135 RBI (second only to the Cardinals' Medwick with 138) and a league-leading 33 home runs. Medwick also led in hits with 223 and total bases with 367.

Dizzy Dean went 24-13 for the Cards, who finished 5 games back, tied with Chicago for second. Fourth-place Pittsburgh, tops in the league in runs with 804, was powered by Waner's circuit-best .373 average.

In the first Subway Series since 1923, only the efforts of pitchers Hubbell and Hal Schumacher made for a respectable 4-2 Giants' defeat at the hands of the Yankees juggernaut. The pinstripers batted .302 and outscored Ott and his teammates 43-23.

1936

- The Yankees take the AL flag by 19½ games, a loop record.

- The Giants win in the NL.

- Yankees take the first Subway Series since 1923 in six games.

- Yankee Jake Powell is the World Series hitting star at .455 with five RBI.

- In game two, the Yanks score a Series record 18 runs.

- Lou Gehrig is AL MVP.

- Carl Hubbell wins his second NL MVP Award.

- Chicago's Luke Appling wins AL bat crown with .388 BA, highest in this century by a shortstop.

- Paul Waner wins his last NL bat crown (.373).

- Gehrig leads majors in homers (49), runs (167), OBP (.478), SA (.696), walks (130), and runs produced (270).

- The Hall of Fame is created; in the first vote for enshrinement, the leading vote-getter is Ty Cobb.

1936

A look at the 1936 World Champion New York Yankees. Joe DiMaggio *(back row, third from the right)* tallied a .323 average, tied for the American League-lead in triples with 15, and nailed 29 home runs in his rookie season. Pitcher Johnny Broaca (wearing cheaters, as "glasses" were then called) and Jake Powell *(to the right of Broaca)* were the Yankees' resident flakes. Broaca jumped the club in 1937 and wrecked his career.

- Babe Ruth, Honus Wagner, Christy Mathewson, and Walter Johnson join Cobb as the first Hall electees.

- Hubbell wins a record 24 straight games over a two-year period.

- Hubbell's 26 wins top majors.

- Ducky Medwick cracks an NL record 64 doubles.

- Cleveland's Hal Trosky leads ML in total bases (405) and RBI (162).

- Trosky's 42 homers set a new Cleveland club record.

- The Yankees have a record five men with 100 or more RBI.

- The Phils commit 252 errors and are last ML team to top 250 in a year.

- On Sept. 23, 17-year-old Indian Bob Feller sets a new AL record (since broken) when he Ks 17 batters in a game.

- Hank Greenberg breaks his arm in April, shelving him for the season and sinking the Tigers' chances.

- Gehrig hits 14 homers vs. Cleveland, a record vs. one team in a season.

Earl Averill

Ott Leads NL in Homers

Mel Ott led the National League in home runs in 1936 with 33. An established star by the time he was 20 years of age, Ott played until he turned 38. It seems that World War II extended a career that otherwise would probably have ended several years sooner. In 1946, with all the top players back from military service, Ott hit .074 in 31 games.

Averill Leads AL in Hits

In 1928, the San Francisco Seals of the Pacific Coast League featured an outfield of Smead Jolley, Roy Johnson, and Earl Averill (pictured). Johnson was rated the best prospect of the three and Jolley the best hitter, but Coast League players told Cleveland scouts that Averill was the real prize. The Indians soon learned they had made the right choice. In 1936, Averill topped the American League in hits with 232 and tied for the lead in triples with 15.

Mel Ott

Tony Lazzeri

Lazzeri: 11 RBI in One Game

Despite clubbing 60 homers one year in the minors, Tony Lazzeri was only a moderate slugging force in the majors, never collecting more than 18 round-trippers in a season. His shining moment in the bigs came on May 24, 1936, when he drove in 11 runs in one game, a record in the American League. One writer said that interviewing the taciturn Lazzeri was "like trying to mine coal with a nail file and a pair of scissors."

1936

- On April 14, Cardinal Eddie Morgan becomes first player to hit a pinch homer in his first ML at-bat.

- Ed Coleman of the Browns sets new AL record with 20 pinch hits (since broken).

- Pirate Woody Jensen's 696 at-bats are a record for a 154-game schedule.

- Joe DiMaggio scores 132 runs, an AL rookie record.

- Chuck Klein, back with the Phils, hits four homers in a ten-inning game on July 10.

- The NL wins the All-Star Game for the first time, 4-3 at Braves Field.

- The Yankees collect an ML record 2,703 total bases.

- Yanks total an ML record 995 RBI.

- The Yankees outscore their opponents by an ML record 434 runs.

- On May 24, Yankee Tony Lazzeri drives in an AL record 11 runs in a game.

Paul Waner

Waner Takes NL Bat Title

Paul Waner captured the batting title in the National League in 1936 with his .373 average, making it the 11th year in a row that he hit .309 or better. He showed no signs of slowing up the following season, rapping .354 with 219 hits, then tumbled to a .280 average in 1938. The timing was unfortunate. Pittsburgh came so close to winning in '38 that even an average season by Waner would probably have meant a flag.

Jake Powell

Powell Excels for Two Clubs

Jake Powell's fine rookie season for the Senators in 1935 caused the Yankees to overlook his hatchet job on Hank Greenberg the following spring and trade Ben Chapman for him. Splitting the 1936 season, Powell tallied a .295 average, one home run, and 30 RBI in 210 at-bats with Washington; he had a .302 mark, seven home runs, and 48 RBI at New York.

Feller, 17, Sets K Record

Bob Feller, the 17-year-old who struck out an American League-record 17 batters on September 23, 1936, was nearly declared a free agent by Kenesaw Mountain Landis after it became clear that Cleveland had signed him illegally. A few months later, Landis got back at the Indians by making farmhand Tommy Henrich a free agent. Henrich signed with the Yankees and played on pennant-winning ballclubs in each of his first three seasons, while Feller had to wait until 1948 to be on a winner.

Bob Feller

- Dizzy Dean is last ML pitcher to lead his league in CGs (28) and saves (11) in the same year.

- Detroit's Tommy Bridges tops AL with 23 wins and 175 Ks.

- Lefty Grove leads AL in shutouts (six) and ERA (2.81).

- Wes Ferrell wins 20 for the Red Sox and tops the AL in innings (301) and CGs (28).

- Dean wins 24, leads NL in innings pitched (315).

- Brooklyn's Van Mungo leads the majors in Ks with 238.

- Medwick paces NL in total bases (367), RBI (138), hits (223), and runs produced (235).

- Cleveland's Earl Averill leads AL in hits (232) and ties in triples (15).

- Pittsburgh's Arky Vaughan leads NL in runs (122), walks (118), and OBP (.453).

New York Giants

Giants Snare Flag

The 1936 New York Giants pose in center field for the camera, with the upper deck of the Polo Grounds and the Manhattan skyline behind them. Although other National League teams scored more runs and fielded better, Bill Terry's crew had Carl Hubbell. The Giants, who finished 92–62 in 1936, had just a 66–56 record for games in which Hubbell did not figure in the decision.

Arky Vaughan

Gehrig Named MVP

In 1935, the one year that Lou Gehrig played with neither Babe Ruth nor Joe DiMaggio, he had his lowest RBI total of any season between 1926 and 1938. In 1936, Gehrig was named the American League's Most Valuable Player with 49 home runs, 167 runs, a .696 slugging average, 130 walks, and 270 runs produced—all top marks in both circuits.

Lou Gehrig

Vaughan Sets SS Record

Arky Vaughan has the highest career batting average (.318) of any shortstop who played exclusively in this century (he placed fourth overall in the National League in 1936 with his .335 mark). Indeed, he may well have been the best of all the shortstops who played exclusively in this century. It hurt him, however, to play in Pittsburgh, where he couldn't escape the inevitable comparison to Honus Wagner.

1936

- Mel Ott tops NL in homers (33) and SA (.588).

- Lyn Lary of the Browns leads the majors in steals with 37.

- Cleveland's Bruce Campbell goes 6-for-6 on July 2.

- Rip Radcliff of the White Sox goes 6-for-7 on July 18.

- Cincinnati's Ival Goodman leads the NL in triples (14).

- The Cubs trade Lon Warneke to the Cards for Ripper Collins and Roy Parmelee.

- A's send Doc Cramer and Boob McNair to the Red Sox for two players and $75,000.

- In April, Yankees trade Ben Chapman to Washington for Jake Powell.

- Pirate Hal Finney sets an ML record for nonpitchers by going 0-for-35 during the season.

- Babe Phelps of Brooklyn hits .367, a modern ML record for catchers.

Yankees Over Giants in Six

Mel Ott hits a bases-loaded shot at Lou Gehrig in the first inning of game six of the 1936 World Series. The Giants scored two runs in the frame to get off to an early lead, but the Yankees put seven tallies across in the top of the ninth to sew up the Series.

World Series

Joe Medwick

Medwick: 64 Doubles

Joe Medwick hated to be called "Ducky" nearly as much as National League hurlers hated what he did to their best pitches, even when they were not strikes. Medwick racked up 64 doubles in 1936, a record in the NL. He paced the circuit with 367 total bases, 138 RBI, and 223 hits.

Luke Appling

Appling Collects 128 RBI

Luke Appling (pictured) knocked home 128 runs in 1936, and teammate Zeke Bonura tallied 138 RBI. Between them, though, they collected just 18 home runs. Just two years earlier, Bonura had been the first White Sox player to hit as many as 20 four-baggers with 27; and in 1935, he collected 21 dingers. Appling, in 20 years with the Sox, never had more than eight.

- The Yankees' Bill Dickey hits .362, a record for AL catchers.
- Detroit's Charlie Gehringer leads the AL in doubles with 60.
- Gehrig is the first player to score five runs in a game twice in a season.
- The AL has a composite 5.04 ERA, worst in ML history.

- The Browns have the worst ERA in AL history—6.24.
- Jack Knott of the Browns has a 7.27 ERA in 193 innings.
- The Yankees' 4.17 ERA is the highest in major league history by a loop leader.

- For the second straight year, the Browns' Russ Van Atta leads the league in mound appearances (52).
- Brooklyn's Buddy Hassett sets a rookie record when he fans just 17 times.
- Giants top NL in ERA (3.46).

DIZZY SQUAWKS; DUCKY LETS BAT DO TALKING

The 1937 season broke open with one of the many controversies in the career of St. Louis Cardinals pitcher Dizzy Dean. In a preview of the 1988 balk brouhaha, baseball commissioner Ford Frick had ordered umpires to enforce the rule requiring pitchers to come to a discernible stop in the stretch position. During a Giants-Cardinals matchup on May 19, a balk of this type was called against Dizzy in the sixth; he became enraged and began throwing at the New York batters. The result was a bench-clearing brawl and a $50 fine for Dean.

In his next start, Dean made a mockery of the balk rule by coming to a several-second stop in his delivery. When he publicly called Frick a "crook" a few days later, he was suspended indefinitely. To add to his troubles, Dean broke his big toe in the 1937 All-Star Game, an injury that led to an unconscious change in his delivery and, in turn, arm trouble. He never again pitched in a regular rotation and retired soon after with a 150-83 record and a 3.04 lifetime ERA.

Without their ace, the Cardinals slipped to an 81-73 record, 15 games out, in spite of an MVP performance by Ducky Medwick. The muscular left fielder was "Mr. Everything" for the St. Louis offense, leading the NL in batting at .374, RBI with 154, doubles with 56, hits with 237, and runs with 111; he tied New York's Mel Ott for the league lead in homers

with 31. Medwick won the Triple Crown that year, the last National League player to do so. Teammate Johnny Mize drove in 113 runs, hit 40 doubles (second in the NL), and batted .364 (also second-best).

Third-place Pittsburgh featured the three top triples hitters in the NL; Arky Vaughan with 17, Gus Suhr with 14, and Lee Handley with 12. Outfielder Paul Waner was third in batting at .354.

Runner-up Chicago scored the most runs of any NL team, 811, and finished 3 games out. Four Cubs—Billy Herman, Stan Hack, Augie Galan, and Frank Demaree—made the top five in runs scored, and Galan and Hack were first and second in stolen bases with 23 and 16.

The New York Giants successfully defended their NL flag, thanks to Ott's 95 RBI and great defense from shortstop Dick Bar-

tell, who also hit .306 with 38 doubles, 14 homers, and 91 runs scored. Carl Hubbell went 22-8 and fellow lefty Cliff Melton turned in a 2.61 ERA, second only to Boston's Jim Turner at 2.38.

In the AL race, monster seasons from the Tigers' pure hitter Charlie Gehringer and slugger Hank Greenberg couldn't prevent another Yankee pennant. Gehringer won the batting title at .371 and scored 133 runs. Greenberg led the AL in RBI with 183—the third-highest total of all-time—and also had 40 homers, 49 doubles, and 102 walks.

The Yankees machine scored the most runs in the league (979), allowed the fewest (671), and finished at 102-52, 13 games up on Detroit. Lou Gehrig hit .351 with 159 RBI and 37 homers; Joe DiMaggio hit .346 with an AL-high 151 runs, 15 triples, and a league-leading 46 homers. Lefty Gomez and Red Ruffing led the AL in wins with 21 and 20, and Gomez took the ERA title at 2.33; reliever Johnny Murphy worked 39 games and saved ten. Ex-Yankee Johnny Allen, pitching for Cleveland, went 15-1 with a 2.55 ERA.

The Yankees made short work of the Giants in their second consecutive October meeting, outscoring them 28-12 in five games. Lefty Gomez went 2-0 with a 1.50 ERA; no Giants starter had an ERA lower than Carl Hubbell's 3.77.

1937

- Yanks take AL flag by 13 games.
- Giants repeat in NL.
- Yanks win World Series in five games.
- Carl Hubbell's win in game four averts a humiliating sweep.
- Lefty Gomez wins two CGs for Yanks in World Series.

- Giant Jo-Jo Moore leads all Series hitters with a .391 mark.
- Ducky Medwick named NL MVP.
- Charlie Gehringer is AL MVP.
- Medwick wins last Triple Crown in NL, batting .374 with 31 homers and 154 RBI.

- Medwick leads NL in runs (111), hits (237), doubles (56), SA (.641), runs produced (234), and total bases (406).
- Hubbell again leads majors in wins with 22.
- The ease with which Yankees again win pennant earns Joe McCarthy the nickname "Push-Button Manager."

Joe Medwick was age 26 when he became the last National League player to win a Triple Crown; he racked up a .374 average, 31 home runs, and 154 RBI in 1937. In keeping with Branch Rickey's philosophy of dealing a player before he slipped, Medwick was traded to Brooklyn before age 29.

- Gehringer wins AL bat title at .371.

- Lou Gehrig is runner-up for AL bat crown (.351), hitting .300 for the last time.

- Pirate Gus Suhr's NL record streak of 822 consecutive games ends (record since broken).

- Detroit's Rudy York hits a record 18 homers in a month, August.

- On June 15, Boston's Ben Chapman makes seven putouts on seven consecutive fly balls.

- Medwick is the first player to collect four hits in an All-Star Game.

- The NL loses the All-Star Game 8-3 at Washington.

- On May 25, Mickey Cochrane is beaned by Yankee Bump Hadley, ending Cochrane's career.

- The Braves have two rookie 20-game winners, Lou Fette and Jim Turner; both are over age 30.

Dickey: .332 BA, 133 RBI

Over a 17-year career in which he played no other position other than catcher, Bill Dickey hit .313 and collected 202 home runs and 1,209 RBI. In 1937, he hit .332 with 29 home runs and 133 RBI. Although there were other receivers who had more flair, he had a quality that was the envy of all. As Charlie Gehringer put it, "Bill Dickey made catching look easy."

Bill Dickey

Charlie Gehringer

Gehringer Tops in BA

Charlie Gehringer became the oldest player in American League history to win a first batting title when he scored a .371 average in 1937 at the age of 34. A year earlier, he had rapped .354. Mickey Cochrane, Gehringer's manager, described him by saying, "He says hello on opening day and good-bye on closing day, and in between he hits .350."

The Heart of New York

Joe McCarthy (far left) sits in the Yankees dugout with his No. 1 star in 1937, Lou Gehrig (beside McCarthy), and the heir apparent, Joe DiMaggio (fourth from the left). During McCarthy's regime, neither the Yankees dugout nor the clubhouse after the game was a place for frivolity. Baseball was strictly business to McCarthy, and the entire park was his office.

New York Yankees

1937

- Cleveland's Johnny Allen tops AL with loop record .938 win pct.
- Allen wins his first 15 starts of the season, then loses on the season's closing day.
- Chicago's Bill Dietrich no-hits Browns on June 1.

- Pirate pitcher Red Lucas leads the NL in pinch hits for the fourth time.
- Mel Ott ties for the NL homer crown (31) and leads in walks (102).
- Hubbell tops NL in win pct. (.733) and Ks (159).
- Turner leads NL in ERA (2.38) and ties for lead in shutouts (five).

- Joe DiMaggio tops AL in runs (151) and total bases (418).
- Hank Greenberg tops AL in RBI (183) and runs produced (280).
- Greenberg's RBI total is one off the AL record.
- Beau Bell of Browns leads AL in hits (218) and doubles (51).

Cochrane Beaned Down

Mickey Cochrane is taken away by an ambulance after being beaned by Bump Hadley on May 25, 1937. Cochrane, who was in and out of consciousness for ten days with a fractured skull, was the victim of a pitcher who had almost everything going for him except control. Hadley averaged nearly 100 walks a season during his career. Cochrane never played in the majors again.

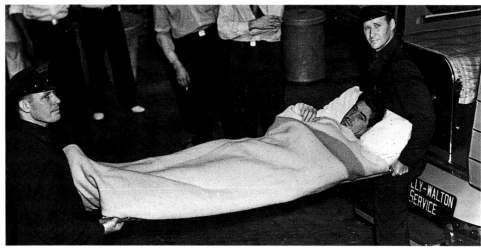

Mickey Cochrane

Vaughan Tops NL in Triples

Arky Vaughan never again approached his .385 average of 1935, though he did hit .318 over his career. In 1937, he hit .322 and led the National League with 17 triples. Arky, who was named after his home state of Arkansas, always had an outstanding walk-to-strikeout ratio. Over his career, he walked 937 times and fanned just 276 times. He fanned a mere 22 times in the 1937 season.

Arky Vaughan

Johnny Allen

Allen Nearly 16–0

Although Johnny Allen was long on talent, he had a short fuse. Guarding a 15–0 record for Cleveland on the last day of the 1937 season, Allen lost a potential 16th straight win when Detroit beat him 1–0 on a hit he thought his third baseman, Bad News Hale, should have handled. Allen wanted to fight Hale after the game.

- Gomez tops AL in wins (21), shutouts (six), Ks (194), and ERA (2.33).

- Gomez's teammate Red Ruffing is the only other 20-game winner in AL.

- Braves have best ERA in NL (3.22), but post worst BA in majors (.247).

- Cleveland's Bob Feller, in his first full season, Ks 150 batters in 149 innings.

- The Yankees have three men with 130-plus RBI—DiMaggio (167), Gehrig (159), and Bill Dickey (133).

- Giants have no one with 100 RBI.

- Cincinnati's Ernie Lombardi goes 6-for-6 on May 9.

- Cub Frank Demaree goes 6-for-7 in a 14-inning game on July 5.

- DiMaggio is second in the AL MVP vote as a sophomore.

- The Cubs' Gabby Hartnett hits .354 and is second in the NL MVP vote.

- Dizzy Dean breaks his toe in the All-Star Game, never recovers his blazing fastball.

- Browns lose a club record 108 games.

AL SLUGGERS NO MATCH FOR BRONX BOMBERS

The Yankees marched on in 1938, this time winning by 9½ games over Boston and 13 over Cleveland. Neither of the AL's top two hitters, however, wore pinstripes.

Third-time MVP Award-winner Jimmie Foxx of Boston had what is probably the best non-Triple Crown season in AL history, driving in a league-leading 175 runs (tied for fourth on the all-time list), banging out 50 home runs, and winning the batting title at .349. Detroit's Hank Greenberg made the first serious challenge in years to Babe Ruth's single-season home run record before finishing at 58 homers, which tied him for second most ever; Greenberg also led the AL in runs scored with 144 and was second in RBI with 146. Greenberg and Foxx were each issued 119 free passes by terrified AL pitchers.

Other highlights of the decade's top home run hitting year—and one of the best for offense in general—were Cleveland outfielder Jeff Heath's .343 batting average and league-leading 18 triples and Red Sox shortstop Joe Cronin's circuit-topping 51 doubles. Cleveland's strikeout king Bob Feller set the modern record for walks issued in a season with 208; Bobo Newsom, the St. Louis Browns pitcher, walked 192, the fifth-highest total in modern history.

Although the Yankees placed few hitters among the league-leaders, their offense blended beautifully to produce 966 runs,

the most in the AL. Gehrig hit .295 with 29 homers, Joe DiMaggio batted .324 and drove in 140 runs on 32 home runs, and Bill Dickey hit .313 with 27 round-trippers. Joe Gordon took over from veteran second baseman Tony Lazzeri and contributed 25 homers and 97 RBI.

Yankee pitching was also the league's best, compiling a 3.91 ERA (the only AL team mark under 4.00), compliments of the 21-7 Red Ruffing and 18-12 Lefty Gomez, second and third in ERA at 3.32 and 3.35; Boston's Lefty Grove was limited by injury to only 21 starts, but led all AL hurlers with a 3.07 ERA. New York's third and fourth starters, Spud Chandler and Monte Pearson, combined for a 30-12 record.

The Depression-inspired phenomenon of night baseball contributed to one of baseball's most famous records in 1938, when Cincinnati's Johnny Vander Meer threw his second consecutive no-hitter in the first under-the-lights game ever held in Brooklyn. (The

novelty of the Ebbets Field lights, which drew a capacity crowd as well as the Dodgers hitters' unfamiliarity with night baseball, contributed to the occasion.)

Vander Meer's feat has never been equaled, although Howard Ehmke came within one hit in 1923 as did Ewell Blackwell in 1947. A wild lefthander with an overpowering fastball, Vander Meer led the NL in strikeouts three times, but was never a consistent winner; he went on to finish his 13-year career with a 119-121 record.

The Chicago Cubs won a close NL race over Pittsburgh, New York, and Cincinnati that came down to a late-season Cubs-Pirates meeting. The game was decided by catcher/manager Gabby Hartnett's ninth-inning, two out, two-strike homer and capped a nine-game winning streak, part of a 20-3 stretch run that vaulted the Cubs over the top.

Mel Ott won another home run title with 36 and Cincinnati catcher Ernie Lombardi, who caught Vander Meer's no-hitters and won the batting title at .342, was voted NL MVP. Cubs ace Bill Lee went 22-9 to lead the league in wins, and Lee and teammate Charlie Root finished first and second in ERA at 2.66 and 2.85.

The World Series was an utter mismatch, as the New York ballclub swept the Cubs in four straight by a combined score of 22-9. The Yankees pitchers recorded an ERA of 1.75 to their opponents' 5.03.

1938

- Yanks win third straight AL flag, tying loop record.
- Cubs win in NL.
- Yanks sweep World Series.
- Red Ruffing wins two complete games in Series.
- Stan Hack of Cubs leads all Series players in BA (.471) and hits (eight)—first member of losing team to do so.
- Yanks have now lost a total of three games in their last six World Series.
- Jimmie Foxx is AL MVP.
- Cincinnati's Ernie Lombardi is NL MVP.
- Lombardi is first catcher to win a consensus bat title (Bubbles Hargrave in 1926 had less than 400 at-bats).
- Hank Greenberg hits 58 homers to lead the AL.

Hank Greenberg came into Cleveland on the last weekend of 1938 needing two home runs to tie Babe Ruth's season record of 60. He didn't stand a chance. The first game was played in League Park, which was 375 feet down the line in left field. The next day, Greenberg was no match for Bob Feller, who fanned 18 Tigers.

- Lou Gehrig has 100 or more RBI for ML record 13th consecutive season.

- Cincinnati's Johnny Vander Meer no-hits Boston on June 11.

- Vander Meer becomes only pitcher in ML history to throw back-to-back no-hitters, as he blanks the Dodgers on June 15.

- Bob Feller fans modern record (since broken) 18 batters in a game.

- Feller's 240 Ks top the majors.

- NL strikeout leader Clay Bryant of Chicago has just 135.

- Feller gives up a 20th-century record 208 walks.

- Feller sets teenager records for Ks, walks, starts (36), CGs (20), and innings (278).

- Cub Bill Lee leads the majors with 22 wins.

- Gabby Hartnett's homer vs. Pittsburgh on Sept. 28 puts Cubs in first to stay.

Bill McKechnie

McKechnie Boosts Reds

In last place in 1937, manager Bill McKechnie pushed the Reds to fourth in 1938, their first season under his command. McKechnie won flags with a record three different National League teams, and some analysts credit him with an American League pennant, too.

Dizzy Dean

Dean Done In

Dizzy Dean's spectacular career took a nose dive in the summer of 1937, when an Earl Averill line drive broke his toe. Dizzy, pitching with the injured foot, altered his motion and hurt his arm; he pitched a 13–10 record that year. He was never the same again. He would win only nine more games in his career.

Stan Hack

Hack Posts .320 BA

The Cubs' Stan Hack was unique in that he was a third baseman who could run but had little power. In recent years, several authorities on the game have mounted a case that he belongs in the Hall of Fame, but testament is against him. Fellow players do not remember Hack as having been anything exceptional, and the record books support them. In 1938, Hack hit .320 with 67 RBI. For his career, he hit .301 with no power. He averaged ten steals a year.

Simmons Has Final Hurrah

After knocking in 100 or more runs in his first 11 seasons, Al Simmons began to fade. However, he enjoyed one last big year with Washington in 1938, when he hit .302 with 21 homers and 95 RBI. In his later years, Simmons drove to reach 3,000 hits, and he bounced from team to team trying to reach his goal. He fell 73 short. Simmons was a hard hitter on the field and off. He loved to party and often hit the booze the night before a game. If he lived a cleaner life, he may have reached his 3,000th hit.

Al Simmons

1938

- Cardinal Frenchy Bordagaray hits record .465 as a pinch hitter and gets 20 pinch hits.
- Reds rise from last in 1937 to fourth in 1938 in first year under Bill McKechnie.
- NL wins All-Star Game 4-1 at Cincinnati.
- Phils move to Shibe Park on July 4.
- Gehrig hits the last of his career record 23 grandslams.
- Greenberg hits a record 39 homers at home.
- On April 19, Dodger Ernie Koy and Phillie Heinie Mueller each homer in their first ML at-bat in same game.
- Hartnett is the last full-time player/manager to win an NL pennant.
- Yankee Monte Pearson no-hits Cleveland on August 27.
- Red Sox Pinky Higgins collects an ML record 12 hits in 12 consecutive at-bats.

Kiki Cuyler

Foxx Nails 50 Dingers

Jimmie Foxx holds the season franchise home run record for both the Athletics and the Red Sox. Like Pinky Higgins, though, he had better slugging marks in Shibe Park than in Fenway. In 1938, Foxx blasted 50 homers and drove in 175 run, however—numbers Higgins never approached.

Jimmie Foxx

Cuyler Retires

Kiki Cuyler finally hung up his spikes in 1938. He hit .273 his last season with 23 RBI. Over his career, he hit .321 and led the league in steals four times. Kiki has one of the most mispronounced names in baseball. His nickname was once "Cuy," which then became "Cuy-Cuy." Though his name is pronounced "Ky-ky," it is often said as "Kee-kee."

Johnny Vander Meer

Vander Meer: Two No-Nos

During his minor league apprenticeship, Johnny Vander Meer looked liked another wild lefthander. His performance for the Reds in 1938 made believers of his skeptics, as he hurled back-to-back no-hitters in June. In his next start, he hurled three no-hit innings before yielding a hit to Boston's Debs Garms. However, Vander Meer had to return later to the minors before he became a finished pitcher. For his career, he was a mediocre 119-121. He was always tough to hit, but had serious problems with control.

- Lombardi grounds into an NL record 30 DPs.

- The Giants, Dodgers, and Yankees allow their home games to be broadcast on a regular basis.

- Foxx wins the AL bat crown (.349) and also leads in RBI (175), and total bases (398).

- Greenberg leads AL in runs (144) and ties for lead in walks (119).

- Hack's 16 steals are an all-time low by an NL leader.

- Ruffing tops AL in wins (21).

- Pitcher Red Lucas retires with 114 career pinch hits, an ML record to this juncture.

- Mel Ott tops NL in homers (36) and runs (116).

- For the seventh straight year, Ott plays 150 or more games in a 154-game season.

- Ducky Medwick paces NL in doubles (47), RBI (122), and runs produced (201).

Yanks Score Opening Run

An overflow crowd of 43,642 at Wrigley Field is about to see the first run of the 1938 World Series cross the plate. Twinkletoes Selkirk of the Yankees has just hit a bouncer toward second base, which Billy Herman will fumble, allowing Lou Gehrig, on third, to score. Bill Dickey moved from second to third on the play and scored moments later on Joe Gordon's smash through Stan Hack at third base.

World Series

Bill Dickey

Dickey Best Behind Plate

In 1938, Bill Dickey hit .313 with 27 home runs and 115 RBI. He also hit .400 in New York's World Series sweep of the Cubs. Dickey, considered by some as the greatest catcher in American League history, caught 1,712 games in his career. He never played another position, not even for a single inning. Dickey saw it all with the Yankees. He played with Babe Ruth during the tail end of Ruth's career. He teamed with Lou Gehrig for many years and played with Joe DiMaggio for a few. And even when New York won five straight World Titles in the late 1940s and early '50s, Dickey helped the team as a coach.

1938

- Johnny Mize leads NL in triples (16), SA (.614), and total bases (326).

- Lee tops majors in shutouts (nine) and ERA (2.66).

- Hank Steinbacher of the White Sox goes 6-for-6 on June 22.

- Bobo Newsom wins 20 games for the Browns despite a 5.08 ERA.

- Boston finishes 9½ games behind the Yankees—closest any AL team finishes from 1936–1939.

- Hall of Fame inducts Pete Alexander, Alexander Cartwright, and Henry Chadwick.

- Phils trade Dolph Camilli to Dodgers for Eddie Morgan and cash.

- In December, Giants swap Dick Bartell, Hank Leiber, and Gus Mancuso to Cubs for Bill Jurges, Frank Demaree, and Ken O'Dea.

- In April, the Cards send Dizzy Dean to the Cubs for three players and $185,000.

- Washington trades Joe Kuhel to the White Sox for Zeke Bonura.

Ernie Lombardi

Lombardi Takes NL Bat Title

Ernie Lombardi was the only catcher in major league history to win an undisputed batting title. In 1938, he hit .342 and had well over the number of plate appearances that modern rules require for a hitting leader. Another Reds catcher, Bubbles Hargrave, had just 326 at-bats when he won in 1926. Lombardi took a second crown in 1942 with a mere 309 at-bats.

Lee Tops NL in Wins

In 1938, Bill Lee got good support from his Cubs teammates during the regular season (22 wins, best in the National League), but next to none in the World Series. He made two starts and pitched well, yet lost both when his teammates scored just one run in his 12 innings on the mound and made two critical boots behind him. Lee was brilliant during the season, leading the league in winning pct. (.710), ERA (2.66), starts (37), and shutouts (nine). At one point, he posted 32 consecutive scoreless innings. His trademark was his extremely high leg kick.

Bill Lee

Bob Feller

Feller Racks Up 240 Ks

Bob Feller, who joined the Indians in 1936 as a 17-year-old, became the team's ace as a 19-year-old. In 1938, Feller went 17–11 and led the American League in strikeouts (240). He also limited opponents to a .220 batting average—the best mark in the AL. By the age of 21, Rapid Robert would win 82 games. Feller probably missed out on between 80 and 90 wins due to the war.

- The Reds send Eddie Miller to the Braves for five players.

- The Dodgers hire Larry MacPhail as general manager.

- Monty Stratton, a 15-game winner with the White Sox, loses his leg after the season in a hunting accident.

- TB forces Washington's John Stone to quit the game and enter a sanitarium.

- Detroit hits a record ten grandslams.

- Virgil "Fire" Trucks of Andalusia in the Alabama-Florida League fans 418 batters.

- George McQuinn of the Browns has a 34-game hitting streak.

- Mace Brown of Pittsburgh wins 15 games in relief to set a major league record.

- Vince DiMaggio of the Braves sets an ML record by fanning 134 times.

- On June 16, the Browns walk Foxx a record six times in one game.

A TEARY GEHRIG BIDS FAREWELL

The 1939 year marked a turning point in the history of the American League, as it lost one of its greatest players, Lou Gehrig, and gained another, Ted Williams.

Gehrig's teammates had noticed something wrong with their 35-year-old leader early in the 1938 season, when the ball no longer jumped off his bat. He had rallied to finish with only slightly sub-par numbers: a .295 batting average, 114 RBI, and 29 homers. Steadily deteriorating from the start of spring training in 1939 through eight games into the regular season, the "Iron Horse" finally called it quits, ending baseball's longest consecutive-game streak at 2,130. Shortly afterward, he was diagnosed with the disease that carries his name.

On July 4, Gehrig was given the day at Yankee Stadium at which he delivered his famous line: "Today, I consider myself the luckiest man on the face of the earth." He was dead by 1941. Gehrig retired with a .340 lifetime batting average, 1,990 RBI, 493 homers—a record 23 of them grandslams—and a slugging average of .632, third on the all-time list behind Babe Ruth and Williams.

A very deep Yankees team replaced Gehrig with Babe Dahlgren and returned to the business of baseball. They were in a close pennant race with Boston, which stayed within striking distance of the lead until the All-Star break. In late July, however, New York kicked into high gear and left the

Red Sox in the dust, finally winning its fourth consecutive pennant by 17 games.

The New York attack was led by MVP Joe DiMaggio (who won the batting title at .381 and drove in 126 runs, second-best in the AL), Red Rolfe (who scored 139 runs and hit 46 doubles, both league-leading figures), and 22-year-old outfielder Charlie Keller (who was fifth in hitting at .334).

As usual, New York pitchers allowed the fewest runs in the AL, behind 21-7 Red Ruffing and 12-6 Bump Hadley (who were fourth and fifth in ERA at 2.94 and 2.98) and Atley Donald and Lefty Gomez (who went a combined 25-11). Even Johnny Murphy had a great showing, redeeming his performance with a record 19 saves in late-inning relief duty.

The Red Sox relied on Lefty Grove, who won a record ninth ERA title, slugger Jimmie Foxx, and Williams. Foxx led the AL with 35 homers while the rookie Williams batted .327 and spearheaded the league in RBI with 145 (he also scored 131 runs and knocked 44 doubles and 31 homers).

Cincinnati celebrated the 70th anniversary of the champion 1869 Reds, baseball's first openly professional team, and the 20th anniversary of their 1919 World Championship by winning the 1939 NL pennant. Only two years removed from the cellar, the Reds were led by MVP pitcher Bucky Walters, who went 27-11 with a league-low 2.29 ERA. Teammate Paul Derringer won 25, second-best in the league, and recorded the fourth-best ERA at 2.93.

The Reds pitched their way to the NL flag by 4 1/2 games over a hard-hitting St. Louis team that featured Johnny Mize, the batting champ at .349 and home run leader at 28. Ducky Medwick batted .332 and had 48 doubles (second only to teammate Enos Slaughter's 52 doubles) and 117 RBI.

Cincinnati became the fourth NL champion in four years to run into the New York Yankees' World Series buzz saw, falling in four games by a combined score of 20-8. After losing 2-1 in a game one pitchers' duel between Derringer and Ruffing, the Reds lost by scores of 4-0, 7-3, and 7-4. The Yankees outhomered their opponents 7-0.

Baseball's Hall of Fame was dedicated in Cooperstown, New York, to celebrate the game's mythical centennial in 1939. Twenty-six players were inducted into the Hall; the first five to be voted in (in 1936) were Ruth, Ty Cobb, Honus Wagner, Christy Mathewson, and Walter Johnson.

1939

- Yanks win AL flag by 17 games for AL record fourth straight pennant.

- Reds win in NL two years after finishing in cellar.

- Yanks sweep Series, and have now won 28 of their last 31 World Series games.

- Rookie Charlie Keller is the Series hero, hitting .438 with six RBI.

- Four different Yankees pitchers win a Series game, the first time this has happened.

- Reds manager Bill McKechnie has now won flags for three different teams.

- Joe DiMaggio is AL MVP.

- Cincinnati's Bucky Walters is NL MVP.

- Walters leads majors with 27 wins; teammate Paul Derringer wins 25.

- DiMaggio leads majors with .381 BA.

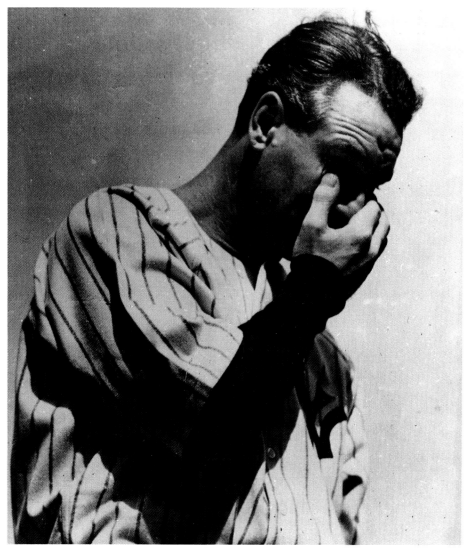

A tearful Lou Gehrig bids farewell to fans at Yankee Stadium on July 4, 1939.
Modest to an extreme, painfully shy, Gehrig was the most durable man to ever wear
a major league uniform. He was still a month short of his 36th birthday when his
fatal disease ended his skein of 2,130 consecutive games.

- Lou Gehrig's string of 2,130 straight games played ends on May 2.

- Gehrig gives his famous farewell address at Yankee Stadium after he learns he has amyotrophic lateral sclerosis.

- On August 26, the first major league game is televised—Reds vs. Dodgers at Ebbets Field.

- The Hall of Fame is officially dedicated and opens on June 12.

- Gehrig is voted into the Hall in 1939 by special ballot.

- On May 16, the first AL night game is played—Indians vs. A's at Shibe Park.

- Lefty Grove wins the last of his ML record nine ERA crowns.

- Boston rookie Ted Williams leads majors in RBI with 145—most ever by an ML rookie.

- DiMaggio is last righty hitter to top .380 in a season.

Hall of Famers

Hall of Fame Inducts 17

Ten of the original 17 men inducted into the Hall of Fame in 1939 pose for posterity. First row *(left to right)*: Eddie Collins, Babe Ruth, Connie Mack, and Cy Young. Second row: Honus Wagner, Pete Alexander, Tris Speaker, Nap Lajoie, George Sisler, and Walter Johnson. Missing is Ty Cobb; the other six were deceased.

Joe DiMaggio

Hall of Fame Dedicated

Ford Frick, president of the National League, cuts the ribbon to dedicate the Hall of Fame in 1939. Looking on *(left to right)* are Kenesaw Mountain Landis, the commissioner of baseball; Will Harridge, the president of the American League; and William Bramham, the president of the National Association, which embraces the minor leagues.

Hall of Fame Dedication

DiMaggio Takes Over

"He never offered the appearance of either gaiety, or anger, or tremendous self-effort. His smile was self-conscious, his manner withdrawn to the point of a chill." So said Robert Smith of Joe DiMaggio, who, with the departure of Lou Gehrig in 1939, became the consummate Yankee (he hit .381 that year).

1939

- Detroit swaps six players to Browns for Bobo Newsom and three other players.

- The use of netting in gloves is outlawed—only leather webbing allowed.

- Radio income now represents 7.3 percent of the average club's revenue.

- The 25-player limit, reduced to 23 during the Depression, is restored.

- Gehrig is first player to have his uniform number retired.

- AL wins All-Star Game 3-1 at Yankee Stadium.

- On August 4, White Sox Mike Kreevich grounds into four DPs.

- Red Rolfe scores at least one run in a record 18 consecutive games.

- Red Sox Jim Tabor hits record two grandslams in a game on July 4.

- Eighteen years after his ML debut, Brave Johnny Cooney hits his first ML homer on Sept. 24; he hits another the next day.

Williams: Star of the Show

Overshadowed by his dazzling slugging stats (131 runs scored, 31 home runs, 145 RBI) was the fact that Ted Williams collected 107 walks in 1939, a 20th-century rookie record. The following year, he dipped to 96 free passes. After that he averaged well over 100 walks per season. Largely because Williams walked so often, he never had a campaign in which he made 200 hits.

Johnny Mize

Mize Tops NL in Homers

In 1939 with St. Louis, Johnny Mize led the National League in home runs with 28. As was the case with virtually every Cardinals star in the 1930s, Mize was traded when he approached age 30. But in this instance, Branch Rickey miscalculated. Mize still had several gigantic seasons left in him, whereas the three players the Cards got in return from the Giants did little in St. Louis.

Ted Williams

Derringer Back on Track

Paul Derringer, the last pitcher to lose 25 or more games in a season, had a 7–25 record for Cincinnati after coming to the Reds from the Cardinals early in the 1932 season. With the pennant-winning Reds in 1939, Derringer was 25–7, the exact reverse of his 1932 figures. Despite his outstanding record, Derringer yielded 321 hits in 301 innings.

Paul Derringer

Jimmie Foxx

Foxx Tops AL in Home Runs

During his career, Jimmie Foxx played every position except second base. Not only did Foxx lead the American League in homers in 1939 (35), he also made his first mound appearance. His perfect relief inning remained his only hurling experience until 1945, when he toed the rubber nine times for the last-place Phillies and registered a 1.59 ERA in $22^{2}/_{3}$ innings, yielding just 13 hits.

- Jimmie Foxx leads AL in homers (35), SA (.694), and OBP (.464).
- Rolfe tops AL in runs (139), hits (213), and doubles (46).
- Pirate Lee Handley and Cub Stan Hack tie for the NL theft lead with just 17.

- Johnny Mize leads NL in homers (28), BA (.349), SA (.626), and total bases (353).
- Williams tops majors in runs produced with 245.
- Bob Feller leads AL in wins (24), innings (297), and Ks (246), and ties in CGs (24).

- Walters tops ML in innings (319), CGs (31), and ERA (2.29).
- Red Frank McCormick again leads NL in hits (209), and also leads in RBI (128) and runs produced (209).
- Brooklyn's Cookie Lavagetto goes 6-for-6 on Sept. 23.

Joe's Hit Triggers Bizarre Play

Shown here in sequential order are four photos of one of the most famous moments in World Series history. In photo No. 1, Yankees rookie star Charlie Keller sprints plateward in the tenth inning of game four of the 1939 Series as Reds catcher Ernie Lombardi awaits the throw. At right is Frank Crosetti, who had already scored on Joe Dimaggio's single. The umpire is former major league third baseman Babe Pinelli.

World Series, Photo 1

World Series, Photo 2

Keller Crosses the Plate

Photo No. 2 shows Keller scoring after he slammed into Lombardi and jarred the ball loose. There are, unfortunately, no photos of the actual instant of impact, which left the 230-pound Lombardi so stunned that he nearly lost consciousness. Keller weighed only 185 pounds, but was so strong that his nickname was "King Kong."

1939

- The Browns finish at 43-111, an AL record 64 1/2 games out of first.

- Average player's salary in 1939 is about $7,300.

- George Sisler, Eddie Collins, Willie Keeler, Cap Anson, Charles Comiskey, Candy Cummings, Buck Ewing, Hoss Radbourn, and Al Spalding enter Hall.

- Williams sets AL rookie records for SA (.609) and walks (107).

- Earl Whitehill retires with a 4.36 career ERA, highest in ML history by a 200-game winner.

- Bob Schmidt of Duluth in the Northern League hits an OB record .441.

- Yankees go 54-20 on the road to set an AL record.

- Browns go 18-59 at home to set AL record for worst home performance in a season.

- Washington's Buddy Lewis is the AL triples leader with 16.

Lombardi Languishes in Dust

In photo No. 3, Lombardi is still sprawled beside the plate as DiMaggio slides across it. One cannot resist wondering where the other Reds players were while DiMaggio circled the bases. In any event, his tally enabled the Yankees to take a 7–4 lead in the contest. The Reds committed three errors in the fateful tenth inning.

Yankees Walk Away Winning

Finally, in photo No. 4, another Reds player appears on the scene. Third baseman Billy Werber comes to the assistance of the stricken Lombardi, as does Crosetti. Meanwhile, DiMaggio walks away and Bill Dickey, the on deck hitter, exhorts on the amazing occurrences he has just witnessed. New York shut down the Reds in the bottom of the inning to win its fourth consecutive World Championship.

World Series, Photo 3

World Series, Photo 4

- Washington's George Case wins his first AL steals crown (51).
- Johnny Murphy of the Yankees leads the majors with 19 saves.
- The Cardinals' Curt Davis wins 22 games and bats .381.
- Billy Werber tops the NL in runs (115).
- Cardinal Enos Slaughter leads the NL in doubles with 52.
- Billy Herman of the Cubs leads the majors with 18 triples.
- Mel Ott tops the NL in OBP (.449).
- Dutch Leonard wins 20 games for sixth-place Senators.
- Yankees have a record eight pitchers who work 116 or more innings and a ninth, Murphy, who appears in 38 games.
- For second year in a row, the Red Sox have no pitchers who work 200 innings.
- The Cards lead the majors with a .294 batting average.

FELLER SHINES, BUT REDS COME OUT ON TOP

Already a veteran of four big-league seasons by 1940, 21-year-old Bob Feller had achieved almost every pitching distinction possible. He had led the AL in strikeouts twice and in innings pitched once. In 1939, he went 24-9 to lead the AL in wins and complete games with 24. Three times—once in 1938 and twice in 1939—he had thrown one-hitters. Just about the only thing Feller hadn't done was to throw a no-hit game, an omission he remedied on Opening Day, 1940, when he no-hit the Chicago White Sox 1-0. It was the only Opening Day no-hitter in AL history.

The 1940 season ended much less happily for the Cleveland ace, as he lost the game that clinched the pennant for Detroit on the next-to-last day of the season. Cleveland finished with an 89-65 record, 1 game behind the 90-64 Tigers. Feller had no reason to hang his head; the Indians would never have come that close to a pennant without his 27-11, 2.62 ERA virtuoso performance. He led the league in wins, ERA, games, complete games, strike-outs, and innings pitched.

Cleveland's mediocre offense was led by young shortstop Lou Boudreau, who hit .295 and drove in 101 runs, and first base-man Hal Trosky, who led the team in home runs with 25. The team's chances were undermined by a palace revolution against manager Ossie Vitt in the closing days of the race. The uprising culminated with the players pre-senting a petition to management demanding, unsuccessfully, that Vitt be fired.

New Detroit manager Del Baker was a more positive factor. He made the managerial move of the year by putting Hank Green-berg in left field in order to open up first base for young, poor-fielding slugger Rudy York. Greenberg responded with an MVP season, hitting .340 and leading the league in home runs (41), RBI (150), and doubles (50). York contributed 134 RBI and 33 home runs, and the Tigers as a whole scored a league-leading 888 runs. On the pitching side, Detroit featured 21-5 Bobo New-som, who was runner-up to Feller in ERA at 2.83; 16-3 Schoolboy Rowe; and 12-9 Tommy Bridges.

Both Detroit and Cleveland were momentarily distracted from their neck-and-neck race down the stretch by the hard-charging New York Yankees, who rose from dead last in May to within 2 games of the flag by season's end. Joe DiMaggio won the batting title at .352, hit 31 home runs, and drove in 133.

The Cincinnati Reds took the NL pennant by 12 games over Brooklyn, but it was no cake-walk. With starting catcher Ernie Lombardi out with an injury in August, backup catcher Willard Hershberger became overwhelmed by the pennant-race pressure and committed suicide. A month later, Lombardi reinjured himself. Coach Jimmy Wilson, who was 40 years old and hadn't caught regularly for five years, was acti-vated and guided the Reds pitchers into the World Series.

First baseman Frank McCor-mick was the Reds' big gun on offense, with a league-leading 191 hits, as well as 44 doubles and 127 RBI. He was named NL MVP. Cincinnati relied heavily on its pitching staff, which was led by Bucky Walters and Paul Der-ringer (who combined for 42 wins).

The Reds won the World Series in seven games to give the NL its first victory since 1934, when Detroit was also the loser. Walters and Derringer continued their good work, each winning two games. But an unexpected hero of the Series was catcher Wilson, who was brilliant defen-sively and hit .353. Wilson re-retired the following year to manage the Chicago Cubs.

1940

- Tigers temporarily break the Yankee dynasty, cop AL flag.

- Reds score second straight NL flag.

- Reds win their first untainted World Championship in seven games.

- Bucky Walters and Paul Derringer both collect two CG wins for Reds in Series.

- Forty-year-old catcher Jimmy Wilson, playing for injured Ernie Lombardi, is unlikely World Series hero, hitting .353.

- Sub outfielder Jimmy Ripple hits .333 with six RBI for Reds in Series.

- The Reds win NL flag by 12 games, largest margin in NL since 1931.

- Frank McCormick is NL MVP—third-different Red in three years to win award.

- Hank Greenberg wins the AL MVP Award.

- Joe DiMaggio takes second consecutive AL bat crown as he collects a .352 BA.

The victorious Reds swamp winning pitcher Paul Derringer after the last out of the 1940 World Series. The Reds' twin aces, Derringer and Buck Walters, between them notched four complete-game wins. In the 2–1 finale, Derringer bested Detroit's Bobo Newsom, who was shooting for his third Series victory.

- Bob Feller pitches only AL Opening Day no-hitter on April 16 vs. Chicago.

- Brooklyn's Tex Carleton no-hits Cincinnati on April 30.

- Johnny Mize tops NL in RBI (137) and homers (43).

- Feller's 27 wins top majors.

- Tigers win pennant by edging Cleveland by 1 game and New York by 2 games.

- Indians nicknamed "The Cry Babies" when they go to club owner Alva Bradley and demand he fire manager Ossie Vitt.

- Bradley retains Vitt as manager.

- On Sept. 27, Detroit no-name Floyd Giebell beats Cleveland's Feller 2-0 to clinch flag.

- Feller's 261 Ks are the most by any pitcher in ML since 1924.

- Greenberg tops AL in homers (41) and RBI (150).

Floyd Giebell

Giebell Secures AL Pennant

Floyd Giebell (pictured) beat Bob Feller 2–0 on the last weekend of the season to clinch the 1940 American League flag for Detroit. It was Ladies Day in Cleveland and thousands of women came to the park armed with fruit and vegetables, prepared to bombard the Tigers into submission. Instead they saw Giebell win for the last time in the majors.

Lou Boudreau

Boudreau Wins Fielding Title

In 1940, his final full season, Lou Boudreau was already a polished shortstop, good enough to cop his first of five consecutive fielding crowns. Boudreau topped the American League in fielding average every year between 1940 and 1948, except 1945 when he played only 97 games owing to an injury.

Keller's a Killer in Pinstripes

Charlie Keller, who led the American League in walks with 106 in 1940, was one of New York's biggest Bombers from 1939 through 1943. As a rookie in the '39 World Series, Keller batted .438 with three home runs. And from 1940 through '43, he averaged 28 homers, 102 RBI, 102 runs, and 107 walks per season.

Charlie Keller

1940

- After the season, Greenberg becomes first MLer to enlist in armed services in preparation for WWII.
- Cub Stan Hack tops NL in BA at .317, lowest in NL history to this juncture by leader.
- NL wins All-Star Game by a score of 4-0 at St. Louis.
- NL also beats AL 2-1 in impromptu All-Star Game on St. Patrick's Day for benefit of Finnish Relief Fund.
- McCormick ties NL record when he leads loop in hits (191) for third consecutive season.
- Reds win an ML record 41 one-run games.
- Willis Hudlin is the first player since 1904 to play with four different teams in the same year.
- The sacrifice fly rule is again abolished.
- Mize paces NL in every major slugging department except OBP.

Ruffing Falls to 15–12

In 1940, Red Ruffing completed his 11th year as a mainstay of the Yankees pitching staff. It was the first time in five years he didn't win 20 games, as he finished 15–12. Ruffing was a durable hurler, going 273–225 in his career, but was never truly exceptional, as evidenced by his 3.80 career ERA. Nevertheless, Ruffing won seven World Series games, second-most of all time.

Stan Hack

Red Ruffing

Hack Posts .317 BA

According to the current rule to determine a batting leader, Stan Hack (pictured) would have won the 1940 National League hitting crown (.317 in 603 at-bats). At the time, however, Debs Garms of the Pirates, who had just 358 at-bats, was declared the victor (.355). Despite leading the NL in pinch hits the following year, Garms was back in the minors in 1942. Hack would again hit .317 in 1941, but would finish only fourth in the NL bat race.

Jimmy Ripple

Ripple on the Wane

Although just age 30, Jimmy Ripple was on the decline by 1940. That year's World Series—in which he totaled six RBI—was the final mark he left on the game. Ripple had to play six seasons with the Montreal Royals in the International League before the Giants finally gave him his first major league look in 1936.

- Ted Williams leads AL in runs (134) and OBP (.442) and is third in batting (.344).
- Greenberg tops majors in RBI (150), doubles (50), runs produced (238), SA (.670), and total bases (384).
- Feller tops majors in CGs (31) and AL in ERA (2.62).
- Walters tops the NL in wins (22) for the second year in a row.
- Walters leads NL in CGs (29), innings (305), and ERA (2.48).
- Detroit's Rudy York, second in AL in RBI with 134, combines with teammate Greenberg for 284 RBI.
- Phils and A's both lose 100 or more games and finish last.
- Cleveland shortstop Lou Boudreau has 101 RBI and tops AL shortstops in assists, DPs, and FA.
- On Sept. 24, Red Sox become first AL team to club four homers in one inning.

Hank Greenberg

Greenberg Serves AL, Army

Hank Greenberg *(second from the right)* takes the oath of allegiance prior to his induction into the Army in May 1941. The American League MVP in 1940 (129 runs scored, 41 home runs, 384 total bases, 150 RBI, .670 slugging average) played just 19 games the following year before departing to start his military training. Greenberg missed over four full seasons while he served in World War II.

Hudlin: A Travelin' Man

Willis Hudlin pitched just eight games in a Washington uniform. In fact, all but 16 of his 491 major league appearances came with Cleveland, for whom he won 157 games over 15 seasons. In 1929, Hudlin beat the Yankees 4-3 in the first major league game involving two teams wearing numbered uniforms. In 1940, he became the first player since 1904 to play for four teams in one year.

Willis Hudlin

Joe DiMaggio

Joe Continues to Reign

Joe DiMaggio (pictured) terrorized virtually every American League pitcher except Cleveland's Mel Harder. Unable to account for his success, Harder said, "I'm just grateful I had good luck against him. It kept me around for a long time." In his 20 seasons with the Tribe, Harder won 223 games (a dozen in 1940). DiMaggio led the circuit in batting in '40 with a .352 average.

1940

- On April 30, Dom DiMaggio of the Red Sox ties AL record by scoring five runs in a game.

- The Cards swap Mickey Owen to Brooklyn for Gus Mancuso and $65,000.

- The Cards send Ducky Medwick and Curt Davis to Brooklyn for four players and $125,000.

- Cubs finish below .500 for the first time in 15 years.

- Walt Judnich's 24 homers set a record for a St. Louis Browns rookie.

- Yankee Frank Crosetti leads the AL in being hit by the pitch a record fifth consecutive year.

- Forty-three minor leagues begin the season—a new record.

- Cincinnati's Harry Craft sets an ML record for outfielders with a .997 fielding average.

- Reds catcher Willard Hershberger commits suicide.

Ernie Lombardi

Injuries Bench Lombardi

Injuries curtailed the playing time of Ernie Lombardi (pictured) for much of the 1940 regular season and again in the World Series. His unavailability forced the Reds to activate 40-year-old coach Jimmy Wilson for the fall classic. Behind the plate in six of the seven contests, Wilson hit .353 and nabbed the only stolen base in the Series.

Del Baker

Mize Misses Triple Crown

Johnny Mize paced the National League in every major slugging department in 1940, including home runs (43) and RBI (137). Moreover, his .314 batting average was just three points behind that of Stan Hack, now recognized by some historians as the bat leader that year. If their view is accepted, Mize's 1940 season is the closest any NL player has come to winning a Triple Crown since 1937.

Johnny Mize

Baker Scales New Heights

Del Baker waves to the camera after shinnying up a pipe to celebrate Detroit's clinching of the American League flag in 1940. Baker, a former catcher and long-time coach, piloted the Tigers for four and a half seasons before being canned following a fifth-place finish in 1942.

- Pittsburgh's Arky Vaughan leads the NL in triples (15) and runs (113).

- Hack ties McCormick for NL lead in hits (191).

- McCormick tops NL in doubles (44).

- Pittsburgh's Elbie Fletcher leads the NL in OBP (.418) after walking an ML-leading 119 times.

- Cincinnati's Lonnie Frey leads the NL in thefts with 22.

- Washington's George Case again leads the AL in steals (35).

- Brownie Rip Radcliff and Tiger Barney McCosky tie for AL lead in hits with an even 200.

- McCosky's 19 triples lead the majors.

- McCosky and Greenberg both hit .340 for Detroit.

- Yankee Charlie Keller leads the AL in walks with 106.

- Detroit's Schoolboy Rowe leads the AL in win pct. (.842).

- Brooklyn's Freddie Fitzsimmons tops the NL in win pct. (.889).

The New York Yankees won the 1941 pennant by 17 games over Boston, but the pennant race was overshadowed by the personal heroics of two superstars. New York's AL MVP Joe DiMaggio put together a record 56-game hitting streak, and Boston's Ted Williams batted .406.

DiMaggio, who had shown a predilection for hitting streaks since his minor league days, started his 1941 streak with a hit against the White Sox on May 15. This was ironic because DiMaggio struggled against Chicago pitching throughout the season. Twice he prolonged the streak with bad-hop singles off Sox shortstop Luke Appling, and once with an infield dribbler in front of Sox third baseman Bob Kennedy. DiMaggio faced White Sox righty Johnny Rigney four times during the streak and went 1-for-3, 1-for-5, 1-for-4, and 1-for-3.

DiMaggio hit half of his 30 homers and drove in 55 runs during the streak to lift the Yankees out of a team slump and into the driver's seat in the 1941 race. On July 2, a DiMaggio homer broke Wee Willie Keeler's 44-year-old, major league hitting-streak record of 44. And on July 17, his streak was ended at 56 by two terrific backhanded stops by Indians third baseman Ken Keltner.

DiMaggio finished the season third in the AL in batting at .357, first in RBI with 125, second in doubles with 43, and fourth in home runs. But his season was dwarfed—statistically, at least—by

HERE'S TO YOU, JOE DIMAGGIO: 56 STRAIGHT!

that of Williams, who led him in runs 135 to 122, homers 37 to 30, on-base average .551 to .440, and slugging average .735 to .643. Williams also batted .406, the highest batting average in either league since Rogers Hornsby's .424 in 1924.

To put Williams's feat in perspective, consider that DiMaggio hit .409 during his hitting streak—just three points higher than Williams's season mark. At one point in June, Williams was hitting .436, but then began to fade. On the final day of the season, he found himself at .3995—technically .400 by baseball scoring rules. Nevertheless, Williams refused to play it safe and played both ends of a doubleheader. He went 6-for-8.

In another historical moment, 41-year-old Red Sox pitcher Lefty Grove won his 300th game and promptly retired with a 300-141 lifetime record. Grove had a 3.06 career ERA compiled exclusively in hitters' parks and in a hitter's era. He won an unap-

proachable nine ERA titles, and led the league in strikeouts seven times in a row.

In the NL, Brooklyn won by 2 1/2 games over St. Louis in a tight race that was decided by the Dodgers' two hitting heroes. MVP Dolph Camilli led the league with 34 homers and 120 RBI, and rookie Pete Reiser hit an NL-high .343, scored 117 runs, and cracked 39 doubles. Dodgers Whitlow Wyatt and Kirby Higbe tied for the NL lead in wins with 22, and Wyatt was second in ERA to the Reds' Elmer Riddle at 2.34. Ironically, the Dodgers' roster was loaded with ex-Cardinals, including Ducky Medwick, manager Leo Durocher, and catcher Mickey Owen. Reiser was plucked from the St. Louis farm system.

The first Dodgers-Yankees World Series looked like it was headed for at least six games. New York was leading two games to one, and Brooklyn's Hugh Casey took a 4-3 lead into the ninth inning of game four. With two outs and nobody on, he struck out Tommy Henrich, seemingly ending the game. However, Owen let the ball get by him, and Henrich reached first safely. The Dodgers had cracked the door open and the Yankees proceeded to kick it in. DiMaggio singled, Charlie Keller doubled, Bill Dickey walked, and Joe Gordon doubled to win the game 7-4. The next day, the Yankees clinched the Series 3-1 on Tiny Bonham's four-hitter.

1941

- Yankees return to top in AL, win by 17 games.

- Dodgers win their first NL flag since 1920.

- Yanks win World Series in five games, but it's the most competitive five-game Series in history.

- Dodgers lose game three of Series when Freddie Fitzsimmons leaves with a fractured kneecap after hurling seven scoreless innings.

- Dodgers lose game four on Mickey Owen's missed third strike in the ninth inning with two out.

- Joe Gordon of the Yanks is Series hero, hitting .500 with five RBI.

- Brooklyn's Dolph Camilli is the NL MVP.

- Joe DiMaggio wins the AL MVP.

- DiMaggio strings together ML record 56-game hitting streak.

- Ted Williams hits .406—remains the last ML player to hit .400.

1941

In the summer of 1941, Joe DiMaggio hit safely in a record 56 consecutive games. Analysts of the streak are of diverse opinions. One is that it was an inimitable achievement; the other is that it was heavily tainted by several extremely charitable scorer's decisions.

- Brooklyn's Pete Reiser, age 22, becomes the youngest in history to win NL bat crown.
- Lou Gehrig dies.
- Jimmie Foxx notches his 13th consecutive 100-RBI season to tie Gehrig's record.
- Phils lose franchise record 111 games.

- Yankees clinch flag in AL record 136 games.
- Tigers give $52,000 to Dick Wakefield; becomes the first of what will soon become a flurry of big-bucks bonus babies.
- Williams hits three-run homer with two out in ninth to give AL 7-5 win in All-Star Game at Detroit.

- Arky Vaughan is first to hit two homers in an All-Star Game.
- On March 8, Hugh Mulcahy of Phils becomes first MLer to be drafted in WWII.
- Bob Feller tops ML in wins with 25.
- Feller's 343 innings pitched are most in ML since 1923.

Brooklyn Dodger Fans

Ted Williams

Williams Hits Highs

Although fans still talk about the .406 average Ted Williams tallied in 1941, he boasted other stats that were equally phenomenal. His .551 on-base percentage was the greatest until 2002. He also slugged .735.

Casey Saves Seven

Hugh Casey was the National League's premier relief pitcher both before and after World War II. Casey won 14 games (seven saves) in 1941. After excelling in the 1947 World Series, he lost his effectiveness and was in the minors by 1950. The following summer, when a return to the majors failed to materialize, Casey committed suicide.

Dodger Fans Disappointed

Brooklyn Dodger fans, perhaps the most famous group of boosters of all time, wait to see a 1941 World Series game. It's unknown which game they're waiting for, but it really doesn't matter. The Bums lost all three of their home meetings to the Yankees, dropping the Series in five games. Dodger fans would have to "wait 'til next year."

Hugh Casey

1941

- Feller tops majors again with 260 Ks, and also leads AL in shutouts (six).

- Feller enlists in Navy at end of season.

- Williams is batting .3995 on last day of season; closes with 6-for-8 performance in doubleheader to finish at .406.

- Cardinal Lon Warneke no-hits Reds on August 30.

- Lloyd Waner plays an NL record 77 straight games without striking out.

- The Dodgers become first team to wear plastic batting helmets after Reiser and Pee Wee Reese are beaned.

- Cleveland's Jeff Heath is first in AL history to hit at least 20 homers, 20 triples, and 20 doubles in a season.

- Heath's 20 triples lead the majors.

- Wes Ferrell leaves majors with career record 38 homers by a pitcher.

- White Sox Taffy Wright collects RBI in 13 straight games.

New York Yankees

Yankees Win Championship

A shot of the 1941 World Champion New York Yankees. Rookie first baseman Johnny Sturm *(second row, fourth from the right)* played every game in the World Series against Brooklyn, but was not invited back after he hit .239 during the regular season. Also a rookie, Phil Rizzuto *(front row, second from the left)* lasted until 1956. Along with powerful hitting and excellent pitching, the Yankees set a major league record by turning 196 double plays.

Camilli Named NL MVP

Dolph Camilli won the 1941 National League MVP Award, leading the league with 34 homers and 120 RBI. Two of Camilli's Brooklyn teammates, Pete Reiser and Whit Wyatt, finished second and third in the balloting, and three other Dodgers were among the top 11 vote-getters. The Dodgers were quite potent. Brooklyn led the NL in runs (800), doubles (286), triples (69), homers (101), batting (.272), and slugging (.405). The pitching staff led the NL in ERA (3.14).

Dolph Camilli

Pee Wee Reese

Pee Wee Shines

Pee Wee Reese (pictured) arrived in Brooklyn in 1940, the same season that Lou Boudreau first made his mark and a year before Phil Rizzuto came alive. In 1941, Reese tallied 136 hits and 46 RBI.

- Camilli leads NL in homers (34) and RBI (120).
- Reiser paces NL in runs (117), doubles (39), triples (17), runs produced (179), SA (.558), and total bases (299).
- Cincinnati's Bucky Walters tops NL in both innings (302) and CGs (27) for third year in a row.
- Cincinnati's Elmer Riddle tops NL in both win pct. (.826) and ERA (2.24).
- Williams leads AL in runs (135), homers (37), OBP (.551), runs produced (218), walks (145), and SA (.735).
- DiMaggio leads only in RBI (125) and total bases (348).
- Thornton Lee of White Sox wins 22 games, tops AL in CGs (30) and ERA (2.37).
- Lefty Grove wins 300th game, last to do it until 1963.
- Grove's streak of 20 consecutive wins at Fenway Park ends.

Pete Reiser

Reiser Knocked Out

An all-too-familiar sight during the early 1940s was that of Pete Reiser being carried off the field on a stretcher. In this instance, he was the victim of a beaning, but he also frequently collided with outfield walls while chasing fly balls. Reiser led the NL in batting average (.343) in 1941.

Bob Feller

Dodgers Win NL Pennant

A look at the 1941 Brooklyn Dodgers. A series of shrewd trades by Brooklyn general manager Larry MacPhail made a pennant-winner out of a team that had finished seventh two years earlier. Second baseman Billy Herman *(second row, second from the right)* was stolen from the Cubs for two utility infielders and $65,000.

Brooklyn Dodgers

Feller Carries the Tribe

Thanks in large part to Bob Feller (25–13), Cleveland finished with a 75–79 record in 1941. The only club in the majors that was as disappointing in 1941 as Cleveland was the defending American League Champion Tigers, who tied the Tribe for fourth place.

1941

- In December, Pirates send Vaughan to Brooklyn for four players.
- Cards ship Johnny Mize to Giants for three players and $50,000.
- Foxx leads AL in batter Ks a record seventh time.
- Browns leave a record 1,334 men on base during the season.

- Bill Klem retires after 40 years as an umpire.
- Infielder Al Brancato of the A's is the last player to make 60 errors in a season.
- On May 7, Eddie Joost of the Reds sets an ML record for shortstops by handling 19 chances in a game.

- The Giants host the first-ever "Ladies Night" game.
- Pittsburgh's Elbie Fletcher again tops the NL in walks (118) and OBP (.421).
- Phillie Danny Murtaugh tops the NL in steals (18) but hits just .219— lowest BA ever by a theft leader.

Owen's Flub Loses Game

The most famous passed ball in history: Tommy Henrich of the Yankees swings for the third strike that would have ended the fourth game of the 1941 World Series—had the pitch not eluded Mickey Owen. Given unexpected life, the Yankees tallied four runs to win the game and forever immortalize the Dodgers catcher.

World Series

Dick Wakefield

Wakefield: First Bonus Baby

In 1941, a young Dick Wakefield inked a $52,000 contract with the Tigers, thus becoming baseball's first renowned bonus baby. Wakefield sparkled in his rookie season, 1943, when he led the American League in hits (200) and doubles (38), but he quickly fizzled out. Other bonus babies, namely pitchers Paul Pettit of the Pirates and Billy Joe Davidson of the Indians, were bigger busts. The two combined for one major league win.

The Iron Horse is Laid to Rest

Babe Ruth pays his last respects to Lou Gehrig. The two great teammates were friends and fellow admirers for many years. After Ruth made the mistake in 1933 of mildly criticizing Gehrig's mother, however, the pair never spoke to one another again. Ironically, both of these great heroes died young. Gehrig, nicknamed "The Iron Horse," died at the tender age of 37. Ruth, nicknamed "The Sultan of Swat," never made it to his 54th birthday. Ruth passed away in August of 1948.

Lou Gehrig, Babe Ruth

- Brooklyn teammates Whit Wyatt and Kirby Higbe tie for the NL lead in wins with 22.

- Wyatt leads the ML in shutouts with seven.

- Cincinnati's Johnny Vander Meer leads the NL in Ks (202).

- Lou Boudreau tops the majors in doubles (45) and again leads AL shortstops in FA.

- Washington's Cecil Travis tops the AL in hits with 218.

- In contrast, Chicago's Stan Hack leads the NL in hits with just 186.

- Yankee Johnny Murphy tops majors with 15 saves.

- Three Yankees have 30 or more homers: Charlie Keller (33), Tommy Henrich (31), and DiMaggio (30).

- With Hank Greenberg lost to the service, the Tigers fall to 75-79.

COOPER COPS MVP; CARDS TAKE TITLE

The Yankees lost Tommy Henrich to the Army in 1942, as World War II increasingly affected baseball rosters. Still, the Bronx Bombers managed a near-repeat of their 1941 performance. With a deep and versatile attack, they led the AL in runs scored and fewest runs allowed, and went 103-51 to come in 9 games ahead of second-place Boston.

Joe DiMaggio batted .305 with 123 runs (second to Ted Williams), 114 RBI (also second to Williams), 21 homers, and 13 triples. Outfielder Charlie Keller scored 106 runs, drove in 108, and drew 114 walks (again, second to Williams). Sophomore Phil Rizzuto stole 22 bases, and his double-play partner Joe Gordon hit .322 with 103 RBI, fourth in the AL.

The Yankees' pitching was just as strong, as pitchers Tiny Bonham, Spud Chandler, and Hank Borowy were second, third, and fifth in the AL in ERA at 2.27, 2.37, and 2.53. Bonham went 21-5 and was second in wins to Boston's Tex Hughson, who had a 22-6 record.

Boston was second in team runs on the strength of good years from Williams, who won the Triple Crown by hitting .356 with 36 homers and 137 RBI; Johnny Pesky, who hit .331; Bobby Doerr, who hit 35 doubles and 15 homers; and Dom DiMaggio, who scored 110 runs. Show-

ing how disliked Williams was by the sportswriters, he lost the MVP vote to the Yankees' Gordon, 270 to 249, even though Gordon led the American League in strikeouts with 95 and errors with 28.

The 1942 NL race was a mirror image of 1941, as the St. Louis Cardinals won a squeaker over Brooklyn by 2 games. Foreshadowing many famous fades, Brooklyn built a 10½ game-lead by August, only to be overtaken by a 43-8 Cardinals run.

The '42 St. Louis team represented the finest hour for Branch Rickey, the architect of the modern farm system. St. Louis was paced by home-grown products Stan Musial, who hit .315; Enos Slaughter, who hit .318; shortstop Marty Marion, who led the league in doubles with 38; outfielder Terry Moore; and catcher Walker Cooper.

Walker Cooper's teammate and brother—Mort Cooper—

copped the MVP Award, winning 22 games and leading the league with a 1.77 ERA. And 24-year-old Johnny Beazley, who was second to Cooper in wins with 21 and in ERA at 2.13, led the league's finest pitching staff to a team ERA of only 2.55. Whit Wyatt did his part for the Dodgers, posting a 19-7 record.

Dodger Dolph Camilli drove in 109 runs and hit 26 home runs, tied for second with New York's Johnny Mize. Teammate Pete Reiser (who had collided with an outfield fence on July 2nd and suffered a severe concussion) was third in hitting at .310 (down from .390) and first in stolen bases with 20. The Giants' Mel Ott led in homers with 30, runs with 118, and walks with 109.

The Yankees took the opening game of the World Series 7-4 behind veteran Red Ruffing, but St. Louis rallied to win the Series in five games. It was the first time New York had lost in October since the 1926 Cardinals defeated them. St. Louis rookies Musial and Whitey Kurowski had key hits in the '42 Series, but young Beazley was the hero with a 2-0, 2.50 ERA performance. Another young pitcher, 26-year-old Ernie White, defeated Spud Chandler on a six-hit shutout in game three. The Cardinals turned in a staff ERA of 2.60 to the Yankees' 4.50.

1942

- The Cards triumph in the NL.
- Yankees repeat in AL.
- Cards are first team since 1926 to beat Yanks in World Series, winning in five games.
- The Yankees are spared from being swept in Series only because Red Ruffing wins the opener.

- Cardinal Johnny Beazley is the Series hero with two CG wins.
- Yankee Phil Rizzuto is top hitter in Series with .381 BA and eight hits.
- Mort Cooper of Cards wins NL MVP Award.
- Joe Gordon of Yanks is AL MVP.

- Ted Williams wins Triple Crown (.356 BA, 36 homers, 137 RBI), but once again loses out on the MVP Award.
- Williams also leads AL in runs (141), walks (145), runs produced (242), total bases (338), OBP (.499), and SA (.648).

Johnny Beazley, the winning pitcher for the Cards in game two of the 1942 World Series, is congratulated by teammates Max Lanier *(left)*, Creepy Crespi *(center)*, and Coaker Triplett *(right)*. Beazley's victory was the first ever by a rookie pitcher in fall play against the Yankees.

- Gordon leads league in errors at his position, strikeouts, and double plays grounded into, though he hits .322 with 103 RBI.

- The Phils finish last for NL record fifth consecutive year.

- Cleveland's Lou Boudreau, age 24, is youngest manager to begin season at helm of team.

- Cooper tops NL with 22 wins and majors with 1.77 ERA and ten shutouts.

- Beazley wins 21 games as a rookie, enters the armed services, and is never again an effective pitcher.

- Boston's Tex Hughson tops AL in wins (22), innings (281), and CGs (22), and ties for lead in Ks (113).

- Dodgers' 104 wins tie ML record for most wins by an also-ran.

- Mel Ott wins his last NL home run crown (30).

- Ott tops the NL in runs (118) and walks (109).

- Ott walks 100 times for a record seventh consecutive year.

Warren Spahn

Spahn's Career Interrupted

Warren Spahn was one of the many promising young players whose career was interrupted after the 1942 season by a stint in the armed services. Put on hold until 1946, Spahn did not win his first game until he was 25 years old. Despite his belated start, he collected 363 career wins. If his career hadn't been interrupted by the war, he probably would have won 400 career games. Only Cy Young and Walter Johnson have ever won 400.

Mort Cooper

Cooper Named NL MVP

Mort Cooper fell just a fraction of a season short in joining Carl Hubbell and Harry Brecheen in a unique category. He would have been one of three pitchers active exclusively between 1920 and the onset of expansion (1961) to post career ERAs under 3.00 (minimum ten years pitched). Cooper finished his career with a 2.97 ERA and 128 wins. He was the National League MVP in '42, posting 22 victories.

Williams Powers Sox

Ted Williams (.356, 36 home runs, 137 RBI) sparked the Red Sox to 93 wins in 1942, their most in any season since 1915. Boston was never really in the race, however, owing to a lack of depth and a need for a front-line catcher. When Williams went into the service in 1943, the Sox tumbled to seventh place.

Ted Williams

1942

- Ernie Lombardi, now with the Braves, is awarded bat title with .330 BA but only 309 at-bats.

- Most sources credit Enos Slaughter as the NL BA leader (.318 in 591 at-bats).

- Hall of Fame inducts Rogers Hornsby.

- The Braves trade Eddie Miller to the Reds for Eddie Joost, Nate Andrews, and cash.

- The Braves trade Buddy Hassett and Gene Moore to the Yankees for Tommy Holmes.

- Branch Rickey is fired as the Cards' general manager.

- The Phils' 354 RBI are the fewest by any team since the dead-ball era.

- Danny Litwhiler tops the Phils with just 56 RBI.

- Cleveland's Clint Brown sets a record when he pitches 220 straight games in relief roles.

Enos Slaughter

Rookie Pesky Nets 200 Hits

Johnny Pesky is the only American League player to make 200 or more hits in each of his first three seasons (1942, '46, and '47). Like many contact hitters of his era, Pesky used a long, heavy bat and choked up on the handle.

Johnny Pesky

Slaughter Hits .318

Some authorities credit Enos Slaughter with winning the 1942 National League bat title (.318). In any event, he ranked at or near the top in almost every major hitting department that season. Slaughter was a throwback, both in his style of play and in his ability to hit as many triples as home runs (17 and 13, respectively, in 1942).

Reiser Boosts Dodgers

In 1942, the Dodgers led the Cardinals by 10 1/2 games in mid-August, but had their seemingly comfortable margin gradually eaten away while Pete Reiser recovered from a fractured skull. Reiser had been hitting .390 that year. With a healthy Reiser, Brooklyn probably would have been able to hold off St. Louis' late charge and win a second straight flag. Reiser, who made a habit of running into fences, was seemingly always disabled. In his ten-year career, he played in only 861 games.

Pete Reiser

- Run production in both leagues is the lowest since 1919, the last year of the dead-ball era.

- The Cardinals' 2.55 ERA is the best by an ML team from 1920 through 1966.

- Cardinal Howie Krist has a 10-0 record, giving him the NL mark for most wins in a season without a loss.

- In his last ML start before going into the Navy, Brooklyn's Larry French pitches a one-hitter.

- French leads the NL with .789 win pct.—highest in history by a pitcher in his final ML season.

- French leaves majors with 197 wins— most at this juncture by any pitcher who never won 20 in a season.

- Hans Lobert of the Phils is the first rookie manager in ML history who's past the age of 60.

- Washington's George Case tops the AL in steals with 44 in 50 attempts.

- Johnny Mize leads the NL in RBI (110).

St. Louis Cardinals

Cards Loaded with Characters

A shot of the 1942 World Champion St. Louis Cardinals. On the team were Estel Crabtree, a pinch hitter from Crabtree, Ohio; Howie Krist, a pitcher who had a 23–3 record over a two-year span; and second baseman Creepy Crespi, who broke a leg while serving in World War II.

Johnny Beazley

Cochrane Serves in War

Like many former stars, Mickey Cochrane was a precious commodity during World War II. Although done as a player, he served his country well as an organizer and manager of service baseball teams. After the war, Cochrane coached and scouted for several years, then was the A's general manager in Connie Mack's last season.

Mickey Cochrane

Beazley Takes NL By Storm

Johnny Beazley was an unnecessary casualty of World War II. Inducted after his brilliant rookie season of '42 (21–6, 2.13 ERA), he encountered arm trouble while playing on a service team. His commanding officer ordered Beazley to pitch despite the pain, and he permanently wrecked his arm. After the war, Beazley won just nine games in the remainder of his career. He retired at age 30.

1942

- Red Sox rookie Johnny Pesky hits .331, tops majors with 205 hits.

- White Sox Ted Lyons goes 14-6 as he makes just 20 mound appearances, all of them CGs.

- AL wins All-Star Game 3-1 at Polo Grounds on July 6.

- Detroit's Al Benton pitches a full five innings to get the save.

- The next night, the AL wins 5-0 over the Service All-Stars, made up mostly of major leaguers in the armed forces.

- Paul Waner collects his 3,000th hit, the last to do it until 1957.

- The average player's salary is down to $6,400.

- The Phils score just 394 runs in 151 games.

- Phillie outfielder Danny Litwhiler is the first ML regular to play a whole season without an error.

Tommy Henrich

Boudreau, Harris: Baby Skippers

Lou Boudreau (right), the "Boy Wonder," talks with Bucky Harris, the original Boy Wonder. Harris was age 27 in 1924 when he became the skipper of the Senators. Boudreau was age 24 in 1942, his first season at the Cleveland helm.

Bucky Harris, Lou Boudreau

Gordon Named AL MVP

In 1942, Joe Gordon *(right)* led all American League batters in strikeouts and grounding into the most double plays and he led all AL second basemen in errors. He was nonetheless voted the AL MVP (.322, 18 home runs, 103 RBI), and it was a solid choice. In his career, Gordon averaged 4.43 home runs per 100 at-bats, the highest average in history by a second baseman.

Joe Gordon

Henrich's Season Ends

Tommy Henrich's late-season military call-up (he had collected 13 home runs and 67 RBI to that point) allowed Yankees sub outfielder Roy Cullenbine to play in the 1942 World Series. The Cardinals, in contrast, had all of their starting cast available. Although Henrich played on eight Yankees pennant-winners, he saw action in only four World Series.

- On August 14, the Yankees make a record seven DPs vs. the A's.

- On May 13, Brave Jim Tobin becomes the only pitcher in this century to hit three homers in a game.

- Gordon and Rizzuto set an AL keystone record (since broken) when they total a combined 234 DPs.

- Pittsburgh's Elbie Fletcher leads the NL in OBP (.417) for the third consecutive year.

- Slaughter leads the NL in hits (188), triples (17), total bases (292), and runs produced (185).

- Giant reliever Ace Adams appears in 61 games, a new NL mound record.

- A's and Phils both finish last for third year in a row.

- In July, with the Dodgers 13½ games ahead of the Cards, Pete Reiser crashes into a fence and fractures his skull.

- Cardinals catch up to the Dodgers while Reiser's out with injury.

YANKS, CARDS WEATHER WAR, MEET IN SERIES

Nearly every major league team lost key personnel to the armed forces in 1943. Baseball itself was allowed to continue because of its morale value, although Washington asked that travel be curtailed and that games be scheduled for the maximum convenience of fans who worked in war-related industries. For the most part, that meant more night games—including the first twi-night doubleheaders—but teams also scheduled early-morning contests for those on night shifts.

Restricted travel meant changing not only the regular-season schedule but spring training sites as well. Instead of sunny Florida, California, and Cuba, major league teams limbered up in exotic locations like Wallingford, Connecticut; Muncie, Indiana; and Asbury Park, New Jersey. Moreover, wartime rubber rationing adversely affected the quality of major league baseballs, and batting averages plummeted into the .240s.

Not surprisingly, the two clubs with the deepest talent and richest farm systems, the Yankees and Cardinals, weathered the storm best and won pennants in 1943. The Cardinals replaced Enos Slaughter, Terry Moore, Johnny Beazley, and Howie Pollet with the likes of Lou Klein, Alpha Brazle, and Harry Brecheen. Walker Cooper hit .318 and Harry Walker .294, but St. Louis' biggest weapon was a blossoming Stan Musial, who at age 22 led the NL in hitting at .357, triples with 20, doubles with 48, hits with 220, and total bases with 347. He also scored 108 runs, drove in a team-leading 81, and was voted NL MVP.

St. Louis had the league's two top pitchers in ERA with 15-7 Max Lanier at 1.90 and 21-8 Mort Cooper at 2.30. As a whole, the Cardinals' staff led in ERA at 2.57, shutouts with 21, and strikeouts with 639.

Cincinnati came in second, 18 games out, and Brooklyn finished third under ex-Cardinal GM Branch Rickey. The pitching-poor Dodgers had the NL's strongest offense, led by stolen-base leader Arky Vaughan with 20; .330-hitting Billy Herman; and Augie Galan, who drew a league-leading 103 walks. Chicago's Swish Nicholson led the league with 29 home runs and 128 RBI.

Pittsburgh's 36-year-old pitching ace Rip Sewell invented the blooper pitch, which he nicknamed the "eephus," and went 21-9 to lead the NL in wins. And in Philadelphia, owner Bill Cox ran afoul of baseball's anti-gambling laws. He was caught betting on his own team (to win), and was forced to sell the team.

The AL race was another laugher, as the Yankees smoked runner-up Washington by 13½ games with a second-half surge. Bill Dickey, age 36, led the Yanks in hitting at .351; Charlie Keller hit 31 home runs, second only to Rudy York's 34; and first baseman Nick Etten totaled 107 RBI, second to York's 118. Thirty-two-year-old Frank Crosetti took over at short, as Phil Rizzuto joined Joe DiMaggio, Tommy Henrich, and Red Ruffing overseas. Pitcher Spud Chandler, age 35, went 20-4 with a league-low 1.64 ERA for the Bronx Bombers.

Chicago's Luke Appling took over the batting title vacated by the absent Ted Williams with a .328 average. Detroit's Dick Wakefield was second in hitting at .316 and first in doubles with 38.

In the 1943 World Series, New York got its revenge for 1942 by beating St. Louis in five games. Chandler, the regular-season's MVP, was the pitching hero, winning game one 4-2 and game five 2-0, and recording an ERA of 0.50. Bill Dickey was the batting hero of New York's tenth World Championship, leading all hitters with four RBI. Dickey homered to account for both Yankee runs in the deciding game. Cooper got the win in game two, the sole Card victory, despite mourning the loss of his father, who died earlier that day.

1943

- Yanks repeat in AL, their seventh flag in eight years.
- Cards also repeat in NL.
- Yanks turn tables on Cards in World Series, win in five games.
- Yankee Spud Chandler's two CG wins is top Series performance.
- Yankee Billy Johnson leads World Series players in hits with just six.
- St. Louis and New York have lost players to armed forces; Yanks are without Joe DiMaggio, Cards without Enos Slaughter.
- Joe McCarthy collects the last of his record seven World Series wins.
- McCarthy takes the last of his AL record (since broken) eight pennants.
- Chandler is AL MVP.
- Stan Musial is NL MVP, beating out Cardinal teammate Walker Cooper.
- Musial wins his first NL bat crown (.357).

Pictured are the Cooper brothers, Walker *(left)* and Mort. In 1943, they became the only sibling teammates in history to both finish among the top five in MVP voting. Walker was the leading catcher in the majors that year (.318, nine home runs, 81 RBI) and Mort tied for the major league-lead in wins (21).

- Musial leads NL in OBP (.425), SA (.562), hits (220), doubles (48), triples (20), and total bases (347).

- Chicago's Luke Appling becomes lone AL shortstop to win two bat crowns (.328).

- Appling leads the AL in OBP (.419).

- Detroit's Rudy York tops AL in homers (34) and RBI (118).

- York leads AL in runs produced (174), SA (.527), and total bases (301).

- Chicago's Bill Nicholson leads NL in homers (29), RBI (128), and runs produced (194).

- Major league teams are forced to conduct spring training in northern sectors due to World War II travel restrictions.

- The Browns add to their on-going ML record when they complete their 42nd season without having won a pennant.

McCarthy Finishes On Top Again

Joe McCarthy guided the Yankees to their third straight American League pennant and second World Championship in 1943. He was so miffed that the club sold pitcher Hank Borowy to the Cubs against his wishes that he left the team for three weeks in 1945 and even offered to resign. A month and a half into the 1946 season, with the Yankees off to a slow start, McCarthy's resignation was accepted.

St. Louis Cardinals

Cards Move Training Digs

The Cardinals, as did all 16 major league teams, had to forsake their regular training site in St. Petersburg, Florida, and conduct their preseason drills closer to home during the war. The Indians, for one, trained at Purdue University.

Yankees Miss Rizzuto, Joe

The temporary departure of stars like Phil Rizzuto *(left)* and Joe DiMaggio ended the Yankees' run of seven pennants in eight seasons. In 1944, and even more in 1945, Joe McCarthy had to do some of his best managing just to preserve his record of never finishing out of the first division.

Joe McCarthy

Phil Rizzuto, Joe DiMaggio

1943

- Ace Adams is the first pitcher to appear in 60 or more games two years in a row.

- Washington finishes second in AL—its best showing since 1933.

- On May 2, Phillie Schoolboy Rowe becomes the first pitcher to hit a grandslam in each league.

- Red Sox Jim Tabor leads AL third basemen in errors for a fifth straight year.

- Dodgers start season with Branch Rickey as their GM, replacing Larry MacPhail who's in the armed forces.

- Yankee Nick Etten goes 77 at-bats without hitting a single (though he does get other hits).

- Prior to the season, the Yanks get Etten from the Phils for four players and $10,000.

- The Twin Ports League, the only Class E league in OB history, disbands on July 13.

- On June 17, Joe Cronin becomes the first to pinch-hit a homer in both games of a doubleheader.

Vaughan Quits the Dodgers

Still at his peak—.305 average, 66 RBI, and a National League-leading 112 runs scored—Arky Vaughan quit the Dodgers rather than play under Leo Durocher. Nowadays, he could have become a free agent, but in 1943 Vaughan had no other choice. He came out of retirement in 1947 to play again for Brooklyn after Durocher was suspended for the season.

Arky Vaughan

Nicholson: 29 HRs, 128 RBI

Purchased from Chattanooga of the Southern Association, Bill Nicholson joined the Cubs in July 1939 and almost immediately demonstrated that he would soon be one of the National League's top sluggers. During World War II, he twice led the NL in both home runs and RBI. In 1943, he led the league with 29 dingers and 128 RBI.

Stan Musial

Musial Slugs .562

Stan Musial participated in four World Series in his first four full seasons in the majors. He then played 17 more years without ever appearing in another. In 1943, Musial led the National League in slugging average at .562 despite hitting just 13 home runs. The following year, he repeated as the NL slugging leader, although his home run total fell to 12.

Bill Nicholson

- Chicago's Wally Moses and New York's Johnny Lindell tie for the AL lead in triples with 12—new record-low for loop leader.
- Chandler and Detroit's Dizzy Trout tie for the AL lead in wins (20).
- Chandler leads in win pct. (.833) and ERA (1.64) and ties for the lead in shutouts (five).

- Jim Bagby Jr.—son of 30-game winner Jim Sr.—tops AL in innings (273).
- No pitcher in the AL has more than 20 complete games.
- Cleveland's Allie Reynolds leads the AL in Ks with 151.

- Cincinnati's Johnny Vander Meer repeats as NL K leader (174).
- ML homer total falls below 1,000 for the first time since 1927.
- The Cards hit .279 while no regular on the Yankees hits above .280.
- The Cards' Max Lanier leads the NL in ERA at 1.90.

Spud Chandler

Chandler Leads AL in Wins

Spud Chandler's .717 career winning percentage is the highest in history for a 100-game winner. All of Chandler's 152 decisions came with the Yankees. A lackluster record in the minors delayed his major league debut, and a fragile arm idled him for long stretches after he made it. Chandler went 20–4 in '43, leading the American League in wins and ERA (1.64).

Bill Cox

Cox Goes Down in Disgrace

Few owners are so brazen as to be photographed wearing their team's uniform. Then again there have been few owners like the Phil's Bill Cox. He was barred in 1943 by the commissioner for betting on his own team. Not only was Cox foolish, he was also apparently a masochist. The Phils that year won just 64 games.

Wakefield Arouses AL

Dick Wakefield led the American League in hits (200) and doubles (38) as a rookie in 1943. He was also second in the league in batting (.316) and total bases (275) and third in runs (91). In 1944, he hit .355 for a half-season and nearly carried the Tigers to the pennant. Baseball came so easily to Wakefield that he adopted a lackadaisical attitude—one which he couldn't shed even when his career began to go down the drain.

Dick Wakefield

1943

- Cardinal Mort Cooper leads NL in win pct. (.724) and ties for lead in wins (21).
- Washington's George Case wins his fifth consecutive AL theft crown (61).
- Case leads the AL in runs (102).
- Giants finish last for first time since 1915.

- To save on rubber, a new balata baseball is introduced.
- There are no homers in the first 11 games of the season, and the new ball is shelved.
- Mel Ott is second in NL with 18 homers—all 18 are hit in his home park.

- White Sox play 44 doubleheaders.
- Phils play an NL record 43 doubleheaders.
- Bankrupt Phils franchise sold to NL for $50,000; Bill Cox becomes owner.
- Guy Curtwright of Chicago hits in 26 straight games, an AL rookie record.

Case Swipes 61 Bases

George Case

George Case was an anachronism. He stole bases by the carload (61 in 1943) yet his home runs could be counted on the fingers of one hand (one homer in '43). His talents made him invaluable to the Senators, who played during the war years as if it were still the dead-ball era. In 1943, the Senators stole 142 bases but clubbed just 47 home runs. In 1944, they smacked just 33 homers.

Harry Walker

Yankees Earn World Title

A look at the 1943 World Champion New York Yankees. Missing from the picture are Joe DiMaggio, Phil Rizzuto, Tommy Henrich, and Red Ruffing, all of whom were in the armed services. Among the new Yankees was rookie Snuffy Stirnweiss *(second row, far right),* who hit .219 in 1943, fielded .938, and gave no hint that he would be the club's biggest war-time star.

New York Yankees

Walker Brother Falters

There were two sets of Walker brothers playing in the majors during the war years. All four of them were outfielders. Harry (pictured) and Dixie Walker were the better known of the two sibling acts. A Series hero in 1946, Harry hit just .143 for the Cardinals in the 1943 fall classic. Harry was nicknamed "The Hat" because he had a habit of tugging at his cap when he was in the batter's box.

- A's lose an AL record (since broken) 20 straight games.
- Commissioner Kenesaw Mountain Landis bans Phils' new owner Cox for life for betting on his own team.
- On Sept. 16, Philly's Carl Scheib, age 16, is youngest ever to pitch in an AL game.

- The AL wins the first All-Star Game played at night, 5-3 at Shibe Park.
- Arky Vaughan quits Dodgers at end of season rather than continue to play under manager Leo Durocher.
- During the season, Vaughan leads the NL in runs (112).

- Detroit rookie Dick Wakefield tops AL in hits (200) and doubles (38), and is second in batting (.316).
- AL has only three .300 hitters and only five above .290.
- Adams sets new modern ML record with 70 mound appearances.

The 1944 season was the peak—or, to look at it another way, the nadir—of wartime baseball. The National League didn't embarrass itself; the Cardinals won their third straight pennant behind respectable ballplayers like Marty Marion, Walker Cooper, Johnny Hopp, and especially Stan Musial.

But in the AL, the acute shortage of players dragged the entire league down to the level of the St. Louis Browns, perennial doormats who had finished in the second division nine out of the previous ten seasons. The dismal Browns had never won a pennant in 43 years of AL competition.

The '44 Browns were relatively untouched by the military draft, as they featured an all-4F infield, nine players on the roster 34 years old or older, and a motley collection of notorious characters, such as Tex Shirley and Mike Kreevich. Fourth starter Sig Jakucki, who went 13-9 with a 3.55 ERA, had retired in 1936 with an 0-3 major league record; he was rediscovered pitching for a Houston industrial-league team.

Rounding out the staff were old men Nels Potter (who went 19-7 with a 2.83 ERA) and Denny Galehouse (9-10), and youngsters Jack Kramer (who finished 17-13 with a 2.49 ERA) and Bob Muncrief (13-8). The big hitters for the Browns were 23-year-old shortstop Vern Stephens, who hit .293 and was second in homers with 20 and first in RBI with 109, and Kreevich, the

SAD-SACK BROWNIES TAKE AL FLAG

team's only .300 hitter at .301.

St. Louis won its first nine games of the season, and continued to surprise the baseball world by hanging tough in a four-team race with Detroit, Boston, and the Yankees. The race came down to the final week, when the Browns defeated New York five times, winning the pennant by 1 game over Detroit. St. Louis clinched the flag with a come-from-behind 5-2 victory over New York on two home runs by Chet Laabs and one by Stephens. The Browns finished with a record of 89-65, which was, at the time, the worst record ever by an AL pennant-winner.

The sportswriters couldn't bring themselves to name one of the Browns AL MVP, so the award went to Detroit lefthander Hal Newhouser, who had a record of 29-9. Newhouser and teammate Dizzy Trout were first and second in both wins and ERA. Cleveland's Lou Boudreau took the batting title at .327, and New York's Nick Etten led in homers with 22.

The Cards slipped from first for just four days during the season. Their 105 triumphs made

them the first NL team to win over 100 games for three straight years.

The NL MVP went to Cardinals shortstop Marty Marion. Musial hit .347 (second only to Brooklyn's Dixie Walker at .357) with 51 doubles, 112 runs, and 94 RBI. Leadoff man Johnny Hopp hit .336, stole 15 bases, and scored 106 runs.

MVP runner-up Swish Nicholson of the Cubs had another big power-hitting year, leading the league with 33 homers and 122 RBI. The Reds' wartime search for talent reached an extreme when they used 15-year-old pitcher Joe Nuxhall in one game. He returned to high school with a major league ERA of 45.00.

The surprising Browns put up a good fight in the 1944 World Series—especially by the pitchers—but were undone by poor defense. The St. Louis double-play combo of Don Gutteridge and Stephens made three errors apiece, as their team lost the Series in six.

A month after the World Series, 78-year-old commissioner Kenesaw Mountain Landis died. His 35-year tenure was characterized by a strong and successful stand against gambling-related corruption, and surprising sympathy for the players' side in disputes with owners. The baseball owners have made sure never to give any other commissioner the power that they regretted giving to Landis. Landis was replaced by Happy Chandler.

1944

- Browns win first and only flag in their history.
- Cards grab third straight flag in NL.
- Cards take all-Mound City World Series in six games.
- George McQuinn of Browns leads all World Series players with .438 BA and five RBI.

- Emil Verban hits .412 to lead the Cards in Series.
- Cards get Series wins from four different pitchers.
- Blix Donnelly wins the key game of Series, game two, in 13 innings after Cards drop the opener.
- Cardinal Marty Marion is NL MVP.

- Detroit's Hal Newhouser wins AL MVP.
- Newhouser wins 29 games for second-place Tigers, most since 1931 by an ML lefty.
- Newhouser leads the AL in strikeouts (187).

Sig Jakucki's 13th win on the closing day of the 1944 season gave the Browns the pennant. Trailing the Yankees 2-0 in the fourth inning, Jakucki got a pair of two-run homers from Chet Laabs to seal the win.

- Dizzy Trout wins 27 for Tigers to give the club a post-dead-ball tandem record of 56 wins from two pitchers.

- Trout is second to Newhouser in MVP vote—only time pitchers from same team have finished one-two.

- Trout and Newhouser are the top two in the league in wins, ERA, innings, strikeouts, CGs, and shutouts.

- Trout tops AL in CGs (33), innings (352), ERA (2.12), and shutouts (seven).

- Brooklyn's Dixie Walker tops NL in batting at .357.

- Cleveland's Lou Boudreau wins AL bat title at .327.

- Cub Bill Nicholson tops majors in homers with 33 and RBI with 122.

- AL homer leader Nick Etten of the Yankees has just 22.

- Giant rookie Bill Voiselle wins 21; is the last rookie in ML history to pitch 300 or more innings, as he works 313.

Snuffy Leads AL in Runs

Snuffy Stirnweiss totaled 290 MVP votes in 1944 and 1945 and never received another. (In 1944, he led the American League with 125 runs scored and 205 hits.) Although he is lumped now among the war-time players who had a couple of fluky good seasons, in one respect—fielding—he did his best work after the war.

Marty Marion

Snuffy Stirnweiss

Marion Named NL MVP

Marty Marion (pictured) was regarded by sportswriters as the National League's best shortstop during the 1940s, but most NL players felt that Eddie Miller was his superior—at least in the field. A .267 hitter in 1944, Marion won the NL MVP Award by a scant one-vote margin over Bill Nicholson of the Cubs.

1944

- Voiselle leads the NL in Ks (161).

- The Giants' Ace Adams appears in 60 or more games as a pitcher for a record third consecutive year.

- Adams leads the majors in saves with 13.

- Snuffy Stirnweiss, a .219 hitter in 1943, tops the majors with 205 hits.

- Commissioner Kenesaw Mountain Landis dies, is voted immediately into Hall of Fame.

- Elmer Gedeon becomes the first former major leaguer to be killed in action in WWII.

- On June 10, the Reds use 15-year-old pitcher Joe Nuxhall, the youngest player in this century.

- Cards sweep 17 doubleheaders.

- Boudreau is involved in 134 DPs, a record for shortstops in a 154-game season.

- Ray Mueller sets NL record when he participates in 217 consecutive games as a catcher.

Etten Leads AL in HRs

If asked to rattle off the names of all the Yankees' home run and RBI kings, few will remember to mention Nick Etten. But his anonymity today notwithstanding, Etten was the Yankees' top slugger from 1943 to 1945, blasting an American League-high 22 home runs in 1944. He later played in the high minors until he was nearly age 40.

Joe DiMaggio

Joe Serves in Military

Staff sergeant Joe DiMaggio has his unit patch sewn on his uniform by Brigadier General William Floos. In DiMaggio's absence, Johnny Lindell manned center field for the Yankees in 1944. Lindell was drafted the following season, and the job fell to Tuck Stainback, who had not played regularly in the majors since 1934.

Nick Etten

McQuinn Tops Series Hitters

George McQuinn hit .438 for the Browns in the 1944 World Series. McQuinn had the dimmest future imaginable in the early 1930s. He played first base in the Yankees farm chain while Lou Gehrig played the position every day for the parent club.

George McQuinn

- Mueller sets an NL record for a 154-game season by catching in 155 games.
- At the end of August, the Cards have a 91-30 mark, but are only 14-19 the rest of the way.
- Tom Sunkel, the most successful one-eyed player in ML history, appears in his last ML game.

- Detroit rookie Chuck Hostetler, age 41, hits .298 in 90 games.
- NL wins All-Star Game 7-1 at Pittsburgh.
- On April 27 vs. Dodgers, Jim Tobin of Braves becomes first pitcher to hit a homer while tossing a no-hitter.

- On August 10, Red Barrett of Braves throws record-low 58 pitches in a CG shutout of Reds.
- Cincinnati's Clyde Shoun no-hits Braves on May 15.
- Stan Musial tops NL in doubles (51) and SA (.549), and ties for lead in hits (197).

Walker Tops NL at .357

The favorite player of many Brooklyn fans in the 1940s, Dixie Walker was nicknamed "The People's Cherce." He earned the most cheers in 1944 when he led the National League with a .357 average. However, Dixie overestimated his popularity with the Brooklyn management. When Walker declared in 1947 that he would not play on the same team with Jackie Robinson, Branch Rickey traded him to Pittsburgh.

World Series

Marion Homers in Game Two

Mort Cooper greets Marty Marion after the Cardinals shortstop's solo home run in game two of the 1943 World Series. Marion, who led the Cards in hitting in the 1943 classic, nonetheless batted eighth in the order for much of the 1944 season. The first eighth-place hitter to win an MVP Award, Marion collected 63 RBI while hitting .267.

Trout Shuts 'Em Out

Irv Haag wrote that Dizzy Trout "came by his nickname naturally." In 1944, striving to overhaul the Browns, Tigers manager Steve O'Neill started Trout in 40 games and used him in relief in nine more. The hurler won 27 games that year, posting an American League-high seven shutouts. Trout and his son Steve lead all father-son pairs in combined career wins.

Dizzy Trout

Dixie Walker

1944

- Nicholson leads NL in runs (116), runs produced (205), and total bases (317).

- Stirnweiss tops AL in runs (125) and ties for lead in triples (16).

- The Cards lead the majors in batting (.275), runs (772), homers (100), fielding (.982), and ERA (2.68).

- Washington's George Myatt goes 6-for-6 on May 1.

- Washington's Stan Spence goes 6-for-6 on June 1.

- Browns' pennant-clinching game is hurled by Sig Jakucki, out of majors since 1936.

- The Carpenter family assumes ownership of the Phillies.

- On August 29, the Braves' Damon Phillips is first third baseman since 1890 to make 11 assists in a nine-inning game.

- Hal Gregg of Brooklyn is first pitcher in ML history to fail to finish as many as 25 starts in a season.

World Series

Cards Win Series

Cardinals pitcher Ted Wilks (capless) is congratulated by teammates Walker Cooper *(right)* and Whitey Kurowski after his scoreless relief stint in game six handed the Cardinals the 1944 World Series. Wilks was 17–4 as a rookie that year. In 1946 and again in 1947, he pitched the entire season for the Cards without suffering a single loss (12–0 total).

World Series

Sanders Heads for Home

Cardinals on-deck hitter Augie Bergamo uses body language to speed teammate Ray Sanders across home plate in game two of the 1944 World Series. Sanders scored on a fly ball by Emil Verban for the Cards' second run in the contest. The umpire is Bill McGowan, who officiated a record 2,541 consecutive games over a 16½-year period without missing so much as a single inning.

Sportsman's Hosts Series

More than 30,000 fans pack Sportsman's Park to see the 1944 World Series, featuring the St. Louis Cardinals and the St. Louis Browns. Both teams played in the stadium during the regular season and, consequently, all of the World Series games were played there. Though the Browns owned the ballpark, the Cardinals won the Series, four games to two.

Kenesaw Mountain Landis

Commissioner Landis Dies

For years prior to his death in 1944, commissioner Kenesaw Mountain Landis had been regarded as the players' best friend, yet that did not mean all players. When asked by a chauffeur when he was going to let blacks play in the major leagues, the commissioner replied, "I can't do a damn thing about it, Art. It's up to the club owners."

Sportsman's Park

- The Senators finish last but only 25 games out of first—an AL record for closest margin between first place and last.

- Ed Heusser of Cincinnati leads the NL in ERA (2.38).

- Pirate Johnny Barrett leads the NL in steals (28) and triples (19).

- Yankee Johnny Lindell ties Stirnweiss for AL lead in triples (16) and edges him for league lead in total bases (297-296).

- Red Sox Bob Johnson leads the AL in OBP (.431) and runs produced (195).

- Johnson is edged by teammate Bobby Doerr for the SA lead, as both slug .528.

- Browns shortstop Vern Stephens leads the AL in RBI (109).

- Dick Wakefield returns from the armed forces and hits .355 for the Tigers, almost carrying them to the pennant.

- Stan Spence hits 18 of Washington's 33 home runs.

As in 1944, the Yankees, Senators, Browns, and Tigers were all still alive in the pennant race as summer turned to fall. But the balance of power shifted with the return of some of baseball's biggest stars from the war. Bob Feller returned to Cleveland, and Charlie Keller rejoined New York; but the player with the biggest impact on the '45 race was Detroit's Hank Greenberg.

The Tigers had been barely hanging on by the efforts of MVP Hal Newhouser, who went 25-9 with a 1.81 ERA to lead the league in wins and ERA, and fellow moundsmen Dizzy Trout and Al Benton, who was runner-up in ERA at 2.02. Greenberg homered in his first game and went on to swat 13 homers, score 47 runs, and drive in 60 in only 270 at-bats. He also batted .311 to lead his team into first place with two games to go in the season. Detroit needed one more victory against the Browns to clinch the flag.

Young Virgil Trucks, three days out of the Navy, pitched for the Tigers, and ace Nels Potter for St. Louis. It was 3-2 Browns in the ninth, when Potter walked the bases loaded to try for the double play with Greenberg. The 34-year-old slugger clouted his 11th career grandslam and Detroit finished at 88-65, 1^1/$_2$ games up on Washington, 6 ahead of St. Louis, and 6^1/$_2$ over the Yanks.

GREENBERG'S A HERO AS TIGERS TAKE TITLE

Despite the return of several big-name players, baseball 1945-style was still a ragged affair. Yankees second baseman Snuffy Stirnweiss took the batting title at .309, the lowest figure to lead either league since Elmer Flick did it with a .308 mark in 1905. St. Louis played a one-armed outfielder, Pete Gray, who hit .218 with six doubles in 77 games. Gray was no publicity stunt; he had been named Southern Association MVP in 1944 when he batted .333 with 68 stolen bases. Perhaps even more amazing than Gray was Senators pitcher Bert Shepard, who pitched five innings of one-run ball in 1945 after having lost his right leg in a wartime plane crash.

American League great Jimmie Foxx retired 89 games into the 1945 season with a .325 lifetime batting average. Foxx still ranks among the all-time leaders in home runs with 534 and RBI with 1,922, and he holds one of the highest slugging averages ever at .609.

The Chicago Cubs took the NL flag by 3 games over St. Louis, with lost Stan Musial to the Army for the entire season. The Cubs boasted MVP Phil Cavarretta, who hit a league-leading .355, scored 94 runs, and knocked in 97, as well as Stan Hack, who batted .323 and scored 110 times. The key to the Cubs' success was a pitching staff comprised of Ray Prim, Claude Passeau, and 22-10 Hank Wyse, who were first, second, and fifth in ERA. Right-hander Hank Borowy came via trade from the Yankees and went 11-2 with a 2.14 ERA in 14 starts.

As the teams prepared for the World Series, fans speculated on its outcome. When asked for his prediction, Chicago sportswriter Warren Brown said, "I don't think either of them can win."

As it turned out, the Cubs pitching failed them in a close, seven-game Series loss to Detroit. Tigers ace Newhouser went 2-1 with an ugly 6.10 ERA in his three starts, but Prim and Wyse were even worse for Chicago, going 0-1 with a 9.00 ERA and 0-1 with a 7.04 mark. Borowy won the opener 9-0 over Newhouser, but slumped to a 2-2 overall record and an ERA of 4.00 in his three starts and one relief outing. Greenberg was the Tigers' hitting hero, batting .304 with two homers and seven runs batted in.

1945

- Tigers win AL flag by 1^1/$_2$ games.
- Cubs triumph in NL.
- Tigers take World Series in seven games.
- Chicago's Phil Cavarretta leads all World Series hitters with .423 average.

- Hal Newhouser is knocked out of box in Series opener, but comes back to win two games, including decisive game seven.
- Hank Greenberg returns from service on July 1, hits grandslam on season's final day to clinch pennant for Detroit.
- Cavarretta named NL MVP.

- Newhouser wins second straight AL MVP.
- Boston's Tommy Holmes hits in 37 consecutive games, new modern NL record.
- Holmes is only player ever to lead league in homers (28) and fewest batter Ks (nine).

Hank Greenberg's three-run dinger provides the margin of victory in Detroit's 4–1 triumph in the second game of the 1945 World Series. On hand to welcome the Tigers slugger are Eddie Mayo (3), Doc Cramer (8), and Roy Cullenbine (6). Meanwhile, Cubs catcher Paul Gillespie jaws with umpire Lou Jordan.

- Yankee Snuffy Stirnweiss tops AL in BA at just .309.

- One-armed outfielder Pete Gray plays the full season for Browns, hitting .218.

- Washington is second in AL, loses shot at pennant when outfielder Bingo Binks loses fly ball in sun in season's final game.

- Brooklyn's Dixie Walker tops majors with 124 RBI and 218 runs produced.

- Walker is last RBI leader to hit fewer than ten homers.

- Stirnweiss tops AL with .476 SA, lowest in AL history by a leader.

- Stirnweiss leads AL in runs (107), hits (195), and triples (22).

- Newhouser tops majors with 25 wins, 1.81 ERA, 212 Ks, and 29 CGs.

- Newhouser tops AL in every major department for starting pitchers, and majors in all but win pct.

- Brooklyn's Branch Rickey signs Jackie Robinson to a contract.

Tommy Holmes

Hank Greenberg

Musial Gone, Cards Endure

With Stan Musial (pictured) gone in 1945, the Cardinals moved Johnny Hopp from center field to Musial's slot in right, stationed Buster Adams in center, and replaced the also-departed Danny Litwhiler in left with a rookie shortstop. The rookie was Red Schoendienst, who topped the National League in stolen bases in 1945 with 26. The following year, Red was moved to second base. Had Musial played in 1945, he probably would have tallied at least 170 hits. If so, he would have finished his career with more than 3,800 hits.

Greenberg Leads Tigers

Hank Greenberg's return from the army spelled a pennant for Detroit, as he racked up 13 home runs and 60 RBI in just 270 at-bats in 1945. The man who had been occupying Greenberg's left field post in the interim—Jimmy Outlaw—hit just 34 RBI in 446 at-bats.

Skein Ends for Holmes

Braves outfielder Tommy Holmes went hitless against the Cubs at Wrigley Field on July 12, 1945. His then-modern National League record streak of 37 consecutive games in which he hit safely came to an end that day against Hank Wyse. The previous pitcher to cipher Holmes was also a Cub—Claude Passeau, on June 2.

Stan Musial

1945

- Happy Chandler named new commissioner of baseball.

- All-Star Game not held due to war—only cancellation in history.

- On August 20, Dodgers shortstop Tommy Brown, age 17, becomes the youngest player in ML history to homer.

- Dick Fowler of A's no-hits Browns on Sept. 9.

- Cubs beat Cincinnati 21 times.

- Brooklyn's Eddie Stanky sets new NL record for walks with 148.

- Bert Shepard, a one-legged pitcher, appears in game for Washington.

- Senators hit only one home run in their home park—and that's an inside-the-park homer by Joe Kuhel.

- Boston's Boo Ferriss wins 21 games as a rookie, is second in AL in innings (265) and CGs (26).

- Ferriss sets an AL record when he's unscored upon in his first 22 innings in the majors.

Charlie Keller

One-Armed Gray Debuts, Hits .218

Pete Gray poses with his parents prior to a game in 1945. The one-armed outfielder was the Southern League's MVP in 1944, but could not cut it in the majors. He hit just .218 in his sole season in the bigs. Outfielders played him so shallow that many of his line drives and potential bloop hits were caught. When the stars returned from the armed forces in 1946, Gray was let go. Pete lost his arm in a truck accident as a child.

Keller Sparks Yankees

After two years of war duty, Charlie Keller's late-season return to the Yankees was an instant tonic. He hit .301 in 163 at-bats to finish out the season.

Shepard Pitches with One Leg

Bert Shepard was the only one-legged player in major league history. A pilot in World War II, he was outfitted with an artificial limb after losing his leg in combat. He allowed just one earned run in a five-and-one-third-inning relief stint for the Senators in 1945. It was the only major league game he ever pitched.

Bert Shepard

Pete Gray

- Philly's Andy Karl pitches 167 innings in relief to set NL record that will last until 1974.

- Karl ties with the Giants' Ace Adams for the most saves in ML (15).

- Jim Turner of the Yankees is the only AL player with more than five saves; he has ten.

- On July 21, Tigers and A's play to 1-1 tie in 24 innings—Les Mueller pitches 19^{2}/$_3$ innings for Detroit.

- Cubs sweep 20 doubleheaders to break their own year-old record.

- Cards lose Stan Musial and Walker Cooper to armed services prior to season, finish 3 games back of Cubs without them.

- Holmes tops NL in hits (224), doubles (47), total bases (367), and SA (.577).

- A's and Phils both end war years as they began them in 1941—in last place.

- AL hits just 430 homers—147 fewer than NL.

Snuffy Stirnweiss

Hal Newhouser

Newhouser Takes AL MVP

Before joining the Indians, Hal Newhouser toiled 15 seasons with the Tigers. Newhouser won his second straight MVP Award in 1945, going 25–9 and leading the American League in wins, complete games (29), innings (313), shutouts (eight), strikeouts (212), and ERA (1.81). He remains the only pitcher ever to win back-to-back MVP Awards.

Stirnweiss Takes AL Bat Title

Snuffy Stirnweiss won the 1945 American League batting crown by a single point over Tony Cuccinello of the White Sox (with a .309 average). Six points in back of Cuccinello was White Sox outfielder Johnny Dickshot, followed by Bobby Estalella of the A's and George Myatt of Washington. None of Stirnweiss's four closest pursuers ever again played enough in the majors to qualify for a batting title.

Happy's Term Not Much Fun

Happy Chandler's term as commissioner of baseball (1945 to 1951) was marred by several player insurrections that club owners thought he mishandled. When his time was up, they replaced him with Ford Frick, a man who could be counted on to do as they wanted.

Happy Chandler

1945

- Red Barrett, pitching for the Braves and Cardinals, leads the NL in wins with 23.

- Former major leaguer Harry O'Neill killed in Iwo Jima assault.

- Hall of Fame inducts Roger Bresnahan, Dan Brouthers, Fred Clarke, Jimmy Collins, Ed Delahanty, Hugh Duffy, and Hugh Jennings.

- Mike Kelly, Jim O'Rourke, and Wilbert Robinson inducted into Hall.

- Steve Gerkin of the A's, in his only season in the ML, sets AL season record for losses without a win when he goes 0-12.

- The A's score just 494 runs on the year.

- A rule is put in that says a player must have 400 at-bats to qualify for a bat title.

- Phillie Vince DiMaggio leads NL batters in Ks a record fourth straight year.

- Cincinnati's Eddie Miller leads NL shortstops in FA for the fifth time to tie the NL record.

1945

Stanky Tallies 148 Walks

Eddie Stanky hit .258 in 1945, led all National League second basemen in errors, and accumulated just 39 RBI. Nevertheless, he got an MVP vote, and he should have gotten a bunch more. In 1945, he became the first major league leader in walks to total more bases on balls (148) than hits (143). He also paced the NL in runs (128).

Eddie Stanky

Rickey Signs Robinson

Branch Rickey, one of the most progressive executives baseball has ever seen, made his boldest move ever in 1945. Rickey, then with the Dodgers, signed the first black player, Jackie Robinson, to a major league contract. Rickey soon signed other black stars—Roy Campanella and Don Newcombe among them—who contributed to the Dodger dynasty.

Branch Rickey

Fowler Hurls a No-Hitter

Chief Bender *(left)* joins Connie Mack in congratulating Dick Fowler *(right)* after his no-hitter against the Browns on September 9, 1945. Fowler's gem was the first hitless game by an A's pitcher since 1916. A severe bursitis condition plagued him all during his career and caused his early exit from the majors. His no-hitter was his only victory in 1945.

Chief Bender, Connie Mack, Dick Fowler

- On Sept. 17, Bill Nicholson makes an NL record ten putouts by a right fielder.

- Lon Warneke retires at end of the season with an ML record skein of 163 errorless games by a pitcher.

- Cleveland plays only 147 games, the fewest in history by a team on a 154-game schedule.

- Early in the season, Cards swap Mort Cooper to Braves for Barrett and $100,000.

- In July, Cubs buy Hank Borowy from the Yankees for $97,000.

- Borowy wins 21 games—ten in the AL and 11 in the NL.

- In December, Cleveland sends Jeff Heath to Washington for George Case.

- Brooklyn has three of the four top run-scorers in the majors: Stanky (128), Goody Rosen (126), and Augie Galan (114).

- Dodgers lead ML in runs (795).

WILLIAMS
SHIFT TIES TED
IN KNOTS

Coming off four years of military service, Ted Williams started the 1946 season on fire, as the Red Sox built a huge lead before coasting to a 12-game lead over Detroit at the wire. Even though Williams's final stats look good (.342 average, 38 home runs, and 123 RBI), the Red Sox MVP did most of his damage early.

Cleveland manager Lou Boudreau contributed to Williams's poor second half when he introduced the "Ted Williams over-shift" in the second game of a July 14 doubleheader. Williams had homered three times in the opener, and when he came to bat in the second game, he faced a defense in which every man was stationed to the right of second base except the left fielder, who played deep short. Williams was laughing so hard that he had to step out of the batter's box to regain his composure.

The shift became less funny as the season wore on and other managers copied it—though the Red Sox slugger did get a measure of revenge by clinching the AL flag for Boston with an opposite-field, inside-the-park homer against Cleveland on September 13. Many AL teams simply pitched around Williams, as evidenced by his 156 walks. Other Red Soxers picked up the slack. Johnny Pesky and Dom DiMaggio batted over .300 (.335 and .316, respectively); Rudy York and Bobby Doerr knocked in over 100 RBI (119, 116).

Washington's Mickey Vernon took the AL batting title at .353, and Detroit's Hank Greenberg led in homers with 44 and RBI with 127. The Tigers' Hal Newhouser won his second straight ERA title at 1.94, and Bob Feller struck out 348, the most in the majors since 1904.

The National League race was disrupted when several players from contending teams jumped to the Mexican League, where the Pasquel brothers were offering underpaid American major leaguers huge increases in salary. Brooklyn's Mickey Owen and Luis Olmo and Giants Danny Gardella and Sal Maglie were among the first to go. The Cardinals lost pitcher Max Lanier, who started the 1946 season 6-0 with a 1.93 ERA, and came close to losing hitting star Stan Musial. Commissioner Happy Chandler discouraged others from leaving by threatening the jumping players with five-year suspensions from the majors. He later issued an amnesty in 1949.

The NL race came down to a season-long battle between St. Louis and Brooklyn. The Dodgers led by 7 1/2 in July, but again faded down the stretch. The two teams finished in a tie to set the stage for the first NL pennant playoff, a best-of-three affair.

MVP Musial and Enos Slaughter were the twin engines that powered the Cardinals' attack. Musial batted a league-leading .365, and also led in runs with 124, doubles with 50, and triples with 20; the .300-hitting Slaughter scored 100 runs and drove in a league-high 130. With Lanier gone, Howie Pollet became St. Louis' ace, going 21-10 with an NL-low 2.10 ERA.

The Dodgers were led by Pete Reiser, who stole a league-leading 34 bases; Dixie Walker, who had 116 RBI; and second baseman Eddie Stanky, who drew 137 walks to lead the NL in on-base average at .436. But it was all for naught. St. Louis won the playoff in two games on Pollet's 4-2 complete-game defeat of Ralph Branca in game one, and an 8-1 drubbing in game two.

The Cardinals also won the World Series in seven well-pitched games. York's tenth-inning homer won game one for the Red Sox, and the teams exchanged victories until the final game. With the score 3-3 in the top of the eighth, the slumping Williams popped up to leave the go-ahead run on second. In the bottom half, Slaughter singled and scored the winning run on a two-out single to left-center by Harry Walker.

1946

- Red Sox win their first flag since 1918.
- Cards cop their fourth NL flag in five years.
- Cards defeat Dodgers two games to none in first pennant playoff in ML history.

- Cards win most exciting World Series since 1926 in seven games.
- Harry Brecheen wins three Series games for Cards.
- Enos Slaughter scores winning run in game seven of Series by coming all the way home from first on a single by Harry Walker.

- Ted Williams and Stan Musial hit .200 and .222, respectively, in their only fall confrontation.
- Walker leads all World Series players with a .412 BA and six RBI.
- Williams is selected AL MVP.
- Musial named NL MVP.

The Cardinals use the "Williams Shift," devised by Cleveland manager Lou Boudreau, to combat pull-hitter Ted Williams in the 1946 World Series. In actuality, the Williams Shift, which featured three infielders stationed on the right side of the diamond, had first been used back in 1922—to combat lefty pull-hitters Cy Williams of the Phillies and Ken Williams of the Browns.

- AL wins most one-sided All-Star Game in history 12-0 at Fenway, as Williams hits two homers.

- Bob Feller fans 348 in first full year back from Navy.

- Hal Newhouser and Feller tie for ML lead with 26 wins.

- Feller's 36 CGs are the most by an ML pitcher since the end of the dead-ball era.

- Boo Ferriss of the Red Sox wins 25 games.

- Washington's Mickey Vernon leads AL in batting at .353.

- Pirate Ralph Kiner is first rookie to lead NL in homers, hits just 23.

- Hank Greenberg leads majors with 44 homers and AL with 127 RBI.

- Greenberg is the first in ML history to hit 40 homers with under a .300 average.

Pirates Owners

Forbes Field Gets Facelift

The new Pirates owners and manager Billy Herman *(right)* look over the plans for renovating Forbes Field. Principal owner John Galbreath is at far left, and Bing Crosby beside him. Both were astute enough to realize that, with the coming of Ralph Kiner, it was time to bring in the left-field wall of Forbes Field.

Mickey Vernon

Brecheen Rises in Series

In the 1946 World Series, Harry Brecheen ceded the Red Sox just one run in 20 innings and became the last National League lefty to win three games in a fall classic. Brecheen was a consistent winner during his eight seasons in the minors, but was judged too small to succeed up top. However, the war-time pitching shortage caused the Cards to reconsider. He went 15-15 for them during the 1946 regular season.

Harry Brecheen

Vernon Wins AL Bat Title

In the 20 seasons Mickey Vernon played, he won two batting titles (.353 in 1946, .337 in 1953) yet cleared the .300 mark just five times. Four of them came when he was past 35 years old. Asked about Vernon, Satchel Paige said, "I've faced the best in the world just about, but I never could get Mickey out."

1946

- Musial tops majors in batting (.365), hits (228), and triples (20).

- Musial tops NL in runs (124), doubles (50), total bases (366), and SA (.587).

- Mexican League lures several ML stars by offering them more money than majors are paying.

- Jackie Robinson becomes first black American to play a full season in OB in this century.

- In January, the Giants buy Walker Cooper from Cards for $175,000.

- A four-man group, including John Galbreath and Bing Crosby, buy Pirates.

- Buddy Rosar of the A's becomes the first regular catcher with a perfect 1.000 FA for a season.

- Buddy Kerr of the Giants sets a new FA record for shortstops (.982).

- On May 28, the first night game is played at Yankee Stadium.

Kiner Leads NL in Homers

Ralph Kiner's minor league performance offered no hint that he would win the National League home run crown his rookie year. Furthermore, his 23 round-trippers tied Johnny Rizzo's club record, set in 1938 when Rizzo was also a rookie. Ironically, Rizzo was back in the minors in 1946 and was never heard from again.

Stan Musial

Musial Posts Three Highs

In 1946, home runs were so scarce in the National League that Stan Musial tied for fifth in the four-bagger derby with just 16. But he led the circuit in hits (228), doubles (50), and triples (20) by such a wide margin that his 366 total bases were 83 more than the NL runner-up, teammate Enos Slaughter, collected. Musial also led the league in batting at a robust .365.

Ralph Kiner

- Larry MacPhail is named the new Yankees general manager.

- On July 27, Rudy York of the Red Sox hits two grandslams.

- Johnny Schmitz of the Cubs tops the NL with just 135 Ks.

- Players form the American Baseball Guild in fourth attempt to unionize.

- Guild helps raise minimum ML salary to $5,000.

- Bill Kennedy of Rocky Mount in the Coastal Plains League fans 456 hitters and has a 28-3 record with a 1.03 ERA.

- On June 9, the Giants' Mel Ott becomes first manager to be ejected from both games of a doubleheader.

- Brooklyn's Pete Reiser steals home an NL record seven times in a season.

- Reiser breaks an ankle with two weeks left in the season, possibly costing the Dodgers the pennant.

- Joe Cronin of Red Sox is first to manage two different AL teams to flags.

Cards Take NL Flag

Dodger catcher Bruce Edwards sheds his mask as Marty Marion of the Cardinals lifts a pop fly in the 1946 playoff series for the National League pennant. The Cardinals had to watch the scoreboard when they lost to the Cubs on closing day of the season; St. Louis had to hope that former Cardinal Mort Cooper could beat the Dodgers and get them a tie. He did, 4–0. The Cards also won the playoff.

National League Pennant Playoff Series

Williams Hits Through Shift

One has to wonder how much the "Williams Shift" affected the lifetime stats of Ted Williams. From 1946 on, opponents regularly applied the shift, and Williams still pulled the ball in their direction, hitting .342 in '46. Williams was also hurt by the deep right field fence in Fenway Park, as well as the nearly five years he lost to armed service. Still, he hit .344 with 525 homers in his career.

Bob Feller

Feller Racks Up 348 Strikeouts

Bob Feller struck out 348 batters in 1946. He would have fanned even more had he been able to pitch against his teammates. In 1946, Cleveland batters fanned only 16 fewer times than the Browns, the most strikeout-prone team in the majors. Feller, who won 26 games and spun a no-hitter in 1946, overpowered hitters with his curve, his slider, and, of course, his blazing fastball. Manager Bucky Harris once told his team how to bat against Feller: "Go up and hit what you see. And if you don't see anything, come on back."

Ted Williams

1946

- Red Sox win 104 games in 1946 after winning just 71 in 1945.
- Feller no-hits Yankees on April 30.
- Ed Head of Brooklyn no-hits Braves on April 23.
- Newhouser tops ML in ERA (1.94), is second in AL MVP vote.

- Cardinal Howie Pollet is NL ERA king (2.10) and also tops the NL in wins (21).
- Williams tops AL in SA (.677), total bases (343), runs (142), runs produced (227), OBP (.497), and walks (156).
- Detroit's George Kell goes 6-for-6 on Sept. 20.

- Bill Veeck serves his first full season as owner of the Indians.
- Walter Johnson dies.
- Braves get Bob Elliott from Pirates for four players.
- Cleveland trades Allie Reynolds to the Yankees for Joe Gordon and Eddie Bockman.

Walker Hits .412 in Series

Harry Walker hit .412 in the 1946 World Series and got the hit that won the championship for the Cardinals, but his performance failed to atone for his .236 average during the season. The following spring, he was shipped to the Phils. Walker became the first player to win a batting crown during a season in which he was traded (.363 in the '47 season).

Harry Walker

Mexican Prexy Manages Too

Mexican League president Jorge Pasquel holds seven-year-old Charley Owen. Pasquel sits on the bench of his Vera Cruz team after he took over as manager from Charley's father, former Brooklyn catcher Mickey Owen. On Pasquel's right is Danny Gardella, whose suit against organized baseball resulted in the reinstatement of most of the disbarred players.

Warren Spahn, Johnny Sain

Spahn, Sain: Boston's Best

Both Warren Spahn *(left)* and Johnny Sain debuted with the Braves in 1942, missed 1943 through 1945 due to the war, and rejoined the Braves in 1946. From 1946 through 1951, Boston boasted a 20-game winner—be it Spahn or Sain. The rest of the staff, unfortunately, never measured up to the two aces, inspiring fans to chant, "Spahn and Sain and pray for rain."

Jorge Pasquel

- Cleveland trades Sherm Lollar and Ray Mack to the Yankees for Gene Bearden, Hal Peck, and Al Gettel.

- Tigers trade Barney McCosky to the A's for Kell.

- McCosky is the only AL regular who Feller fails to fan in 1946.

- A group headed by Lou Perini buys the Braves.

- Bill Thomas, winningest pitcher in minor league history, is banned after the season in a gambling probe (he's later reinstated).

- On May 8, Boston's Johnny Pesky becomes the first ALer to score six runs in a game.

- Pesky leads AL in hits (208) in his first year back from armed service.

- On July 14, Lou Boudreau becomes the first player in the 20th century to collect five extra-base hits in a nine-inning game.

- An all-time record 52 minor leagues begin the season.

Nineteen-forty-seven, the year of Jackie Robinson and the first televised World Series, began with another controversy—the Leo Durocher affair. Although he was the fall guy in an ongoing feud between Dodgers GM Branch Rickey and Yankees executive Larry MacPhail, Durocher also got himself in trouble with the commissioner's office for associating with gamblers and unsavory types like actor George Raft and gangster Bugsy Siegel. Durocher received a year's suspension for "an accumulation of unpleasant incidents." Burt Shotton took over as Brooklyn's manager for the 1947 season, and Durocher's career as a Dodger came to an end in mid-1948, when he moved to New York as manager of the Giants.

All this momentarily distracted baseball fans from the Dodgers' purchase of first baseman Robinson from Montreal. Robinson opened the season as the first black major leaguer since the Walker brothers, Fleet and Welday, who played in the American Association in the 1880s. To add to the obvious pressure on Robinson, many of his teammates were initially malevolent. After a group of them signed a protest petition during spring training—to which Rickey and Durocher responded by offering to trade any player who wished to go—the general attitude of the team mellowed to cold indifference. For weeks, none of them sat near

JACKIE'S A SMASH IN BIG LEAGUE DEBUT

Robinson; some refused even to speak to him. Things changed when Robinson's aggressive, running brand of baseball helped move Brooklyn into first.

Robinson hit .297, scored a team-high 125 runs, and led the NL in stolen bases with 29. He was voted Rookie of the Year. With Robinson, Pee Wee Reese, and .300 hitters Dixie Walker and Pete Reiser—and without a legitimate power threat—the Dodgers led the league in stolen bases and on-base average on their way to a 94-60 record.

Philadelphia's Harry Walker (Dixie's brother) won the batting title at .363, and New York's Johnny Mize and Pittsburgh's Ralph Kiner shared the league lead in homers with 51. Boston third baseman Bob Elliott, who hit .317 and drove in 113 runs, was named NL MVP.

A reunited Yankees team scored the most runs in the AL (794), allowed the fewest (568), and ran away with the flag by 12 games over Detroit. While defending champion Boston stumbled due to injuries, New York tied an

AL record with a 19-game winning streak and never looked back. MVP Joe DiMaggio hit .315 with 97 runs, 97 RBI, and 61 extra-base hits, and Tommy Henrich drove in 98 runs on 35 doubles and an AL-high 13 triples. Allie Reynolds went 19-8, and reliever Joe Page compiled a 2.49 ERA and 17 saves.

Another great Ted Williams season went for naught; he won the Triple Crown with a .343 average, 32 home runs, and 114 RBI. He also led in runs with 125 and drew the most walks, 162. Cleveland debuted the first black player in American League history, Larry Doby, on July 4, and the St. Louis Browns followed suit with Hank Thompson and Willard Brown.

Yankees pitcher Spud Chandler retired in 1947 with the highest winning percentage in history, .717. Also retiring were Mel Ott, who ranked among all-time leaders in homers (511), walks (1,708), runs (1,859), and RBI (1,860); and Hank Greenberg, who owned a career slugging mark of .605.

New York defeated Brooklyn in a seven-game World Series, as Spec Shea went 2-0 with an ERA of 2.35 and Johnny Lindell drove in seven runs. The highlight of the Series was game four, when Bill Bevens took a no-hitter into the ninth inning. With two outs and two on, pinch hitter Cookie Lavagetto doubled to win the game for Brooklyn, 3-2.

1947

- Yanks take AL flag by 12 games.
- Dodgers win NL pennant.
- Yanks win exciting, but erratically played, World Series in seven games.
- Yankee Bill Bevens comes within one out of no-hitter in game four of Series, loses game on two-run double by Cookie Lavagetto.

- Dodger Al Gionfriddo makes great catch to rob Joe DiMaggio of homer in game five of Series.
- Reliever Hugh Casey wins two games in Series for Dodgers, saves their third win.
- Johnny Lindell leads Yanks in Series with a .500 average and seven RBI.

- On Oct. 2, Yankee Yogi Berra hits the first pinch homer in World Series history.
- DiMaggio wins AL MVP by one vote over Ted Williams, 202 to 201.
- Bob Elliott wins the NL MVP—the first Brave to do so since 1914.

Jackie Robinson catches even the Dodgers hitter by surprise with his steal
of home. Despite tremendous adversity, Robinson hit .297 in 1947, led the league
in steals with 29, was named National League Rookie of the Year,
and sparked the Dodgers to the pennant.

- Williams again wins Triple Crown, batting .343 with 32 homers and 114 RBI.
- Williams leads AL in runs (125), total bases (335), runs produced (207), walks (162), OBP (.499), and slugging (.634).
- Yanks tie AL record by winning 19 straight games.

- Brooklyn's Jackie Robinson, the first black American to play in an ML game in this century, goes 0-for-3 in his debut.
- Robinson wins Baseball Writers Association of America's first Rookie of the Year Award, as he posts a .297 average.

- Harry Walker of Phils, sent to them by the Cards, becomes first player traded in midseason to win NL bat crown (.363).
- Cincinnati's Ewell Blackwell no-hits Braves on June 18, pitches eight hitless innings in his next start.
- Johnny Mize and Ralph Kiner again tie for NL homer crown with 51.

DiMaggio Named AL MVP

Joe DiMaggio (.315, 20 home runs, 97 RBI) displays his 1947 American League MVP Award. Triple Crown-winner Ted Williams lost the plaque to DiMaggio by a single vote. Williams would have won the award had he not personally alienated many of the voters. In 1947, the Yankee Clipper became the first outfielder or first baseman to win the prize without leading his league in any of the Triple Crown departments.

Ewell Blackwell

Joe DiMaggio

Blackwell Triumphs in 22

Ewell "The Whip" Blackwell had a sidearm delivery so devastating that righthanded hitters begged out by the hordes on days he pitched. Blackwell went 22–8 in 1947. A kidney ailment sidelined him in 1948, and he was never the same. Like many former National League stars, he was acquired on waivers by the Yankees to aid them in a late-season pennant drive.

1947

- Kiner hits a record eight home runs in a four-game stretch.

- Mize scores at least one run in an NL record 16 straight games.

- Giant teammates Mize and Willard Marshall combine for 87 homers, setting NL teammate tandem record.

- Walker Cooper hits 35 homers for the Giants.

- Bobby Thomson chips in 29 homers for the Giants, a new club rookie record.

- Giants hit 221 homers, a new ML record (since broken).

- Giants rookie Larry Jansen goes 21-5, topping the NL in win pct. (.808).

- Brooklyn manager Leo Durocher suspended for year by commissioner Happy Chandler for associating with gamblers.

- Larry Doby debuts with Cleveland on July 5 to break color line in AL.

Boudreau: 45 Doubles

Lou Boudreau

Thirty-year-old Lou Boudreau, completing his sixth year as Cleveland's player/manager, led the American League in doubles with 45 in 1947. After buying the Indians in '46, Bill Veeck had planned to fire Boudreau as manager, but public sentiment changed his mind. It's a good thing. Boudreau led the Tribe to a flag in 1948.

Harry Walker

Ralph Kiner, Johnny Mize

Kiner, Mize Hit 51 HRs

In 1947, both Ralph Kiner (*left*) and Johnny Mize made a run at Hack Wilson's National League home run record of 56 dingers before ending in a tie for the crown with 51 four-baggers apiece. Three of Mize's New York Giants teammates—Willard Marshall, Walker Cooper, and rookie Bobby Thomson—rounded out the top five finishers.

Walker Takes NL Bat Title

After hitting .237 in 1946, the Cardinals were looking to dump Harry Walker. And on May 3, 1947, they shipped him and Freddy Schmidt to the Phillies for Ron Northey. Walker's bat caught fire in Philly and he ended up leading the National League in batting (.363). It was the only time in his career that he hit above .318.

- Dodgers set new NL attendance record.

- Attendance everywhere is at an all-time high as post-war baseball boom is in full swing.

- AL wins All-Star Game 2-1 at Wrigley.

- Hank Greenberg, AL reigning homer and RBI king, sold prior to 1947 season to Pittsburgh for $75,000.

- Greenberg ties for the NL lead in walks (104) in his final season.

- Greenberg persuades Pittsburgh brass to shorten the fences in Forbes Field, which boosts Kiner's career.

- Red Sox get Vern Stephens and Jack Kramer from Browns for six players and $310,000.

- Spud Chandler retires holding ML record for the highest career win pct. (.717)—minimum 100 career wins.

- Don Black of Cleveland no-hits A's on July 10.

World Series

Yankees Win in Seven

Yankees players race for the dugout as ushers set up a protective cordon after the last out of the 1947 World Series. Despite the see-saw quality of the Series and its many memorable moments, the crowd at Yankee Stadium for the seventh game fell several thousand short of being a sellout.

Wynn Just Breaks Even

Early Wynn managed a 17–15 record on a Washington team that went 64–90 in 1947. For the most part, Wynn pitched well for his six-plus seasons with the Senators, though he fell apart in 1948 (8–19, 5.82 ERA).

Early Wynn

Bob Elliott

Elliott Named NL MVP

In 1947, Bob Elliott of the Braves became the first third sacker in history to win an MVP Award. He hit .317 with 22 homers and 113 RBI that year. Elliott was a right fielder until 1942 when the Pirates needed a replacement for Jeep Handley, who had been drafted.

1947

- Bill McCahan of A's no-hits Washington on Sept. 3.
- Dan Bankhead of Dodgers is first black to pitch in ML.
- Blackwell wins 16 straight games, a Cincinnati club record.
- Las Vegas team in the Sunset League hits OB record 270 home runs.

- Mize tops NL in RBI (138), runs (137), and runs produced (224).
- Blackwell leads NL in wins (22), CGs (23), and Ks (193).
- Warren Spahn tops NL in ERA (2.33), innings (290), and shutouts (seven), and posts 21 wins.

- The Hall of Fame inducts Carl Hubbell, Lefty Grove, Frankie Frisch, and Mickey Cochrane.
- Athletic Hank Majeski's .988 FA is a new ML record for third basemen.
- Phils trade Ken Raffensberger and Hugh Poland to the Reds for Al Lakeman.

Casey Alone Can't Stop Yanks

Reliever Hugh Casey worked in six of the seven games in the 1947 World Series and tallied an 0.87 ERA. The other Dodger hurlers were not nearly so baffling to the Yankees. Joe DiMaggio and George McQuinn (scoring here) and the other Yankees combed the rest of the Brooklyn staff for 6.52 earned runs per game.

World Series

World Series

Berra Miffed in Series

Dodger Hugh Casey stands impassively as Yogi Berra heatedly argues with umpire Ed Rommel. Rommel ruled that Casey did not interfere with the Yankee catcher's effort to catch his pop fly bunt in game three of the 1947 World Series. New York skipper Bucky Harris *(to Berra's right)* is adding his two cents worth. Berra had a frustrating Series, as he batted a mere .158 (3-for-19) with two RBI. This was the first of a record 14 fall classics in which Berra participated. He hit just .150 in his first three Series, but .306 in his last 11. He holds the all-time Series records for games played (75), at-bats (71), hits (71), and doubles (ten).

- Phils trade Ron Northey to the Cards for Harry Walker and Freddy Schmidt.

- Red Sox swap Rudy York to the White Sox for Jake Jones.

- Prior to the season, the Dodgers send five players to Pittsburgh for Al Gionfriddo and cash.

- Pirates send Billy Cox, Preacher Roe, and Gene Mauch to Brooklyn for Dixie Walker and two pitchers.

- In spring of 1947, the Dodgers train in Cuba for the last time.

- After the World Series, GM Larry MacPhail is fired by the Yankees for brawling in public.

- Al Lopez retires holding the record for most games at catcher—1,918 (since broken).

- Bob Feller tops the AL in wins (20), Ks (196), innings (299), and shutouts (five).

- Detroit's Roy Cullenbine walks in an ML record 22 straight games.

Baseball came within one game of having an all-Boston World Series in 1948, as the Braves went 91-62 to take the NL flag by 6 1/2 games over St. Louis, and the Red Sox finished the regular season tied with Cleveland at 96-58.

The star of the National League was 27-year-old, second-time MVP Stan Musial, who turned in the finest all-around year of his career. "Stan the Man" led the NL in batting at .376, runs with 135, and RBI with 131. He also led the league in hits with 230, total bases with 429, doubles with 46, triples with 18, on-base average at .450, and slugging at .702. He came within one home run of leading the NL in every major offensive category, as Johnny Mize and Ralph Kiner tied for the league lead in homers with 40.

The Braves were led by Bob Elliott—who hit 23 homers and drew 131 walks—and .300 hitters Eddie Stanky, Al Dark, Tommy Holmes, Mike McCormick, and Jeff Heath. On the pitching side, the Boston fans' cry was "Spahn and Sain and two days of rain." Thirty-year-old righty Johnny Sain went 24-15 to lead the NL in wins, complete games with 28, and innings with 315. Warren Spahn, 27, went 15-12 with 16 complete games and 257 innings. No other Braves pitcher won more than 13 games. Apparently, there were enough rain-outs that Boston led the NL in team ERA,

IT'S SPAHN AND SAIN, BUT INDIANS REIGN

complete games, and fewest walks allowed.

The AL race was still up for grabs at the All-Star break among Cleveland, Philadelphia, New York, and Boston. New York's Joe DiMaggio led the AL in home runs with 39 and RBI with 155, and the Yanks' Tommy Henrich led in runs with 138 and triples with 14. But as the second half wore on, the best hitting team, Boston, and the best pitching team, Cleveland, rose to the top.

The Red Sox featured batting champion Ted Williams, whose home run total slipped to 25, third on his own team behind Bobby Doerr's 27 and Vern Stephens's 29. The Sox also fielded Dom DiMaggio, who hit 40 doubles and scored 127 runs, and Johnny Pesky, who was tied with Williams for third in the AL in runs with 124.

Williams batted .369, but lost out in the MVP voting to Cleveland shortstop Lou Boudreau, who was runner-up in batting at .355. Cleveland also boasted second baseman Joe Gordon, who hit 32 home runs; third baseman Ken Keltner, who had

his peak year with 31 homers and 119 RBI; and outfielder Dale Mitchell, who batted .336.

But the Indians main strength, like the Braves', was pitching. Unlike their NL rivals, however, the Indians staff was a deep one. The Tribe featured two 20-game winners in Gene Bearden and Bob Lemon, a 19-game winner in Bob Feller, and spot starters Steve Gromek, Sam Zoldak, and Satchel Paige (who went a combined 24-10). Cleveland owner Bill Veeck was widely ridiculed for pitching Paige, the former Negro League star (his exact age is unknown, but he was definitely pitching for the Birmingham Black Barons in 1928). Paige quieted his critics, however, by going 6-1 with a 2.47 ERA.

A coin flip determined that the one-game AL pennant playoff would be played at Boston's Fenway Park. And almost 30 years to the day before Bucky Dent's famous home run over the Green Monster, shortstop Boudreau won the pennant for the Indians with two home runs.

Cleveland then proceeded to make it a clean sweep of Boston, polishing off the Braves in the World Series. Cleveland's Feller went 0-2, but the Indians beat the Braves in six games on great pitching performances by Bearden (who pitched a shutout in game three), Gromek (who posted one win and a 1.00 ERA), and Lemon (who triumphed in two games).

1948

- Indians win first flag since 1920.

- Braves take first NL flag since 1914.

- Indians ruin all-Boston World Series by defeating Red Sox in first pennant playoff game in AL history.

- Indians win World Series in six games.

- Johnny Sain beats Bob Feller 1-0 in game one of Series.

- In game one of Series, Boston's Phil Masi scores the lone run after being ruled safe on a pickoff play at second, though replays show he's out.

- Gene Bearden is Series hero, winning game three and saving the final game in relief of Bob Lemon.

- Indians win Series despite team BA of .199.

- Cleveland's Lou Boudreau is AL MVP—last player/manager to win the award and the last to win a World Series.

- Stan Musial named NL MVP.

Lou Boudreau, the player/manager of the victorious Indians, is surrounded by writers following the 1948 World Series. The final game, played at Boston on October 11, was Cleveland's last win in postseason action and also the last postseason contest the Braves played while in Boston.

- Brave Al Dark named Rookie of the Year and is third in NL MVP vote.
- Musial misses Triple Crown by margin of just one home run.
- Ralph Kiner and Johnny Mize again tie for NL homer crown with 40.
- Sain tops majors with 24 wins.

- Ted Williams tops AL in BA (.369), SA (.615), and OBP (.497).
- Rookie Bearden wins 20 games for Cleveland, tops AL in ERA (2.43), and wins the pennant playoff game vs. Red Sox.
- Indians become first team in ML history to draw more than two million at home.

- The Negro National League disbands, as most of its top players have jumped to the majors.
- Boudreau tops AL shortstops in FA for the eighth time to tie a loop record.
- AL wins All-Star Game 5-2 at St. Louis.

Stan the Man Shines Again

Stan Musial's 1948 season ranks among the ten greatest in history (.376 average, 39 home runs, 131 RBI). What made it even more amazing was that, with the exception of Enos Slaughter, Musial got very little help from other Cardinals batters. On the mound, Harry Brecheen (20–7, 2.24 ERA) had a similar kind of year for the Redbirds.

Last Respects to Babe Ruth

World Mourns Death of Ruth

Baseball fans, young and old, file past the bier of Babe Ruth in the rotunda of Yankee Stadium on August 18, 1948, to say farewell to the greatest slugger in the game's history. Ruth died of throat cancer at the age of 53. At Ruth's burial, on a hot day, ex-teammate Joe Dugan whispered, "I'd give a lot for a cold beer about now." Waite Hoyt confided, "So would the Babe."

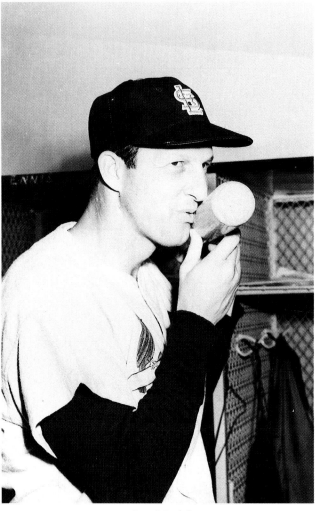

Stan Musial

1948

- The Pirates make a record 19 outfield putouts on July 5.

- Eddie Joost of the A's sets a new AL record when he leads off six games with home runs.

- Pittsburgh's Johnny Riddle, age 42, catches for his brother Elmer in an ML game for the first time.

- Phillies rookie Richie Ashburn leads NL in steals (32).

- Cleveland's Russ Christopher, the AL's saves leader with 17, retires after the season because of a heart condition.

- Hal Newhouser leads the AL in wins with 21.

- Yankee Tommy Henrich leads the AL in runs (138) and triples (14).

- Feller leads majors in Ks with 164.

- Boudreau is first shortstop in AL history to hit over .350 and drive in more than 100 runs in the same season.

Gene Bearden

Bearden Wins AL Flag

Indians lefthander Gene Bearden is airborne after his stunning 8–3 win over the Red Sox in the first pennant playoff game in American League history. Johnny Berardino, later a star of the soap opera *General Hospital,* is to Bearden's rear right. In the background, Larry Doby shakes hands with catcher Jim Hegan.

Ted, Doerr: Unbeatable Duo

Ted Williams *(left)* and Bobby Doerr combined with shortstop Vern Stephens to produce 81 home runs and 375 RBI for the Red Sox in 1948. The trio was largely responsible for Boston tallying 67 more runs than Cleveland, even though the Tribe both outhit and outhomered the Red Sox by a substantial margin.

Ted Williams, Bobby Doerr

Pat Seerey

Seerey Smacks Four HRs

Pat Seerey smooches the bat that produced four home runs for him on July 18, 1948. Teammate Luke Appling *(left of Seerey)* pats Pat on the back. Seerey, a 200-pound slugger with a 200-inch hole in his swing, was the American League whiff leader in every one of the four seasons that he played 100 or more games. Though he cracked four four-baggers in this game, he hit just 15 more during the rest of the season.

- In the AL playoff game, Boudreau goes 4-for-4.

- Cleveland owner Bill Veeck signs Satchel Paige.

- Paige is the first black American to pitch in the AL and the first to pitch in a World Series game.

- Veeck holds a special night for a fan, Joe Early, after Early writes Veeck inquiring why players are always honored and not the fans.

- Babe Ruth dies of throat cancer.

- Casey Stengel, manager of the Oakland Oaks of the PCL, is hired to manage Yankees in 1949.

- White Sox Pat Seerey hits four homers in an 11-inning game on July 18.

- Boston's Dom DiMaggio sets an AL record (since broken) with 503 outfield putouts.

- Musial gets 429 total bases, the most by any ML player since Jimmie Foxx's 438 in 1932.

World Series Heroes

Tribe Wins Series in Six

A shot of the heroes of Cleveland's World Series-clinching win in 1948 *(left to right):* Joe Gordon, who hit a key home run; winning pitcher Bob Lemon; shortstop/manager Lou Boudreau; and Gene Bearden, who relieved Lemon in the eighth inning and stifled a Braves rally to earn the save.

World Series

Mitchell Scores in Series

Cleveland on-deck hitter Joe Gordon signals to Dale Mitchell that he can score standing up on Lou Boudreau's double. The tally was the Indians' first run in game four of the 1948 World Series, won by the Tribe 2–1 behind Steve Gromek. A record 81,897 attended the game; the next day, a new record of 86,288 was set.

Dark Named ROTY

Shortstop Alvin Dark, who batted .322 with 39 doubles and 85 runs, was the controversial choice for Rookie of the Year in 1948. With only one award given for both leagues, Dark beat out Richie Ashburn, who hit .333 and led the majors in steals, as well as Gene Bearden, who won 20 games for Cleveland.

Alvin Dark

1948

- Musial gets five hits in a game four times during the season.

- Cleveland's Joe Gordon hits an AL record 32 homers by a second baseman.

- Snuffy Stirnweiss's .993 FA is a new ML record for second basemen.

- Lemon no-hits Detroit on June 30.

- Brooklyn's Rex Barney no-hits the Giants on Sept. 9.

- The A's win 84 games, their best season between 1933 and 1969.

- Cardinal Harry Brecheen tops NL in win pct. (.741), ERA (2.24), Ks (149), and shutouts (seven).

- Lemon leads AL in innings (294), CGs (20), and shutouts (ten).

- Joe DiMaggio tops AL in RBI (155), homers (39), and total bases (355).

- St. Louis' Bob Dillinger paces AL in hits (207) and steals (28).

- Cleveland tops AL in BA (.282), ERA (3.22), and FA (.982).

Ashburn Hits .333 in Debut

Richie Ashburn

Few players have batted .300 in both their first season and their last season. Richie Ashburn was one of them. Ashburn debuted with a .333 average in 1948, leading the National League in steals (32). He led the league in batting twice. In his final season, 1962, he hit .306 with the Mets.

Barney Enjoys Final Thrill

After years of struggling to acquire control, Rex Barney seemed right on the verge of putting it all together in a big way in 1948 (he went 15–13 that season with a 3.10 ERA). Instead, he regressed—so enormously that he was gone from the majors by 1950. In the 1949 World Series, Barney started the final game but was lifted in the third inning after issuing six walks. Barney's big moment came on September 9, 1948, when he no-hit the Giants.

Rex Barney

Satchel Paige

Paige, 42, Goes 6–1

Cynics were convinced that Cleveland owner Bill Veeck signed the ancient Satchel Paige midway through the 1948 season solely as a gate attraction. The 42-year-old "rookie" went 6–1 with a 2.48 ERA that season. Five years later, he pitched in 57 games for Veeck's St. Louis Browns and was fourth in the American League in saves.

- Cleveland's four infielders have a combined 432 RBI and 97 homers.

- Braves manager Billy Southworth wins his fourth pennant as a helmsman.

- The Hall of Fame inducts Herb Pennock and Pie Traynor.

- Cleveland pitcher Don Black suffers a brain aneurysm while batting in a game and nearly dies.

- Frank "Trader" Lane hired as White Sox general manager.

- White Sox send Eddie Lopat to the Yanks for Aaron Robinson, Bill Wight, and Fred Bradley.

- White Sox trade Bob Kennedy to Cleveland for Seerey and Al Gettel.

- Browns trade Sam Zoldak to Cleveland for Bill Kennedy and cash.

- Cleveland swaps Eddie Robinson, Joe Haynes, and Ed Klieman to Washington for Mickey Vernon and Early Wynn.

Ted Williams won his second MVP Award in 1949, batting .343 with 150 runs, 159 RBI, and 43 home runs. Barely nosed out for the batting title by Detroit's George Kell, Williams led all AL hitters in on-base average at .490 and slugging at .650.

The Boston offense improved around him. Dom DiMaggio, Vern Stephens, and Johnny Pesky were third, fourth, and fifth in runs. Stephens tied Williams with 159 RBI and was second in home runs with 39. And Williams, DiMaggio, Al Zarilla, and Stephens were first, third, fourth, and fifth in doubles. The Red Sox won 96 games and scored the most runs in the major leagues, 896, yet they lost the pennant by 1 game to the Yankees.

Rookie manager Casey Stengel did it with mirrors, as none of the Yankees' three best hitters—Joe DiMaggio, Tommy Henrich, or Phil Rizzuto—led the AL in any major hitting category. Only Henrich, with the third-best slugging mark of .526, appeared in the top five. Stengel overcame injuries to DiMaggio (who missed half of the season with a heel injury and a case of pneumonia), Yogi Berra, and even late-season acquisition Johnny Mize with deft platooning and substituting. Among everyday players, only shortstop Rizzuto was steady.

The Yanks featured solid pitchers in 21-10 Vic Raschi, 17-6 Allie Reynolds, and super reliever

CASEY PLATOONS THE YANKS TO WORLD TITLE

Joe Page, who went 13-8 with 27 saves and a 2.60 ERA in 60 appearances. However, no Yankee made the top five in ERA, and only Raschi (fourth place) cracked the top five in wins.

Still, the Yankees gutted it out. With two days to go in the season and New York trailing Boston by 1 game, a sick DiMaggio doubled and singled and Johnny Lindell smacked a key homer to lead New York to a 5-4 victory and a tie for the pennant. On the season's last day, the Yanks clinched the pennant 5-3, thanks to Jerry Coleman's three-run double.

The race for the NL flag was also decided by a single game, as St. Louis and Brooklyn fought all season long before the young Dodgers came out on top. The Cardinals featured their usual recipe of Stan Musial and tough pitching. Musial hit .338 and chalked up 41 doubles, 128 runs, and 123 RBI. Cardinals ace Howie Pollet went 20-9 with a 2.77 ERA, and five other St.

Louis hurlers won in double figures.

Burt Shotton took over the Dodger reins as Leo Durocher went off to manage the Giants. Shotton's philosophy was to let the new recruits—and the veterans—show their stuff at various stations. He put Duke Snider, for example, in center field. The rookie responded by batting .292 with 23 home runs and 92 RBI. Brooklyn's Jackie Robinson, now moved to his natural position at second base, put on an MVP performance, hitting .342 to lead the league, scoring 122 runs, and surpassing Musial in RBI 124 to 123. Robinson also cracked 38 doubles and 12 triples. Teamed with fellow former Negro Leaguers Don Newcombe (who went 17-8) and Roy Campanella (who hit 22 homers), as well as Carl Furillo, Pee Wee Reese, and Gil Hodges, Robinson gave Brooklyn the NL's best offense.

For the first two games of the 1949 World Series, the Dodgers and Yankees were like two heavyweight fighters feeling each other out. Reynolds won game one 1-0, and Preacher Roe evened things up in game two by the same score. Then the veteran New Yorkers began to land telling blows. In game three, the Yankees rallied for three in the ninth to win 4-3. In game four, Ed Lopat beat Newcombe 6-4. In game five, New York scored ten runs in the first six innings to win 10-6.

1949

- Yankees cop first flag under Casey Stengel.

- Dodgers edge the Cards by 1 game in NL.

- Red Sox lose second AL flag in row by 1 game when they lose last two games of season to Yankees.

- Yankees win World Series in five games.

- Yankee Tommy Henrich homers in bottom of the ninth of game one of Series, winning game 1-0.

- Dodgers win game two of Series 1-0 on a Preacher Roe shutout.

- No one in Series collects more than six hits.

- Jackie Robinson selected NL MVP.

- Ted Williams is AL MVP.

- Williams tops AL in homers (43), ties for lead in RBI (159).

A drenched and disheveled Casey Stengel celebrates with Yogi Berra *(left)*, Hank Bauer *(center)*, and the rest of his team, after the Yankees captured the American League flag on the final day of the 1949 season. Stengel's triumph was not only his first in ten tries as a major league manager, but also the first time a club of his finished in the first division.

- Williams loses Triple Crown when he finishes a fraction behind Detroit's George Kell in batting, as both hit .343.

- Williams tops AL in runs (150), doubles (39), total bases (368), SA (.650), OBP (.490), and walks (162).

- Robinson tops NL in hitting (.342) and steals (37).

- Mel Parnell of Red Sox tops majors with 25 wins.

- Parnell leads the AL in innings (295) and CGs (27).

- Ellis Kinder of Boston wins 23, giving club 48 wins by top tandem, easily the best in majors.

- Ralph Kiner wins fourth consecutive NL homer crown with 54, threatening NL record.

- Williams is last ML player until 1999 to produce 250 or more runs in a season.

- Boston's Vern Stephens ties Williams for AL RBI lead with 159, an ML record for shortstops.

Brooklyn Dodgers Infield

Reese Heads Dodger Infield

The Brooklyn Dodgers infield crew looked solid in 1947. By 1949, however, only shortstop Pee Wee Reese *(second from left)* was still with Brooklyn at the same station. The others in the picture are *(from left to right)* third baseman Spider Jorgensen, second baseman Eddie Stanky, and first sacker Jackie Robinson, who was at second in 1949.

Robinson Hits Zenith

In 1949, Jackie Robinson hit .342, scored 122 runs, knocked in 124 more, and was named National League MVP. Robinson also stole 37 bases in '49, the most by any NL player between 1930 and 1956.

Ted Williams

Ted Tops AL in Runs, RBI

Ted Williams was never known for his baserunning, but he was not a load on the basepaths, either. Even though he pilfered the fewest sacks of any great hitter, he was perennially among the leaders in runs scored. In 1949, he scored 150 runs—to go along with his 159 RBI (both American League-bests).

Jackie Robinson

1949

- Yankee Joe Page sets a new ML record with 27 saves.
- Dale Mitchell of Cleveland hits 23 triples, the most by any player since 1930.
- AL wins wild All-Star Game 11-7 at Brooklyn.
- This marks the first appearance of black players in an All-Star Game.
- Joe DiMaggio signs first $100,000 contract in ML history.
- Browns use nine different pitchers, one in each inning, in season finale vs. White Sox.
- Bob Lemon's seven homers tie AL record for most homers by a pitcher during a 154-game schedule.
- A's perform ML record 217 double plays.
- New York's Dave Koslo tops NL in ERA (2.50) and is the first leader without a shutout.

Joe DiMaggio

DiMaggio Hangs Tough

Idled by an ailing heel, Joe DiMaggio played in only half of the Yankees' games in 1949. His production, however, continued to be so extraordinary that writers maintained he would again have denied Ted Williams an MVP Award if he had played a full season.

Lemon Sweet with 22 Wins

Bob Lemon never had a spectacular season, but he sure was consistent. From 1948 through 1956, Lemon didn't win more than 23 games in a season, yet *averaged* 21 wins per year. In that period, he led the league in complete games five times and innings pitched four times. He went 22–10 in 1949.

Bob Lemon

Ralph Kiner

Kiner Has Career Year

Ralph Kiner had his finest overall season at the plate in 1949, as he smacked 54 home runs and drove in 127 runs. The Pirates usually just tried to ignore his fielding. Enos Slaughter said he could score on a fly ball to Kiner hit 30 feet behind third base.

- A's and Phils both finish above .500 for the first time since 1913.

- Cards have only 17 stolen bases, record low for NL team.

- Boston's Dom DiMaggio has a 34-game hitting streak.

- The Red Sox collect ML record 835 walks.

- Kiner hits 25 homers on road, new NL record.

- Stan Musial tops NL in hits (207), doubles (41), total bases (382), and OBP (.438), and ties in triples (13).

- Kiner paces NL in RBI (127), walks (117), and SA (.658).

- Warren Spahn tops NL in wins (21), innings (302), CGs (25), and Ks (151).

- Williams and Stephens combine for 499 runs produced, most since 1932 by pair of teammates.

- Roy Sievers of Browns wins AL Rookie of the Year honor.

Yankees Take Championship

The scene in the visiting team dressing room at Ebbets Field after the Yankees claim their first World Championship under Casey Stengel. The Yankees skipper holds the ball that Joe Page *(center foreground)* threw for the final out in game six. To Stengel's right is Phil Rizzuto.

Casey Stengel, Joe Page

Campy Catches Full Series

Roy Campanella nips Yankees hurler Ed Lopat at the plate in the 1949 World Series. Campanella shared the Dodgers' catching load with incumbent Bruce Edwards as a rookie in 1948; but by spring of 1949, the job was his. In five World Series with Brooklyn, Campanella caught every inning of every game.

World Series

DiMaggio Dives in Series

Joe DiMaggio swings away in the 1949 World Series. DiMaggio, so exceptional in all phases of the game, so consistently productive in every season he played, flopped in the '49 Series. Joltin' Joe hit just .111, collecting two hits in 18 at-bats. The Yankees, however, won the Series in five games. DiMaggio missed the first half of the 1949 season due to an injured foot. However, he was awesome in the second half. Despite totaling just 272 at-bats on the year, he hit .346 with 67 RBI.

World Series

1949

- Cards finish second, 1 game back of Brooklyn, after losing four games in the final week.

- Phillie Eddie Waitkus shot and nearly killed in Chicago hotel room by female admirer.

- Brooklyn's Pee Wee Reese leads the NL in runs (132).

- Mitchell leads the AL in hits (203).

- Kinder leads the AL in win pct. (.793) and ties for top in shutouts (six).

- Cleveland rookie Mike Garcia leads the AL in ERA at 2.35.

- Detroit's Virgil Trucks tops the majors in Ks with 153.

- The Yankees yield an AL record 812 walks.

- Brooklyn's Don Newcombe voted NL Rookie of the Year.

- On July 6, Cincinnati's Walker Cooper goes 6-for-7 and hits three homers in a nine-inning game.

Reese Tops NL in Runs

It's hard to imagine that the great Dodgers teams of the 1940s and '50s would have a captain named "Pee Wee," but it's true. Pee Wee Reese spearheaded the Dodgers to seven pennants. A slick-fielding shortstop, he led the National League in runs with 132 in 1949.

Mel Parnell

Pee Wee Reese

Parnell Tops AL in Victories

Mel Parnell's superb season in 1949 (25–7) contributed heavily to his .621 career win percentage, one of the highest ever by a pitcher who never played on a pennant-winner. Parnell battled control problems throughout his ten-year stint with the Red Sox. He walked 134 batters in '49.

- A record 59 minor leagues begin season, and the minors attract a record 40 million fans.

- The Hall of Fame inducts Charlie Gehringer, Three Finger Brown, and Kid Nichols.

- The A's trade Nellie Fox to the White Sox for Joe Tipton.

- Reds send Hank Sauer and Frankie Baumholtz to the Cubs for Harry Walker and Peanuts Lowrey.

- Braves ship Al Dark and Eddie Stanky to the Giants for Sid Gordon, Willard Marshall, and two others.

- The Cards sell Murry Dickson to the Pirates for $125,000.

- Jimmy Stewart stars as Monty Stratton in *The Stratton Story*.

- Howie Judson of the White Sox loses 14 games in a row.

- Paul Calvert of Washington also loses 14 games in a row.

- Rookie Alex Kellner of the A's wins 20 games.

VETERAN YANKS TEACH WHIZ KIDS A LESSON

New York teams dominated the decade of the 1950s: There were five Subway Series; 14 of the 20 teams to play in the World Series were from the Big Apple; and the Yankees were champs six times, the Giants and Brooklyn Dodgers once apiece.

Just as the town was bubbling over with baseball, the Giants and the Dodgers departed for California before the 1958 season broke open, leaving behind the Yankees and many a broken heart.

The majority of the thrills in 1950, however, were produced by a team from Philadelphia. The story of the year was that the Phillies (also known as the "Whiz Kids," since they won the National League with a starting lineup of players under 30 years of age) had even made it to the Series.

On the final day of the regular season, the first-place Phils (90-63) faced the Dodgers (89-64) at Ebbets Field. Philadelphia's 7-game lead over Brooklyn nine days before had been whittled down to a single-game edge. After losing ace lefty Curt Simmons and his 17-8 record to military duty on September 10, the Phils began to fade. Injuries to rookie hurlers Bubba Church and Bob Miller forced manager Eddie Sawyer to give the ball to righthander Robin Roberts in the closing day game (it was his third start in five days).

Brooklyn had a chance for victory in the bottom of the ninth, but Roberts weathered a bases-loaded jam to send the game into overtime. In the tenth, Dick Sisler hit a three-run homer to give the Phils their first flag since 1915.

The Philly pitching star of the year, however, was Jim Konstanty. Named MVP, he appeared in a league-high 74 games with a circuit-topping 22 saves. Another Philadelphia standout, Del Ennis led the league with 126 RBI.

As for the rest of the National League, Ralph Kiner gave last-place Pittsburgh hope for next year as he nailed 47 home runs (tops in both leagues) and 118 RBI (second in the circuit). Warren Spahn and Johnny Sain, ranked first and second in the league in wins, wowed Boston with their 41 combined victories. Sal Maglie of New York posted the best ERA in both circuits with a 2.71 mark.

The Yankees followed a smoother path to October, finishing the regular season with a 98-56 record, 3 games ahead of Detroit. Nine wins from rookie southpaw Whitey Ford (called up by manager Casey Stengel in late June), a strong finish from Joe DiMaggio, and an MVP year from Phil Rizzuto (.324 average) guided the Yankees to the pennant. Detroit might have made the race for the flag interesting if not for the season-long injury to ace Virgil Trucks.

The third-place Red Sox were headed up by Vern Stephens and Rookie of the Year Walt Dropo (each knocked in a league-leading 144 runs) and by Billy Goodman (the batting leader with a .354 average). Ted Williams, however, missed most of the second half of the season due to an All-Star Game injury, very likely costing Boston the flag.

Cleveland produced the other stars in the American League: Al Rosen, the home run king with 37 round-trippers; Bob Lemon, the leader in wins with 23; and Early Wynn, the top ERA man at 3.20.

New York's pitching staff made short work of the Whiz Kids in the Series, allowing Philadelphia just five runs in the four-game sweep, to become champs for the second straight season.

The 1950 campaign also marked the end of two long careers. Luke Appling, who had played shortstop for the White Sox since 1931, retired. And after 53 years, 7,755 games, and 3,731 wins, Connie Mack stepped down as manager of the Athletics at age 88; he died six years later.

1950

- Yankees triumph again in AL under Casey Stengel.
- Phils win first flag since 1915, edging out Brooklyn by 2 games.
- Phils clinch flag on last day of season, as Dick Sisler's tenth-inning homer beats Dodgers.
- Yanks sweep Phils in World Series.

- Relief ace Jim Konstanty, the Phils' surprise starter in game one of Series, is beaten 1-0 on a sacrifice fly.
- Phils' Granny Hamner tops all Series players in hits (six) and BA (.429), even though his team is swept.
- Phils score five runs in Series.

- Most competitive World Series sweep ever, as Phils are beaten three times by one run and are in every game until the final out.
- Yankee Phil Rizzuto selected AL MVP.
- Konstanty is NL MVP, becoming the first reliever to win award.

Dizzy Dean *(left)* tells Jim Konstanty how he handled the pressure of starting a World Series opener. Konstanty made a record 74 mound appearances during the regular season in 1950, none of them starts. Yet he was called upon to start the opener of the '50 Series. He pitched eight innings and lost 1–0.

- Konstanty wins an ML record 16 games in relief, and also leads the ML in saves with 22.

- Stan Musial tops NL in hitting (.346).

- Red Sox Billy Goodman wins AL bat crown (.354)—only player ever to win hit title without having a regular position.

- Bob Lemon tops majors with 23 wins.

- Brooklyn's Gil Hodges hits four homers in a game on August 31.

- Red Sox Walt Dropo wins Rookie of the Year Award.

- Dropo hits 34 homers and posts a rookie record 144 RBI.

- Sam Jethroe of the Braves voted NL Rookie of the Year.

- Cleveland's Early Wynn tops AL with 3.20 ERA, highest ERA in ML history by leader.

- NL wins All-Star Game 4-3 at Comiskey, as St. Louis' Red Schoendienst homers in the 14th inning to win it.

Appling Calls It Quits

Luke Appling set a record in 1949 when he played 141 games at shortstop at the age of 42. He hit .301, scored 82 runs, and even stole seven bases. It was a typical year for Appling. The White Sox, too, had one of their typical years during his sojourn with them. They finished sixth. Appling played in just 50 games in 1950, collecting a .234 average.

George Kell

Kell Cracks 56 Doubles

Until the last fortnight of the 1950 season, there was considerable doubt whether Billy Goodman would accumulate enough at-bats to qualify for the American League hitting title. Had he fallen short, George Kell (pictured) would have won his second straight crown. Kell, who led the league with 218 hits and 56 doubles in 1950, had one of the best seasons ever by a third baseman.

Luke Appling

Joe DiMaggio

DiMaggio Dominates

If he had to do it over again, Joe DiMaggio probably would have retired after the 1950 season, instead of after '51. In 1950, DiMaggio hit .301 with 32 home runs and 122 RBI. His secret to hitting? "There's no skill involved," he said. "Just go up there and swing at the ball."

1950

- Ted Williams breaks his elbow in the All-Star Game and is lost until September, possibly costing Boston the flag.

- Connie Mack retires after finishing last in final season at A's helm.

- All Mexican League jumpers are reinstated by OB for the 1950 season.

- Sal Maglie, one of the jumpers, wins 18 games for Giants and tops NL in win pct. (.818) and ERA (2.71).

- Boston's Dom DiMaggio leads AL with 15 steals—fewest ever by a loop leader.

- On May 18 vs. Brooklyn, Cardinal third sacker Tommy Glaviano makes errors on three straight plays.

- Musial hits in 30 consecutive games.

- On Sept. 10, Joe DiMaggio becomes first to hit three homers in a game in Washington's Griffith Stadium.

- Browns hire hypnotist David Tracy during the season to rid team of its defeatist complex.

Hodges Hits Four HRs

Gil Hodges was the first National League player in this century to hit four round-trippers in a regulation-length game (August 31, 1950). He accomplished it at Ebbets Field, which also made him the first in this century to pull off the feat at home.

Pee Wee Reese

Gil Hodges

Pee Wee Falls Short

Pee Wee Reese (shown here surprising the Pirates with a bunt) was the only one of the four regular Dodgers infielders who did not have the top fielding average at his position in 1950. (He did, however, compile 11 home runs, 52 RBI, and 21 doubles.) Brooklyn led the National League in every important department except pitching.

Red, Marion Play Finale

Red Schoendienst *(left)* and Marty Marion were one of the best keystone combos in the late 1940s. In 1950, they played together for the last time. Schoendienst topped the NL with 43 doubles; Marion was good for 40 RBI. By August, Marion's aching back had benched him most days.

Red Schoendienst, Marty Marion

- On June 8, Browns are beaten 29-4 by Red Sox at Fenway—most lopsided game in century.
- Vern Bickford of Braves no-hits Brooklyn on August 11.
- Bickford tops majors in both innings (312) and CGs (27).

- On April 18 at St. Louis, Cards and Pirates play first "Opening Night" game in ML history.
- TV provides baseball with an extra $2.3 million in new revenues in 1950.
- Yankee Vic Raschi sets ML record (since broken) when he retires 32 batters in a row.

- Brooklyn's Duke Snider tops NL in hits (199) and total bases (343).
- Ralph Kiner wins fifth consecutive NL homer crown (47).
- Warren Spahn tops NL in wins (21) and Ks (191).
- Detroit's George Kell leads AL in hits (218) and doubles (56).

Ted Williams

Red Sox Obliterate Browns

Ted Williams surveys the Fenway Park scoreboard on June 8, 1950. The Browns tallied a run in the top of the ninth to make the final 29–4. The Red Sox would have loved to have batted in the bottom half and added to their modern record for the most runs scored by one team in a game.

Phil Rizzuto

Rizzuto Cops AL MVP

American League MVP Phil Rizzuto had his finest season in 1950—.324 average, seven home runs, 66 RBI—and the Yankees needed it all. Detroit and Boston were in the race until the last week of the season, and fourth-place Cleveland finished only 6 games back. It was the only time during the 16-team era that four clubs in one league won more than 90 games.

Roberts Clinches NL Flag

Robin Roberts won exactly 20 games in 1950, the first of six straight 20-win seasons. His gutty victory on the final day of the 1950 season brought the Phillies their first flag since 1915. In the 35 years between pennants, the Phils finished in the first division only four times—and just once between 1917 and 1949.

Robin Roberts

1950

- Pittsburgh's Johnny Hopp goes 6-for-6 on May 14.

- Cleveland finishes fourth in AL with a better record than the Phils.

- AL boasts four excellent teams and four bad teams—fourth-place Cleveland finishes 25 games ahead of fifth-place Washington.

- Cleveland's Al Rosen leads the AL in homers with 37, which is also an AL rookie record.

- Robin Roberts is the Phils' first 20-game winner since 1917, as he wins exactly 20.

- The Braves finish above .500 for the last time in Boston.

- Indians trade Mickey Vernon to Washington for Dick Weik.

- In September, the Yanks buy Hopp from Pittsburgh for bench strength.

- White Sox send Cass Michaels and two other players to Washington for Eddie Robinson, Al Kozar, and Ray Scarborough.

Berra Nails HR in Finale

After cracking a home run, Yogi Berra crosses the plate in the sixth inning of game four of the 1950 World Series. If Berra seems ho-hum about his accomplishment, it's understandable. Not only did the Yankees sweep the Phils, but this was just one of 12 dingers that Berra slammed in his 259 World Series at-bats.

World Series

Vern Bickford

Bickford: A Braves Ace

In 1950, the Braves got 60 wins from their top three starters. Led by Vern Bickford (pictured), the trio enabled the Braves to pace the majors in complete games (88). In fact, the three accounted for more complete games (77) than the entire staff of any other team in the majors.

Konstanty Named NL MVP

National League MVP Jim Konstanty (22 saves) is the center of attention as he warms up before the first game of the 1950 World Series. A year earlier, his name had been virtually unknown to fans everywhere—even in Philadelphia. Konstanty never played a full season in the majors until he was past age 31. After 1950, Konstanty again fell into obscurity. In '51, he went 4-11 with a 4.05 ERA. Konstanty is the classic case of a one-hit wonder.

Jim Konstanty

- A new balk rule is instituted.
- On May 3, Raschi commits four balks in one game.
- White Sox set new AL record for fewest steals in a season (19).
- Called up from the minors in June, Yankee rookie Whitey Ford goes 9-1.

- Yogi Berra's 192 hits set a record for an AL catcher.
- Yankee Jackie Jensen plays in both a Rose Bowl and a World Series.
- The A's allow 6.6 runs per game on the road.
- Red Sox score an ML record 625 runs at home.

- Red Sox score 216 runs in 22 games against the Browns.
- Pitcher Bill Wight sets an AL record for futility when he goes 0-for-61 at the plate.
- Detroit's Jerry Priddy helps turn 150 DPs to set an AL record for second basemen.

THOMSON'S SHOT HEARD 'ROUND THE WORLD

It was one of many "next years" for the Dodgers. After almost catching the Phillies the previous season, the city of Brooklyn renewed its hope in the fresh slate of 1951. It was the dawning of an era (Ford Frick succeeded Happy Chandler as commissioner), and the Dodgers came flying out of the gate behind Most Valuable Player Roy Campanella.

It became a slow season all around. With the Yankees coasting to another American League pennant by 5 games over Cleveland and with the Giants 13½ games behind the Dodgers in the National, there wasn't a race in sight.

There were highlights that year, of course. In the National League, the Cardinals' Stan Musial won the batting title with a .355 average. Ralph Kiner of the Pirates clubbed a league-leading 42 homers. Brooklyn's Preacher Roe racked up a 22-3 season with a winning percentage that ranks sixth on the all-time single-season list. Monte Irvin totaled 121 RBI, the best in the league, for New York. Boston's Chet Nichols posted a league-low 2.88 ERA.

In the American League, Gus Zernial came to Philadelphia via Chicago early in the season to blast 33 home runs and 129 RBI, both league-bests; teammate Ferris Fain topped all batters with a .344 average. Cleveland's Bob Feller spearheaded the league with 22 victories and a .733 winning percentage. Saul Rogovin responded to an early-season trade

to Chicago with a league-leading 2.78 ERA.

The brightest of highlights—and one of the most dramatic comebacks ever—was the 16-game winning streak that Leo Durocher's Giants kicked off on August 12. Led by Willie Mays (the 20-year-old Rookie of the Year) and Sal Maglie (a 2.93 ERA and a league-leading 23 wins), New York won 39 of its last 47 (including the final seven) to pull into a first-place tie with the Dodgers.

A split of the first two playoff contests set up a dramatic deciding game at the Polo Grounds on October 3. The Dodgers took a 4-1 lead into the bottom of the ninth. With Don Newcombe cruising along, three outs did not seem to be a tall order. Al Dark and Don Mueller then opened the inning with singles. After the heavy-hitting Irvin popped out, Whitey Lockman ripped a double to left, scoring Dark and sending Mueller to third and Newcombe to the showers.

Owning a 4-2 lead with the tying run in scoring position, Dodger skipper Chuck Dressen called for the righthander Ralph Branca. With Bobby Thomson at bat, Mays on deck, and first base open, Dressen chose to pitch to Thomson (who collected 32 round-trippers on the year). On the second pitch, the outfielder lined a game-winning, three-run homer to left—the "shot heard 'round the world"—giving the Giants the pennant and forever linking himself with Branca as baseball's classic hero-and-goat duo.

Although the Yankees featured no .300 hitters, they did have clutch-hitting catcher Yogi Berra (who won the MVP) and pitching ace Eddie Lopat (21 wins and 2.91 ERA). Allie Reynolds hurled a pair of no-hitters for New York along the way to the AL flag.

The high-flying Giants won the first game of the World Series 5-1 and the third 6-2. But behind the fine pitching of Reynolds, Lopat (who allowed one earned run in 18 Series innings), and Vic Raschi, the Bronx Bombers took the next three matches and, in the process, their third consecutive championship.

Perhaps more noteworthy than the Yankees' victory was a changing of the guard in the Bronx: As Joe DiMaggio ended his Hall of Fame career in pinstripes, a fleet-footed, 19-year-old outfielder named Mickey Mantle made his debut.

1951

- Yanks take third straight flag under Casey Stengel.
- Giants edge Dodgers by 1 game in NL, beating them in a pennant playoff.
- Giants win NL playoff 5-4 on Bobby Thomson's ninth-inning three-run homer—the "shot heard 'round the world."

- For the third time in six years, Dodgers lose pennant on last day of season.
- Yanks win World Series in six games.
- Yankee Ed Lopat is pitching star of Series with two CG wins.
- Giant Monte Irvin leads all hitters in Series with 11 hits and .458 average.

- Joe DiMaggio retires after Series.
- Yankee catcher Yogi Berra is AL MVP.
- Dodger catcher Roy Campanella named NL MVP.
- Dodgers force playoff on final day of regular season, as Jackie Robinson's 14th-inning homer beats Phils.

Bobby Thomson is seen the instant before a sea of Giants players, coaches, and club officials wash over him after his historic playoff homer in the 1951 race for the National League flag. Giants pitcher Carl Hubbell said of the event, "We won't live long enough to see anything like it again." It was yet another highlight in Thomson's spectacular season (.293 average, 32 home runs, 101 RBI).The following year, Thomson was the only Giants player to total more than 17 home runs or 73 RBI.

- On August 12, Giants begin 16-game win streak and take 39 of last 47 games to overhaul Dodgers at the wire.

- Giant teammates Sal Maglie and Larry Jansen tie for ML lead in wins with 23.

- Stan Musial tops NL in batting (.355).

- Ferris Fain of the A's leads the AL in batting (.344).

- Ralph Kiner wins sixth consecutive NL homer crown (42).

- Kiner leads the NL in walks (137), SA (.627), and OBP (.452).

- Bill Veeck buys the Browns after having sold the Indians.

- Veeck signs midget Eddie Gaedel; Gaedel appears in game as pinch hitter on August 19 and draws a walk.

- Ford Frick named new commissioner after Happy Chandler's contract is not renewed by ML owners.

- Yankee Allie Reynolds no-hits Cleveland on July 12.

Ralph Kiner

Veeck Buys Browns

In 1951, Bill Veeck bought the Browns after selling the Indians. This photo was taken in 1943 when he was still owner of the minor league Milwaukee Brewers, but his office at Sportsman's Park in '51 looked much the same. Veeck, in a word, was casual. More people have seen World Series games at Wrigley Field than have seen Veeck in a coat and tie.

Bill Veeck

Kiner Bests Majors in HRs

Lacking a first baseman in 1951, the Pirates tried Ralph Kiner at the gateway post as first base was the only position he could even remotely play. The fourth slot in the batting order, though, was all his. He led the majors in home runs (42).

Mays Selected NL ROTY

Willie Mays (photographed sliding home ahead of Cardinals catcher Bill Sarni's tag) was the National League's Rookie of the Year in 1951. Mays scored just 59 runs in 1951, but it was the last time until 1966 that he played a full season without scoring at least 101.

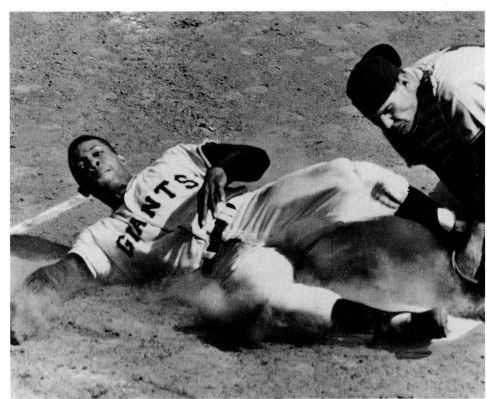

Willie Mays

1951

- Reynolds no-hits Boston on Sept. 28.

- On July 1, Bob Feller becomes first in 20th century to throw three career no-hitters, as he blanks Detroit.

- Cliff Chambers of Pittsburgh no-hits Braves on May 6.

- Preacher Roe's .880 win pct. is highest ever by NL 20-game winner.

- Kiner leads NL in walks (137), SA (.627), and OBP (.452).

- Warren Spahn leads NL in CGs (26), Ks (164), and shutouts (seven).

- On Sept. 14, Bob Nieman of Browns becomes only player in ML history to homer in his first two ML at-bats.

- Paul Lehner ties AL record when he plays for four teams in the same year.

- On Sept. 13, due to rainouts, Cards play Giants at home in afternoon and Braves at home at night.

- Cleveland has three 20-game winners—Feller (22), Early Wynn (20), and Mike Garcia (20).

Irvin Tops NL in RBI

Monte Irvin was age 30 before he played his first game in organized baseball. Early in the 1950 season, the Giants recalled him from Jersey City, where he was hitting .510, and installed him in left field. In 1951, he led the National League in RBI (121).

Monte Irvin

Stan Musial

Musial Still Unbeatable

In 1951, Stan Musial was nearly as much of a one-man gang in St. Louis as Ralph Kiner was in Pittsburgh. The third-place Cards scored even fewer runs than the seventh-place Pirates. Musial, though, couldn't be stopped. He led the National League in batting (.355), runs (124), triples (12), and total bases (355).

Campy Named MVP

Roy Campanella copped the 1951 National League MVP Award. The Brooklyn catcher topped Stan Musial in the voting and was the first NL backstopper since 1938 to be honored. Along with being the top defensive receiver in the senior loop in '51, Campanella was fourth in batting (.325) and third in homers (33).

Roy Campanella

Eddie Lopat

Lopat Is on the Money

Eddie Lopat's salary negotiations with Yankees general manager George Weiss are reported as being along the lines of the following: "Don't forget you'll make six or eight grand in Series money," said Weiss. "If we don't win, will you make up the difference?" asked Lopat. "We'll win," said Weiss. That was the end of it. The Yankees did indeed win the 1951 Series, with Lopat allowing just one run in two starts. As for the rest of the season, Lopat went 21–9 with a 2.91 ERA.

- Musial tops NL in runs (124), triples (12), total bases (355), and runs produced (200).

- Yankee Gil McDougald named AL Rookie of the Year.

- Willie Mays is NL Rookie of the Year after beginning year in minors.

- NL wins All-Star Game 8-3 at Detroit.

- Ned Garver wins 20 games for last-place Browns, who win just 52 times.

- Chicago's Go-Go Sox lead majors with 99 steals a year after setting the AL record for fewest steals.

- Yankee Clint Courtney is the first ML catcher to wear eyeglasses.

- Roy Smalley of the Cubs is the last player to make 50 errors in a season.

- A rule is put in that says a pitcher must work at least one inning per every scheduled game to qualify for the ERA title.

Mantle, Mays Fall Short

Mickey Mantle *(left)* and Willie Mays collected just one RBI and no home runs between them in the 1951 World Series. When they next opposed each other in earnest—in the 1962 World Series—they again had just one RBI and no home runs between them.

Yogi Berra

Berra Named AL MVP

The 1951 season was the first time that the MVP in each league was a catcher. Yogi Berra not only outdistanced all other American League catchers at the plate (.294 average, 27 home runs), but he also led them in assists and double plays. Apart from Berra and National League MVP Roy Campanella, no catcher in either league received a single MVP vote.

Feller Posts .733 Win Pct.

Gone by 1951 was Bob Feller's legendary fastball. But what he had lost in speed he compensated with guile, finishing the season at 22–8. Feller gave up a lot of hits and a lot of runs in the latter part of his career, but remained a winner until nearly the end. His .733 win percentage in 1951 was his career-high.

Mickey Mantle, Willie Mays

Bob Feller

1951

- The Hall of Fame inducts Mel Ott and Jimmie Foxx.
- Gus Zernial is traded by the White Sox to the A's in a three-team deal involving the Indians, who give up Minnie Minoso and get Lou Brissie.
- Zernial, in A's garb, tops AL in homers with 33 and RBI with 129.
- Minoso, in Sox garb, leads AL in triples (14) and steals (31).
- The Cubs send Smoky Burgess and Bob Borkowski to the Reds for Johnny Pramesa and Bob Usher.
- Burgess and two other players are shipped to the Phils for Andy Seminick, Dick Sisler, and two others.
- The Browns trade Sherm Lollar, Al Widmar, and Tom Upton to the White Sox for Jim Rivera and four others.
- The Cubs trade Andy Pafko, Johnny Schmitz, Rube Walker, and Wayne Terwilliger to the Dodgers for four players.

World Series

Giants Take Opening Game

Giants batter Bobby Thomson hurls himself out of the way, as Monte Irvin stuns the Yankees by stealing home in the first inning of the opening game of the 1951 World Series. Irvin's run, the Giants' second of the contest, was all the team needed, as Dave Koslo cruised to a 5–1 win.

Eddie Gaedel

Gaedel Pinch Hits—Once

On view here is the only player in this book who had just one plate appearance in the major leagues. He pinch-hit for St. Louis Browns leadoff man Frank Saucier in the second game of a doubleheader against the Tigers on August 19, 1951. His name was Eddie Gaedel, and he stood about $2^{1}/_{2}$ feet shorter than his discoverer, Bill Veeck.

Teary DiMaggio Departs

In a rare display of emotion, Joe DiMaggio announces his retirement after the 1951 season. Former Yankees teammate Red Ruffing, skeptical of DiMaggio at first, subsequently said, "You saw him standing there and you knew you had a pretty damn good chance to win the baseball game."

Joe DiMaggio

- The Yankees send minor leaguer Lew Burdette and $50,000 to the Braves for Johnny Sain.

- On August 22, Yankee Tommy Byrne yields 16 walks in a 13-inning game.

- Irvin leads the NL in RBI (121).

- Phillie Richie Ashburn tops the majors in hits (221).

- Brave rookie Chet Nichols tops NL in ERA (2.88).

- Detroit's George Kell tops AL in hits (191) and ties in doubles (36).

- Ted Williams paces AL in total bases (295), SA (.556), OBP (.464), walks (144), and runs produced (205).

- Boston's Dom DiMaggio again leads AL in runs (113).

- White Sox Saul Rogovin leads the AL in ERA (2.78).

- Yankee rookie Mickey Mantle hits .267, suffers knee injury when he steps on a sprinkler unit in the outfield during the World Series.

MANTLE'S MIGHT POWERS YANKS TO TITLE

The Yankees had won three rings in a row—a string that Cleveland fans thought could be broken in 1952. There was indeed reason for optimism on the shores of Lake Erie: The Indians had a lineup filled with heavy lumber and what looked to be the best hurlers in the league. Meanwhile, over in the Bronx, the Yankees were without Joe DiMaggio (who had retired) and starting infielders Bobby Brown and Jerry Coleman (who were lost to the military).

The Tribe was the team to beat. Outfielder Larry Doby tallied 104 RBI and a league-leading 32 home runs; first baseman Luke Easter was just one behind in round-trippers. Third baseman Al Rosen knocked in a circuit-topping 105 RBI and belted 28 homers. Outfielder Dale Mitchell hit .323, just second to the league-leading .327 average turned in by Philadelphia's Ferris Fain. On the hill, Early Wynn won 23 games while Bob Lemon and Mike Garcia took 22 apiece.

The Casey Stengel-led Yankees, however, had a 2 1/2-game cushion on Labor Day, thanks to the substitution of fiery Billy Martin at second base, the insertion of solid Gil McDougald at third, and the emergence of outfielder Mickey Mantle as a star.

With just over a week remaining in the season, the Yanks were blanked 2-0 by Philadelphia southpaw Bobby Shantz (who collected a league-topping 24-7 record, a 2.48 ERA, and the

MVP Award) and the Tribe pulled to within 1 1/2 games. The Yankees went on to take the pennant with a 95-59 record, 2 games ahead of Al Lopez's Indians.

An unusually poor season from Cleveland ace Bob Feller may have been the Indians' undoing. Feller had compiled a 230-131 record in his first 13 seasons (a 17-10 average per year), then went 9-13 in '52. If he had won just three more games, Cleveland would have come out on top.

An especially good year from Philadelphia hurler Robin Roberts—28 wins, the most in the National League since Dizzy Dean's 28 triumphs in 1935—wasn't enough to drive the Phillies to the pennant; Philadelphia finished 9 1/2 games back. Allie Reynolds also had a sound season, posting a league-leading 2.07 ERA, 160 strikeouts, and six shutouts for New York.

After coming close to the flag two consecutive years, Brooklyn won the NL title. Although the Giants had a running 16-2 start, the Dodgers steadily took control. Joe Black, the Rookie of the Year

at age 28, was the heart of the Dodgers pitching staff, going 15-4 with a 2.15 ERA. St. Louis, which had batting champ Stan Musial (a .336 average), came in third. Fifth-place Chicago had the league MVP in Hank Sauer (37 home runs, 121 RBI).

New York began to miss Monte Irvin, who sat out nearly the entire year with a broken ankle. When super sophomore Willie Mays was called into military service and ace Sal Maglie had back trouble, the Giants began to fade. If it wasn't for rookie knuckleballer Hoyt Wilhelm, who posted a 15-3 record and a league-best 2.43 ERA, the Giants might have dropped below second. By season's end, they were 4 1/2 behind the first-place Dodgers (96-57).

The Dodgers pushed the Yanks to a full seven games in the World Series. In game five, Duke Snider's single drove in the winning run in the top of the 11th to give the Dodgers a 6-5 victory and a 3-2 Series edge. Snider nearly won game six single-handedly with homers accounting for both Brooklyn runs, but the Yankees and Vic Raschi came out on top 3-2 after Yogi Berra and Mantle homered in the seventh and eighth.

In the deciding game, Mantle's sixth-inning solo shot secured the lead, reliever Bob Kuzava retired the last eight Dodger batters, and the Yanks took a fourth straight World Championship.

1952

- Yankees take their fourth straight flag.
- Brooklyn wins pennant in National League.
- Yanks win World Series in seven games to claim their fourth straight title.

- Dodgers lead World Series three games to two with final two games in Brooklyn, but Yankees go to Ebbets and win both.
- Vic Raschi and Allie Reynolds both win two Series games for New York—Reynolds also gets a save in game six.

- New York's Mickey Mantle and Brooklyn's Pee Wee Reese tie for Series hitting lead at .345, as each has ten hits.
- Brooklyn's Joe Black is first black pitcher to win World Series game (game one) after going 15-4 on the year.

Casey Stengel and his three pitching aces—Allie Reynolds *(to the right of Stengel)*,
Eddie Lopat *(behind Stengel)*, and Vic Raschi *(to the left of Lopat)*—celebrate the
Yankees' fourth straight world championship. The seemingly unsaddened member of
the losing team is Dodgers skipper Chuck Dressen.

- Johnny Mize plays in only five games for New York, but tops Series hitters with six RBI and three homers.

- Cub Hank Sauer is NL MVP.

- Robin Roberts wins 28 games for Phils, most in NL since 1934, but doesn't get MVP.

- Roberts leads the NL in innings (330) and CGs (30).

- Philly's Bobby Shantz wins AL MVP Award.

- Shantz tops AL with 24 wins.

- Stan Musial tops majors with .336 average.

- Musial leads NL in hits (194), doubles (42), total bases (311), and SA (.538), and ties in runs (105).

- Philly's Ferris Fain wins second consecutive AL bat crown (.327).

- Ralph Kiner ties Sauer for NL homer crown to give him seventh consecutive NL title (37).

Reynolds Tops in Ks, ERA

Allie Reynolds was age 28 when the war-time manpower shortage forced Cleveland to issue him a major league uniform. Despite his belated start, he won 182 games and saved 49 others. In World Series play, he was 7-2 with four saves. Reynolds had his best season ever in 1952, collecting a 20-8 record, a league-high 160 strikeouts, and a circuit-best 2.07 ERA.

Allie Reynolds

Monte Irvin

Irvin Injury Hurts Giants

The Giants were dealt a critical blow in their attempt to repeat as National League champs when Monte Irvin broke his ankle in a 1952 spring training game against Cleveland. Giants supporters falsely accused Al Rosen, the Indians third sacker, of causing Irvin to slide unnecessarily by faking a tag.

Fain: .327

Ferris Fain (shown here sliding safely past lunging Red Sox catcher Sammy White) led the American League in 1952 with a .327 batting average. Fain was the first two-time batting champ to retire with a career batting average below .300 and one of the few players in this century whose on-base percentage was higher than his slugging average.

Ferris Fain

1952

- Ted Williams is taken by the military to fight in Korean War; Red Sox tumble to sixth place.

- On April 23, Giant Hoyt Wilhelm homers in first ML at-bat; never homers again.

- Wilhelm tops the NL in win pct. (.833) and ERA (2.43).

- Pirates lose 112 games under new GM Branch Rickey, who was ousted by Dodgers owner Walter O'Malley the previous year.

- Cleveland has three 20-game winners plus the American League's homer and RBI kings, but does not win pennant.

- Indians dominate individual leaders board in runs, slugging, triples, wins, innings, and CGs.

- Rogers Hornsby is hired by Bill Veeck to manage Browns, is soon fired, and is then hired by Reds.

- NL wins All-Star Game 3-2 at Philadelphia.

Dodgers an Arm Short

The Brooklyn Dodgers had the best offensive and defensive team in the majors in 1952, yet they were unable to fill the pitching hole Don Newcombe left when he was called into military service. Rookie Joe Black *(middle row, third from the right)* led the staff in both wins (15) and saves (15). Carl Erskine *(back row, fourth from the left)* was the only member of the mound crew to work more than 187 innings.

Brooklyn Dodgers

Stan Musial

Musial Takes Six Honors

With the exception of the 1947 campaign during which he was plagued by appendicitis, Stan Musial had his poorest season in 1952 since his rookie year. Nevertheless, his .336 average still won the National League batting title by 16 points. Musial also topped the circuit in hits (194), doubles (42), total bases (311), and slugging average (.538), and tied for first place in runs scored (105). Catcher Joe Garagiola, a one-time teammate of Musial's, once said, "What's the best way to pitch to Stan Musial? That's easy. Walk him and then try to pick him off first base."

Robin Roberts

Roberts: 23-2 vs. Five Teams

Robin Roberts had a 2-2 record against the Cubs and a 3-3 record against the Giants in 1952. Against the other five National League clubs, including the pennant-winning Dodgers, he was 23-2 that season. With Roberts, the Phils posted an 87-67 mark in '52; without him, they would have finished below .500.

- Black is NL Rookie of the Year.
- Philadelphia's Harry Byrd is AL ROTY.
- Virgil Trucks of Detroit no-hits Washington 1-0 on May 15.
- Trucks no-hits the Yankees 1-0 on August 25.

- In game against Washington, Trucks allows a single to the first batter and then no-hits the Senators the rest of the way.
- Trucks goes just 5-19 overall.
- Tiger pitcher Fred Hutchinson named team manager—is the last pitcher to serve as player/manager.

- On May 21, a record 19 straight Dodgers reach base safely vs. Reds in the first inning.
- Brooklyn's Carl Erskine no-hits Cubs on June 19.
- Walt Dropo ties ML record with 12 hits in 12 consecutive at-bats.

Bobby Shantz

Shantz Wins MVP

The smallest MVP selection in major league history at 139 pounds, Bobby Shantz was also one of the best all-around athletes to win the award. He posted an American League-leading 24 triumphs and a .774 winning percentage in 1952. Shantz was so talented a hitter and fielder that, had he not been lefthanded, he might have been a shortstop.

Gil McDougald

McDougald an Unsung Hero

Apart from Mickey Mantle and Yogi Berra, Gil McDougald was the Yankees' most valuable player during the 1950s. Able to play second, third, and short equally well, he is one of the few players in this century to be a regular at three different infield positions. In 1952, McDougald hit 16 doubles, five triples, and 11 home runs.

Doby Leads AL in Slugging

Larry Doby was the American League's top slugger in 1952 with his .541 mark, yet he finished just 12th in the MVP vote. Two years later, when he again paced all AL sluggers, he climbed to second in the balloting. Most students of the era agree that Doby should have been the first black player in the junior circuit to cop the award.

Larry Doby

1952

- On August 6, the Browns' Satchel Paige, at age 47, shuts out Detroit 1-0 in 12 innings.

- Cardinal Peanuts Lowrey collects an ML record seven straight pinch hits.

- Cleveland's Larry Doby tops AL in runs (104), homers (32), and slugging (.541).

- Cleveland's Al Rosen leads AL in RBI (105), total bases (297), and runs produced (178).

- Reynolds paces AL in ERA (2.07) and Ks (160).

- Cleveland's Jim Fridley goes 6-for-6 on April 29.

- The Hall of Fame inducts Harry Heilmann and Paul Waner.

- Braves draw only 281,278 in their last year in Boston.

- The Tigers finish last for the first time in their history and post their worst won-loss record ever (50-104).

Satchel Paige

Paige, 47, Best on the Browns

Satchel Paige led the Browns in wins (12), saves (ten), ERA (3.07), and MVP votes (12) in 1952. In addition, he fanned 91 hitters in 138 innings and had the American League's second-best strikeouts-per-game ratio (5.9). He was 47 years of age at the time.

Snider Shines in Series

Duke Snider slides across the plate with one of his five runs in the 1952 World Series. The Brooklyn center fielder collected ten hits, four home runs, and eight RBI in the fray. The Dodgers' other two slugging greats, Gil Hodges and Roy Campanella, accounted for only six hits and a mere two RBI between them.

Carl Erskine

Erskine: 14-6, .270 ERA

Mainly a reliever early in his career, Carl Erskine continued to be used as an occasional stopper throughout the 1950s by both Chuck Dressen and Walter Alston. A Brooklyn rookie in 1948, Erskine was the only pitcher still with the Dodgers ten years later when they played their first season in Los Angeles. In 1952, he went 14-6 with a 2.70 ERA and four shutouts.

World Series

- On June 13, Ron Necciai of Bristol of the Appalachian League throws a no-hitter and fans 27 batters.

- Giant Monte Irvin breaks an ankle in spring training, never regains his old ability.

- Toby Atwell of the Cubs is the first NLer to catch 100 games as a rookie.

- Bob Neighbors, ex-Browns shortstop, is the only former major leaguer to be killed in action in the Korean War.

- Yankee Phil Rizzuto leads the majors in sacrifice hits a record fourth straight year.

- Philly's Eddie Joost has 100 or more walks for sixth straight year.

- The Yankees trade four players to Cincinnati for Ewell Blackwell to give them help in the pennant stretch.

- Yankees trade Jackie Jensen and three other players for Irv Noren and Tommy Upton.

- Reese leads the ML in steals with 30.

YANKEES WIN FIFTH STRAIGHT WORLD SERIES

Although the Yankees and the Dodgers cruised to pennants on the skill of their outstanding squads, baseball's most watched team in 1953 was the Braves—the *Milwaukee* Braves. With air transportation facilitating travel, owner Lou Perini chose to move his Braves from Boston to Milwaukee. It was the first franchise shift since 1903.

The success of the Braves in their new hometown, both on the field and at the gate, prompted other owners to consider changing cities. The Braves finished second to the Dodgers with a 92-62 record and drew a record 1,826,397 fans. Warren Spahn led the staff, topping the National League with 23 wins (tied with Robin Roberts of Philadelphia) and a 2.10 ERA, while sophomore third baseman Eddie Mathews broke Ralph Kiner's seven-year hold on the league's home run crown with 47 homers.

The Dodgers, however, fielded a remarkable team. MVP Roy Campanella had a .312 batting average, 41 homers, and a league-high 142 RBI. Duke Snider added a .336 average, 42 homers, and 126 RBI. It was the first time in NL history two players from the same team belted 40 or more home runs.

The Dodger attack didn't end there. Carl Furillo won the batting title with a .344 average; Jackie Robinson hit .329 with 95 RBI; Gil Hodges hit .302 with 31 homers and 122 RBI; and second

baseman Junior Gilliam was named Rookie of the Year. Brooklyn won a club-record 105 games, becoming the first team to repeat in the National League since the 1944 Cardinals.

Awaiting the powerhouse Dodgers in the World Series were the dreaded Yankees, who had a fine season themselves in the American League. New York won nine of its first 11 games, triumphed in 18 straight in May (one win shy of the American League record set by the White Sox in 1906), and took the pennant by 8½ games over Cleveland with a 99-52 record.

Casey Stengel became the first to manage five consecutive flag-winners. He did so with a sharp pitching staff. Twenty-four-year-old Whitey Ford returned from two years of military service to win 18 games, and Eddie Lopat led the league with a 2.43 ERA. Along with Allie Reynolds (38 years old), Vic Raschi (34), and Johnny Sain (35), the five hurlers combined for a 74-30 record. The hitting was strong as

well. Yogi Berra racked up 27 home runs and 108 RBI, and Mickey Mantle clubbed 21 round-trippers, including a 565-foot mammoth shot off Chuck Stobbs in Washington.

The Yankees were not the only story in the American League, however. Cleveland's Al Rosen won the MVP Award after leading the junior circuit in home runs (43) and RBI (145) and finishing second in batting at .336. Bobo Holloman of the Browns hurled a no-hitter in his first major league start on May 6; with a 3-7 record in July, however, he was optioned to the minors, never to return to the bigs. Despite having a roster that boasted the batting champ (Mickey Vernon with a .337 average) and the pitcher with the most wins (Bob Porterfield with 22 victories), Washington placed fifth.

New York took a two-game lead in the World Series, winning game two on Mantle's two-run homer in the bottom of the eighth. The Dodgers fought back, winning the next games 3-2 and 7-3, but Mantle's grandslam won game five for the Yankees.

In game six, Brooklyn tied the score three-all with two runs in the top of the ninth. But Billy Martin's 12th hit of the Series—he finished with two homers, eight RBI, and a .500 average—scored Hank Bauer in the bottom of the inning to give the Yankees an all-time record fifth consecutive World Championship.

1953

- Yanks win ML record fifth consecutive flag.
- Brooklyn repeats in NL.
- Yanks take World Series in six games.
- Yankee Billy Martin hits .500 in World Series, ties Series record with 12 hits, and has eight RBI.

- Brooklyn's Carl Erskine fans World Series record (since broken) 14 hitters in game three.
- Dodgers win club record 105 games.
- Roy Campanella wins second NL MVP.
- Cleveland's Al Rosen named AL MVP.

- Rosen misses Triple Crown when he loses bat title by failing to beat out a ground ball in final at-bat of season.
- Rosen hits .336 with 43 homers and 145 RBI.
- Brooklyn's Carl Furillo takes NL bat crown at .344.

Yogi Berra and two other Yankees applaud Mickey Mantle for hitting a home run in the 1953 World Series. Although Berra hit .429 in the fray and Mantle notched seven RBI, both took a back seat to Billy Martin, who set numerous records for a six-game Series, including most total bases (23).

- Braves move to Milwaukee—first franchise shift in ML since 1903.

- Braves set new NL attendance record in their first year in Milwaukee.

- Braves surpass their previous year's attendance in Boston by their 13th game.

- Dodgers tie ML record with six men scoring 100 runs or more.

- Dodgers homer in record 24 straight games.

- Vic Janowicz of Pirates becomes first Heisman Trophy winner to play in majors.

- Phillie Robin Roberts again tops ML in CGs (33) and innings (347), and ties for ML lead in wins (23).

- Detroit rookie Harvey Kuenn tops majors in hits with 209.

- Walter Alston named new Dodgers manager after another devastating Brooklyn World Series loss.

Joe Garagiola, Ralph Kiner

Joe, Ralph Dealt to Cubs

Both Joe Garagiola *(left)* and Ralph Kiner were traded by the Pirates to the Cubs in a blockbuster deal early in the season that helped neither team in 1953. The Cubs dropped from fifth place to seventh and the Pirates finished last for the second year in a row.

Blue Furillo Hits .344

Carl Furillo never played a game at any position other than outfield or in any uniform other than that of the Dodgers. On seven pennant-winners in his first 14 years with the club, he was released at the beginning of his 15th season and remained bitter toward the organization until his death in 1988. In 1953, he claimed the National League batting title with a .344 average.

Carl Furillo

Roy Campanella

Campy: 41 HRs as a Catcher

Roy Campanella (shown in action against the Phillies) had possibly the greatest offensive season ever by a catcher in 1953. In addition to setting a new backstopper record for home runs (41) and pacing in the National League in RBI (142), he tallied 103 runs and stroked .556 as a pinch hitter.

1953

- On May 6, Brown Bobo Holloman becomes only pitcher this century to toss no-hitter in first ML start, as he blanks Philly.

- Mickey Vernon wins his second AL bat title (.337).

- NL wins All-Star Game 5-1 at Cincinnati.

- Paul Pettit, Pirates' $100,000 bonus baby, wins his only ML game.

- Cleveland's $100,000 bonus baby, Billy Joe Davidson, never even throws a single pitch in an ML game.

- On June 18, Red Sox send a record 23 men to plate in seventh inning, scoring a record 17 runs.

- On June 18, Red Sox Gene Stephens becomes only player in modern ML history to get three hits in an inning.

- On May 25, Max Surkont of Braves becomes first in this century to fan eight batters in a row in a game.

- Cardinal Peanuts Lowrey ties ML record with 22 pinch hits.

Ford Back to Bolster Yanks

Whitey Ford returned from a two-year military hitch in 1953 to top the Yankees in wins (18) and innings pitched (207). With Vic Raschi, Ed Lopat, and Allie Reynolds all aging rapidly, Ford and NL castoff Johnny Sain, who both relieved and started, were key figures in New York's fifth straight flag drive.

Whitey Ford

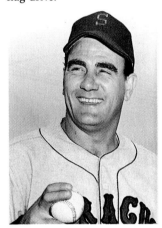

Bobo Holloman

Rookie Bobo Tosses No-No

Bobo Holloman tossed a no-hitter for the Browns on May 6, 1953. It was his first major league start and the only complete game he ever pitched. A few weeks later, he was back in the minors, posting a 5.07 ERA at Toronto of the International League.

Walter Alston, Walter O'Malley

Alston Takes Over Dodgers

Dodgers owner Walter O'Malley demonstrates what he thinks new manager Walter Alston will mean to the club. Alston, who replaced Charlie Dressen at the conclusion of the 1953 season, brought the Dodgers home second in 1954. The following year, he lived up to O'Malley's forecast.

Harvey Kuenn

Kuenn: All Hit, No Field

Harvey Kuenn was a polished hitter from the first day he played in the majors—his 209 hits led both loops in 1953, his rookie season—yet his offensive contributions were diminished by his lack of power and low walk totals. In the field, he was a liability regardless of where he played. Rather amazingly, he began as a shortstop.

- Campanella's 41 homers set an ML record for catchers.

- Pittsburgh's O'Brien twins, Johnny and Eddie, become the second brother keystone combo in the ML.

- On April 17 in Washington, Mickey Mantle hits longest measured home run in history—565 feet.

- Brooklyn's Jim Gilliam is NL Rookie of the Year.

- Kuenn is AL ROTY.

- Rosen tops AL in SA (.613), runs (115), and runs produced (217).

- Washington's Bob Porterfield leads the AL in wins (22), CGs (24), and shutouts (nine).

- Yankee Ed Lopat paces AL in win pct. (.800) and ERA (2.43).

- Warren Spahn tops NL in ERA (2.10) and ties Roberts for lead in wins (23).

- Brooklyn's Duke Snider leads NL in runs (132), total bases (370), SA (.627), and runs produced (216).

Mickey Mantle

Eddie Mathews

Mantle Hits One out of Sight

The arrow follows the flight of Mickey Mantle's gargantuan home run in 1953 at Washington's Griffith Stadium. In his third season with the Yankees, Mantle had yet to realize his full potential as a slugger. He collected just 21 four-baggers that year.

Roe Passes Torch to Podres

Preacher Roe *(left)* had an 11-3 record for the Dodgers in 1953, giving him a three-year mark of 44-8. Rookie Johnny Podres was 9-4 that season and would replace Roe the following year as the club's top southpaw hurler.

Preacher Roe, Johnny Podres

Mathews, 21, Clubs 47 HRs

In 1953, Eddie Mathews became the first third baseman since the end of the dead-ball era to lead the National League in home runs that year (47). Moreover, his 135 RBI set a 20th-century record in the Braves franchise. Only 21 years old at the time, Mathews never again matched his 1953 slugging figures.

1953

- Stan Musial leads NL in walks (105), on-base percentage (.437), and doubles (53).

- The Phillies' Connie Ryan goes 6-for-6 on April 16.

- Jimmy Piersall of the Red Sox goes 6-for-6 on June 10.

- The Hall of Fame inducts Dizzy Dean, Al Simmons, Ed Barrow, Chief Bender, Tommy Connolly, Bill Klem, Bobby Wallace, and Harry Wright.

- Browns lose 20 straight at home.

- The Pirates send Ralph Kiner and Joe Garagiola to Cubs for five players and $150,000.

- A's send Ferris Fain to White Sox for Eddie Robinson and two others.

- The Yanks trade Vic Power and five other players to the A's for Robinson and Harry Byrd.

- Pittsburgh swaps Danny O'Connell to Milwaukee for Sid Gordon and five other players.

Brooklyn Dodger Runs Scored Leaders

Four Dodgers Score at Will

The Dodgers had six players who scored over 100 runs in 1953. The four club leaders were *(left to right)* Junior Gilliam (125), Pee Wee Reese (108), Duke Snider (132), and Jackie Robinson (109). All four also finished among the top five in the National League in stolen bases, totaling 76 swipes.

Jackie Robinson

Jackie Still Has Magic

Jackie Robinson (shown here being congratulated by Stan Musial and the Phillies bat boy after homering in the 1952 All-Star Game) was switched to left field in 1953 after Andy Pafko was traded to the Braves. He was 34 years of age and near the end of his career, yet he still managed to hit .329 and knock in 95 runs.

- Washington ships Jackie Jensen to the Red Sox for Tommy Umphlett and Mickey McDermott.

- Tigers trade Art Houtteman and three others to Cleveland for Ray Boone, Steve Gromek, and two others.

- The Braves, Dodgers, Phils, and Reds pull a complex four-player deal.

- Cards owner Fred Saigh forced to sell the club to Augie Busch when he's handed a 15-month sentence for income tax evasion.

- Cards rookie Ray Jablonski totals 21 homers and 112 RBI.

- Cards rookie Harvey Haddix wins 20 games.

- Milwaukee's Eddie Mathews leads NL with 47 homers.

- Phillie Richie Ashburn leads the NL in hits with 205.

- Brooklyn rookie Jim Gilliam walks 100 times, becomes the first NL rookie to do so.

The Yankees won 103 games in 1954—more than they had in any of their five previous pennant seasons—only to finish 8 games behind the Indians, who won a league-record 111. The absence of the Yanks from postseason play was just one of several changes in '54.

Dodger skipper Chuck Dressen after winning two pennants demanded a three-year contract and was fired. Financially troubled, Bill Veeck sold the Browns to a group that moved the team to Baltimore. Arnold Johnson purchased the Athletics from Connie Mack, then took them to Kansas City after the season.

There were new faces that would become legends. Hank Aaron took over left field for the Braves, launching a 23-year career that would include 755 home runs. Ernie Banks played his first full season as the Cubs shortstop; 19 years later, he would retire, as a Cub, with 512 homers. Al Kaline played the first full season of 22 with the Tigers.

The story of the year, though, was the Tribe, who bested the seemingly invincible Yanks. Although Larry Doby led the league in home runs (32) and RBI (126) and Bobby Avila placed second in the league behind Boston's Ted Williams with a .341 average, it was Cleveland's pitching that won it. Early Wynn and Bob Lemon each took 23 games to share the league lead. Mike Garcia had the league's best ERA

STRONG-ARMED INDIANS CAN'T OUTHIT GIANTS

at 2.64, and rookie hurlers Don Mossi and Ray Narleski combined for nine wins and 20 saves.

The Yankees got an MVP year from Yogi Berra, and Bob Grim was Rookie of the Year with 20 wins. Age was taking its toll on the rest of the pitching staff, however, and they couldn't catch the Tribe.

The Dodgers were expected to win the National League for a third straight year, but the Giants, coming off a fifth-place finish, ended up taking the flag by 5 games. Willie Mays returned from two years of service and won the MVP, hitting a league-high .345 (right fielder Don Mueller finished second in the NL with a .342 average); he also hammered in 41 home runs to tie with Hank Sauer of Chicago for third place. A trade, however, was what really powered New York.

The Giants shipped Bobby Thomson to the Braves for pitcher Johnny Antonelli, who was 21-7 with a league-leading 2.29 ERA. The trade haunted

Dodger fans, who had been trying to forget about Thomson since his pennant-winning homer in 1951. Giants starters Sal Maglie and Ruben Gomez combined for 31 wins, and relievers Marv Grissom and Hoyt Wilhelm teamed up for 22 wins and 26 saves.

Although Ted Kluszewski provided Cincinnati with a league-topping 49 homers and 141 RBI and Robin Roberts won a circuit-best 23 games for Philadelphia for the third consecutive year, both teams posed little threat to the Giants.

The World Series had some memorable moments. With the score tied two-all in the eighth inning of game one, the Tribe had two men on and Vic Wertz at the plate. He launched a rocket into center field of the Polo Grounds. The legendary Mays turned, sprinted straight back, and made an astonishing over-the-shoulder catch some 440 feet from the plate, preserving the tie. Dusty Rhodes broke the deadlock in the bottom of the tenth with a pinch-hit homer off Lemon.

Antonelli beat Wynn 3-1 in the second game, as Rhodes tied it in the fifth with a pinch-hit single and homered in the seventh. In the third inning of game three, Rhodes delivered a two-run, pinch single to give the Giants a 3-0 lead in a match they finally won 6-2.

The Giants then swept the Series with a 7-4 win in game four.

1954

- Indians break Yankees' choke-hold on AL flag, win AL record 111 games.

- Giants return to top in NL.

- Giants sweep World Series in huge upset.

- Willie Mays makes most famous catch in Series history in game one on long drive by Vic Wertz.

- Giant Dusty Rhodes hits two game-winning homers, drives in seven runs in only six Series at-bats.

- Wertz leads all regular players in Series with .500 BA and eight hits.

- Yankees win 103 games, most in any season under Casey Stengel, but finish a distant second.

- Mays wins National League MVP.

- Yogi Berra takes MVP Award in the American League.

- AL wins All-Star Game 11-9 in Cleveland, as hometown star Al Rosen hits two homers and knocks in five runs.

Willie Mays makes his historic catch of Vic Wertz's booming 460-foot drive
in game one of the 1954 World Series, played at the Polo Grounds. The Giants
took the game 5-2 over the Indians. Wertz hit .500 in the four-game fray; the
rest of the Indians batted .149.

- Mays tops NL in batting (.345) and slugging (.667) after spending past two years in armed service.

- Cleveland pitchers Mike Garcia (2.64), Bob Lemon, and Early Wynn rank one-two-three in ERA.

- Wynn and Lemon tie for the AL lead in wins with 23.

- On August 1, Milwaukee's Joe Adcock hits four homers and collects ML record 18 total bases.

- Players no longer allowed to leave their gloves on playing field while their team is batting.

- Ted Williams returns from Korean War duty and hits .345.

- Cleveland's Bobby Avila awarded AL bat crown (.341) because Williams has fewer than 400 at-bats.

- Cleveland's Larry Doby tops AL in homers (32) and RBI (126).

- The Tribe outscores its opponents by 242 runs.

Bobby Avila, Willie Mays

Avila, Mays Hit .340-Plus

Bobby Avila *(left)* came in second in the American League with a .341 batting average in 1954; Willie Mays topped the National League with his .345 mark that year. Avila was the last Indian to win a hitting crown. Two years later, he hit .224 and had just 115 hits in 138 games.

Browns Head East

Bill Veeck might have remained the St. Louis Browns owner if the franchise could have been shifted to the West Coast or even to Kansas City. The team's move to Baltimore after the 1953 season seemed against the grain to him, and events proved him right. Apart from the Browns and the ill-conceived Seattle Pilots, every franchise shift since 1954 has resulted in a move from a city east of the Mississippi to one in either the West or South.

Bill Veeck

Duke Snider

Snider Can't Carry Dodgers

Duke Snider had his finest all-around season in 1954, as he finished at or near the top in virtually every major batting department—a .341 average, 130 RBI, 120 runs scored. Dismal pitching and a year below par by Roy Campanella, however, doomed the Dodgers. Rookie skipper Walter Alston may have done his best managing job ever to get the club a second-place finish.

1954

- Giants newcomer Johnny Antonelli tops NL in win pct. (.750) and ERA (2.29), and ties for second place in wins (21).

- Robin Roberts leads the NL in wins (23), Ks (185), CGs (29), and innings (337).

- St. Louis' Wally Moon is NL Rookie of the Year.

- Yankee Bob Grim is AL ROTY.

- Grim becomes the only pitcher in ML history to win 20 games while pitching fewer than 200 innings.

- Browns are sold and move to Baltimore, becoming first American League franchise to be moved since 1903.

- On August 8, in the eighth inning, the Dodgers score 12 runs with two out and the bases empty.

- Cards rookie Rip Repulski collects an ML record two-or-more hits in ten consecutive games.

- The sacrifice fly rule is reinstated once again.

New York Giants

Mays, Mueller Fuel Giants

A look at the 1954 World Champion New York Giants. Willie Mays and Don Mueller *(middle row, fourth and fifth from the left)* finished first and second in the National League batting race. Mueller, who also paced the loop in hits, walked so rarely that his career on-base percentage was only 28 points above his batting average.

Early Wynn

Hodges Nets 130 RBI

Gil Hodges, like Duke Snider, also had his top season in 1954, racking up a .304 average, 23 doubles, 42 home runs, and 130 RBI. Between them, Hodges and Snider collected 82 home runs, 260 RBI, and 713 total bases. All three totals were easily the best in the majors that year by a pair of teammates. The Orioles, in contrast, got just 91 combined RBI and 14 home runs from their strongest duo—Vern Stephens and Bob Kennedy, who split time at third base. In 1955, Hodges would knock in 100 runs for the seventh consecutive season.

Gil Hodges

Wynn Dusts Off Giants

Early Wynn maintained that he would dust off his own mother if she came up to bat against him with the game on the line. In game two of the 1954 World Series, he gave up just four hits, two of them to Dusty Rhodes. Cleveland fans waited in vain for Wynn to dust Dusty.

- Cincy's Ted Kluszewski breaks Johnny Mize's NL record when he scores at least one run in 17 straight games.

- Karl Spooner of the Dodgers hurls shutouts in his first two ML starts.

- Spooner sets an ML record by fanning 15 batters in his big league debut.

- Jim Wilson of Milwaukee no-hits the Phils on June 12.

- After the season, the Yankees and Baltimore make a record 18-player swap.

- On May 2, Stan Musial becomes first player to hit five homers in a doubleheader.

- Bobby Thomson's injury frees a spot in the Braves outfield for rookie second baseman Hank Aaron, who hits .280.

- Duke Snider leads NL in runs (120) and total bases (378).

- Kluszewski tops NL in homers (49) and RBI (141).

AL's All-Star Heroes

A shot of the American League heroes of the 1954 All-Star Game *(left to right)*: Larry Doby, Ray Boone, Al Rosen, Bobby Avila, and Nellie Fox. Rosen nailed two home runs that day; Doby and Boone had one apiece. Boone, traded to Detroit in 1953, began his career with Cleveland as Lou Boudreau's much-maligned replacement at shortstop. The Tigers made him a third baseman, and for four years he was the best in the AL.

All-Star Game Heroes

Larry Doby

Doby: Lots of HRs, Lots of Strikeouts

The rap on Larry Doby was that he chased bad pitches and struck out too often. In 1954, he led the American League with 32 home runs and 126 RBI. Upon retirement in 1959, he held the major league career record for the most strikeouts (18.9) per 100 at-bats; by 1990, Doby barely ranked among the top 50 in Ks per 100 at-bats.

Ted Williams

Ted Robbed of BA Title

By today's rules, Ted Williams would have won the American League batting title in 1954. Although he had just 386 at-bats, his 136 walks would have given him well over the minimum number of plate appearances needed to currently qualify. He was, however, conceded the slugging crown, as his .635 slugging average was a full 100 points better than runner-up Minnie Minoso's mark.

1954

- Musial leads NL in doubles (41) and ties in runs (120).

- The Hall of Fame inducts Rabbit Maranville, Bill Dickey, and Bill Terry.

- Ray Jablonski of the Cards becomes second player in ML history to drive in 100 runs in first two seasons.

- After the season, St. Louis trades Jablonski and Gerry Staley to Cincinnati for Frank Smith.

- Baltimore trades Roy Sievers to Washington for Gil Coan.

- The Cards deal Enos Slaughter to the Yankees for Bill Virdon, Mel Wright, and Emil Tellinger.

- The Orioles ship Wertz to Cleveland for Bob Chakales.

- In August, the Yanks buy Jim Konstanty from the Phils.

- Prior to the season, the Braves trade Antonelli, Don Liddle, and two other players to the Giants for Thomson and Sam Calderon.

Eddie Stanky, Stan Musial

Stan is *Real*'s Main Man

Cardinals manager Eddie Stanky *(left)* and Stan Musial scan *Real* magazine, which polled all 16 major league managers to name Musial the greatest player in baseball in 1954. That year, Musial played on a second division team for the first time. The Cards finished in sixth place despite topping the National League in runs and hitting.

World Series

Yogi Berra

Yogi: Two Awards, Two Sons

Yogi Berra displays his second MVP Award as well as his two sons, Tim *(left)* and Larry. In 1954, Berra hit .307 and knocked home 125 runs; he also caught 149 games. Two years later, Dale—the only Berra to follow in his father's footsteps—was born.

Rhodes Homers Again

For the second day in a row, backup outfielder and pinch-hitter Dusty Rhodes of the Giants rounds the bases after hitting a home run during the 1954 World Series. His 280-foot fly ball in game two hit the upper facing of the right-field stands at the Polo Grounds, just inside the foul pole.

- Cass Michaels of the White Sox is beaned and his skull is fractured; he's forced to retire at age 28.

- Gil Hodges of the Dodgers sets an ML record with 19 sacrifice flies.

- Only three AL teams win more than 69 games—Cleveland, New York, and Chicago (94).

- Cleveland is only 22-22 against New York and Chicago, but goes 89-21 against the rest of the AL.

- The Yankees' 103 wins are the most ever by an AL also-ran.

- Red Sox finish fourth in AL with a .448 win pct.

- The Pirates lose 100 or more games for the third year in a row.

- The World Series winner's share tops $10,000 per player for the first time.

- Joe Bauman of Roswell in the Longhorn League hits an OB record 72 home runs.

THE 1955 BASEBALL CHRONICLE

HEARTBREAK IS OVER: DODGERS WIN IT ALL

After a heartbreaking string of near-misses that began in 1947, the Dodgers would finally have their year in 1955, breezing to the pennant and nipping the Yanks in seven tough games to win it all.

It was the most balanced Dodger team in years. Roy Campanella fully recovered from the hand injury that hampered him in 1954 and once again led Brooklyn, batting .318 with 32 home runs en route to a third MVP Award. Duke Snider belted 42 round-trippers with a .309 average and topped the league with 136 RBI and 126 runs scored. Don Newcombe rebounded from a poor season and pitched to a masterful 20-5 record, while Clem Labine was reliable out of the bullpen with 13 wins and 11 saves.

Sophomore skipper Walter Alston had the Dodgers flying out of the starting gate. They won their first ten—20 of their first 22—and were ahead by 12½ on July 4. Eddie Mathews's 41 homers weren't enough for the Braves and Willie Mays's 51 dingers and .319 average weren't enough for the Giants as the Dodgers won the pennant by 13½ games over Milwaukee and 18½ over New York (the Giants were also hurt by weak performances from Johnny Antonelli and Ruben Gomez).

Although Philadelphia had Robin Roberts (the winner of 23 games, the most in the league for the fourth straight year) and

Richie Ashburn (the batting champ at .338), they couldn't catch the Dodgers either, finishing a whopping 21½ games back. The most that last-place Pittsburgh could do was come up with the ERA champ in Bob Friend, who posted a 2.84 mark.

The Yankees and Yogi Berra, who won his third MVP, took a sixth American League flag in seven years. The Bronx Bombers, able to survive pitching problems with good years from Bob Turley and Don Larsen and with Mickey Mantle (a league-high 37 homers), held off Cleveland by 3 games with a 96-58 record. The Indians got 16 victories and a league-topping 245 strikeouts from Rookie of the Year Herb Score, but they lacked offensive punch and never really made a run for it.

Third-place Chicago took consolation in Billy Pierce and his 1.97 ERA, best in the majors. Jackie Jensen's 116 RBI (tops in the league) and Frank Sullivan's 18 wins (tied for first) took Boston to fourth place. Detroit fin-

ished fifth, as sophomore right fielder Al Kaline, age 20, won the batting title with a .340 average to become the youngest batting champion ever (he was younger than Ty Cobb by one day).

But far and away, the highlight of 1955 was the World Series. The Yankees took the first two games 6-5 and 4-2. The Dodgers came back in the next three: Campanella had three hits and three RBI, including a two-run homer, to give Brooklyn and Johnny Podres an 8-3 win in game three. Campanella, Gil Hodges, and Snider all homered in the following contest and Labine pitched the final four frames, as the Dodgers evened the Series with an 8-5 victory in game four.

In game five, Snider hammered two more home runs and Sandy Amoros hit one, as the Dodgers won 5-3. The Yankees dominated the Dodgers in game six, winning 5-1 behind Whitey Ford's four-hitter.

Podres took a 2-0 lead into the bottom of the sixth of game seven, but Billy Martin led off with a walk and then Gil Mc-Dougald bounced an infield single. Berra strode to the plate for the go-ahead run. He lofted a fly ball deep into the left field corner. Amoros made the catch with an outstretched arm at the last second, then got the ball back to the infield to double up McDougald. Podres completed the eight-hit shutout that, at long last, crowned the Dodgers World Champions.

1955

- Yankees return to top in AL.
- Dodgers likewise in NL.
- Dodgers win their first World Series in seven games.
- Johnny Podres is Brooklyn hero with two CG wins and a shutout in game seven.

- Yogi Berra is leading hitter in World Series with ten hits and .417 BA.
- Dodgers rally from a two-game Series deficit, as they drop the first two games in Yankee Stadium.
- Berra named AL MVP for third time in five years.

- Roy Campanella is NL MVP for second time in three years.
- Detroit's Al Kaline wins AL bat title at age 20—youngest bat crown winner in ML history.
- Cleveland rookie Herb Score tops AL in Ks with 245, setting ML rookie record for Ks.

Johnny Podres swings from the roof of his locker in the visitors' dressing room at Yankee Stadium on October 4, 1955. Podres's 2-0 win that afternoon not only brought the Dodgers their first World Championship; his triumph also marked the first time since 1926 that the Yankees had lost a seven-game Series.

- Dodger pitcher Don Newcombe cracks 42 hits.

- Rookie pitcher Toothpick Sam Jones of the Cubs sets NL record with 185 walks.

- Jones also tops the NL in strikeouts with 198.

- Jones no-hits Pirates on May 12 after walking the bases full in the ninth and then fanning the side.

- Phillie Richie Ashburn leads NL in batting (.338).

- Robin Roberts again tops NL in wins, as he earns 23.

- Roberts leads the NL in CGs (26) and innings (305).

- Roberts leads the NL in starts a record sixth straight year.

- Yankee Mickey Mantle wins AL homer crown (37), his first of four such titles.

Banks Sets HR Record

Ernie Banks hit his first major league home run on September 23, 1953. Less than two years later, he became the first shortstop in history to slam 40 four-baggers in a season, nailing 44 round-trippers in 1955. Banks also was the first slugger to hit 500 or more home runs and never play on a pennant-winner.

Ernie Banks

Don Newcombe

Newcombe Emerges

Don Newcombe won 47 games and lost just 12 for the Dodgers in the 1955 and '56 seasons. In 1955, he topped the National League with his .800 winning percentage; in 1956, he led the circuit with his .794 winning percentage. In three World Series starts during those two seasons, however, Newcombe had two losses.

Yogi Berra

Berra Cops Third MVP

Yogi Berra picked up his third MVP plaque in 1955 for a season performance that included 20 doubles, 27 home runs, and 108 RBI. Berra also finished second in the balloting in 1953 and again in 1956, third in 1950, and fourth in 1952. No other player has ever been so highly regarded by MVP voters for a seven-year span.

1955

- Mantle leads AL in OBP (.433), walks (113), and SA (.611), and ties in triples (11).

- Willie Mays hits 51 homers to pace the NL.

- Duke Snider leads majors in runs (126), RBI (136), and runs produced (220).

- Elston Howard is the first black American to play for Yankees, one of last teams to break the color line.

- Down 5-0 at one point, the NL rallies to win All-Star Game 6-5 in 12 innings at Milwaukee.

- Score is AL Rookie of the Year.

- Bill Virdon of Cards is NL ROTY.

- Cincinnati's Ted Kluszewski slams 47 home runs, giving him 136 homers and only 109 strikeouts from 1953 through 1955.

- Kluszewski leads the NL in hits with 192.

- Newcombe wins 20 games, tops NL in win pct. (.800).

Klu Clubs 47 HRs

Over the four-year span between 1953 and 1956, Ted Kluszewski drilled 171 home runs while fanning just 140 times, about the same amount that the typical home run leader nowadays whiffs in a single season. In 1955, "Klu" led the National League in hits with 192, came in second in home runs with 47 and total bases with 358, tied for third in runs scored with 116, and placed fifth in RBI with 113.

Ted Kluszewski

Campy Again NL MVP

Upon receiving his third Most Valuable Player Award in 1955, Roy Campanella (.318 average, 32 home runs, 107 RBI) said, "When you win the first award, you're happy. When you win the second, you're very happy. When you win the third, you're overwhelmed." Campanella and Yogi Berra are the only catchers to be honored as three-time MVPs.

Roy Campanella

Mickey Mantle

Mantle Tops AL in HRs, Triples

In 1955, Mickey Mantle led the American League in home runs with 37 and tied for first place in triples with 11. Although Mantle would have a few more seasons in which he would top the circuit in home runs, he never again hit more than six triples in a season. Following a serious knee injury in 1962, he hit just a half-dozen three-baggers in his last seven seasons. Mantle also collected remarkably few doubles during his career.

- Pirate Bob Friend leads NL in ERA (2.84).

- Calvin Griffith, adopted son of Clark, takes over as Senators president upon his father's death.

- Washington's Harmon Killebrew hits his first ML home run on June 24 at age 18.

- Ernie Banks of Cubs hits five grandslams.

- Banks becomes the first shortstop to hit 40 homers in a season, as he cracks 44.

- Dodgers open season with ten consecutive wins.

- Milwaukee's Bill Bruton takes third consecutive NL theft crown (25).

- Kaline leads AL in hits (200), total bases (321), and runs produced (196).

- Bob Lemon, Whitey Ford, and Boston's Frank Sullivan tie for AL lead in wins with 18.

Campanella on the Run

Roy Campanella narrowly avoids toppling over the railing as he chases a foul pop in the 1955 World Series. The hatless gray-haired man who is trying to get out of Campanella's path *(front row)* is Ford Frick, the then-commissioner of baseball.

Al Kaline

World Series

Kaline Wins AL Bat Title

As a teenager in Baltimore, Al Kaline rooted for the Washington Senators and hoped to sign with them. When the Nats showed little interest, he went with the Tigers instead. Kaline made his major league debut just a couple of weeks after he graduated from high school and never played a day in the minors. He hit for a career-high .340 in 1955, the best average in the majors.

Walter O'Malley, Walter Alston

Dodgers Celebrate

Owner Walter O'Malley *(left)* and manager Walter Alston embrace in the Brooklyn dressing room after Johnny Podres brings an end to the Dodgers' long World Championship drought. Prior to 1955, the closest a Brooklyn team had come to winning a postseason affair was in 1890. This would be Brooklyn's only World Title. The Dodgers would win four crowns in LA.

1955

- For the first time in history, no AL pitcher wins 20 games.

- Ford leads the AL in CGs with just 18—fewest by a loop leader to this juncture.

- Sullivan paces the AL in innings with just 260.

- Yankee Tommy Byrne, back from the minors, leads AL in win pct. (.762).

- White Sox Billy Pierce's 1.97 ERA tops majors.

- Enos Slaughter of A's tops majors with 16 pinch hits; has .322 BA in 267 at-bats at age 39.

- Boston's Jackie Jensen and Detroit's Ray Boone tie for AL RBI lead (116).

- Joe DeMaestri of the A's goes 6-for-7 in an 11-inning game on July 8.

- The Hall of Fame inducts Joe DiMaggio, Ted Lyons, Dazzy Vance, Gabby Hartnett, Home Run Baker, and Ray Schalk.

Roy Campanella

Campy Belts 32 HRs

A common scene in the Brooklyn dugout in 1955. Four Dodgers hit 26 or more home runs, and the club topped the majors in four-baggers with 201. The slugger being congratulated in this instance is Roy Campanella, who ripped 32 circuit-clouts that season.

World Series

Furillo Clinches Game Five

Carl Furillo of the Dodgers slides safely back into second as a Yankees' pickoff attempt fails in the eighth inning of game five of the 1955 World Series. Moments later, Furillo scored the final run of the contest on a single by Jackie Robinson to give Brooklyn a 5-3 victory and a 3-2 lead in games.

Roberts Wins 23

Robin Roberts was a 20-game winner for the sixth consecutive season in 1955, spearheading the National League with 23 victories and 305 innings pitched. Although only 29 years of age that year, Roberts never had another 20-victory campaign. For the remaining 11 seasons of his career, he was a sub-.500 pitcher and a loop leader in only one department—losses.

Robin Roberts

- The Pirates finish last for the fourth consecutive year.

- The A's move to Kansas City—the first franchise shift that is not an immediate financial success.

- Six AL teams begin the 1955 season with managers who were not at their helm at the start of the 1954 season.

- In a four-inning relief stint on July 19, Detroit's Babe Birrer hits two home runs in his only two at-bats.

- Braves teammates Hank Aaron and Johnny Logan tie for the NL lead in doubles with 37.

- Mantle and teammate Andy Carey tie for the AL triples lead with 11.

- The Phils swap Smoky Burgess and two other players to the Reds for Andy Seminick, Jim Greengrass, and Glen Gorbous.

- Al Smith of Cleveland leads the AL in runs with 123.

- Ray Narleski of Cleveland tops the majors with 19 saves.

NEWK IS GOOD, BUT LARSEN'S PERFECT

The Yankees opened the 1956 season wanting revenge. Their target: The Dodgers, who had beaten them the year before.

New York took hold of first place on May 16 and never looked back, giving Casey Stengel his seventh flag in eight tries. Mickey Mantle, age 24, became the newest Yankee Stadium legend, winning the Triple Crown and the Most Valuable Player Award with 52 home runs, 130 RBI, and a .353 average. Yogi Berra totaled 30 homers and 105 RBI, Hank Bauer knocked 26 homers, Gil McDougald batted .311, and Bill Skowron averaged .308. Pitcher and ERA champ Whitey Ford won 19 games, Johnny Kucks claimed 18, and Tom Sturdivant took 16.

With Bob Lemon, Herb Score, and Early Wynn all winning 20 games, the Yankees might have been caught—if strong-armed Cleveland could hit. The Indians finished 9 games out.

The Tigers won just 82 games, but featured Frank Lary, the league-leader with 21 triumphs. Lary became known as the "Yankee Killer," going 5-1 against the Yanks in 1956 and 7-0 in 1958.

The National League battle was waged by Brooklyn, Milwaukee, and, surprisingly, Cincinnati. The defending champion Dodgers were carried by Don Newcombe, whose 27 wins earned him MVP honors and baseball's first Cy Young Award. Dodger Sal Maglie, obtained off waivers early in the season, won 13 and tossed a no-hitter against the Phils in September. Duke Snider clubbed a league-high 43 homers, teammate Gil Hodges belted 32 round-trippers, and Junior Gilliam hit .300 to pace the offense.

The Braves were led by Hank Aaron (the batting champ with a .328 average along with 26 homers) and Warren Spahn (20-11), Lew Burdette (19-10, a league-low 2.71 ERA), and Bob Buhl (18-8). Rookie of the Year Frank Robinson supplied 38 of Cincinnati's 221 homers (tied with the 1947 Giants for the most home runs by a team in a season) and scored a league-high 122 runs.

As Brooklyn swept the Pirates, the Braves lost two of three to the Cardinals and finished 1 game back. Cincinnati ended up 2 games off. The Dodgers closed with a 93-61 record. Even with RBI leader Stan Musial, St. Louis couldn't get above fourth.

The Bums cruised to a 6-3 victory in the World Series opener behind Maglie, then roughed up Don Larsen in their 13-8 game two win. As the Series shifted to the Bronx, so did the tide. Ford and Sturdivant notched wins in the next two games.

On October 8, Larsen made headlines by hurling a perfect game—the only no-hitter in Series history. Using a no-windup style, the righthander cut down 27 consecutive batters and struck out seven. There were some close calls: A deflected Jackie Robinson line drive in the second inning was saved by McDougald; Mantle caught Hodges's long drive with a sensational backhand move in the fifth; and in the eighth, Andy Carey snapped up Hodges's line drive inches from the ground.

In the ninth inning, Carl Furillo flied out and Roy Campanella bounced out. Up came pinch hitter Dale Mitchell. Larsen's first pitch was wide. His second, a slider, rendered a called strike. Mitchell swung and missed on the third pitch and fouled off the fourth. Hitting the outside corner, the last pitch was declared a called strike. The pitcher who claimed a 30-40 record over four major league seasons had himself a record-setting feat.

Clem Labine threw a scoreless ten frames and Jackie Robinson, in his last season, singled in the bottom of the tenth to give the Dodgers a 1-0 win in game six. The Yanks scored off five Dodger hurlers in the seventh game to make the Series finale a 9-0 blowout.

1956

- Yanks cop AL flag by 9 games.
- Dodgers repeat in NL, squeaking past Braves by 1 game.
- Yankee Don Larsen pitches only perfect game in World Series history in game five to put Yankees up three games to two.
- Yanks win World Series in seven games.
- Brooklyn's Clem Labine, normally a relief pitcher, beats the Yankees 1-0 in ten innings in game six of Series.
- Yogi Berra tops all hitters in Series with .360 BA and ten RBI.
- Don Newcombe wins NL MVP.
- Newcombe also wins first-ever Cy Young Award (only one given each year until 1967).
- Mickey Mantle is AL MVP.
- Mantle wins Triple Crown, hitting .353 with 52 homers and 130 RBI.

Yogi Berra leaps into Don Larsen's arms after Larsen seals his perfect game in the 1956 World Series by fanning Dale Mitchell. The feat won Larsen everlasting fame—and a token raise (nothing compared to the financial reward he would have gotten had he thrown a perfect game today).

- Reds hit 221 homers to set ML record (since broken).

- Cincinnati fans stuff ballot boxes; all the Reds regulars are voted All-Star starters.

- Commissioner Ford Frick disallows vote and replaces some of the Reds with more deserving players.

- Dale Long of Pirates hits home runs in record eight consecutive games.

- The Reds' Frank Robinson clubs 38 homers to tie NL rookie record (also ML record at the time).

- Mantle is first switch-hitter to lead a major league in batting since 1889.

- Newcombe leads majors in wins (27) and in win pct. (.794).

- Milwaukee's Hank Aaron wins NL batting crown (.328).

- Willie Mays tops NL with 40 steals, most in majors since 1944.

- NL wins All-Star Game 7-3 at Washington.

Clem Labine

Don Newcombe

Newk Grabs Cy Young, MVP

Dan Daniel, president of the Baseball Writers Association of America, presents Don Newcombe with the first Cy Young Award, while National League president Warren Giles hands Newk the 1956 MVP plaque. The dual ceremony preceded the Dodgers' 1957 home opener, the last one ever played at Ebbets Field. Newcombe's 1956 performance included a major league-topping 27 victories, five shutouts (tied for second in the circuit), and a 3.06 ERA (fifth in the loop).

Labine: Brooklyn's MVP

Clem Labine was quite probably Brooklyn's most valuable pitcher during the mid-1950s. In 1956, Labine led the majors with 19 saves. His 1-0 shutout of the Yankees in game six of the 1956 World Series was eclipsed by Don Larsen's perfect game the day before and by the blowout of the Dodgers in game seven. It was his last complete game in the majors. Labine had some rather notable accomplishments in his career: He shut out the Giants in the second game of the 1951 NL playoff; he retired Stan Musial 49 straight times; and he collected three hits in 1951—all home runs.

Duke Snider

Snider: Last Dodger HR King

In 1956, Duke Snider became the sixth Dodgers player since 1900—and the last to date—to win the National League home run crown, hitting 43 dingers that season. In 1957, he became the first player ever to hit 40 or more round-trippers and net less than 100 RBI.

1956

- On Sept. 21, Yankees leave an ML record 20 men on base in nine-inning game vs. Boston.

- Jim Derrington of White Sox, age 16, becomes youngest pitcher in this century to start a game.

- Carl Erskine of Brooklyn no-hits Giants on May 12.

- On May 26, three Reds pitchers throw a combined no-hitter vs. Milwaukee for nine innings, but lose 2-1 in 11 innings.

- Boston's Mel Parnell no-hits White Sox on July 14.

- Sal Maglie of Brooklyn no-hits Phils on Sept. 25.

- Maglie is released by Cleveland, signs with Brooklyn, and is voted NL MVP runner-up.

- Braves lead NL race by 1 game with three to play, but drop two of three while Dodgers win three straight.

- Aaron tops the NL in hits (200), doubles (34), and runs produced (172).

Mickey Mantle

Mantle: 52 HRs, 130 RBI

By racking up a .353 average, 52 home runs, and 130 RBI in 1956, Mickey Mantle became the first switch-hitter in modern history to win a batting crown and the only one ever to win a Triple Crown. He also set all-time switch-hitter records for slugging average (.705) and total bases (376), and the modern RBI mark for switch-hitters.

Series Fails to Sell Out

A crowd shot at Yankee Stadium during a 1956 World Series game. Of the three games played there, only the first drew close to a sellout crowd. Game five, the final contest at the stadium and the matchup in which Don Larsen achieved perfection, was played to some 10,000 empty seats.

Aparicio Brings Back the Steal

Luis Aparicio served notice in his rookie season that a dimension that had been missing from the game for some 30 years was about to return. Though he stole only 21 bases in 1956, he was caught swiping just four times. Aparicio's high rate of success induced him to increase his attempts with each passing season.

Luis Aparicio

World Series

- Rookie Robinson tops NL in runs (122).

- Duke Snider tops the NL in homers (43), SA (.598), OBP (.402), and walks (99).

- Mantle leads in runs (132), runs produced (210), SA (.705), and total bases (376).

- Herb Score wins 20 for Cleveland, tops majors in Ks (263) and AL in shutouts (five).

- Cleveland once again has three 20-game winners, but finishes second to New York.

- White Sox Luis Aparicio tops AL in thefts (21), is AL Rookie of the Year.

- Robinson is NL ROTY.

- Whitey Ford leads AL in win pct. (.760) and ERA (2.47).

- The Hall of Fame inducts Hank Greenberg and Joe Cronin.

- Al Lopez leaves as Cleveland's manager and is hired by the White Sox.

1956

Robinson Blooms in a Hurry

Many in the Reds organization doubted that Frank Robinson was ready for the parent club in 1956. The previous year, he had hit just .263 for Columbia in the Class-A Sally League. By midseason of 1956, however, the question became whether National League pitchers were ready for Robinson. He led the loop with 122 runs scored and tied for second place with 38 home runs.

Ford Just Can't Lose

Whitey Ford led the American League with his .760 winning percentage and his 2.47 ERA in 1956. In just one of his first 13 seasons with the Yankees did Ford lose as many as ten games. His career record after the 1964 season, his last great year, was 216-84 for a .720 win percentage. Playing for a losing New York team in his final three campaigns, Ford was 20-22.

Frank Robinson

Whitey Ford

Mays: Speed with Power

Willie Mays (pictured sliding safely into third) became the only player to hit 50 or more home runs one season and lead his league in steals the next by nailing 51 home runs in 1955 and pilfering 40 bases (in 50 attempts) in 1956. Mays swiped 338 cushions in his career, including 23 in 1971, the year he turned 40 years old.

Willie Mays

1956

- The Phils swap Del Ennis to the Cards for Rip Repulski and Bobby Morgan.

- The Giants send Al Dark and three other players to the Cards for Red Schoendienst, Jackie Brandt, and three others.

- Connie Mack dies at age 93.

- Kansas City trades Eddie Robinson and three other players to Detroit for Virgil Trucks, Ned Garver, and two others.

- Kansas City rookie Troy Herriage goes 1-13 with a 6.64 ERA in his only ML season.

- KC's Al Ditmar leads the majors with 22 losses.

- Orioles bonus baby Tom Gastall perishes at sea in a private plane crash.

- Johnny Podres misses the season when he's inducted into the Navy.

- Washington's Eddie Yost leads the majors in walks with a whopping 151.

Yanks Finally Break the Color Line

A look at the 1956 World Champion New York Yankees. What is unique about this picture is that it includes a black player. The Yankees were one of the last teams to continue to field an all-white crew. Pressure on the club to break the color line grew until Elston Howard made the final roster in 1955.

New York Yankees

Jackie Robinson

Jackie Hangs Up His Spikes

Jackie Robinson (pictured escaping a tag to score) chose to retire at the finish of the 1956 season rather than report to the hated Giants to whom he was traded. He wrapped up his career with a ten-home run, 43-RBI year. In Robinson's ten seasons with Brooklyn, the Dodgers won six pennants and their first World Championship. Wrote Roger Kahn: "(Robinson) had intimidating skills, and he burned with a dark fire. He wanted passionately to win. . . . He bore the burden of a pioneer and the weight made him more strong. If one can be certain of anything in baseball, it is that we shall not look upon his like again."

- Washington's Jim Lemon sets an ML record for batter Ks with 138.
- Stan Musial leads the NL in RBI (109).
- Detroit's Harvey Kuenn leads the AL in hits with 196.
- Boston's Jimmy Piersall leads the majors with 40 doubles.

- Detroit's Frank Lary leads the AL in wins (21) and innings (294).
- Billy Hoeft joins Lary to give Detroit two 20-game winners.
- Labine leads the ML in saves with 19.
- Robin Roberts again leads the majors in CGs (22).

- Cubs pitcher Sam Jones again leads the NL in whiffs (176).
- Milwaukee's Lew Burdette tops the NL in ERA at 2.71.
- Detroit manager Bucky Harris retires after 29 years as an ML helmsman.
- Ted Williams leads the ML in OBP (.479).

With the Yankees, Giants, and Dodgers claiming every flag in sight thus far in the 1950s, fans were beginning to feel that baseball existed only in New York. That changed in 1957, however, as the world discovered Hank Aaron and the Milwaukee Braves.

After managing the Pirates to three straight last-place finishes, Fred Haney took over as the Braves skipper midway through the 1956 season. The Braves found the aging Dodgers ripe for the picking in '57. In another of his many magnificent years, Aaron earned the Most Valuable Player Award on his league-leading 44 homers and 132 RBI and his .322 average. Eddie Mathews contributed 32 homers and Red Schoendienst, picked up in a trade, hit .310. Although the Braves lost Bill Bruton and Joe Adcock to injury, they did have Wes Covington (21 homers) and Bob Hazle (.403 in 134 at-bats).

The Braves' pitching staff was strong as well, paced by the Big Three of Cy Young Award-winner Warren Spahn (21-11, 2.69 ERA), Lew Burdette (17-9, 3.71 ERA), and Bob Buhl (18-7, 2.74 ERA). When help was needed in the bullpen, Haney brought out Don McMahon (nine saves, 1.53 ERA). Milwaukee took the flag at 95-59, 8 games ahead of the Cardinals (who had batting champ Stan Musial with a .351 average) and 11 ahead of the Dodgers (who had the top two ERA men in Johnny Podres and Don Drysdale).

BRAVES AND HANK HAMMER THE YANKS

Although superstar Willie Mays hit 35 homers and led the league in steals with 38, New York finished 26 games behind. Last-place Chicago had its own hitting sensation in Ernie Banks, who smacked 43 homers.

In the American League, the White Sox took an early lead, thanks to Luis Aparicio, Nellie Fox, and Minnie Minoso. The Yankee bats then took over, and New York breezed to the pennant. Mickey Mantle won another MVP title with a .365 average and 34 home runs. Yogi Berra went downtown 24 times, while Bill Skowron (.304) and Rookie of the Year Tony Kubek (.297) were reliable bats.

With Whitey Ford having a sub-par year on the hill, manager Casey Stengel needed steady hurling from Tom Sturdivant (16-6, 2.54 ERA), a strong comeback of Bob Turley (13-6, 2.71 ERA), and the acquisition of Kansas City's Bobby Shantz (11-5, a league-best 2.45 ERA). The Yankees, 98-56 on the season, took the flag from the White Sox—and 20-game winner Billy Pierce, who tied with

Detroit's Jim Bunning for the lead in victories—by 8 games.

Although Boston finished a distant third, 39-year-old Ted Williams hit a loop-high .388 with 38 home runs to become the oldest batting champion ever. Cleveland, which had lost Al Rosen and Bob Feller to retirement, lost southpaw phenom Herb Score on May 7 when he was hit in the face by Gil McDougald's line drive. Although Washington's Roy Sievers led the league with 42 homers and 114 RBI, the Senators brought up the rear.

The Series opened in New York, with Ford tossing a five-hitter and the Yankees winning 3-1. The Braves took the second game in Yankee Stadium behind Burdette's 4-2 complete game triumph. Kubek hit two homers as the Yanks romped to a 12-3 score in game three, and the Braves took game four 7-5 on Mathews's three-run homer in the tenth inning.

Although Burdette out-dueled Ford by one in game five, the Yanks evened the Series with a 3-2 win in game six. Burdette pitched his third complete game of the Series in game seven, as the Braves won 5-0 to take the Championship flag out of the Big Apple for the first time since 1948.

The title was not all that New York lost that year. Citing inefficient ballparks and a lack of parking facilities, the owners of the Dodgers and Giants ballclubs moved their teams to California at season's end.

1957

- Braves win NL flag.
- Yanks take third in row in AL.
- Braves triumph in World Series in seven games.
- Brave Lew Burdette has three CG World Series wins, including two shutouts.

- Hank Aaron leads Series batters with 11 hits, seven RBI, and .393 BA.
- Fred Haney manages World Champs two years after piloting Pirates to third straight cellar finish.
- Aaron named NL MVP.
- Mickey Mantle repeats as AL MVP.

- Ted Williams tops AL with .388 BA, highest in ML since his own .406 in 1941.
- For second time in his career, Williams loses the MVP by one vote.
- Aaron wins his first NL homer crown with 44.

Lew Burdette *(left)* hugs Braves skipper Fred Haney after Burdette's 5-0 shutout brings Milwaukee the franchise's first World Championship since 1914. Moments later, when asked by reporters how it felt to be victorious, Haney said, "If Lew could cook, I'd marry him."

- Warren Spahn leads majors with 21 wins.

- Stan Musial wins his last bat crown (.351).

- Musial bats over .300 for the 15th consecutive year.

- Senators steal 13 bases, fewest ever by an ML team.

- Herb Score is hit in eye by line drive, nearly killed, and never regains his overpowering fastball.

- Brooklyn's Danny McDevitt shuts out Pirates 3-0 on Sept. 28 in last ML game at Ebbets Field.

- Giants and Dodgers play their final games as New York-based teams.

- For first time in ML history, no pitcher in either league completes as many as 20 games.

- AL wins All-Star Game 6-5 at St. Louis.

- Spahn wins Cy Young Award.

- Tony Kubek is AL Rookie of the Year.

Yogi Berra, Don Larsen

Yogi, Larsen Relive Glory

Yogi Berra *(left)* and Don Larsen hold a replica of the glove Berra used to catch Larsen's perfect game in the 1956 World Series. The following season, Larsen was 10-4 as a spot starter. Called on in desperation by Casey Stengel in the final game of the 1957 World Series, he was kayoed by the Braves in the third inning. In his career, Larsen pitched for nine big league teams and compiled a mere 81-91 record.

Hank Aaron

Kubek Earns Job at Shortstop

Like Mickey Mantle, Tony Kubek was a shortstop during his minor league apprenticeship. Unwilling to trust such an important job to a recruit, Casey Stengel stationed Gil McDougald at short in 1957 and used Kubek in utility roles. Kubek hit .297 as a rookie, making the shortstop post his in 1958. Despite hitting a light .266 in his nine-year career, Kubek was an excellent defensive shortstop who helped New York to six World Series. In game seven of the 1960 Series, he was struck in the throat by a bad-hop grounder, which opened the gates for a Pittsburgh victory.

Tony Kubek

Aaron is Named MVP

Hank Aaron (pictured) was the National League's Most Valuable Player in 1957, winning by a nine-vote margin over Stan Musial. Aaron hit .322 that year, racking up a league-leading 44 home runs, 132 RBI, and 118 runs scored. Two other Braves, Warren Spahn and Red Schoendienst, also finished among the top five in the balloting. The Dodgers, who had dominated the MVP voting for the past decade, placed only one player—Gil Hodges—among the top 15.

1957

- Jack Sanford of Phils is NL ROTY.
- Gold Glove Awards are originated, but only one given at each position in 1957.
- Willie Mays, Al Kaline, and White Sox Minnie Minoso win first three Gold Gloves for outfielders.
- Gold Gloves go to White Sox Nellie Fox (second base), Red Sox Frank Malzone (third), and Red Roy McMillan (short).
- Gold Gloves go to Dodger Gil Hodges (first base), White Sox Sherm Lollar (catcher), and Yankee Bobby Shantz (pitcher).
- Williams reaches base a record 16 times in 16 consecutive plate appearances.
- Bob Keegan of the White Sox no-hits Washington on August 20.
- Black infielder John Kennedy debuts with Phils, the last NL team to break the color line.

Giants Bid Last Farewell

A shot of the closing ceremony held at the final game played by the Giants at the Polo Grounds (the ballclub moved to San Francisco for the 1958 season). Giants manager Bill Rigney and John McGraw's widow pose for the cameras. The Pirates, the Giants' foes that day, also opposed the Dodgers in the last game ever played at Ebbets Field.

New York Giants, Closing Ceremony

Turley, 13-6, Finally Blooms

Once the most promising prospect in the Browns' farm system, Bob Turley still had not begun to realize his vast potential in 1957 (he finished the year at 13-6). The following season, almost magically, it all came together for him. He went 21-7 and won the Cy Young Award. It would be his only great season.

Bob Turley

Mickey Mantle

Mantle Hits Peak at .365

Mickey Mantle was at his peak in 1957. He led the American League in runs scored with 121, placed second in batting with a .365 average and in total bases with 315, and came in third in home runs with 34. Just 25 years of age, he seemed destined to shatter records for years to come. Casey Stengel called Mantle the purest talent he ever saw: "He had it in his body to be great." By 1957, however, Mantle's body had already taken so much abuse that the predicted records never materialized.

- Ernie Banks's record streak of 424 consecutive games played at start of career ends (record since broken).
- Eddie Robinson leaves majors having played for every AL franchise except the Red Sox.
- Aaron tops NL in runs (118), RBI (132), and total bases (369).

- Mays tops NL in triples (20) and steals (38).
- Mantle leads AL in runs (121) and walks (146).
- Williams, at age 39, leads AL in SA (.731) and OBP (.528).
- Minoso leads AL in doubles (36) and runs produced (187).

- Washington's Roy Sievers leads AL in homers (42), RBI (114), and total bases (331).
- Sievers sets Senators records for home runs and total bases.
- The Braves hit an ML record 1.61 homers per game on the road.

Stan Musial

Musial Captures BA Title

National League president Warren Giles presents Stan Musial with his seventh and final batting award to honor the player's .351 average in 1957. Musial played until 1963, hitting above .288 just once in his last five seasons. As a result, his career average dropped from .340 to .331.

Malzone: Good as Gold

Although Frank Malzone began his pro career at age 18, he did not stick with the Red Sox until he was past 27. With such a lengthy maturation, many thought he would be, at best, a marginal big leaguer. They undersold him. For nearly a decade, Malzone was one of the finest third basemen in the game. In 1957, he won the Gold Glove Award.

Frank Malzone

Gil McDougald

McDougald Bats .289

Gil McDougald showcases the odd batting stance that many teenage players tried to emulate during the 1950s, much to the horror of their coaches. Apart from McDougald, few hitters who cocked their bats below shoulder level have been successful at the major league level. McDougald hit .289 in 1957, collecting nine triples (tied for tops in the league) and 13 home runs.

1957

- The A's become the first team in ML history to have no pitchers with enough innings to qualify for the ERA title.
- The Hall of Fame inducts Sam Crawford and Joe McCarthy.
- Ted Kluszewski is injured and is never again a top-notch slugger.

- After the season, the Reds trade Kluszewski to Pittsburgh for Dee Fondy.
- KC sends Art Ditmar, Clete Boyer, Shantz, and three others to the Yankees for Billy Hunter and five others.
- The Giants trade Red Schoendienst to the Braves for three players.

- The White Sox trade Minoso and Fred Hatfield to Cleveland for Al Smith and Early Wynn.
- The Yankees ship Billy Martin and three other players to KC for Ryne Duren and three players.
- KC sends Martin and five players to the Tigers for seven players.

Minnie, Luis Light Up Sox

Flanking former baseball executive Larry MacPhail are Minnie Minoso *(left)* and Luis Aparicio. Both players were instrumental in the rise of the White Sox to second place in 1957—their highest finish since 1920. Minoso hit .310 that year, with 36 doubles (tied for tops in the American League) and 103 RBI, while Aparicio stole 28 bases (the circuit-high) in his second season. The ballclub also got help from Nellie Fox, the first White Sox player to lead the loop in hits (196), and southpaw Billy Pierce (20 wins, 3.26 ERA).

Casey Stengel

Casey Mulls Over Loss

Casey Stengel contemplates his second World Series loss in three seasons. A master at assembling teams that were better than the sum of their parts, Stengel saw his patchwork 1957 crew out-hit and out-pitch the Braves, yet falter because they could only score two runs in 27 innings against Lew Burdette.

Minnie Minoso, Luis Aparicio

World Series

Roy Sievers

Sievers Adds Dimensions

Part of the reason the Senators (the slowest team in the majors) tinkered with Griffith Stadium, shortening its dimensions, was the acquisition of slugger Roy Sievers. In 1957, Sievers became the first Washington player to lead the American League in home runs, clubbing 42 round-trippers. He also led the loop in RBI that year with 114.

Covington Nails Yogi

Yogi Berra is nailed at the plate by Braves catcher Del Rice while trying to score on Jerry Lumpe's fly out to Wes Covington during the 1957 World Series. An injury to center fielder Bill Bruton forced the Braves to play Covington, who had been platooned during the regular season, in all seven games of the fall classic.

- Duke Snider is first ML player to post 40 homers and post less than 100 RBI.

- A new rule states that a batter needs 3.1 plate appearances per scheduled game to qualify for the BA title.

- Bob Riesener of Alexandria in the Evangeline League sets an OB record when he has a perfect 20-0 season.

- Anthony Perkins stars as Jimmy Piersall in *Fear Strikes Out.*

- Washington's Pete Ramos dishes up 43 homers, a new AL record.

- The AL makes batting helmets mandatory for all players.

- Fox leads the AL in hits (196).

- Schoendienst, playing for two teams, leads the NL in hits with 200.

- For the first time in history, no one in the AL reaches double figures in triples.

- Brooklyn's Johnny Podres returns from the Navy to lead the NL in ERA (2.66) and shutouts (six).

YANKEES LEFT ALONE IN NY, WIN ANYWAY

The geography of baseball changed dramatically during the 1950s. The Braves moved from Boston to Milwaukee, the Browns from St. Louis to Baltimore, the Athletics from Philadelphia to Kansas City, and for the '58 season—in the most shocking moves of all—the Dodgers and the Giants from New York to California.

Ebbets Field was leveled (the Polo Grounds stood for several additional years), as the Dodgers made a home of Los Angeles Memorial Coliseum and the Giants set up shop at Seals Stadium in San Francisco. A record 78,672 attendees saw the Giants down the Dodgers on Opening Day at the Coliseum; the teams went on to pull in 167,204 supporters for the three-game series. The Dodgers drew 1,845,556 fans by year's end. Both teams would soon build new stadiums.

As the Dodgers dropped to a humiliating seventh place, tragedy struck. A car accident in New York left three-time Dodger MVP Roy Campanella permanently paralyzed. Old mainstays Pee Wee Reese and Carl Erskine saw limited action and Don Newcombe was traded. Duke Snider, who hit 40 home runs in 1957, managed only 15 in '58.

Milwaukee took the pennant again, this time on a 92-62 record. Hank Aaron had another outstanding year with 30 homers and a .326 average, but the keys were Warren Spahn (a league-high 22 wins) and Lew Burdette (20-

10). The surprising Pirates—with solid years from pitcher Bob Friend (22-14) and third baseman Frank Thomas (35 home runs, 109 RBI)—finished strong and wound up in second, 8 games back.

Rookie of the Year Orlando Cepeda racked up 25 homers and 96 RBI, Willie Mays hit .347, and Stu Miller turned in a league-best 2.47 ERA to spur San Francisco to third. Cubs shortstop Ernie Banks led the league with 47 homers and 129 RBI and was named MVP, even though Chicago finished fifth. Richie Ashburn won the batting crown at .350 for the last-place Phillies.

The Yankees won the American League flag, their eighth in nine seasons of the decade. Leading the way were Mickey Mantle (a league-high 42 homers), Bob Turley (the junior loop's first Cy Young Award-winner with a 21-7 record), and Whitey Ford (the ERA leader with 2.01). New York outdistanced the second-place White Sox by 10 games. Although the Red Sox placed third, the 40-year-old Ted Williams won the batting crown again with a .328

average. Teammate Jackie Jensen was awarded the MVP title for 35 homers and a circuit-topping 122 RBI.

The Yankees, winners of six of the last nine World Series, met the Braves with an axe to grind—Milwaukee had dropped the Yanks in seven games in '57. Revenge, however, didn't come easy. The Braves stormed to a 3-1 lead with wins of 4-3 and 13-5 in games one and two and a 3-0 whitewashing in game four.

Things looked bleak for New York's only team. With their backs to the wall in game five, they started Turley, who had been shelled in the opener. The right-hander responded with a masterpiece five-hitter, and the Yanks beat Burdette 7-0.

The Braves still held an advantage going into the final two games. With game six tied two-all after nine innings, the Yanks scored twice in the top of the tenth on a homer by Gil McDougald and three singles. The Braves rallied in the bottom half, scoring once and having the tying run on third when Casey Stengel brought Turley in from the bullpen. He retired Frank Torre for the final out.

The Yanks took game seven with four runs in the eighth (three on Bill Skowron's homer). Turley, the star of the Series, pitched the final 6²/3 innings as New York defeated the Braves 6-2 to become the first team since 1925 to win a World Series after being down three games to one.

1958

- Yanks reel off their fourth straight flag.

- Braves repeat as pennant-winners in NL.

- Yanks take World Series in seven games; are first team since 1925 Pirates to win after trailing three games to one.

- In Series, Bob Turley wins two of last three Yankees victories and saves the third, all in the space of four days.

- Yankee Hank Bauer leads all Series hitters with ten hits, four homers, and eight RBI.

- Milwaukee's Billy Bruton has top BA among Series regulars (.412).

- Warren Spahn wins two of three starts for Braves in Series, losing game six 4-3 in ten innings.

- Dodgers and Giants move to LA and San Francisco, respectively.

- Ernie Banks is NL MVP.

- Boston's Jackie Jensen is AL MVP.

In 1958, Mickey Mantle was the only Yankee to play more than 138 games as Casey Stengel, the master platooner, juggled his lineup almost daily. Bill Skowron and Marv Throneberry alternated at first base, Gil McDougald and Bobby Richardson at second, and Andy Carey and Jerry Lumpe at third. Mantle was the lone constant, occupying center field virtually every day. Mantle spearheaded the American League that year in home runs (42) and runs scored (127).

- Turley wins Cy Young and is second in AL MVP vote.

- San Francisco's Orlando Cepeda is unanimous choice as NL's top rookie.

- Washington's Albie Pearson wins AL ROTY; is the first winner from a last-place team.

- Roy Campanella's career ends when he's left paralyzed by a car crash.

- Phillie Richie Ashburn is second player on a last-place team to win NL bat title (.350).

- Banks tops NL in homers (47), RBI (129), total bases (379), runs produced (201), and SA (.614).

- Banks sets ML records for most homers and highest SA by a shortstop.

- Spahn and Pittsburgh's Bob Friend tie for ML lead with 22 wins.

- Ashburn ties NL record by leading outfielders in chances for ninth time.

Aparicio Tops at DPs

Luis Aparicio leaps high above a sliding Gene Woodling as he gets off a throw to first to complete a double play. Aparicio and White Sox second sacker Nellie Fox took part in 207 twin killings between them in 1958, tops among keystone combinations in the American League.

Billy Bruton

Bruton Hits .412 in Series

A knee injury shelved Billy Bruton for much of the 1957 and 1958 seasons. He was almost fully recovered, however, by the end of the latter campaign, hitting the Braves' first home run in the 1958 World Series. He went on to rack up a .412 batting average, the best among Series regulars. Two years later, Bruton had his finest season.

Luis Aparicio

Mickey Mantle, Elston Howard, Hank Bauer

The Yankee Power Supply

A look at the heart of the 1958 New York Yankees *(left to right)*: Mickey Mantle, Elston Howard, and Hank Bauer. Mantle (.304 average, 42 home runs, 97 RBI) led the circuit in total bases with 307 and walks with 129 that season. Howard (.314 average, 11 home runs, 66 RBI) had the skill to play the outfield, first base, and catch stations. Bauer (.268 average, 12 home runs, 50 RBI) was the team's first sergeant.

1958

- White Sox Billy Pierce loses perfect game when Washington's Ed Fitzgerald doubles with two out in ninth.

- Nellie Fox plays ML record 98 consecutive games without fanning.

- Ted Williams wins AL bat crown (.328) at age 40.

- AL wins All-Star Game 4-3 in Baltimore; game features no extra-base hits.

- Gold Glove selections made for first time in both leagues.

- On April 15, Giants defeat Dodgers in first West Coast game in ML history.

- On Sept. 20, Oriole Hoyt Wilhelm wins first game as a starting pitcher when he no-hits the Yankees.

- On June 15, 18-year-old Von McDaniel of Cards debuts with two-hit shutout of Dodgers.

- Willie Mays leads NL in runs (121) and steals (31).

Cepeda Tops Rookie List

Orlando Cepeda was only one of the many brilliant rookies the Giants unveiled in the late 1950s. Arriving in 1958 along with Jim Davenport, Felipe Alou, Willie Kirkland, and Leon Wagner, Cepeda hit .312 and led the National League with 38 doubles as a recruit. It was only the beginning of what would for years be a steady flow of young talent running through San Francisco.

Orlando Cepeda

Williams, 40, Cops BA Title

In 1958, Ted Williams became the oldest player ever to win a batting title, hitting .328 at 40 years of age. There were, however, subtle signs that he was slipping. He fanned 11.9 times per every 100 at-bats, the highest ratio of his career to that point, and collected fewer walks (98) than he had in any full season since 1940.

Ted Williams

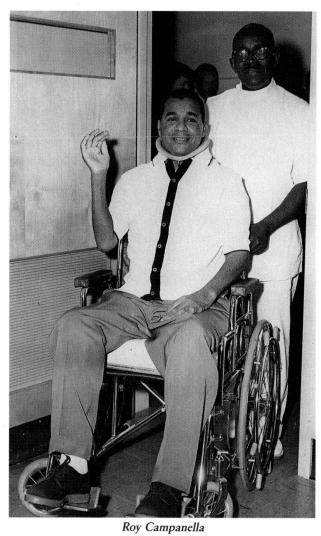

Roy Campanella

Car Wreck Paralyzes Roy

Confined for life to a wheelchair, Roy Campanella gives a quiet wave. Injured in an auto accident in January of 1958, Campanella was pinned in the wreckage. He suffered two fractured vertebrae and was permanently paralyzed below the waist. His career was over before the Dodgers played their first game in Los Angeles.

- Ashburn tops majors in hits (215), triples (13), and BA (.350), and leads NL in walks (97) and OBP (.441).

- Rookie Cepeda tops NL in doubles (38), and hits .312 with 25 homers and 96 RBI.

- Giant Stu Miller leads NL in ERA (2.47).

- Mickey Mantle leads AL in homers (42), runs (127), runs produced (182), total bases (307), and walks (129).

- Reds make just 100 errors to set new ML record.

- Yankee Ryne Duren tops AL with 20 saves and fans 87 in 75²/₃ innings.

- Turley leads AL in wins (21) and win pct. (.750), and ties in CGs (19).

- Spahn tops NL in CGs (23) and innings (290), and ties for lead in win pct. (.667).

- On August 14, Cleveland's Vic Power steals home twice in a game; he steals a total of three bases all season.

Jim Bunning

Richie Ashburn was one of the best fielding flycatchers of all time. Six of the ten highest season putout totals in history by an outfielder were achieved by him. In 1958, Ashburn took the batting title with a .350 average and topped the loop in on-base percentage with a .441 mark, hits with 215, triples with 13, and walks with 97.

Richie Ashburn

Bunning Throws a No-No

Jim Bunning won 20 games for the Tigers in 1957, his first full season in the majors, then pitched 14 more years without ever reaching that circle again. In 1958, Bunning finished with a 14-12 record and a 3.52 ERA—though he did manage a no-hitter on July 20. During the early to mid-1960s, he collected 19 victories, one short of the coveted figure, four times in five seasons.

Pearson Named ROTY

Albie Pearson was the smallest Rookie of the Year honoree in history. The 5′ 5″-recruit hit .275 in 1958, collecting 25 doubles, five triples, 63 runs scored, and 64 walks. A bad case of the sophomore jinx reduced Pearson to a benchwarmer by his third season. Expansion then saved his career. Drafted by the Los Angeles Angels, he turned into one of the American League's best leadoff hitters in the early 1960s.

Albie Pearson

1958

- Sam Jones of St. Louis becomes the first NL pitcher to fan 200 or more batters since 1941, as he Ks 225.

- The Braves set an ML record when they're caught stealing just eight times all year (in only 34 attempts.)

- The A's post their highest win pct. while in Kansas City—.474.

- Pittsburgh's Dick Stuart, "Dr. Strangeglove," leads NL first basemen in errors despite playing only 64 games in the field.

- Lee MacPhail, son of Larry, becomes Baltimore's GM and president.

- Gwen Verdon and Tab Hunter star in *Damn Yankees*.

- Cards trade Wally Moon and Phil Paine to LA for Gino Cimoli.

- KC trades Woodie Held and Vic Power to Cleveland for Roger Maris, Dick Tomanek, and Preston Ward.

- Washington sends Pete Runnels to Boston for Norm Zauchin and Albie Pearson.

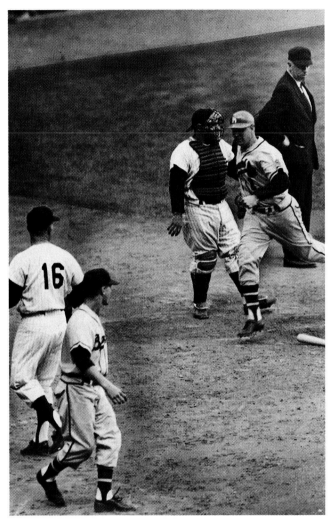

World Series

Crandall Scores in Series

Del Crandall scores the second run of game four of the 1958 World Series on a single by Warren Spahn. Crandall caught every inning of the fall classic for the Braves. Spahn won two games and nearly copped a third, which would have given the Braves their second consecutive championship. The Braves, however, lost the game 4-3 in ten innings.

Ernie Banks

Banks Powers Hapless Cubs

Ernie Banks played with the Cubs for ten years before the club had a season in which it finished above .500. In 1958, as Chicago finished at .468, Banks led the National League in home runs with 47 and RBI with 129. Even with his efforts, however, the team was so poor during most of those ten seasons that Jimmy Dykes remarked, "Without him, the Cubs would finish in Albuquerque."

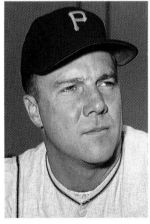

Bob Friend

Friend's 22 Wins Lead NL

Bob Friend tied for the National League wins lead in 1958 with 22 victories. Three years earlier, he had been the first pitcher from a last-place team to cop an ERA crown. In 1959 and again in 1961, he topped the NL in losses. When he retired, Friend posted a .461 career win percentage, the lowest of any pitcher involved in 400 or more decisions.

- Detroit ships Billy Martin and Al Cicotte to Cleveland for Don Mossi, Ray Narleski, and Ossie Alvarez.

- Washington sends Eddie Yost and two other players to Detroit for Reno Bertoia and two others.

- Pittsburgh's Elroy Face leads the NL in saves with 20.

- Milwaukee's Carlton Willey heads the NL in shutouts with just four.

- Cleveland's Rocky Colavito leads the majors in SA (.620) and is second in homers (41) and RBI (113).

- Fox tops the AL in hits with 187.

- Detroit's Harvey Kuenn leads the majors in doubles with 39.

- Luis Aparicio again leads the AL in steals (29).

- Whitey Ford tops the AL in ERA (2.01) and shutouts (seven).

- Chicago's Early Wynn tops the AL in Ks with 179.

- Every team in the NL bats between .251 and .266.

The 1959 season featured several accomplishments—and nonaccomplishments—of note. Ted Williams hit just .254 and Stan Musial dropped to .255 in the twilight of their extraordinary careers. The Pirates' Harvey Haddix threw a 12-inning perfect game only to lose in the 13th, and teammate Roy Face went 18-1 in relief. The Dodgers got back into the thick of it after finishing seventh in 1958 and won the National League. But the biggest surprise of all in 1959 was delivered by the Yankees.

The Bronx Bombers, winners of nine American League flags in ten years, were in last place on May 20. New York's pitching woes weighed the team down and it was never able to join the race, which the White Sox eventually won by 5 games over the Indians.

Detroit placed fourth despite the efforts of Harvey Kuenn and Al Kaline, the top two batting men with averages of .353 and .327. Boston and Jackie Jensen, the RBI leader at 112, came in fifth. The ERA champ couldn't do it on his own, as Hoyt Wilhelm (a 2.19 mark) and Baltimore finished sixth. Harmon Killebrew's league-leading 42 home runs were for naught as Washington finished last.

The NL pennant race was far more dramatic. San Francisco appeared to have the flag locked up with a 2-game lead over the Dodgers and Braves and one week to play. The Dodgers then came

GO-GO SOX RUN OUT OF GAS IN LA

into town and swept San Francisco in three games.

The Giants never recovered, dropping four of their last five to the Cubs and Cards. San Fran came in third, despite great years from Willie Mays (.313 average, 34 homers, and 104 RBI) and Orlando Cepeda (.317 average, 27 homers, and 105 RBI) and a solid performance from Sam Jones (who posted the best ERA in the league at 2.82 and tied with Milwaukee's Warren Spahn and Lew Burdette for the lead with 21 wins).

The Dodgers and the Braves ended up tied for first place, as both teams won on the last Sunday. In a best-of-three playoff, the Dodgers swept Eddie Mathews (who led the league with 46 homers), Hank Aaron (who launched 39 and led the circuit with a .355 average), and the rest of the Braves.

Los Angeles boasted a balanced attack which combined experience and youth. Duke Snider and Gil Hodges combined for 48 homers, while ex-Cardinal Wally Moon hit .302. Speedy Maury Wills took over at shortstop, and 23-year-old Don Drys-

dale won 17 games to anchor the pitching staff.

Ernie Banks won his second-straight MVP with 45 homers (second in the circuit) and 143 RBI (tops in the league) for the fifth-place Cubs. His American League MVP counterpart, Nellie Fox, led the White Sox to a first-place finish with his .306 batting average.

The Go-Go Sox also featured catcher Sherm Lollar (22 homers, 84 RBI) and shortstop Luis Aparicio (the stolen base leader with 56). Cy Young Award-winner Early Wynn, age 39, was 22-10 while Bob Shaw went 18-6 to stabilize the starting pitching. Gerry Staley and Turk Lown were solid out of the pen.

In the first game of the Series, Ted Kluszewski belted a pair of two-run homers to lead Chicago to an 11-0 victory over Los Angeles. The Dodgers came back behind Johnny Podres, taking game two 4-3 and sending a tied Series to Los Angeles.

Although the Sox stroked 12 hits in game three, they lost to Los Angeles 3-1. The Dodgers then took game four 5-4 on Hodges's eighth-inning home run.

A record crowd of 92,706 showed up in the Coliseum the next day with hopes of seeing California's first World Series winner, but Chicago spoiled the party with a 1-0 win. The Dodgers then took game six 9-3 in Chicago for their first of many World Series crowns.

1959

- White Sox win their first flag in 40 years.
- Dodgers take their first West Coast flag.
- Dodgers beat Braves in playoff to capture pennant.
- LA wins World Series in six games.

- Chicago's Ted Kluszewski is Series hitting star with three homers, ten RBI, and .391 BA.
- Charlie Neal leads Dodgers in Series with .370 BA and six RBI.
- Larry Sherry of Dodgers is Series MVP, winning two games and saving two others.

- Chuck Essegian of LA hits two pinch homers in Series.
- In game five, Dodgers set World Series attendance record of 92,706.
- White Sox Nellie Fox is AL MVP.
- Ernie Banks again voted NL MVP—only player from second-division team to win twice.

Dodgers outfielder Wally Moon scores as Chicago catcher Sherm Lollar waits on a late throw in the 1959 World Series. Upon joining the Dodgers in 1959, Moon, a lefthanded hitter, tailored his swing so that he could take advantage of the short left-field screen in the Los Angeles Coliseum (the club's first West Coast home).

- Banks tops majors in RBI (143), loses NL homer crown by one to Eddie Mathews (46-45).

- Hank Aaron tops the majors in BA at .355.

- Detroit's Harvey Kuenn hits .353 to lead AL.

- White Sox Early Wynn leads majors with 22 wins, takes Cy Young Award.

- Pumpsie Green is first black player to join Red Sox, the last ML team to break the color line.

- Banks sets NL shortstop records with 143 RBI and .985 FA.

- On August 31, Dodger Sandy Koufax becomes first NL hurler in this century to fan 18 in a game.

- Pirate Harvey Haddix pitches record 12 perfect innings vs. Milwaukee on May 26, but loses 1-0 in 13 innings.

- Washington's Bob Allison is AL ROTY.

Green: First Black BoSox

Pumpsie Green (shown getting an encouraging pat from Boston manager Billy Jurges) was the first black player to wear a Red Sox uniform. In 1959, Green was only a utility infielder for the Red Sox, the last major league team to break the color line. Boston's first black regular was Willie Tasby, who joined the club in 1960.

Pumpsie Green, Billy Jurges

Ernie Banks

Bunning: Ace of Star Staff

The Tigers had the best four-man starting rotation in the American League in 1959. Staff leader Jim Bunning (pictured), Frank Lary, Paul Foytack, and Don Mossi had a composite 65-46 record (Bunning contributed a 17-13 mark). Detroit nevertheless finished below .500, as the club's second-line pitchers contributed only 11 wins.

Jim Bunning

Banks Wins Second MVP

An erratic fielder early in his career, Ernie Banks had become an excellent shortstop by the close of the 1950s. In 1959, he took his second MVP Award, setting shortstop records with a .985 fielding average and 143 RBI. Banks later made himself into a more than adequate first baseman.

1959

- Willie McCovey hits .354 with 38 RBI in just 192 at-bats.
- McCovey goes 4-for-4 in ML debut on July 30.
- Reds rookie Vada Pinson hits .316 with 20 homers and a league-leading 131 runs scored, but is not ROTY.
- San Francisco's McCovey named NL ROTY.
- Boston's Jackie Jensen repeats as AL RBI champ (112), but hits no triples for second year in row.
- Jensen quits baseball at age 32 because he refuses to fly to games.
- For the first time, there are two All-Star Games; NL wins first game 5-4 at Pittsburgh, and AL takes second 5-3 at LA.
- Joe Cronin named AL president—first ex-player to reach that pinnacle.
- Cleveland's Rocky Colavito hits four homers on June 10.

Eddie Mathews

Mathews Blasts 46 HRs

In Eddie Mathews (pictured), the Braves had the best third baseman in the majors in 1959. Mathews's 46 home runs snared the crown that year. The Braves also had the top right fielder in Hank Aaron and, indeed, were solid at every position but second base. The Braves experimented with Felix Mantilla, then Johnny O'Brien, and finally Bobby Avila at second. All flopped.

Aparicio, Fox Keys for Sox

Luis Aparicio played 152 games at short for the White Sox in 1959. His keystone partner, Nellie Fox, was at second for 156 games. They made the difference. Chicago finished the year 94-60. Down the stretch, the second-place Indians had to go with career minor leaguer Jim Baxes at second and Woodie Held, a converted outfielder, at short.

Luis Aparicio

Johnny Podres

Podres Finally Back in Shape

Johnny Podres's career was interrupted by a military call-up in 1956, and it took him awhile to get back on track. "I'd been 4-F until I won the seventh game of the World Series in 1955," Podres said later. "They reclassified me 1-A that winter." In 1958, he went 13-15 and posted a 3.73 ERA. In 1959, he had a 14-9 season.

- Bill Veeck buys the White Sox.

- Elroy Face wins a season record 17 straight games in relief (22 games over two-year period).

- Face finishes 18-1 with a win pct. of .947.

- Baltimore's Dave Philley collects a record nine consecutive pinch hits.

- Detroit's Eddie Yost tops AL in runs (115), walks (135), and OBP (.437).

- Yogi Berra's record streak of 148 consecutive errorless games at catcher ends.

- Baltimore beats Chicago 2-1 on May 19 on a 120-foot homer by pitcher Billy O'Dell.

- Washington's Harmon Killebrew ties Colavito for AL lead in homers (42).

- Kuenn leads AL in hits (198) and doubles (42).

- Aaron leads NL in hits (223), total bases (400), SA (.636), and runs produced (200).

Kuenn Wins BA Crown

Harvey Kuenn was one of the last righthanded batters to win an American League hitting title. His chief competition in 1959 came from Cleveland's Tito Francona, who hit .363 (ten points higher than Kuenn) only to fall a few plate appearances short of the requisite number. The two were teammates the following year.

Harvey Kuenn

Nellie Fox

Fox Hits .306; Tipton, .236

The White Sox acquired Nellie Fox (pictured) prior to the 1950 season from the A's in a swap for backup catcher Joe Tipton. It was one of the worst deals the A's ever made. Over the next 14 years, Fox averaged .291 and four times led the American League in hits. In 1959, he batted .306 and tallied 191 hits. Tipton played just 417 games in the majors and hit .236.

Face Wins 22 in a Row

The 18-1 mark Elroy Face posted in 1959 is the best single-season pitching record in history. He also won 22 consecutive games over two seasons—a record for relief pitchers. When Face retired after the 1969 season, he ranked behind just Hoyt Wilhelm in career saves.

Elroy Face

1959

- Finally getting a chance to play, Cleveland's Tito Francona hits .363, but lacks enough at-bats to qualify for BA title.

- Ted Williams and Stan Musial both hit below .300 for the first time in their careers.

- Hall of Fame inducts Zach Wheat.

- A record crowd of 93,103 attends the LA Coliseum for a Yankees-Dodgers exhibition, which is also Roy Campanella Night.

- The Phils' Sparky Anderson has just 119 total bases, fewest in history by a player with 500 or more at-bats.

- Warren Spahn leads the NL in CGs (21) and ties in wins (21).

- Sam Jones of the Giants leads the NL in ERA (2.82) and ties in wins (21).

- LA's Don Drysdale leads the majors in Ks with 242.

- On April 22 vs. KC, the White Sox score 11 runs on just one hit in the seventh inning.

Aging Wynn Wins 22

Despite frequent debilitating bouts with gout, Early Wynn pitched until he was age 43. His 22 triumphs in 1959 topped the American League (he pitched a circuit-high 256 innings). At the conclusion of the 1962 season, when he was just one victory short of 300, Wynn was released by the White Sox. Signed by Cleveland on June 21, 1963, he lost 1-0 in his first start for the Tribe and took a month to join the 300-win circle. He finished with a career record of 300-244 with a hefty 3.54 ERA.

Larry Sherry

Early Wynn

Sherry Earns Series MVP

Dodgers pitcher Larry Sherry holds the Babe Ruth Award he received for being the Most Valuable Player of the 1959 World Series. Los Angeles won all four of the games in which Sherry appeared in relief. The hurler won two of the four contests, saved the other two, and allowed just one earned run in 12²/₃ innings.

- Pittsburgh deals Frank Thomas, Whammy Douglas, Jim Pendleton, and Johnny Powers to the Reds for Haddix, Don Hoak, and Smoky Burgess.

- With interleague trading now allowed, the Giants send Jackie Brandt and two others to Baltimore for Billy Loes and Billy O'Dell.

- Cleveland sends Minnie Minoso and three other players to the White Sox for John Romano, Bubba Phillips, and Norm Cash.

- The Yankees ship Jerry Lumpe, Johnny Kucks, and Tom Sturdivant to KC for Hector Lopez and Ralph Terry.

- Cleveland trades Billy Martin, Cal McLish, and Gordy Coleman to the Reds for Johnny Temple.

- On Sept. 22, the Dodgers collect nine pinch hits.

- Red Schoendienst is shelved for the season by TB, possibly costing the Braves a pennant.

Over the winter that followed the 1959 season, in which the Yankees finished third, general manager George Weiss acquired Roger Maris via Kansas City for Hank Bauer, Don Larsen, Norm Siebern, and Marv Throneberry. Voted the Most Valuable Player, the 25-year-old lefthanded-hitter turned the trade into one of the century's greatest heists.

With Mickey Mantle contributing a league-high 40 round-trippers and Maris pounding the short right field porch in Yankee Stadium for 39 homers and a loop-best 112 RBI, New York had baseball's most devastating one-two power punch since Babe Ruth and Lou Gehrig. Another 26 homers from Bill "Moose" Skowron boosted the team to a major league-high 193 homers.

The Yankees needed all the offense they could get, as not one pitcher won more than 15 games. Even the great Whitey Ford was limited to just a dozen triumphs. Ten different pitchers won five or more (for a pennant-winner, the Yanks had an unusually high 16 hurlers). The Yankees won their last 15 contests to take the flag.

Chuck Estrada of Baltimore, which finished 8 games behind New York, and Jim Perry of fourth-place Cleveland tied for tops in the American League with 18 wins. Ranked third, Chicago owned league ERA leader Frank Baumann, who posted a 2.68 mark. Batting champ Pete Runnels hit .320 for seventh-place

BUCS BEAT YANKS ON MAZ'S HEROIC HOMER

Boston. Baltimore's Ron Hansen (22 homers, 86 RBI) was voted Rookie of the Year.

The National League champion Pittsburgh Pirates had a 20-game winner in Vern Law, who took Cy Young honors, and an 18-game victor in Bob Friend. The savior of the staff, however, was reliever Elroy Face, who won ten games and saved 24 others.

On the other side of the ball, Pittsburgh shortstop Dick Groat led the league in batting with a .325 average and won the MVP title. Groat beat out some tough competition—Willie Mays (.319, 103 RBI), Hank Aaron (40 homers, a circuit-high 126 RBI), and Ernie Banks (a league-best 41 homers, 117 RBI). Budding superstar Roberto Clemente also sparked the Bucs offense with a .314 average and 16 home runs. Pittsburgh's unsung hero was 23-year-old second baseman Bill Mazeroski, who anchored the defense with flashy fielding.

Finishing 7 games behind Pittsburgh, Milwaukee had vet-

eran Warren Spahn, who tied with Ernie Broglio of third-place St. Louis for most wins with 21. Mike McCormick posted a league-low 2.70 ERA playing for fifth-place San Francisco. Rookie Frank Howard of Los Angeles emerged with 23 homers.

Over the first six games of the World Series, the Yankees outscored the Pirates 46-17 but couldn't win more than three contests. Law took games one and four with relief from Face, and veteran Harvey Haddix won game five. Ford posted shutouts in games three and six.

Game seven turned out to be a classic. The Pirates blew an early 4-0 lead as the Yanks went up 7-4. The Bucs' five-run eighth inning was highlighted by reserve catcher Hal Smith's three-run homer. The explosive Yankee offense then notched two runs in the ninth to tie the game at nine.

Mazeroski led off the bottom of the ninth against Ralph Terry, who had stopped the Pirates' rally in the eighth. Up to that point, Mazeroski (.273 with 11 homers during the season) had knocked seven hits in 24 at-bats for the Series, hitting a game-winning two-run homer in the first contest. Maz belted Terry's second pitch over Yogi Berra's head and the left-field fence for the win.

The Yankees, not taking defeat well, fired manager Casey Stengel, the 71-year-old master who had engineered all those flags in the decade of the 1950s.

1960

- Yanks back on top in AL.
- Pirates win first NL flag since 1927.
- Pirates capture World Series in seven games.
- Bill Mazeroski cracks a ninth-inning homer to win game seven of Series 10-9—it's the only home run in history to end a Series.
- Harvey Haddix and Vern Law each win two Series games for Pirates.
- Yanks outhit Pirates .338-.256, outscore them 55-27, saddle Pirate pitchers with 7.11 ERA, yet lose.
- Manager Casey Stengel is fired after World Series loss despite winning nine World Series in 12 seasons at New York helm.
- Yankee Roger Maris is AL MVP.
- Pirate Dick Groat named NL MVP.
- For first time in ML history, both batting leaders hit under .330.
- Detroit's Frank Lary tops AL with 15 CGs, lowest total to that juncture to lead a league.

1960

Holding his right arm aloft in victory, Bill Mazeroski nears the plate after leading off the bottom of the ninth inning with a home run to end the 1960 World Series. "I was too excited and too thrilled to think," he said. "It was the greatest moment of my life."

- On April 17, on the eve of the season's first game, Cleveland swaps Rocky Colavito to Detroit for Harvey Kuenn.

- Branch Rickey's proposed rival major league, the Continental League, forces majors to expand for first time since 1901.

- Annual income from television tops $12 million for the first time in ML history.

- Lindy McDaniel of the Cards records 26 saves, new NL record.

- Jim Brosnan writes *The Long Season*, probably the best book on the game written by a player.

- NL wins first of two All-Star Games, 5-3 at KC.

- NL wins the second All-Star Game two days later, 6-0 at Yankee Stadium; McDaniel earns a save in both games.

- White Sox owner Bill Veeck is first to put names on his team's uniforms.

Lindy McDaniel

Lindy Saves 26 Games

No pitcher during the past 40 years was more underrated than Lindy McDaniel. He was effective for nearly 21 years as both a closer and a long reliever; on occasion, he even took a turn as a starter. In 1960, he racked up 26 saves, a record in the National League. That McDaniel was never on a pennant-winner is the only black mark on what was otherwise a brilliant career.

Four Prime AL Sluggers

A look at four of the American League's top five home run hitters in 1960 *(left to right)*: Harmon Killebrew (31 homers), Mickey Mantle (40), Jim Lemon (38), and Roger Maris (39). Rocky Colavito (35 home runs) is the missing slugger.

Jim Brosnan

Brosnan Tells All

Jim Brosnan's first book, *The Long Season* (Harper & Row, 1960), was a genuine literary work, yet the baseball community still reacted negatively. The novel was a tell-all chronicle of the life of a pitcher during a season, from spring training through the end of the then-regular schedule of 154 games. In 1988, Brosnan found that ex-Cardinals general manager Bing Devine remained upset by the book. The pitcher's second novel, *Pennant Race*, was a record of his stint with the 1961 National League Champion Reds.

American League Home Run Leaders

1960

- Veeck unveils the first exploding scoreboard.
- Baltimore's Ron Hansen selected AL Rookie of the Year.
- Dodger Frank Howard is NL ROTY.
- Ted Williams hits his 500th homer on June 17.

- San Francisco's Juan Marichal debuts on July 19 with one-hit shutout of Phils.
- On August 10, Detroit trades manager Jimmy Dykes for Cleveland manager Joe Gordon.
- Williams homers in his last ML at-bat on Sept. 28.

- AL approves transfer of Washington franchise to Minneapolis-St. Paul.
- AL grants expansion franchises for 1961 season to Washington and LA.
- Reds second baseman Billy Martin punches Cubs pitcher Jim Brewer in an on-the-field fight, breaking his cheekbone.

New York Yankees

Yanks Come Again

The 1960 American League Champion New York Yankees had the best offensive attack and the best pitching in the league, but both were group efforts. Art Ditmar *(back row, third from the right)* led the team in wins with just 15. Jim Coates *(back row, sixth from the left)* won 13 for the ballclub.

Howard Best NL Frosh

During his junior year at Ohio State, 6' 7"-Frank Howard was an All-America candidate in both basketball and baseball. To the chagrin of NBA scouts, he went on to sign with the Dodgers. In 1960, he was the National League Rookie of the Year, hitting .268.

Frank Howard

Tony Kubek, Mike de la Hoz

DP Duo Spark Yanks

Yankees second sacker Bobby Richardson watches as shortstop Tony Kubek leaps over Cleveland's Mike de la Hoz after firing to first to complete a double play. Kubek totaled 77 runs scored that season while Richardson came up with 45 runs to help the Yankees win 97 games in 1960. The Indians lost 78 games that year, their worst showing since 1946. It was only the beginning of their descent.

Dick Groat

Groat Tallies .325 BA

Dick Groat, the National League batting champ in 1960 with a .325 average, was the third Pirates shortstop since 1900 to win a hitting crown. No other NL team has had a shortstop win a batting title. Luke Appling, Lou Boudreau, Alex Rodriguez, and Nomar Garciaparra have won the crown in the American League.

- Orioles manager Paul Richards devises a catcher's mitt 50 inches in circumference to handle Hoyt Wilhelm's knucklers.

- Milwaukee's Lew Burdette no-hits Phils on August 18.

- Warren Spahn no-hits the Phillies on Sept. 16.

- Ernie Banks leads majors with 41 homers.

- Mickey Mantle leads AL in homers (40), runs (119), and total bases (294).

- Don Cardwell of the Cubs no-hits Cards on May 15.

- Spahn and Cardinal Ernie Broglio top majors with 21 wins.

- For the first time in ML history, war-shortened seasons excepted, no one in either league makes more than 190 hits.

- Yankees allow ML record-low 2.83 runs per game on road.

Banks Excels at Plate, Short

Ernie Banks in 1960 became the only shortstop ever to lead his league in home runs (41) and win a Gold Glove in the same season. He was virtually a one-man gang for the Cubs that year. Being that Banks and Richie Ashburn were the only two team members to score more than 58 runs, the RBI total of 117 turned in by Banks is incredible.

Ernie Banks

Maris Edges Mick for MVP

Three votes separated Roger Maris *(left)* and Mickey Mantle in the voting for the American League's Most Valuable Player in 1960. Maris, who topped the circuit in slugging with a .581 mark and RBI with 112, took the title. Mantle led the loop in home runs with 40, runs scored with 119, and total bases with 294.

Rocky Colavito

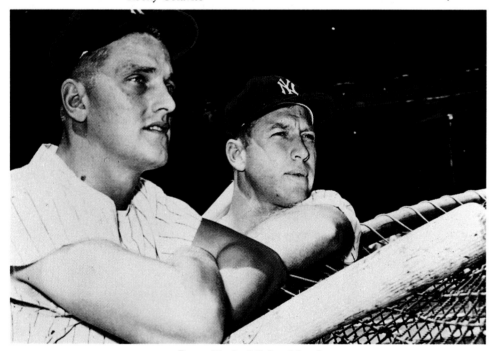

Roger Maris, Mickey Mantle

Rock Clubs 35 HRs

Like most home run hitters, Rocky Colavito had serious weaknesses at the plate. He may have had the strongest arm, though, of any slugger in history. Traded from Cleveland to Detroit for the 1960 season, Colavito posted a .474 slugging average, 35 home runs, and 87 RBI that year. In 1968, his last season, the Yankees brought Colavito on in relief in a tight game. When he got the win, he became the last AL nonpitcher to date to be credited with a victory.

1960

- Indians score ML record-low 2.65 runs per game on road.

- Arnold Johnson dies; Charley Finley buys the A's from his heirs.

- Jerry Holtzman of the *Chicago Sun-Times* helps initiate the crediting of saves to relief pitchers for first time in ML history.

- Haddix wins third straight Gold Glove as NL pitcher.

- Bobby Shantz of the Yankees wins fourth straight Gold Glove as AL pitcher.

- The Braves' Del Crandall wins third straight Gold Glove as NL catcher.

- Cardinal Bill White wins first of seven straight Gold Gloves as NL first baseman.

- Oriole Brooks Robinson wins first Gold Glove as AL third baseman.

- Banks wins his only Gold Glove as NL shortstop.

Law, 20-9, Nabs Cy Young Award

Vern Law received eight of the 14 votes cast for the 1960 Cy Young Award as he went 20-9 in 1960. The runner-up with four mentions was Warren Spahn of the Braves, who produced a 21-10 season. Ernie Broglio (21-9) and Lindy McDaniel (12-4) of the Cardinals both got one vote each. The reason no American League hurlers were cited is that none won more than 18 games. Law was probably the right choice for the award. He was second in the NL in wins, second in win pct. (.690), and tied for first in complete games. Without Law, the Pirates would have struggled to win the pennant.

Vern Law

Pittsburgh Pirates

Ted Goes Out in Style

As a rookie in 1939, Ted Williams said, "All I want out of life is that when I walk down the street folks will say, 'There goes the greatest hitter who ever lived.' " Long before Williams retired in 1960, the year he hit his 500th home run, millions were saying just that.

Ted Williams

Pirates a Mix of Talent

The 1960 World Champion Pittsburgh Pirates were a mix of home-grown talent and clever trade acquisitions. Team star Roberto Clemente *(third row, third from the right)*, for example, was pilfered from the Dodgers' farm chain. Clemente hit .314 with 16 home runs and 94 RBI that season.

- Willie Mays is the only outfielder to win fourth straight Gold Glove.

- Law wins Cy Young Award.

- Cubs trade Ron Perranoski and two other players to Dodgers for Don Zimmer.

- The Indians trade Norm Cash to the Tigers for Steve Demeter.

- Expansion Senators trade Shantz to Pittsburgh for Harry Bright, Benny Daniels, and R.C. Stevens.

- Braves deal Billy Bruton and three other players to Detroit for Frank Bolling and Neil Chrisley.

- Phils trade Harry Anderson and Wally Post to Cincinnati for Lee Walls and Tony Gonzalez.

- Cleveland trades Kuenn to the Giants for Johnny Antonelli and Willie Kirkland.

- Cincinnati trades Roy McMillan to the Braves for Joey Jay and Juan Pizarro.

- Buddy Daley wins nine games in a row to set KC A's record.

World Series

Smith Nails HR in Series

Pittsburgh catcher Hal Smith crosses the plate after blasting a three-run homer in the eighth inning of the final game of the 1960 World Series. The Pirates held a 9-7 lead in the top of the ninth; the Yankees, however, were not quite finished. A heady bit of baserunning by Mickey Mantle allowed the tying run to score and set the stage for Bill Mazeroski to win it.

Richardson Slams Pirates

Gil McDougald (12), Elston Howard (32), and Bill Skowron (14) wait their turn to greet Bobby Richardson after his grandslam in game three of the 1960 World Series. The second baseman had 12 RBI in the Series.

Harvey Haddix, Art Ditmar

Haddix, Ditmar Face Off

Harvey Haddix *(left)* of Pittsburgh and Art Ditmar of New York shake hands prior to game five of the 1960 World Series. Neither of the two starting pitchers that day was around at the end of the clash. Haddix got the win, however, lasting until the seventh inning of the Pirates' 5-2 triumph.

World Series

1960

- Bobby Wallace dies.
- Fred Clarke dies at age 87.
- Phillie Pancho Herrera fans 136 times, an NL record for a 154-game season.
- Banks leads NL in games played a record fourth consecutive season.

- Elmer Valo receives an ML record 18 walks as a pinch hitter.
- Giants skipper Tom Sheehan, at age 66, becomes baseball's oldest rookie manager.
- Candlestick Park opens on April 12, Cards vs. Giants.

- Pete Runnels of Boston goes 6-for-7 in a 15-inning game on August 30.
- Groat goes 6-for-6 on May 13.
- Runnels tops AL in batting at .320.
- Groat leads NL in BA (.325).
- Howard sets LA Dodgers rookie record with 23 homers.

Maz, Skip Reminisce

Pirates manager Danny Murtaugh *(left)* and hero Bill Mazeroski celebrate after the 1960 World Series. Jim Coates, who had been relieved in the eighth inning by Ralph Terry, told the losing Yankees pitcher that he hated to see Mazeroski's home run but that Terry had taken him "off the hook."

Bucs Celebrate

Roberto Clemente hoists Dick Groat, the NL's MVP, during World Series action. Obscured by Clemente is catcher Hal Smith. Smith had been traded from the Yankees because, with backstops Yogi Berra and Elston Howard, New York had no need for him.

Danny Murtaugh, Bill Mazeroski

Roberto Clemente, Dick Groat

Sub Cimoli Boosts Bucs

In this shot from the 1960 World Series, Pittsburgh outfielder Gino Cimoli slides into second ahead of the throw to Yankees shortstop Tony Kubek as umpire John Stevens prepares to make the call. A sub during the regular season, Cimoli scored four runs in the Series to tie Pirates second sacker Bill Mazeroski for the club lead. This was his only bright moment in his ten-year, eight-team career.

World Series

- Hank Aaron tops NL in total bases (334) and RBI (126).
- Chicago's Richie Ashburn paces NL in walks (116) and OBP (.416).
- Cincinnati's Vada Pinson leads majors with 37 doubles.
- Maris tops AL in RBI (112).

- Luis Aparicio leads AL with 51 steals, one more than NL leader Maury Wills of the Dodgers.
- Eddie Mathews leads majors with 193 runs produced.
- The Dodgers' Don Drysdale (246) and Detroit's Jim Bunning (201) repeat as league leaders in Ks.

- Cardinal Larry Jackson tops majors in innings with 282.
- Pittsburgh leads the NL in runs scored (734) and ties for fewest runs allowed (593).
- Yankees lead AL in runs scored (746), homers (193), ERA (3.52), and saves (42).

MARIS OUTDOES THE BABE, CRACKS 61 HRs

The Yankees of 1961, now under the leadership of manager Ralph Houk, were even more awesome than the previous year's edition, winning 109 games and the American League pennant by 8 games.

The Bombers set a new team record with their 240 home runs, a statistic aided greatly by the league's expansion to ten teams (the Los Angeles Angels and the Washington Senators had been added) and an increase to a 162-game schedule.

The eight extra games and watered-down pitching enabled Roger Maris to break Babe Ruth's single-season record of 60 home runs. Maris, again the league's MVP, had waged a summer-long assault on a mark deemed so sacred that commissioner Ford Frick issued a decree: If Maris didn't shatter the record during the first 154 games, the feat would have an asterisk assigned to it. Maris hit his 59th homer in game 154, matched the mark five games later, then broke the record on the last day of the season at Yankee Stadium with a homer against Boston's Tracy Stallard.

Mickey Mantle also flirted with Ruth's record, but a September injury stalled him at 54. Bill Skowron, Elston Howard, Yogi Berra, and Johnny Blanchard each belted 20 or more homers for New York.

Cy Young Award-winner Whitey Ford claimed a circuit-topping 25 of 29 decisions while screwball reliever Luis Arroyo won 15 games and saved a league-leading 29 for New York.

In any other year, the Tigers' 101 wins would have been pennant-caliber. Notable seasons were turned in by Norm Cash (41 homers, a league-high .361 average), Al Kaline (.324), Rocky Colavito (45 homers, 140 RBI), and pitcher Frank Lary (23 wins). Dick Donovan spearheaded the majors with his 2.40 ERA for Washington, which tied with Kansas City for last place. Don Schwall of Boston (15–7, 3.22 ERA) was Rookie of the Year.

The Reds won the National League pennant by 4 games over the Dodgers with strong performances by 25-year-old Frank Robinson (the league MVP with 37 homers, 124 RBI, and a .323 average), Vada Pinson (.343), Joey Jay (a league-high 21 wins), and Jim O'Toole (19 victories).

Wally Moon hit .328 (fourth-best in the league) and Johnny Podres posted a circuit-topping .783 winning percentage for second-place Los Angeles. Although Willie Mays belted four home runs in one game while teammate Orlando Cepeda led the league with 46 homers and 142 RBI, the Giants couldn't get past third. For the fifth consecutive year, 40-year-old Warren Spahn of the fourth-place Braves racked up enough wins to rank at the top; this time, his 21 victories matched those of Cincinnati's Jay. Spahn also took the ERA title at 3.01. Roberto Clemente of sixth-place Pittsburgh led the league in batting with a .351 average. Billy Williams of Chicago (.278, 25 homers, 86 RBI) was named Rookie of the Year.

The arms of the Reds couldn't stave off the Yankees' latest edition of Murderer's Row. Ford's shutout in game four broke Ruth's 29 2/3 consecutive scoreless-innings record in Series play. The ace hurler ran his streak to 32 innings before leaving the sixth with an ankle injury.

The Yankees offense burst open in game five with 15 hits in the 13–5 trouncing of the Reds. New York had won convincingly despite the fact that the M&M boys—Mantle and Maris—drove in just two runs between them for the entire Series. Most of the damage was caused by second baseman Bobby Richardson, who set a five-game Series record with nine hits, and Moose Skowron, who batted .353.

1961

- Reds triumph in NL for first time since 1940 as they edge out the Dodgers by 4 games.
- Yanks win their second AL flag in a row.
- Yankees set record for 162-game season by winning 109.
- Yanks rout Reds in World Series in five games.
- New York's Bobby Richardson leads all Series batters with nine hits and .391 BA.
- Whitey Ford breaks Babe Ruth's record for consecutive scoreless innings hurled in World Series play.
- The AL now has ten teams, becoming the first ML loop to have that many since 1899.
- AL plays a 162-game schedule.
- Frank Robinson wins the MVP Award in the NL.
- Roger Maris is AL MVP.

After the 1961 season, New York columnist Jimmy Cannon wrote of the M&M boys, "The community of baseball feels Mickey Mantle *(left)* is a great player. They consider Roger Maris a thrilling freak who batted .269." Mantle led the American League in slugging with a .687 average, came in second in home runs with 54 and on-base percentage with a .452 mark, and tied Maris for the lead in runs scored with 132. Maris topped the loop with 61 home runs, 366 total bases, and 142 RBI. His 159 hits that year are the fewest by a player who hit 50 or more homers in a season.

- Maris breaks Ruth's ML season record by hitting 61 homers.

- Mickey Mantle hits 54 homers, giving Yankees teammate record of 115 four-baggers.

- Cubs owner William Wrigley, tired of second-division finishes, decides the team will be managed by eight coaches.

- Willie Mays hits four homers on April 30 vs. Braves.

- Detroit's Norm Cash tops expanded AL in batting with .361 BA.

- Yankees hit 240 homers to set new ML record.

- Ford tops majors with 25 victories and wins Cy Young.

- Phillies lose ML record 23 straight games.

- Pittsburgh's Roberto Clemente wins his first National League bat crown (.351).

- Giant Orlando Cepeda tops NL with 46 homers and 142 RBI.

Reds Cruise to NL Flag

A shot of the 1961 National League Champion Cincinnati Reds. Although no match for the Yankees in the World Series, the Reds won the flag by a comfortable four-game margin. The following year, the Reds actually had a higher winning percentage yet could finish no better than third place.

Cincinnati Reds

Warren Spahn

Spahn Wins 21 at Age 40

Age 40 in 1961, Warren Spahn won 21 games, tying for first place in victories in the National League; in 1963, after turning 42 years old, he won 23 games. His phenomenal durability caused Stan Musial to remark that he doubted Spahn would ever get into the Hall of Fame because it seemed Spahn would never stop pitching.

Joe Cunningham

Cunningham Nabs Liner in Stick

St. Louis left fielder Joe Cunningham spears a liner off Orlando Cepeda's bat in a 1961 game against the Giants at Candlestick Park. A few weeks later, the Stick, in its second year of existence, introduced a national TV audience to its infamous wind when Stu Miller was blown off the mound in an All-Star Game. Cunningham, a nondescript player for a dozen years, was actually a darn good hitter: He batted .345 in 1959 to finish second in the batting race. In 1961, he hit .286.

1961

- Warren Spahn tops NL in wins an ML record eighth time, as he and the Reds' Joey Jay win 21.

- Jay ties Spahn for NL top spot in shutouts with just four.

- Spahn leads NL in CGs (21) and ERA (3.01).

- NL wins first All-Star Game of the year, 5-4 in ten innings at San Francisco.

- Second All-Star Game ends in 1-1 tie at Boston, as rain stops play after nine innings.

- Chicago's Billy Williams named NL Rookie of the Year.

- Boston's Don Schwall selected AL ROTY by one vote over KC's Dick Howser.

- Ty Cobb dies.

- On May 9, Jim Gentile hits grandslams in two consecutive innings for Baltimore.

Aaron Leads Proud Braves

The Braves were still in Milwaukee in 1961 and showed no signs of moving, as Hank Aaron spearheaded the club to its ninth first-division finish in the nine years it had been in Wisconsin. Aaron hit .327 that year with 39 doubles (tops in the loop), 34 home runs, and 120 RBI. The Braves' skein continued through the 1965 season, the club's last year in Milwaukee.

Bob Allison, Ted Lepcio

Allison Catches Sox Fly

Twins utility infielder Ted Lepcio ducks out of the way as outfielder Bob Allison calls him off of a fly ball in a 1961 game against the Red Sox. Lepcio began his career in 1952 with Boston as the heir apparent to Bobby Doerr's second base job, then never developed. He split the 1961 season, his last in the majors, between Chicago and Minnesota. Allison collected 21 doubles, 29 home runs, 105 RBI, and 103 walks in '61.

Hank Aaron

- Braves hit four consecutive homers on June 8 vs. Reds.

- Maris hits 61st homer in final game of season, Oct. 1, off Boston's Tracy Stallard.

- NL opts to expand to ten teams in 1962, placing franchises in New York and Houston.

- Spahn no-hits Giants on April 28.

- Spahn wins 300th game—first NL southpaw to do so.

- Baltimore's Dave Philley sets new ML record when he collects 24 pinch hits.

- Luis Arroyo of Yankees sets new ML record when he notches 29 saves.

- Detroit rookie Jake Wood fans 141 times to set new ML record.

- Milwaukee's Eddie Mathews hits 30 or more homers for NL record ninth consecutive year.

- Yankees have ML record six players who hit 20 or more homers.

Roger Maris

Maris: 61 HRs a Nightmare

Roger Maris later revealed to writer Joe Reichler that his baseball career would have been a lot more fun if he had never hit those 61 home runs in 1961. About all that breaking Babe Ruth's record brought him, he said, was headaches. The controversy of the accomplishment centered on the fact that Ruth had nailed 60 home runs playing in 151 of his team's 155 games while Maris had 161 of 163 games to collect dingers.

Charley Finley

Cepeda No. 1 at First

The Giants had an enviable problem in the early 1960s: They had two great first basemen in Orlando Cepeda (pictured) and Willie McCovey. (In 1961, Cepeda tallied 46 home runs and 142 RBI.) The Giants came up with a solution: They waited until Cepeda's value had been reduced by an injury and then traded him.

Orlando Cepeda

Finley Lacks Horse Sense

By the close of the 1961 season, A's followers had already begun believing that new owner Charley Finley (pictured with team member Charlie O.) had about as much baseball sense as his mascot. The A's tied the expansion Senators for last place in the American League that year.

1961

- Though the '61 Yankees are widely acclaimed for their great offense, the Tigers actually score more runs (841-827).
- Mays leads NL in runs (129) and runs produced (212).
- Maris leads AL in RBI (142) and total bases (366), and ties in runs (132).

- The Hall of Fame inducts Max Carey and Billy Hamilton.
- Bobby Shantz is first to win Gold Gloves in each league when he takes prize while pitching for Pirates.
- Richardson breaks Nellie Fox's monopoly on AL Gold Glove at second base.

- Clemente wins his first Gold Glove as NL outfielder.
- Dazzy Vance dies.
- On August 23, five Giants homer in one inning to tie the ML record.
- Gentile ties ML season record with five grandslams.

Six Yanks Hit 207 HRs

A shot of the Yankees' 1961 version of their "Murderer's Row" *(left to right)*: Roger Maris, Yogi Berra, Mickey Mantle, Elston Howard, Bill Skowron, and Johnny Blanchard. All hit at least 21 home runs for a combined total of 207. Blanchard, a backup catcher and pinch hitter deluxe, nailed his dingers in only 243 at-bats.

Murderer's Row

Brooks Robinson

Brooks Can't Help O's

Brooks Robinson was the infield fulcrum on a team that in 1961 was a preseason favorite to win the American League pennant (he hit .287 that season). When it grew evident in September that Baltimore was out of the race, manager Paul Richards was replaced by Lum Harris. A fine pilot, Richards did not manage again in the majors until 1976.

Frank Robinson

Robby Slugs Way to MVP

Frank Robinson led the National League in one category in 1961—slugging, with a .611 average—yet ran away with the award for Most Valuable Player. The emergence of Gordy Coleman allowed Reds skipper Fred Hutchinson to move Robinson from first base back to his normal post in right field; consequently, Cincy vaulted from sixth place in 1960 to a pennant in 1961, its first flag since 1940.

- Gentile sets O's franchise record with 46 home runs and 141 RBI.

- By hitting his 50th homer on August 22, Maris becomes the first to have 50 homers by the end of August.

- Minnesota's Pete Ramos tops AL in losses a record fourth consecutive time (20).

- Minnie Minoso leads the majors a record ninth time in being hit by the pitch.

- Dummy Hoy dies at 99.

- Lee Thomas sets Angels record that still stands for most homers by a rookie (24).

- Cash sets record for most home runs by a Tigers lefty hitter (41).

- In the All-Star Game at Candlestick Park in SF, pitcher Stu Miller at one point is blown off the mound by the park's infamous wind.

- Bill Dewitt becomes new owner of the Reds.

Cash Boasts Best BA of '60s

The extraordinary 1961 season of Norm Cash was overshadowed by the home run feats of Roger Maris and Mickey Mantle, but historians are now beginning to recognize its true significance. That year, Cash had the highest batting average (.361) of any player during the 1960s and the highest on-base percentage (.488) since 1957. Cash went on to club 377 home runs in his 17-year career yet, oddly, never came within 75 points of his .361 mark. In 1962, his average plummeted to .243. The 118-point fall-off is the worst ever by a batting champion.

Willie Mays

Norm Cash

Willie Thrills Giants Fans

Willie Mays (pictured waving good-bye to New York fans before serving a military hitch in 1952) ranked high in every major slugging department in 1961. He topped the National League with 129 runs scored, came in second with 40 home runs, and placed third with 334 total bases, 123 RBI, and 81 walks. Oddly, never once in his 22-year career did Mays lead the NL in RBI.

1961

- Mathews tops NL in walks (93).
- Williams's 25 homers set a Cubs rookie record.
- Lew Burdette tops the NL in innings with 272.
- Johnny Podres leads NL in win pct. (.783).

- Red Vada Pinson, playing a 154-game schedule in the NL, has 208 hits—15 more than Cash, the AL leader, who plays a 162-game schedule.
- Wood tops AL and majors with 14 triples.
- Mantle leads AL in walks (126) and SA (.687).

- Cash has top OBP in majors (.488).
- LA's Wally Moon leads NL in OBP (.438).
- Maury Wills and Luis Aparicio once again lead their leagues in steals with 35 and 53, respectively.
- Detroit's Rocky Colavito tops AL and majors with 234 runs produced.

Vada, Robby Rev Up Reds

Vada Pinson *(left)* and Frank Robinson were the offensive leaders for the Reds in 1961. Pinson posted a .343 average that season, leading the National League with 208 hits. Robinson led the circuit with a .611 slugging average that year, with 37 homers and 124 RBI.

Burdette Wins 18

Lew Burdette was a master at never working any harder than he had to. Given one run, he'd pitch a shutout. Given nine runs, he'd win 9-6. The end result was that he always finished among the leaders in runs surrendered. In 1956, however, with his team in a down-to-the-wire flag race, he led the National League with a 2.71 ERA. In 1961, he led the league in innings (272) and went 18-11.

Vada Pinson, Frank Robinson

Chairman Goes 25-4

By the early 1960s, Whitey Ford had acquired the nickname "The Chairman of the Board." It was somewhat misleading. Ford and Mickey Mantle were probably the Yankees' two leading free spirits in that era. On the field, though, Ford was all business; his 25-4 record in 1961 was the best performance by a Yankees pitcher prior to 1978. Ford paced the American League in wins, win pct. (.862), starts (39), and innings pitched (283).

Lew Burdette

Whitey Ford

- Al Kaline leads American League in doubles (41), is second in batting (.324).
- Chicago's George Altman leads the NL in triples with 12.
- Ford tops ML in win pct. (.862) and innings (283).
- Dick Donovan, with the expansion Senators, posts AL's top ERA (2.40).
- Camilo Pascual leads the AL in Ks with 221.
- Pascual ties Baltimore's Steve Barber for AL lead in shutouts with eight.
- Frank Lary wins 23 games for Detroit, tops majors with 22 CGs.
- Miller and Pittsburgh's Roy Face tie for the NL lead in saves with 17.
- MVP Robinson tops NL only in SA (.611), but is second in several other departments.
- Despite the expanded schedule, only two AL hurlers, Ford and Lary, win more than 18 games.

YANKS WIN, BUT WILLS STEALS THE SHOW

Following the American League's lead, the National League expanded to ten teams in 1962, adding the New York Mets—thus returning National League baseball to the Big Apple and the Polo Grounds after a four-year absence—and the Houston Colt .45s. Houston won a respectable 64 games to finish in eighth place; the Casey Stengel-led "Amazin' Mets" lost a record 120 contests.

The Dodgers picked up several awards in their quest for the National League pennant. Maury Wills broke Ty Cobb's record of 96 stolen bases in 1915 with 104 swipes and was voted MVP. Tommy Davis topped the circuit with his .346 average and 153 RBI. Don Drysdale won a league-high 25 games and the Cy Young Award; Sandy Koufax, who pitched a no-hitter against the Mets on June 30, was the ERA champ at 2.54. All this talent made for an exciting first season at the new Chevez Ravine stadium. The Los Angeles fans responded with a record-setting attendance of 2,755,184.

With Koufax sidelined with an injury, however, the Dodgers won just three of their last 13 games. The Giants—led by Willie Mays's league-high 49 homers and second-best 141 RBI—forced a three-game tie-breaking playoff. As in 1951, the Giants beat the Dodgers in come-from-behind style, overcoming a 4–2 deficit in the ninth inning of game three to win the pennant.

The Indians led the American League at the All-Star break, then fell to sixth place by season's end as the Yankees took first again. Mickey Mantle missed 39 contests, yet still belted 30 homers and seized the MVP title. Roger Maris followed his 61-homer season with 33 round-trippers and 100 RBI. Shortstop/outfielder Tom Tresh hit 20 homers and won Rookie of the Year honors (Chicago's Ken Hubbs was the NL's Rookie of the Year with a .260 average). Ralph Terry led the circuit with 23 wins; Whitey Ford won 17.

The Twins made a pennant run behind Harmon Killebrew's league-leading 48 homers and 126 RBI, Camilo Pascual's 20 wins, and Jack Kralick's no-hitter against Kansas City on August 26; they ended the season five games back. In third place, the second-year Angels surprisingly won 86 games on the strength of Leon Wagner's 37 homers and 107 RBI and the pitching of youngsters Dean Chance (14–10,

2.96 ERA) and Bo Belinsky (10–11, 3.56 ERA, a no-hitter against Baltimore on May 5).

The most that Boston could do with batting champ Pete Runnels (.326) and a pair of no-hitters—Earl Wilson no-hit Los Angeles on June 26 and Bill Monbouquette no-hit Chicago on August 1—was tie with Baltimore for seventh place. Detroit, ranked fourth, had the ERA champ in Hank Aguirre (2.21).

Ford took the first game of the World Series 6–2, although his scoreless-innings Series streak was stopped at 33²/₃ when the Giants scored in the second. The teams traded victories before ex-Yankee Don Larsen won game four. New York went up three games to two behind Ralph Terry's 5–3 victory.

When play resumed after three straight days of rain, the Giants and their 16-game winner Billy Pierce finally pinned a Series loss on Ford, winning 5–2.

In the tense seventh game at San Francisco, Terry and 24-game winner Jack Sanford locked in a pitcher's duel that had the Yankees up 1–0 after seven innings. Billy O'Dell, San Fran's 19-game winner, took over in the eighth and held the Yankees down until his team had one last shot in the ninth. A Mays double gave the Giants runners at second and third and two outs. Willie McCovey then hit a scorching line drive and second baseman Bobby Richardson snagged it for another Yankee World Championship.

1962

- Yanks off on another run, taking third consecutive AL flag.
- Giants win NL pennant in playoff.
- Dodgers involved in fourth pennant playoff since 1946 and lose for third time.
- Yankees eke out World Series win in seven games.

- New York's Ralph Terry wins 1-0 over Jack Sanford in game seven.
- Bobby Richardson ends Series by spearing Willie McCovey's line drive, leaving tying and winning runs in scoring position.
- Yanks win 20th World Title in last 40 years.

- Yankees hit just .199, lowest BA by winning team in seven-game Series.
- Dodger Maury Wills is NL MVP, edging out Willie Mays.
- Mickey Mantle named AL MVP.
- Dodger Don Drysdale tops majors with 25 wins and captures the Cy Young Award.

According to this photo, someone went to the trouble of collecting all 104 bases
Maury Wills pilfered in 1962. His thievery brought Wills the MVP Award, as he did
not pace the National League in any other department. He did, however, tie for the
top spot in triples (ten) and for second in runs scored (130).

- Tommy Davis of LA wins NL bat crown (.346) and knocks home 153 runs, most by anyone in majors since 1949.

- Wills steals ML record 104 bases.

- Mays leads majors with 49 homers and 382 total bases.

- Expansion New York Mets lose modern major league record 120 games.

- Jackie Robinson becomes the first black player inducted into the Hall of Fame.

- Sanford wins 16 straight games.

- Expansion Los Angeles Angels finish third in AL, lead loop as late as July 4.

- NL wins first All-Star Game of year, 3-1 at Washington.

- AL wins year's second All-Star Game, played almost three weeks after first one, 9-4 at Wrigley Field.

1962

San Francisco Giants

Giants Led by Old Hands

A look at the 1962 San Francisco Giants. Manager Alvin Dark (front row, center), coach Larry Jansen (to the right of Dark), and coaches Whitey Lockman and Wes Westrum (to the left of Dark) all played on the 1954 World Champion New York Giants. The only member of that club who was still an active player with the 1962 Giants was Willie Mays (seated beside Westrum).

Harmon Killebrew

Harmon Tops in HRs, RBI

Harmon Killebrew paced the American League in major slugging departments in 1962 with 48 home runs and 126 RBI. He led the league in home runs while playing each of the three different positions he served at as a regular for at least one full season.

Speedy Davis Ties in Triples

Willie Davis tied with three other players for the title of triples king in the National League in 1962; all four had ten apiece. Davis was also the circuit's second-best base thief that year, swiping 32 cushions (72 less than teammate Maury Wills). After 17 years in the majors, Davis left after the 1976 season to play in Japan.

Willie Davis

1962

- Minnesota pitcher Jim Kaat wins first of record 14 consecutive GGs.

- On Sept. 12, Washington's Tom Cheney Ks 21 Orioles in 16-inning game, winning 2-1.

- Bo Belinsky of Angels no-hits Baltimore on May 5.

- Earl Wilson of Red Sox no-hits Angels on June 26.

- Sandy Koufax of LA no-hits Mets on June 30.

- Bill Monbouquette of Boston no-hits Chicago on August 1.

- Jack Kralick of Minnesota no-hits KC on August 26.

- The three Sadowskis—Ted, Ed, and Bob—are last trio of brothers to all be active in AL in same year.

- Dodger Stadium opens on April 10, LA vs. Cincinnati.

- Harmon Killebrew sets ML record when he fans 142 times.

Sandy Koufax

Veteran Friend Wins 18

Although he was just age 31 at the end of the 1962 season, Bob Friend had already put in 12 full years in the majors. He debuted with the 1951 Pirates, who finished in next-to-last place, then pitched for five cellar-dwellers in the next six seasons, thus accounting for his poor career-win percentage. He had an 18-14 season in 1962, tying for the league-lead with five shutouts.

Bob Friend

Koufax No-Hits Hapless Mets

A shot of Sandy Koufax in action on June 30, 1962, the night he threw his first no-hitter. His victims, the Mets, were everyone's patsies that year. New York's five main starters had a combined 30-92 record. Reliever Ken MacKenzie somehow managed to collect five wins and just four losses for the Mets.

Elroy Face

Face Saves NL-High 28

Elroy Face topped the National League in saves for the third and final time in 1962, tallying 28. His work helped the Pirates triumph in 93 games. In 1962, however, with the circuit so unbalanced by expansion that seven teams finished above .500, 93 victories was good only for a fourth-place spot.

- Pittsburgh reliever Diomedes Olivo, age 43, is the oldest rookie in ML history.

- Cub pitcher Bob Buhl is hitless for the full season in 70 at-bats to set ML record for futility.

- Detroit's Hank Aguirre has best ERA in majors.

- On Oct. 2, Dodgers and Giants play for four hours and 18 minutes, setting ML record for longest nine-inning game.

- Cincinnati's Frank Robinson tops the majors in runs (134), doubles (51), and SA (.624), and leads NL in OBP (.424).

- Davis leads majors with 230 hits and 246 runs produced.

- Pirate Elroy Face sets new NL save record with 28.

- Mantle tops AL in OBP (.488), slugging average (.605), and walks (122).

Drysdale Goes 25-9

Don Drysdale was the National League's top pitcher in 1962, posting a 25-9 record. He led a mound staff that, for the sixth year in a row, topped the majors in strikeouts (1,104 that season). The Dodgers' skein was ended at seven seasons in 1964 by the Reds. Drysdale's personal high of 251 Ks came in 1963.

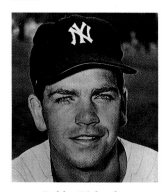

Bobby Richardson

Bobby Bats 692 Times

Bobby Richardson set a Yankees club record in 1962 by collecting 692 at-bats. Most Bomber fans will be hard-pressed, though, to recall even one of his plate appearances that season. What Yankees fans remember is the moment, forever frozen in time, when he snagged the World Series-ending line drive.

Don Drysdale

Elston Howard

Howard, 33, Finally Starts

In 1962, for the first time in his major league career, Elston Howard played just one position—catcher. He was already 33 years of age then, and on the downside of the hill (.279 average, 21 home runs, 91 RBI). With any team other than the Yankees (who were led for years by All-Star backstop Yogi Berra), Howard would probably have been a full-time regular ten years sooner. He would not, however, have cashed ten World Series checks. Howard played in 54 Series games in his career—third most in history.

1962

- Boston's Pete Runnels wins his second AL bat crown (.326) and is first to win bat titles at two positions—second base and first base.

- Terry tops AL with 23 wins.

- The Hall of Fame inducts Bob Feller, Bill McKechnie, and Edd Roush.

- Yankee Tom Tresh is AL Rookie of the Year.

- Cincinnati's Ken Hubbs is NL Rookie of the Year.

- Milwaukee's Del Crandall and Minnesota's Earl Battey win their final Gold Gloves at catcher.

- Hubbs interrupts, for one year only, Bill Mazeroski's grip on NL Gold Glove prize at second base.

- Wills wins second Gold Glove for NL shortstops; Luis Aparicio continues to be the only AL shortstop to win a Gold Glove.

- Mets play first game on April 11, lose 11-4 to Cards.

Jackie: First Black in Hall

Jackie Robinson was the first black player to be inducted into the Baseball Hall of Fame. Robinson trailed only Bob Feller in the 1962 voting. Between 1956 and 1966, the balloting for selection was conducted every other year rather than each winter.

Jackie Robinson

Jim Bunning

Bunning Wins 19

Jim Bunning spearheaded the fourth-place Tigers and placed among the American League's top five leaders with 19 victories in 1962. In December of the following year, he was traded to the Phils in one of the first big interleague deals. Interleague trading, which for years had been prohibited except via the waiver route, was kicked off by a 1959 swap between the Giants and Orioles.

Yanks Wear World Crown

A look at the 1962 World Champion New York Yankees. Jack Reed *(back row, third from the left)*, who was primarily used as a late-inning replacement for Mickey Mantle, played 194 games with the Yankees in 1962 and '63 and had only 116 at-bats. Serving the same role in 1965, Ross Moschitto had just 27 at-bats in 96 games. New York again led the league in runs (817). This marked the 37th straight year in which they ranked in the top half of the AL in runs.

New York Yankees

- Mets get off to 0-9 start, don't win first game in franchise history until April 23, 9-1 over Pittsburgh.

- Reliever Pete Richert of LA debuts in majors on April 12 by fanning the first six batters he faces.

- Detroit's Rocky Colavito goes 7-for-10 in a 22-inning game on June 24.

- Floyd Robinson of the White Sox goes 6-for-6 on July 22.

- Bill Fischer of KC pitches an ML record $84\frac{1}{3}$ consecutive innings without issuing a walk.

- Detroit's Norm Cash sets ML record that still stands for the largest drop in BA—118 points—by a previous year's bat crown winner.

- Nellie Fox plays 150 or more games for an AL record 11th consecutive season.

- Eddie Yost retires with a record 28 homers as the leadoff batter in a game (since broken).

- Hubbs sets new ML record for second basemen by handling 418 consecutive errorless chances.

Terry Wins Close Series

Ralph Terry is the only pitcher to throw the last pitch in two World Series, both of which ended dramatically. In each instance, Terry's delivery was hit hard. On the second occasion, however, he was lucky. Had Willie McCovey's line drive escaped Bobby Richardson in the 1962 Series finale, Terry would have lost the game 2-1.

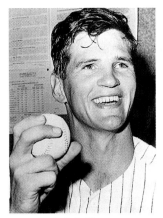

Ralph Terry

Radatz Hot in Relief

Dick Radatz made 62 relief appearances as a rookie with the 1962 Red Sox and notched 24 saves on a 2.24 ERA. For three years, he was nearly untouchable, registering well over a strikeout an inning. Then in 1965, his fastball lost a little of its kick and he began to get blasted.

Dick Radatz

Clemente: .312, Ten HRs

Perhaps the closest parallel Roberto Clemente had in terms of hitting was Harry Heilmann, who also started extremely slowly. Clemente had a .282 career average after his first five seasons. In 1962, he hit .312 with ten home runs and 74 RBI. When he died in 1972, his average was up to .317.

Roberto Clemente

World Series

Yanks Rejoice After Big Win

The scene on the field at Candlestick Park after the last out of the 1962 World Series. Yankees catcher Elston Howard embraces winning pitcher Ralph Terry. Partaking in the celebration are Bill Skowron *(to the left of Howard)*, Tony Kubek *(behind Terry)*, and a hatless Bobby Richardson.

1962

- Paul Waner dies.

- The majors adopt a Player Development Plan to address the problems of a shrinking talent pool and the collapse of the minor leagues.

- At season's end, Pirates trade Dick Groat and Olivo to the Cards for Don Cardwell and Julio Gotay.

- Pittsburgh's Groat and Mazeroski participate in a combined NL keystone record 264 double plays (since broken).

- At Candlestick, the Giants' Billy Pierce has a 12-0 record in 12 starts— an ML record for most home wins without a loss in a season.

- Craig Anderson loses 16 straight games for Mets, setting a new ML post-dead-ball record.

- Yankees send Bill Skowron to Dodgers for Stan Williams.

- Eddie Mathews leads NL again in walks (101).

World Series

Stafford Wins Game Three

A moment from game three of the 1962 World Series, which was won 3-2 by Yankee Bill Stafford, the man on the mound. Crouched in readiness at third base is Clete Boyer.

Jim Kaat

Kaat Pumps Up Twins

Twins teammates Jim Kaat (caught in a jubilant moment during the 1962 season) and Camilo Pascual won 38 games between them that year, the most of any American League mound duo except Ralph Terry and Whitey Ford of the Yankees. Kaat and Pascual also tied with Cleveland's Dick Donovan for the lead in shutouts with five apiece.

Chuck Hiller

Hiller Cracks Series Slam

Chuck Hiller returns to the Giants dugout in the seventh inning of game four of the 1962 World Series after his grandslam breaks a two-all tie. Nicknamed "Iron Hands" for his shaky fielding, Hiller lost his second base job the following year when his average dipped to .223. He never again played regularly.

Tommy Davis

Davis: NL's Toughest Out

In addition to leading the circuit with 153 RBI and 230 hits, Tommy Davis was the 1962 National League batting champ with a .346 average. He won a repeat hitting crown in 1963, had an off year in 1964, then broke an ankle the following spring. Soon after returning to full-time action, Davis was traded to the Mets, beginning a ten-year stretch in which he played for nine different teams.

- Four players tie for NL lead in triples (ten).
- KC's Gino Cimoli leads AL with 15 triples.
- Bob Purkey has 23 wins for Reds, tops NL in win pct. (.821).
- Koufax leads NL in ERA (2.54).

- Drysdale tops NL and majors in innings (314) and Ks (232).
- Warren Spahn leads NL again in CGs with 22.
- Richardson leads AL in hits (209).
- Colavito tops AL in total bases (309).

- AL and NL showing great disparity in developing black talent.
- NL offensive leader board is dominated by blacks, while the AL's is dominated by whites.
- Minnesota's Camilo Pascual again leads AL in Ks (206), also leads in CGs (18) and ties for lead in shutouts (five).

The 1963 season was the year of southpaw sensation Sandy Koufax. The 27-year-old hurler had one of the greatest seasons in history, winning a "quadruple crown" of pitching with 25 victories, 306 strikeouts, 11 shutouts, and a 1.88 ERA. Koufax took the Most Valuable Player and Cy Young Awards.

Koufax's marvelous hurling overshadowed the strong seasons of his Dodger teammates. Don Drysdale contributed 19 wins in 315 innings; relief ace Ron Perranoski, another 16 triumphs and 21 saves. On offense, outfielder Tommy Davis hit a league-high .326. Frank Howard smashed 28 homers in just 123 games. Maury Wills hit .302 and led the league with 40 stolen bases.

The most threatening rivals to the Los Angeles ballclub were the Cardinals. Featuring batsmen Bill White, Ken Boyer, Curt Flood, Tim McCarver, and 42-year-old Stan Musial (in his final year), the Cards led the league in scoring, hits, doubles, and triples. Inconsistent all season, St. Louis connected in September, winning 19 of 20 to come within a game of the first-place Dodgers.

The two teams went head-to-head in a critical late-season, three-game series in St. Louis. With Los Angeles winning the first two games of the series, the Cardinals blew a 5-1 lead in the seventh inning of the finale and fell 6-5 in 13 innings. The Dodgers took the league by 6 games.

SANDY'S SMOKE UNHITTABLE; LA BLOWS BY YANKS

San Francisco came in third, despite banner seasons from the Giants' Willie Mays (.314 average, 38 home runs, and 103 RBI), Willie McCovey (44 homers—tied with the legendary Hank Aaron for the crown—and 102 RBI), and Juan Marichal (25 triumphs—tied with Koufax for the league-best—and 2.41 ERA).

The Giants' old home, the Polo Grounds, saw its last season of play as the ballpark for the Mets. Despite losing 111 games, the Mets drew more than a million spectators.

The Yankees won their fourth consecutive American League pennant, beating the White Sox by 10 1/2 games. Despite prolonged injuries to Mickey Mantle and Roger Maris, the Bombers won the league, scoring the second-most runs and allowing the second-fewest runs. Solid pitching came from 34-year-old Whitey Ford (a league-best 24 wins, 2.74 ERA) and 24-year-old Jim Bouton (21-7, 2.53 ERA).

Other notable feats: Harmon Killebrew of Minnesota led the AL with 45 homers. Boston's Carl Yastrzemski hit .321 for the title, while teammate Dick Stuart racked up 118 RBI to top the loop. Milwaukee's Aaron paced the NL with 130 RBI. Cincinnati's Pete Rose, the Rookie of the Year, batted his first major league hit.

Due to baseball's recent expansions, many pitchers made the major leagues when they should have been throwing in the minors. To compensate, the strike zone was expanded in '63. The extension allowed the best pitchers—the Reds' Jim Maloney (23-7, 2.77 ERA, 265 Ks), the White Sox' Gary Peters (19-8, a league-best 2.33 ERA), the Twins' Camilo Pascual (21-9, 2.47), the Cubs' Dick Ellsworth (22-10, 2.10), the Braves' 42-year-old Warren Spahn (23-7, 2.60)—to get even better. Another older pitcher, 43-year-old Early Wynn, finally won his 300th game.

Ford went up against Koufax in the first game of the World Series. Koufax's record-setting 15 strikeouts were the talk of the 5-2 Los Angeles victory. The Dodgers, aided by a homer courtesy of ex-Yankee Bill Skowron and 8 1/3 scoreless innings by pitcher Johnny Podres, took game two 4-1. Drysdale was the star of game three with a three-hit, nine-strikeout, complete game victory. The Dodgers finished the sweep the next day with a 2-1 Koufax triumph over Ford.

1963

- Yanks cop fourth straight flag in AL.
- Dodgers triumph in NL.
- Dodgers sweep Yanks—first time New York is swept since 1922.
- Sandy Koufax wins two games in World Series; Dodgers pitchers have 1.00 ERA.
- Dodger Tommy Davis leads all batters in Series with .400 BA.
- Dodger Bill Skowron comes back to haunt Yankees, hitting .385 in the Series.
- Yankees skipper Ralph Houk, Casey Stengel's replacement, wins flags in each of his first three seasons as pilot.
- Ellie Howard is first black player to win AL MVP.
- Koufax wins NL MVP.
- Koufax is first unanimous choice for Cy Young Award.
- Koufax sets new modern NL record with 306 Ks.

Sandy Koufax springs into the air after notching the last out of the 1963 World Series. Koufax won the opening and closing games of the stunning Dodgers' sweep, 5-2 and 2-1. Los Angeles collected just 25 hits in the four-game fray and only a half-dozen in the last two contests.

- Koufax sets modern record for southpaws with 11 shutouts.

- Koufax leads majors with a 1.88 ERA.

- Carl Yastrzemski wins first AL bat crown (.321).

- Yaz leads AL in hits (183), doubles (40), walks (95), and OBP (.419).

- Davis repeats as NL bat crown winner (.326).

- Roger Craig of Mets ties NL single-season record when he loses 18 consecutive games.

- Warren Spahn breaks Eddie Plank's record for most career wins by a southpaw when he collects his 328th victory.

- Mets lose ML record 22 straight games on the road.

- White Sox Dave Nicholson fans 175 times, breaking the ML record by 33.

- Twins lead majors in runs (767) and hit 225 home runs—most homers in history by a non-pennant winner.

Luis Sparkles at Short

Luis Aparicio never got the kind of attention in his time that Ozzie Smith currently enjoys, but he was every bit as good a shortstop. Aparicio either holds or shares almost every major career fielding record for American League shortstops, as well as the major league mark for most games by a shortstop (2,599). In 1963, Aparicio topped the circuit with 40 stolen bases.

Luis Aparicio

Elston Howard

Roger Craig

Howard Catches MVP Award

Elston Howard was voted the Most Valuable Player in the American League in 1963. He batted .287 that year with 28 home runs and 85 RBI. Neither Mickey Mantle, who was hurt much of the season, nor Roger Maris got a single vote that year. Howard also finished third in the balloting in 1964, yet only in tenth place in 1961 (his best season).

Helpless Craig Goes 5-22

Owing to a poor year in 1961, Roger Craig was left unprotected by the Dodgers and claimed by the Mets from the pool of players designed to stock the two new National League expansion teams. Consequently, he became the last pitcher in major league history to lose 20 or more games in two consecutive seasons. Craig posted a .185 winning percentage in 1963, going 5-22.

1963

- Harmon Killebrew leads AL in homers (45) and SA (.555).
- On July 6, Marichal beats Spahn 1-0 in 16 innings on a homer by Willie Mays.
- The Hall of Fame inducts John Clarkson, Elmer Flick, Sam Rice, and Eppa Rixey.
- On March 30, Rose, a nonroster player for the Reds, goes 2-for-2 in his first major league exhibition game.
- White Sox Gary Peters is AL Rookie of the Year.
- Peters has AL's best ERA (2.33).
- Minnesota's Zoilo Versalles breaks Luis Aparicio's reign as AL's Gold Glove shortstop.
- Minnesota's Vic Power continues to be the only AL first baseman to win a Gold Glove.
- Cardinal Curt Flood wins first of seven consecutive Gold Gloves.

Steady Ford Wins 24

Whitey Ford has the top career ERA—2.74—of any pitcher active exclusively since the end of the dead-ball era for ten or more seasons. He was so consistently effective that his highest ERA in the 16 seasons he pitched was 3.24 in 1965. His lowest, a 1.64 mark, came in his final season. In 1963, Ford led the American League with 24 wins and a .774 winning percentage.

Whitey Ford

Bob Allison

Willie McCovey

Stretch Returns with 44 HRs

Even though he won the National League Rookie of the Year Award in 1959, Willie McCovey was not altogether ready for the majors. He had to return to the Pacific Coast League the following year for more seasoning. The 1963 campaign was the first in which he held a regular job for the entire season. He tied with Hank Aaron for the home run crown that year, racking up 44 round-trippers.

Allison Part of Twins' HR Trio

Twins right fielder Bob Allison belonged to the only outfield trio whose members each hit 30 or more home runs in 1963. Allison clubbed 35 dingers, left fielder Harmon Killebrew led the American League with 45, and rookie center fielder Jimmie Hall contributed 33.

- Rogers Hornsby dies.
- Home Run Baker dies.
- The Pirates trade Bob Skinner to Reds for Jerry Lynch.
- The Tigers deal Jim Bunning and Gus Triandos to Phils for Don Demeter and Jack Hamilton.

- Cleveland swaps Jim Perry to Twins for Jack Kralick.
- White Sox send Al Smith and Aparicio to the O's for Hoyt Wilhelm and three other players.
- SF trades Felipe Alou and three other players to Milwaukee for Del Crandall and two pitchers.

- Jimmie Hall hits 33 homers to set Twins rookie record.
- On June 9 in Houston, the Colt .45s beat the Giants in the first Sunday night game in ML history.
- Dick Stuart is the first player to hit 30 or more homers in a season in both leagues, as he clubs 42 for Boston.

LA Polishes Off Yanks

The Dodgers celebrate their third World Championship in nine years. LA's sweep of the 1963 World Series was so one-sided that the Yankees were held to just four runs in the four-game tournament, the lowest of any team in the fall classic since the 1905 Philadelphia Athletics.

Harmon Clouts 45 HRs

Never an acclaimed fielder, Harmon Killebrew was nevertheless one of the most versatile players in recent years. He began as a second baseman, was converted to third sacker in his second season, and later also played regularly as both a first baseman and an outfielder. In 1963, Killebrew bested the AL with 45 homers.

World Series

Harmon Killebrew

Ken Boyer

Boyer Keeps Cards in Pennant Race

Ken Boyer's bat and steady glove at third base was a significant reason the Cardinals were able to stay in the National League pennant race until the final week of the 1963 season, Stan Musial's last. Boyer hit .285 that season with 24 home runs and 111 RBI. The following year, the Cards won their first flag without Musial since 1934. Again, Boyer would be the big bat. His 119 RBI would lead the league in 1964 and would earn him the National League Most Valuable Player Award.

1963

- In the final game of the season, Houston's John Paciorek goes 3-for-3 with two walks, three RBI, and four runs scored in his first ML game.
- After going 3-for-3 in debut, Paciorek never plays another ML game.
- Vada Pinson tops majors with 204 hits and 14 triples.
- Versalles tops AL in triples with 13.
- Eddie Mathews leads majors in walks (124) and is only NL player to have a .400 OBP.
- Albie Pearson of the Angels is second in AL in OBP (.403), runs (92), and walks (92).
- Stuart tops AL in RBI (118) and total bases (319).
- Al Kaline leads AL in runs produced with just 163.
- Cardinal Dick Groat tops majors with 43 doubles.
- Maury Wills and Luis Aparicio again are stolen base kings, each with 40.

Sandy Quiets the Yankees

Sandy Koufax had a superb season in 1963. He tied for the National League-lead in wins with 25 and topped the circuit with 11 shutouts, 306 strikeouts, and a 1.88 ERA. Yet he said that he felt somewhat ambivalent before he pitched the first game of that season's World Series. "I felt that I had to show myself and my team and the Yankees too that they were just a team of baseball players, not a pride of supermen," he said.

Sandy Koufax

World Series

Hank Misses Triple Crown

In 1963, Hank Aaron came the closest of any National League player since 1948 to winning the Triple Crown. He led in RBI with 130, tied Willie McCovey for the top spot in home runs with 44, and finished third in the batting race, just seven points behind the winner, with a .319 average.

Hank Aaron

Bright Ks to End Game One

Yankees pinch hitter Harry Bright ends game one of the 1963 World Series by fanning. Bright's strikeout was the 15th K registered by Dodgers ace Sandy Koufax (a Series record at the time). Johnny Roseboro is the catcher for Los Angeles.

- Whitey Ford leads AL in wins (24), win pct. (.774), and innings (269).
- Stu Miller tops majors with 27 saves for Baltimore.
- Camilo Pascual again tops AL in Ks (202) and wins 21 for Twins.
- Chicago's Ray Herbert leads AL with seven shutouts.

- Marichal ties Koufax for ML lead in wins (25) and also tops majors in innings (321).
- Reliever Ron Perranoski leads majors in win pct. (.842) and has 21 saves for the Dodgers.
- Lindy McDaniel tops NL with 22 saves for Cubs.

- Spahn tops the NL for the last time in CGs (22).
- The White Sox lead the AL in ERA with a 2.97 mark.
- LA leads the NL in ERA, strikeouts (1,095), and shutouts (24).
- Cards finish in second place after leading NL in runs (747).

Down by 6¹/₂ games to the White Sox, the Yankees won 30 of their last 40 to earn their fifth straight World Series appearance in 1964. They propelled themselves to championship contention without any pitcher winning as many as 19 games and by leading the league in one major category, hits with 1,442, and tying with Chicago for most saves at 45. Falling 1 game short to the New York onslaught, the Sox led in ERA at 2.72. Their 41-year-old ace reliever Hoyt Wilhelm posted a 12-9 record with 27 saves and a 1.99 ERA.

Also in the hunt the final weekend were the Orioles, whose third baseman Brooks Robinson (.317 average, 28 homers, and circuit-topping 118 RBI) led the league in four fielding categories and was named its Most Valuable Player. Minnesota led in home runs and runs scored, courtesy of round-tripping champ Harmon Killebrew (49 homers) and Rookie of the Year and batting champion Tony Oliva (.323 average). Dean Chance of the Los Angeles Angels grabbed the Cy Young Award with 20 wins (tied for first place in the league with Chicago's Gary Peters) and a circuit-best 1.65 ERA.

As wild as the American League finish was, it was outdone by the National League. Gene Mauch's Phillies, with help from Rookie of the Year third baseman Dick Allen (.318 average, 29

PHILLIES FOLD; CARDS HOLD THE WINNING HAND

homers, 91 RBI) and pitcher Jim Bunning, whose 19 wins included a perfect game against the Mets, led the pack by 6¹/₂ games with two weeks to go. They unexpectedly lost ten straight to hand the pennant to the Cardinals.

Four teams still had a chance to win it going into the final weekend, but first San Francisco and then Cincinnati (which lost to the Phils on the second-to-last day of the season) were eliminated. Needing to win only one of three games from the Mets (who christened their brand-new field, Shea Stadium, by losing 109 games), the Cardinals lost the first two 1-0 and 15-5 then trailed on the final Sunday. They rallied to beat the Mets, however, for their first pennant since 1946. St. Louis was led by league MVP and third baseman Ken Boyer, who topped the league with 119 RBI, and Lou Brock, a midseason pickup who batted .315 and was second in the NL in stolen bases.

Willie Mays of San Francisco took the home run crown with 47

round-trippers and Roberto Clemente of Pittsburgh won the batting title with a .339 average. Los Angeles lefthander Sandy Koufax went 19-5 with a league-best 1.74 ERA. Chicago's Larry Jackson topped the circuit with 24 wins.

Though they outslugged and outpitched their rivals, the Yankees lost the World Series in seven games to the Cardinals. Bob Gibson won two out of three games, including the clincher, while the sore-armed Yankee ace Whitey Ford was uncharacteristically hit hard in game one and did not appear again in the Series. Twenty-two-year-old Mel Stottlemyre, who was called up in August and went 9-3 down the stretch, beat Gibson in game two to even the Series; Jim Bouton won game three.

St. Louis won it, however, with timely hitting and stout pitching. Boyer's grandslam won game four 4-3 and Gibson went the distance in the ten-inning, 5-2 fifth game, won on Tim McCarver's three-run homer. Bouton squared the Series in game six, but an exhausted Gibson proved worthy to the end, beating the Yankees 7-5 in the final game. Bobby Richardson of New York set a Series record with 13 hits before making the last out.

The day after the Series ended, St. Louis manager Johnny Keane resigned and replaced fired Yankee manager Yogi Berra.

1964

- Yanks tie own record by winning fifth consecutive flag in AL.

- Cards emerge on top in NL by 1-game margin in five-team race.

- Cards win World Series in seven games—first time since 1921–22 that Yankees have been beaten twice in a row in fall play.

- Tired Bob Gibson beats tired Mel Stottlemyre in game seven, as both start third Series game on only three-days rest.

- Gibson fans 13 men in ten innings in game five of Series.

- Tim McCarver of Cards leads all Series hitters with .478 BA.

- Mickey Mantle has three homers and eight RBI in his last World Series.

- Yankee Bobby Richardson sets Series record with 13 hits.

- Yogi Berra is fired as Yankees pilot after winning flag as rookie manager; Cards manager Johnny Keane hired to replace him.

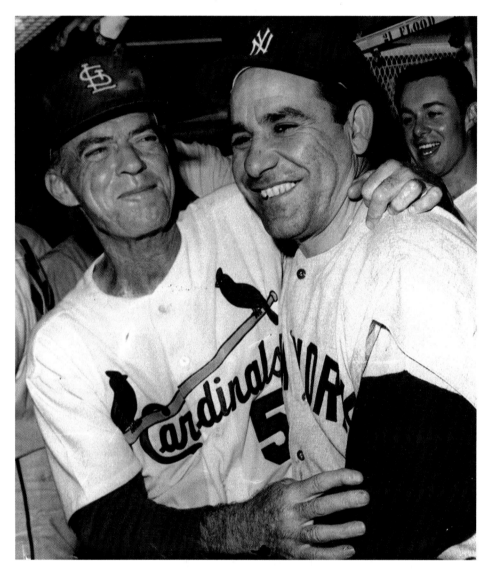

Beaming Cardinals skipper Johnny Keane *(left)* clasps Yogi Berra after St. Louis triumphed in the seventh game of the World Series on October 15, 1964. Unbeknownst to Berra, Keane was already ticketed to take over his job as Yankees manager.

- St. Louis' Ken Boyer wins NL MVP Award.

- Brooks Robinson of Baltimore is named AL MVP.

- Tony Oliva of Twins named AL Rookie of the Year, as he wins bat title (.323).

- Philly's Dick Allen named NL ROTY, as he tops NL in total bases (352) and runs (125), and ties in triples with 13.

- Phils lose National League flag after leading by 6 1/2 games with 12 to play as they lose ten straight games down the stretch.

- Boston's Dick Radatz has 16 wins and ML top 29 saves for team that wins only 72 games.

- On May 31, Mets and Giants play twinbill that lasts record 10 1/2 hours—Mets lose both games.

- Yankees sold to CBS.

Santo Slugs in Vain

In 1964, Ron Santo placed second in the National League in RBI (114) and slugging average (.564). Although he may have been the most valuable player in the NL that year, the standings did not reflect it. After breaking .500 in 1963 for the first time since 1946, the Cubs dropped back into the pack again the following season, finishing eighth.

Hoyt Wilhelm

Wilhelm, 41, Saves 27

Turning 41 years old in 1964, Hoyt Wilhelm seemed only to improve with age as he notched 27 saves for the White Sox on a 1.99 ERA. In the five-year span between 1964 and 1968, Wilhelm's saves totaled 77 and his ERA stayed under 2.00 each season, with a personal career-low of 1.31 in 1967.

Tony Oliva

Ron Santo

Brooks Hits and Fields

Brooks Robinson once said, "I could field as long as I can remember. But hitting has been a struggle all my life." In 1964, Robinson posted career-highs in home runs (28), RBI (118), and batting average (.317). Although he played 14 additional years, he never again hit .300.

Brooks Robinson

Oliva Takes Five Titles

Pedro Oliva used his brother's birth certificate when he applied for a passport to enter the United States, and thereafter kept the name of his sibling Tony. In 1964, he set several American League rookie records and topped the circuit in runs scored (109), hits (217), doubles (43), total bases (374), and batting average (.323). Until suffering a crippling knee injury in 1972, Oliva was almost unquestionably bound for the Hall of Fame.

1964

- Wally Bunker, age 19, wins 19 games for Orioles—most in the 20th century by a teenage pitcher.

- New York's Shea Stadium opens on April 17—Mets vs. Pittsburgh.

- NL wins All-Star Game 7-4 at Shea Stadium.

- Jim Bunning pitches a perfect game vs. Mets on June 21—first perfect game in NL in the 20th century.

- Houston's Ken Johnson becomes lone ML hurler to lose a CG no-hitter in nine innings, as Reds beat him 1-0 on April 23.

- Sandy Koufax no-hits Philadelphia on June 4.

- Koufax Ks 18 Cubs on April 24.

- Koufax held to 223 innings by arm trouble, but still leads NL in shutouts (seven), win pct. (.792), and ERA (1.74).

- Mantle receives his first $100,000 contract.

Gary Peters

Peters Wins 20 Games

Gary Peters struggled for seven years in the minors before earning a permanent spot on the White Sox roster in 1963. For the next nine seasons, he was one of the top southpaws in the American League. In 1964, he tied for the league-lead in wins with 20. Peters was also frequently utilized in the pinch-hitting capacity.

Richardson Nets 13 Hits

Bobby Richardson played in five World Series between 1960 and 1964. He was the top RBI man in the '60 Series and the leading hitter in the '61 affair. In 1964, he set a Series record with 13 hits. Only once during the period did he hit above .267 or total more than 50 RBI in the season.

Jim Bunning

Bobby Richardson

Bunning Perfect on Father's Day

Jim Bunning retires pinch hitter Johnny Stephenson of the Mets to nail down his perfect game on Father's Day in 1964. That season, Bunning posted a 19-8 record and Stephenson, a rookie, hit .158. The rest of the Mets lineup was not as inept as before and even had two .300 hitters—Ron Hunt and Joe Christopher.

- Boston's Tony Conigliaro, age 19, hits 24 homers and has .530 SA—both records for a teenage player.

- Baltimore's Luis Aparicio leads AL in steals (57) a record ninth consecutive year.

- Don Drysdale tops majors in innings pitched (321).

- Johnny Wyatt of KC is first pitcher in ML history to appear in at least half of his team's games (81 of 162).

- Oliva leads majors in hits (217) and total bases (374), AL in runs (109) and doubles (43).

- Oliva sets AL rookie record for hits.

- Oliva ties ML rookie record with 374 total bases.

- Allen sets NL rookie record with 352 total bases.

- Mets finish last for third consecutive year under Casey Stengel, losing ML record 340 games over a three-year period.

Bob Gibson

Gibson Earns Clutch Wins

Bob Gibson's career win percentage came in below .500 after his first four seasons in the majors. For the remaining 13 years of his career, it ranked above .600. In World Series action, Gibson holds virtually every significant career record for a pitcher who played for a team other than the Yankees. In 1964, the hurler posted a 19-12 record, yet was on the money when it counted, pitching to victories in games five and seven of the fall classic.

Ken Boyer

Flood Finds His Niche

In 1957, Curt Flood was a scatter-armed third baseman in the Reds farm system who was not about to supplant Don Hoak, the hot corner man on the parent club. Acquired over the winter by the Cardinals for three pitchers of limited worth, Flood was installed in center field and remained there for 12 years. In 1964, he batted .311 and posted 211 hits (tied for the lead in the NL).

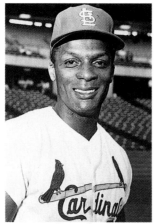

Curt Flood

Speedy Boyer Tops in RBI

Ken Boyer (shown here legging out a hit in a spring training game) swiped 22 bases as a rookie in 1955, an astounding total in that era for a third baseman. He was so fleet afoot early in his career that in 1957 the Cardinals moved him to center field, where he led all National League gardeners in fielding average. In 1964, Boyer spearheaded the majors with 119 RBI.

1964

- Willie Mays tops NL in homers (47) and SA (.607).

- Dean Chance of the Angels wins Cy Young.

- Chance tops AL in ERA (1.65), shutouts (11), innings (278), and CGs (15).

- Larry Jackson of the Cubs tops majors with 24 wins.

- Cubs trade Lou Brock and two other players to Cards for Ernie Broglio, Bobby Shantz, and Doug Clemens.

- The Hall of Fame inducts Luke Appling, Red Faber, Burleigh Grimes, Miller Huggins, Tim Keefe, Heinie Manush, and Monte Ward.

- Shantz wins last of eight consecutive Gold Gloves.

- Catchers Elston Howard of the Yankees and Johnny Edwards of the Reds both win second consecutive Gold Gloves.

- Vic Power wins last of seven straight Gold Gloves as AL first baseman.

Roberto Clemente

Roberto Takes NL Crown

Roberto Clemente claimed his second National League batting title in 1964, posting a .339 average. When he repeated the feat in 1965, it was the seventh year in a row that the NL batting king was righthanded. The period between 1959 and 1965 in the NL is the longest run of dominance in either loop by righty swingers since the end of the dead-ball era.

Cards Better Ford in Series

This sequence of shots shows Whitey Ford in the opening game of the 1964 World Series, trying unsuccessfully to wrest home plate away from Cardinals catcher Tim McCarver. Ford was also battered on the mound during the contest. A 9-5 loser in the opener, he failed to make another appearance in the Series.

Mauch Goes Down

The jury is still out on whether Gene Mauch was the victim of bad luck or his own panic-stricken managing in the collapse of the Phillies. In any event, his club won on the season's final day to knock the Reds out of a tie for the flag.

Gene Mauch

World Series

- Chicago's Ron Santo replaces Ken Boyer as NL Gold Glove champ at third base; Santo will win five Gold Gloves in a row.

- Ruben Amaro takes Bobby Wine's job as Phils shortstop and also replaces him as reigning NL Gold Glove champ.

- Chicago's Jim Landis wins his last of five consecutive Gold Gloves given to AL outfielders.

- Jesus Alou of the Giants goes 6-for-6 on July 10.

- Oriole Jerry Adair's .994 FA sets a new ML record for second basemen.

- For first time in ML history, third basemen win both MVP Awards.

- On Sept. 21, Reds beat Phils on steal of home by Chico Ruiz; the game starts the Phils' incredible slide from the top.

- Joe Stanka is selected the MVP of Japan's Pacific League, the first American player to be so honored.

1964

Boyers Face Off in Series

Ken Boyer bags a pop foul in the 1964 World Series. Among the enemy force the third baseman faced in that year's fall classic was his younger brother Clete. It marked the first time that two siblings who played the same position opposed each other in a World Series.

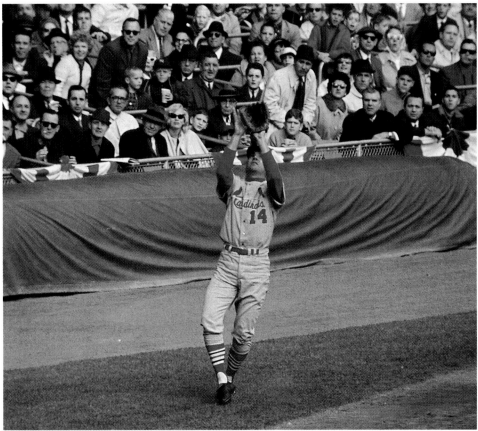

World Series

Mel Stottlemyre

Mel Starts Three Games

Mel Stottlemyre began the 1964 season with Triple-A Richmond in the International League and was not called up by the Yankees until August. With Whitey Ford idled, manager Yogi Berra was forced to start Stottlemyre in three World Series games. The rookie won his first fall classic contest 8-3, then lost 5-2 and 7-5. Never again in his 11-year career did he pitch in postseason play.

PH Warwick Sets Marks

Cardinals outfielder Carl Warwick slaps a single in the 1964 World Series. Warwick tied both a single and a career Series record when he garnered three pinch blows in the 1964 classic. For the remainder of his career, he batted just .140 as a pinch hitter.

World Series

1964

- Masanori Murakami of the Giants becomes the first Japanese-born player to play in the majors.

- White Sox give up an AL record-low 2.63 runs per game at home.

- Cleveland deals Mudcat Grant to Twins for George Banks and Lee Stange.

- LA sends Frank Howard and four others to Washington for Claude Osteen, John Kennedy, and cash.

- Milwaukee deals Roy McMillan to Mets for Jay Hook and Adrian Garrett.

- Houston pitcher Jim Umbricht dies of cancer.

- Ken Hubbs of the Cubs dies in a private plane crash prior to the season.

- Reds manager Fred Hutchinson dies of cancer.

- Brooks Robinson leads AL in games played for fourth consecutive year to tie the loop record.

Mick Wins Game Three

World Series

Mickey Mantle stands in against Cards reliever Barney Schultz. In the bottom of the ninth of game three of the 1964 World Series, Mantle tagged Schultz's first pitch for a home run to win the contest 2-1. Schultz, the Cards' bullpen ace during the regular season, had little success in the Series. He went 0-1 with an 18.00 ERA.

Jim Bouton

Bouton Wins Two in Series

Not yet a writer in 1964, Jim Bouton was still a pitcher—and a good one. He topped the American League with 37 starts that season, posting 18 victories, then won games three and six in the World Series. Bouton nose-dived to a 4-15 record the following year, joining in the overall Yankees collapse.

Gibson Beats the Yankees

Tim McCarver sprints from behind the plate to congratulate Bob Gibson on his seventh-game triumph after the last out in the 1964 World Series. The hurler started three games in an eight-day period and was hit freely by the Yankees throughout. Only in Gibson's first outing, however, was New York able to administer a knockout punch.

World Series

- Twins tie record of 1961 Yankees when they have six players who hit 20 or more homers.
- Reds blow chance to win NL flag by losing the last two games of the season to Phils.
- Cards nearly blow pennant by losing next-to-last game to Mets.

- Jim Ray Hart sets a Giants franchise rookie record with 31 homers.
- Roberto Clemente tops NL in batting (.339), ties St. Louis' Curt Flood for lead in hits (211).
- Ken Boyer is NL RBI leader (119) and is tops in runs produced (195).

- Maury Wills cops fourth NL steals crown in a row (53).
- Santo leads NL in walks (86) and OBP (.401), and ties in triples (13).
- Lee Maye of the Braves tops majors with 44 doubles.
- Juan Marichal tops the majors with 22 complete games.

KOUFAX'S HEAT COOLS OFF ZOILO'S TWINS

The seeds of parity were sown in the 1965 season, as the collapse of the Yankees after decades of domination was followed by the first-ever rookie draft (Rick Monday was the No. 1 pick of the Kansas City A's). After a one-year hiatus, the Dodgers again made and won the World Series, establishing themselves as potential heirs to the Yankee throne.

Sandy Koufax had another dominating year, leading the National League in wins (26), strikeouts (382—a major league record), and ERA (2.04), and winning his second Cy Young Award. His perfect game against the Cubs in September was the fourth no-hitter of his career. With the aid of Don Drysdale's 23 wins, Los Angeles' pitching was strong enough to offset its extremely weak offense—which fourth-place Cincinnati outscored 825-608 while finishing 8 games back. (Los Angeles second baseman Jim Lefebvre seized the league's Rookie of the Year Award with his season performance of .250, 12 home runs, and 69 RBI.)

The broad-based attack of the Reds included league RBI champ Deron Johnson (.287 average, 32 homers, 130 RBI) and Frank Robinson (whose season of a .296 average, 33 homers, and 113 RBI earned him a trade to the Orioles).

Willie Mays took MVP honors for batting .317 with a league-leading 52 home runs (including a record-breaking 17 round-trippers in August) and Willie McCovey knocked in a second-best 39 homers as San Francisco finished 2 games in back of Los Angeles. Roberto Clemente of third-place Pittsburgh won his second straight batting title and third overall with a .329 average. The Houston Astrodome opened with much fanfare—but the hometown fans had little to cheer as their team lost 97 games to finish ninth.

Wresting the American League crown from the Yankees—not difficult, since New York finished sixth—were the Twins. Minnesota won 102 games with the help of batting champion Tony Oliva (.321 average—his second title in two years in the majors), Most Valuable Player Zoilo Versalles (.273 average, 19 homers, 77 RBI), and Jim Grant (a league-high 21 victories).

Curt Blefary of Baltimore took top rookie honors with a .260 average, 22 homers, and 70 RBI. Ninth-place Boston racked up the most homers in the league, courtesy of home run king Tony Conigliaro, who hammered 32. Rocky Colavito's league-best 108 RBI and Sam McDowell's circuit-leading 2.18 ERA got Cleveland as far as fifth place.

Jim Maloney of the Reds nearly pitched two no-hitters: On June 14, the 25-year-old righty struck out 18 Mets (tying a league record) then gave up a homer in the 11th to lose 1-0. On August 19, he set down the Cubs in ten innings to win it 1-0.

Although San Francisco's Juan Marichal won 22 games with a 2.14 ERA, the pennant race headlines concentrated on Marichal's encounter with Dodgers catcher John Roseboro. Marichal clobbered Roseboro in the head with his bat after Roseboro returned a pitch to the mound close to the pitcher's head. The Giants won that day, beating Koufax. Although the Giants led the Dodgers and Reds by 3¹/₂ games on September 17, they finished the season 2 games behind LA. The Dodgers had their third pennant in seven years.

The Los Angeles hitters came alive in the World Series after Minnesota took the first two games at home. Koufax and Claude Osteen hurled shutouts as Los Angeles swept the Twins at home, 4-0, 7-2, and 7-0. After Minnesota won game six behind Grant, Koufax returned to shut out the Twins 2-0, the only game of the Series won by the visiting team.

1965

- Dodgers win NL flag by 2 games over Giants.
- Twins take franchise's first AL flag since 1933.
- LA wins World Series in seven games after dropping first two contests in Minnesota.
- Sandy Koufax wins two CG shutouts in Series, including crucial seventh game 2-0 over Jim Kaat.
- Koufax fans 29 Twins in three games in Series.
- Ron Fairly of LA leads all Series hitters with .379 BA, 11 hits, and six RBI.
- Mudcat Grant wins two games for Twins in Series.
- Willie Mays named NL MVP.
- Minnesota's Zoilo Versalles is chosen AL MVP over teammate Tony Oliva.
- Mays leads majors in homers (52), total bases (360), SA (.645), and OBP (.399).

National League batters hit only .179 against Sandy Koufax in 1965, as the ace hurler averaged 10.2 strikeouts and less than two walks per nine innings. He was used as a reliever in two crucial situations and got a save both times. Over his 12-year career, Koufax held opposing hitters to a composite average of .205.

- For the second time, Koufax is unanimous choice for Cy Young, as he Ks 382 to set new ML record.
- Koufax tops majors with 26 wins, 336 innings, 27 CGs, and 2.04 ERA.
- Majors adopt an annual free agent (rookie) draft.

- Minnesota wins 102 games after winning 79 the year before.
- LA manager Walter Alston wins NL record fourth World Series.
- Jim Maloney of Reds pitches no-hitter for ten innings over Mets on June 14, but loses in 14 innings.

- Pittsburgh's Bob Veale tops majors with 250 Ks.
- Maloney has to go ten hitless innings to win no-hitter, 1-0 over Chicago on August 19.
- NL wins All-Star Game 6-5 in Minnesota, and for first time takes lead in All-Star victories.

Yaz Paces Sox Attack

In 1965, Carl Yastrzemski led a Red Sox team that paced the American League in home runs and slugging average and was second only to the Twins in batting. He hit .312 with 45 doubles (tied for the league-lead), 20 home runs, and 72 RBI. Boston nevertheless narrowly escaped finishing in the AL cellar when its hurlers were tagged for a circuit-high 791 runs.

Carl Yastrzemski

Mays Tallies Giant Stats

Willie Mays racked up 52 home runs and a mammoth .645 slugging average in 1965, keeping the Giants in the National League race until the final weekend of the season. Between them, Mays and Willie McCovey tallied 91 round-trippers, 13 more than the first-place Dodgers.

Willie Mays

The Mick Is Honored

Robert Kennedy was just one of the luminaries to take part in Mickey Mantle Day at Yankee Stadium in 1965. The Yankees' tumble to sixth place that year was caused in small part by an off year for some stars (including Mantle, who posted a .255 average, 19 home runs, and 46 RBI) and in large part by the club's failure to keep pace with other teams in developing talented young black players.

Mickey Mantle

1965

- At 65, Satchel Paige is oldest to play in an ML game when he hurls three scoreless innings for KC vs. Boston on Sept. 25.
- Koufax pitches a perfect game and his major league record fourth no-hitter in four years, beating Chicago 1-0 on Sept. 9.
- First indoor stadium, the Astrodome, opens on April 9—Houston vs. Yankees in an exhibition game.
- Mets lose 112 games for four-year ML record of 452 losses.
- Bert Campaneris plays all nine positions for A's on Sept. 8.
- Spike Eckert replaces Ford Frick as baseball's commissioner.
- Jerry Kindall leaves majors with .213 career BA, lowest in 20th century by infielder or outfielder.
- Ted Abernathy's 31 saves for Cubs set new ML record.

Don Drysdale

Campy Shines for A's

Bert Campaneris was virtually the lone bright spot for the last-place A's in 1965. In topping the American League in steals with 51 and tying for the lead in triples with 12 that year, he became the only player in the club's history to pace the loop in more than one major offensive department.

Bert Campaneris

Drysdale, Koufax Win 49

Don Drysdale (pictured) and Sandy Koufax won 49 games between them for the 1965 Dodgers—the most victories by any mound duo since the beginning of the expansion era in 1961. The American League postexpansion record is 48 triumphs, held by Denny McLain and Mickey Lolich of the 1968 Tigers and Mike Cuellar and Dave McNally of the 1970 Orioles.

Workhorse Mel Leads Yanks

Mel Stottlemyre is the only pitcher since 1920 to win 20 or more games three times for the Yankees without notching 20 victories on a pennant-winning team. After copping the American League flag in 1964, Stottlemyre's rookie season, the New York ballclub went a dozen years before claiming another. The hurler's rotator cuff had given out by then.

Mel Stottlemyre

- Dave Morehead of Boston no-hits Cleveland on September 16.

- Oliva again leads AL in batting (.321), and also leads in hits (185) and runs produced (189).

- Carl Yastrzemski tops AL in OBP (.398) and SA (.536), and ties for lead in doubles (45).

- Boston's Tony Conigliaro leads AL with 32 homers, and at 20 is youngest ever to win a league homer crown.

- Versalles tops American League in runs (126) and total bases (308), and ties for lead in doubles (45) and triples (12).

- Cleveland's Sam McDowell leads AL in ERA (2.18) and sets new AL southpaw record for Ks (325).

- Mays hits NL record 17 homers in a month en route to setting Giants club record with 52 homers.

- Abernathy appears in new ML record 84 games as a pitcher.

Champion Twins Soft at Second

A shot of the 1965 American League Champion Minnesota Twins. Rookie Frank Quilici (*back row, second from the left*), a .208 hitter during the regular season and later a Twins manager, played every inning of the 1965 World Series at second base. He replaced Jerry Kindall (*middle row, far left*), a .196 hitter that season who retired to become a high school teacher.

Minnesota Twins

Soph Oliva Nabs Second BA Crown

Tony Oliva is the only player in major league history to win a batting title in each of his first two seasons, hitting .323 in 1964 and .321 in '65. Although some sources credit Paul Waner with the same feat, most still give the National League hitting title in 1926, Waner's rookie year, to Bubbles Hargrave.

Zoilo Versalles

Tony Oliva

Versalles Cops MVP in AL

The lone shortstop between 1950 and 1982 to win the MVP Award in the American League, Zoilo Versalles was just 25 years of age in 1965. He spearheaded the loop in runs scored (126) and tied for the lead in doubles (45) and triples (12) that year. When he hit .249 the following season and again topped the circuit in errors, it was attributed to an off year. As it turned out, 1966 was his last decent season.

1965

- Yankees finish in second division for first time since 1925.

- Emmett Ashford, first black ump in ML history, debuts in AL.

- Leo Durocher hired to manage the Cubs, ending Wrigley's college of coaches scheme and four years of chaos.

- The Hall of Fame inducts Pud Galvin.

- Jim Lefebvre of LA is NL Rookie of the Year.

- Curt Blefary of Baltimore named AL Rookie of the Year, as he hits 22 home runs.

- Bob Gibson wins first of nine consecutive Gold Gloves given to NL pitchers.

- Detroit catcher Bill Freehan wins first of five consecutive Gold Gloves.

- Bobby Richardson wins last of five straight Gold Gloves given to AL second basemen.

Wills Off and Running

Maury Wills (shown here stealing his 72nd base in 1962) committed 94 thefts in 1965, the second-most number of swipes in modern National League history at the time. He was caught a career-high 31 times that season.

Willie Horton

Horton Nets 104 RBI

Had Willie Horton not narrowly missed qualifying as a rookie in 1965, he would have been the hands-down winner of the American League frosh award. His 104 RBI ranked second and his 29 home runs placed third in the loop. In his 18-year career, Horton never led the junior loop in a single major offensive department.

Maury Wills

Tony Conigliaro

Phenom Tony Clubs 32 HRs

In 1964, Tony Conigliaro set three major league batting records for teenage players and, in addition, five American League marks. When he became the youngest home run leader in history in 1965 with 32 dingers, he seemed destined to be one of the supreme sluggers of all time. Conigliaro instead joined Pete Reiser and Herb Score, two other potential greats who were cut down young by devastating injuries.

- Yankee Joe Pepitone wins first of three career Gold Gloves at first base.
- Branch Rickey dies.
- Bill McKechnie dies.
- The Cards send Ken Boyer to Mets for Al Jackson and Charley Smith.
- The Giants deal Randy Hundley and Bill Hands to Cubs for Lindy McDaniel, Don Landrum, and Jim Rittwage.
- The Cards swap Dick Groat, Bill White, and Bob Uecker to Phils for Alex Johnson, Art Mahaffey, and Pat Corrales.
- Indians send Tommie Agee, John Romano, and Tommy John to White Sox; Tribe gets Rocky Colavito and Cam Carreon in three-way deal with Kansas City.
- Versalles sets a major league record for shortstops when he strikes out 122 times.

Paige Offers His Advice

Satchel Paige (ball in hand) imparts some of his pitching savvy to four members of the A's mound staff late in the 1965 season. The oldest man ever to pitch in a major league game, Paige held the Red Sox to one hit and no runs in a three-inning relief stint on September 25, 1965.

Satchel Paige

Kaat Dips to 18-11 Mark

The Twins won the American League pennant easily in 1965, even though Jim Kaat (pictured) and Camilo Pascual, its two best pitchers the previous year, won fewer games between them in '65. Kaat posted an 18-11 record with a 2.83 ERA; Pascual went 9-3 with a 3.35 ERA. Several other regulars had mediocre years.

Houston Astrodome

Jim Kaat

Astrodome Opens

A mole's-eye view of a grounds keeper rolling the infield prior to the official opening of the Houston Astrodome. The first stadium to feature artificial surface and sky cost $31.6 million to build. The coliseum was inaugurated on April 9, 1965, in an exhibition game between the Astros and the Yankees.

1965

- Versalles ties AL record by leading loop in triples for third consecutive year, as he ties for lead with 12.

- The Braves have an NL record six players with 20 or more homers.

- J.C. Martin sets 20th-century record for catchers with 33 passed balls for White Sox.

- Average ML salary in 1965 is around $17,000.

- Dodgers feature first all-switch-hitting infield in ML history: Wes Parker, Lefebvre, Maury Wills, and Jim Gilliam.

- Yankees legend Yogi Berra plays four games for the Mets.

- Washington's Eddie Brinkman hits .185, tying Johnny Gochnauer's AL record for lowest BA by shortstop with a minimum of 400 at-bats.

- Gus Triandos retires with an ML record 1,206 consecutive games without being caught stealing—though he stole only one base.

World Series

Wills Scores in Dodger Blowout

Maury Wills scores for the Dodgers in game five of the 1965 World Series. The contest, a 7-0 Los Angeles victory, marked the third straight one-sided Dodger triumph in the Coliseum. Back at Metropolitan Stadium two days later, Los Angeles lost 5-1 to the Twins.

World Series

Koufax Stymies Twins

Sandy Koufax (center) held the Twins to three hits in the seventh game of the 1965 World Series to bring the Dodgers the World Title. Koufax struck out ten hitters in his second Series shutout. No. 24 is Los Angeles manager Walter Alston.

World Series

Kaat Puts Twins Up 2-0

Jim Kaat starts off the field after beating the Dodgers 5-1 in the second game of the 1965 World Series. Catcher Earl Battey gives him a pat while first baseman Don Mincher seizes his hand. Kaat's win gave the Twins a seemingly commanding 2-0 lead in the fall classic.

- Joe Morgan of Houston goes 6-for-6 on July 8.

- After the season, the Reds deal Frank Robinson to Baltimore for Milt Pappas and two other players.

- On Sept. 3, the Dodgers use four pitchers to shut out the Astros the day after they used three pitchers to shut them out.

- Campaneris ends Luis Aparicio's reign as AL theft king, as he swipes 51.

- Cleveland's Colavito tops AL in RBI (108) and walks (93).

- Grant leads AL in wins (21), shutouts (six), and win pct. (.750).

- Mel Stottlemyre tops AL in innings (291) and CGs (18).

- Ron Kline of Washington tops the AL with 29 saves.

- Roberto Clemente repeats as NL batting leader (.329).

- Pete Rose tops majors with 209 hits.

- Cincinnati's Tommy Harper leads NL in runs (126).

For the second straight year, the Los Angeles Dodgers won the National League behind the Cy Young form of Sandy Koufax, who led the league with 27 wins, a 1.73 ERA, and 317 strikeouts. The Baltimore Orioles—especially Frank Robinson, the Triple Crown winner and the American League's Most Valuable Player—however, had a few surprises for the Dodgers in the fall classic.

Baltimore depended on a deep but average pitching corps, the sterling infield defense of Brooks Robinson and Luis Aparicio, and a decidedly huge "Big Three" in the middle of their lineup: the two Robinsons—Frank, the ex-Red (.316 average, 49 home runs, 122 RBI, all league-bests), and Brooks (.269 average, 23 home runs, 100 RBI)—and Boog Powell (.287 average, 34 home runs, 109 RBI).

Minnesota finished in second place behind the hitting of Harmon Killebrew (.281 average, 39 home runs, 110 RBI) and Tony Oliva (.307 average, 25 home runs, 87 RBI) and the pitching of Jim Kaat, who had a 2.74 ERA and led the league with 25 wins.

Willie Horton hit 100 RBI (tied for fourth-best in the league), Al Kaline averaged .288 (third-best), and Denny McLain won 20 games (second-best), yet Detroit couldn't do any better than third.

Tommie Agee of the fourth-place White Sox was the American League's top rookie with a .273 average, 22 home runs, and

THREE O'S FIRE BLANKS TO SNUFF OUT DODGERS

86 RBI. Chicago also had three of the top five ERA leaders in Gary Peters (first with 1.98), Joe Horlen (second with 2.43), and Tommy John (fifth with 2.62), yet finished fourth, 15 games behind the Orioles.

While the Orioles coasted to the title, however, the Dodgers had to outlast San Francisco and Pittsburgh. The Giants had Willie Mays (.288 average, 37 home runs, 103 RBI) and Willie McCovey (.295 average, 36 home runs, 96 RBI) and a fine pitching staff anchored by Juan Marichal (25-6, 2.23 ERA) and Gaylord Perry (21-8, 2.99 ERA).

Although Roberto Clemente of Pittsburgh was the National League's Most Valuable Player with a .317 average, 29 home runs, and 119 RBI, he didn't top any offensive categories. Teammate Matty Alou won the batting title with a .342 average. Willie Stargell (.315 average, 33 home runs, 102 RBI) and Donn Clendenon (.299 average, 28 home runs, 98 RBI) were also reliable Pirates.

Hank Aaron, in the Braves' first season in Atlanta, blasted 44 homers and knocked in 127 runs to lead the league. Aaron's teammate (and Matty's brother) Felipe Alou was second in batting at .327. Tommy Helms of Cincinnati (.284 average, 49 RBI) was Rookie of the Year.

The biggest worry for the Dodgers down the stretch, though, was St. Louis rookie Larry Jaster, a 22-year-old who shut them out five consecutive times during the season. Koufax saved the day for Los Angeles when he returned on two days' rest to beat Philadelphia 6-3 in the season finale. San Francisco fell just $1^1/_2$ games short; Pittsburgh, 3.

The World Series was concluded briskly. The Dodgers knocked out an uncharacteristically wild Dave McNally in the third inning of game one, when they scored once to cut Baltimore's lead to 4-2. Moe Drabowsky shut them down the rest of the way, striking out 11, as the O's won it 5-2. The Dodgers didn't score again in the Series, as first Jim Palmer then Wally Bunker and McNally shut them out 6-0, 1-0, and 1-0 for the upset sweep.

Two homers, courtesy of Paul Blair and Frank Robinson, accounted for the only runs in games three and four. Robinson's round-tripper in the fourth inning of game four capped an amazing turnaround for the right fielder and won the Series for Baltimore.

1966

- Dodgers repeat as NL champs.
- Orioles take first flag since move to Baltimore.
- Orioles sweep World Series.
- Dodgers are blanked for Series record 33 consecutive innings after scoring two runs in game one.

- Jim Palmer, Wally Bunker, and Dave McNally shut out the Dodgers in succession in Series.
- In Series, Paul Blair and Frank Robinson win back-to-back 1-0 games for Orioles with home runs.
- The Dodgers bat .142 in the Series.

- At age 20, Palmer becomes the youngest pitcher in history to hurl a World Series shutout, as he wins 6-0 in game two.
- Robinson earns the American League MVP Award after winning the Triple Crown (.316 BA, 49 homers, 122 RBI).

Baltimore manager Hank Bauer *(left)* hugs pitcher Dave McNally after McNally bested the Dodgers 1-0 in the fourth game. The win gave the Orioles a sweep of the 1966 World Series and the franchise's first championship since its inception in 1902. When the O's failed to repeat, Bauer was replaced by Earl Weaver midway through the 1968 season.

1966

- Robinson leads the AL in runs (122), total bases (367), runs produced (195), OBP (.415), and slugging (.637).

- Roberto Clemente cops the NL MVP Award.

- Arthritic elbow forces Sandy Koufax to retire after season.

- In his final season, Koufax tops majors with 27 wins, 27 CGs, 317 Ks, 323 innings, and 1.73 ERA.

- Yankees tumble into cellar for first time since 1912.

- Prior to season, Koufax and Don Drysdale stage first dual holdout by teammates in ML history.

- Marvin Miller elected president of Major League Players Association.

- The Yankees fire broadcaster Red Barber after he calls attention on television to a sparse crowd in Yankee Stadium.

- Pitcher Tony Cloninger of Braves hits two grandslams in game on July 3.

Brooks, Clete Best at Third

Brooks Robinson (*left*) and Clete Boyer were the best defensive third basemen in the American League during the decade of the '60s. Robinson hit .269 in 1966, with 23 home runs and 100 RBI. Boyer, the younger brother of Cardinals star Ken, was hampered by a weak bat. He hit above .251 just once in his 16 seasons in the majors. In '66, he batted .240 with 14 homers.

Brooks Robinson, Clete Boyer

Sandy Koufax

Koufax Wins 27, Bows Out

Forced to retire following the 1966 World Series because of a bum elbow, Sandy Koufax set or tied five records by pitchers in their final seasons. Among them were most wins (27), Ks (317), and innings (323).

1966

- Braves move to Atlanta; first game in Dixie on April 12 at Fulton County Stadium, Pirates vs. Braves.

- Willie Mays plays 150 or more games for ML record 13th consecutive year.

- Pittsburgh's Matty Alou leads NL in BA (.342); brother Felipe Alou of Atlanta is second (.327).

- Tony Oliva tops AL in hits in each of his first three seasons in majors, as he collects 191 in '66.

- Cards rookie Larry Jaster ties for NL lead in shutouts with five, and all five are achieved vs. Dodgers.

- Koufax wins third unanimous Cy Young Award in last four years.

- Koufax tops NL in ERA a record fifth consecutive time, and he wins the '66 title by 49 points.

- Sonny Siebert of Cleveland no-hits Washington on June 10.

- First game in Anaheim Stadium— White Sox vs. Angels on April 19.

1966

Don Drysdale

Drysdale Wins When It Counts

Don Drysdale collected a 13-16 record for the Dodgers in 1966, one of the poorest seasons ever by a pitcher on a pennant-winning club. He was nevertheless named by manager Walter Alston to start the first game of the World Series. Knocked out early by the Orioles, Drysdale returned to pitch brilliantly in the final contest, allowing four hits and one run.

Willie McCovey

McCovey Cracks 36 Homers

Willie McCovey (pictured), Willie Mays, Jim Ray Hart, and catcher Tom Haller hit a total of 133 home runs for the Giants in 1966 (McCovey tallied 36 home runs and 96 RBI for a .295 average that season). The rest of the club accounted for just 48 round-trippers, however, and the team as a whole hit .248, the next-to-lowest average in the National League.

- First game in Busch Stadium—Braves vs. Cards on May 16.
- Jack Aker's 32 saves for KC set new ML record.
- California pitcher Dean Chance fans 54 times in 76 at-bats for Angels.
- NL wins All-Star Game 2-1 at St. Louis.

- Felipe Alou leads NL in runs (122) and total bases (355), and majors in hits (218).
- Hank Aaron paces NL in homers (44), and majors in RBI (127) and runs produced (200).
- Juan Marichal wins 25 for SF, tops majors in win pct. (.806).

- AL has only two hitters above .288—Robinson (.317) and Oliva (.307).
- Jim Kaat leads AL with 25 wins, 305 innings, and 19 CGs.
- Pirates Gene Alley and Bill Mazeroski participate in an ML keystone record 289 combined DPs.

THE BASEBALL CHRONICLE

Boog Powell

Powell: 34 HRs, 109 RBI

In 1966, Boog Powell placed third in the American League in home runs with 34 and RBI with 109. He also fanned 125 times, a career-high. Powell was one of the few sluggers during the 1960s and 1970s who walked nearly as often as he struck out.

Aaron's HRs Keep Braves Afloat

Thanks to Hank Aaron, the Braves continued their skein of consecutive first-division finishes in 1966, their initial year in Atlanta. Aaron tallied 44 home runs (best in the National League) and 127 RBI (best in the majors) that year. The streak was in jeopardy in late August, however, before manager Bobby Bragan was replaced by Billy Hitchcock.

Hank Aaron

- Alley and Maz both win Gold Gloves for first of two consecutive years.

- Mets finish a heady ninth as the Leo Durocher-led Cubs fall into NL basement.

- The Hall of Fame inducts Ted Williams and Casey Stengel.

- Cincinnati's Tommy Helms is NL Rookie of the Year.

- Chicago's Tommie Agee named AL ROTY.

- Phillie Bill White wins the last of seven consecutive Gold Gloves as NL first baseman.

- Angel Bobby Knoop wins first of three consecutive Gold Gloves as AL second baseman.

- The Phils trade Fergie Jenkins and two other players to the Cubs for Larry Jackson and Bob Buhl.

- Giants trade Orlando Cepeda to the Cards for Ray Sadecki.

John Finds Home in Chicago

Tommy John was part of the price the Indians had to pay in order to reobtain slugger Rocky Colavito following the 1964 season. With Cleveland, John was 2-11 and looked to be another in a long line of promising young Tribe hurlers who ultimately flopped. With the White Sox in 1966, he was 14-11 and tied for the American League-lead in shutouts with five. Some 20 years later, he had 286 career wins.

Tommy John

Roberto Clemente

Clemente Nearly Perfect

Roger Angell wrote that Roberto Clemente performed "at close to the level of absolute perfection, playing to win but also playing the game almost as if it were a form of punishment for everyone else on the field." Clemente sparked the Pirates to a near pennant in 1966, hitting .317 with 29 home runs and 119 RBI.

- Yanks trade Clete Boyer to Atlanta for Bill Robinson and Chi-Chi Olivo.
- Dodgers trade Tommy Davis to the Mets for Ron Hunt and Jim Hickman.
- Knoop sets record for AL second basemen with 144 Ks.

- On May 1, Knoop participates in a single-game record six DPs by a second baseman.
- Maz performs an ML record 166 DPs by a second baseman.
- Donn Clendenon sets NL record for first basemen by participating in 182 double plays.

- Luis Aparicio leads AL shortstops in FA a record eighth straight year.
- On August 12, Art Shamsky of the Reds enters the game as a pinch hitter and hits three homers.
- St. Louis' Tim McCarver becomes the only NL catcher ever to top loop in triples (13).

Koufax Bids Farewell

A tearful Sandy Koufax announces his retirement from baseball on November 18, 1966, in Beverly Hills, California. In his last major league appearance—game two of the 1966 World Series—the Dodgers were blanked 6-0 and made six errors, three of them in one inning by center fielder Willie Davis. Koufax posted a 1.50 ERA for the game.

Paul Blair

Sandy Koufax

Blair Blossoms

Paul Blair was one of three standout rookie outfielders the Orioles came up with in the mid-1960s. But unlike Sam Bowens and Curt Blefary, who arrived in 1964 and 1965, Blair did not regress after his rookie campaign in '64. In 1966, he batted .277, scored 35 runs, and nailed a dinger to win game three of the fall classic.

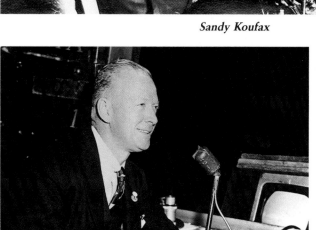

Red Barber

Barber Axed for Telling the Truth

For years the voice of the Brooklyn Dodgers, Red Barber joined the Yankees' broadcasting team after the Dodgers moved to Los Angeles. However, when he told it like it was as a television camera panned the empty seats in Yankee Stadium late in the 1966 season, he was swiftly axed.

1966

- Yanks fire Johnny Keane after a 4-16 start, bring Ralph Houk out of front office to replace him.

- Yanks finish last to ruin Houk's perfect record of three flags in three years as a manager.

- Yankee workhorse Mel Stottlemyre goes 12-20.

- On August 26, Orioles Vic Roznovsky and Boog Powell hit the first back-to-back pinch homers in AL history.

- Frank Delahanty, last surviving member of the five baseball-playing Delahanty brothers, dies at 83 years of age.

- Cub Ron Santo's NL record streak of 364 consecutive games played at third base comes to an end.

- Santo tops NL in walks (95) and OBP (.417).

- Phillie Johnny Callison tops majors with 40 doubles.

Bunker Blanks LA

Wally Bunker unleashes the first pitch of game three of the 1966 World Series to Dodgers leadoff hitter Maury Wills. Andy Etchebarren is the Baltimore catcher and Chris Pelekoudas is the plate umpire. Bunker, who logged just three complete games and no shutouts during the regular season, checkmated the Dodgers 1-0 that day.

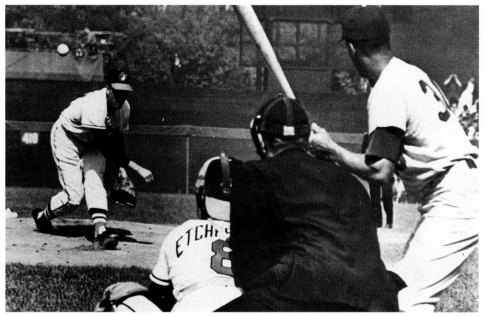

World Series

Jim Kaat

Kaat Sets Twins Mark

Jim Kaat was an atypical southpaw—he had excellent control—in addition to being an extraordinary fielder and a decent hitter. He topped American League hurlers in several departments in 1966, including complete games (19) and fewest walks per game (1.62). His circuit-high 25 victories that season are still a record for the Twins.

Fleet Robby Scores 122 Times

Frank Robinson was nearly as fine a baserunner as he was a hitter. He ranks tenth on the all-time list in runs, topping the National League in tallies twice before coming to the Orioles in 1966. When Robinson crossed the plate 122 times in his first year with the Birds, he set a new club record that still stands. He also topped the American League that season in slugging average (.637), on-base percentage (.415), and total bases (367).

Frank Robinson

- Phillie Richie Allen tops NL in SA (.632), is second in homers (40).
- St. Louis' Lou Brock replaces Maury Wills as NL steals king (74).
- Bert Campaneris replaces Aparicio as AL theft leader (52).
- Dodger Phil Regan leads NL in saves with 21.

- Carl Yastrzemski tops AL in doubles with 39.
- Knoop leads AL in triples (11), tops AL second basemen in every major fielding department.
- Harmon Killebrew tops majors with 103 walks and is second in homers (39) and RBI (110).

- Siebert (16-8) is the only AL pitcher to win as many as two-thirds of his decisions.
- Chicago's Gary Peters wins AL ERA crown again (1.98).
- Detroit's Denny McLain is second in AL with 20 wins and 14 CGs.

GIBSON RETURNS TO KNOCK OFF YAZ'S SOX

More than anyone, Carl Yastrzemski made the Red Sox' Impossible Dream a reality in 1967. Ninth-place finishers a year earlier, the Sox owed much of their success in '67 to a midseason transformation that brought them pitcher Gary Bell, infielder Jerry Adair, catcher Elston Howard, and outfielder Ken Harrelson. It was, however, Yaz who defined the team. His .326 season with 44 home runs and 121 RBI all led the American League, and he took both the Triple Crown and the Most Valuable Player Award.

But even though Yaz & Co. pushed the World Series to the full seven games, they couldn't beat the Cardinals' ace, Bob Gibson, in the year's biggest game.

Gibson had to overcome adversity to even get to the Series that year, as he missed the second half of the season after having his leg broken by a Roberto Clemente line drive. In his absence, San Francisco journeyman Mike McCormick (22-10, 2.85 ERA) won the National League's Cy Young Award.

St. Louis had an award-winner in MVP Orlando Cepeda (.325 average, 25 homers, a league-high 111 RBI). Pittsburgh's Clemente led in batting with a .357 average. Legend Hank Aaron topped the league with 39 homers. Phil Niekro of Atlanta led the circuit with his 1.87 ERA. Houston's Don Wilson pitched a no-hit game against Atlanta on June 18. The league's top rookie was Tom Seaver of the Mets (16-13, 2.76 ERA).

With the collapse of the defending champion Orioles, four teams in the American League slugged it out in the closest pennant race in history. Boston's Jim Lonborg won the Cy Young Award with a 22-9 record and a 3.16 ERA. The Twins had Harmon Killebrew (.269 average, a league-leading 44 home runs, 113 RBI), Dean Chance (20-14, 2.73 ERA, and a no-hitter in August), and Rookie of the Year Rod Carew (.292 average, eight homers, 51 RBI).

The balanced Tigers were spearheaded by future Hall of Famer Al Kaline (.308 average, 25 home runs, 78 RBI) and Earl Wilson (tied for the circuit-lead in wins with Lonborg at 22).

ERA champ Joe Horlen (19-7, 2.06 ERA) led the White Sox to a league-low 2.45 team mark. Meanwhile, Mickey Mantle of New York hit his 500th homer on May 14.

Down the stretch went the four teams. On September 7, there was a four-way tie for first. The White Sox then fell from the race while the Red Sox, who had lost star right fielder Tony Conigliaro to a near-fatal beaning in August, could have been eliminated by losing either of its two games to the Twins. Yastrzemski went 7-for-8 in those two contests, executing a game-winning homer and a game-saving throw, and the Red Sox won them both. Yaz clinched the MVP Award by going 23-for-46 with five home runs and 16 RBI down the stretch. Detroit could still have tied it by sweeping California during a final-day doubleheader. The Tigers won the first game but lost the second, 8-5. The Red Sox won the pennant by 1 game over Detroit and Minnesota.

The Series unexpectedly went the full seven, though the Cards, winners of 101 games during the season, clearly were superior. In the end, Gibson was the difference, winning three complete games 2-1, 6-0, and 7-2 while striking out 26 and walking only five. Lonborg won his first two games 5-0 and 3-1, but could not beat Gibson in the 7-2 seventh game.

Lou Brock (.414 average) and Roger Maris (.385 average, seven RBI) were the hitting stars for St. Louis; Brock stole a Series-record seven bases and scored eight runs. Yastrzemski, not surprisingly, led the Red Sox with a .400 average, three home runs, and five RBI.

1967

- Cards breeze to NL pennant.
- Red Sox win AL flag on last day in four-team race.
- Cards win World Series in seven games.
- Bob Gibson wins three Series games for the Cards despite missing a third of the season with a broken leg.

- Jim Lonborg wins two games for Red Sox in Series, is beaten in game seven when he pitches on three-days rest.
- Cardinal Lou Brock hits .414, steals Series record seven bases, and scores eight runs.
- Carl Yastrzemski hits .400 for Red Sox, cracks three homers.

- Yaz is near-unanimous AL MVP after winning Triple Crown (.326 BA, 44 homers, 121 RBI).
- Yaz leads AL in runs (112), hits (189), total bases (360), runs produced (189), OBP (.421), and SA (.622).
- St. Louis' Orlando Cepeda wins the NL MVP Award.

Lou Brock *(left)*, Julian Javier *(center)*, and Bob Gibson voice their joy following the triumph of the Cardinals in the final game of the 1967 World Series. Javier's three-run homer in the sixth inning gave St. Louis an insurmountable 7-1 lead in the finale. Gibson had nailed a round-tripper an inning earlier.

- Tom Seaver wins a club record 16 games for the Mets.

- Seaver named NL Rookie of the Year.

- Boston's Tony Conigliaro is beaned by Angel Jack Hamilton; his vision is impaired and he's out of the game until 1969.

- Twins lead American League by 1 game with two to play, but they lose their last two games to Boston in Fenway.

- Tigers also finish 1 game out, as they split two doubleheaders with the Angels on the last two days of the season.

- The Red Sox jump from ninth place in 1966 to first in '67—the first team to do so in this century.

- Two Cy Young Awards given for the first time.

- Lonborg is easy Cy Young winner in the AL.

Yaz Leads Across the Board

Although Carl Yastrzemski led the American League in almost every major offensive department in 1967—.326 batting average, .622 slugging average, 112 runs scored, 189 hits, 44 home runs (tied for first), 360 total bases, 121 RBI, .421 on-base percentage—he was not a unanimous MVP selection. One New York writer voted for Cesar Tovar of the Twins. Some observers felt the reason for the renegade choice was that the Red Sox took the flag while the Yankees finished ninth.

Hank Aaron

Carl Yastrzemski

Aaron Zeroes In on 500 HRs

In the mid-1960s, Hank Aaron said that he hoped to hit around 500 home runs in his career. He had nailed 481 dingers at the end of the 1967 season, his fourth and last as the National League-leader in home runs. Aaron cleared the 500-mark the following year, hitting 29 dingers.

1967

- SF's Mike McCormick wins NL Cy Young and leads loop with 22 wins.

- NL wins longest game in All-Star history, 2-1 in 15 innings at Anaheim, as Red Tony Perez homers to win it.

- Al Kaline wins last of ten GGs as AL outfielder.

- Mickey Mantle hits his 500th homer on May 13.

- Mets trade Bill Denehy and $100,000 to Washington in order to obtain Gil Hodges as their manager.

- Don Wilson of Houston no-hits Atlanta on June 18.

- Dean Chance of Minnesota no-hits Cleveland on August 25.

- Joe Horlen of Chicago no-hits Detroit on Sept. 10.

- On April 30, Orioles Steve Barber and Stu Miller lose combined no-hitter to Detroit 2-1 in nine innings.

Brock: Best in Runs, Steals

Lou Brock not only topped the National League in thefts in 1967 with 52, he also tied for first in runs scored with 113 and was second in total bases with 325 and hits with 206. Defense was another story: For the fourth year in a row, Brock led NL outfielders in errors.

Lou Brock

Dick Williams

Williams Wins AL Pennant

Dick Williams of the Red Sox joined a select fraternity in 1967 when he won a pennant in his first season managing. Three years earlier, in his last season as a player, Williams hit .159 for the Crimson Hose. He then managed the minor league affiliate for the Sox in Toronto for two campaigns before assuming the Boston helm.

Orlando Cepeda

Cepeda Wins Unanimous MVP Vote

Reaping the rewards that came with playing on a pennant-winning team, Orlando Cepeda was a unanimous choice for the National League MVP Award in 1967. He hit .325 that year, tallying 25 home runs and a league-high 111 RBI. Six years earlier, he posted a better season (.311 with 46 home runs and 142 RBI) yet finished second in the voting because his team at the time (the Giants) was an also-ran.

- Whitey Ford retires with .690 career win pct., best in history among 200-game winners, as he compiles a 236-106 record.

- Ford retires with a 2.74 career ERA, lowest of any pitcher active exclusively since the end of the dead-ball era.

- While on leave during military service, Cubs pitcher Ken Holtzman posts a 9-0 record.

- Cleveland pitchers fan AL record 1,189 hitters.

- Eddie Mathews hits his 500th homer on July 14.

- Television revenue is now up to $25 million.

- Roberto Clemente leads ML with 209 hits and 190 runs produced.

- Hank Aaron leads NL in home runs (39), slugging (.573), and total bases (344).

Jim Lonborg

Lonborg Leads Loop in Wins, Ks

A skiing accident deprived Jim Lonborg of the greatness that might have been his. He was the top pitcher in the American League in 1967 at age 24, tying for most wins in the circuit with 22 and topping the loop with 246 strikeouts. He did not again hurl more than 200 innings in a season until five years later. In 1978, his final full season, Lonborg logged 22 starts yet just 114 innings.

Ron Santo

Santo's 96 Walks Lead NL

Although Ron Santo led the National League in bases on balls four times during the 1960s, he never walked more than 100 times in a season. Between 1964 and 1968, no NL player broke the 100-walk barrier. In 1964, Santo topped the senior circuit with just 86 walks, the fewest since 1933 by a leader in either league. In 1967, he posted a loop-high 96 walks, 35 fewer than the AL-high.

John: 2.47 ERA, Ten Wins

Although Tommy John placed fourth in the American League in 1967 with a 2.47 ERA, he had only a 10-13 record. His team, the White Sox, batted .225 and scored just 531 runs that year, making life miserable for all the club's hurlers. No regular on the Pale Hose hit above .241 that season.

Tommy John

1967

- White Sox pitchers Horlen, Gary Peters, and Tommy John finish one-two-four in ERA in AL, Horlen leading at 2.06.

- Yankees finish ninth in 1967 and are last in the AL in runs (522).

- AL BA is down to .236, as Red Sox are only team to hit above .243.

- Charley Finley is called a "menace to baseball" by KC's Hawk Harrelson; Finley then lets Harrelson leave as a free agent.

- White Sox finish only 3 games out with a club that has a .225 team average and no regulars who hit above .241.

- Ninth-place Astros are the only team in ML with a staff ERA above 4.00.

- Owners create Player Relations Committee to cope with burgeoning Players Association.

- The Hall of Fame inducts Red Ruffing, Branch Rickey, and Lloyd Waner.

1967

Harmon Killebrew

Mike McCormick

McCormick Nabs Cy Young Award

Signed for a large bonus by the Giants while they were still in New York, Mike McCormick made his major league debut in 1956 when he was just 17 years of age. Traded back to the Giants in 1967 by Washington, McCormick went 22-10 with five shutouts and a 2.85 ERA to unexpectedly snare the Cy Young Award.

Harmon Nails 44 Homers

Harmon Killebrew tied Carl Yastrzemski for the American League home run crown in 1967 with 44 and came in third in the circuit with a .413 on-base percentage (despite hitting just .269). Three years earlier, Killebrew had led the junior loop with 49 home runs yet collected only 61 extra-base hits (one triple and a mere 11 doubles).

Lew Burdette

Burdette Winds Up Career in Pen

Lew Burdette ended his career in 1967 as he began it 17 years earlier—in the bullpen. His 203rd and last victory came as a reliever with the Angels. Burdette, one of the few 200-game winners who gave up more than a hit an inning, seemed an unlikely stopper but was actually quite successful.

- Minnesota's Rod Carew is AL ROTY.

- Boston's George Scott wins first of AL record eight Gold Gloves by a first baseman.

- Bill Mazeroski wins last of NL record eight Gold Gloves by a second baseman.

- Mazeroski tops NL second basemen in DPs a record eighth consecutive year.

- Cardinal Curt Flood's record streak of 568 consecutive errorless chances in the outfield ends.

- Clemente tops NL outfielders in assists a record fifth consecutive year.

- Jimmie Foxx dies.

- Mets use NL record 54 players in a vain effort to escape the cellar.

- White Sox use a record four pinch runners in an inning on Sept. 16.

- Boston trades Tony Horton and Don Demeter to Cleveland for Gary Bell.

Brock Scores in Series

Lou Brock scores the Cardinals' first run in game six of the 1967 World Series. The Red Sox catcher is Elston Howard. Brock totaled eight runs scored in the event, batting .414 and stealing seven bases. Howard was behind the plate in all seven contests, despite hitting a meager .147 after joining Boston in August. He replaced Mike Ryan, who hit .199 during the regular season.

World Series

Tony Perez

Maz Nabs Every Ball in Sight

In his early teens, Bill Mazeroski was a shortstop. He never played a single inning at that position in the majors, however. Mazeroski's fielding prowess as a second baseman was such that batters despaired when they hit the ball anywhere near him. In 1967, he accepted 158 more chances than any other second sacker in the NL.

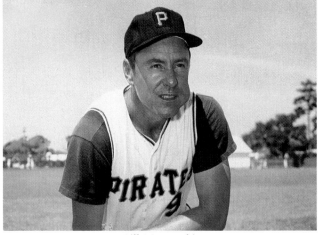

Bill Mazeroski

Perez Stars at Third

To free a spot for Tony Perez in 1967, the Reds moved Pete Rose to left field and switched Tommy Helms to second base, Rose's former position. The shift paid immediate dividends. Perez knocked home 102 runs to lead all third basemen and nailed 26 home runs to top the Reds that season.

1967

- Pittsburgh trades Don Money and three other players to the Phils for Jim Bunning.

- World Series winner's share is below $10,000 for the last time.

- Chance wins 20 games and tops AL in CGs (18) and innings (284).

- Lonborg leads AL in Ks (246).

- Jim Wynn sets Astros record with 37 homers.

- Mickey Lolich loses ten in a row, a Tigers record.

- Brock tops NL in runs (113) and steals (52).

- Cepeda paces NL in RBI (111).

- Rusty Staub of Houston tops ML with 44 doubles.

- Vada Pinson leads majors with 13 triples.

- Chicago's Ron Santo leads NL in walks with 96.

- Phillie Dick Allen has NL's top OBP (.404).

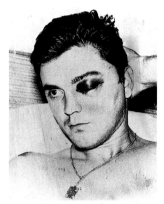

Tony Conigliaro

Tony Beaned

Tony Conigliaro had a .287 average and 20 home runs when he was struck by a pitch thrown by Jack Hamilton of the Angels in mid-August, 1967. His place was taken by Jose Tartabull, who averaged .223 and didn't hit a single homer all season.

Yaz Hits HR in Game Two

Carl Yastrzemski unloads his second home run in game two of the 1967 World Series. The Cardinal catcher is Tim McCarver. Yaz's clout came in the seventh inning and cemented the 5-0 win for Sox ace Jim Lonborg. Boston clubbed a total of eight home runs in the tournament, including a dinger by pitcher Jose Santiago in his first Series at-bat.

Bob Gibson

Injured Gibson Stars in Series

Shelved for much of the regular season due to a broken leg, Bob Gibson acquired just 13 wins in 1967. The previous year, he had been the first pitcher since the end of the dead-ball era to win 20 games two years in a row for a second-division team. Gibson more than made up for the '67 season in that fall's World Series, collecting a trio of triumphs, a 1.00 ERA, and 26 strikeouts in 27 innings pitched.

World Series

- Harmon Killebrew ties Yaz for homer crown (44), leads ML in walks (131).
- Tony Oliva tops AL in doubles (34).
- Oriole Paul Blair's 12 triples lead AL.
- Bert Campaneris repeats as steals champ in AL (55).

- Bunning, pitching for the Phils, leads ML with 302 innings and 253 Ks, and ties for ML lead with six shutouts.
- Atlanta's Phil Niekro tops NL in ERA (1.87).
- Rookie Dick Hughes of Cards leads NL in win pct. (.727).

- Ted Abernathy, now with the Reds, paces ML with 28 saves.
- Minnie Rojas of the Angels leads AL with 27 saves.
- Fergie Jenkins of the Cubs tops ML with 20 CGs.
- Horlen leads AL in win pct. (.731) and ERA (2.06).

Forever known as "The Year of the Pitcher," the long hot summer of 1968 had Carl Yastrzemski taking a batting title at .301—the lowest winning average ever—Boston teammate Ken Harrelson leading the American League with 109 RBI, and Frank Howard of Washington topping the circuit with 44 homers.

The numbers the pitchers put up were astounding: Luis Tiant of Cleveland led the American League with nine shutouts and a 1.60 ERA. Detroit's Denny McLain, the first pitcher since Dizzy Dean in 1934 to win 30 games, totaled a 31-6 record and a 1.96 ERA—numbers that seized the league's Cy Young and MVP Awards. Bob Gibson's 1.12 ERA set a post-1920 major league record in the National League; the righty threw 13 shutouts and managed, incredibly, to lose nine games. His 22 victories were enough for the Cy Young Award, the Most Valuable Player Award, and a trip to the World Series with the St. Louis Cardinals.

The Cards went 97-65 with only two players hitting as many as seven home runs (Orlando Cepeda had 16, Mike Shannon had 15). Willie McCovey of the second-place Giants led the National League with 36 homers and 105 RBI and teammate Juan Marichal led in wins with 26. Pete Rose of the Reds took the batting title with a .335 average and teammate Johnny Bench was named Rookie of the Year for his .275 average, 15 home runs, and 82 RBI. The Rookie of the Year

DENNY'S GOLDEN ARM CARRIES TIGERS TO TITLE

in the American League was Stan Bahnsen of the Yankees, who went 17-12 with a 2.06 ERA.

Five pitchers hurled no-hitters for the year (Catfish Hunter's being a perfect game). Two came in Candlestick Park on successive days, as Gaylord Perry of the Giants no-hit the Cardinals on September 17 to beat Gibson 1-0 and Ray Washburn of St. Louis returned the favor by blanking San Francisco 2-0 the following day. Don Drysdale of Los Angeles threw a record 58²/₃ consecutive scoreless innings. Even the All-Star Game was dominated by the pitchers. The National League won the contest 1-0, with the only run the result of a first-inning double play.

Both pennant races were decided early. Defending World Champion St. Louis came in 9 games ahead of the Giants in the National League and Detroit claimed the American League title

by finishing 12 games over the Orioles.

Each team was led by its respective leagues' most dominating pitchers, Gibson and McLain, but the two teams offered different styles of play. St. Louis, which led the league in only one offensive category (triples), was built on speed and defense (Lou Brock had a league-leading 62 stolen bases). Detroit, on the other hand, depended on the long ball. The Tigers led the league in runs (671), home runs (185), and slugging average (.385); Willie Horton (.285 average, 36 homers, 85 RBI), Bill Freehan (.263 average, 25 homers, 84 RBI), and Jim Northrup (.264 average, 21 homers, 90 RBI) supplied the sock.

That power—and the pitching of Mickey Lolich, McLain's understudy—carried the Tigers to a 4-3 upset of the Cardinals in the World Series.

After St. Louis went ahead 3-1 by beating McLain with lopsided scores of 4-0 and 10-1, Detroit stormed back with Lolich winning games five and seven (the Tigers won game six by a count of 13-1). Though Gibson set a Series record with 35 strikeouts, his 2-1 record and 1.67 ERA were bested by Lolich's 3-0, 1.67 Series-mark. Lolich's stats included his 4-1 win in the finale, the only head-to-head meeting with Gibson. Lolich defused the Cardinals on the bases, too, picking both Curt Flood and Brock off first in the sixth inning of a zero-all game-seven tie.

1968

- Tigers cruise to AL flag by 12-game margin.
- Cards repeat in NL, as Giants finish second for the fourth year in a row.
- Tigers take World Series in seven games after trailing in the Series three games to one.

- Mickey Lolich wins three Series games for Tigers and beats Bob Gibson in the closing contest.
- Gibson sets Series record in game one when he fans 17 Tigers.
- Lou Brock once again tops all Series batters with .464 BA and record-tying seven steals.

- Al Kaline hits .379 and produces a Series-top eight RBI.
- Detroit triumphs in game seven of Series by breaking up scoreless duel with three runs in the seventh inning.
- Detroit's Denny McLain, first 30-game winner in NL since 1934, cops boy AL MVP and Cy Young by racking up 31 wins.

The victorious Tigers and their followers storm into the field after capturing the 1968 World Series. As had happened in 1945, when Detroit last won a World Championship, the Tigers landed the deciding seventh-game victory on the road. When they copped their next title at home, in 1984, there was a near riot in the Motor City.

- Gibson posts a 1.12 ERA, lowest in the ML since 1914, and is named the NL MVP and Cy Young winner.

- Gibson has 13 shutouts, most in ML since 1916.

- The A's move to Oakland and top AL with .240 BA, lowest in ML history by a loop leader.

- Houston beats Mets 1-0 in 24 innings on April 15, the longest 1-0 game in ML history.

- Don Drysdale sets new ML record when he pitches 58 consecutive scoreless innings.

- Carl Yastrzemski wins AL bat crown with .301 BA, lowest in ML history to lead a league.

- Yankees set post-dead-ball record for lowest team batting average when they hit just .214.

- NL attendance is down to 11.7 million.

- NL wins first indoor All-Star Game 1-0 at Houston, as winning run scores on a double-play grounder.

Brock Steals Show Again

No player has ever been more awesome in back-to-back World Series affairs than Lou Brock. In the fall classics of 1967 and 1968, he made 25 hits in 14 games, stole 14 bases, scored 14 runs, and collected three home runs and eight RBI. For the two regular seasons, he hit a combined .289.

Wilbur Wood

Wood Hurls in Record 88 Games

Wilbur Wood made 241 mound appearances between 1968 and 1970, all but two of them in relief roles. In 1968, he set a record in the majors by pitching in 88 games. In 1971, the White Sox converted him to a starting pitcher and he made 224 starts between 1971 and '75, the highest number over a five-year span by any hurler in this century.

Lou Brock

Carl Yastrzemski

Yaz All Alone at .300

A late-season surge made Carl Yastrzemski (pictured playing pepper) the American League's lone .300 hitter in 1968. There weren't even any subs who topped the mark. Offensive production that year was so minuscule that Mickey Mantle, who hit just .237, had the third-highest on-base percentage in the junior circuit with a .387 mark.

1968

- Willie Mays is first to win two All-Star MVP Awards.

- Cincinnati rookie catcher Johnny Bench wins first of ten consecutive Gold Gloves.

- Mickey Stanley of Tigers is awarded AL Gold Glove as outfielder, but plays shortstop in World Series.

- Luis Tiant strikes out 19 batters for the Indians in a ten-inning game on July 3.

- Player Relations Committee and Players Association hammer out their first "Basic Agreement."

- Cesar Tovar plays all nine positions for Twins on Sept. 22.

- Giant Jim Davenport's record streak of 97 consecutive errorless games at third base ends.

- Hank Aaron hits his 500th homer on July 14.

- On July 29, Senator Ron Hansen performs the first unassisted triple play in ML since 1927.

Detroit Tigers

Tigers Boast Big Bats

A shot of the 1968 World Champion Detroit Tigers. Willie Horton *(front row, far right)* led the team in home runs with 36 and batting with a .285 average. Although Al Kaline *(third row, far left)* had a slightly higher average (.287), he didn't have enough at-bats to be considered a regular. Eddie Mathews *(beside Kaline)* joined the team just in time to play in the World Series.

Bench Catches 154 Games

Rookie of the Year Johnny Bench set a new rookie record in 1968 when he caught 154 games for the Reds. He never again worked so many contests, which contributed heavily to his longevity. Randy Hundley, who caught 160 games for the Cubs in '68 then 151 games in '69, was burned out by age 30.

Johnny Bench

Pete Rose

Rose Flashes Unusual Power

Pete Rose posted a .470 slugging average in 1968, the second-highest mark of his career. He collected just 49 RBI, however—the fewest of any NL outfielder with more than 500 at-bats. Also on the Reds that year was Alex Johnson, another high average hitter (.312) who produced notoriously few RBI (58).

- George Culver of Cincinnati no-hits Phils on July 29.

- Tom Phoebus of Baltimore no-hits Boston on April 27.

- Gaylord Perry of Giants no-hits the Cards on Sept. 17.

- On Sept. 18, Ray Washburn of Cards no-hits the Giants.

- On May 8, Catfish Hunter of A's pitches a perfect game vs. Twins, and collects three hits and four RBI in his own cause.

- Washington's Frank Howard tops majors with 44 homers, 330 total bases, and .552 SA.

- Willie McCovey leads NL in homers (36), RBI (105), and SA (.545).

- Juan Marichal tops NL in wins (26), CGs (30), and innings (326).

- Wilbur Wood of White Sox pitches in 88 games, a new ML record.

- Pete Rose wins his first bat crown (.335) and becomes first switch-hitter in NL history to lead the loop in hitting.

Don: 14 Wins, Eight Shutouts

Despite throwing six consecutive shutouts and eight all told in 1968, Don Drysdale won just 14 games for the Dodgers that year. The following season, when he was hit hard in his first 12 starts, he felt he had lost it and quit. He was barely 33 years old.

Juan Wins 26, But No Cy Young

The Dave Stewart of the 1960s, Juan Marichal won 20 or more games four years in a row and six times altogether, yet he never received a Cy Young Award. He even won 25 or more games on three occasions, with a high of 26 triumphs in 1968, when he also paced the National League in complete games (30) and innings (326).

Juan Marichal

Don Drysdale

Ernie Banks

Banks Regains Old Stroke

Ernie Banks clouted 32 home runs in 1968, the third-highest round-tripper total in the National League. It was the first time since 1962 that he finished among the loop's top five in slugging. Although Banks retired with a .500 career slugging average, he never topped the .469 mark in his last nine seasons.

1968

- Tigers win flag with a third baseman, Don Wert, who hits .200, and a shortstop, Ray Oyler, who hits .135 in 111 games.

- Four teams in the ML score fewer than 500 runs.

- The Hall of Fame inducts Joe Medwick, Kiki Cuyler, and Goose Goslin.

- Bench is NL Rookie of the Year in close vote over Jerry Koosman of the Mets.

- Yankee Stan Bahnsen is AL ROTY.

- Chicago's Glenn Beckert ends Bill Mazeroski's reign as NL Gold Glove champ at second base.

- Chicago's Ron Santo wins the last of his five consecutive Gold Gloves at third base.

- For the sixth straight year, Mays, Roberto Clemente, and Cardinal Curt Flood sweep Gold Gloves given to NL outfielders.

- Angel second baseman Bobby Knoop wins third Gold Glove.

Bob Gibson

Frank Howard

Gibson: 1.12 ERA, 268 Ks

Although Bob Gibson was only the second pitcher in history to strike out more than 3,000 batters in his career, he topped the National League in Ks just once (268 in 1968). Gibson registered personal high marks in every major pitching department in '68 except for wins and strikeouts, as he set a post dead-ball ERA record of 1.12 for the season.

Willie McCovey

McCovey Slugs .545

In 1968, Willie McCovey paced the National League in slugging average for the first of three successive seasons, posting a .545 mark. That same season, his strikeout total dropped to 71 (from 110 the previous year). He collected 100 or more Ks four times in the five seasons prior to 1968 and only once thereafter.

Howard Clouts 44 Homers

The Senators, the worst team in the majors in 1968, were made semi-respectable by slugger Frank Howard. Howard not only topped the American League by a wide margin in home runs (he had 44) and total bases (he had 330), he also hit .274, the eighth-highest average in the loop. Between 1968 and 1970, he collected 136 home runs.

- Koosman is first rookie in 55 years to collect as many as seven shutouts in his frosh season.

- Fergie Jenkins of the Cubs is 20-15 with nine shutout losses, most in this century by a 20-game winner.

- Mets batters strike out an ML record 1,203 times.

- Dick McAuliffe of Detroit ties the ML record when he grounds into no DPs while playing in over 150 games.

- Sam Crawford dies at 83.

- Gates Brown of Detroit hits an ML record .472 as a pinch hitter (since broken).

- Howard hits a record ten homers over a six-game span.

- Pitcher Bill Hands of the Cubs strikes out a record 14 times in a row.

- Backstop Randy Hundley of the Cubs catches a major league record 160 games.

McAuliffe Snuffs Out Cards

Before being dumped by a sliding Orlando Cepeda, Tigers second baseman Dick McAuliffe fires to first to nip Mike Shannon and complete a double play. The action occurred in the sixth inning of game two of the 1968 World Series and terminated the sole Cardinals scoring outburst in the contest.

Dave McNally

McNally Wins 22 Games

Dave McNally's big year—his 22 wins placed second in the American League in 1968—was even more of a surprise than that of Denny McLain. Prior to that season, McNally had hurled only 22 complete games in 128 starts; in '68, however, he went all the way 18 times in 35 outings.

World Series

Tigers Party on the Road

Willie Horton soaks manager Mayo Smith with champagne in the visiting dressing room at Busch Stadium after the Tigers took the 1968 World Series. It was the Tigers' first World Title since 1945 and only their third in history. The Tigers were the fourth team that decade to win the crucial seventh game of a World Series on the road. Only Pittsburgh and St. Louis prevailed on their home turf in a seven-day fray during the '60s.

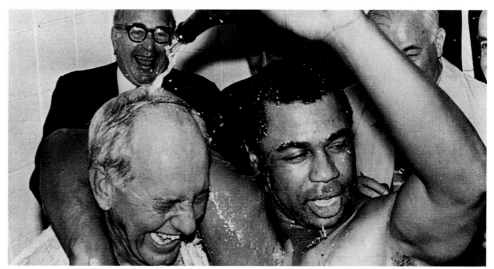

Mayo Smith, Willie Horton

1968

- Curt Blefary, former AL ROTY, hits .200 for Houston—lowest BA in history by an outfielder with 400 or more at-bats.

- Jim McAndrew of Mets loses a record four consecutive games in which his team is shut out.

- McAuliffe, a .249 hitter, tops AL in runs with 95.

- Jim Northrup of Detroit hits a record-tying three grandslams in a five-day period.

- Beckert tops majors in runs scored with 98.

- Brock tops the NL with 46 doubles, 14 triples, and 62 steals.

- Boston's Hawk Harrelson leads majors with 109 RBI.

- Harrelson tops AL with just 153 runs produced, setting a record low for a loop leader.

- Cincinnati's Tony Perez paces ML with 167 runs produced, setting a record low by an ML leader.

Ken Harrelson

Harrelson Tops AL with 109 RBI

Not only was Ken Harrelson the leader in the AL in 1968 with 109 RBI, he also was the circuit's seventh-best hitter at .275. Averages everywhere, not only in the majors, neared all-time lows in '68. Tony Torchia, the Eastern League's top hitter, batted just .294 to finish 24 points ahead of runner-up Carmen Fanzone.

Mickey Lolich

Lolich's Day Finally Comes

In 1968, Mickey Lolich placed second among Tigers pitchers in wins with 17 and third in starts with 32. Following his three victories in the '68 World Series, he said, "All my life somebody else has been the big star and Lolich was No. 2. I figured my day would come."

McLain, Gibson Go Head-to-Head

Denny McLain delivers in game one of the 1968 World Series as his mound opponent, Bob Gibson, squares away to attempt a sacrifice bunt. The Tigers scored just one run for McLain in his first two Series starts. In game six, his third outing, they broke lose for 13 tallies.

World Series

- Yaz tops majors in walks (119) and OBP (.429).
- Rose leads NL with a .394 OBP, lowest to top loop since 1917.
- Rose and Atlanta's Felipe Alou tie for the National League lead in hits with 210.

- Bert Campaneris leads AL with 177 hits, fewest ever by AL leader in season when full schedule is played.
- Campaneris tops AL in stolen bases (62).
- McLain leads AL in innings (336), win pct. (.838), and CGs (28).

- Phil Regan of the Cubs tops majors with 25 saves.
- Minnesota's Al Worthington leads AL with just 18 saves.
- Tiant leads AL in ERA (1.60).
- Cleveland's Sam McDowell leads AL in Ks (283).

New York unexpectedly dominated the news in 1969: The year began with the retirement of Mickey Mantle and ended with the World Series victory of Gil Hodges's Amazin' Mets. In between, Bowie Kuhn was named baseball commissioner and Steve Carlton set a major league record by striking out 19 Mets in a game (he lost the contest 4-3).

In the first year of divisional play, Billy Martin led the Twins to a title then was fired. Martin's lineup boasted batting champion Rod Carew, who had a .332 average, and Most Valuable Player Harmon Killebrew, who had a .276 average and a league-leading 49 round-trippers and 140 RBI. Although the four expansion teams lost a total of 411 games, Lou Piniella of the Kansas City Royals was named Rookie of the Year for his .282 average, 11 home runs, and 68 RBI. The Cy Young Award was shared by Baltimore's Mike Cuellar (23-11, 2.38 ERA) and Detroit's Denny McLain (24-9, 2.80 ERA).

San Francisco's Willie McCovey was the big bopper for the National League: His .320 average and league-leading 45 homers and 126 RBI earned him Most Valuable Player honors. Atlanta seized the West Division crown with hitting hero Hank Aaron (.300 average, 44 home runs, 97 RBI). Los Angeles second baseman Ted Sizemore was the senior circuit's top rookie.

Tom Seaver led the Mets to

AMAZIN' METS BEAT THE BIRDS, SHOCK THE WORLD

their first-ever title and took Cy Young honors with a 25-7 record and a 2.21 ERA. San Francisco's Juan Marichal won the ERA title at 2.10. With the assistance of Lee May (.278 average, 38 home runs, 110 RBI), Tony Perez (.294 average, 37 home runs, 122 RBI), Bobby Tolan (.305 average, 21 home runs, 93 RBI), and Johnny Bench (.293 average, 26 home runs, 90 RBI), the Reds finished in third, 4 games out—despite the hitting of Pete Rose, who had a league-topping .348 average.

The Mets won their division in stirring fashion, coming from both a ninth-place finish in '68 and 9 1/2 games back. The Chicago Cubs, flagless since 1945, helped the Mets by dropping ten of 11 games in early September. The Mets went on to win 38 of their last 49 games, taking the division by 8 contests—thanks to stout pitching, extraordinary fan support (major league-leading attendance of 2,175,373), and a platoon lineup in which only Cleon Jones (.340 average, 12 home runs, 75 RBI) and Tommie

Agee (.271 average, 26 home runs, 76 RBI) garnered 400 official at-bats.

The power corps of the Orioles included Boog Powell (.304 average, 37 home runs, 121 RBI), Frank Robinson (.308 average, 32 home runs, 100 RBI), and Paul Blair (.285 average, 26 home runs, 76 RBI). Although Washington had the ERA champ in Dick Bosman, the Baltimore rotation was anchored by Mike Cuellar (23-11, 2.38 ERA), Dave McNally (20-7, 3.21 ERA), and Jim Palmer (16-4, 2.34 ERA), who tied a league record by winning 15 consecutive games. The O's, winners of 109 games, had the league's best defense and pitching (2.83 team ERA).

The Mets crushed the Atlanta Braves in three straight in the first divisional playoffs, scoring 27 runs and allowing 15; the Orioles, victors in the ALCS over Minnesota in three, scored 16 runs and allowed five.

The Mets stunned Baltimore by taking four straight after Seaver lost the World Series opener 4-1. Jerry Koosman won twice and chalked up an ERA of 2.04; meanwhile, Agee made two spectacular catches in game three to save five runs and Ron Swoboda made a diving catch to help Seaver to his first World Series victory in game four, 2-1 in ten.

New York won game five 5-3 and, in the process, completed one of the greatest upsets in sports history.

1969

- AL and NL both expand to 12 teams and divide into two divisions, with division winners to play best-of-five playoffs.

- Mets become second ML team in three years to win flag after finishing as low as ninth the preceding year.

- Orioles take AL flag.

- Braves win NL West title, bow to Mets in three straight games in first NLCS.

- Twins win first AL West title, are swept by Orioles in first ALCS.

- Mets beat heavily favored Orioles in World Series in five games to top off miracle season.

- Donn Clendenon raps three homers and hits .357 to lead Mets in the World Series.

- Jerry Koosman wins two World Series games for Mets.

- Bowie Kuhn named new commissioner, replacing Spike Eckert.

Mets relief ace Tug McGraw *(left)* and southpaw whiz Jerry Koosman partake in a pregame snack. The shared sandwich was meant to symbolize the pair's roles in the club's incredible theft of the 1969 National League pennant. The Mets did not lead the league in a single major department that season except one—wins (with 100).

- To add more offense, rules are made to reduce the height of the pitcher's mound and the size of the strike zone.

- The NL's batting average jumps seven points and the AL's jumps 16 points.

- Harmon Killebrew leads majors with 49 homers and 140 RBI and is AL MVP.

- Willie McCovey named NL MVP after leading league in homers (45), RBI (126), SA (.656), and OBP (.458).

- The Mets' Tom Seaver tops majors with 25 wins.

- Seaver wins NL Cy Young Award.

- Detroit's Denny McLain leads AL with nine shutouts and 24 wins to repeat as AL Cy Young winner.

- Minnesota's Rod Carew steals home seven times to tie Pete Reiser's ML season record.

- Orioles' 109 wins tie 1961 Yanks for most wins in 162-game season.

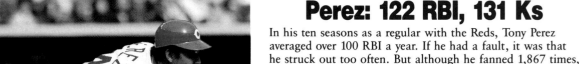

Tom Seaver, Ron Santo

Seaver Nearly Perfect

Ron Santo of the Cubs flies out to center on a pitch from Tom Seaver of the Mets on July 10, 1969. That night, with one out in the ninth, Seaver lost a bid for a perfect game when Chicago pinch hitter Jim Qualls cracked a double. Despite the defeat, the Cubs ended the day still in first place by a comfortable margin. They would eventually blow a 9¹/₂-game lead and lose the title to Seaver's Mets.

Perez: 122 RBI, 131 Ks

In his ten seasons as a regular with the Reds, Tony Perez averaged over 100 RBI a year. If he had a fault, it was that he struck out too often. But although he fanned 1,867 times, the fourth-highest career total in history, he was never a league-leader in whiffs. In 1969, he had 122 RBI and 131 Ks.

Tony Perez

Curt Flood

Flood Trade Ends in Court

Only age 31 in 1969 and still in his prime, Curt Flood chose to quit the game rather than be traded against his will. His act of protest and the legal repercussions that ensued resulted in the most serious threat to baseball's reserve clause since its origin in the late 1870s.

1969

- NL wins All-Star Game 9-3 at Washington.
- Dave McNally sets Orioles franchise record by winning 15 games in a row.
- Ted Williams is hired as Washington manager; the team finishes over .500 for the first time in its nine-year history.
- The Curt Flood case begins vs. OB after Flood is traded to Phils by Cards and refuses to report to new team.
- Twins manager Billy Martin beats up one of his own pitchers, Dave Boswell.
- On August 5, Pirate Willie Stargell becomes first to hit a homer out of Dodger Stadium.
- LA's Willie Davis hits in 31 consecutive games.
- Houston hurlers fan ML record 1,221 hitters.
- Wayne Granger of Reds is first pitcher to appear in 90 games.
- Bobby Bonds of Giants fans ML record 187 times.

Stargell Nails One in LA

Willie Stargell was the first player to hit a home run out of Dodger Stadium, nailing the dinger on August 5, 1969. When Stargell played every day, he hit a ton. As a pinch hitter, though, he was abysmal—as least until the tag end of his career. In his first 16 seasons, he hit just .146 in pinch roles; in his last four seasons, however, he hit .339, lifting his overall pinch average to .206.

Rod Carew

Carew's .332 Best Since '61

With the exception of the 1961 expansion season, Rod Carew's .332 average in 1969 was the AL's highest mark that decade. As it turned out, 1969 was also an expansion year. The only AL players between 1960 and 1973 to hit .330 in a non-expansion season were Tony Oliva and Bobby Murcer, both in 1971.

Willie Stargell

McNally One of Four Aces

With 20 victories for the Orioles in 1969, Dave McNally came in third in the American League in win percentage (.741). Baltimore's four top starters—McNally, Mike Cuellar, Jim Palmer, and Tom Phoebus—had a combined 73-29 mark as the club won 109 games that season, an expansion-era record in the American League.

Dave McNally

- McCovey receives ML record 45 intentional walks.
- McCovey's .656 SA sets record for NL first basemen.
- Boston's Rico Petrocelli sets AL shortstop record with 40 homers.
- Bob Moose of Pittsburgh no-hits Mets on Sept. 20.

- Ken Holtzman of Cubs no-hits Atlanta on August 19.
- Jim Palmer of Baltimore no-hits Oakland on August 13; this comes in the midst of his 15 consecutive wins.
- Bill Stoneman of Montreal no-hits Phils on April 17.

- Jim Maloney of Cincinnati no-hits Houston on April 30; the next day, Houston's Don Wilson no-hits Cincinnati.
- On April 14, in the first major league game played outside the United States, Montreal beats the Cards 8-7.

Mincher Leads Pilots

Don Mincher (shown tumbling second baseman Rod Carew in a game against the Twins) led the Seattle Pilots in both home runs (25) and RBI (78) in 1969, the team's only year of existence. As awful as the expansion club was, it still won two more games than the Indians, who finished last for only the second time in their history.

Don Mincher, Rod Carew

Jerry Koosman

Young Koos Wins 17

At the close of the 1969 season, rival clubs coveted Mets southpaw Jerry Koosman even more than they did Tom Seaver, his righthanded counterpart. That year, Koosman went 17-9. His stats for his first two full seasons included 13 shutouts and a combined 2.18 ERA. In the remaining 16 years of his career, he collected just 20 additional shutouts.

Williams Takes Nats to 86 Wins

Rookie manager Ted Williams piloted the expansion Senators to 86 wins in 1969, easily the club's highest number of triumphs while in the nation's capital. Williams not only seemed able to teach hitting, he turned around a pitching staff that had been the worst in the majors the previous year.

Ted Williams

1969

- Pete Rose wins his second consecutive NL bat crown (.348).

- Carew takes his first AL bat crown (.332).

- For the first time since 1914, Cleveland finishes last in AL, trailing even the Seattle Pilots and KC Royals, two expansion teams.

- Cleveland's Sam McDowell leads ML with 279 Ks.

- Hoyt Wilhelm becomes first pitcher in ML history to achieve 200 career saves.

- The Hall of Fame inducts Stan Musial, Roy Campanella, Stan Coveleski, and Waite Hoyt.

- "The Bleacher Bums" make their official debut in Wrigley Field and root Cubs to their highest finish since 1945.

- Rose breaks up the Flood-Roberto Clemente-Willie Mays NL Gold Glove monopoly as he replaces Mays as an outfield Gold Glover.

First ALCS Game, Photo 1

First ALCS Game, Photo 2

O's Win ALCS Game on Squeeze

These two photographs capture the play that ended the first ever American League Championship Game in 1969. In photo No. 1, with the score knotted at three-all in the bottom of the 12th inning and two out, Orioles outfielder Paul Blair surprises the Twins by laying down a two-strike suicide squeeze bunt. Photo No. 2 shows Minnesota reliever Ron Perranoski, who fielded the bunt, futilely chasing Mark Belanger across the cushion.

- Baltimore's Davy Johnson takes first of three consecutive Gold Gloves as AL second baseman.
- Carl Yastrzemski wins fifth Gold Glove as an AL outfielder.
- Lou Piniella of the expansion Royals is AL ROTY.

Ted Sizemore of LA named NL ROTY.

The Astros trade Rusty Staub to expansion Montreal Expos for four players and $100,000.

Cleveland sends Luis Tiant and Stan Williams to Twins for Graig Nettles, Dean Chance, and two other players.

- Yanks trade Joe Pepitone to the Astros for Curt Blefary.
- St. Louis trades Orlando Cepeda to the Braves for Joe Torre.
- Mets trade Amos Otis and Bob Johnson to Kansas City for Joe Foy.
- Juan Marichal tops ML with 2.10 ERA.

McLain Wins 24

Just age 25 in 1969, Denny McLain already had 114 career victories to his credit, winning 108 games over a five-year period. In 1969, he won 24 games, tops in the American League. If any active pitcher seemed a lock to win 200 games by the time he was 30 years old, it was McLain. Three years later he was gone, his total number of career victories frozen at 131.

Cleon Jones, Tommie Agee, Ron Swoboda

Mets Outfield Fuels Club

A shot of the Mets regular outfield in 1969 *(left to right)*: Cleon Jones, Tommie Agee, and Ron Swoboda. Jones spearheaded the club in hitting, posting a .340 average, 164 hits, and 92 runs scored that year. Agee led the team in home runs with 26 and RBI with 76. Swoboda, for his part, topped the crew in unrealized talent. Swoboda, who hit .235 in '69, platooned with Art Shamsky, who hit .300. In the World Series that fall, however, Swoboda rapped .400 and Shamsky hit .000. Jones and Agee also had abysmal World Series showings. Jones hit .158 and Agee batted .167.

Denny McLain

1969

- Mickey Mantle announces his retirement prior to the season.

- On Sept. 10, the Royals use an ML record 27 men in a nine-inning game.

- Houston's Jim Wynn ties NL record when he receives 148 walks.

- Washington's Dick Bosman has best ERA in AL (2.19).

- Boston's Rico Petrocelli sets an AL record when he hits 40 homers as a shortstop.

- Washington's Del Unser tops AL with eight triples, fewest ever by a loop leader.

- Jim Northrup of Detroit goes 6-for-6 in a 13-inning game on August 28.

- Bob Oliver of the Royals goes 6-for-6 on May 4.

- Steve Carlton of the Cards fans 19 Mets on Sept. 15, but loses 4-3.

- On Sept. 12, Mets Koosman and Don Cardwell both shut out the Pirates 1-0, and each gets a game-winning RBI.

Frank Robinson

Robby and Mates Can't Hit Mets

Frank Robinson hit .333 for Baltimore in the 1969 American League Championship Series and just .188 against the Mets in the '69 World Series. As a team, the Orioles had a meager .146 batting average off New York pitching in the fall classic that year. Four Baltimore regulars—Brooks Robinson, Dave Johnson, Don Buford, and Paul Blair—hit a combined .080.

Davis Hits .311, a Rarity in LA

Willie Davis topped the Dodgers with a .311 batting average in 1969 to become the club's first .300 hitter since 1963. Los Angeles was the National League team with the weakest punch during the late 1960s. In 1968, catcher Tom Haller spearheaded the Dodgers with 53 RBI and substitute outfielder Len Gabrielson was the lone Dodger to hit as many as ten home runs.

Willie Davis

Phil Niekro

Niekro Wins 23 at 30

Phil Niekro had accumulated 31 career victories going into the 1969 season. That year, at age 30, he collected a personal-best 23 wins. Niekro posted 20 or more triumphs on just two additional occasions—the year he turned 35 and the year he turned 40. He finished his 24-year career with a total of 318 wins.

- On July 9, Jim Qualls of the Cubs singles with one out in the ninth to break up a perfect game bid by Seaver.

- The Seattle Pilots, defunct after only one year of existence, at least win their first game in franchise history—7-0 over Chicago.

- Pittsburgh's Matty Alou tops majors in hits (231) and doubles (41).

- Oakland's Reggie Jackson tops AL with 123 runs and a .608 SA.

- Tony Oliva leads AL in hits (197) and doubles (39).

- Tommy Harper of Seattle tops ML with 73 steals.

- Lou Brock leads NL with 53 thefts.

- Clemente tops ML in triples (12), is second in NL in batting (.345).

- Rose and Bonds tie for NL lead in runs with 120.

- Bob Gibson leads the majors in CGs with 28.

On the field, the news was that baseball had returned to Milwaukee, as the Pilots franchise ended its one-year stay in Seattle and became the Brewers.

Off the field, the headlines were made by two big names who sat out most of the year: Curt Flood pursued an antitrust lawsuit challenging baseball's reserve clause, which gives baseball owners the right to trade a player against his wishes; and Denny McLain, the two-time Cy Young Award-winner, was suspended not once but twice for his involvement with gamblers. Additionally, Houston Astros pitcher Jim Bouton was censured by commissioner Bowie Kuhn for writing *Ball Four*, his controversial, now-classic memoir.

Bob Gibson (a 23-7 record, NL-leading winning percentage, and 3.12 ERA) won his second Cy Young Award for St. Louis, while Montreal starter Carl Morton (18-11, 3.60 ERA) was named Rookie of the Year. Hitters continued their resurgence, however, as league MVP Johnny Bench led the Reds to the World Series with a .293 average and league-high totals in home runs (45) and RBI (148). In Atlanta, Rico Carty's .366 average took the NL batting title.

In the AL, Boog Powell won MVP honors on a .297 average, 35 home runs, and 114 RBI. Frank Howard of Washington led the league with 44 home runs and 126 RBI and Alex Johnson of

Orioles' Arms And Bats Batter Reds

California took the batting title at .329. Thurman Munson of the Yankees (.302 average, six home runs, 53 RBI) was named Rookie of the Year. Jim Perry took Minnesota to its second straight division title by winning the Cy Young Award (24-12, 3.03 ERA). The Twins were led at bat by third baseman Harmon Killebrew (.271 average, 41 home runs, 113 RBI) and right fielder Tony Oliva (.325 average, 23 home runs, 107 RBI).

Hank Aaron of Atlanta and Willie Mays of San Francisco both collected their 3,000th hits. New York's Tom Seaver struck out 19 Padres in a game—ten in a row—to tie one record and set another. Sudden Sam McDowell of Cleveland won 20 games and struck out a major league-high 304 batters. And a 21-year-old rookie named Vida Blue pitched a no-hitter for Oakland against division-winning Minnesota.

The Twins matched their 1969 American League Championship Series performance by being swept again by the Orioles in three games. The O's batted

.330 with six home runs in the trio of victories, as they continued their quest to erase the memories of their five-game loss to the Mets in the '69 World Series. Mike Cuellar (24-8) and Dave McNally (24-9) led the way by tying Jim Perry for the league lead in wins.

The Reds took the field against Pittsburgh—after winning their division by 14 1/2 games, leading in home runs (191), and tying for first place in batting (.270)—and promptly swept the Bucs in the National League Championship Series on the strength of their pitching (they turned in a 1.29 team ERA).

The Reds were favored in the Series against Baltimore. The O's, however, slugged ten home runs en route to a 4-1 Series win. The Reds were blown out twice by identical scores of 9-3, one of which featured a grandslam by McNally. The most memorable aspect of the Series was the acrobatic fielding by Baltimore third baseman Brooks Robinson; that is not, however, to downplay Robinson's performance at the plate (he hit .429 with two homers and six RBI).

Cincinnati's only win came in game four, on Lee May's three-run eighth-inning homer, and it broke the O's 17-game winning streak (the final 11 games of the regular season, the three playoff games, and the first three games of the Series). Cuellar shut down the Reds once and for all in game five with a 9-3 triumph.

1970

- Pirates win NL East flag with .549 win pct., lowest in ML history by winner to this juncture.

- Orioles give manager Earl Weaver his second consecutive AL flag.

- NL West champ Reds sweep Pirates in NLCS.

- Orioles sweep AL West champion Twins in ALCS.

- After two years of League Championship Series play, a losing team has yet to win a single game.

- Orioles win World Series, beating Reds in five games.

- Baltimore's Brooks Robinson is Series MVP with .429 BA and a host of brilliant fielding plays.

- Reds avert a sweep in Series by winning game four on three-run homer by Lee May, who hits .389 with eight RBI in Series.

- Boog Powell of Baltimore is AL MVP.

Baltimore manager Earl Weaver imbibes the traditional beverage after the Orioles clinched the American League East title for the second year in a row. Weaver believed that poor players made good managers. In his 13 years as a minor league second baseman, his top batting average was .288.

- Johnny Bench named NL MVP.

- Bob Gibson wins second Cy Young in NL, as he ties Gaylord Perry for NL lead in wins (23).

- Minnesota's Jim Perry is AL Cy Young winner, as he ties two others for AL lead in wins (24).

- The Perrys are the first brothers to ever top their respective leagues in wins.

- Orioles win 108 games, giving them a combined 217 victories over the last two years.

- Atlanta's Rico Carty leads ML with .366 BA.

- Angel Alex Johnson wins AL bat crown (.329) by fraction of a point over Carl Yastrzemski, who also bats .329.

- On April 22, Tom Seaver sets ML record when he fans ten Padres in a row and ties ML record by fanning 19 total.

Cuellar Lands Job, Wins 24

Mike Cuellar knocked around organized ball for 12 years before landing with the Orioles in 1969. In 1970, he tied for the most wins in the majors (24) and topped the American League in win percentage (.750) and complete games (21).

Mike Cuellar

Bench Posts Monster Stats

Had Johnny Bench not played other positions as well in 1970, he would have set major league records for the most home runs (45), RBI (148), and total bases (355) collected by a catcher. If he had been moved soon thereafter to another full-time position, he would probably have made well over 500 home runs.

Johnny Bench

Carter Honors Carty

Georgia governor Jimmy Carter presents a silver bat to Rico Carty for winning the 1970 National League hitting title with a .366 average. Carty received the award prior to a Braves-Mets game in 1971, a season in which he was idled by leg injuries. He was never again an every-day player except in the role of designated hitter.

Rico Carty

1970

- Cub Billy Williams sets new NL record when he plays in his 1,117th consecutive game.
- Willie Mays collects his 3,000th hit.
- NL wins its eighth straight All-Star Game, 5-4 in 12 innings at Cincinnati.

- Yankee Thurman Munson wins AL ROTY Award.
- Carl Morton of Expos is NL ROTY.
- Cincinnati's Wayne Granger sets new ML record with 35 saves.
- Giant Bobby Bonds fans 189 times to set ML record that still stands.

- Carty hits in 31 straight games.
- Three Rivers Stadium opens on July 16, Reds vs. Pirates.
- Riverfront Stadium opens on June 30, Braves vs. Reds.
- Conigliaro brothers, Tony and Billy, hit a sibling record 54 homers for Red Sox.

Jim Palmer

Palmer High in All Depts.

Jim Palmer won 20 games in 1970, tying for third place in the American League in win percentage (.667). He also tied for the circuit-lead in shutouts (five) and innings (305), finished second in ERA (2.71), placed third in complete games (17), and came in fourth in strikeouts (199). Palmer was a distant fifth, however, in the voting for the Cy Young Award.

Thurman Munson

Munson Named AL ROTY

Thurman Munson, the American League Rookie of the Year in 1970, hit .302 for the Yankees in his first full season. Cleveland's Ray Fosse, also in his fledgling year as a regular backstopper, batted .307 in the junior circuit that season. Soph catcher Manny Sanguillen of the Pirates hit .325, the second-best average in the National League.

Jim Perry

Perry Back on Top Again

Jim Perry was the elder member of the Perry brothers, the winningest siblings in history prior to the Niekros. Outstanding with Cleveland in his first two seasons, he won just 76 games over the next eight years before emerging again in 1969 as one of the best pitchers in the American League. In 1970, Perry tied for the circuit-lead in wins with 23 and snared the Cy Young Award.

- The Seattle franchise is moved to Milwaukee just prior to the season; team name changed from "Pilots" to "Brewers."

- Hank Aaron gets his 3,000th hit.

- Cardinal Vic Davalillo ties ML record with 24 pinch hits.

- Detroit's Cesar Gutierrez is first in 20th century to go 7-for-7 when he does it on June 21 in 12-inning game.

- Dock Ellis of Pittsburgh no-hits San Diego on June 12.

- Clyde Wright of California no-hits Oakland on July 3.

- Bill Singer of LA no-hits Philadelphia on July 20.

- Vida Blue of Oakland no-hits Minnesota on Sept. 21.

- Bench tops majors in homers (45) and RBI (148).

- Seaver tops NL in Ks (283) and ERA (2.81).

A Green Blue Fires No-Hitter

Vida Blue won a pair of complete-game shutouts for the A's late in the 1970 season (one of which was a no-hitter), whetting appetites in Oakland for what the future of the rookie might hold. The A's registered 89 victories that year, the franchise's highest total since 1932. Charley Finley suddenly seemed as if he might be more than an inept cousin to Bill Veeck.

Hondo: 44 HRs, 126 RBI

Frank Howard acquired the nickname "Hondo" early in his athletic career. By 1970, however, he was more commonly known as "The Capital Punisher." He clubbed 237 round-trippers for the expansion Senators, a club record. He also set the mark for the most career home runs by a Washington player, original or expansion club. In 1970, Howard led the American League with 44 dingers, 126 RBI, and 132 walks.

Frank Howard

Vida Blue

Brooks: A's for D in Series

Brooks Robinson achieved recognition as perhaps the finest fielding third baseman after his stunning performance in the 1970 World Series. Some, however, felt he was not even the best hot corner gloveman in the American League that year. The debate over whether Robinson or Graig Nettles was the better third sacker raged for the next half-decade.

Brooks Robinson

1970

- Williams tops ML in runs (137), total bases (373), and runs produced (224), and ties for ML lead in hits (205).

- Frank Howard leads AL in homers (44), RBI (126), and walks (132).

- O's have two 24-game winners (Dave McNally and Mike Cuellar) and also a 20-game winner (Jim Palmer).

- Royals end ML record skein of 23 consecutive losses to Orioles.

- The Hall of Fame inducts Lou Boudreau, Earle Combs, Ford Frick, and Jesse Haines.

- Rookie Ray Fosse of Cleveland wins first of two consecutive Gold Gloves given to AL catchers.

- Fosse sustains career-threatening injury in home-plate collision with Pete Rose in All-Star Game when Rose bowls him over to score winning run.

- Cincinnati's Tommy Helms wins first of two consecutive Gold Gloves given to NL second basemen.

Perry, 23 Wins, Leads NL

Gaylord Perry led National League pitchers in several hurling departments in 1970—23 wins (tied for first place), five shutouts, and 329 innings pitched. When he sagged to 16 wins the following year, he was traded to Cleveland for Sam McDowell. Perry went on to take the Cy Young Award in 1972, his first season with the Tribe; McDowell was nearly through that year.

Gaylord Perry

Alex Tops AL in BA

Alex Johnson lived to get his cuts at the plate, and in batting practice he looked as if he ought to be the game's hitting king. There were days when he was. In 1970, for example, Johnson claimed the AL batting crown with a .329 average, beating out Carl Yastrzemski by a fraction of a point. Most of the time, though, Johnson frustrated his managers more than any other player of his era.

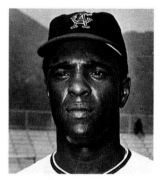

Alex Johnson

Billy Scores 137 Runs

Billy Williams (shown sliding into third in a game against the Phillies) compiled 2,711 hits, 426 home runs, and 1,475 RBI over an 18-year career. In 1970, he led the National League with 137 runs scored and tied for first with 205 hits.

Billy Williams

- Houston's Doug Rader wins first of five consecutive Gold Gloves as NL third baseman.

- White Sox Luis Aparicio wins the last of his nine Gold Gloves at shortstop.

- Mets center fielder Tommie Agee becomes the first outfielder to win a Gold Glove in each league.

- Paul Blair of the O's wins third of what will be eight consecutive Gold Gloves as AL outfielder.

- ML umps refuse to work the LCS games and force a settlement that increases their salaries and benefits.

- Fergie Jenkins sets a Cubs record with 274 strikeouts.

- Cleveland hits an AL record 133 homers at home.

- Official scorer's pay is raised from $30 to $35 per game.

- Average player's salary is up to $25,000.

- Ray Schalk dies.

World Series

Bench Ired by Reds Pitchers

Johnny Bench angrily fires the ball back to a Reds pitcher in the 1970 World Series. The Cincinnati backstopper had reason to be upset: In the five-game fray, the Queen City mound crew surrendered 20 walks and posted a composite 6.70 ERA while the Orioles clubbed ten home runs.

Moe Beats Rose to Bag

Relief hurler Moe Drabowsky scurries to the first base bag in time to retire Pete Rose on a ground ball to first sacker Boog Powell. The 1970 World Series was Drabowsky's second fall appearance with Baltimore, which had reclaimed him earlier in the year after losing him in the 1969 expansion draft.

World Series

1970

- Jim Bouton's book about the 1969 season, *Ball Four*, is a smash success.

- KC's Amos Otis sets AL stolen base pct. record of .943 (33 in 35 attempts).

- Montreal's Bobby Wine sets NL record for shortstops by participating in 137 double plays.

- Yaz is last player to win All-Star MVP Award while playing for the game's losing team.

- Felix Millan of Atlanta goes 6-for-6 on July 6.

- Denny McLain is suspended for part of the season for being involved in a bookmaking operation.

- After the season, Tigers trade McLain and three other players to Washington for Joe Coleman, Ed Brinkman, Aurelio Rodriguez, and Jim Hannan.

- Red Sox trade Tony Conigliaro and two other players to the Angels for Ken Tatum, Jarvis Tatum, and Doug Griffin.

World Series

Powell, O's Batter Reds

Boog Powell passes by Tommy Helms and rounds second base after homering in the 1970 World Series. Baltimore unmercifully hammered every member of the Reds pitching staff except relievers Clay Carroll and Don Gullett. Against the other seven Cincy hurlers who appeared in the Series, the Orioles pounded out 31 earned runs in $27\frac{1}{3}$ innings.

Robby Tags Former Mates

Second baseman Tommy Helms of Cincinnati nabs Frank Robinson at the keystone sack in the 1970 World Series. In his only postseason appearance against his former teammates, Robinson hit just .273 but rapped two pivotal home runs. One dinger came in game three, a contest which also featured a grandslam by Baltimore pitcher Dave McNally; the other round-tripper came in the game-five finale.

World Series

Lee May

May Wins Game Four

Tony Perez and Johnny Bench wait to greet Lee May after he homered with both of them aboard in the eighth inning of game four of the 1970 World Series. May's three-run blow gave the Reds a 6-5 win and averted a sweep by the Orioles. Reliever Eddie Watt, making his lone fall appearance in 1970, was the victim.

- Tom Egan of the Angels sets an AL record when he commits five passed balls on July 28.

- Bill Melton of the White Sox Ks ten consecutive times, an ML record for nonpitchers.

- Willie McCovey tops ML in SA (.612) and walks (137).

- LA's Wes Parker leads ML in doubles with 47.

- Dodger Willie Davis leads ML in triples (16).

- Bobby Tolan of the Reds tops majors with 57 steals; Bert Campaneris leads AL with 42.

- Yaz tops AL in runs (125), runs produced (187), total bases (335), OBP (.453), and SA (.592).

- Minnesota's Cesar Tovar leads AL in triples (13) and ties for lead in doubles (36).

- Tony Oliva leads AL in hits (204) and ties in doubles (36).

It was Vida Blue's year, all right—all the way until October, when the veteran Baltimore Orioles showed the 21-year-old Oakland pitcher what pressure baseball was. They themselves were then taught a lesson by the Pittsburgh Pirates, World Series winners for the first time since Bill Mazeroski's ninth-inning homer threw down the Yankees back in 1960.

Blue's phenomenal first full season—a 24-8 record, 301 strikeouts, a league-leading 1.82 ERA, and eight shutouts—earned him both the American League's Cy Young and Most Valuable Player Awards. The Rookie of the Year was slick-fielding first baseman Chris Chambliss of last-place Cleveland with a .275 average, nine home runs, and 48 RBI. Tony Oliva of Minnesota won the batting title at .337. Detroit's Mickey Lolich led the league with 25 wins, and Chicago's Bill Melton had a circuit-best 33 home runs.

Individual honors in the National League were won by Atlanta's Earl Williams, whose 33 homers and 87 RBI won him the Rookie of the Year Award; Joe Torre of St. Louis, who led the league with a .363 average and 137 RBI and was named Most Valuable Player; Willie Stargell, whose 48 home runs topped the circuit and propelled Pittsburgh to a division title; New York's Tom Seaver, whose 1.76 ERA was best in the league; and Cy Young

A's Sing The Blues; Bucs Have a Blass

Award-winner Ferguson Jenkins, who logged the most innings (325) and won the most games (24) to tally a 2.77 ERA for the Cubs.

Pittsburgh's combination of speed, power, defense, and pitching was too much for the NL East. Roberto Clemente led the Bucs with a .341 average. His 86 RBI ranked second on the team, right behind Stargell's 125. Although no Pirate pitcher won 20 games, the Pittsburgh hurlers were well-balanced and they did have an ace in the hole in Dave Giusti, whose palmball brought in five wins and a loop-high 30 saves.

In the NLCS, the Pirates overpowered the San Francisco Giants, who had ridden the broad back of Bobby Bonds (.288 average, 33 home runs, 102 RBI) to a division title by 1 game over the Los Angeles Dodgers. After losing game one to the Giants, the Pirates turned on the power. They slugged their way to a 3-1 tournament victory that featured a three-homer second game by first baseman Bob Robertson as well as homers by Richie Hebner in games three and four.

With the assistance of Catfish Hunter's 21-11, 2.96 ERA season and the muscle of Reggie Jackson, Sal Bando, Rick Monday, and Mike Epstein, Blue and the A's marched to a 101-60 record and a 16-game edge over Kansas City for the AL West title. The Orioles won 101 games as well, on the stellar pitching of a record-tying four 20-game winners: Dave McNally (21-5), Mike Cuellar (20-9), Pat Dobson (20-8), and Jim Palmer (20-9). The Orioles also led the AL in runs scored for a convincing 12-game lead over second-place Detroit.

The Orioles pitching was the key to their 3-0 sweep of the A's in the ALCS. Baltimore's hitting, however, couldn't keep pace in the World Series, and Pittsburgh took it in seven contests behind two complete game wins by Steve Blass in the third and seventh matches. Blass was called upon to save the day after Baltimore whipped the Bucs at home 5-3 and 11-3. The Pittsburgh pitcher responded with a three-hitter and a 5-1 win.

Baltimore scored three runs in the top of the first inning of the next game—but it would be 22 innings before the O's would score again, as first Bruce Kison and then Nelson Briles and Bob Moose kept them in check (Briles pitched a shutout in game five).

The O's came back to win game six in ten innings, but Blass slammed the door in game seven with a four-hit, 2-1 win.

1971

- Pirates win NL flag under Danny Murtaugh.

- Orioles take their third straight pennant in AL.

- Bucs defeat Giants in four games in NLCS, as Pirate Bob Robertson cracks four homers.

- Orioles again sweep ALCS, this time beating Oakland.

- Pirates win World Series in seven games after trailing two games to none.

- Pirate Steve Blass is Series pitching star with two CG wins, including 2-1 victory over Mike Cuellar in game seven.

- Roberto Clemente is overall Series star, hitting .414 with 12 hits and two homers.

- Game four at Pittsburgh is first night game in Series history.

- Cardinal Joe Torre is NL MVP, as he leads league in BA (.363), hits (230), RBI (137), and total bases (352).

As a rookie in 1970, Vida Blue pitched a no-hit game against Minnesota—no small feat considering the West Division Champion had a lineup of such sluggers as Harmon Killebrew and Tony Oliva. In 1971, the Pride of Mansfield, Louisiana, dominated the American League, capturing 24 victories with 301 strikeouts in 312 innings. His performance earned him the Cy Young and MVP Awards, not to mention an abortive effort by A's owner Charley Finley to change his first name to "True."

- Oakland's Vida Blue wins both MVP and Cy Young in AL.
- Chicago's Ferguson Jenkins cops NL Cy Young, as he leads loop in wins (24), CGs (30), and innings (325).
- Tiger Mickey Lolich leads AL in wins (25), innings (376), CGs (29), and Ks (308).

- Lolich's 45 starts and 376 innings are the most by any hurler since dead-ball era.
- Willie Stargell leads majors with 48 homers.
- Chicago's Bill Melton tops AL in homers with 33.

- Baltimore becomes the only flag winner in ML history to have four 20-game winners.
- Montreal's Ron Hunt sets a modern ML record when he's hit by pitches 50 times.
- Astros play ML record 75 one-run games.

Torre Named NL MVP

Nicknamed "The Godfather," Joe Torre terrorized National League pitchers in 1971. A former All-Star catcher in the 1960s, Torre was relocated to third base in '71. Making the most of the move, he topped the loop with a .363 batting average and 137 RBI that year, capturing the league's MVP Award in the process. It was the only monster year in Torre's career. He dropped to a .289 average in 1972.

Joe Torre

Amos Otis

Amos Cranks Out HRs, RBI

When he left the Royals in 1983, Amos Otis departed as the team career leader in several offensive categories including hits (2,004), runs (1,086), and RBI (997). His graceful fielding helped him capture three Gold Gloves. The Royals obtained Otis from the Mets in December 1969. In 1971, Otis had a .301 average, 15 home runs, and 79 RBI.

Steve Carlton

Carlton Trade Wise for Phils

Following the 1971 season, the Cardinals traded Steve Carlton, the second-winningest lefthanded pitcher of all time, to the Phillies for Rick Wise. Carlton went 20-9 in '71, tying for second place in wins in the National League (Wise went 17-14 that year). The reason for the swap was Carlton's request for a $10,000 raise. The 1972 season would find him sporting a 27-10 record.

1971

- Veterans Stadium opens on April 10, Expos vs. Phils.

- Phillie Larry Bowa's .987 FA is a new ML record for shortstops.

- Cleveland third baseman Graig Nettles compiles an ML record 412 assists.

- Tony Oliva wins third AL bat crown (.337) and leads the league in slugging (.546).

- AL wins All-Star Game 6-4 at Detroit, as Oakland's Reggie Jackson blasts a mammoth home run.

- Chris Chambliss of Cleveland is AL Rookie of the Year.

- Atlanta's Earl Williams is named NL ROTY.

- Williams, a catcher/third baseman, hits 33 homers, an NL rookie record for both catchers and infielders.

- Phillie rookie Willie Montanez cracks 30 homers, setting a team rookie record.

1971

Murcer Has Best Year

Bobby Murcer followed fellow Oklahoman Mickey Mantle as center fielder of the New York Yankees. Although he never measured up to Mantle's daunting standards, Murcer appeared in five All-Star Games during his 17-year major league career. His best season as a Yankee came in 1971, when he batted .331 (second in the American League) and socked 25 home runs.

Bobby Murcer

Sal Bando

Mickey Lolich

Bando Takes A's to First

Ever colorful, Sal Bando was the gritty co-captain of the A's dynasty teams that dominated baseball in the early '70s. In 1971, he helped Oakland to a first-place finish in the American League West with his 24 home runs and 94 RBI.

Lolich Tops AL in Wins, Ks

Portly Mickey Lolich followed his 1968 World Series heroics with a remarkably consistent career that saw him set a major league record for strikeouts by a southpaw (2,832). Lolich spearheaded the American League in victories (25), strikeouts (308), complete games (29), and innings (376) in 1971, only to see the Cy Young Award go to Oakland wunderkind Vida Blue.

- Hank Aaron leads NL with a .669 slugging average.
- On June 23, Rick Wise of the Phils no-hits Reds and hits two home runs.
- Wise homers in four consecutive games he pitches in June.
- Ken Holtzman of Cubs no-hits Cincinnati on June 3.
- Bob Gibson no-hits Pittsburgh on August 14.
- Blue fans 301 in his first full ML season.
- Lou Brock tops majors in runs (126) and steals (64).
- Harmon Killebrew leads AL in RBI (119) and walks (114).
- Tom Seaver tops NL in Ks (289) and ERA (1.76), winning 20 games.
- Earl Weaver is first non-Yankee manager since 1931 to win three consecutive AL flags.
- The Orioles become first team since the 1942–44 Cards to win 100 or more games three consecutive years.

Tom Seaver

Seaver Sizzles for Mets

Tom Seaver was "The Franchise" for the Mets in the late 1960s and early '70s, taking the team to a World Championship in 1969 and a division title in 1973. On April 22, 1970, the ace righty struck out 19 San Diego Padres including a record ten in a row to end the game. Seaver had what he considered his best year in 1971—a 20-10 record (tied for second in wins in the National League) and a 1.76 ERA (best in the majors).

Jenkins Has Career Year

Confronted with pitching in a bandbox of a ballpark and supported by a host of mediocre Chicago Cub nines, Fergie Jenkins merely won 20 or more games for six consecutive years beginning in 1967. His best year was in 1971: Not only did he spearhead the National League in complete games (30), triumphs (24), and innings pitched (325), he batted .243 with six home runs. His effort was rewarded with the Cy Young Award.

Weaver Fails to Repeat

Fiery Earl Weaver ruled the Oriole roost as no other manager had since John McGraw guided the Giants. His 1971 defending champion Orioles featured a pitching staff of four 20-game winners and a combined ERA of 3.00. Despite the efforts of his hurling aces—as well as Brooks Robinson, Frank Robinson, and American League MVP Boog Powell—Weaver and the Orioles dropped a classic seven-game World Series to the Pirates that fall.

Earl Weaver

Fergie Jenkins

1971

- Reds and Braves combine for ten homers on April 21.

- Hall of Fame inducts Jake Beckley, Dave Bancroft, Chick Hafey, Harry Hooper, Joe Kelley, Rube Marquard, George Weiss, and Satchel Paige.

- Dodger Willie Davis wins first of three consecutive Gold Gloves as NL outfielder.

- The Orioles trade Frank Robinson and Pete Richert to the Dodgers for four players.

- The Mets trade Nolan Ryan and three other players to Angels for Jim Fregosi.

- Boston sends George Scott and five other players to Milwaukee for Tommy Harper and three others.

- The Cubs trade Holtzman to the A's for Rick Monday.

- The Dodgers swap Dick Allen to the White Sox for Tommy John and Steve Huntz.

- The Astros trade John Mayberry and a minor leaguer to KC for two minor leaguers.

Willie Stargell

Oliva Wins Batting Title

On a team of such hitters as Rod Carew and Harmon Killebrew, Tony Oliva was considered to be the best pure hitter in Twins history. He won his third American League batting crown in 1971 with a .337 average.

Tony Oliva

Pops a Local Favorite

As Willie Stargell established an April record with 11 home runs in 1971, Bob Prince, a Pirate broadcaster, came up with the phrase "chicken on the hill" in connection with Stargell's fast-food restaurants. "Pops" promised free chicken to patrons every time he hit a home run that season. His 48 homers (best in the NL) and 125 RBI (second in the circuit) helped lead the Pirates to a World Championship and kept Pittsburgh well-fed.

Catfish Reels in 21 Wins

Shortly after he was signed to a $75,000 bonus, North Carolina phenom James Augustus Hunter was nicknamed "Catfish" by team owner Charley Finley, and a legend was born. Hunter was the best and most consistent pitcher on the Oakland A's from 1971 through 1974, baseball's last true dynasty. During that four-year span, he won 88 games and lost just 35. His 21 victories in 1971 were second only to Vida Blue's club-leading 24 and tied for fourth in the American League.

Catfish Hunter

- Astros send Joe Morgan, Denis Menke, Cesar Geronimo, Jack Billingham, and Ed Armbrister to the Reds for Lee May, Tommy Helms, and Jimmy Stewart.

- Heinie Manush dies.

- Goose Goslin dies.

- Elmer Flick dies at age 94.

- Don Kessinger of the Cubs goes 6-for-6 on June 17.

- Enzo Hernandez of the Padres has 12 RBI in 549 at-bats—an ML record for fewest RBI in 500 or more at-bats.

- Atlanta's Rico Carty, reigning NL bat champ, is out all year with injury.

- J.R. Richard of Houston ties Karl Spooner's ML record when he Ks 15 hitters in his first ML start.

- On May 11, Cleveland's Steve Dunning hits the last grandslam by an AL pitcher.

- The current rule to determine rookie status in order to select the two Rookies of the Year is adopted.

Pirates See the Light

In 1971, Danny Murtaugh led the Pirates to their second World Championship during his ten-year stint as manager. On October 13, the Pirates and Orioles played the first night game in Series history. The Bucs tied the fall classic at two games apiece that evening.

Danny Murtaugh

Bobby Bonds

Bonds: 33 HRs, 102 RBI

Tagged as having "unlimited potential," Bobby Bonds hit more than 30 home runs and stole 30 or more bases five times in his career. He is the only player of the 20th century to hit a grandslam as his first major league hit. Bonds posted 110 runs scored in 1971 (second in the National League), totaling 33 home runs and 102 RBI.

Steve Blass, Bob Robertson

Blass Wins Championship

Steve Blass (hugging first baseman Bob Robertson) lets out a cheer as the Pirates take the 1971 World Championship with a 2-1 triumph in game seven. Blass was the pitching hero of the '71 Series, earning three- and four-hit victories in the third and seventh games. He posted a 1.00 ERA, allowing seven hits and striking out 13 batters in 18 innings. A cerebral lanky hurler, Blass pitched with a unique herky-jerky delivery that inexplicably deserted him in 1973. His record plummeted from 19-8 with a 2.49 ERA in 1972 to 3-9 with a 9.81 ERA in '73.

1971

- Baltimore's Mark Belanger is first AL regular since 1958 to go homerless for a full season in 500 or more at-bats.
- Yankee Roy White hits an AL record 17 sacrifice flies.
- Chicago's Ron Santo leads NL third basemen in DPs a record sixth time.

- Houston's Cesar Cedeno tops ML in doubles (40).
- Two Astros, Morgan and Roger Metzger, tie for the NL lead with 11 triples; KC's Freddie Patek likewise tops AL with 11.
- Willie Mays leads NL in walks (112) and OBP (.429).

- Baltimore's Don Buford leads AL in runs with 99.
- Minnesota's Cesar Tovar tops AL with 204 hits, 25 more than any other ALer.
- Yankee Bobby Murcer tops AL in runs produced (163) and OBP (.429).

Billy Williams

Williams Surefire at Plate

Billy Williams continued to endear himself to the Wrigley Field faithful with his sweet swing and quiet, dependable style in 1971. From September 22, 1963, to September 2, 1970, Williams played in 1,117 consecutive games to establish the National League record. Never in 18 years did Williams play in a World Series. In 1971, he posted a .301 average with 28 home runs and 93 RBI.

Mike Cuellar

Cuellar Posts 20 Wins

Most of Mike Cuellar's deliveries could barely break a pane of glass, yet his varied assortment of junk hounded batters and helped him to four seasons with 20 or more wins. In 1971, Cuellar joined fellow Oriole pitchers Jim Palmer, Dave McNally, and Pat Dobson in winning 20 or more games apiece by going 20-9. When the World Series rolled around, however, Cuellar ran out of juice, losing a pair of games.

Clemente Steals Show

A national television audience delighted in the strong batting performance given by Roberto Clemente in the 1971 World Series. The 37-year-old right fielder for the Pirates batted .414 with a pair of home runs to snare Series MVP honors. He is shown here clubbing the sole home run of the seventh game. The '71 fall classic was his greatest triumph.

World Series

- Boston's Reggie Smith leads AL in doubles (33) and total bases (302).

- Royal Amos Otis tops AL in steals (52), and teammate Patek is a close second (49).

- Ken Sanders of the Brewers tops majors with 31 saves; Dave Giusti of the Pirates leads NL with 30.

- Baltimore's Dave McNally tops AL in win pct. (.808).

- Cincinnati's Don Gullett has NL's best win pct. (.727).

- Indians have worst staff ERA in majors (4.28) three years after having the best in the AL.

- Indians finish last in AL for second time in three years after finishing last just once in previous 68 years.

- Padres finish with worst record in NL for third year in a row, as they go 61-100.

- Reds manager Sparky Anderson has his only losing season (79-83) until 1989.

The 1972 year found its heroes in unlikely venues. Only Johnny Bench, the catcher for the National League Champion Cincinnati Reds, played for a division-winning team; his league-leading 40 homers and 125 RBI snared the Most Valuable Player title. Steve Carlton of the last-place Phillies took the Cy Young Award after winning nearly half of his team's games (a 27-10 record with a league-leading 1.98 ERA and 310 Ks). Even with the league's Rookie of the Year in pitcher Jon Matlack (15-10, 2.32 ERA), the Mets could only take third. Billy Williams of the second-place Cubs was the batting champ at .333.

In the American League, Dick Allen celebrated his first year in Chicago by blasting 37 home runs and knocking in 113 runs, both league-leading totals, and earning MVP honors. Gaylord Perry of Cleveland finished at 24-16 with a 1.92 ERA, good enough for the Cy Young Award. Boston's Luis Tiant won the ERA crown with a 1.91 mark. Rod Carew of the 77-77 Twins won his second batting title with a .318 average. Rookie of the Year Carlton Fisk (.293 average, 22 home runs, 61 RBI) caught for the Red Sox, who could not catch the Tigers, losing the East Division by a half-game margin.

That difference was the result of a players' strike that canceled the season's first two weeks.

TENACE STARS IN YEAR OF UNSUNG HEROES

Those missing games came back to haunt the teams vying for the AL East title, as Detroit's 86-70 mark bested Boston's 85-70 record by virtue of having played— and won—one extra game.

In off-the-field news, the Rangers came to Arlington, Texas, from Washington, D.C., in the off-season. Pittsburgh's Roberto Clemente, who had racked up his 3,000th hit near the final day of the regular season, was killed in a plane crash that occurred on December 31. And Curt Flood lost his suit against baseball after the Supreme Court upheld the game's reserve clause, which binds a player to the team that owns his contract.

The playoffs hosted several improbable comebacks in both leagues. In the NL, the Reds and Pirates split the first two games; Pittsburgh then came from behind to win game three. The Reds took game four on a two-hitter by Ross Grimsley. Trailing 3-2 going into the ninth inning of the final game, the Reds tied it on Bench's leadoff homer off Dave Giusti, and singles by Tony Perez and

Denis Menke chased the Pirates' palmballer. The loser of game two, reliever Bob Moose threw a wild pitch to allow the series-winning run to score.

Oakland came back in the 11th inning of game one of the ALCS to beat Mickey Lolich 3-2. A Jim Northrup single won the fourth game 4-3 for the Tigers. Oakland's Blue Moon Odom and Vida Blue combined for the tournament-clinching 2-1 win in game five.

In a year of unlikely heroes, Oakland's Gene Tenace was the most timely. A part-time catcher and utility man with 20 career home runs over four years, Tenace opened the World Series by slugging two round-trippers, the first man ever to homer in both of his first two Series at-bats. The A's won it 3-2, then took game two 2-1.

The Reds came alive in Oakland, winning game three 1-0 behind Jack Billingham and Clay Carroll. After dropping game four on Oakland's two-run, ninth-inning rally, Cincinnati came back to withstand Tenace's fourth home run of the Series—a three-run shot—and win game five 5-4. The Reds took apart the A's 8-1 in the sixth game.

Series MVP Tenace then drove in two runs in the 3-2 Oakland victory, the first World Championship for the A's since 1930, when they hailed from Philadelphia.

1972

- A's end Orioles' reign in AL and capture first pennant since 1931.
- Reds win NL flag.
- Tigers take A's to five games in ALCS.
- Reds beat Pirates in five games, scoring game five's winning run in the bottom of the ninth on a wild pitch by Bob Moose.

- A's take World Series in seven games.
- Oakland wins game seven of Series 3-2, as reliever Rollie Fingers stifles an eighth-inning uprising.
- Oakland's Gene Tenace hits .348 with four homers and nine RBI in Series.
- The Reds' Tony Perez leads all Series players with ten hits and a .435 BA.

- Catfish Hunter wins two games for A's in Series, as does Ross Grimsley for Reds.
- For first time in World Series history, no pitcher on either team turns in a complete game.
- Johnny Bench wins second NL MVP.
- Chicago's Dick Allen is AL MVP.

The 1972 World Series, played out in seven acts, had Gene Tenace (shown here catching) as its hero. Tony Perez (the batter) was one of the few valuable players the Reds had in the Series. Tenace accounted for four of Oakland's five home runs—he was the first player to nail round-trippers in his first two at-bats in the World Series—and nine of the ballclub's 16 RBI. A substitute catcher for most of the '72 season, Tenace and his weak arm were stationed at first base in '73. Perez batted .435 with three runs scored and two RBI in the fall classic.

- Phillie Steve Carlton wins NL Cy Young.

- Carlton wins 15 straight games (and 27 overall) for the Phils, who win only 59 games all told.

- Carlton is responsible for 45.8 percent of his team's wins—a post-1893 ML record.

- Carlton leads majors in wins (27) and CGs (30), and tops NL in Ks (310), innings pitched (346), and ERA (1.98).

- Cleveland's Gaylord Perry wins AL Cy Young after tying for loop lead in wins (24) and leading in complete games (29).

- First players' strike in ML history ends on April 10; several games are not made up, and Boston loses to Tigers by a half-game.

- Roberto Clemente produces his 3,000th hit on Sept. 30, and then dies in a plane crash in late December.

Lolich On Top in 22

Mickey Lolich

Despite losing several starts to the players' strike of 1972, ace lefty Mickey Lolich won 22 games for the Tigers, finishing second in the American League that season, and tallied a 2.50 ERA. Due to an unequal number of games played, the Tigers went on to defeat the Red Sox by a half-game, winning one of the most unusual pennant races in the history of the sport.

Seaver: 21 Wins, 249 Ks

A 21-12 record with 249 strikeouts would constitute a career year for most pitchers. For Tom Seaver, however—a pitcher who would eventually total 311 games—it was a standard season. In addition to his 20-plus victories, the Mets star posted 262 innings, just 77 walks, and a 2.92 ERA in 1972. Despite his excellent performance, he didn't lead the league in a single pitching category that year.

Tom Seaver

Steve Carlton

Carlton Leads Phils

One can only imagine how many games the 1972 Phillies would have lost without the services of Steve Carlton (shown receiving the Cy Young Award from Warren Giles, president emeritus of the National League that year). As it was, the ballclub was victorious in just 59 games, 27 of those triumphs being credited to Carlton. No pitcher before or since has ever won as high a percentage of his team's victories in a single season.

1972

- Billy Williams tops majors in BA (.333), SA (.606), and total bases (348).
- Bench leads majors in homers (40) and RBI (125).
- Fired by Twins after guiding team to two straight division titles, Billy Martin wins AL East for Tigers.

- NL wins All-Star Game 4-3 in Atlanta in ten innings—this is the NL's seventh win in seven overtime games.
- On Sept. 2, Cub Milt Pappas no-hits the Padres; Pappas loses perfect game by walking the 27th man on a 3-2 pitch.

- Burt Hooton of the Cubs no-hits Phils on April 16.
- Bill Stoneman of the Expos no-hits Mets on Oct. 2.
- Boston's Carlton Fisk is a unanimous choice for AL ROTY.
- New York's Jon Matlack is NL ROTY.

Matlack Is NL ROTY

In 1972, lefty Jon Matlack became the second Met to capture Rookie of the Year honors, following Tom Seaver in 1967. The only Met who could better Matlack's record of 15 victories in '72 was Seaver, who collected 21 triumphs that season. Matlack also tallied a 2.32 ERA and four shutouts in his first full season.

Jon Matlack

Willie Stargell

Willie Keeps On Swinging

In 1972, Willie Stargell forged another link on the chain of stellar seasons that led to Cooperstown. He totaled 33 home runs and 112 RBI that season. He had a less-than-spectacular National League Championship Series that year, however, batting a mere .063 as the Pirates dropped a heartbreaking five-game duel with the Reds.

Bob Moose

Moose Blows the NLCS

Bob Moose of the Pirates faces the press after throwing the most infamous pitch in the history of the National League Championship Series. With two out in the bottom of the ninth inning of the fifth and deciding contest of the 1972 playoffs, the Pirate pitcher bounced a pitch past catcher Manny Sanguillen. The wild toss allowed George Foster to score the run that clinched the pennant for the Reds. In two games in the playoffs, Moose retired just two men and recorded a 54.00 ERA.

- Detroit's Ed Brinkman sets new ML FA record of .990 for shortstops, including 72 straight errorless games.

- Washington franchise moved to Texas, renamed the "Rangers."

- Al Kaline's AL record streak of 242 consecutive errorless games in the outfield ends.

- Rod Carew wins AL bat title (.318), and is first bat crown winner to go homerless since Zach Wheat in 1918.

- SF's Jim Barr retires an ML record 41 batters in a row over two games.

- Allen leads AL in homers (37), RBI (113), runs produced (166), OBP (.422), and SA (.603).

- On August 1, Padre Nate Colbert hits ML record-tying five homers in doubleheader and collects ML record 13 RBI.

- California's Nolan Ryan tops AL in strikeouts (329) and sets all-time ML record by allowing only 5.26 hits per game.

Foster Clinches NLCS

While playing a most uncharacteristic role as a pinch runner for Tony Perez, George Foster scored the fourth and deciding run of the 1972 National League Championship Series. Reds manager Sparky Anderson can't contain himself as he relishes his second pennant in his third year as manager of the Cincinnati ballclub.

George Foster, Sparky Anderson

Rod Carew

Carew Wins AL Bat Title

With a swing that looked like the mechanical motion of a spring-wound toy, Panamanian Rod Carew became the first batting champion to win his crown without hitting a single home run in 1972. Along with his .318 average that season, he accumulated 21 doubles, six triples, 51 RBI, and 61 runs scored. His '72 award was the first of four consecutive American League batting titles for Carew, who totaled seven circuit-topping hitting averages over his 19-year career.

Clemente Is Killed

Roberto Clemente died in a plane crash on New Year's Eve in 1972, while on a mission to bring relief aid to earthquake victims in Nicaragua. It seems both eerie and appropriate that Clemente's final hit of the 1972 season was the 3,000th of his fabled career. Just 38 years old when he died, Clemente batted .312 in 1972 and had hit .290-plus in 14 consecutive seasons.

Roberto Clemente

1972

- The Hall of Fame inducts Sandy Koufax, Yogi Berra, Early Wynn, Lefty Gomez, Will Harridge, Ross Youngs, Josh Gibson, and Buck Leonard.

- Pappas becomes first pitcher in history to collect 200 career wins without ever having won 20 games in a season.

- Fisk becomes the only catcher to top the AL in triples, tying Oakland's Joe Rudi for the lead with nine.

- Fisk is second AL rookie catcher in three years to win a Gold Glove.

- Atlanta's Felix Millan wins second Gold Glove as NL second baseman.

- Jackie Robinson dies.

- Pie Traynor dies.

- Zach Wheat dies.

- Gabby Hartnett dies.

- Mets manager Gil Hodges dies of a heart attack.

Murcer Nets 33 Dingers, 102 Runs

Yankee fans couldn't help but compare Bobby Murcer to Mickey Mantle, especially after Murcer's Gold Glove season of 1972. That year, the 26-year-old center fielder hit .292 with 33 home runs (second in the American League), 102 runs scored (first in the circuit), and 96 RBI (third in the loop); he also topped the league in total bases and putouts. His '72 showing earned him his second All-Star Game appearance.

Bobby Murcer

Wilbur Wood

Williams: 37 HRs, 122 RBI

Billy Williams never swung sweeter than in 1972, when he was named the *Sporting News* Major League Player of the Year. Williams batted .333 in '72, nailing 37 home runs and knocking in 122 runs for the second-place Cubs. He finished second in National League MVP balloting that year.

Billy Williams

Wood Wins 24 Games

In his first six major league seasons, Wilbur Wood won just five games. After learning the intricacies of the knuckleball from teammate and future Hall of Famer Hoyt Wilhelm, though, Wood forged a series of great seasons. The highlight year of his career was 1972. The lefty went 24-17 that season, tying for the AL lead in wins.

Dusty Baker

Rookie Baker Hits .321

Dusty Baker batted .321 in 1972, his first full season in the majors, placing third in the batting race. He also mustered 17 home runs and 76 RBI that season. Just a 27th-round draft choice by the Braves, Baker was described by Hank Aaron as having more potential than any outfielder he had seen.

- Freddy Parent, last survivor of the first World Series, dies at 96.
- Oakland uses an ML record 30 men in a 15-inning game against Chicago on Sept. 19.
- The new Rangers score just 461 runs and collect only 424 RBI.
- Prior to the season, St. Louis ships Carlton to Philadelphia for Rick Wise.
- Cleveland trades Graig Nettles and Gerry Moses to the Yankees for four players.
- The Yanks trade Danny Cater to Boston for Sparky Lyle.
- The Reds swap young Hal McRae and Wayne Simpson to Kansas City for Roger Nelson and Richie Scheinblum.
- The Angels send Andy Messersmith and Ken McMullen to the Dodgers for Frank Robinson, Bill Singer, and three other players.

Oakland A's

Rollie Preserves the Win

In 1972, his first full season as a reliever, Rollie Fingers (photographed pitching in the World Series) won 11 games, saved another 21 contests, and cultivated the greatest handlebar moustache since surrealistic painter Salvador Dali. In the seventh game of the '72 World Series, he worked out of a bases-loaded, one-out jam to save a 3-2 victory and the championship trophy for the A's.

Rollie Fingers

A's Celebrate the Win

Charley Finley's Swingin' A's were caught in a trio of World Series mob scenes in the early 1970s. The ballclub's victory in 1972 marked the first franchise triumph for Oakland. The A's remain the only major league team to win three straight World Titles since the Yankee ballclub of 1949 to 1953.

Hunter Is Series Ace

Crafty veteran Catfish Hunter provided both leadership and pitching savvy for the 1972 World Champion A's, as he won a pair of games and compiled a sterling 2.81 ERA over the run of the Series. Hunter sweated through a tense second game in the fall classic: He allowed just a single earned run in 8²/₃ innings as he was saved by a home run and a memorable catch, both courtesy of left fielder Joe Rudi.

Catfish Hunter

1972

- The Giants send Willie Mays to the Mets for Charlie Williams and $50,000.

- Montreal deals Rusty Staub to the Mets for Ken Singleton, Tim Foli, and Mike Jorgensen.

- Yankee Bobby Murcer tops AL in runs (102) and total bases (314).

- The Phils send Don Money and two other players to Milwaukee for Jim Lonborg, Ken Brett, and two others.

- Tigers manager Martin is shown giving the world the finger on his 1972 baseball card.

- Bill Mazeroski retires holding the NL record for most games at second base (2,094).

- On July 14, Bill Haller umps behind the plate in a game which is caught by his brother—Tom Haller of the Tigers.

- Cincinnati's Clay Carroll sets a new ML save record with 37.

- On Oct. 3, Oriole Roric Harrison becomes the last AL pitcher to homer prior to interleague play.

Reds Hang On to Win Game Five

Pinch runner Blue Moon Odom is tagged out by Johnny Bench in a dramatic ninth-inning play at home plate to preserve a 5-4 Cincinnati victory in game five of the 1972 World Series. Odom attempted to score with one out from third base on a drifting pop fly to Joe Morgan in short right field. Umpire Bob Engel is just about to signal an out call.

World Series

Rollie Fingers, Dave Duncan

Fingers Closes Series

Catcher Dave Duncan congratulates Rollie Fingers, who just forced Pete Rose to fly out to Joe Rudi for the last out of the 1972 World Series. Sal Bando heads for the duo. It was the fourth one-run Oakland win of the Series.

Reds Fizzle in Series

Neither Reds shortstop Darrel Chaney nor any of his teammates could stop the relentless march of the A's toward their first of three consecutive World Championships in 1972. Chaney posted a disastrous career record in postseason play, netting just three singles in 35 at-bats. He went 0-for-7 in the '72 Series. As for the rest of the staff, the Reds matched the A's in team batting average (.209) and hits (46) and beat them in runs scored, doubles, triples, RBI, and stolen bases—and yet it was the A's who reigned victorious.

World Series

- White Sox Wilbur Wood's 49 starts are the most in the majors since 1908.

- Tom Seaver receives $172,000 to become the highest-paid hurler in ML history to this juncture.

- Joe Morgan leads NL in runs (122), walks (115), and OBP (.419).

- Philly's Willie Montanez and Houston's Cesar Cedeno top majors in doubles with 39.

- Philly's Larry Bowa leads majors with 13 triples.

- Lou Brock leads NL in steals (63); Bert Campaneris tops AL (52).

- Rudi leads AL in hits (181).

- Boston's Luis Tiant has best ERA in majors (1.91).

- Hunter wins 21 for the A's and ties Cincinnati's Gary Nolan for best win pct. in majors (.750).

- Lyle of New York leads AL with 35 saves.

MEDIOCRE METS CAN'T STEAL CROWN FROM A'S

What was amazing this time around was that the Mets, barely a .500 team, came so close to a World Series victory. Except for Cy Young Award-winner Tom Seaver (19-10, a league-best 2.08 ERA), the Mets had a cast completely worthy of their 82-79 record—their .509 winning percentage was the worst ever for a league or division winner.

Fortunately for them, the rest of the NL East had similar problems. Of the sub-.500 teams still in the race during the last week of the season, only two teams could boast heavy hitters: league home run and RBI champ Willie Stargell of Pittsburgh (.299 average, 44 home runs, 119 RBI) and Ken Singleton (23 home runs, 103 RBI) and Bob Bailey (26 home runs, 86 RBI) of the Expos.

In the West, Sparky Anderson's Reds ran roughshod over everyone, with batting champion and league MVP Pete Rose (a .338 batter who topped the majors with 230 hits) leading the way to a 99-63 record. The league's premier rookie was Gary Matthews of third-place San Francisco, a left fielder who hit an even .300 with 12 homers and 58 RBI.

The American League unveiled its new Designated Hitter Rule as Boston met New York in the season's first game (Ron Blomberg drew a walk off Luis Tiant). The league's Rookie of the Year was Baltimore's Al Bumbry, who hit .337 in a half-

season. Cy Young Award-winner and ERA champ Jim Palmer (22-9, 2.40 ERA), Mike Cuellar (18-13), and Dave McNally (17-17) carried the Orioles to an 8-game edge over Boston. Reggie Jackson of the A's was named league MVP with a .293 average and circuit-leading 32 home runs and 117 RBI. Minnesota's Rod Carew took his second straight batting title (third overall), finishing at .350.

California Angel Nolan Ryan broke Sandy Koufax's single-season strikeout record by whiffing 383 batters (he also threw two no-hitters). Hank Aaron withstood intense media scrutiny and clubbed 40 more homers, bringing him to 713—one dinger short of Babe Ruth's record total.

The defending champion Oakland A's won the West by 6 games over Kansas City, behind the power of Jackson, Sal Bando (.287 average, 29 home runs, 98 RBI), and Gene Tenace (.259, 24, 84) and the pitching of Ken Holtzman (21-13, 2.97 ERA),

Vida Blue (20-9, 3.27), Catfish Hunter (21-5, 3.34), and Rollie Fingers (22 saves, 1.91 ERA).

The A's used the full five games to knock off the Orioles in the ALCS, with Hunter shutting out the O's 3-0 in the final game. The Mets won the NL pennant over the Reds in five complete games. New York outscored Cincinnati 23-8 and sported a team ERA of 1.33 for the NLCS (they also outfought them, with Bud Harrelson outlasting Rose in the infamous game-three brawl which nearly overshadowed the Mets' 9-2 victory).

Oakland defeated New York to, once again, claim the World Series crown. After the A's took game one 2-1, their five errors in game two allowed the Mets to walk away with a 12-inning, 10-7 win. Although Willie Mays won it for New York on the last hit of his career, a single up the middle, the pair of errors by reserve second baseman Mike Andrews in the final frame got most of the press.

Forced by owner Charley O. Finley to undergo a medical exam minutes after game two, Andrews was subsequently dropped from the team. He was reinstated for the next game by commissioner Bowie Kuhn. The A's gave Andrews a rousing send-off by winning the last two matches at home to finally put away the Mets four games to three. Manager Dick Williams left the team at the conclusion of the Series.

1973

- Oakland grabs its second consecutive AL flag.
- Mets win in NL with .509 win pct., lowest ever for ML flag winner.
- Oakland defeats Baltimore in five games in ALCS, as Catfish Hunter shuts out the Orioles in game five.
- Mets beat Reds in five games in NLCS, as Mets pitchers post 1.33 ERA.
- Mets take A's to seven games in World Series before succumbing.
- Ken Holtzman wins two Series games for Oakland.
- New York's Rusty Staub tops all batters in Series with 11 hits, .423 BA, and six RBI.
- The Mets and A's make for first World Series in history without a .300-hitting regular on either team.
- Oakland's Reggie Jackson is AL MVP, leading loop in homers (32), RBI (117), runs (99), and SA (.531).

Oakland pitching coach Wes Stock *(left)* and catcher Ray Fosse greet Rollie Fingers after the ace reliever retired the Mets in a one-two-three ninth inning to win game six of the 1973 World Series. Appearing in six of the seven Series games in '73, Fingers yielded just one run and saved two games.

- Pete Rose cops NL MVP.

- Tom Seaver wins Cy Young in NL although he wins just 19 games, five less than Ron Bryant of Giants.

- Jim Palmer wins Cy Young in AL.

- Willie Stargell tops ML in homers (44), doubles (43), RBI (119), and SA (.646).

- Third "Basic Agreement" gives players the right to salary arbitration and to "five and ten" rule with respect to trades.

- White Sox Wilbur Wood is first pitcher in 57 years to both win and lose 20 games in a season, as he goes 24-20.

- Ship magnate George Steinbrenner buys the Yankees.

- On July 20, Wood becomes last ML hurler to start both games of a doubleheader; he loses both.

- Oriole Bobby Grich's .995 FA sets ML record for second basemen.

DH Blomberg Hits .329

On Opening Day 1973, Ron Blomberg became the first designated hitter in major league history. The oft-injured slugger enjoyed his best year in the '73 season; he batted .329 in 100 games for the Yankees, collecting a dozen home runs in the process.

Willie Mays

Ron Blomberg

Mays Plays Out Final Season

Perhaps the most notorious trade of 1972 was that of aging superstar Willie Mays of the Giants for journeyman pitcher Charlie Williams of the Mets. Always a New York favorite, Mays couldn't produce the magic he wielded in the Polo Grounds in the 1950s. In his last year of play, 1973, Mays tallied a mere .211 average, with a half-dozen home runs and 25 RBI in 209 at-bats.

Tony Perez

Perez Is the Main Cog in the Machine

Many consider Tony Perez to have been the greatest of the great players who comprised the Big Red Machine of the 1970s. He displayed his quiet leadership, steady fielding, and prodigious power hitting in six League Championship Series and five World Series. In 1973, Perez helped take the Reds to a division title on the force of his .314 batting average, 27 home runs, and 101 RBI.

1973

- Detroit's John Hiller sets new ML record with 38 saves.

- Nolan Ryan fans ML record 383.

- Braves have three men with at least 40 homers—Dave Johnson (43), Darrell Evans (41), and Hank Aaron (40).

- Yankee pitchers Mike Kekich and Fritz Peterson swap wives, families, houses, and dogs.

- AL adopts designated hitter rule—pitchers no longer have to bat for themselves.

- On April 6, Yankee Ron Blomberg becomes first DH to bat in ML.

- NL wins All-Star Game 7-1 at Kansas City, as a record 54 players participate.

- Giant Gary Matthews wins the NL ROTY Award.

- Baltimore's Al Bumbry is AL ROTY.

- Steve Busby of KC no-hits Detroit on April 27.

Palmer Wins AL Cy Young

Sporting a 22-9 record and a 2.40 ERA (best in the loop), Jim Palmer captured the 1973 American League Cy Young Award, his first of three such honors in four years. Always a master of control, the unflappable Palmer never surrendered a grandslam during his 16 years as an Oriole. Palmer probably hated to see the new designated hitter rule that started that season; he collected 22 hits in '72.

Jim Palmer

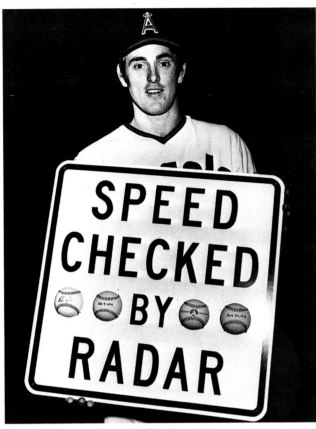

Nolan Ryan

Ryan Tosses Two No-Nos

In 1973, Nolan Ryan became the fifth pitcher in major league history to hurl two no-hitters in one season. Ryan no-hit the Royals on May 15, then turned the trick on Detroit on July 15, striking out 17 Tigers.

Rose Named NL MVP

Pete Rose won his sole National League MVP Award in 1973, batting .338 and gathering 230 hits, both top marks in the circuit. The switch-hitting outfielder also collected 115 runs scored, making the '73 year one of his best seasons of the 1970s. He was rewarded with the title of *Sporting News* Player of the Decade.

Pete Rose

- Ryan no-hits KC on May 15.

- Ryan no-hits the Tigers on July 15.

- Jim Bibby of Texas no-hits Oakland on July 20.

- Rose wins NL bat crown (.338) and leads majors in hits (230).

- Phil Niekro of Atlanta no-hits San Diego on August 5.

- Rod Carew leads AL in BA (.350) and hits (203), and ties for lead in triples (11).

- Giant Bobby Bonds just misses becoming first 40/40 player in ML history, as he hits 39 homers and steals 43 bases.

- Wood ties Bryant for ML lead in wins with 24.

- Seaver leads NL in ERA (2.08) and strikeouts (251), and ties for lead in CGs (18).

- The two leagues steal more than 2,000 bases combined for the first time since the dead-ball era.

Mike Kekich

Kekich Deals Wife, Kids to Peterson

The Bronx Zoo never seemed more weird than early in the 1973 season, when hard-throwing Yankee southpaw Mike Kekich decided to trade wives and families with teammate Fritz Peterson. Kekich would himself be traded to Cleveland midway through the 1973 season—he ended the year 2-5 with a 7.48 ERA—and receive his unconditional release in 1974.

Peterson Fares Better in Swaps

Of their two wife-swapping pitchers, the Yankees held on to Fritz Peterson for the 1973 season while trading teammate Mike Kekich (and Peterson's former wife) to Cleveland. After posting an 8-15 season in 1973 and starting off 1974 with 13 hits in eight innings, Peterson was also given his walking papers. He arrived in Cleveland just as the Tribe was releasing Kekich.

Fritz Peterson

Gary Matthews

Matthews: NL ROTY

Hustling Gary Matthews (pictured in a habitually soiled uniform) proved to be the perfect complement to Giant teammates Bobby Bonds and Garry Maddox, as the trio comprised one of the great National League outfields of the '70s. Matthews won the 1973 National League Rookie of the Year Award, hitting an even .300, nailing a dozen home runs, and scoring 74 runs.

1973

- The Hall of Fame inducts Warren Spahn, Billy Evans, George Kelly, Mickey Welch, Monte Irvin, and Roberto Clemente.
- George Sisler dies.
- Frankie Frisch dies.
- Chick Hafey dies.

- The Cubs deal Fergie Jenkins to Texas for Bill Madlock and Vic Harris.
- Cubs send Ron Santo to ChiSox for four prospects.
- LA sends Willie Davis to Montreal for Mike Marshall.
- Davis, while still with LA, goes 6-for-9 in 19 innings on May 24.

- Johnny Briggs of the Brewers goes 6-for-6 on August 4.
- Paul Lindblad's record streak of 385 consecutive errorless games at pitcher ends.
- Willie Mays retires holding the record for most career chances by an NL outfielder (7,290).

Willie Stargell

Borbon a Joy in Cincy

Always a crowd-pleaser, star reliever Pedro Borbon would show off during pregame practice by throwing strikes from the center field warning track. He pleased the Reds in 1973, collecting an 11-4 record and 14 saves. He capped off his best season by winning one game and saving another in the '73 National League Championship Series.

Pedro Borbon

Stargell Still the Best

Willie Stargell maintained his status as the premier power hitter in the National League in 1973 by racking up circuit-leading figures in doubles (43), home runs (44), RBI (119), and slugging average (.646). No National Leaguer would reach his slugging mark for 20 years. Despite Stargell's heroics, the Pirates finished 2½ games behind the Mets to end the season in third place.

Tom Seaver

Seaver Loses Game One of NLCS

Home runs by Pete Rose and Johnny Bench defeated Tom Seaver (pictured) by a score of 2-1 in the first game of the 1973 National League Championship Series. The Mets ace bounced back in game five, keeping the Reds scoreless after they tied the game at two-all in the top of the fifth inning, to lead the New York team to the flag.

- Luis Aparicio retires with the ML record for most career games at shortstop (2,581).

- California's Frank Robinson homers in a record 32nd ML park in use during his career.

- Seven of the 24 regular ML shortstops go homerless for the entire season.

- Bonds hits a season record 11 homers leading off a game.

- After going 19-8 in 1972, Pirate Steve Blass goes 3-9 with a 9.85 ERA and 84 walks in 89 innings; he never regains his form.

- Royals Stadium opens on April 10, Texas vs. KC.

- The mediocre Mets are first team in history to win pennant without a 20-game winner, .300 hitter, or 100-RBI man.

- Milwaukee's Pedro Garcia and Oakland's Sal Bando tie for AL lead in doubles with 32—an AL record for fewest in a season by leader.

Mets Triumph in NLCS

Pete Rose slides into shortstop Bud Harrelson in the fifth inning of game three of the 1973 National League Championship Series. It was this slide that started a brawl between Rose and Harrelson that cleared both benches and incited attendees in the left-field stands to pelt Rose with garbage. Neither team scored any more runs after the incident, as New York defeated Cincinnati 9-2.

NLCS

Holtzman Measures Up

Christened "The New Koufax" while a 20-year-old rookie in 1966, lefty Ken Holtzman bore the burden of comparison with the Dodger immortal. Although Holtzman seemed to be on the road to record-setting seasons as a Cub—a 9-0 record in 1967, a no-hitter against Atlanta in '69, another no-hitter in '71, a 19-11 record in '72—it was with the A's that he secured lasting fame. He won 21 games for the A's during the 1973 season, took the third contest of the ALCS with an 11-inning complete game, and won games one and seven of the World Series.

Sal Bando

Bando Does Double Duty for the A's

Sal Bando proved to be a leader for Oakland both on and off the field in 1973. Following the forced benching and "firing" of Oakland reserve infielder Mike Andrews, Bando distributed black arm-bands tagged with "17" (the number Andrews wore) to his teammates. His protest flew in the face of team owner Charley Finley and endeared him to fans everywhere. During the regular '73 season, Bando topped the American League with 32 doubles. In World Series action that fall, Bando scored five runs.

Ken Holtzman

1973

- Ryan and Bill Singer of Angels fan 624 men between them—a post-1893 ML teammate record.

- John Mayberry of KC tops AL in walks (122) and OBP (.420).

- Roger Metzger of Houston leads ML with 14 triples.

- Montreal's Ken Singleton leads NL in OBP (.429).

- Lou Brock tops majors with 70 steals.

- Tommy Harper of Boston tops AL in steals (54).

- Hunter leads the majors with an .808 win pct.

- Wood leads ML in innings (359).

- Steve Carlton ties Cincinnati's Jack Billingham for NL lead in innings (293).

- Minnesota's Bert Blyleven leads ML with nine shutouts; Billingham leads NL with seven.

1973

Tug McGraw, Rollie Fingers

McGraw, Rollie Shine in Series

The two bullpen aces of the 1973 World Series, Tug McGraw *(left)* of the Mets and Rollie Fingers of the A's were also two of the game's most spirited characters. McGraw voiced the rallying cry of "Ya Gotta Believe" while flapping his glove on his thigh after each of his 25 saves in '73. In Series action that year, he posted one win, one save, and 14 strikeouts in $13^2/3$ innings. The moustache-twirling Fingers compiled a 1.91 ERA over the season and a 0.66 mark over the Series.

World Series

Mets Fall

Willie Mays makes an appeal as Bud Harrelson of the Mets is declared out in the tenth inning of the second game of the 1973 World Series. Harrelson had tried to score from third on Felix Millan's short fly ball to left. Joe Rudi nailed him to end the threat.

Rusty Staub

Staub Takes Game Four on a Dinger

A legend in Montreal, where he was known to fans as "Le Grande Orange," Rusty Staub played a key role for the Mets in postseason play in 1973. After hurting his shoulder crashing into Shea Stadium's right-field wall in the fourth game of the playoffs, Staub was given cortisone shots and had to throw underhanded in the World Series. He nevertheless hit an opposite-field home run off Oakland's Ken Holtzman to win game four.

- Marshall leads NL in saves with 31 and sets a new ML record with 92 mound appearances.

- Cleveland's Gaylord Perry tops the ML with 29 CGs.

- The AL, in first year of the DH rule, has 167 more CGs than the NL but only seven more shutouts.

- Palmer heads the AL in ERA (2.40).

- The AL outhits the NL .259 to .254—first time since 1963 that the AL has done this.

- A year after winning the AL East, Billy Martin is let go as Tigers manager in September, and is immediately hired by Texas.

- Rookie manager Whitey Herzog is fired by Texas after Rangers go 47-91 under him and finish last in AL.

- The Mets win NL East flag in which five teams finish within 5 games of first place.

- Last-place Phillies finish just $11^1/2$ games out of first.

In his career, Al Downing pitched for four teams and appeared in three World Series. As a Yankee in 1964, he led the American League in strikeouts. Seven seasons later, he went 20-9 with the Dodgers. However, most fans remember the 17-year veteran for something other than his career feats. On April 8 at 9:07 p.m. EST, a national television audience watched Downing serve up the pitch that Hammerin' Hank Aaron hit out of the ballpark for his 715th home run a new major league record.

The shot ended a mini-controversy. Braves owner Bill Bartholomay wanted Aaron to sit out the opening three-game series at Cincinnati, hoping his aging star would break the record before a packed hometown crowd. Commissioner Bowie Kuhn, however, insisted Aaron play. And on the first swing of his first at-bat of the year, the 40-year-old outfielder tied Babe Ruth's seemingly unreachable record. By season's end, the man with the wrists of steel had upped his career total to 733.

Other notable milestones involved Redbirds Bob Gibson and Lou Brock. En route to a disappointing 11-13 season, the 38-year-old Gibson became only the second pitcher to record 3,000 Ks, while the 35-year-old Brock hit .306 and established a new steals record, swiping 118.

HANK'S THE NEW HOME RUN KING, CRACKS NO. 715

In the American League, Detroit star Al Kaline wrapped up an outstanding 22-year career by collecting his 3,000th hit (he also finished with 399 home runs). Angels flamethrower Nolan Ryan notched his third career no-hitter.

The one record-setter who figured in a pennant race was Dodger reliever Mike Marshall. Los Angeles won the NL West, finishing 4 up on Cincinnati, as the Cy Young winner appeared in an unprecedented 106 games, winning 15 and leading the league with 21 saves. Teammate Steve Garvey (.312 average, 21 home runs, 111 RBI) won the MVP Award. Garvey also hit .389 in the NLCS to lead LA over Pittsburgh three games to one. The Pirates had won the NL East on the bats of Richie Zisk (100 RBI), Al Oliver (.321 average), and Willie Stargell (25 home runs).

The Oakland A's displayed the form that made them World Champions in 1972 and '73, fin-

ishing 5 games ahead of Texas. Catfish Hunter (25-12) won the Cy Young Award, and Reggie Jackson (.289 average, 29 home runs, 93 RBI) supplied the pop.

The most compelling pennant race of the season came in the AL East. Baltimore rallied to win 27 of 33 (including 15 one-run games) to edge the Yankees by 2 games. However, the Orioles were no match for the A's in the ALCS, falling three games to one.

Oakland and Los Angeles waged California's version of a Subway Series. The first three games were decided by the identical scores of 3-2. Jackson's homer gave Oakland the edge in game one, and Los Angeles evened the Series in game two when Marshall picked off designated runner Herb Washington to kill a ninth-inning rally. In game three, the A's capitalized on two Dodger errors, giving them a two-games-to-one World Series lead. Oakland won game four 5-2, as pitcher Ken Holtzman, who had logged in two regular seasons without an at-bat, belted a home run.

In game five, with his team trailing 3-2, Dodger Bill Buckner was gunned down trying to stretch a double into a triple in the eighth inning. A's reliever Rollie Fingers preserved the win, giving Oakland its third title in as many years. It was the only non-Yankee three-peat in World Series history.

1974

- Oakland wins its third consecutive AL flag.
- Dodgers triumph in NL.
- A's need only four games to subdue Orioles in ALCS.
- LA likewise dispatches Pittsburgh in four in NLCS.

- A's take third consecutive World Championship in five games.
- LA reliever Mike Marshall appears in every World Series game, saving one and losing one.
- For the third Series in a row, no pitcher turns in a CG.

- Four of the five Series games are 3-2 affairs, and only Oakland's Joe Rudi (four RBI) knocks in more than two runs.
- A's players win championship despite dislike for owner Charley Finley and, in some cases, for one another.
- Dodger Steve Garvey is NL MVP.

No hitter before or since had stronger or quicker wrists than Hank Aaron. Although he never hit 50 dingers in one season, Aaron continues to reign as the all-time home run king, having eclipsed Babe Ruth during the 1974 season (his 21st year in the major leagues); he hit 20 dingers that year, bringing his career total to 733.

- Ranger Jeff Burroughs wins AL MVP after topping the AL in RBI (118) and runs produced (177).

- Catfish Hunter wins AL Cy Young in close vote over Ranger Ferguson Jenkins.

- Both Hunter and Jenkins tie for ML lead in wins with 25.

- NL Cy Young winner Marshall appears in ML record 106 games and is first reliever to cop the award.

- Hank Aaron hits ML record 715th career homer on April 8 off Al Downing of Dodgers.

- Phillie Mike Schmidt tops majors with 36 homers.

- Lou Brock shatters ML record by stealing 118 bases.

- Rod Carew takes AL bat crown (.364).

- White Sox Dick Allen tops AL in homers (32) and SA (.563).

- Pete Rose makes ML record 771 plate appearances.

Steve Garvey

Carew Leads AL in Batting

Rod Carew was the greatest singles hitter of his era. He led the American League in batting seven times in his 19-year career in the majors. In 1974, he had a loop-high .364 average, although he socked just three home runs and knocked in only 55 runs. In his eight-year career to that point, Carew had been named to seven All-Star teams; he lost the 1970 season—and quite possibly the All-Star vote—due to military service.

Rod Carew

Garvey Named NL MVP

Nicknamed "Senator" for his post-baseball career aspirations, Dodgers first baseman Steve Garvey played in his first World Series in 1974. Although his team bowed to the A's in the battle for the World Crown, Garvey achieved an excellent individual season: a .312 average, 21 home runs, and 111 RBI. His performance earned him Most Valuable Player honors in the National League. Voted to a starting position in the All-Star Game by write-in ballots, the powerhouse took the game's MVP honors.

1974

- Ron LeFlore debuts with the Tigers the year after being released from prison.

- On June 4 in Cleveland, 10-cent beer night results in near riot and forfeit of game to Texas.

- Milwaukee's Don Money sets a new ML season FA record for third basemen (.989).

- The Orioles set an AL record when they win five straight games by shutouts.

- Johnny Bench leads NL with 129 RBI and 315 total bases.

- Rose tops ML with 110 runs and 45 doubles.

- Atlanta's Ralph Garr tops the NL with a .353 batting average, 214 hits, and 17 triples.

- NL wins All-Star Game 7-2 at Pittsburgh for 11th win in last 12 games.

- Mike Hargrove of the Rangers named AL ROTY.

Fergie Jenkins

Bench Leads NL in RBI

Johnny Bench knocked in a National League-leading 129 runs in 1974 while taking the Reds to a second-place finish, 4 games behind the Dodgers. It was the third RBI crown for the man considered by many to be the greatest catcher of all time. Bench was voted to the All-Star lineup 13 years in a row and won ten consecutive Gold Gloves.

Johnny Bench

Jenkins Wins 25

Following his worst season with the Cubs (14-16 in 1973), Fergie Jenkins was traded to the Texas Rangers for Bill Madlock and Vic Harris. The Rangers received quick dividends from the deal: Jenkins tallied 25 victories to tie for the lead in the American League in 1974. Ironically, the Cubs picked up Jenkins again in 1982. After pitching two seasons in Wrigley, he retired with 284 career wins.

Schmidt Tops NL in HRs

Mike Schmidt clubbed 36 home runs in 1974, his second full season in the majors, to lead the National League. On his way to knocking in 116 runs that season, he also topped the loop with his .546 slugging average. He is acknowledged as the greatest third baseman of all time.

Mike Schmidt

- Bake McBride of the Cardinals selected NL ROTY.

- Aaron defeats Japanese slugger Sadaharu Oh 10-9 in a specially arranged home run contest in Tokyo.

- Nolan Ryan fires a no-hitter vs. the Twins on Sept. 28.

- Steve Busby of KC no-hits Milwaukee on June 19.

- Dick Bosman of Cleveland no-hits Oakland on July 19.

- Pittsburgh's Richie Zisk has 21 RBI in a ten-game span.

- Ray Kroc buys the Padres.

- George Steinbrenner is suspended by commissioner Bowie Kuhn because of his part in the Watergate scandal.

- Al Kaline gets his 3,000th hit, retires after the season.

- Kaline nearly becomes the first ALer to reach 3,000 hits and 400 homers, as he finishes with 399 home runs.

Burroughs an MVP Surprise

Perhaps the decade's least likely Most Valuable Player, Jeff Burroughs of the Rangers batted .301 with 25 home runs and 118 RBI (tops in the American League) in 1974. As the nation's first draft pick in 1969, the outfielder/first baseman often clashed with Ted Williams, the manager of the Senators, yet later credited Williams with improving his batting.

Jeff Burroughs

Rudi Soars in Series

Joe Rudi was the quiet superstar of the boisterous Swingin' A's. An excellent defensive player, his glovework earned him two Gold Gloves, the first of which he received in 1974. An able hitter, he led the American League in doubles that year with 39. His ability was never more evident than in the seventh game of the '74 World Series. His home run in the seventh inning broke the two-all tie and proved to be the margin of victory for the World Champion A's.

Joe Rudi

Marshall Cops Cy Young

Before achieving fame as the winner of the 1974 National League Cy Young Award, Mike Marshall was known to fans as Jim Bouton's cerebral teammate in the book *Ball Four*, Bouton's anecdotal account of the sport of baseball. As a doctoral candidate in kinesiology, Marshall used his study of human performance to resurrect his pitching career. He went from a 5-8 record with the Expos in 1971 to a 15-12 record with the Dodgers in 1974. His knuckleball carried him to 21 saves in '74, best in the loop.

Mike Marshall

1974

- Cards beat Mets 4-3 on Sept. 11 in 25-inning night game.

- Buzz Capra of Braves tops ML in ERA (2.28).

- Danny Murtaugh hired to manage Pirates an NL record fourth different time.

- Hunter is made a free agent because of a faux pas by owner Finley, signs with Yankees for 1975 season.

- The Hall of Fame inducts Mickey Mantle, Whitey Ford, Jim Bottomley, Jocko Conlan, Sam Thompson, and Cool Papa Bell.

- Cleveland swaps Pedro Guerrero to LA for Bruce Ellingsen.

- The Giants trade Bobby Bonds to the Yankees for Bobby Murcer.

- Cleveland trades Chris Chambliss and two other players to the Yankees for Fritz Peterson and three other players.

- After the season, Atlanta deals Aaron to Milwaukee for Dave May and a minor leaguer.

Lou Brock

Brock Pilfers 105 Bases

On September 10, 1974, Lou Brock slid into the record books as he broke the single-season stolen base mark set by Maury Wills in 1962. In the game that pitted the Cardinals against the Phillies, Brock reached base on singles in the first and seventh innings, on both occasions stealing on an 0-1 pitch to Ron Hunt to rack up swipes No. 104 and 105. Bob Boone was the catcher on both thefts.

Al Oliver

Oliver Posts .321 Average

The license plate on outfielder Al Oliver's car used to simply read "AL HITS." During his first six seasons with the Pirates (through 1974), Oliver had a .294 lifetime average and played in four National League Championship Series. His slashing line drive hitting was the perfect complement to Willie Stargell's power strokes. In 1974, Oliver batted .321 with 11 home runs and 85 RBI. Four seasons later, he batted .324 for the Rangers.

- Ryan wins AL record 22 games for a last-place team.
- Gaylord Perry ties Cleveland club record by winning 15 games in a row.
- The baseball is now made out of cowhide instead of the traditional horsehide.
- Harry Hooper dies.

- Dizzy Dean dies.
- Sam Rice dies.
- Baltimore's Bobby Grich sets an ML record for second basemen with 484 putouts for the year.
- Ron Hunt leads the NL a record seventh consecutive year in being hit by pitches.

- On Sept. 7, Ryan becomes the first to throw a pitch that's clocked at over 100 mph.
- Brooks Robinson tops AL in assists at third base a record eighth time.
- Money's record streak of 261 consecutive errorless chances at third base ends.

Reggie: HR Off the Bat

Reggie Jackson takes Dodgers righty Andy Messersmith downtown as he smacks a home run in his first at-bat in game one of the 1974 World Series. Jackson enjoyed being called "Mr. October" in honor of his myriad heroics in playoff and World Series play. Highlights of his postseason career include a .417 average in the '75 American League Championship Series; a .450 average, five home runs, and eight RBI in the '77 World Series; and a .462 average and six RBI in the '78 ALCS.

World Series

World Series

Garvey Heats Up in Debut

As a kid, Steve Garvey was introduced to the Dodgers by his father, who drove the team bus at Dodgertown in Vero Beach, Florida. Some 15 years later, Garvey was the living embodiment of Dodger blue, winning the National League MVP Award and leading his team to the World Series in 1974. In that fall classic, his first Series, Garvey led the club in batting with a .381 average and in hits with eight. He would go on to play in five World Series and bat a combined .319—though with only one home run.

World Series

Lopes Swift at Second

Davey Lopes erases Joe Rudi then goes for the double play in game two of the 1974 World Series. As a second baseman, Lopes was a member of a Dodger infield that remained intact longer than any infield in major league history. As one of the best basestealers in the game, he matched a major league record as he swiped five bases in one game in 1974.

1974

- Marshall is the only pitcher in history to work over 200 relief innings in a season (208).

- The Mets' Ed Kranepool sets an ML record when he has a .486 BA as a pinch hitter.

- Ryan tops ML in innings with 333 and Ks with 367.

- Phil Niekro and LA's Andy Messersmith lead the NL in wins with 20.

- Niekro leads NL in innings (302) and CGs (18).

- Jenkins tops ML with 29 CGs, one more than Perry.

- Hunter leads AL in ERA (2.49).

- New York's Jon Matlack leads NL with seven shutouts; Boston's Luis Tiant likewise tops AL with seven shutouts.

- White Sox Terry Forster leads ML with 24 saves; Marshall tops NL with only 21 despite being in 106 games.

- Joe Morgan tops NL in OBP (.430).

World Series

A's Edge Out LA

Attempting to score on a fly ball by Reggie Jackson to Joe Ferguson, Sal Bando is nailed in an eighth-inning rundown between third base and home in game one of the 1974 World Series. Bando continued his dismal performance, finishing the five-game tournament with a .063 average, three runs scored, and two RBI. His teammates continued their solid showing to take the opening game 3-2.

Aaron Racks Up No. 715

A national television audience viewed a rare weeknight broadcast—and a part of history—on the evening of April 8, 1974. In a game between the Braves and the Dodgers, Hammerin' Hank Aaron (shown heading for the plate) smacked an Al Downing fastball into the hands of Braves reliever Tom House, who was sitting in Fulton County Stadium's left-field bullpen. It was Aaron's record-shattering 715th home run.

World Series

Rudi Slams the Clincher

Following a six-minute delay in which officials removed debris thrown on the field by Oakland fans, Joe Rudi of the A's stepped in to face Dodger ace Mike Marshall in game five of the 1974 World Series. Rudi proceeded to crush Marshall's first pitch into the left-field stands for the third and winning run of the deciding game. Marshall was the winner of the National League Cy Young Award that season.

Hank Aaron

- Oakland's Bill North leads AL in steals (54).

- Atlanta's Darrell Evans tops ML with 126 walks; Oakland's Gene Tenace leads AL in walks with 110.

- Carew leads ML in hits (218) and OBP (.435).

- Rudi tops AL in total bases (287) and doubles (39).

- Carl Yastrzemski leads AL in runs with just 93; this is the last time Yaz will lead the AL in a major department.

- California's Mickey Rivers leads AL in triples with 11.

- Texas, in its first full year under Billy Martin, finishes second with 84 wins, a 27-game hike over its 1973 performance.

- New York loses AL East race to Orioles by just 2 games—the closest the Yankees have come to first place since 1964.

REDS EDGE RED SOX, DESPITE FISK'S HEROICS

In the early 1960s, Charles O. Finley of the A's signed a teenage country boy named Jim "Catfish" Hunter to a contract. Although Hunter's first five big league seasons were far from spectacular (he went 55-64), the guileful ace turned in blockbuster years from 1970 through 1974, going 106-49.

But after his Cy Young season in '74, Hunter and Finley engaged in a bitter contract dispute. As a result, Hunter became a free agent, and on New Year's Eve, 1974, Catfish celebrated the signing of a five-year, $3.75-million deal with the Yankees. Thus began the era of big-money free agency.

The '75 A's managed to win the AL West without Hunter. Vida Blue stepped in as the staff's ace, going 22-11. Ken Holtzman, the team's workhorse, went 18-14, and reliever extraordinaire Rollie Fingers notched ten wins and 24 saves. Oakland's Reggie Jackson led the league with 36 homers, and a 20-year-old Athletic named Claudell Washington hit .308 with 40 stolen bases.

Baltimore—the unanimous preseason pick in the AL East—won 90 games, but Boston surprised everyone by finishing 4½ games in front of the Orioles. Rookies Fred Lynn (.331 average, 21 home runs, 105 RBI) and Jim Rice (.309 average, 22 home runs, 102 RBI) sparked the Sox, as Lynn became the first player

to win both the MVP and Rookie of the Year Awards in the same season. The Sox also featured established hitters like Carl Yastrzemski and Carlton Fisk, as well as pitchers Rick Wise (19 wins), Luis Tiant (18), and Bill Lee (17).

Elsewhere in the American League, Minnesota's Rod Carew won his fourth consecutive batting title with a .359 average. Hank Aaron, Milwaukee's designated hitter, blasted 12 home runs and upped his total to 745. Angel Nolan Ryan pitched no-hitter No. 4. And 28 years after Jackie Robinson broke baseball's color barrier, Frank Robinson became the first black manager in major league history. The 39-year-old skipper led Cleveland to a fourth-place finish, and also played in 49 games, belting nine home runs.

Two power-hitting lefties carried Pittsburgh to the NL East title. Thirty-five-year-old Willie "Pops" Stargell hit .295 with 90 RBI, and 24-year-old Dave Parker batted .308 with 101 RBI.

Cincinnati's Big Red Machine (108-54) ran away with the West, boasting an All-Star lineup that included league MVP Joe Morgan (.327 average, 94 RBI), Johnny Bench (110 RBI), Pete Rose (210 hits, 47 doubles), Tony Perez (109 RBI), Ken Griffey (.305), Dave Concepcion (.274), and George Foster (.300, 23 home runs). The Reds led the National League by huge margins in runs (840), stolen bases (168), saves (50), and fielding average (.984).

The Reds and the Sox swept their respective League Championship Series, setting the stage for one of the most dramatic World Series in baseball history. Cincinnati crawled out to a three-games-to-two lead, which included three one-run games. But the real fun didn't start until the sixth game in Boston.

The two teams battled into the 12th inning of game six, when Fisk, the Sox leadoff hitter, blasted a long fly ball to left. The ball had home run distance and stayed fair, giving Fisk a home run and Boston a 7-6 come-from-behind victory.

Game seven was almost as intense. Boston jumped to a 3-0 lead, the Reds tied it in the seventh, and Morgan won it in the ninth with a run-scoring bloop single. Many feel the '75 Series helped spark baseball's popularity, which soared in the late 1970s and throughout the 1980s.

1975

- Red Sox end Oakland's reign as AL champs.
- Reds win NL flag.
- Boston sweeps Oakland in ALCS, outscoring the A's 18-7.
- Reds sweep Pirates in NLCS, saddling Pittsburgh with four LCS losses in six years.

- Reds pull out World Series in seven games after trailing 3-0 in sixth inning of finale.
- Pete Rose leads all Series players with ten hits and scores Series' winning run on bloop single by Joe Morgan.
- Carlton Fisk's dramatic 12th-inning homer wins game six of Series for Boston.

- Luis Tiant wins two CGs for Boston; Rawly Eastwick wins two for Reds.
- Boston's Fred Lynn becomes only player in ML history to be named Rookie of the Year and MVP in same season.
- Lynn drives in 105 runs, while rookie teammate Jim Rice knocks in 102.

The fluid stroke of rookie extraordinaire Fred Lynn was good for five RBI (the high for the Red Sox) and a .282 batting average in the 1975 World Series. The recruit stunned the crowd in game six as he clubbed a home run in the first inning to put the Sox ahead of the Reds by three runs. Four innings later, he stunned the audience once again as he collided with the center-field wall while tracking Ken Griffey's triple.

- Morgan wins NL MVP.
- Tom Seaver leads NL with 22 wins and cops Cy Young.
- Jim Palmer wins his second AL Cy Young, as he leads loop in ERA (2.09) and ties for lead in wins (23).
- Chicago's Bill Madlock takes first NL bat crown (.354).

- In historic decision, arbitrator Peter Seitz grants pitchers Dave McNally and Andy Messersmith free agency.
- Frank Robinson named manager of Cleveland—first black manager in major league history.
- Nolan Ryan throws his fourth no-hitter on June 1 vs. Baltimore.

- Catfish Hunter becomes last ML pitcher to toss 30 CGs.
- NL wins All-Star Game 6-3 at Milwaukee.
- SF's John Montefusco wins NL ROTY in close vote over Montreal's Gary Carter.

Hunter on the Prowl

No free agent made more money or more of an impact than did Catfish Hunter in 1975. Signed for the then-phenomenal amount of $3.75 million, Hunter proceeded to turn New York on its ear that season: He won 23 games (tied for tops in the majors), notched a league-leading 30 complete games, earned the American League's Cy Young Award, and brought a winning attitude to the Bronx Bombers clubhouse.

Carlton Fisk

Catfish Hunter

Fisk Makes World Series History

At 12:33 a.m. on October 22, 1975, Carlton Fisk hit one of the most celebrated home runs in World Series history. Fisk smacked Pat Darcy's first offering off the left-field foul pole of Fenway Park in the 12th inning, breaking the six-all stalemate to give the Red Sox the win over the Reds. The contest is cited by some as being the greatest game in World Series history.

Jim Rice

Rice Powers Red Sox

Joining Fred Lynn as the other half of Boston's rookie duo was Jim Rice (pictured). A tremendous power hitter, Rice socked 22 four-baggers and knocked in 102 runs while batting .309 in 144 games in 1975. A broken wrist, injured by a pitch from Vern Ruhle of the Tigers, cut what would have been his first full season in the majors short. Rice got back on the fast track quickly, hitting 25 home runs in 1976 and 39 in 1977. Of the two young stars, Rice would have the greatest career, clubbing nearly 400 homers. Lynn, though, would play more years than Rice.

1975

- Davey Lopes of LA sets new ML record when he steals 38 consecutive bases without being caught.

- Pirates beat Cubs 22-0 on Sept. 16.

- In Sept. 16 game, Rennie Stennett of Pirates becomes first player this century to go 7-for-7 in a nine-inning game.

- Ed Halicki of SF no-hits Mets on August 24.

- Four A's pitchers combine to no-hit California on Sept. 28.

- Hank Aaron breaks Babe Ruth's career RBI record of 2,211.

- Bob Watson of Astros scores the millionth run in ML history.

- Harmon Killebrew retires with 8,147 at-bats, no sacrifice bunts, and no bunt hits.

- Dave Cash of Phils sets new ML record when he has 699 at-bats.

- Rose leads NL in runs (112) and doubles (47).

Fans Appeal to Twins Execs

Ever the managerial nomad, Billy Martin won supporters in every city in which he stepped behind the helm. Shown here are fans at Metropolitan Stadium in Bloomington, Minnesota, letting their sentiments for Martin be known. Martin skippered the Twins in 1969, taking them all the way to first place in the American League West. After two-year stints in Detroit and Texas, Martin made tracks to New York, as the Yankees finished in third place in the American League East in 1975. Martin took four Manager of the Year Awards during his career.

Minnesota Twins Fans

Harmon Killebrew

Harmon Hangs It Up

Signed as a free agent by Kansas City in January 1975, Harmon Killebrew finished his career in less-than-spectacular fashion as a designated hitter/first baseman for the Royals; he batted .199 with 14 home runs and 44 RBI in 1975. What was spectacular, however, was that he retired with no sacrifice bunts and no bunt hits in 8,147 at-bats.

George Brett

Little Brett Grows Up

Although George Brett was known as the kid brother of pitcher Ken Brett for several seasons, it didn't take the younger Brett long to establish himself in his own right. He batted for a respectable .308 average in 1975, posting 195 hits (tops in the American League) and 13 triples (tied for first in the loop) in his second full season.

- Mike Schmidt leads majors with 38 homers.

- Brewer George Scott leads the AL in RBI (109) and total bases (318), and ties Reggie Jackson for lead in home runs (36).

- Lynn tops AL in runs (103), runs produced (187), and SA (.566).

- Lynn's 47 doubles lead AL and set loop rookie record.

- Billy Martin is fired as Texas manager, hired by Yankees to replace Bill Virdon.

- The Reds set an NL record for 162-game season with 108 wins.

- Brooks Robinson tops AL third basemen in FA a record 11th time.

- The Hall of Fame inducts Ralph Kiner, Bucky Harris, Earl Averill, Billy Herman, and Judy Johnson.

- Casey Stengel dies.

- Lefty Grove dies.

Thurman Munson

Lopes Lifts 77 Bases

One of the masters of thievery, Davey Lopes stole a total of 77 bases in 1975, best in the National League. Additionally, he racked up 38 consecutive steals without being caught to set a then-major league record. The scrappy Lopes retired after 1987 with 557 swipes, 19th on the all-time list. He was generally viewed as one of the most underrated players in the senior circuit.

Davey Lopes

Munson: .318, 102 Runs

Gruff, taciturn, and competitive to the point of nastiness, Thurman Munson was the heart and soul of the World Champion New York Yankees in 1977 and 1978. During the decade of the '70s, Munson and Carlton Fisk were considered the top two catchers in the American League. Munson knew how to handle the bat as well, hitting .318 while driving in 102 runs in 1975.

Seaver Takes NL Cy Young

Tom Seaver claimed the last of his three Cy Young Awards in 1975, as he reigned victorious in a National League-leading 22 games. The ace righty fashioned a 2.38 ERA (third in the loop) while striking out 243 batters (tops in the circuit) that year. Never again would Tom Terrific win as many games in a season.

Tom Seaver

1975

- Ducky Medwick dies.
- Astros pitcher Don Wilson commits suicide prior to season.
- Tigers lose 19 games in a row.
- The Dodgers trade Geoff Zahn and Eddie Solomon to the Cubs for Burt Hooton.

- Cleveland swaps Gaylord Perry to Texas for three pitchers and $100,000.
- Phils send Willie Montanez to SF for Garry Maddox.
- Tigers trade Mickey Lolich and Bobby Baldwin to Mets for Rusty Staub and Bill Laxton.

- Yanks send Bobby Bonds to Angels for Mickey Rivers and Ed Figueroa.
- Yanks trade Doc Medich to Pittsburgh for Willie Randolph, Ken Brett, and Dock Ellis.
- On July 21, Joe Torre of the Mets grounds into four double plays, each time following a single by Felix Millan, who's promptly erased.

Frank Robinson

Simmons Has His Best Year

Ted Simmons was one of the game's greatest offensive catchers. He had extraordinary switch-hitting power, whacking home runs from both sides of the plate in a game on three separate occasions. His greatest season was in 1975, when he batted .332 (second in the National League).

Ted Simmons

Robby Named Manager

Not since Jackie Robinson crossed the color line in 1947 had such a progressive move been made in baseball as when Frank Robinson became player/manager of the Indians—the sport's first black manager. On Opening Day, Robinson thrilled a crowd of 56,715 by hitting a home run off Yankee pitcher Doc Medich to lead the Tribe to a 5-3 victory. On the last day of the season, Robinson and the Indians left the fans somewhat discontented as they finished in fourth place in the East Division (15½ games out).

Bobby Bonds

Bonds Is a 30/30 Man

Bobby Bonds was one of the most talented and traveled outfielders in the game. Traded to the Yankees prior to the 1975 season, Bonds played one year with the New York ballclub. He reached the 30/30 plateau with 32 home runs and 30 stolen bases. He played under the California sunshine in 1976, his home run total dropping to ten and his swipes holding at 30.

Ron Cey

Cey Lets Bat Do Talking

Christened the "Penguin" due to his stocky stature and jerky running style, Ron Cey put in ten years at third base for the Dodgers. During that decade, he clubbed 228 moon shots and played in six All-Star Games. In 1975, Cey hit .283 with 25 home runs and 101 RBI. Oddly, in his 16-year National League career, Cey never played a position other than third base.

- On August 21, Rick and Paul Reuschel of the Cubs become only brothers in ML history to pitch a combined shutout.

- Lopes sets an NL record for second basemen with 77 steals.

- Schmidt's 180 Ks set new ML record for third basemen.

- Cardinal Ted Simmons sets new ML record for catchers with 193 hits.

- Cardinal Mike Garman sets new ML record when he issues 23 intentional walks.

- Madlock goes 6-for-6 in ten innings on July 26.

- Brewer Mike Hegan's record streak of 178 consecutive errorless games at first base ends.

- The World Series winner's share is below $20,000 for the last time.

- An estimated record 75 million fans watch the seventh World Series game on television.

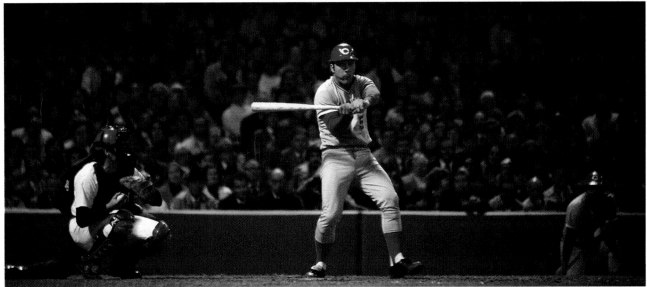

Johnny Bench

Bench Saves Face in World Series

The 1975 World Series was not, to say the least, Johnny Bench's finest hour. The legendary catcher batted a meager .207 in the seven-game affair. The Pride of the Reds did, however, flirt with a moment of greatness, as he drilled a home run to help his team to a 6-5 victory in game three. During the '75 season, Bench drove in 110 runs and stole 11 bases. The following season would be a reversal for Bench. He would have his worst season of the decade, but would hit .533 in the Series.

Joe Morgan

Morgan Brings Series to an End

The 5′ 7″, 150-pound Joe Morgan brought the seven-game 1975 World Series to an end with the single stroke of a bat. Little Joe lined the game-winning hit off reliever Jim Burton to score Ken Griffey with the clinching run of the fall classic. Morgan enjoyed the first of two consecutive MVP seasons as well as two straight World Titles for the Big Red Machine in '75. During the '75 season, Morgan walked 132 times, stole 67 bases, hit 17 homers, and drove in 94 runs.

1975

- Willie McCovey ties an ML record by hitting his third pinch grandslam.

- Mike Vail of the Mets ties the NL rookie record by hitting safely in 23 straight games.

- Danny Goodwin becomes the first man to be chosen No. 1 twice in the free agent draft of amateur players.

- Hunter ties for AL lead in wins (23) and leads in innings (328).

- Mike Torrez wins 20 for Baltimore, tops AL in win pct. (.690).

- Frank Tanana of California tops AL in Ks (269), breaking teammate Ryan's skein.

- White Sox Goose Gossage leads ML with 26 saves; Al Hrabosky and Rawly Eastwick lead NL with 22.

- San Diego's Randy Jones leads NL in ERA (2.24).

- Messersmith tops NL in CGs with 19 and shutouts with seven.

- Seaver leads NL in Ks (243).

Rose Hits His Peak

Pete Rose

The 1975 season was the zenith of a 24-year career for Pete Rose. Prolific and sassy, Rose put up typical Charlie Hustle numbers to top the National League in runs scored (112), doubles (47), and dirty uniforms that year. The human hitting machine racked up 210 hits, just three shy of the circuit-high. The 1975 season marked Rose's move to third base, which turned out to be the third of four defensive positions he would play in his career.

Carlton Fisk

Luis Tiant

Tiant Wins One for Tiant

One of the most moving moments of the 1975 season came to pass just prior to the opening game of the 1975 World Series, as Luis Tiant was reunited with his father, Luis Sr., who made the trip from Cuba to Fenway Park in Boston. The younger Tiant responded to the presence of his father by hurling a five-hit shutout that day.

Fisk Dynamic in Series

Carlton Fisk is a prime example of the adage that most baseball heroes hail from small-town America. Fisk put his hometown of Charlestown, New Hampshire, on the map even before the final out of the 1975 World Series. Known for his supreme catching skill, Fisk proved his offensive worth by batting a pair of crucial home runs in the fall classic that season.

- Morgan tops NL in walks (132), OBP (.471), and runs produced (184).
- Atlanta's Ralph Garr again leads NL in triples (11).
- Rivers and KC's George Brett tie for ML lead in triples with 13.
- Brett leads AL with 195 hits, three more than runner-up Rod Carew.

- Cash leads ML with 213 hits.
- Philly's Greg Luzinski tops ML with 120 RBI and 322 total bases.
- KC's John Mayberry again leads AL in walks (119), is second in RBI (106), and third in homers (34).
- Tigers lose 100 games for the first time since 1952.

- Boston's 796 runs are 108 more than anyone else's in the AL East.
- Cincinnati's 840 runs lead the NL East by 176.
- Reds lead the NL in saves (50) and FA (.984).
- LA's 2.92 ERA tops the majors.

REDS CELEBRATE CENTENNIAL BY ROUTING YANKS

Fireworks reigned in 1976, as the United States celebrated its bicentennial and baseball's National League honored its 100th season.

The year also marked Marvin Miller's tenth anniversary as executive director of the Players Association. After the 1975 season, Miller went to bat for pitchers Andy Messersmith and Dave McNally, who were declared "free agents" by an arbitrator. The ruling so angered the owners that they locked the players out of spring training. The season did begin on schedule—thanks to the intervention of commissioner Bowie Kuhn—but the sport of baseball had been irrevocably changed. Free agents would become commonplace and baseball salaries would skyrocket.

Mike Schmidt, the Phillies' third baseman, opened the season with a bang, slugging four of his major league-leading 38 home runs in an 18-16 shootout with Chicago. Schmidt led a team loaded with recently acquired veterans, including outfielders Bobby Tolan, Jay Johnstone, and Garry Maddox; second baseman Dave Cash; and pitchers Jim Lonborg and Tug McGraw. They joined vets Schmidt (107 RBI), Greg Luzinski (.304 average, 21 home runs, 95 RBI), slick-fielding shortstop Larry Bowa, and lefty Steve Carlton (20-7). Cellar-dwellers in 1972 and '73, Philly won 101 games in '76, finishing 9 up on Pittsburgh.

Cincinnati continued to roll mightily along in the West, winning 102 games. Baseball's best second baseman, Joe Morgan (.320 average, 27 home runs, 111 RBI), walked away with his second consecutive MVP trophy. Morgan and the rest of the Big Red Machine—including Pete Rose, Johnny Bench, Tony Perez, Dave Concepcion, and George Foster—scored 857 runs, 232 more than any other NL West team. Cincinnati led the NL in runs, batting, hits, doubles, triples, homers, steals, walks, on-base percentage, and slugging—all by substantial margins.

After a two-year hiatus, the once-dominant Yankees returned to a renovated Yankee Stadium and played like the Bombers of old. With Chris Chambliss, Willie Randolph, Graig Nettles, and Thurman Munson guarding the infield; speedster Mickey Rivers patrolling in center; and Sparky Lyle leading the AL with 23 saves, the Yanks finished first in the East, 10 1/2 up on the Orioles.

The most talked-about bird in baseball was 21-year-old Mark Fidrych. Nicknamed "The Bird" (he resembled Big Bird on the TV show *Sesame Street*), the Tiger rookie went 19-9, sported an AL-best 2.34 ERA, and packed stadiums with his flaky antics.

Kansas City's 23-year-old George Brett led the AL with a .333 average, winning a disputed batting title over teammate Hal McRae by one point. Brett won the crown on the last day of the season against Minnesota; he smacked one to outfielder Steve Brye, who seemed to deliberately misplay the ball, allowing Brett to get his needed hit. The hit didn't affect the AL West standings, though, as Kansas City finished 2 1/2 up on the second-place A's.

The Reds swept the Phils in the NLCS in three games. The ALCS, however, was a classic five-game series. Although Kansas City's Brett hit a sizzling .444, the spotlight was on Chambliss, New York's first baseman. Chambliss hit .524 with eight RBI, including a homer in the bottom of the ninth of game five—a shot fans still talk about.

The World Series, however, was a disappointment. Billy Martin's Bombers had little left against the powerful Big Red Machine, as the Reds won in four. Bench ripped the Yankees' pitching for a .533 average, making Cincinnati the first NL team since 1922 to repeat as World Series Champions.

1976

- Reds win again in NL.
- Yankees garner first AL flag since 1964.
- Reds blow Phils out in three games in NLCS.
- Yankees beat KC in five games in ALCS, as Chris Chambliss wins game five on a homer in the ninth.

- Reds sweep Yankees in most one-sided World Series ever to this juncture.
- Catfish Hunter's complete game 4-3 loss in game two of Series is New York's lone competitive effort.
- Johnny Bench leads all World Series hitters with .533 BA and six RBI.

- Joe Morgan is again NL MVP, hitting .320 and stealing 60 bases.
- Morgan tops ML in OBP (.453), SA (.576), and runs produced (197).
- Thurman Munson is AL MVP, and also tops Yankee hitters in Series with .529 BA.

The 1976 Reds (102-60) were the best edition of the Big Red Machine and are considered one of the great teams of the past 50 years. The main cogs of the apparatus were *(left to right)* Tony Perez, Johnny Bench, Joe Morgan, and Pete Rose. Morgan was a standout with 197 runs produced, a .453 on-base percentage, and a .576 slugging average, all highs in the National League that year. Rose excelled with circuit-topping figures in runs (130), hits (215), and doubles (42).

- San Diego's Randy Jones takes NL Cy Young, topping NL with 22 wins.

- Jones ties an NL record when he pitches 68 consecutive innings without allowing a walk.

- Jim Palmer claims his third AL Cy Young in four years, as he leads AL with 22 wins.

- A's set record with 341 stolen bases.

- In June, Charley Finley tries to sell Joe Rudi, Rollie Fingers, and Vida Blue, but commissioner Bowie Kuhn vetoes the deals.

- Free agency bidding begins in earnest after 1976 season; Yankees sign Reggie Jackson for $3.5 million.

- George Brett wins bat crown over teammate Hal McRae, .333 to .332.

- Brett wins BA title on his last at-bat of season, as Twins outfielder Steve Brye seems to deliberately misplay the ball.

- Mike Schmidt leads majors in homers (38) and total bases (306).

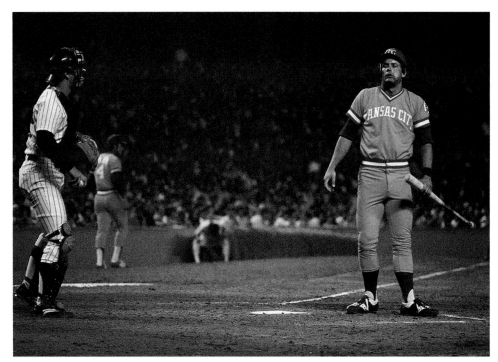

George Brett

Brett Is Breathtaking

George Brett achieved superstar status in the 1976 American League Championship Series, batting .444 with five RBI for the Royals. His sole moon shot tied the fifth and deciding game at six-all and set the stage for the pennant-clinching homer off the bat of Chris Chambliss.

Gary Matthews

Palmer Wins Cy Young

Jim Palmer won the third and last of his Cy Young Awards in 1976 as he compiled a record of 22-13 with a 2.51 ERA. A workhorse, Palmer topped the American League with 315 innings that season. In time, the righty's stint as a spokesman and model for Jockey Underwear would win him more popular acclaim than any of his awards.

Jim Palmer

Matthews Distracted

Gary Matthews was yet another great outfielder who got away from the Giants, joining such players as George Foster, Garry Maddox, and Bobby Bonds in exile. A contract dispute marred his 1976 season as he batted .279 with 20 home runs and 84 RBI. A free agent, he signed with the Braves in time for the '77 season.

1976

- NL wins All-Star Game 7-1 at Philadelphia, as Detroit rookie Mark Fidrych starts for AL and takes the loss.

- Fidrych is AL ROTY, winning 19 for Detroit.

- Fidrych leads AL in ERA (2.34) and CGs (24).

- Butch Metzger of San Diego and Pat Zachry of Cincinnati tie for NL ROTY Award.

- Ted Turner buys Braves.

- Hank Aaron retires; still holds ML records for homers (755), RBI (2,297), and total bases (6,856).

- Schmidt hits four homers in ten-inning game on April 17.

- Only "rainout" in Astrodome history occurs on June 15 when heavy rains prevent fans and umps from getting to the dome.

- John Montefusco of SF no-hits Atlanta on Sept. 29.

Mike Schmidt

Schmidt: 38 HRs, 107 RBI

Mike Schmidt whacked 38 round-trippers in 1976 to capture the third of eight home run titles in his 18-year career. The National League's leader in total bases (306) that season, Schmidt placed third in RBI (107), runs produced (181), slugging average (.524), and walks (100). That season, Schmidt also won his first of ten Gold Gloves—nine of which were consecutive—at third base.

Nolan Ryan

Ryan Collects 327 Ks

On August 20, 1974, a Nolan Ryan fastball was clocked at a sizzling speed of 100.9 mph, the material of which entries in the *Guinness Book of World Records* are made. Almost one year to the day later, Ryan underwent surgery on his elbow. In 1976, the pitching prodigy notched 327 strikeouts and allowed just 6.12 hits per game, both bests in the American League.

Madlock Hits .339 for Title

Bill Madlock captured the second of his four National League batting titles in 1976, hitting .339 for the Cubs. Madlock was the premier player to capture two batting titles with two different ballclubs and the only righthanded hitter to top the senior circuit in batting average from 1971 through 1989.

Bill Madlock

- John Candelaria of Pittsburgh no-hits LA on August 9—first no-hitter thrown by Pirates pitcher at home since 1907.

- Blue Moon Odom and Francisco Barrios of White Sox pitch a combined no-hitter vs. Oakland on July 28.

- Larry Dierker of Houston no-hits Expos on July 9.

- On Sept. 12, at age 54, Minnie Minoso of White Sox becomes oldest player to get a hit in an ML game.

- Pete Rose tops NL in hits (215), doubles (42), and runs (130).

- Brett leads AL in hits (215), total bases (298), and triples (14).

- Chicago's Bill Madlock wins NL bat crown (.339).

- The A's have three players who steal 50 or more bases each: Bill North (75), Bert Campaneris (54), and Don Baylor (52).

1976

Carlton Tops NL in Win Pct.

An alteration in stance cast Steve Carlton from a .517 winning percentage in 1975 to a whopping .741 winning percentage in 1976, best in the NL that year. A southpaw with a devastating fastball, Carlton racked up 20 victories that season to boost the Phillies to their first NL East title.

Steve Carlton

Greg Luzinski

Luzinski Bats .304

Although Greg "The Bull" Luzinski may have looked more like a tight end than an outfielder, his power hitting kept him in the majors for 14 seasons. Batting .304 in 1976, he led the Phillies to the first of three straight division titles.

Mark Fidrych

A Goofy Bird Wins 19

"The Bird" was the word around Detroit in 1976, as rookie phenom Mark Fidrych won 19 games for a Tiger team that placed fifth in the American League East, 24 games back. In between his chats with baseballs, the hurler racked up 24 complete games and a 2.34 ERA, both top marks in the circuit. Fidrych's bubble burst within two years and several comeback attempts proved fruitless.

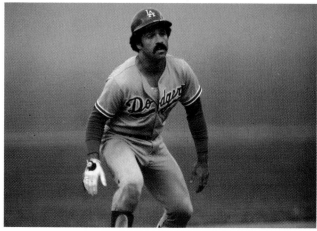

Davey Lopes

Lopes Leads NL in Swipes

National League catchers hated to see Davey Lopes on the basepaths in 1976. The second baseman topped the league in steals for the second consecutive year with 63 thefts that season. Always an efficient basestealer, he was nabbed just ten times.

1976

- Tom Seaver fans at least 200 batters for ML record ninth consecutive season and leads the NL in Ks for the fifth time.
- The Hall of Fame inducts Robin Roberts, Bob Lemon, Roger Connor, Fred Lindstrom, Cal Hubbard, and Oscar Charleston.
- ChiSox deal Goose Gossage and Terry Forster to Pittsburgh for Richie Zisk and Silvio Martinez.
- Texas sends Jeff Burroughs to Atlanta for five players and $250,000.
- Cincinnati trades Tony Perez and Will McEnaney to Expos for Woodie Fryman and Dale Murray.
- The Giants send Willie Montanez, Craig Robinson, and two other players to Atlanta for Darrell Evans and Marty Perez.
- Minnesota sends Bert Blyleven and Danny Thompson to Texas for Bill Singer, Roy Smalley, two other players, and $250,000.

Hendrick: 25 HRs, 81 RBI

George Hendrick had a couple of nicknames, depending on who was doing the talking: Those who didn't appreciate his laid-back style of play dubbed him "Jogging George"; members of the press found the alias "Silent George" more fitting. Hendrick spent his last season with the Indians in 1976, posting 25 home runs and 81 RBI. In his four seasons with the Tribe, he averaged 22 home runs and 74 RBI per season.

George Hendrick

Thurman Munson

Munson Named AL MVP

Thurman Munson was in his prime from 1976 to 1978. His 1976 stats—a .302 average, 17 home runs, 105 RBI—earned him the American League MVP Award. Although the starting catcher for the Yankees was well-respected throughout the majors, he was not without his quirks. Detroit's Norm Cash didn't care for his grooming habits, for example. "Where'd ya get that haircut," Cash once asked Munson. "In a pet shop?"

Nettles Leads AL in Dingers

Graig Nettles once remarked that as a kid he wanted to either join the circus or become a big league player. As a member of the Yankees, he fulfilled both ambitions. In 1976, he led the American League in home runs with 32. By 1988, the year he retired, he had collected 390 home runs (including an American League-record 319 dingers by a third baseman).

Graig Nettles

- The A's swap Jackson, Ken Holtzman, and Bill Van Bommell to the O's for Baylor, Mike Torrez, and Paul Mitchell prior to season.

- The O's send Holtzman, Grant Jackson, Doyle Alexander, Ellie Hendricks, and Jimmy Freeman to the Yanks.

- The Yanks send Scott McGregor, Tippy Martinez, Rudy May, Dave Pagan, and Rick Dempsey to the O's.

- Danny Thompson dies of leukemia.

- Bob Moose of the Pirates dies in an auto accident.

- Earle Combs dies.

- Max Carey dies.

- Red Faber dies.

- Cub Jose Cardenal goes 6-for-7 in a 14-inning game on May 2.

- The minimum player's salary is raised to $19,000; average player makes around $52,000.

Joe Morgan

Foster on Fire

After taking seven major league years to warm up, George Foster finally got hot in 1976. Showcasing his awesome power that season, Foster bested the National League in RBI with 121 to take the first of three consecutive RBI titles (tying a major league record). He also whacked 29 home runs that year (fourth in the circuit).

George Foster

Morgan: Tops Across Board

No second baseman since the immortal Rogers Hornsby had better overall offensive statistics than Joe Morgan. Enjoying his best season ever in 1976, Morgan batted .320 with 27 home runs and 111 RBI to win his second consecutive MVP Award. For good measure, he topped the National League in runs produced (197), on-base percentage (.453), slugging average (.576), and stolen base percentage (87.0) that season.

Hunter Bags 17 Triumphs

Catfish Hunter hauled his bag of pitching tricks from Oakland to the Big Apple in 1975, then helped lead the Yankees to a pennant in 1976. His 17 wins in '76 brought his total to 40 victories in his first two seasons with the Yankees. Inducted into the Hall of Fame in 1987, Hunter said in his speech that merely playing for both Charley Finley and George Steinbrenner qualified him for enshrinement.

Catfish Hunter

1976

- Reds leave an NL record 1,328 men on base during the season.

- Nolan Ryan is 17-18 for California with eight shutout losses.

- Ryan leads the majors with seven shutout wins.

- Detroit's Ron LeFlore hits safely in 30 consecutive games.

- Rose sets NL record for most runs by a third baseman since 1901 (130).

- Alex Johnson plays for Detroit, the seventh team with which he's played at least one full season during his career.

- Detroit's Bill Freehan retires with a .993 career FA, a record for catchers.

- Cincinnati's George Foster leads ML in RBI (121).

- Atlanta's Jim Wynn tops ML with 127 walks.

- Baltimore's Lee May tops AL in RBI (109).

- Rod Carew tops AL in runs produced with 178.

Reds Roll Over Yanks

Even the fiery protest of Yankee skipper Billy Martin couldn't hold back the onslaught of the Red juggernaut in the 1976 World Series. Martin's ballclub was blown away in almost every category over the course of the four-game tournament: The Reds scored 22 runs, whacked four home runs, and posted a .313 team average; the Yankees scored eight runs, nailed a single home run, and tallied a .222 average.

World Series

Munson Shines in Series

Thurman Munson slides under the throw to Johnny Bench in game four of the 1976 World Series. The fall classic was, in many respects, Munson's finest hour, as the clutch hitting of the Yankee captain was matched only by Bench, the Series MVP. Munson hit .529, with nine hits in 17 at-bats.

Rose Shuts Down Phillies

With Pete Rose in high gear and the Big Red Machine humming on all cylinders, the Phillies never had a chance in the National League Championship Series. Though the Phillies outhit the Reds in games two and three, the Reds outscored the Phillies 19 runs to 11. Rose, for his part, hit .429 in the sweep to lead all regulars on the Reds team.

Pete Rose

- Carew finishes third in AL in batting at .331, making this the closest three-way bat race since 1931.

- Ranger Mike Hargrove leads AL in walks (97), is second in OBP (.401).

- McRae tops AL in OBP (.412); teammate Amos Otis leads the league in doubles with 40.

- Yankee Graig Nettles leads AL with just 32 homers; teammate Roy White leads AL in runs with 104.

- Ryan leads ML with 327 Ks; Seaver leads NL in Ks with 235.

- Cardinal John Denny is the NL ERA champ (2.52).

- Minnesota's Bill Campbell leads AL in win pct. (.773), is third in saves (20), and tops AL pitchers in mound appearances (78).

- Rawly Eastwick of the Reds leads ML with 26 saves.

- Jones tops ML in CGs with (25), ties Palmer for most innings in ML (315).

Mix together an arrogant slugger, a tempestuous manager, and an impatient owner and, well, anything can happen. Prior to 1977, free agent Reggie Jackson (the slugger) left the Baltimore Orioles and joined the Yankee roster. During the season, Reggie fought with New York manager Billy Martin, who clashed with owner George Steinbrenner, who didn't get along with anyone. Yankeeland quickly became known as the "Bronx Zoo."

At the start of 1977, it looked like the Yankees would breeze to the playoffs. After all, they won 97 in 1976, and now they added Jackson, Don Gullett, Mike Torrez, and Bucky Dent—not to mention rookie phenom Ron Guidry. Jackson did indeed have a big year in '77 with a .286 average, 32 home runs, and 110 RBI. The new pitchers performed well too, as Gullett went 14-4, Torrez went 14-12, and Guidry finished 16-7. But the Yanks' season wasn't easy. New York won the AL East with 100 victories, but had to weather serious challenges from Baltimore and Boston, which both finished 2½ games behind.

In the AL West, Kansas City won 102 games and took the division by 8 games over Texas. Dennis Leonard (20-12) and Paul Splittorff (16-6) anchored a solid staff, and George Brett (.312 average, 22 home runs, 88 RBI) continued to establish himself as one of baseball's brightest stars.

REGGIE'S DRAMATIC HRS DO IN DODGERS

The hitter that everyone was talking about, however, was Minnesota's six-time batting champion, Rod Carew. The first baseman with the sweet stroke threatened to become the first man since Ted Williams to hit over .400 in a season. Carew finished at .388 on 239 hits, drove in 100 runs, and was voted the league's MVP.

In the National League, the big news was the trading of the most Amazin' Met of all, Tom Seaver, to Cincinnati (a trade that still angers Mets fans). The 32-year-old righthander posted a 14-3 record with the Reds, 21-6 overall. Tom Terrific's teammate, George Foster, posted some of the biggest numbers of the generation—.320 average, 52 home runs, 149 RBI—and walked away with the NL MVP.

Foster's Reds, however, finished 10 games behind the heavy-hitting Dodgers. Steve Garvey (.297 average, 33 home runs, 115 RBI), Reggie Smith (.307 average, 32 home runs), Ron Cey (30

home runs, 110 RBI), and Dusty Baker (.291 average, 30 home runs) did the damage. The Dodgers became the only team in history to boast four players with at least 30 homers.

In the NL East, Lou Brock of the Cardinals swiped 35 bases to break Ty Cobb's all-time base-stealing record, but St. Louis finished well in back of Philadelphia. Phillie southpaw Steve Carlton (23-10) won his second Cy Young Award, and the bullish Greg Luzinski (.309 average, 39 home runs, 130 RBI) carried the 101-61 Phillies to their second straight divisional title.

In the NLCS, Los Angeles downed Philly in four games, with Baker blasting two key homers. Garry Maddox made a valiant attempt on the part of the Phillies, hitting .429 before Dodger Tommy John wrapped it up by pitching a one-run seven-hitter in game four. The ALCS, meanwhile, went down to the last inning of game five. New York burned KC pitchers for three runs in the top of the ninth to win the deciding game 5-3.

The bi-coastal World Series between Los Angeles and New York became Jackson's private stage. In the sixth and final game, Mr. October launched three homers on three successive pitches to join another Yankee, Babe Ruth, as the only other player to hit three round-trippers in one Series game. Jackson batted .450 and belted a record five home runs for the Series.

1977

- Dodgers win NL flag.
- Yankees repeat as AL champs.
- NL East champ Phils again put up little resistance in LCS, bowing in four games.
- Yanks again edge KC in five games in ALCS, as New York rallies for three in the ninth to win game five 5-3.
- Yankees best Dodgers in six games in World Series.
- Reggie Jackson leads all Series hitters with a .450 BA and five home runs, including three in game six.
- Mike Torrez fashions two CG wins for New York in Series.
- Billy Martin wins his only World Championship as manager.
- Cincinnati's George Foster is NL MVP, as he leads the majors with 52 homers and 149 RBI.
- Foster leads NL in runs (124), total bases (388), and runs produced (221).

Reggie Jackson pauses to hug his father in the Yankee Stadium clubhouse following his home run heroics in game six of the 1977 World Series. Martinez Jackson, a Philadelphia tailor, had played semi-professional baseball in his youth and helped direct his son to the majors.

- Rod Carew wins AL MVP after hitting .388, top BA in majors since expansion.

- The AL swells to 14 teams, taking on two new franchises—Toronto Blue Jays and Seattle Mariners.

- Steve Carlton wins Cy Young in NL, as he leads majors with 23 wins.

- Yankee Sparky Lyle becomes first reliever to win AL Cy Young.

- Nolan Ryan fans an ML high 341 batters in 299 innings.

- Boston's Jim Rice leads AL in homers (39), SA (.593), and total bases (382).

- Dodgers become only team in history with four 30-homer men—Ron Cey, Steve Garvey, Dusty Baker, and Reggie Smith.

- The Mets, frustrated by salary disputes with star pitcher Tom Seaver, trade him to Cincinnati for four players.

Ted Simmons

Simmons Bats .318

Ted Simmons solidified his reputation as one of the best hitting catchers of all time in 1977, batting .318 with 21 home runs and 95 RBI. As one of the resident intellectuals of baseball, Simmons began collecting art and antiques while with the Cardinals; he eventually was elected as a trustee of the St. Louis Museum of Art.

Cey Tallies 30 HRs, 110 RBI

Ron Cey achieved career-high totals in home runs (30) and RBI (110) in 1977 as he helped lead the Dodgers to their second pennant in four seasons. Although he possessed a physique that drew comparisons to that of a penguin, the squat third baseman was extremely quick and was solid defensively.

Ron Cey

Billy Martin

Martin Wins His Only Ring

Billy Martin, the most temperamental of baseball figures, won several World Championships as a player and just one as a manager. The Yankees won the crown for Martin in 1977, his second full season at the helm. His volatile nature compelled him to change uniforms six times in his 16-year career as manager.

1977

- NL wins All-Star Game 7-5 at Yankee Stadium.

- Chicago's Chet Lemon sets AL record for outfielders with 512 putouts.

- Montreal's Andre Dawson edges New York's Steve Henderson by one vote for NL ROTY honors.

- Baltimore's Eddie Murray beats out Oakland's Mitchell Page for AL ROTY.

- Jim Colborn of KC no-hits Texas on May 14.

- Dennis Eckersley of Cleveland no-hits California on May 30.

- Bert Blyleven of Texas no-hits California on Sept. 22.

- Merv Rettenmund of Padres sets new ML record with 86 plate appearances as a pinch hitter.

- On April 10, Cleveland and Boston combine to score ML record 19 runs in one inning.

Steve Carlton

Carlton Takes NL Cy Young

Steve Carlton copped his second National League Cy Young Award in 1977, as he posted a record of 23-10 for the East Division Champion Phillies. He also tossed 17 complete games and posted a 2.64 ERA. After a newspaper allegedly misquoted him, the Philly ace refused to grant interviews to the press for nearly a decade. A player who took his job seriously, the lefty stuffed cotton in his ears when on the mound to block out noise and maximize concentration.

Tom Seaver

Mets Cut Seaver

On June 15, 1977, Mets general manager M. Donald Grant traded Tom Seaver to the Reds for Doug Flynn, Steve Henderson, Pat Zachry, and Dan Norman. In his decade with the ballclub, Seaver won 189 games for the Mets. Despite the shakeup of the swap, Seaver still managed to win 21 games between his two teams in '77. The Mets came in dead last that season, 37 games back.

Rookie Sutter Saves 31 for Cubs

Long before the split-finger fastball became as common as domed stadia, Bruce Sutter was the only pitcher throwing the difficult pitch for fun and profit. As the stopper for some pretty mediocre Cub teams, Sutter dazzled the National League and was close to unhittable for a half-dozen years. In 1977, Sutter was 7-3 with 31 saves (second in the loop). Moreover, his other totals were phenomenal. He allowed just 69 hits in 107 innings. He fanned 129 batters while walking a mere 23. His ERA? A paltry 1.35.

Bruce Sutter

- On July 4, Red Sox beat Toronto 9-6 on the strength of eight homers.

- KC's Hal McRae leads ML with 54 doubles.

- Pirate Dave Parker tops the NL in batting (.338), hits (215), and doubles (44).

- Pirate John Candelaria tops ML with 2.34 ERA and .800 win pct.

- Carew leads ML with 239 hits, 128 runs, and .452 OBP, and AL in triples (16) and runs produced (214).

- Royals are first expansion team in history to top majors in wins, as they net 102.

- LA sends Bill Buckner, Ivan DeJesus, and Jeff Albert to the Cubs for Rick Monday and Mike Garman.

- Pittsburgh ships Tony Armas, Rick Langford, Doc Medich, and three other players to Oakland for Phil Garner and two other players.

Andre Dawson

Dawson Named NL ROTY

In 1977, Andre Dawson became the second Expo to win the National League Rookie of the Year Award, as he batted .282 while smacking 19 home runs and driving in 65 runs. Despite being overshadowed by catcher Gary Carter, the outfielder called "Awesome" became the greatest all-around player in the history of the franchise.

Murcer: 27 HRs, 89 RBI

The Cubs were Bobby Murcer's third major league address. The friendly confines of Wrigley Field were ideal for his compact lefthanded power swing, as he totaled 27 home runs and 89 RBI in 1977, his last great season. Murcer broke into broadcasting after retiring in 1983.

Niekro Puts Up a Mixed Year

Phil Niekro lost 20 games in 1977 to tie for first in defeats in the National League; in addition, he topped the loop in hits allowed (315), runs allowed (166), and walks (164). A workhorse for the Braves, Niekro also spearheaded the circuit in innings pitched (330), strikeouts (262), complete games (20), and—naturally for a knuckleballer—wild pitches (17). Niekro got a lot of his mileage out of his trademark toss, pitching in the majors until age 48.

Phil Niekro

Bobby Murcer

1977

- The AL revises its schedule: each team now plays divisional opponents only 13 times each per year.

- Gene Richards of San Diego goes 6-for-7 in 15 innings on July 26.

- The Cubs swap Bill Madlock and Rob Sperring to the Giants for Bobby Murcer and two other players.

- Detroit's Mark Fidrych hurts his knee in a spring training game; the injury alters his delivery and he is never again much of a factor.

- The Hall of Fame inducts Ernie Banks, Joe Sewell, Al Lopez, Amos Rusie, Martin Dihigo, and John Henry Lloyd.

- Rangers swap Willie Montanez to Mets for Jon Matlack and John Milner.

- Minors are stabilized at 17 leagues and 121 teams.

- Danny Frisella of Atlanta is killed in a dune buggy accident.

Ryan Racks Up 341 Ks

Named Pitcher of the Year by *The Sporting News*, Nolan Ryan compiled a 19-16 record in 1977 while leading the American League in strikeouts with 341 (almost 100 more than the runner-up), walks (204), and wild pitches (21). The pitching sensation also bred a disease dubbed the "Ryan flu"—a malady which infected batters in four- to five-day intervals, causing them to sit out games in which they were to face the righty. Batters simply couldn't touch Ryan's 100-mph fastball; their best strategy was waiting for a walk. In fact, in 1977, Ryan yielded fewer hits than walks (204-198)—an extreme rarity in baseball.

Nolan Ryan

Carew Peaks at .388

In the 36 years since Ted Williams hit .406, only Williams himself and Rod Carew had approached the lofty .400 plateau. Both batting machines got as high as .388 (Williams in 1957, Carew in '77). Carew compiled an American League-best 239 hits, 16 triples, and 128 runs scored in 1977. By permanently moving from second base to first in '76, Carew became one of only a handful of players in the history of the sport to play 1,000 games at two different positions.

Rod Carew

Garvey's Streak Ends

In 1977, Steve Garvey blasted 33 home runs during a season in which he fell below 200 hits and a .300 average for the first time in four years. It was this kind of slugging that kept his teammates from openly criticizing the image-conscious first baseman who many thought was a phony and a politician.

Guidry Posts 16-7 Mark

Born in the bayou of Louisiana, Ron Guidry threw a baseball harder than anyone weighing 160 pounds should be allowed. His "Louisiana Lightning" pitch yielded a 16-7 record in 1977, his first full season in the majors (he was 26 years old). At the conclusion of his career 11 years later, Guidry had accumulated 170 triumphs, fourth on the all-time Yankee list.

Ron Guidry

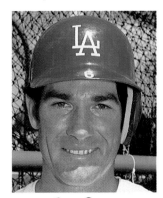

Steve Garvey

- Bucky Harris dies.

- Ernie Lombardi dies.

- Olympic Stadium opens on April 15, Phils vs. Montreal.

- AL teams combine for more than 10,000 runs scored, the first time a major league tops that mark.

- Padre Gene Tenace sets ML record for walks by a catcher with 125.

- Brooks Robinson retires as holder of many career fielding records, including top FA for a third baseman and most games played at third base.

- Robinson retires after an ML record 23 years with the same team.

- On June 24, Don Money of Milwaukee makes an AL record 12 assists by a second baseman in a nine-inning game.

- St. Louis' Garry Templeton leads ML with 18 triples.

- Boston's Ted Cox starts ML career with six straight hits.

George Foster

Foster Fires 52 Homers

In 1977, George Foster became the first batter since Willie Mays in 1965 to whack 50 or more home runs, as he blasted 52 dingers (31 of those round-trippers were hit on the road, which set a major league record for righties). Even more impressive is Foster's accumulation of a .320 average and 149 RBI for the Reds that season. He captured the MVP Award for his efforts.

Sparky Lyle

Lyle Takes AL Cy Young

Albert "Sparky" Lyle was more than one of the game's great characters. His flaky exterior belied an inner strength that helped him capture the 1977 American League Cy Young Award, becoming the first reliever to cop the title. His 26 saves ranked second in the circuit that season, and his record was an outstanding 13-5.

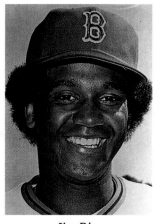

Jim Rice

Rice Is Sensational

Jim Rice (shown without his moustache and without a frown—a rare photograph) enjoyed a spectacular season in 1977. The moody Rice batted .320 with 39 home runs (tops in the American League) and 114 RBI (third in the circuit). His .593 slugging average and 382 total bases placed first in the junior circuit. He hit three homers in one game that season.

1977

- Minnesota's Larry Hisle tops AL in RBI (119).

- Ranger Toby Harrah leads AL in walks (109).

- Smith has National League's top OBP (.432) and is third in slugging (.576).

- Jim Palmer, KC's Dennis Leonard, and Minnesota's Dave Goltz tie for AL lead in wins with 20.

- Palmer paces AL in innings (319) and ties Ryan for most CGs in ML (22).

- California's Frank Tanana has AL's top ERA (2.54).

- Phil Niekro tops NL in Ks (262) and CGs (20).

- Ryan leads ML in fewest hits allowed per game with 5.96—nearly a hit per game less than any other ML pitcher.

- Rollie Fingers of San Diego tops ML with 35 saves.

1977

World Series

Randolph, Russell Flop in Series

In an action shot from the 1977 World Series, Willie Randolph dives for second base while shortstop Billy Russell lunges for the toss. Randolph gave a dismal performance in the fall classic that year, batting only .160. He did, however, manage to outhit Russell by six points, as the Yankees beat the Dodgers in six games.

Jackson on Fire in Series

Such is the stuff of which legends are made...Reggie Jackson *(left)* whacked three home runs to put the Yankees out of reach in the sixth and decisive game of the 1977 World Series. His third home run, a solo shot in the eighth inning, rocked Yankee Stadium and wowed TV viewers throughout the country. No one since the immortal Babe Ruth had ever hit three homers in a Series game. Teammate Chris Chambliss (shown greeting Jackson at the plate) also blasted his lone home run of the Series in that game. Jackson wrapped up the affair with a .450 average, five home runs, and eight RBI.

Reggie Jackson, Chris Chambliss

- Boston's Bill Campbell leads AL with 31 saves.

- Seaver tops NL with seven shutouts; Tanana likewise tops AL with seven shutouts.

- Kansas City's Paul Splittorff has best win pct. in AL (.727), as he goes 16-6.

- Twins lead ML with .282 team BA, as Carew hits .388 and teammate Lyman Bostock bats .336.

- Frank Taveras of Pittsburgh tops majors with 70 steals.

- Phils win 101 games for second year in a row to tie own club record.

- Tommy John of LA, out all of 1975 after elbow reconstruction surgery, rebounds to win 20 games for first time in his career.

- The expansion Seattle Mariners finish sixth in AL West, ahead of Oakland, only two years after the A's won their fifth straight division flag.

YANKS MASSACRE BOSTON, DOWN DODGERS AGAIN

In 1978, the baseball world revolved around the American League East. For the final ten weeks of the season, the Red Sox and the Yankees were involved in a wild, exciting race, full of memorable moments on and off the field.

Through mid-July, it was all Red Sox. They were enjoying a 13½-game lead over the second-place Brewers and were getting outstanding performances from a host of players, especially Jim Rice. Rice was on his way to an MVP season, in which he would bat .315 with 46 home runs and 139 RBI.

To make life even better for Red Sox rooters, the disliked Yankees—two-time defending pennant-winners—were in the midst of intense turmoil. Reggie Jackson had been suspended for five games by manager Billy Martin, and a week later Martin was forced to resign after making derogatory remarks about Jackson and owner George Steinbrenner.

Amid all the pandemonium, the Yankees began to play good baseball, showing up at Fenway in early September down by only 4 games. The Bronx Bombers went on to rock the Sox by scores of 15-3, 13-2, 7-0, and 7-4 in what became known as the "Boston Massacre."

There were exciting moments in other parks as well. Not only did Pete Rose get his 3,000th career hit, he also ran a 44-game hitting streak through June and July. His efforts couldn't carry the Reds, though, as they fell 2½ games short of the Dodgers in the NL West. The Phillies, led by Greg Luzinski's 35 homers, edged out the Pirates to capture their third straight NL East title.

The Kansas City Royals, led by manager Whitey Herzog, won the AL West. Herzog, always a lover of team speed, had his team on the run, as they led the league with 216 stolen bases. Even George Brett got into the act, with a career-high 23 thefts.

Back in Boston, the turbulent battle between the Sox and Yanks was reaching its climax. Tied after the regulation 162 games, the two squads played a single game at Fenway to determine the division champ. The star-crossed Red Sox went into the seventh inning with a slim 2-0 lead, but then Yankee shortstop Bucky Dent swatted a three-run homer into the left-field netting. The Yanks never relinquished the lead.

Set against the dramatic one-game playoff, postseason play paled in comparison. The Yankees beat the Royals for the third year running, three games to one. Game three featured three home runs by Brett, but Thurman Munson belted a two-run homer to win the game 6-5. A Roy White solo shot in game four secured the AL flag for the Yanks.

The Dodgers also won their playoffs three to one, beating Danny Ozark's Phillies. A tenth-inning single by shortstop Bill Russell drove in the winning run in the final game and put the Dodgers back in the World Series, setting the stage for a rematch of the 1977 Series.

Although the conclusion was a repeat of last year's World Series—the Yankees beat the Dodgers in six games—the storyline was different. After the Dodgers busted out of the starting gate, winning the first two contests, the Yankees shut them down the rest of the way.

The left side of the Yankees' infield was spectacular in the fall classic. Anyone who watched game three will never forget the amazing defensive might of Graig Nettles, who made several diving stops. Cy Young winner Ron Guidry, 25-3 during the regular season, went the distance in game three to earn the win.

The Yankees wrapped it up in game six. Dent, the Series MVP, banged out three hits, lifting the Bombers to a 7-2 victory and to their 22nd World Title.

1978

- Yanks repeat in AL to give them three consecutive flags.
- Dodgers triumph again in NL, setting up the majors' first World Series rematch since 1958.
- Phils bow in LCS for third year in a row, as LA beats them in four games on Steve Garvey's four homers.

- Royals lose to New York for third year in a row in ALCS, this time in four games.
- Yanks again beat Dodgers in six games in the World Series.
- Reggie Jackson has another big World Series, hitting .391 with two home runs.

- Yankee second baseman Brian Doyle, playing for injured Willie Randolph, leads all Series players with .438 batting average.
- Yanks win AL East crown by defeating Red Sox in one-game playoff at Fenway, as Bucky Dent's three-run homer wins it 5-4.

Bucky Dent launched one of the most famous home runs in Yankee—and perhaps American League—history in 1978. The dinger came during the showdown game between the Yanks and Red Sox for first place in the AL East. Lofting a Mike Torrez pitch into the left-field screen at Fenway Park, Dent's three-run homer in the seventh inning erased a 2-0 edge for Boston. Dent is pictured being greeted by teammates Roy White (No. 6) and Chris Chambliss, who scored on his epic blast.

- Red Sox blow 14-game lead over Yankees as late as July 17.

- Billy Martin resigns as Yankees manager in midseason under pressure from owner George Steinbrenner.

- Martin punches out a *Nevada State Journal* reporter.

- New manager Bob Lemon leads Yanks to AL flag.

- Lemon is first manager in AL history to pilot a team to a World Championship after taking over the team in midseason.

- Pete Rose sets modern NL record by hitting in 44 consecutive games.

- Ron Guidry is 25-3, sets win pct. record for 25-game winner at .893, and tops ML with 1.74 ERA.

- Guidry is unanimous choice for AL Cy Young.

- Padre Gaylord Perry wins NL Cy Young, becoming only hurler to win award in both leagues.

Ron Guidry

Lou Whitaker

Whitaker Named AL ROTY

His slick fielding, speed, and .285 batting average helped Lou Whitaker win the American League Rookie of the Year Award in 1978, making him the first Tiger who wasn't a pitcher to win the title since Harvey Kuenn in 1953. "Sweet Lou," who debuted with keystone mate Alan Trammell in September 1977, continued to turn two with his pal until 1995. Whitaker became the team's best second baseman since Charlie Gehringer.

Guidry Goes Off on Rampage

Had Jim Rice not established his Cooperstown credentials with a career year in 1978, Ron Guidry would have been a sure bet as American League MVP that season. As it was, the slender lefty won the Cy Young Award for his 25-3 record hands down. The Ragin' Cajun set three Yankees records in '78: most consecutive wins to start a season (13), most Ks in a year (248), and most strikeouts in a game (18, against the Angels on June 17).

Amos Otis

Otis Hits .429 in ALCS

Amos Otis put on a dazzling performance in the 1978 American League Championship Series, leading his team with a .429 batting average. Otis also set the then-record of four stolen bases in a five-game playoff event. His postseason heroics capped a solid '78 season in which he hit .298 with 22 home runs and 96 RBI.

1978

- Jim Rice edges out Guidry for AL MVP.

- Rice leads AL in hits (213), home runs (46), RBI (139), triples (15), total bases (406), SA (.600), and runs produced (214).

- Rice is the last MLer to reach 400 total bases until 1998.

- Pirate Dave Parker named NL MVP.

- Parker repeats as NL bat champ (.334), and also leads loop in total bases (340), SA (.585), and runs produced (189).

- Rod Carew takes second consecutive AL bat crown (.333) and leads loop in OBP (.415).

- Cincinnati's George Foster again tops NL in homers (40) and RBI (120).

- Giant Bobby Bonds is a member of 30/30 club (30 homers/30 steals) for ML record fifth time.

- California's Lyman Bostock, AL bat crown runner-up in 1977, is shot to death.

Pete Rose

Rose Breaks, Ties Batting Streaks in NL

In 1978, Pete Rose (pictured being congratulated by former Braves great Tommy Holmes) bettered the modern National League batting streak of 37 games set by Holmes in 1945. Rose went on to hit in 44 straight games, tying Willie Keeler's all-time National League mark. On May 5, 1978, Rose became the youngest player to reach 3,000 hits. He was 37 years old at the time.

Billy Martin

Steinbrenner Kicks Billy Out of NY

Billy Martin sealed his fate in July of 1978, while still at the Yankee helm, when he spouted off about owner George Steinbrenner and outfielder Reggie Jackson. Said Martin: "The two of them deserve each other: One's a born liar; the other's convicted." Martin was forced to resign shortly after making the remarks. He returned to the Yankees in July 1979.

- Dodgers become the first team to draw more than three million fans in a season.
- Joe Morgan's record skein of 91 consecutive errorless games ends.
- NL wins All-Star Game 7-3 at San Diego for its seventh consecutive victory.
- On July 30, the Braves suffer worst loss by a home team in NL history, as they're blown out by Expos 19-0.
- Giants get Vida Blue from A's for five players and $390,000.
- Average player's salary is up to $90,000.
- Rose leads ML with 51 doubles.
- Detroit's Ron LeFlore tops AL in steals (68) and runs (126).
- Atlanta's Bob Horner is NL ROTY.
- Detroit's Lou Whitaker is AL ROTY.
- Rose gets his 3,000th hit.
- Bob Forsch of the Cards no-hits Phils on April 16.

Horner Is NL ROTY

Expectations for Bob Horner ran high in 1978. After signing with the Braves off the campus of Arizona State University, Horner slugged his way to the National League Rookie of the Year Award in '78. Smacking a dinger in his first game in the majors, he went on to tally 23 home runs and 63 RBI in only 89 games that season. In the next two years, despite limited duty, he would club 68 home runs. In 1987, he was playing the game in Japan.

Eddie Murray

Murray Clubs 27 HRs Again

In 1977, Eddie Murray became the first designated hitter to win the American League Rookie of the Year Award. Hitting .283 that season, he racked up 27 home runs and 88 RBI. As a sophomore in '78, Murray was switched to first base, where he batted .285 with 27 home runs and 95 RBI. The all-time home run king for the Orioles ranks among the all-time leaders in grandslams (he nailed at least one in each season from 1980 through 1986).

Bob Horner

Parker Named NL MVP

In 1978, Dave Parker was made the leader of the superstar-studded team that was often known as the "Pittsburgh Lumber Company." Parker followed on the heels of Roberto Clemente and Willie Stargell by winning the National League MVP Award in 1978 with a .334 batting average, .585 slugging average, 30 home runs, and 117 RBI. Parker achieved most of this success with a wired broken jaw which required him to wear a football-type helmet while at bat.

Dave Parker

1978

- Tom Seaver of Cincinnati no-hits Cards on June 16.

- Cardinal Keith Hernandez wins first of ML record ten consecutive Gold Gloves at first base.

- The Hall of Fame inducts Eddie Mathews, Addie Joss, and Larry MacPhail.

- The Yanks trade Sparky Lyle and four other players to Texas for Dave Righetti and four other players.

- The Mets send Jerry Koosman to Twins for Jesse Orosco and a minor leaguer.

- Texas ships Perry to San Diego for Dave Tomlin and $125,000.

- Cleveland trades Buddy Bell to Texas for Toby Harrah.

- Texas swaps Bobby Bonds and Len Barker to Cleveland for Jim Kern and Larvell Blanks.

- Ray Grebey named head of the owners' Player Relations Committee.

Perry, 42, Takes Cy Young

Gaylord Perry captured the second Cy Young Award of his career in 1978—at the age of 42. His 21-6 record and .778 winning percentage that year (both highs in the National League) made the veteran righty the first hurler to capture the title in both circuits. For years, Perry was criticized for doctoring the ball—using grease, jellies, Vaseline. Said Billy Martin: "When you stand next to Perry, he smells like a drugstore."

Steinbrenner: Pure Yankee

George Steinbrenner symbolized the Yankees. He represented grit—like the club's plucky comeback in 1978—and arrogance—by involving himself in the everyday affairs of managing a ballclub. Steinbrenner changed managers in the middle of '78, and the move seemed to spark New York to the World Crown. Although he tried this maneuver several more times in his career, it never again brought success.

George Steinbrenner

Gaylord Perry

George Foster

Foster Tops NL in RBI

Although he didn't quite measure up to his epic 1977 season, George Foster still had plenty to smile about in 1978, as he whacked 40 home runs, batted .281, and spearheaded the National League with 120 RBI. For the remainder of his 18-year career, the outfielder would be expected to duplicate his heroics in 1977—a goal he never achieved.

- Don Gullett's career ends at age 27 by a bum arm.

- Jesse Haines dies.

- Dodgers coach Jim Gilliam dies.

- O's rookie Sammy Stewart fans seven consecutive Cleveland hitters in his ML debut on Sept 1.

- Third baseman Butch Hobson of Boston is first ML regular in 62 years to post a FA below .900.

- Guidry's nine shutouts top ML and tie the AL record for a lefthander.

- Ross Grimsley becomes first Expos pitcher to win 20 games in a season, as he wins 20 even.

- Baltimore's Eddie Murray is second in AL in total bases (293) but with 113 less than leader Rice.

- Ivan DeJesus of the Cubs leads NL in runs (104).

- Garvey tops NL with 202 hits.

- Atlanta's Jeff Burroughs paces ML with 117 walks and .436 OBP.

Richard Fans 303

J.R. Richard showcased his incredible fastball in 1978 while fanning a National League-high 303 batters. The Astro ace surpassed his personal record for strikeouts by 89, while also topping the loop in walks with 141. The 6′ 8″ righty, when poised to pitch, appeared to hitters to be a power forward with a bazooka.

Jim Rice

Rice Named AL MVP

Not since Joe DiMaggio garnered a total of 418 bases in 1937 had an American League player tallied 400 total bases until Jim Rice (pictured) led the league with 406 in 1978. Rice batted .315 that season, leading the circuit in home runs (46), triples (15), hits (213), RBI (139), and slugging percentage (.600). His performance earned him the 1978 American League MVP Award. Rice ranks third on the all-time Red Sox list in round-trippers (379), RBI (1,423), and hits (2,403).

J.R. Richard

1978

- Cardinal Garry Templeton leads NL in triples with 13.
- Pirate Omar Moreno leads ML with 71 steals.
- Ranger Mike Hargrove, known as the "Human Rain Delay" for taking so much time in the box, paces AL in walks with 107.

- George Brett leads AL in doubles (45).
- Perry leads NL pitchers in wins (21) and win pct. (.778).
- Houston's J.R. Richard tops ML with 303 Ks.
- Phil Niekro leads NL in innings (334) and CGs (22).

- Craig Swan of the Mets has best ERA in the NL (2.43), narrowly beating out Montreal's Steve Rogers.
- Bob Knepper of the Giants paces NL with six shutouts.
- Rollie Fingers of San Diego leads majors with 37 saves.

1978

Welch Saves Game Two

Twenty-one-year-old Bob Welch of the Dodgers became a household name the instant he struck out Reggie Jackson to end game two of the 1978 World Series. With runners on first and second and two out, the righthanded reliever fanned Mr. October, blazing a 3-2 fastball by Jackson to preserve the one-run margin of victory. Welch paid the price of instant fame three days later, when he couldn't save the Dodgers in another 4-3 game.

Bill Russell

Yanks Cash in on Flub by Russell

Although Bill Russell was a solid member of the Dodger infield that comprised Steve Garvey, Ron Cey, and Davey Lopes, he may be best remembered for his weak composure during game five of the 1978 World Series. The deafening crowd noise in Yankee Stadium that day caused the usually unflappable Russell to bobble Roy White's routine first-inning grounder for an error. The Yankees went on to win the contest—a game they had trailed 2-0—by a score of 12-2, setting a Series record with 16 singles.

Bob Welch

Graig Nettles

Graig Stars at Third

Not since Brooks Robinson did his best imitation of a vacuum cleaner in the 1970 fall classic had a third baseman so dominated a World Series as did Graig Nettles in 1978. Although the slugger hit just .160 over the six-game tournament, his remarkable fielding more than made up for his weak bat. He was sensational in game three, making four incredible stops. After winning that contest largely on Puff's fielding, the Yankees went on to take the World Championship. On the season, Nettles whacked 27 homers and drove in 93 runs.

- Mike Caldwell of Milwaukee tops ML with 23 complete games and wins 22 games.

- Jim Palmer leads AL in innings (296), wins 21 for O's.

- Goose Gossage of the Yankees leads AL in saves (27).

- Brewers top ML in runs (804), homers (173), BA (.276), SA (.432), and OBP (.342), as they finish just 6½ back of Yankees in AL East.

- The Mariners and Blue Jays, both in their second year of existence, finish last in their divisions and lose over 100 games apiece.

- Kent Tekulve saves 31 games for Pittsburgh and pitches in an ML top 91 games.

- Oriole Mark Belanger wins sixth consecutive Gold Glove at short.

- Three Oakland pitchers lead AL in games: Bob Lacey (74), Dave Heaverlo (69), and Elias Sosa (68).

PIRATES, POPS DANCE TO WORLD CROWN

In 1979, the Pittsburgh Pirates led the league in outfits. Their arsenal of uniforms was so vast—black caps and yellow jerseys, yellow caps and white jerseys, and so on—that they had 64 possible combinations at their disposal.

The Pirates' lineup of players was just as varied as their line of garb. They featured an outfielder who looked like a Pittsburgh Steelers linebacker (the 6' 5", 230-pound Dave Parker), and a pitcher who looked more like a placekicker (the 6' 4", 170-pound Kent Tekulve). And, of course, they had Willie "Pops" Stargell, an inspiring presence at bat and in the clubhouse. The Pirates, whose theme song was "We Are Family," won the NL East by 2 games over Montreal.

The World Champion Yankees didn't even come close to repeating, as they lost two of their key players. Relief ace Goose Gossage was sidelined for two months due to an injury he incurred in a fight with teammate Cliff Johnson. And gritty catcher Thurman Munson was killed in an airplane crash in August.

The Baltimore Orioles ended the Yankees' three-year divisional reign, winning 102 games. Cy Young winner Mike Flanagan (23-9) paced the pitching staff, while veteran Ken Singleton (111 RBI) spearheaded the offense. They beat the Brewers by 8 games and the Red Sox by 11 1/2.

Boston boasted a fearsome offense, as Fred Lynn and Jim Rice tied for second in the league in home runs with 39. However, the pitching, hurt by the departure of Luis Tiant to the Yankees, was too weak to beat the Orioles.

The American League West was tight to the end, as four teams ranked within 6 games of first place. The California Angels, starring MVP Don Baylor and his 139 RBI, took their first division crown. The Twins, who finished just 6 back, were pleasantly surprised by their off-season pickup of Jerry Koosman. Koosman, 11-35 in his previous two years with the Mets, won 20 games for the Twins.

The big news in the senior circuit was Pete Rose's preseason defection to the Philadelphia Phillies. His arrival, however, did not promote the Phils to champs just yet, as they settled for fourth place. In St. Louis, first baseman Keith Hernandez won the batting crown (.344) and shared the MVP honors with Stargell (.281, 32 home runs, 82 RBI). Lou

Brock retired, having stolen more bases (938) than any player in history. The Cubs boasted a Cy Young winner with Bruce Sutter, who saved 37 games.

The Rose-less Reds were still good enough to win the NL West. Though the Big Red Machine was losing its hitting punch, its pitching was as strong as ever—Tom Seaver went 16-6. Cincinnati edged out the strong-armed Houston Astros, whose staff included Joe Niekro (21-11), J.R. Richard (313 strikeouts), and Ken Forsch (who pitched a no-hitter April 7 against the Expos).

Pittsburgh swept Cincinnati in the National League Championship Series, though it took two extra-inning wins to do it. Stargell cracked two key homers as the Pirates outscored the Reds 15 runs to five. Baltimore defeated California in four games in the American League Championship Series, which included three nail-biting finishes and a shutout.

The Orioles and the Bucs battled through a seven-game World Series. After losing the opener, Pittsburgh evened it up at one game apiece when Manny Sanguillen drove in Ed Ott with a ninth-inning single off Don Stanhouse. Baltimore won the next two games to go up three games to one, but the Pirates stormed back. They won the final three games—7-1, 4-0, 4-1—to take the World Title.

1979

- Orioles return to top in AL.

- Pirates win in NL to set up repeat of exciting 1971 World Series.

- Angels succumb to Orioles in four games in ALCS after winning first division crown.

- Pirates sweep Reds in NLCS.

- Pirates snatch World Series after trailing three games to one—second time in franchise history they've pulled off this feat.

- Willie Stargell is World Series hitting star for Pittsburgh with .400 batting average, three homers, and seven runs batted in.

- Pirates keystone combo of Phil Garner and Tim Foli combine for 22 hits and ten runs scored in Series; Garner bats .500 in the affair.

- Stargell, age 39, becomes oldest MVP in history, as he and Cardinal Keith Hernandez finish in flat tie for NL award.

Willie Stargell (shown in the center of the trio of Pirate team members) was a man with a mission in the 1979 World Series. "Pops" batted .400 in the fall classic, racking up a trio of home runs and seven RBI. His most sterling moment of the seven-game affair came in the finale. The Series MVP went 4-for-5 in that game, hitting a home run in the sixth inning to take the lead.

- Angel Don Baylor wins AL MVP after leading ML in runs (120), RBI (139), and runs produced (223).

- Boston's Fred Lynn wins AL bat crown (.333), and also leads in SA (.637).

- Baltimore's Mike Flanagan leads ML in wins with 23, cops AL Cy Young.

- Cubs reliever Bruce Sutter wins NL Cy Young, as he tops the majors with 37 saves.

- After 1979 season, Astros sign free agent Nolan Ryan for estimated $1 million.

- Cub Dave Kingman tops ML in homers (48) and NL in SA (.613).

- San Diego's Dave Winfield tops National League in RBI (118) and total bases (333).

- Yankees star Thurman Munson dies in plane crash on August 2.

- Phillie Larry Bowa sets ML record for shortstops with .991 FA.

Larry Bowa

Bowa Makes Marks on Field

In 1979, Larry Bowa established a major league record for highest career fielding percentage for a shortstop (1,000 or more games) with a .982 mark. He also set the single-season fielding mark at .991. Some critics, however, consider these marks to be tainted and claim that Bowa was helped by a generous official scorer in Philadelphia who rarely credited fielders with errors.

Stargell Posts Glittering Year

The leader of the Pirate "Fam-a-lee," Willie Stargell was an inspiration to his teammates both on and off the field. As team captain, Willie dispensed "Stargell Stars" to his teammates for great plays and key hits. Sharing National League MVP honors with Keith Hernandez in 1979, Stargell hit .281 with 32 home runs and 82 RBI. He was also named MVP in both the Championship Series and the World Series that season.

Yaz Reaches a Milestone

American League history was made in 1979 as Carl Yastrzemski, the captain of the Red Sox, became the only player in the junior circuit to hit 400 home runs and gather 3,000 hits. Prior to Yastrzemski, the only player to come close to the milestone was former Tiger right fielder Al Kaline, who retired in 1974 with 399 home runs and 3,007 hits.

Carl Yastrzemski

Willie Stargell 8

Willie Stargell

1979

- Pete Rose gets 200 or more hits for record tenth time in career.

- Billy Martin takes over from Bob Lemon as Yankees skipper 64 games into season, only to be fired again after season.

- NL wins the All-Star Game 7-6 at Seattle.

- Rick Sutcliffe of the Dodgers wins NL ROTY.

- John Castino of Minnesota named AL ROTY.

- Lou Brock gets his 3,000th hit.

- Brock retires with ML record for career stolen bases (938).

- Carl Yastrzemski collects his 3,000th career hit.

- Phillie Del Unser homers in three consecutive pinch-hit plate appearances.

- Cardinal Garry Templeton is first switch-hitter to get 100 hits from each side of the plate in a season.

Niekro Breaks Even

A player whose name became synonymous with the Braves franchise in the 1970s, Phil Niekro was the winner of the 1979 Lou Gehrig Award, which honored his exemplary character and plentiful contributions to the Atlanta community. A pitcher whose name became synonymous with the knuckleball, the 40-year-old Niekro won 21 games and lost 20 in '79.

Phil Niekro

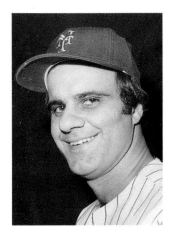

Joe Torre

Torre Stuck in Cellar

In his first three years as manager (1977 to 1979), Joe Torre guided the Mets to three consecutive last-place finishes. The former slugger's three-year won-lost record totaled 178-263.

Funeral of Thurman Munson

Munson Dies in Crash

Baseball lost a fiery competitor, one destined for the Hall of Fame, when Thurman Munson died in the crash of his private jet in Canton, Ohio, on August 2, 1979. The Yankee captain/catcher was in his prime, having just turned 32 years of age. His 11-year career totals boast a .292 batting average, 113 home runs, and 701 RBI.

- The Astros are last team in the majors to hit more triples (52) than home runs (49).

- On May 31, Detroit's Pat Underwood makes ML debut against brother Tom of Toronto; Pat beats Tom 1-0.

- Ken Forsch of Astros no-hits Atlanta on April 7.

- Hernandez tops NL in batting (.344), doubles (48), runs (116), runs produced (210), and OBP (.421).

- Phil Niekro of Atlanta and his brother Joe of Houston tie for NL lead in wins (21).

- Phil Niekro both wins and loses 20 games as he goes 21-20.

- Phil Niekro makes 44 starts, most by any NL pitcher in a season since 1917.

- Milwaukee's Gorman Thomas leads AL with 45 homers; he also has 123 RBI.

- Houston's J.R. Richard leads ML in Ks (313) and ERA (2.71).

Dave Kingman

Kingman Slugs 48 HRs

In 1979, Dave Kingman became known as the new "Mayor of Waveland Avenue" in honor of his National League-leading 48 home runs, many of which landed on front yards and door stoops in the Wrigleyville region of Chicago. Kingman's 115 RBI and loop-high .613 slugging average that year also earned him the nickname of "Kong." Kingman tied a major league record by smacking five homers in two consecutive games in '79.

Ron Guidry

Guidry Mows Down Hitters

Although Ron Guidry didn't match in 1979 what he had accomplished the previous season, the cagey southpaw did sport a record of 18-8 while leading the American League with a 2.78 ERA. Guidry, who would continue on into the 1980s, could "bring it" with the best of them.

Fred Lynn

Lynn Reaches His Peak

In the year that followed his fullest season (150 games in 1978), oft-injured Fred Lynn enjoyed his greatest performance. Leading the American League with a .333 batting average and a .637 slugging mark, he smacked 39 home runs and drove in 122 runs.

1979

- The Hall of Fame inducts Willie Mays, Warren Giles, and Hack Wilson.

- Ranger Buddy Bell wins first of six consecutive Gold Gloves given to AL third basemen.

- KC's Willie Wilson leads the AL in steals with 83.

- Omar Moreno tops the NL with 77 swipes.

- Phillie Bob Boone, after ending Johnny Bench's skein of ten straight Gold Gloves in 1978, wins second Gold Glove as an NL catcher.

- Templeton leads NL with 211 hits.

- Oakland's Matt Keough loses 14 straight games and finishes the season at 2-17.

- Joe Niekro sets an Astros record when he wins nine consecutive games.

- Detroit sends Ron LeFlore to Montreal for Dan Schatzeder.

Winfield Knows RBI

Drafted by four ballclubs in three sports (baseball, basketball, and football) after his senior year at the University of Minnesota, Dave Winfield was a decade ahead of Bo Jackson in the versatility department. In 1979, Winfield hit .308 (for the second consecutive year) with 34 home runs (third in the National League) and 118 RBI (tops in the circuit). The 12-time All-Star also led the loop with 333 total bases and came in fourth with a .558 slugging average that year.

Bruce Sutter

Dave Winfield

Sutter Wins NL Cy Young

In 1979, Bruce Sutter saved 37 games for the fifth-place Cubs and won his second consecutive All-Star Game, as he mastered what some considered at the time to be a spitter or a trick pitch. His efforts earned him the '79 National League Cy Young Award. Sutter took the Cubs to arbitration that year, winning a $700,000 salary—a staggering amount for that era.

- Twins send Rod Carew to the Angels for four players.

- Dodgers play an ML record 11 straight errorless games in May.

- Atlanta's Gene Garber loses an ML record 16 games in relief.

- Rob Picciolo of the A's has just three walks in 348 at-bats.

- KC's Darrell Porter tops AL with 121 walks and sets loop record for most walks by a catcher.

- Porter becomes the first catcher since Mickey Cochrane in 1933 to top AL in OBP (.429).

- Rangers play an AL record 135 night games.

- An umpire strike on March 7 forces teams to use sandlot and semipro umps in spring training games.

- Walter O'Malley dies.

- The average player's salary shoots up to $113,500, as salaries approach $1 million for the first time.

Niekro Wins 21 Games

Despite being viewed as the lesser of the two knuckleballing Niekros, Joe fashioned a career year in 1979, winning 21 games to tie brother Phil for the lead in the National League. Unlike his older sibling, however, the Astro hurler lost just 11 games to yield a .656 winning percentage (second in the loop).

Joe Niekro

Don Baylor

Baylor Named AL MVP

Don Baylor enjoyed his greatest season in 1979, winning the American League Most Valuable Player Award while leading the Angels to a West Division title. Batting .296 and smacking 36 home runs that season, Groove headed the loop with 139 RBI and 120 runs scored.

World Series

Kent Tekulve

Tekulve Saves Pirates

Following an eight-year apprenticeship in the minors, Kent Tekulve emerged in the mid-1970s as the bullpen stopper for the Pirates. In 1979, the stork-like righty saved 31 games and set a World Series record by protecting the lead in games two, six, and seven of the fall classic.

Stargell Shines on D

Willie Stargell stretches to retire Dave Skaggs in this action shot from the 1979 World Series. Although his bat did most of his talking during his career, Stargell was a better than average fielder who won more than a few of the stars pictured on his cap for outstanding defensive play.

1979

- Bell is first in AL history to make 200 or more hits and not hit .300.

- George Brett becomes second player in AL history to collect 20 or more homers, doubles, and triples in a season.

- Brett tops the majors with exactly 20 three-baggers.

- Brett paces ML with 212 hits, is second in AL in batting (.329).

- Templeton leads NL with 19 triples—first time since 1931 that both leaders have amassed that many.

- Mike Schmidt tops NL in walks (120) and is second in homers (45).

- Chicago's Chet Lemon and Brewer Cecil Cooper tie for AL lead in doubles with 44.

- Phil Niekro tops NL in innings (342) and CGs (23).

- Phil's brother Joe ties with Tom Seaver and Montreal's Steve Rogers for loop-lead in shutouts with five.

Flanagan Wins Cy Young

Following in the footsteps of Mike Cuellar and Jim Palmer, Mike Flanagan in 1979 became the third Oriole pitcher to win the American League Cy Young Award. The lefty's 23-9 record led the loop and his five shutouts tied for first place that season. Traveling to the World Title in '79, Flanagan won one game in both the Championship Series and the World Series.

Garner Heats Up in Series

Phil "Scrap Iron" Garner posted a solid regular season in 1979, batting .293 with 11 home runs and 59 RBI. It was in postseason action, however, that Garner hit full stride. He batted .417 in the National League Championship Series, finishing second on the Pirates. He went all out in the '79 World Series, leading the team with a .500 batting average.

Phil Garner

Mike Flanagan

Brock Hangs Up Spikes

Lou Brock topped off his 19-year career with a .304 average and 21 stolen bases in 1979. While becoming the career leader in swipes (938), Brock stole 50 or more cushions for a record 12 consecutive seasons. At the plate and on the bases, he usually won the psychological battle against the pitcher. Perhaps the message taped to his locker reflects the mind games he played with hurlers.

Lou Brock

- Seaver leads NL in win pct. (.727).

- Milwaukee's Mike Caldwell is AL win pct. leader (.727).

- Ron Guidry tops AL in ERA (2.78).

- Mike Marshall of the Twins leads AL with 32 saves.

- Dennis Martinez of the O's paces AL with 18 CGs and 292 innings.

- Ryan leads AL with 223 Ks in his last season with California.

- Tommy John wins 21 for Yankees, is second in AL in wins, ERA (2.97), innings (276), and CGs (17).

- Jim Rice tops AL in total bases (369) and is second in homers (39), hits (201), RBI (130), and runs produced (208).

- Oakland tumbles into AL West cellar again with a 54-108 record.

- Toronto loses 109 games—the most in the AL on a 162-game schedule.

As good as Philadelphia's Mike Schmidt had been in the 1970s, some Philly fans still considered him an underachiever. Although he had taken three consecutive NL home run crowns and traveled to the playoffs three times, he had not claimed an MVP Award or a league pennant.

The 1980 season, however, proved to be a different kind of year for the 31-year-old Schmidt. He set career-highs with 48 home runs and 121 RBI, won the MVP Award, and, most importantly, led the Phillies to a win over Kansas City in the World Series.

Managed by Dallas Green, the Phillies were a veteran club extremely strong up the middle. Their pitchers included Cy Young-winner Steve Carlton (24-9), Dick Ruthven (17-10), and Tug McGraw (20 saves). The Phillies beat the Expos in the penultimate game of the season, on Schmidt's two-run homer in the top of the 11th, to clinch the division crown.

As good as that race was, it wasn't half as exciting as the NL West dogfight. The Los Angeles Dodgers beat the Houston Astros in the season's last three games to force a one-game playoff between the two teams. Houston won the playoff 7-1, and was on the way to its first postseason series.

A tragedy kept the Astros' celebration in check, however. Their great hurler, the 6' 8" J.R. Richard, suffered a near-fatal

PHILLIES ROMP TO THEIR FIRST-EVER WORLD TITLE

stroke in July. Although he returned to good health, he never pitched in the majors again.

In the American League East, the Yankees took the division crown under manager Dick Howser. The Yanks got great years out of Reggie Jackson, who hit .300 with 41 homers and 111 RBI; catcher Rick Cerone, who batted .277 with 85 RBI; and Tommy John, who won 22 games. The Orioles, winners of 100 games, came in a close second.

The most spectacular player of the year was MVP George Brett, who batted .390 and had 118 RBI in 117 games. The Royals had plenty of other talent as well; Willie Wilson stole 79 bases and Willie Aikens powered 20 home runs and 98 RBI. Dennis Leonard led the staff with 20 wins and Larry Gura added 18. Rickey Henderson's 100 stolen bases were not enough for the Oakland A's, who finished in second place, 14 games behind Kansas City.

The National League playoffs provided their own drama, as the last four games all went into extra

innings. In game three, Houston's Denny Walling drove home Joe Morgan with a sacrifice fly in the bottom of the 11th to break a scoreless tie. In game four, tenth-inning hits from Philadelphia's Pete Rose, Greg Luzinski, and Manny Trillo gave the visitors a 5-3 win. And in the deciding match, Philly overcame a three-run, eighth-inning deficit to send the game into extra frames. Garry Maddox's double in the tenth inning drove home Del Unser to give the Phils their first pennant in 30 years.

There was a surprise finish in the AL. The Royals, who had lost to the Yanks three straight times in the playoffs, scored a quick knockout and swept the Bombers. Second baseman Frank White of the Royals spearheaded all hitters in the tournament, racking up a .545 average and three RBI.

In the World Series, the Phils utilized the strengths that got them there, namely Schmidt and Carlton. Schmidt hit .381 and had seven RBI; Carlton won two games with a 2.40 ERA. The moment that will always be remembered, however, came in the ninth inning of game six. A pop-up squirted out of the mitt of Philly catcher Bob Boone, and Rose—the 39-year-old "Charlie Hustle"—charged over to grab the ricochet. McGraw then struck out Wilson to give the Phillies their first-ever World Championship.

1980

- Phils snag their first NL flag since 1950.

- Kansas City wins its premier AL pennant.

- Phils win dramatic five-game NLCS over Houston, as the last four games go into extra innings.

- Houston's Terry Puhl collects an NL record ten hits in LCS.

- Yankees stunned in ALCS, falling to KC in three straight games.

- Frank White is first winner of newly created ALCS MVP Award (Dusty Baker was first NL winner in 1977).

- Phils win first World Series in club history in six games.

- Royals Amos Otis and Willie Aikens each hit .400-plus in Series, but Mike Schmidt's key blows and Tug McGraw's relief work spark Phils.

- Steve Carlton becomes first NL starting pitcher to win two Series games since Steve Blass in 1971.

Reliever Tug McGraw was instrumental in the 1980 World Series triumph of the Phillies, as he won one game and saved two and held his ERA to 1.17. Not to be slighted was his enthusiastic cheerleading, which set the tone of victory for the Phillies. McGraw saved 20 games and posted a 1.47 ERA during the season.

- Dodgers force playoff in NL West by sweeping Houston on season's final weekend; Astros win the playoff, though, 7-1.

- George Brett named AL MVP, as he hits .390 after flirting with .400 much of the season.

- Brett also leads AL in SA (.664) and OBP (.461) by wide margins.

- Schmidt sets ML record for third basemen with 48 home runs; leads ML in homers and grabs NL MVP.

- Oriole Steve Stone wins AL Cy Young, as he leads ML with 25 wins.

- Carlton wins NL Cy Young, as he wins 24 games.

- On Oct. 5, LA's Manny Mota collects ML record 150th career pinch hit.

- Orioles finish second in AL East with 100 wins.

- Mike Parrott of Seattle loses 16 straight games.

- Houston pitching star J.R. Richard's career is ended by a stroke.

Nolan Ryan

Ryan Whiffs 3,000 Batters

Jumping at the chance to return to his native Texas in 1980, Nolan Ryan signed a contract with the Astros which made him baseball's first million-dollar-per-year player. Although Ryan gained his 3,000th career strikeout in '80, he sported a mediocre record of 11-10.

James Rodney Richard

Boone Solid Behind Plate

In 1980, Bob Boone started for his third consecutive division-winner. The Philly catcher more than made up for his weak bat that season (.229 average, nine home runs, 55 RBI) with a powerful throwing arm, a quick glove, and an unmatched rapport with his pitching staff. By the time postseason play rolled around, Boone had raised his level of hitting; he batted .412 with four RBI in the 1980 World Series.

George Hendrick

Hendrick Hits .302

His .302 batting average, 25 home runs, and 109 RBI earned George Hendrick a spot on the 1980 National League All-Star team (his third in a total of four appearances). The 1980 year was Hendrick's sixth season in which he hit 20 or more home runs.

J.R. Felled by Stroke

The most tragic moment of the 1980 baseball season occurred when James Rodney Richard was felled by a stroke shortly after his appearance as a starter for the National League in the All-Star Game. To recuperate, the ace righty took two years off before spending time in the minors. As it turned out, he never pitched another inning in the majors.

Bob Boone

1980

- Major league attendance soars to record 43 million.

- Cubs relief ace Bruce Sutter awarded staggering salary of $700,000 when he takes club to arbitration.

- Yankees manager Dick Howser is fired after leading the club to 103 wins in first year with New York.

- Padre Ozzie Smith sets ML record for shortstops with 621 assists.

- NL wins All-Star Game 4-2 at LA.

- Steve Howe of LA named NL ROTY.

- Super Joe Charboneau of Cleveland is AL ROTY.

- Willie Wilson of Royals sets new ML record with 705 at-bats.

- Income from TV accounts for record 30 percent of game's $500 million in revenues.

- Average player now makes about $185,000.

Super Cooper Hits .352

Cecil Cooper posted his best season in 1980. The Brewer first baseman batted 38 points behind George Brett, the leader in the American League, and still managed to collect a career-high .352 average that year. Cooper also tallied a circuit-high 122 RBI and socked 25 home runs to earn a spot on the 1980 AL All-Star team.

Cecil Cooper

Fisk Changes His Sox

Carlton Fisk served at third, first, and the outfield—as well as fulfilling his regular duty as catcher—in an attempt to shake the effects of lingering shoulder trouble. He seemed in great shape in 1980, hitting .289 with 18 home runs and 62 RBI. Little did Red Sox fans know that they would lose their All-Star receiver to free agency at season's end, due to an error by the front office (Fisk's contract was not postmarked by the deadline date). Though age 33 at the time of his free agency, Fisk was hardly washed up. In fact, he would go on to play more than a decade with the White Sox, actually setting the Pale Hose career home run record.

Steve Carlton

Carlton Fisk

Carlton Takes NL Cy Young

Steve Carlton added a third National League Cy Young Award to his trophy case in 1980 with a loop-high 24-9 record. The Phillie mainstay topped the league that season with 286 strikeouts and 304 innings pitched. In World Series action that fall, Carlton won both games he started and posted a 2.40 ERA. Long a devotee of the martial arts, Carlton claimed he maintained his arm strength by twisting his left limb in a large vat of uncooked rice for extended periods of time.

- KC is first AL expansion team to win a pennant.

- Jerry Reuss of LA no-hits the Giants on June 27.

- In first year under Billy Martin, A's rise to second in AL West and post 94 CGs, most in majors since 1946.

- Bill Buckner leads NL in BA (.324).

- Cardinal Keith Hernandez tops NL in runs (111), runs produced (194), and OBP (.410).

- Wilson leads AL in hits (230) and runs (133), and ties in triples (15).

- Brewer Cecil Cooper leads AL in RBI (122) and total bases (335).

- On August 25, Fergie Jenkins becomes the first ML player to be arrested on a drug-related charge.

- The Hall of Fame inducts Al Kaline, Duke Snider, Chuck Klein, and Tom Yawkey.

- Smith wins first of what will become a record number of Gold Gloves as NL shortstop.

Brett Wins AL Bat Title

George Brett batted .390 in 1980 to win the American League batting title with the highest average since Ted Williams hit .406 in 1941. The 27-year-old Royals third baseman also clubbed 24 home runs and tallied 118 RBI. The superstar was joined for part of the '80 season by his older brother, pitcher Ken Brett, who appeared in only eight games for the Royals before retiring from baseball.

George Brett

Stone Wins AL Cy Young

Steve Stone

Known primarily as a journeyman pitcher, Steve Stone had tossed for three clubs in eight years before arriving in Baltimore in 1979. The righty crafted a career year in 1980, winning 25 games and losing just seven to take the American League Cy Young Award. One year later, he was retired from the sport and had joined Harry Caray in the Cubs broadcasting booth.

Andre Dawson

Dawson Stalks His Prey

Andre Dawson led the Expos to within 1 game of first place in the National League East Division in 1980. The Hawk batted .308 that season with 17 home runs and 87 RBI while capturing his first Gold Glove. One of the most feared hitters in the senior circuit, Dawson could hit line drives, with power, to left, center, and right fields.

1980

- Montreal's Andre Dawson wins first of six consecutive Gold Gloves.

- The Padres swap Gaylord Perry back to Texas with two other players for much-traveled Willie Montanez.

- The Angels send Carney Lansford, Rick Miller, and Mark Clear to Boston for Rick Burleson and Butch Hobson.

- The Padres send Rollie Fingers and three other players to Cards for Terry Kennedy and six other players.

- Cards send Fingers, Pete Vuckovich, and Ted Simmons to Milwaukee for Sixto Lezcano and three others.

- The Giants send John Montefusco and a minor leaguer to Atlanta for Doyle Alexander.

- Free agent Dave Winfield signs with Yankees in December.

- Rich Gale wins 11 in a row to set Royals club record.

- The Royals lead the AL in triples (59) a record sixth consecutive year.

- Jorge Orta of Cleveland goes 6-for-6 on June 15.

Bill Buckner

Sutton: The Right Stuff

By the time he left the Dodger organization at the conclusion of the 1980 season—a year in which he went 13-5 with a 2.21 ERA (best in the National League) and just 6.92 hits allowed per game (second-fewest in the loop)—Don Sutton had set nearly every Los Angeles franchise pitching record. Yet the righty is still considered the third or fourth best pitcher in franchise history. He nevertheless won 230 games over 15 years for the Blue, pitching in three World Series.

Don Sutton

Buckner Wins NL Bat Title

Bill Buckner will go down in the books as one of the game's great underrated hitters. In 1980, Billy Bucks opened his third decade in the majors by winning the National League batting title with a .324 mark and tying for second in doubles (41). For the second time in eight consecutive seasons, he reached double figures in home runs (ten). Also quite a fielder, he set a major league record for assists by a first baseman (184) in 1983.

Jerry Reuss

Reuss on the Rebound

Dodger lefty Jerry Reuss was named *Sporting News* National League Comeback Player of the Year in 1980, winning 18 games while losing only six with an excellent 2.52 ERA. In 1980, Reuss won eight more games and lost ten fewer games than he had posted for the two previous seasons combined. Rolls finished second in the voting for the National League Cy Young Award that season. Though a journeyman who never won 20 games in a season, Reuss would go on to win 200-plus games in his career.

- Bob Welch of the Dodgers publicly acknowledges that he has an alcohol abuse problem.
- Yankees coach Ellie Howard dies.
- On Sept. 10, Montreal's Bill Gullickson sets rookie record when he fans 18 in a game.

- Brett's .390 BA is the highest this century by an ML third baseman, as is his .664 SA.
- Padres are first team in NL history to have three players who steal 50 bases: Gene Richards (61), Smith (57), and Jerry Mumphrey (52).
- Boston's Burleson participates in a record 147 DPs by a shortstop.

- White Sox Mike Squires is the first lefthanded major leaguer to catch in a game since the Cubs' Dale Long in 1958.
- Rick Langford of the A's tops ML with 28 CGs and becomes last pitcher to post more than 25 CGs in a season.

Dale Murphy

Murphy Hits 33 HRs

Dale Murphy finally moved out from behind home plate to assume his rightful place in the Braves outfield in 1980. The defensive switch also helped his offensive production, as Murphy tallied 89 RBI while batting .281 that season. His 33 home runs, 98 runs scored, and .510 slugging average all finished in third place in the National League that year.

Tug McGraw

Amos Otis

Otis Finishes With a Bang

Kansas City veteran Amos Otis saved his best for last in 1980 as he enjoyed a superb World Series. Not only did he hit a home run in his first Series at-bat, he also racked up a .478 average for the six-game tournament. Leading all fall classic players with 11 hits, Otis blasted three home runs and seven RBI during the affair.

McGraw Saves Two in NLCS

Tug McGraw exults after saving the dramatic ten-inning Phillie victory in game four of the 1980 National League Championship Series. The lefty was particularly happy about this save, his second of the playoff series, as he had been tagged with the previous night's 1-0 loss. McGraw loved the limelight, and it wasn't a coincidence that three of his best seasons came on pennant-winning teams: the 1969 Mets, the '73 Mets, and the '80 Phillies.

1980

- On April 12, Milwaukee's Cooper and Don Money each hit a grandslam in the second inning of the Brewers' 18-1 win over Boston.

- Joe Morgan leads NL in walks (93).

- Steve Garvey leads NL in hits (200).

- Pete Rose, now with the Phils, tops the NL in doubles (42).

- Montreal's Ron LeFlore wins NL theft crown, 97 to 96, over Pittsburgh's Omar Moreno.

- Rickey Henderson tops AL with 100 steals.

- Carlton leads ML in innings (304) and Ks (286).

- LA's Don Sutton tops the majors in ERA at 2.21.

- AL strikeout leader Len Barker of Cleveland has just 187.

- Pirate Jim Bibby leads NL in win pct. (.760); Stone is AL win pct. leader (.781).

Brett Royal in Series

George Brett continued burning up the basepaths throughout the 1980 regular season and into the fall classic. The Royals third baseman racked up a .375 average in the '80 World Series, tallying nine hits and three RBI. Brett is shown here breaking open game three by lofting a Larry Christenson pitch into the night.

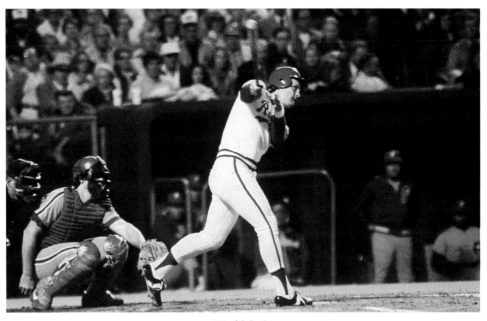

World Series

Manny Mota

Mota Shines in Finale

Dodger coach and pinch hitter extraordinaire Manny Mota retired in 1980 as baseball's all-time pinch-hit leader with 150. His .315 career batting average is the best mark among Los Angeles batters with 1,800 or more at-bats, and his lifetime pinch-hitting average is .297.

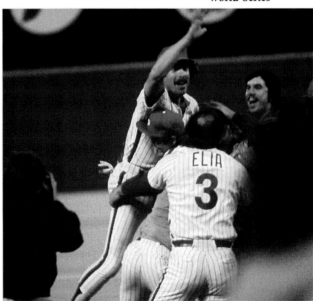

Mike Schmidt

Schmidt Carries Phils

The Phillies ended 97 years of frustration in 1980 as they beat out the Royals in six games to capture their first World Championship. Raising his arm in victory is Mike Schmidt, a Series hero with a .381 batting average and seven RBI. Schmidt collected a pair of home runs in that fall classic: one dinger tied up game three in the fifth inning; the other sparked the Phillies in game five. Schmidt was brilliant in 1980, leading the league in homers (48), RBI (121), and slugging (.624). Only in the playoffs, in which he hit .208, did he fail to produce.

- Goose Gossage and KC's Dan Quisenberry share AL lead with 33 saves.

- The Cubs' Sutter tops NL with 28 saves.

- Mike Norris wins 22 games for A's, is second in innings (284), CGs (24), and ERA (2.54).

- Yankee Rudy May leads AL in ERA (2.47).

- Tommy John leads AL with six shutouts and Yanks with 22 wins.

- Reuss leads NL with six shutouts.

- Montreal's Rodney Scott and Moreno tie for NL lead in triples with 13.

- Ben Oglivie of Milwaukee ties Reggie Jackson for AL homer crown (41) and is second in RBI (118) and total bases (333).

- Ranger Al Oliver leads AL in runs produced (194).

- Fifth-place Detroit leads majors in runs with 830.

The 1981 season is, unfortunately, best remembered for the ten-week players' strike that canceled 713 games and put America through a disorientating summer. The players' union walked out because the league's owners, worried about rising salaries, were trying to cut back on free agency.

Major league baseball eventually resumed, but under an unpopular "split-season" format. According to the format, those teams in first place before the strike began were declared first-half winners. The teams that finished atop their divisions *after* the strike would be declared second-half winners. The first-half winners would then play the second-half winners in divisional playoffs.

The format garnered more playoff revenue for the league, but it turned out to be an unfair and embarrassing creation. Cincinnati and St. Louis, the National League teams with the best overall records, didn't even make the playoffs.

The NL East playoffs instead featured the Phillies and Expos, with Montreal winning three games to two. Philadelphia got another MVP year from Mike Schmidt, who spearheaded the league in home runs with 31 and RBI with 91. Montreal was led by Gary Carter, who hit a pair of homers in the All-Star Game at Cleveland, the first game played

LA WINS TITLE, BUT BASEBALL STRIKES OUT

after the strike ended. Rookie Tim Raines, the league leader in steals with 71, was another Expo asset.

The Dodgers beat the Astros in five games in the NL West playoffs. Dodger Fernando Valenzuela, the Rookie of the Year and Cy Young winner, was backed by a great Los Angeles staff, including Jerry Reuss, Bob Welch, Burt Hooton, and Dave Stewart. The Astros pitching was more than adequate, too, with Nolan Ryan (1.69 ERA), Don Sutton, Joe Niekro, and Bob Knepper.

In the AL East, Buck Rodgers's Brewers faced the Yankees in the postseason playoff. Milwaukee boasted relief ace Rollie Fingers, who won both the Cy Young and MVP titles. But the Yankees, who had picked up free agent Dave Winfield over the winter, beat the Brewers in five.

Billy Martin's Athletics swept Kansas City in the AL West playoffs. The A's had led the league with 60 complete games (the next

highest total was 33), but a few years later, pitching staff leaders Rick Langford, Steve McCatty, and Mike Norris would retire from baseball as the result of arm injuries.

Among other notable events, Ryan fired his fifth career no-hitter, a new major league record. Pete Rose got his 3,631st hit, breaking Stan Musial's NL record. Tom Seaver struck out No. 3,000. And Toronto's Danny Ainge wisely retired from baseball to pursue a career in the NBA.

The National League Championship Series wasn't decided until the last inning of the fifth game, when LA's Rick Monday blasted a two-out homer off Steve Rogers to break a 1-1 tie. Rogers, who had pitched a complete game just three days earlier, was making only his third relief appearance in nine seasons.

In the American League Championship Series, the Yankees beat the A's in three straight games. The A's scored just four runs over the tournament; the Yanks racked up 20 runs.

The Yankees won the first two games of the World Series, beating the Dodgers 5-3 and 3-0. But the Dodgers, sparked by strong play from Pedro Guerrero, Ron Cey, and Steve Yeager, went on to win the next four for the World Championship. Yankee reliever George Frazier was the Series goat, going 0-3 with a 17.18 ERA.

1981

- Players' strike cancels eight weeks of the season.
- Strike settlement results in first split-season campaign in majors since 1892.
- Owing to split-season format, the team with baseball's best record, Cincinnati, doesn't qualify for postseason play.

- In NL East, first-half winner Phils are beaten by second-half winner Expos in five-game division playoff.
- In NL West, first-half winner LA bests second-half winner Houston in five games.
- Dodgers beat Expos in NLCS, as Rick Monday wins game five 2-1 with a ninth-inning homer.

- In AL East, first-half winner New York tops second-half winner Milwaukee in five games.
- In AL West, first-half winner Oakland sweeps second-half winner KC, which made the playoffs with a 50-53 overall record.
- Yanks sweep A's in ALCS.

Steve Howe takes to the air after the six-game Dodger victory over the Yankees in the 1981 World Series. Joining in the celebration are first baseman Steve Garvey *(right)* and catcher Steve Yeager. Howe was 1-0 with a 3.86 ERA for the affair. Garvey batted a whopping .417 while Yeager was good for a pair of home runs and four RBI.

- Dodgers win World Series in six games after losing opening two games in New York.

- Yankees bullpen flops in Series, especially George Frazier (0-3).

- LA's Fernando Valenzuela wins NL ROTY and Cy Young, as he tops NL in innings (192), CGs (11), shutouts (eight), and Ks (180).

- Rollie Fingers named MVP and Cy Young winner in AL.

- Mike Schmidt named NL MVP.

- Dave Righetti wins AL ROTY.

- Pete Rose tops ML in hits (140) to become only 40-year-old player ever to accomplish this.

- Rose collects his 3,631st hit, breaking Stan Musial's NL record.

- Steve Carlton becomes first lefthander to collect 3,000 career strikeouts.

- On Sept. 20, Minnesota's Gary Gaetti, Kent Hrbek, and Tim Laudner all homer in their first ML game.

Ryan Hurls No-No No. 5

A national television audience witnessed the highlight of Nolan Ryan's 1981 season—and the establishment of a major league record—as The Express hurled his fifth career no-hitter on September 26, at the Astrodome, in a game against the Dodgers. Ryan went 11-5 that season, leading the National League in ERA (1.69) and fewest hits per game (5.98).

Nolan Ryan

Gaetti Cracks Open Career

On September 20, 1981, rookie Gary Gaetti of the Twins homered off Charlie Hough of Texas in his first major league at-bat to signal the beginning of an All-Star career. Gaetti became the 47th player in major league history to accomplish the feat. Amazingly, fellow rookie teammates Kent Hrbek and Tim Laudner, who were also playing in their first major league game, homered in the same contest.

Gary Gaetti

Dwight Evans

Evans Clubs 22 Home Runs

Dwight Evans put up impressive numbers during the strike season, as he tied for the lead in the American League in home runs with 22, batted .296, drove in 71 runs, and won his fourth Gold Glove. One of the most misunderstood players in club history, the right fielder gained some respectability—and a little insurance for his future with the team—once his offensive output began to match his superb fielding and throwing.

1981

- Schmidt leads the majors in home runs (31), RBI (91), total bases (228), slugging (.644), runs produced (138), and OBP (.439).
- Schmidt leads NL in walks (73) and runs (78).
- NL wins its tenth straight All-Star Game, 5-4 in Cleveland.

- Charley Finley sells A's to Levi's jeans magnates.
- Bill Veeck sells White Sox for second time in his life.
- Cubs are sold to Chicago Tribune Co.
- Len Barker of Cleveland pitches a perfect game vs. Toronto on May 15.

- Nolan Ryan throws ML record fifth no-hitter on Sept. 26 vs. LA.
- Charlie Lea of Montreal no-hits SF on May 10.
- Rochester and Pawtucket of the International League play 33-inning game—longest in OB history—over a two-day period.

Bill Madlock

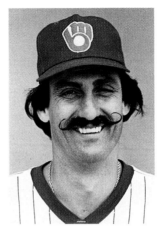

Rollie Fingers

Valenzuela Is a Star

Fernando Mania swept America in 1981 as Fernando Valenzuela, the Mexican rookie sensation for the Dodgers, led the National League in innings pitched (192), strikeouts (180), and complete games (11). The first rookie to win the Cy Young Award, Valenzuela compiled a 13-7 record in a strike-shortened season and won a World Series game.

Fingers Wins AL MVP

No reliever with the possible exception of Willie Hernandez has ever had a season like that which Rollie Fingers turned in in 1981. Cited by many as being the greatest reliever in the history of the game, Fingers figured in 55 percent of all the Brewer victories during the season (hurling in 13 of the team's final 15 triumphs that year). Fingers captured both the American League MVP Award and the Cy Young Award in '81, compiling a 6-3 record with 28 saves and an incredible 1.04 ERA while leading the Brewers to their first-ever postseason appearance. In the divisional playoffs, Fingers won one game and saved another, though his team lost in five to the Yankees.

Fernando Valenzuela

Madlock Wins NL Bat Title

Bill Madlock won his third National League batting crown in 1981, hitting .341 in 82 games. Mad Dog won four batting titles in his career, was an All-Star three times, and spearheaded three teams into postseason action over the course of his 15-year stint. In his spare time, the quick-handed Madlock became an outstanding pingpong player.

- Expo Tim Raines sets ML rookie record with 71 steals despite abbreviated season (record since broken).
- Boston's Carney Lansford wins AL bat crown at .336.
- Pirate Bill Madlock barely qualifies for BA crown, winning at .341.
- Ryan has best ERA in majors (1.69).
- Tom Seaver leads NL with 14 wins and .875 win pct.
- Oakland, managed by Billy Martin, plays in manner that is labeled "Billy Ball" and finishes with the best record in AL (64-45).
- Martin sets ML record for most franchises managed to a division title (four).
- The Hall of Fame inducts Bob Gibson, Johnny Mize, and Rube Foster.
- Valenzuela is third consecutive Dodgers pitcher to win NL ROTY honor.

Steve Carlton

Carlton Wins 13 Games

Despite winning an equal number of games and having a better winning percentage than Fernando Valenzuela, Steve Carlton finished third in the voting for the National League Cy Young Award in 1981. His 13-4 record led the Phillies to a strike-induced first playoff round against the Expos; once there, Carlton lost two games as the Phillies fell in five.

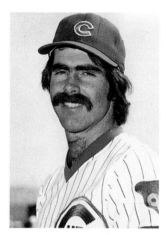

Bill Buckner

Buckner Tops in Doubles

Bill Buckner missed out on a career year in 1981 due to the strike. That is not to say that the first baseman did not have an impressive showing. Buckner batted .311, drove in 75 runs in 106 games, and topped the National League in doubles with 35. He banged out 498 two-baggers over his career, 28th on the all-time list and just eight fewer than Babe Ruth's total.

Raines Sets Record with 71 Swipes

It took a great player to finish second in National League Rookie of the Year balloting to Fernando Valenzuela, and Montreal outfielder Tim Raines more than justified his position. The recruit batted .304 while stealing 71 bases (a major league rookie record). Despite his steady performance, the Expos—with their best team in franchise history—lost the pennant to the Dodgers. Raines would go on to become one of the most exciting players of the 1980s. He would lead the league in such departments as batting, runs, doubles, and, of course, steals.

Tim Raines

Tom Seaver

Seaver Racks Up 14 Wins

Tom Seaver had a superb season in 1981, silencing critics who said the righty was nearing the end of the road. Seaver finished second to Fernando Valenzuela in balloting for the Cy Young Award, as he led the National League with 14 wins against two defeats and posted a 2.55 ERA.

1981

- Ranger Jim Sundberg wins last of six consecutive Gold Gloves awarded to AL catchers.
- Oakland outfielder Rickey Henderson wins his only Gold Glove to date.
- The Yankees send Willie McGee to St. Louis for Bob Sykes.

- Boston trades Fred Lynn and Steve Renko to California for Frank Tanana, Joe Rudi, and Jim Dorsey.
- Cincinnati swaps Ray Knight for Houston's Cesar Cedeno.
- Detroit sends Steve Kemp to ChiSox for Chet Lemon.

- St. Louis deals Tony Scott to Houston for Joaquin Andujar.
- The Mets trade Jeff Reardon and Dan Norman to Expos for Ellis Valentine.
- St. Louis deals Garry Templeton to San Diego for Ozzie Smith.
- The Carpenter family sells the Phillies.

Dave Winfield

Winfield: 13 HRs, 68 RBI

Dave Winfield put up numbers during the 1981 season which justified his expensive free agent contract—a minimum of $23 million for ten years. The Yankee outfielder batted .294 with 13 home runs and 68 RBI in 105 games in 1981. For most of the 1980s, Winfield was probably one of the top ten players in the game. He could run, field, throw, and hit for both average and power.

Pete Rose

Rose Breaks Hit Record

Pete Rose topped the National League in hits with 140 in 1981. Tied with Stan Musial for the loop's all-time mark with 3,630 hits when the players' strike began in June, Rose finally broke the record on August 10, the night after the strike ended. At age 40, Charlie Hustle had his last .300 season, batting .325.

Bobby Grich

Grich Slugs Way to Top

Bobby Grich made the most of the strike-shortened season of 1981, batting a career-high .304 and topping the American League in slugging average at .543. He also placed himself in a four-way tie for the lead in the American League in home runs (22). Also a Gold Glover at second base, Grich was ranked as one of the 40 greatest players ever by *Total Baseball*.

- George Argyros buys control of the Mariners.
- The Astros allow ML record-low 2.08 runs per game at home.
- Houston's Art Howe hits in 23 consecutive games to set Astros team record.

- Former Astros GM Tal Smith hired by several owners to help advise them in an escalating number of salary arbitration cases.
- Fred Lindstrom dies.
- Vida Blue of the Giants is first to be an All-Star Game winning pitcher in both leagues.

- Schmidt's .644 SA is a record high for NL third basemen.
- Ranger Bill Stein sets AL record with seven consecutive pinch hits.
- Ranger Buddy Bell makes a modern ML record 2.93 assists per game by a third baseman.

Martin Wins with Billy Ball

Billy Martin traveled to his fifth major league managerial stop in 1980 when he took over the A's. In 1981, his charges took the West Division Championship only to fall to Martin's previous employers, the Yankees, in three straight in the American League Championship Series. The A's won with a style known as "Billy Ball," which included bunting, stealing, and hit-and-running.

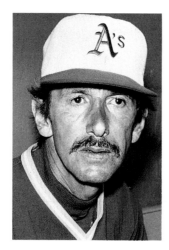

Billy Martin

Fernando Valenzuela

Fernando Is a Sensation

Fernando Valenzuela toasts to his game-three victory in the 1981 World Series, as his triumph gave the Dodgers their first win in the six-game affair. The pitching virtuosity and incredible farm-to-baseball-field story of the Dodger rookie piqued the interest of a nation. Valenzuela was the *Sporting News* Player of the Year in 1981.

Morris Wins 14 Games

With a bag of tricks that included a fastball, a slider, and a split-finger fastball, Jack Morris became the winningest pitcher of the 1980s. In 1981, the righty tied for the American League-lead in victories with 14, pitched two shutout innings in the All-Star Game, and was named *Sporting News* Pitcher of the Year in the junior circuit.

Jack Morris

1981

- Frank Robinson of the Giants is first black manager in NL.

- Chicago's Bill Buckner tops NL in doubles (35).

- Padre Gene Richards and Astro Craig Reynolds tie for NL lead in triples with 12.

- Henderson leads AL in swipes (56), hits (135), and runs (89).

- Milwaukee's Cecil Cooper tops AL with 35 doubles.

- Eddie Murray, Oakland's Tony Armas, California's Bobby Grich, and Boston's Dwight Evans all tie for AL homer crown with 22.

- Murray tops AL in RBI (78).

- Grich leads AL in SA (.543).

- Evans tops AL in walks (85) and runs produced (133).

- Cleveland's Mike Hargrove leads AL in OBP (.432).

Pedro Guerrero

Guerrero Ties for Series MVP Honors

Playing in his first full season for the Dodgers, Pedro Guerrero batted an even .300 (and hit a dozen home runs) in 1981. An outstanding contributor in that fall's World Series, he batted .333, smacking two home runs and leading the ballclub with seven RBI. Giving the performance of his life in the final contest of that six-game Series, he batted in five runs. For his efforts, Guerrero was named co-MVP of the Series along with Steve Yeager and Ron Cey.

Bob Welch

Winfield Ends with a Dive

Although Dave Winfield had much to do with helping the Yankees make it to the 1981 World Series, the outfielder suffered through a terrible slump once he got there. Batting just .045 in the fall classic, Winfield posted a lone hit and a single RBI over the six-game tournament. His Series performance left New Yorkers expecting more from the multimillion-dollar man.

Dave Winfield

Welch Bombs in Series

Bob Welch compiled a record of 9-5 during the 1981 season, tallying a 3.45 ERA. In that year's postseason play, the righty suffered a disastrous start in game four of the World Series, where he surrendered a triple, a double, a walk, and a single to the first four Yankee batters he faced before being pulled from action.

- Oakland's Steve McCatty wins AL ERA crown (2.32).
- KC's Dennis Leonard tops ML with 202 innings.
- Barker leads AL in strikeouts with just 127.
- Oakland's Rick Langford leads ML with 18 CGs.

- Fingers tops ML with 28 saves.
- Cardinal Bruce Sutter's 25 saves are tops in the NL.
- Seattle's Tom Paciorek is runner-up for AL bat crown (.326) and also stands high in several other offensive departments.

- Every team in AL East finishes above .500 except last-place Blue Jays, who have the worst record in majors (37-69).
- No pitcher in the AL has more than four shutouts.
- Minnesota's John Castino leads AL in triples with just nine.

The Atlanta Braves were the talk of baseball in April 1982, when they won their first 13 games. Just a mediocre team in the first two years of the 1980s, few thought Atlanta would make a run for the pennant in '82. The record of Joe Torre, their new manager, was no winner, either. The Mets, from whom he was fired in the off-season, had never finished higher than fifth under his tenure.

But Torre's '82 Braves were for real, as they led the league in runs and homers, hung tough in the pennant race, and made the playoffs for the first time since 1969. Atlanta center fielder Dale Murphy won the MVP, hitting 36 homers and driving in 109 runs.

Another exciting club was Harvey Kuenn's Milwaukee Brewers, a.k.a. "Harvey's Wallbangers." The Brewers were loaded with menacing hitters, including Robin Yount (.331 average, 29 homers, 114 RBI), Paul Molitor (.302, 19 homers, 136 runs), Cecil Cooper (.313, 32 homers, 121 RBI), Ted Simmons (23 homers, 97 RBI), Ben Oglivie (34 homers, 102 RBI), and Gorman Thomas (39 homers, 112 RBI). They also featured Cy Young winner Pete Vuckovich, who went 18-6, and Rollie Fingers, who saved 29.

Milwaukee, however, didn't coast to the AL East title. In fact, the regular season went down to the final series. The Orioles, four

BRAVES AND BREWERS BOTH BOW TO CARDS

games out of first, beat the Brew Crew three straight times at Memorial Stadium. If the Orioles had won again, a one-game play-off would have decided the division-winner. It never came to that, though, as Don Sutton beat Jim Palmer in game 162 and Milwaukee took the AL East crown.

Prior to 1982, free agent Reggie Jackson left the Yankees to join the Angels. With four former MVPs now on its squad (Jackson, Don Baylor, Fred Lynn, and Rod Carew), California won the West Division by 3 games over Kansas City.

Whitey Herzog's speedy St. Louis Cardinals edged out the Phillies to win the NL East flag, thanks in part to recent arrivals Ozzie Smith (obtained from San Diego), Lonnie Smith (picked up from Philadelphia), and rookie Willie McGee. Steve Carlton won another Cy Young Award by going 23-11.

Dave Kingman of the Mets led the league with 37 home runs, though he hit all of .204 and was a butcher in the field. Al Oliver of Montreal took the batting title

with a .331 average and also led the league in RBI, hits, doubles, and total bases.

With the Reds' dismissal of Ken Griffey, Ray Knight, George Foster, and Dave Collins in the off-season, its dynasty collapsed and the team fell into the cellar. A couple of infielders, Baltimore's Cal Ripken and Los Angeles' Steve Sax, were named Rookies of the Year. Sax represented the fourth straight year a Dodger won the award.

In the NLCS, St. Louis flattened Atlanta in three games. The Braves mustered only one extra-base hit—a double—in the Series. In the junior circuit playoffs, the Brewers beat the Angels in five, coming back from a two-game deficit. California, though, featured the best hitter in Lynn, who batted .611 (11-for-18).

The World Series had its share of exceptional individual performances. In game one, Molitor became the first player to get five hits in a Series game, as Milwaukee won 10-0. Yount had four hits in that same game, then repeated the feat four games later. Game three was a showcase for McGee, who not only cracked two home runs, but made a circus catch at the center-field wall.

The Series boiled down to the seventh game. Milwaukee built a 3-1 lead in the contest, but the Cardinals scored three in the sixth and two in the eighth to win it 6-3.

1982

- Cards win their first NL flag since 1968.
- Brewers become second AL expansion team in three years to win its first flag.
- Cards sweep Braves in League Championship Series.

- Angels lose LCS after leading two games to none—first club to suffer this fate.
- Cards win World Series in seven games.
- Brewer Paul Molitor gets Series record five hits in opener.

- Joaquin Andujar leads Cards with two Series victories.
- Braves win NL West by 1 game when LA is beaten 5-3 by Giants on last day of season.
- Orioles could force playoff in AL East by sweeping Milwaukee on season's final weekend, but lose to Brewers on Sunday 10-2.

World Series MVP Darrel Porter *(right)* jumps into the arms of Bruce Sutter, as Keith Hernandez rushes in to join the crowd after the Cardinals defeated the Brewers 6-3 in the seventh game of the 1982 World Series. The Cards racked up 15 hits to the Brewers' seven in the finale. Porter finished the tournament with a .286 batting average, one home run, and five RBI; Sutter went 1-0 with a pair of saves.

- Steve Carlton wins record fourth Cy Young.
- Milwaukee's Pete Vuckovich wins controversial Cy Young vote in AL.
- Atlanta's Dale Murphy named NL MVP.
- Milwaukee's Robin Yount is AL MVP.

- Braves open season with 13 consecutive wins, an NL record.
- Carlton tops ML in wins (23), innings (296), CGs (19), Ks (286), and shutouts (six).
- Harvey Kuenn takes over a 23-24 Brewers team and manages it to the pennant.

- Oakland's Rickey Henderson steals ML record 130 bases.
- Reggie Jackson's tumultuous tenure with the Yankees ends, as he signs with the Angels.
- Billy Martin fired as A's manager after team tumbles to 68-94 record.

Yount Named AL MVP

Robin Yount (pictured with glove) won the first of his American League MVP Awards—and his premier Gold Glove—in 1982, tallying a .331 batting average, 29 home runs, 46 doubles, and 114 RBI (all career-bests). To cap his All-Star season, Yount batted .414 in World Series play that year, collecting 12 hits in 29 at-bats.

Dan Quisenberry

Quiz Saves 35 Games, Goes 9-7

In 1982, Dan Quisenberry was American League Fireman of the Year for the second time and an All-Star for the first time. With a quirky underhanded delivery that aggravated hitters while preserving his arm from undue strain, the reliever saved a circuit-high 35 games while compiling a 9-7 record that season.

Robin Yount

Yaz Knows No Bounds

Carl Yastrzemski entered the homestretch of his storied career in 1982. Batting .275 that year, he tallied 72 RBI and 16 home runs. A left fielder for 12 seasons, Yaz was shifted to the center-field station on July 21, where he went 2-for-3 with a run and an RBI. It is likely that, as he was approaching age 43, he is the oldest major leaguer to play the position. He was elected to the Hall of Fame in 1989, his first year of eligibility.

Carl Yastrzemski

1982

- Rollie Fingers becomes first in history to collect 300 saves.
- NL wins its 11th straight All-Star Game, 4-1 at Montreal.
- Baltimore's Cal Ripken is AL ROTY.
- Dodger Steve Sax is NL ROTY.

- Phillie Garry Maddox wins last of eight consecutive GGs as NL outfielder.
- Joel Youngblood gets hits for two different teams in two different cities in same day when he's traded from Mets to Expos.
- Metrodome opens on April 6, Mariners vs. Twins.

- Royal Hal McRae tops majors with 133 RBI, most RBI ever by a DH.
- Gaylord Perry wins his 300th game on May 6.
- In August, Perry is ejected for the only time in his career for throwing a spitball.

Jackson: 39 HRs, 101 RBI

Upon being stripped of all his power in 1990 as owner of the Yankees, George Steinbrenner said that his chief regret over his 17-year proprietorship was letting Reggie Jackson defect to the Angels once his option was unclaimed. Jackson, in the twilight of his career in 1982, batted .275, nailed 39 home runs (tied for the lead in the American League), and racked up 101 RBI to spearhead the Angels to the West Division title.

Reggie Jackson

Harold Baines

Baines: 25 HRs, 105 RBI

White Sox owner Bill Veeck first scouted Harold Baines when he was just a 12-year-old sandlot star on Maryland's Eastern Shore. Baines played his first full season with the Sox in 1982, batting .271 while socking 25 dingers and driving in 105 runs. Baines went on to set the all-time White Sox record for round-trippers with 173.

Brewers Win AL Pennant

Baseball fans in Milwaukee hadn't seen a championship game since the 1958 Braves pennant when the Brew Crew of 1982 sent the beer city into orbit. Nearly two million fans flocked to County Stadium over the course of the season to watch the slugging team they nicknamed "Harvey's Wallbangers" for manager Harvey Kuenn and the club's 216 home runs. The Brewers finished 1 game ahead of the Orioles in the AL East in '82.

Milwaukee Brewers Fans

- Royal John Wathan sets ML record for catchers with 36 stolen bases.
- Montreal's Al Oliver leads NL in BA (.331), hits (204), and doubles (43), and ties in RBI (109).
- Mike Schmidt leads NL in walks (107), OBP (.407), and SA (.547).

- Yount leads AL in hits (210), total bases (367), runs produced (214), and SA (.578), and ties in doubles (46).
- New York's Dave Kingman leads NL with 37 homers.
- Kingman's .204 BA is lowest since 1901 by a first baseman in 400 or more at-bats.

- Willie Wilson tops AL in batting (.332) and triples (15).
- Angel Reggie Jackson and Brewer Gorman Thomas tie for AL homer lead with 39.
- Boston's Bob Stanley sets AL record by pitching 168 innings in relief.

Rickey Sets Mark with 130 Swipes

In 1982, Rickey Henderson demolished the single-season major league stolen base record set by Lou Brock by swiping 130 bases. Flourishing under the guidance of A's manager Billy Martin, who appreciated the speedster's unique gifts, Henderson hit .267 in 1982. The All-Star tallied 119 runs scored (fourth in the American League), 116 walks (best in the majors), and a .399 on-base percentage (third in the circuit) that season.

Rickey Henderson

Carter Stars as All-Star

Gold Glove-winning catcher Gary Carter of the Expos displayed his usual All-Star form in 1982, batting .293, clubbing 29 four-baggers, and driving in 97 runs. His single knocked in a run in the All-Star Game, played in his home park of Olympic Stadium. Probably the most avid baseball card collector among his contemporaries, Carter is unlike many professional ballplayers in his unabashed love for the game.

Fernando: No Fluke

Fernando Mania grew in stature in 1982, as did the man who started it all. Avoiding the sophomore jinx, the lefty sported a 19-13 record with a 2.87 ERA in '82. Valenzuela was still logging lots of innings into the 1990s.

Fernando Valenzuela

Gary Carter

1982

- Terry Felton leaves baseball with an 0-16 lifetime record—worst mark ever.
- The Hall of Fame inducts Hank Aaron, Frank Robinson, Travis Jackson, and Happy Chandler.
- Ron Guidry wins first of five consecutive Gold Gloves awarded to AL pitchers.

- KC's Frank White wins sixth consecutive Gold Glove as American League second baseman; he also bats a career-high .298.
- Yankee Dave Winfield wins first of four consecutive Gold Gloves as AL outfielder after having won two Gold Gloves in NL.

- California sends Tom Brunansky, Mike Walters, and $400,000 to Twins for Doug Corbett and Rob Wilfong.
- Texas trades Oliver to Montreal for Larry Parrish and Dave Hostetler.
- Oakland sends Tony Armas and Jeff Newman to Boston for Carney Lansford and two other players.

Andujar Carries Cards

Joaquin Andujar blossomed under the wing of Redbird pitching coach Hub Kittle, as the temperamental Dominican went 15-10 for a 2.47 ERA during the regular 1982 season. In postseason play, the righty became the stopper for the Cardinals, winning both the National League pennant-clinching game against the Braves and capturing the seventh game of the World Series against the Brewers. When asked to describe life in the majors, Andujar once remarked that everything could be summed up in one word: "youneverknow."

Joaquin Andujar

Murphy Named NL MVP

Dale Murphy enjoyed his best season to date in 1982, batting .281 with 36 home runs and 109 RBI to lead the Braves to the National League West Division title. He was named the circuit's MVP for his efforts. Unlike most superstars, Murphy spent most of his off-season deciding which products *not* to endorse. The one product he did agree to promote? Milk.

Dale Murphy

Tim Raines

Raines Leads NL in Steals

In 1982, Tim Raines led the National League in stolen bases for the second consecutive season, swiping 78 cushions. The former *Sporting News* Rookie of the Year also played in his second All-Star Game in as many years. Although Raines lacked Rickey Henderson's power, the two were often described as the most talented players in their respective leagues.

Dave Kingman

Kingman Is NL HR King

In the second year of his second tour of duty with the Mets, Dave Kingman led the National League in home runs with 37 while driving in 99 runs and batting an anemic .204. In the process, Kong set a major league record for the lowest batting average by a home run champion. His .204 mark was also the lowest ever for a first baseman with 400 or more at-bats.

- The Mets trade Lee Mazzilli to Texas for Walt Terrell and Ron Darling.

- Mets re-acquire Tom Seaver from Reds for three players.

- The Phils deal Ryne Sandberg and Larry Bowa to the Cubs for Ivan DeJesus.

- Phils deal Julio Franco, Manny Trillo, and three other players to Cleveland for Von Hayes.

- For the first time in history, the Yankees' home opener is cancelled by a blizzard.

- Brewers hit an AL record 1.57 homers per game on the road.

- Ripken sets O's record for most homers by a rookie (32).

- Lloyd Waner dies.

- Satchel Paige dies.

- Trillo sets new record for second basemen when he handles 479 consecutive chances without an error.

Brewers Win Game Five

After executing a force out on Lonnie Smith of the Cardinals at second base, Brewers shortstop Robin Yount tries in vain to get Keith Hernandez out at first in game five of the 1982 World Series. The Brewers defeated the Cardinals 6-4 that day to take a one-game edge in fall classic action; it was their last victory in the tournament.

Oliver Posts .331 Average

Traded to Montreal for third baseman Larry Parrish of Texas in March 1982, Al Oliver gained a lot of popularity as the new kid on the block. He responded by winning the National League batting title with a career-high .331 average. Topping the circuit in hits (204) and doubles (43), he tied Dale Murphy for the RBI title with 109.

World Series

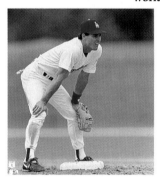

Steve Sax

Sax Named NL ROTY

In 1982, Steve Sax became the fourth consecutive Dodger to capture National League Rookie of the Year honors. The second baseman hit .282 and set a Dodger rookie record with 49 stolen bases that season.

Smith Wields Some Magic

In 1982, the Padres and Cardinals swapped shortstops, as Garry Templeton was shipped to San Diego and Ozzie Smith (pictured) headed for St. Louis. At the time, Smith was considered an offensive liability despite his amazing glovework. The Wizard of Oz proved his critics only partly right, however, as he batted .248 for the '82 season and then hit an impressive .556 in the three-game playoff sweep of the Braves.

Ozzie Smith

Al Oliver

1982

- Yount sets records for AL shortstops with a .578 SA and 367 total bases.

- In a game vs. Omaha, Denver draws 65,666—a minor league record.

- This season's ALCS is the first time in ML history that two expansion teams oppose each other in postseason play.

- Oakland's Jimmy Sexton sets AL record for most stolen bases in a season without being caught (16).

- Mark Belanger leaves majors with only 389 RBI in 2,016 games—the worst ratio in history by a player with ten or more years in the majors.

- Willie Stargell retires after 21 years with the Pirates, a club record.

- Padre Joe Lefebvre goes 6-for-8 in a 16-inning game on Sept. 13.

- Cardinal Lonnie Smith tops NL in runs (120), is fourth in hits (182) and BA (.307).

- Dickie Thon of Houston leads NL in triples (ten).

1982

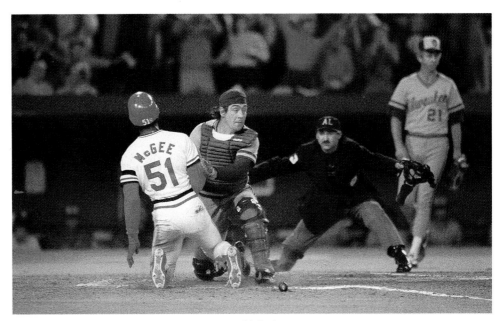

World Series

Cards Bomb the Brewers

Ted Simmons, the Brewers catcher, almost needs a calculator to count the Cardinal baserunners crossing his threshold in game six of the 1982 World Series. Bringing home the run here is Willie McGee. Before the night was over, 13 Redbirds—and one Brewer—had scored.

Paul Molitor

Molitor Heats Up to .302

Nicknamed the "Ignitor" for his ability to spark rallies, Paul Molitor batted .302 in 1982, spearheading the American League and setting a Brewers record by scoring 136 runs. Capping his prolific season with a spectacular World Series, the third baseman set a record with five hits in game one, sparking the Brew Crew to a 10-0 pasting of the Cardinals.

Cooper's Bat Catches Fire

Cecil Cooper could do no wrong in 1982, racking up a .313 batting average, a .528 slugging average, 32 home runs, and 121 RBI. Finishing out the year in style, the Brewers first baseman led his team to a dramatic come-from-behind victory in the fifth and decisive game of the 1982 American League Championship Series. In the seventh inning, he singled home the tying and winning runs as the Brewers completed a three-game sweep of the Angels after having been down in the Series two games to none.

Cecil Cooper

- Montreal's Tim Raines tops NL in steals (78) while Smith finishes second (68).

- Murphy tops NL in runs produced (186), is second in homers (36).

- Montreal's Steve Rogers leads NL in ERA (2.40), is second in wins (19).

- Phil Niekro has top win pct. in NL (.810).

- Vuckovich and Jim Palmer tie for best win pct. in AL (.750).

- Molitor tops majors with 136 runs.

- Boston's Dwight Evans tops AL in OBP (.403), is second in walks (112).

- Toronto's Dave Stieb leads AL in innings (288) and CGs (19).

- Floyd Bannister is first Mariners pitcher to top AL in Ks (209).

- With 19 wins, LaMarr Hoyt is first White Sox hurler to top AL in that department since 1973.

Johnny Bench, Carl Yastrzemski, and Gaylord Perry—all great players of the generation—retired after the 1983 season. Bench, with the Reds since 1967, finished his career with a total of 389 home runs and four World Series appearances. Yaz, who had worn the Red Sox uniform for 23 years, slugged the last of his 3,419 hits. And Perry left with 314 wins for eight different teams, although he never made it to the World Series.

Some other aged players had no intentions of retiring. Philadelphia's Steve Carlton, 38 years of age, and Houston's Nolan Ryan, 36, spent the spring battling for the all-time strikeout crown. Ryan passed longtime strikeout king Walter Johnson in April, only to be overtaken by Carlton in June. Ryan wound up the winner and Carlton wound up getting his 300th career victory. Tom Seaver, anchor of the Mets' staff in their heyday, returned to Shea Stadium and won nine games for New York.

And there were bright moments for other players across the league. Yankee Dave Righetti had a July 4 no-hitter against Boston. The Cardinals' Bob Forsch and Oakland's Mike Warren also fired no-hitters. Playing his first complete season, Boston third baseman Wade Boggs won the batting title with a .361 average. Boston teammates Jim Rice and Tony Armas led the league in homers, hitting 39 and 36.

AGING STARS HAVE ONE LAST DAY IN THE SUN

The story in the NL East was Philadelphia, a team loaded with aging stars, including: Pete Rose (42 years of age), Joe Morgan (40), Tony Perez (41), Tug McGraw (39), and Carlton. But the Phillies—or "the Wheeze Kids," as they were called—still had enough spring in their legs to win the NL East. In the playoffs, the Phillies would meet a Dodgers team that featured no pitchers who won more than 15 games and only one hitter (Pedro Guerrero) who knocked in more than 73 runs.

Joe Altobelli replaced the legendary Earl Weaver as manager of the Orioles and—with the solid performances of MVP Cal Ripken (.318 average, 27 home runs, 102 RBI) and near-MVP Eddie Murray (.306 average, 33 home runs, 111 RBI)—took them to their first World Championship since 1970. Although none of the Baltimore pitchers won 20 games, the staff was strong and consistent.

The once-hapless Chicago White Sox won the West Division with 99 games. Their offense lived by the long ball, as skipper

Tony LaRussa had four players who blasted at least 20 home runs: Greg Luzinski, Harold Baines, Carlton Fisk, and Rookie of the Year Ron Kittle. The team led the league in runs. Its pitching staff, which relied on control, was spearheaded by Cy Young winner LaMarr Hoyt, a 24-game winner.

The Mets finished just 68-94, but they did lay the groundwork for future success. They traded pitchers Neil Allen and Rick Ownbey to St. Louis for standout first baseman Keith Hernandez, and they introduced young slugger Darryl Strawberry, who slammed 26 home runs, collected 74 RBI, and took Rookie of the Year honors.

The Phillies defeated the Dodgers three games to one in the National League Championship Series. Carlton won two of the games, allowing a total of just one earned run. The Orioles shot down the White Sox' hopes of a championship in the American League Championship Series. Chicago, which had such a potent offense during the season, scored a measly three runs in four games against Baltimore.

And in the World Series, the Orioles took care of the Phillies in five games. No Baltimore pitcher won more than one game, but together they limited Philadelphia to a .195 average and 1.8 runs per game. Oriole catcher Rick Dempsey, who batted .385, was named Series MVP.

1983

- Orioles win AL flag for new manager Joe Altobelli.

- Phils triumph in NL.

- Orioles need just four games to beat White Sox in LCS.

- Phils beat LA in four games in LCS, as Steve Carlton wins two.

- Orioles win World Series in five games after dropping opener to John Denny.

- Pete Rose, oldest Series regular ever at 42, hits .313 in Series.

- Denny awarded NL Cy Young after topping loop with 19 wins.

- LaMarr Hoyt of Chicago wins American League Cy Young, tops loop with 24 wins.

- Atlanta's Dale Murphy wins second consecutive NL MVP.

- Baltimore's Cal Ripken wins AL MVP.

Scott McGregor is hugged by catcher Rick Dempsey after McGregor shut out the Phillies 5-0 in the fifth and decisive game of the 1983 World Series. The Oriole southpaw posted a 1.06 ERA in the fall classic, striking out a dozen players in 17 innings. Finishing the tournament with a .385 batting average, Dempsey was named Series MVP.

- Steve Garvey's NL record streak of 1,207 consecutive games ends when he breaks his thumb.

- KC's Dan Quisenberry sets new ML record with 45 saves.

- Nolan Ryan and Carlton both surpass Walter Johnson's career K record of 3,509.

- Jim Rice leads AL in homers (39) and total bases (344), and ties in RBI (126).

- Boston's Wade Boggs wins his first bat crown in AL (.361) and also leads in OBP (.449).

- Bill Madlock wins fourth and final bat crown in NL (.323).

- White Sox win their division by 20 games.

- With 108 steals, Rickey Henderson becomes the first to swipe at least 100 bases in consecutive years.

- Louisville Redbirds become first team in minor league history to draw one million fans in a season.

Murray: 33 HRs, 111 RBI

Eddie Murray didn't lead the American League in a single offensive category in 1983, yet he was probably the most feared power hitter in either league. He batted .306 that season, tallying 33 four-baggers and 111 RBI. The all-time home run leader for the Orioles, Murray nailed a pair of dingers in the fifth and final game of the 1983 World Series.

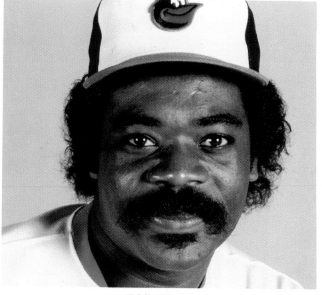

Strawberry Ripens in NY

Few rookies have ever arrived in New York with as much potential and hoopla as did Darryl Strawberry in 1983. In his 122 appearances in '83, the 21-year-old outfielder batted .257 with 26 home runs and 74 RBI to capture the National League Rookie of the Year Award.

Darryl Strawberry

Eddie Murray

Rice Tops AL in HRs

Jim Rice enjoyed a monster season at the plate in 1983, as he led or tied for the lead in the American League in round-trippers (39), RBI (126), and total bases (344). With that kind of season, many had high hopes for huge career numbers from the left fielder. However, he fizzled out at age 34 and retired after 1989. A player who shunned the press, Rice was once quoted as saying, "Privacy is important to everyone. People say you owe the public this or that. You don't owe the public anything."

Jim Rice

1983

- George Brett hits his famous "Pine Tar" homer vs. Yankees on July 24.
- AL breaks skein of 11 consecutive losses in All-Star Game by beating NL 13-3 at Comiskey Park.
- New York's Darryl Strawberry named NL ROTY.
- Chicago's Ron Kittle is AL ROTY.

- Strawberry sets Mets rookie record when he hits 26 homers.
- Kittle sets ChiSox rookie record when he hits 35 homers.
- On April 23, Tiger Milt Wilcox misses a perfect game vs. Chicago when he gives up a single with two out in ninth inning.

- On July 3, Texas beats A's with 12 runs in 15th inning—an ML record for most runs scored in an overtime frame.
- Mariners are the first major league team in this century to go through a season without playing a doubleheader.

Gaylord Perry

Dale Murphy

Murphy Cops MVP Award

Dale Murphy won his second consecutive National League MVP Award in 1983, at the age of 27, to become the youngest player ever to win back-to-back MVP honors. To capture the title, he combined his Gold Glove fielding skills with a .302 batting average, a league-leading .540 slugging average, and a loop-high 121 RBI. His 36 home runs (second in the circuit) and 30 stolen bases that season gained him admission to the 30/30 club.

Dr. Perry Wins 314th

Gaylord Perry (shown as a Brave) played out his 22-year major league career with eight teams, splitting the 1983 season between Seattle and Kansas City. He totaled seven victories that season, bringing his career wins to 314 games. Perry's stellar stint in baseball was marred when he was ejected from a game late in his career for doctoring the baseball.

Boggs Leads AL at .361

In his first full major league season, Wade Boggs continued the torrid hitting that marked his rookie campaign, seizing the American League batting title with a .361 average. The superstitious third baseman achieved further press when it was discovered that he ate chicken prior to each game. He eventually wrote a cookbook entitled *Fowl Tips*, which was illustrated with drawings by his father, Win Boggs.

Wade Boggs

- Dodger Steve Howe and Royal Willie Aikens are first players to be suspended for a full year for drug abuse.

- Dave Righetti of Yankees no-hits Boston on July 4.

- Bob Forsch of Cards no-hits Expos on Sept. 26.

- Mike Warren of Oakland no-hits Chicago on Sept. 29.

- Expo Tim Raines sets NL record when he scores 19.6 percent of his team's runs, as he leads ML with 133 runs.

- Raines also tops NL with 90 steals.

- Raines has a steals success rate of 86.5 percent, setting an NL record for players who've attempted 100 or more steals in a season.

- Mike Schmidt tops NL in homers (40), walks (128), and OBP (.402).

- Murphy leads NL in RBI (121) and SA (.540).

Quiz Saves a Record 45

Dan Quisenberry enjoyed his best season in 1983, as the Royals reliever set a then-major league record of 45 saves. Originally undrafted and signed out of La Verne College by the Royals as a free agent in '75, the righty adopted his submarine style of pitching because of a sore arm caused by hurling 194 innings his senior year.

Dan Quisenberry

Cal Ripken Jr.

Ripken Named AL MVP

Cal Ripken Jr. followed up his stellar 1982 rookie season with an American League MVP year in 1983. Spearheading the Orioles to a World Championship that season, the shortstop batted .318 with 27 home runs and 102 RBI. He achieved circuit-topping totals for runs (121), hits (211), and doubles (47).

Steve Garvey

Garvey Ends CG Streak at 1,207

In December 1982, veteran first baseman Steve Garvey bade farewell to the Dodgers and signed a five-year, $6.5-million contract with the Padres. His power hitting and overall professionalism were of great value to the Padres. In 1983, Garvey brought his consecutive game streak to an end at 1,207, a record in the National League. He finished the season with a .294 batting mark, a .459 slugging average, and 76 runs scored.

1983

- Ripken tops ML in hits (211) and doubles (47), and leads AL in runs (121).

- Atlee Hammaker of Giants paces majors with 2.25 ERA.

- The Hall of Fame inducts Brooks Robinson, Juan Marichal, George Kell, and Walter Alston.

- Phil Niekro wins the last of his five Gold Gloves for NL pitchers.

- Detroit's Lance Parrish wins the first of his three consecutive Gold Gloves as AL's top fielding catcher.

- Detroit's Lou Whitaker wins the first of his three consecutive Gold Gloves as AL's best fielding second baseman.

- Alan Trammell joins keystone mate Whitaker by winning Gold Glove at shortstop.

- Cubs second baseman Ryne Sandberg wins his first Gold Glove.

- Dwayne Murphy of the A's wins fourth of six consecutive Gold Gloves as AL outfielder.

Fernando Wins NL West

Backup catcher Jack Fimple administers a congratulatory dousing to teammate Fernando Valenzuela, who clinched the National League Division title for the Dodgers in an October 1 game with the Braves. It was the ballclub's second division championship in three years. Despite losing the services of such veterans as Ron Cey and Steve Garvey, the Dodgers still managed to win 91 games in 1983.

Jack Fimple, Fernando Valenzuela

Righetti Sparkles on July 4

The highlight of Dave Righetti's 14-8 season in 1983 was greeted by fireworks. On July 4, 1983, Rags thrilled a packed Yankee Stadium by pitching a no-hitter against the Red Sox. It was the first no-no for the Yankees since Don Larsen made World Series history with his perfect game in 1956. The lefty administered the final stroke to his masterpiece by striking out American League batting champion Wade Boggs.

Staub Is a PH Deluxe

In 1983, Rusty Staub utilized his skills as a pure hitter while playing the role of pinch hitter deluxe for the Mets. Batting .296 that season, he matched major league records for consecutive pinch hits (eight) and RBI (25) while setting the mark for pinch at-bats (81).

Dave Righetti   *Rusty Staub*

- Phillie Pete Rose is first first sacker since the dead-ball era to play a full season for a pennant winner without hitting a home run.

- St. Louis ships Keith Hernandez to Mets for Neil Allen and Rick Ownbey—a trade which will help New York to a World Crown.

- Braves send Rick Behenna, Brook Jacoby, Brett Butler, and $150,000 to Cleveland for Len Barker.

- White Sox trade Pat Tabler to Cleveland for Jerry Dybzinski.

- Cleveland sends Rick Manning and Rick Waits to Milwaukee for Gorman Thomas and two other players.

- Hoyt sets ChiSox club record when he wins 13 games in a row.

- Pittsburgh's Dale Berra reaches base an ML season record seven times on catcher's interference.

- Chicago's Harold Baines sets a new AL record with 22 game-winning RBI.

George Brett, Joe Garagiola

Pine Tar Erases Brett Home Run

No occurrence sparked more controversy in 1983 than the infamous pine tar incident. The dispute centered on the ninth-inning, two-run home run George Brett hit off Yankee reliever Goose Gossage to give the Royals a 5-4 lead in a July 24 game. Because the third baseman's bat had pine tar beyond the legal limit of 18 inches, the round-tripper was disallowed—hence the furor. Brett *(center)* is shown here being interviewed about the incident by Joe Garagiola (with bat and microphone).

Hoyt Wins AL Cy Young

LaMarr Hoyt gave the performance of his career in 1983, placing first in the American League with 24 triumphs and 1.07 walks per game. On his way to leading the White Sox to their first American League West Division crown, Dewey copped the Cy Young Award. To wrap up his banner season, the ace pitcher hurled the Sox to their sole victory in the League Championship Series against the Orioles.

LaMarr Hoyt

Fisk Adds Sock to Sox

Power hitters have always been a rare commodity at Comiskey Park. In 1983, however, the city of Chicago was shaken up as Carlton Fisk helped lead the Sox to the American League West Division title. Posting a .518 slugging average in 1983, Pudge socked 26 home runs and tallied 86 RBI. Fisk went on to set the all-time White Sox record for home runs (161). Fisk disappeared in the playoffs, though, as he batted .176 with no runs or RBI.

Carlton Fisk

1983

- The Mets' Rusty Staub sets new ML record when he has 81 at-bats as a pinch hitter.

- Earl Averill dies.

- Andre Dawson paces NL in total bases (341) and ties for lead in hits (189).

- Butler of the Braves leads majors with 13 triples.

- Milwaukee's Cecil Cooper leads AL in runs produced (202).

- Brett leads ML with a .563 SA.

- Robin Yount paces AL with ten triples.

- Henderson leads AL in walks (103) and is second in OBP (.415).

- Carlton leads NL in Ks (275) and innings (284).

- Cincinnati's Mario Soto leads NL with 18 CGs, is second in wins with 17, and also second in innings with 274.

World Series

Dwyer Scores in Game Four

Jim "Pigpen" Dwyer scores the winning run in the seventh inning of game four of the 1983 World Series, as Baltimore beat Philadelphia 5-4. Rich Dauer was credited with the RBI on a base hit. The catcher is Bo Diaz. Dwyer hit .375 in the fall classic that year, breaking open game one of the tournament with a first-inning home run.

World Series

Dempsey Homers in Game Five

Gary Matthews, the left fielder for the Phillies, can't reach Rick Dempsey's third-inning home run in game five of the 1983 World Series. The dinger, which was socked off Philly starter Charles Hudson, put the Orioles up 2-0 in the finale. Dempsey had hit just four home runs that year.

Lou Whitaker

Whitaker Bats .320

Sweet Lou Whitaker had a watershed year in 1983. Securing his position as one of the game's great middle infielders, the second baseman captured his premier Gold Glove that year. Securing his position as one of the ballclub's greatest hitters, he was named Tiger of the Year that season. Whitaker batted .320 with a dozen home runs and 72 RBI in '83, and became the first lefthanded Tiger batter since 1943 to get 200 hits.

- Ranger Rick Honeycutt wins AL ERA crown (2.42.)
- Chicago's Lee Smith tops NL with 29 saves.
- Montreal's Steve Rogers paces NL with five shutouts; AL leader Mike Boddicker of the O's also has five.

- Jack Morris leads AL in Ks (232) and innings (294), wins 20 for Tigers.
- Ron Guidry wins 21 games and tops ML with 21 CGs.
- Hoyt tops majors in fewest walks issued per game at 1.07—lowest total in AL since Tiny Bonham's 0.96 in 1942.

- Blue Jays break .500 for first time with an 89-73 record.
- Reds improve by 13 games over 1982 showing, but still finish last in NL West for second consecutive year.
- Phils win NL flag despite having oldest team in majors and posting a sub-par BA (.249) and FA (.976).

The best teams of 1984 were ballclubs that had posed little, if any, threat of contention over the years. The San Diego Padres, who would close the year as winners of the NL West, had just one winning season in their 15-year existence. Neither the Cubs nor Mets, who at season's end would be duking it out in the NL East, had challenged for the pennant in over a decade. And the Detroit Tigers, who would become the World Champions in '84, hadn't been to the playoffs since 1972.

The most exciting player of the year was Met rookie Dwight Gooden, age 19, who struck out five straight batters in the All-Star Game. Gooden finished the season 17-9 with a 2.60 ERA and a league-leading 276 strikeouts, a record for rookies. He kept the Mets in a season-long race with the Cubs, who had their own great pitcher, Cy Young winner Rick Sutcliffe. Picked up in an early season trade with Cleveland, Sutcliffe went 16-1 for the Cubs.

The North Siders also had MVP winner Ryne Sandberg, a slick-fielding, heavy-hitting second baseman. The Cubs trailed the Mets by 4 1/2 games at the end of July, then rallied to beat them in seven of their next eight games. Chicago won the division by 6 1/2.

The Padres, with 92 victories, ran away with the NL West. They featured not only a strong pitching staff, but batting champion Tony Gwynn (.351) as well.

TIGERS OPEN AT 35–5, ROAR TO WORLD TITLE

Dale Murphy and Mike Schmidt shared the NL home run title with 36, while Montreal's Gary Carter tied Schmidt in RBI with 106. Cardinal Joaquin Andujar was the NL's only 20-game winner, while teammate Bruce Sutter led the league with 45 saves.

The Tigers were the premier team of 1984, going 104-58. Their pitching was solid, with Jack Morris, Dan Petry, and Milt Wilcox all winning at least 17 games (Morris even pitched a no-hitter in April against Chicago). Reliever Willie Hernandez won both the Cy Young and MVP Awards, posting 32 saves in his first 32 save opportunities.

The Detroit offense, powered by Kirk Gibson, Lance Parrish, Alan Trammell, and Chet Lemon, led the league in home runs (187) and runs scored (829). Their up-the-middle defense, with Parrish, Trammell, Lemon, and Lou Whitaker, was the best in baseball. With this well-rounded attack, the Tigers opened the season 35-5, easily capturing the division.

In the West, Kansas City edged out the Angels and Twins, despite winning only 84 games. The Royals' only standout player was Dan Quisenberry, who notched 44 saves.

Yankee teammates Don Mattingly and Dave Winfield led the league in batting much of the season, with Mattingly taking the title on the season's final day (.343). Boston outfielder Tony Armas led the league in homers with 43 and RBI with 123, while Seattle rookie Alvin Davis posted 27 homers and 116 RBI. Mike Witt of the Angels pitched a perfect game September 30 against Texas.

The AL playoffs were a yawner, as Detroit swept the overpowered Royals. In the NL, however, an exciting series was taking shape. In the opener, the Cubs hammered the Padres 13-0, thanks to five home runs (including one by pitcher Sutcliffe). In game two, Steve Trout and Lee Smith combined to win 4-2, and Chicago was now only one victory from its first World Series in 39 years. That victory never came, however, as the Padres won three straight at Jack Murphy Stadium and captured the flag.

The World Series was a formality. Detroit rolled right through the Padres' starting pitching and won the Series four games to one. To show how dominant Detroit was in 1984, check out this stat: Including the postseason, the Tigers were 100-0 when leading after eight innings.

1984

- Tigers win their first AL flag since 1968.

- Padres become first second-wave expansion team to win flag in NL.

- Down two games to none in NLCS, Padres rally to beat Cubs in five games.

- Tigers sweep Royals in ALCS, winning finale 1-0.

- Tigers defeat Padres in World Series in five games, as Kirk Gibson clouts two homers in game five to clinch it.

- Tiger Jack Morris wins two CG victories in Series.

- Detroit's Alan Trammell leads all World Series players with .450 batting average and collects two homers and six RBI.

- Tigers reliever Willie Hernandez wins Cy Young and MVP, as he earns 32 saves in his first 32 save opportunities.

Kirk Gibson celebrates after hitting the first of his two round-trippers—a two-run, first-inning blast—in the fifth and decisive game of the 1984 World Series. The right fielder tallied a .333 average and seven RBI in the Tiger triumph over the Padres.

- Cub Rick Sutcliffe is only Cy Young winner who began year with another team.
- Chicago's Ryne Sandberg takes NL MVP.
- Met Dwight Gooden is NL ROTY, as he sets new rookie K record with 276.

- Seattle's Alvin Davis is AL ROTY.
- Tony Armas of Boston leads ML in homers (43), RBI (123), and total bases (339).
- Tigers win 26 of their first 30 games, and 35 of their first 40—best starts for any ML team this century.

- Tigers win AL record 17 straight games on the road.
- Sutcliffe goes 4-5 with Cleveland, is traded, and goes 16-1 with the Cubs.
- Dick Williams ties Bill McKechnie's record when he takes third different team, the Padres, to a pennant.

Lee Smith

Smith Tallies 33 Saves

Co-Fireman of the Year in the National League in 1984, burly Lee Smith saved 33 games and won another nine for the East Division Champion Cubs. It was the first of a four-year streak in which the righty saved 30-plus games. Fizzling out by the time postseason play rolled around, the reliever lost a game in the '84 Championship Series, posting a 9.00 ERA. Smith is the all-time leader in saves for the Cubs (180).

Gwynn Takes NL Bat Title

When general manager Jack McKeon drafted Tony Gwynn in the third round of the free agent draft in 1981, everyone thought the Padres had wasted their choice on a pudgy ex-college basketball star who didn't stand a chance at making the majors. Gwynn proved his critics wrong in 1984, as he won the National League batting championship with a .351 average—.30 more than the runner-up—and topped the circuit with 213 hits (it was the first time a Padre had accomplished either feat). Hitting .368 in the League Championship Series that year, he clinched the fifth game with his third RBI to carry the Padres to their premier World Series.

Tony Gwynn

Darrell Evans

Evans Off With a Bang

The first free agent signed by new Tiger owner Tom Monaghan, Darrell Evans busted out of the starting gate in 1984, then settled into a comfortable pace. The first baseman/designated hitter socked an Opening Day home run to spark the Tigers to their 35-5 start that year, then finished the season with a .232 batting average and 16 home runs. Bouncing back the following season, the 37-year-old veteran finished the year with 40 round-trippers and a new lease on his career.

1984

- Pete Rose gets his 4,000th hit on April 21.

- NL wins All-Star Game 3-1 at SF, as 19-year-old Gooden strikes out the side in the first inning he pitches.

- Montreal's Gary Carter becomes first player since 1968 to win two All-Star MVP Awards.

- On April 7, Morris throws first no-hitter by Detroit pitcher in 26 years, 4-0 over Chicago.

- Reggie Jackson hits his 500th homer on Sept. 17.

- Cardinal Bruce Sutter ties ML record with 45 saves.

- Sandberg leads the NL in runs (114), and ties in runs produced (179) and triples (19).

- Dale Murphy leads NL in total bases (332) and SA (.547).

- Boston's Dwight Evans tops ML in runs (121) and runs produced (193).

Jim Palmer

Carter: .294 BA, 106 RBI

With the retirement of Johnny Bench after the 1983 season, the mantle for the ultimate National League catcher was passed over to Gary Carter in 1984. The Kid posted his best season that year, cranking out a career-high 106 RBI (tied for the lead in the National League) and a .294 batting average. A perennial All-Star, he won his second All-Star MVP Award in '84 on a second-inning home run, as he caught future battery mate Dwight Gooden for the first time. Carter spent the second half of the 1980s with the Mets before signing with San Francisco in 1990. Carter is one of a handful of catchers to club 300 homers in his career.

Gary Carter

Palmer Hangs Up Glove

Jim Palmer had barely pitched one month of the 1984 season before he received notice on May 17 that the Orioles had released him. Thus ended the career of one of the greatest pitchers in American League history. His lifetime record of 268-152 was marked with eight seasons with 20 or more wins. Palmer soon became a baseball analyst for ABC-TV. For the most part, he was insightful as a commentator; he did, however, have a few klutzy moments. He once remarked, "When you stop throwing good pitches, you start throwing bad pitches."

Dennis Boyd

Boyd Breaks Even with 12

Dennis "Oil Can" Boyd evoked memories of the late Satchel Paige, as the young Red Sox pitcher spoke with a continuous singsong banter while both winning and losing 12 games in 1984. The son of an ex-Negro Leagues player, Boyd was as controversial as he was entertaining, often criticizing both teammates and management.

- Yankee Don Mattingly leads the AL in BA (.343), hits (207), and doubles (44).

- Sparky Anderson becomes first manager to win World Championships in both leagues.

- Rose achieves 100 or more hits for 22nd consecutive year, an ML record.

- Rose sets new ML record when he plays in his 3,309th game.

- Steve Carlton wins his 300th game.

- Mike Witt of Angels pitches a perfect game over Texas on Sept. 30, the final day of the season.

- Peter Ueberroth replaces Bowie Kuhn as commissioner.

- Padre Tony Gwynn wins his first NL bat crown with a .351 average, and tops ML with 213 hits.

- Mike Schmidt ties Murphy for NL homer crown (36) and Carter for RBI crown (106).

- Baltimore's Mike Boddicker tops AL with 20 wins.

Sandberg Carries Cubs

The improbable rise of the 1984 Cubs as champs of the National League East Division was fueled by Ryne Sandberg. Capturing MVP honors that season, the second baseman batted .314 with 19 home runs and 84 RBI and tied for the lead in the circuit with 19 triples. His valiant effort in the League Championship Series, a .368 average, was all in vain as the Cubs lost to the Padres 3-2.

Ryne Sandberg

Dwight Gooden

Gooden: Best at K'ing

Described by some as the Mozart of baseball, the precocious Dwight Gooden won 17 games with a 2.60 ERA in 1984. In the process, the 19-year-old hurler set a pair of major league records: One was for most strikeouts by a rookie (276 batters in just 218 innings); the other was for most strikeouts in two consecutive games (32). Gooden's fanning feats earned him the nickname "Dr. K."

Dave Winfield

Mattingly Wins AL Bat Title at .343

Don Mattingly won his first American League batting championship in 1984, on the final day of the season, by hitting .343. Along with the title, Mattingly received the distinction of being the first lefthanded Yankee hitter to bat over .340 since Lou Gehrig batted .351 in 1937. Posting a strong year all around, the first baseman topped the circuit with 207 hits and 44 doubles, came in second with a .537 slugging average, and placed fourth in total bases with 324.

Winfield Has .340 BA

Dave Winfield shortened his stroke in 1984 in a conscious effort to elevate his average and possibly win a batting title. His average jumped from .283 the year before to .340 that season. As for any crowns, the outfielder was edged out by teammate Don Mattingly, who hit .343. Off the field, the Yankee superstar continued to battle with owner George Steinbrenner, who had refused to honor his contractual obligation to support Winfield's charitable foundation.

Don Mattingly

1984

- St. Louis' Joaquin Andujar leads the NL with 20 wins.

- Average player's salary is now $363,000.

- The Hall of Fame inducts Luis Aparicio, Harmon Killebrew, Don Drysdale, Rick Ferrell, and Pee Wee Reese.

- Jim Rice sets new ML record when he grounds into 36 DPs.

- Eddie Murray wins third of his three consecutive Gold Gloves as AL first baseman.

- Pittsburgh's Tony Pena wins second of three straight Gold Gloves as NL catcher.

- Gooden fans 16 batters in two consecutive starts to set new modern record for most Ks in two straight starts (32).

- Stanley Coveleski dies at age 94.

- Waite Hoyt dies.

- Joe Cronin dies.

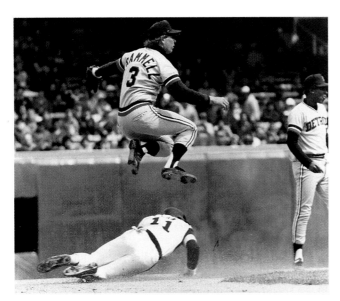

Alan Trammell

Trammell Hits .314

Alan Trammell established himself as the best overall shortstop in baseball in 1984, as he batted .314 with 14 home runs and 69 RBI. The Gold Glove shortstop came to the fore during postseason play that year. Superb in the American League Championship Series, he turned in a .364 average and three RBI. Spectacular in the World Series, he racked up a .450 average, two home runs, and six RBI to cop Series MVP honors.

Rick Sutcliffe

Sutcliffe Wins 16

Dallas Green, general manager for the Cubs, made the trade of the year when he obtained Rick Sutcliffe from the Indians in exchange for outfielders Mel Hall and Joe Carter. Sutcliffe went 16-1 for the Cubs after having started the 1984 season with a 4-5 record for the Indians.

Cey: 25 HRs, 97 RBI

Despite having lost a step in the field, Ron Cey still wielded a potent bat. In 1984, he helped the Cubs to the National League East Division title by hitting 25 homers and driving in 97 runs. In the League Championship Series, he was good for one home run and a trio of RBI. His glovework, however, was off the mark. At one point during the '84 season, a Chicago sportswriter wrote that a sheet of propped-up plywood would have provided better defense at Wrigley's hot corner.

Ron Cey

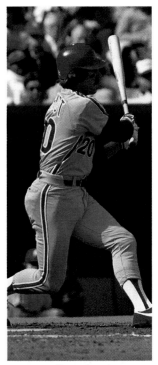

Mike Schmidt

Schmidt: 36 HRs, 106 RBI

Mike Schmidt had a typical season for a budding Hall of Famer in 1984. Tying for first place in the National League in home runs with 36 and RBI with 106, the third baseman's slugging proficiency had him nailing a round-tripper in seven percent of his total at-bats. Capturing his ninth consecutive Gold Glove Award that year, he exhibited a defensive prowess that was matched only by Brooks Robinson.

- George Kelly dies at age 89.
- Houston's Dickie Thon is beaned, suffers damaged vision, and never regains hitting ability.
- Cleveland trades Sutcliffe, Ron Hassey, and George Frazier to the Cubs for Joe Carter, Mel Hall, and a minor leaguer.
- Oakland swaps Rickey Henderson, Bert Bradley, and cash to the Yankees for Jay Howell, Stan Javier, Tim Birtsas, Jose Rijo, and Eric Plunk.
- Boston ships Dennis Eckersley to the Cubs for Bill Buckner and Mike Brumley.
- Montreal deals Carter to the Mets for Hubie Brooks and three other players.
- Prior to the season, the Phils deal Hernandez and Dave Bergman to Detroit for John Wockenfuss and Glenn Wilson.
- Carl Pohlad buys Twins from Calvin Griffith.
- Pittsburgh's Johnny Ray sets ML record when he has game-winning RBI in six straight games.

Lloyd Moseby

Moseby: 18 HRs, 92 RBI

Uniting with George Bell and Jesse Barfield to form the American League's best outfield of the late 1980s, Lloyd Moseby put up some impressive offensive numbers in 1984. He batted .280 with 18 home runs and 92 RBI, tying for first place in the circuit in triples with 15. Shaker heads up the Blue Jay list in career games (1,392), at-bats (5,124), runs (768), hits (1,319), extra-base hits (451), doubles (242), and stolen bases (255).

Hernandez Saves 32

In 1984, Willie Hernandez became only the second reliever, right behind Rollie Fingers, to capture league MVP and Cy Young honors in the same season. While helping the Tigers to their greatest season in two decades, the lefty saved 32 games in 33 chances, won another nine, and sported a 1.92 ERA. Giving an encore of his spectacular performance in that fall's World Series, he tallied a pair of saves and a 1.69 ERA.

Willie Hernandez

Carmelo Martinez, Tony Gwynn, Kevin McReynolds

Outfield Carries Padres

The youthful outfield of Carmelo Martinez *(left)*, Tony Gwynn *(center)*, and Kevin McReynolds helped the Dick Williams-led Padres to their first National League pennant ever. Gwynn spearheaded the trio with his circuit-topping .351 batting average. McReynolds contributed 20 home runs and 75 RBI to the cause, while Martinez tallied 13 round-trippers and 66 RBI. The three disappeared in the World Series. Martinez and Gwynn hit a combined .222 with no extra-base hits and no RBI. McReynolds missed the action because of an injury.

1984

- Joe Morgan's 265th career homer breaks Rogers Hornsby's record for second basemen.

- Phillie Juan Samuel sets record for both NL second basemen and NL rookies when he fans 168 times.

- Steve Garvey's 1.000 FA sets new ML record for first basemen.

- Jim Frey, who piloted the Royals to a division title in his first year in KC, does the same in his first year with the Cubs.

- Boddicker, a breaking-ball specialist, establishes a major league record for pitchers when he averages 1.44 putouts per game he pitches.

- Gary Matthews of the Cubs tops NL in walks (103) and OBP (.417).

- Ray and Tim Raines tie for NL lead in doubles (38).

- Raines tops Samuel in steals (75-72) to lead ML.

- Murray paces AL in walks (107) and OBP (.415).

Jack Morris

Chet Lemon

Lemon: 20 HRs, 76 RBI

Chet Lemon was a solid contributor to the Tigers in 1984, as he batted .287 with 20 home runs and 76 RBI. Baseball guru Bill James ranked Lemon the second-best center fielder in the American League behind Lloyd Moseby of the Blue Jays.

Gibby One-Ups Garvey

Kirk Gibson avoids a pickoff attempt by Steve Garvey at first base in the third inning of game five of the 1984 World Series. Although Garvey led the Padres to their incredible National League Championship Series comeback against the Cubs, he couldn't stem the Tiger tide in the fall classic. Batting just .200, Garvey was good for just a pair of RBI. Gibson, on the other hand, hit two four-baggers in the fifth and final game to bring the Tigers their first World Title since 1968.

Morris Blanks ChiSox

A national television audience witnessed the spectacle of Jack Morris twirling a no-hitter against the White Sox on April 7, 1984, as he made a bit of history in the process. Not only did Morris match Ken Forsch's 1979 feat for throwing the season's earliest no-no in the history of the game, he also became the first Tiger to throw a no-hitter since Jim Bunning in 1958. The ballclub's leading victor from 1979 through 1987, Morris finished the '84 season at 19-11. The hurler posted an excellent 2.00 ERA in the 1984 World Series, winning games one and four.

Kirk Gibson, Steve Garvey

- Chicago's Harold Baines has AL's top SA (.541).

- Teammates Lloyd Moseby and Dave Collins of Toronto lead AL in triples with 15.

- Henderson, playing for Oakland, leads AL in steals (66).

- KC's Dan Quisenberry leads AL with 44 saves.

- Alejandro Pena of LA has best ERA in ML (2.49); Boddicker has best ERA in AL (2.79).

- Toronto's Dave Stieb leads ML in innings with 267.

- Charlie Hough of Texas tops majors with 17 CGs.

- Cincinnati's Mario Soto leads the National League with just 13 complete games.

- Seattle rookie Mark Langston tops AL in Ks (204), wins 17 games to set new Mariners club record.

Milestones toppled like dominoes in 1985. Nolan Ryan racked up his 4,000th strikeout, Rod Carew collected his 3,000th hit, and Tom Seaver and Phil Niekro each earned their 300th victory (Seaver and Carew accomplished their respective feats on the same day). And in the biggest moment of all, Pete Rose cracked his 4,192nd hit on September 11, breaking Ty Cobb's major league record.

Three of the four divisions offered close contests. In the AL East, Toronto edged Billy Martin's Yankees by 2 games. The Blue Jays were led by the fantastic outfield of Lloyd Moseby, Jesse Barfield, and George Bell, who combined for 73 home runs. Barfield also had a lethal arm, racking up 27 assists.

The Yankees boasted a devastating lineup with MVP Don Mattingly (48 doubles, 145 RBI), Dave Winfield (114 RBI), Rickey Henderson (146 runs, 80 steals), and Don Baylor. Ron Guidry had a strong season, too, winning 22 games. The Yankees chased Toronto throughout the summer, never quite able to overtake them, then replaced Martin with Lou Piniella in the off-season.

The Royals won their division with a deep pitching staff, spearheaded by Cy Young winner Bret Saberhagen, who went 20-6 with a 2.87 ERA. George Brett had one of his finest seasons, batting .335 and driving in 112 runs.

KC PULLS OFF BACK-TO-BACK COMEBACKS

The Cardinals won the NL East, thanks to MVP Willie McGee and his NL-best .353 average. St. Louis edged out the Mets, who were led by phenom Dwight Gooden. Gooden won the Cy Young Award with a league-leading 24 wins, 268 strikeouts, and 1.53 ERA.

In the NL West, Tommy Lasorda's Dodgers won the division on the pitching of Orel Hershiser (who went 19-3) and the offense of Pedro Guerrero and Mike Marshall, who combined for 61 homers.

A few dark moments blemished the banner year. A players' strike in August halted the season for two days. In September, several major leaguers—including Keith Hernandez and Dave Parker—testified in court that they had used cocaine. And in their never-ending quest for money, the owners expanded the playoffs to a best-of-seven series.

St. Louis defeated the Dodgers in six games to win the NL pennant. Ozzie Smith was the hero of game five, hitting a bottom-of-the-ninth solo shot to give his club a 3-2 win. In game six, the big hit came from Jack Clark, as he blasted a ninth-inning, three-run homer off Tom Niedenfuer (who also gave up Smith's homer) to give the Cards a 7-5 win.

In the ALCS, Toronto won three of the first four games, but the Royals came back and won three straight, pitting them against cross-state rival St. Louis in the World Series.

The "I-70 Series" proved exciting. The strong starting pitching of John Tudor and Danny Cox put the favored Cards up two games to none. Frank White's three RBI, however, helped KC win game three. Tudor shut out KC in game four, and the Royals took game five 6-1.

KC trailed three games to two, and were trailing 1-0 in the ninth in game six. But then the tide turned KC's way. Royal Jorge Orta led off the ninth with an infield single, which on video replay indicated a bad call by the umpire. Clark then misplayed a foul ball hit by Steve Balboni, and, given a second life, Balboni singled. A passed ball and an intentional walk loaded the bases, and Dane Iorg singled over first base to win the game 2-1, forcing game seven.

The Royals won the final game 11-0, knocking Tudor out after 2 1/3 innings. The victory gave the Royals their first World Championship.

1985

- Cards win second flag in '80s under Whitey Herzog.

- Royals win AL dogfight.

- The LCS format is expanded to best-of-seven; in ALCS, KC rallies from three-to-one deficit to beat Toronto.

- In NLCS, Cards sink Dodgers in six games, as Ozzie Smith wins game six with his first homer ever lefthanded.

- Royals beat Cards in World Series.

- In bottom of ninth of game six of Series, ump Don Denkinger rules KC pinch hitter Jorge Orta safe at first, though TV cameras show Orta out.

- Royals parlay Denkinger's miscue into two runs and win the game 2-1 to even the Series.

- Bret Saberhagen wins two Series games for KC, including a shutout in game seven.

- George Brett leads KC with ten hits in Series.

1985

George Brett led the Royals to the 1985 World Crown by batting .335 with 30 home runs and 112 RBI during the season. Continuing his hot hitting in the American League Championship Series, he racked up a .348 average with three home runs in seven games. Remaining true to form in the World Series, he batted .370 as the Royals came from behind to snare a seven-game triumph over the cross-state rival Cardinals. Commenting on the most prolific player in the history of the Royals franchise, umpire Steve Palermo said, "If God had him no balls and two strikes, he'd still get a hit."

- Willie McGee of Cards voted NL MVP, as he leads league in BA (.353), hits (216), and triples (18).

- Don Mattingly is AL MVP.

- Dwight Gooden wins NL Cy Young, as he leads NL in wins (24), ERA (1.53), Ks (268), CGs (16), and innings (277).

- Gooden's 1.53 ERA is best in majors during the 1980s.

- Saberhagen wins AL Cy Young.

- On Sept. 11, Pete Rose cracks his 4,192nd career hit, breaking Ty Cobb's ML record.

- Mattingly's 145 RBI lead ML by 20.

- Vince Coleman of Cards steals rookie record 110 bases.

- Wade Boggs leads ML with 240 hits, most in majors since 1930.

- Boggs also leads ML in BA (.368) and OBP (.452).

- Rickey Henderson scores 146 runs, most in majors since 1949.

Bert Blyleven

Blyleven: 17 Wins, 206 Ks

Dividing his 1985 season between the Indians and the Twins (where he returned after an eight-year absence), Bert Blyleven spearheaded the American League in innings pitched (293²/₃) and strikeouts (206) while compiling a 17-16 record. He also topped the circuit in shutouts (five) and complete games (24). Yielding a major league record 50 gopher balls in 1986, the righty helped the Twins to a World Championship in 1987. During the American League Championship Series of that year, a Twins fan held up a banner that read, "Bert will have us home Blyleven."

Winfield: 26 HRs, 114 RBI

In 1985, Dave Winfield hit .275 with 26 home runs and 114 RBI and helped the Yankees with his speed, defense, and throwing ability. It's only fitting that he is tied with Roger Maris on the Yankees' all-time home run list (203), because neither star ever got the recognition they deserved in New York. When Winfield signed a multi-million-dollar contract in 1981, Yankee fans expected him to produce the numbers of Mickey Mantle and the drama of Reggie Jackson. When he fell below their expectations, they got on his case.

Dave Winfield

Wade Boggs

Boggs Posts .368 Average

Batting an American League-leading .368 average in 1985, Wade Boggs began a four-year streak in which he would top the circuit in batting. An above-average fielder, he also led all circuit third basemen in chances that year with 486. Boggs was named to his first All-Star Game in '85. Tallying a .356 career average at the end of the 1988 season, he tied with Joe Jackson for the third-highest mark in the history of the game, behind Ty Cobb (.366) and Rogers Hornsby (.358).

1985

- Cal Ripken breaks Buck Freeman's record for consecutive innings played, as he reaches 5,342 innings without respite.

- NL wins All-Star Game 6-1 at Metrodome, taking 17-game lead in All-Star competition; NL has won 21 of last 23 games.

- Don Sutton becomes first pitcher in ML history to fan 100 or more hitters in 20 consecutive seasons.

- Steve Garvey's record streak of 193 consecutive errorless games at first base ends.

- Angel Bobby Grich's .997 FA sets new ML record for second basemen.

- Larry Bowa retires with record for highest career FA by a shortstop (.980).

- Nolan Ryan fans his 4,000th batter on July 11.

- Rod Carew collects his 3,000th hit.

- Phil Niekro picks up his 300th win.

Ripken: 26 HRs, 110 RBI

Cal Ripken Jr. was the top American League All-Star vote-getter in 1985 (his third of seven consecutive years as an All-Star selection), as he continued to produce stellar numbers. Despite the demise of the Orioles, the shortstop tallied a .282 batting average, 26 home runs, and 110 RBI while leading the loop in putouts and double plays that season. His stature both on and off the field made Ripken the most popular Oriole since Brooks Robinson.

Cal Ripken Jr.

Keith Hernandez, Pete Rose

Keith, Rose Best at First

Keith Hernandez (*left*) and Pete Rose were two of the greatest, if not more controversial, hitters of the past quarter-century. One of the best fielding first basemen in the history of the game, Hernandez hit .309 in 1985, collecting ten home runs and 91 RBI. Rose, the all-time hit man, batted .264 with 107 hits and 60 runs scored that season. In '85, it was revealed that Hernandez was using drugs and he was suspended; he put his career back together to be named team captain in 1987. Rose is still rebuilding his gambling-tarnished reputation.

Dwight Gooden

Gooden: 24 Victories, 1.53 ERA

Dwight Gooden built upon the heroics of his rookie season by reaching new heights in 1985. Not only did he garner the "pitcher's triple crown" by leading the National League in wins (24-4), ERA (1.53), and strikeouts (268), he also placed first in complete games (16). Fanning 16 batters in a 3-0 win over the Giants on August 20, 1985, the ace righty became the first pitcher in the senior circuit to strike out 200 batters in each of his first two years. The 20-year-old won that year's AL Cy Young Award hands down.

- Tom Seaver gets win No. 300.
- Darrell Evans is first to hit 40 or more homers in a season in each league, as he cracks an ML-leading 40 for Detroit.
- Pirate Jose DeLeon goes 2-19, posting the lowest win pct. in NL history (.095).

- The players strike on August 6 for two days.
- Cubs are first National League team since 1901 to play no doubleheaders in a season.
- Dale Murphy leads NL in homers (37), runs (118), and walks (90).

- A rejuvenated Dave Parker, now with the Reds, tops NL in RBI (125), total bases (350), and doubles (42).
- LA's Pedro Guerrero paces NL in SA (.577) and OBP (.425).
- Mattingly leads the AL in runs produced (217), total bases (370), and doubles (48).

Pete Rose

Henderson Goes 20/50

In 1985, Rickey Henderson became the first American League player ever to post a 20 home run/50 steal season (24 dingers, 80 swipes); in 1986, he became the circuit's first player to post back-to-back 20/50 seasons (28 dingers, 87 swipes). In 1985, he had himself one of the greatest seasons ever by a leadoff man: a .314 average, 99 walks, 146 runs scored (the best showing in the majors since 1949), and an average of over a run scored per game (the best since 1939). Despite all his heroics, he lost the loop's MVP Award to teammate Don Mattingly.

Rickey Henderson

Rose Breaks Cobb's Mark

At Riverfront Stadium on September 11, 1985, Pete Rose surpassed Ty Cobb as baseball's all-time leading hitter by stroking No. 4,193 off Eric Show, the starter for the Padres. To reach the milestone, Rose recorded over 100 hits a season past the age of 38. When asked to suggest his epitaph, Rose said, "Here lies the man who could hit forever."

Dale Murphy

Murphy: 37 HRs, 111 RBI

Dale Murphy continued his string of fabulous seasons in 1985, batting .300 with 111 RBI while leading the National League with 37 home runs, 118 runs scored, and 90 walks. A seven-time All-Star selection and a five-time (consecutive) Gold Glove-winner, the slugger for the Braves received the Lou Gehrig Award that year for his generous off-field activities. On the downside, Murphy led the National League in strikeouts (141) for the third time in his career.

1985

- Bert Blyleven, traded by Cleveland to Minnesota in midseason, tops AL in CGs (24), innings (294), and Ks (206).

- Dale Berra becomes second player in major league history to be managed by his father—Yogi Berra of the Yankees.

- The Hall of Fame inducts Hoyt Wilhelm, Lou Brock, Arky Vaughan, and Enos Slaughter.

- Chicago's Ozzie Guillen is AL ROTY.

- Coleman is NL ROTY.

- Brett wins the only Gold Glove of his long career.

- Mattingly wins his first Gold Glove as AL's top fielding first baseman.

- Boston's Bill Buckner sets new ML record for first basemen with 184 assists.

- KC's Steve Balboni fans 166 times to set a new ML record for first basemen.

Orel Hershiser

Hershiser Triumphs in 19

Nicknamed "Bulldog" by Tommy Lasorda, the manager of the Dodgers, Orel Hershiser made 1985 his breakthrough year. The righty spearheaded all National League pitchers in winning percentage at .864 as he went 19-3 and posted a 2.03 ERA for the season. In the League Championship Series, he won one game and hit .286.

Don Mattingly

Mattingly Named AL MVP

Batting third in the Yankee lineup in 1985, Don Mattingly showed a marked increase in his power statistics as he amassed a career-high 35 home runs and an American League-leading 145 RBI. The performance snared the junior circuit's MVP Award that year. Mattingly also displayed power at first base, winning his first of four consecutive Gold Gloves that season. In the mid-1980s, many experts considered him the game's best all-around player.

Evans Leads AL in HRs

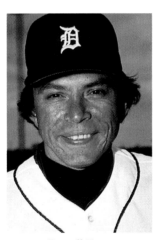

In 1985, 38-year-old Darrell Evans led the American League in home runs with 40. Not only did the feat make him the oldest home run champion in the history of the game, it also made him the only player ever to hit 40 or more home runs in both leagues. For good measure, Evans also racked up 94 RBI that season. Evans was the only bright spot on the '85 Tigers.

Darrell Evans

- Steve Bedrosian of Atlanta makes major league record 37 starts without registering a single complete game all season.

- Tommy Herr of the Cards is first ML player since 1950 to amass 100 or more RBI with fewer than ten homers.

- Rob Picciolo leaves majors with 25 walks in 1,628 career at-bats—poorest walk ratio in ML history.

- Duane Kuiper retires with one homer in 3,379 career at-bats—worst home run ratio in 20th century among players active ten or more seasons.

- Chicago's Carlton Fisk sets AL record for catchers with 37 homers.

- Henderson sets ML record for players with 90 or more steal attempts when he has 88.9-percent success.

- LaMarr Hoyt of San Diego allows just 0.86 walks per game.

- Dennis Lamp has a perfect 11-0 record for Blue Jays—most wins without a loss by a pitcher since 1928.

McGee Sets Record with .353 Average

Willie McGee, the National League MVP in 1985, tallied the highest average by a switch-hitter in history, as he racked up a .353 mark. In leading the Cardinals to the senior circuit's pennant, the outfielder garnered a circuit-high 216 hits and 18 triples. In the World Series that year, he homered in game four to give the Cardinals their last win in the fall classic.

Willie McGee

Niekro Racks Up 300 Wins

The most celebrated game in the long career of Phil Niekro came on the final day of the 1985 season, when the 46-year-old pitcher won his 300th game as the Yankees defeated the Blue Jays. The ageless wonder went 16-12 for the Bronx Bombers in '85. Said Bobby Murcer, the outfielder: "Trying to hit Phil Niekro is like trying to eat JELL-O® with chopsticks. Sometimes you might get a piece, but most of the time you get hungry."

Coleman Named NL ROTY

Vince Coleman captured National League Rookie of the Year honors in 1985, stealing 110 bases while scoring 107 runs. In his first seven years of professional baseball, the speedster led every league he had ever played in in stolen bases. He became the first player in the history of the game to swipe 100 cushions in each of his first three seasons in the majors. Coleman missed most of the 1985 postseason due to a freakish injury (his foot got caught in an automatic tarp dispenser). He played in just three playoff games and stole just one base that year.

Vince Coleman

Phil Niekro

1985

- A record 458 games are played in majors before the first rainout of the year occurs on May 20 in Cleveland.

- Giants trade Jack Clark to St. Louis for Jose Uribe and three other players.

- Local group buys Pirates, installs Syd Thrift as GM.

- Cincinnati auto dealer Marge Schott becomes principal owner of the Reds.

- Boggs sets AL record when he makes one or more hits in 135 games.

- Boggs also sets major league season record for most hits by a third baseman (240).

- Joe Wood dies at age 95.

- Roger Maris dies at age 51.

- Burleigh Grimes dies.

- Billy Martin replaces Berra as Yankees manager in late April, guides club to 91-54 record under him, and has a fight with pitcher Ed Whitson.

Bret Saberhagen

Carew Hits No. 3,000

Rod Carew became the 16th member of the exclusive 3,000-hit club on August 4, 1985, as he stroked a single off Frank Viola, the starter for the Twins, at Anaheim Stadium. He hit .280 in 1985, his last year, to retire with a .328 career average and 1,015 RBI. Carew's 3,053 hits rank 12th on the all-time list, while his .328 lifetime average ranks 27th. No one since Stan Musial has retired with a higher average. Though fans were sad to see Carew leave the game, many sportswriters were glad to see him go. At times, he was downright nasty with reporters.

Rod Carew

Bret Wins Cy Young

In 1985, while Dwight Gooden was establishing himself as the best young pitcher in the National League, Bret Saberhagen was building a similar case for himself in the American League. The youngest pitcher ever to win the Cy Young Award, the 21-year-old Saberhagen went 20-6 with a 2.87 ERA that year. Stunning in the '85 World Series, the righty won games three and seven and posted a 0.50 ERA.

Ozzie Smith

Smith Clinches Game Five

The Wizard of Oz, alias Ozzie Smith, celebrates his game-winning home run in the fifth contest of the National League Championship Series. Hit off Tom Niedenfuer, the Dodger reliever, the dinger was only the 14th round-tripper in the eight-year-old career of the tiny switch-hitter. It was, moreover, his first homer hit lefthanded. Smith also collected a .435 average and three RBI in the tournament.

- Astros play NL record 126 night games.

- Andy Hawkins sets Padres club record when he wins 15 consecutive games.

- McGee's .353 BA is highest since 1901 by a switch-hitter in the NL.

- Ron Guidry leads AL with 22 wins and .786 win pct.

- KC's Willie Wilson leads majors with 21 triples—most since Dale Mitchell's 23 in 1949.

- Expo Jeff Reardon leads majors with 41 saves; Royal Dan Quisenberry tops AL with 37.

- John Tudor of the Cards tops majors with ten shutouts—one short of modern record for southpaws.

- Brewers are last in American League with 101 homers after topping majors with 216 four-baggers as recently as 1982.

- Angels fall 1 game short of winning AL West, adding to Gene Mauch's record of most years as a manager without winning a pennant (24).

The Amazin' Mets of 1969 stunned the baseball world with great pitching and timely hitting. The Macho Mets of 1986 dominated the sport with a dazzling combination of power, speed, and pitching.

Twenty-one-year-old flamethrower Dwight "Doctor K" Gooden (17-6), Ron Darling (15-6), Bobby Ojeda (18-5), and Sid Fernandez (16-6) created the soundest starting staff in the majors. Scrappy tablesetters Lenny Dykstra (.295, 31 stolen bases), Wally Backman (.320), and Ray Knight (.298) and RBI men Gary Carter (24 home runs, 105 RBI), Darryl Strawberry (27 home runs, 93 RBI), and Keith Hernandez (.310 average, 83 RBI) provided solid hitting.

Houston took the NL West by storm, going 96-66. Cy Young Award-winner Mike Scott (18-10) baffled hitters with his split-fingered fastball, no-hitting San Francisco on September 25 and leading the majors in innings (275), ERA (2.23), and strikeouts (306). Slugger Glenn Davis belted 31 home runs—no small feat in the Astrodome—and Kevin Bass hit .311 with 20 homers.

On the other side of the majors, Boston had its own established stars in Wade Boggs (a circuit-topping .357 average), Dwight Evans (26 home runs, 97 RBI), Jim Rice (.324, 20 home runs, 110 RBI), and 23-year-old Cy Young Award-winner and MVP Roger Clemens (a league-leading 24 wins).

SOX LET SERIES SCOOT THROUGH THEIR LEGS

Veteran stars Don Sutton, Reggie Jackson, Bob Boone, and Bobby Grich combined to give California a 92-70 season and a first-place finish in the American League West.

There were other notable deeds around the circuits. In the National League, Philadelphia's Mike Schmidt took MVP honors on his 37 round-trippers, 119 RBI, and .547 slugging average. Fernando Valenzuela of Los Angeles had a 21-11 season and three shutouts. Montreal's Tim Raines posted a league-leading .334 average. Toronto outfielder Jesse Barfield topped the American League with 40 homers. Joe Cowley of the White Sox had his own no-hitter against the Angels on September 19. Cleveland finished fifth in the East, two spots up from last year, with a league-leading .284 team average.

The Mets and Astros faced off in the NLCS. Trailing by three for most of game six, the Mets tied it in the ninth. In the 16th frame, New York took a 7-4 advantage. Houston trimmed the lead to one; then, with two out

and two on, Jesse Orosco fanned Bass, ending the longest postseason game.

The ALCS between the Angels and the Red Sox was almost as exciting. California had a tournament-lead of three games to one and a 5-2 advantage in the top of the ninth inning of game five when Boston designated hitter Don Baylor slashed the gap with a two-run homer; Dave Henderson's two-run dinger rung up a 6-5 BoSox lead. California went on to lose 7-6 in 11 innings. Boston took games six and seven.

New York and Boston staged a memorable World Series. The Red Sox swept the first two games in Shea Stadium; the Mets, the next two in Fenway Park. Boston took game five at home.

The Sox took a 5-3 lead into the bottom of the tenth of game six, the key blow being Henderson's home run. Reliever Calvin Schiraldi retired the first two Mets. One out separated Boston from its first title in 68 years. Gary Carter and Kevin Mitchell singled. Knight brought Carter home and Mitchell went to third. Up came Mookie Wilson. Reliever Bob Stanley's wild pitch allowed Mitchell to tie the game at five-all. Wilson ended it by sending a slow roller to first, a certain out—until Bill Buckner let it squirt through his legs. Knight raced home with the winning run.

Two days later, the celebration was official, as Orosco recorded the last out in the 8-5 New York win in game seven.

1986

- Mets take pennant after winning NL East by 21 1/2 games, a record margin since majors went into division play.

- Red Sox win first AL flag since 1975.

- In NLCS, Mets best Astros in tight six-game Series, winning clincher 7-6 in 16 innings.

- Jesse Orosco wins LCS record three games for Mets, all in relief.

- In ALCS, Red Sox rally from three-games-to-one deficit to defeat Angels.

- Dave Henderson's two-out, two-strike, two-run homer in ninth inning of game five saves Red Sox.

- Mets win World Series in seven games, nabbing the clincher after trailing 3-0 in the sixth inning of the finale.

- Red Sox drop game six after leading 5-3 in tenth inning, as Met Mookie Wilson hits a grounder through Bill Buckner's legs.

Rocket Roger Clemens became the third American League pitcher in four years to capture both the Cy Young Award as well as MVP honors as he turned the trick in 1986. While leading the Red Sox to the World Series that year, he triumphed in 24 games, topped the loop in both winning percentage (.857) and ERA (2.48), and won the All-Star Game in his adopted hometown of Houston. Fans knew to expect a red-hot season from the righty when, on April 29, he fanned 20 Mariners in the 3-1 Sox victory to set the record for most strikeouts in a nine-inning game.

- Boston's Roger Clemens wins AL Cy Young and MVP, as he leads ML in wins (24) and win pct. (.857).

- Mike Schmidt captures NL MVP Award.

- Houston's Mike Scott wins NL Cy Young.

- Oakland's Jose Canseco named AL ROTY, as he hits 33 homers and has 117 RBI.

- Clemens fans ML record 20 Mariners on April 29.

- Schmidt sets NL record by leading his league in homers for the eighth time, as he clubs 37.

- For first time in history, every club in majors exceeds one million in attendance.

- Don Mattingly hits .352 and sets Yankees franchise records with 238 hits and 53 doubles.

- Mattingly tops ML in hits, doubles, and total bases (388).

1986

Mike Scott

Scott's No-No Wins Flag

Mike Scott achieved a major league first on September 25, 1986, as he clinched the National League West Division title for the Astros by hurling a no-hitter in a game against the Giants. Wrapping up the season with 18 wins, the stopper topped the loop in innings pitched (275), strikeouts (306), strikeouts per game (10.01), and ERA (2.23), and tied for first place in shutouts (five) and fewest hits per game (5.96). The second NL righty (11th hurler overall) to notch 300 Ks, he captured the Cy Young Award that year. Almost unhittable in postseason action against the Mets, Scott posted a 0.50 playoff ERA.

Bob Horner

Pete Rose

Horner Hits Four HRs

On July 6, 1986, Bob Horner of the Braves socked four home runs in a game against the Expos to tie the major league record. The National League's 1978 Rookie of the Year was the first slugger to achieve the feat since Mike Schmidt in 1976. Upon becoming a free agent in '87, the third baseman went to play ball in Japan. Although he was back in the States in '88, playing with the Cards, injuries forced him to call it quits in midseason.

Rose Lays Down Bat

"I'd walk through hell in a gasoline suit to keep playing baseball," Pete Rose once remarked. The end for Rose came in 1986. The Reds player/manager closed his 24-year career by rapping his 4,256th hit, the all-time record (Rose recorded 80 additional hits in postseason play). Rose retired as the all-time leader in games (3,562), at-bats (14,053), and singles (3,510), placed second in doubles (746), and came in fourth in runs scored (2,165). He was named to the All-Star Game at five different positions in his career (first base, second base, third base, left field, and right field).

1986

- Wade Boggs leads ML in BA (.357), walks (105), and OBP (.455).

- On August 11, at age 45, Pete Rose becomes the oldest player ever to go 5-for-5.

- Rose retires holding ML career records for hits (4,256), games (3,562), and at-bats (14,053).

- AL wins All-Star Game 3-2 at Houston, as Fernando Valenzuela Ks five AL hitters in a row to match Carl Hubbell's 1934 feat.

- Cardinal Todd Worrell is NL ROTY, as he sets ML rookie record with 36 saves.

- Schmidt wins last of his ten Gold Gloves.

- Joe Cowley of White Sox no-hits California on Sept. 19.

- Scott no-hits Giants on Sept. 25—the only no-hitter in NL history to clinch a pennant or division crown.

- KC's Bo Jackson becomes second Heisman Trophy winner to play in majors.

Grich Calls It Quits After 17 Years

Bobby Grich ended his 17-year career in the major leagues in 1986 having played in the American League Championship Series five times without making it to the World Series. He came closest to fall classic contention in '86, when the Angels led the Red Sox three games to one in the playoffs before choking. Grich tallied one home run and three RBI for the seven-game affair. One of the league's top all-around second basemen for more than 15 years, he was a six-time All-Star.

Bobby Grich

Dave Righetti

Rags Saves 46 Games, Sets a Record

In 1986, Dave Righetti saved 46 games—an all-time single-season record. Previously, Bruce Sutter and Dan Quisenberry held the record with 45 saves, but Rags went all out to surpass that total. The Yankee bullpen ace converted on 29 of his final 30 save opportunities in 1986; his last two saves came on the closing day of the season, when he slammed the door on the Red Sox in both games of a doubleheader.

Tony Gwynn

Gwynn Tops in Hits, Runs

Continuing his hot hitting in 1986, Tony Gwynn tallied a .329 batting average and National League-leading totals for hits (211) and runs scored (107). Showing marked improvement in his fielding, he copped his first Gold Glove that season. More than doubling his stolen base total of the previous year, the outfielder swiped five cushions in a game against the Astros. A gifted all-around athlete, Gwynn starred in basketball at San Diego State.

- On July 6, Atlanta's Bob Horner becomes first player in this century to hit four homers in a game lost by his team.

- Yankee Dave Righetti sets new ML record with 46 saves, as he breaks the record with two saves during the closing-day doubleheader.

- Steve Carlton is first lefty to collect 4,000 career Ks.

- Don Sutton wins his 300th game.

- Mariners set ML team record when they fan 1,148 times.

- Average player's salary reaches $412,000; the minimum salary is now $62,500.

- Minnesota's Bert Blyleven gives up ML record 50 home runs.

- Schmidt leads NL in SA (.547) and RBI (119).

- Toronto's Jesse Barfield leads majors with 40 homers.

- Valenzuela tops NL with 21 wins and majors with 20 CGs.

Raines Wins NL Bat Title

Tim "Rock" Raines bested the National League with a .334 batting average and a .415 on-base percentage in 1986. The fleet left fielder stole 70 bases that year (his sixth season with 70 or more swipes). Raines is currently the all-time leader in stolen base average (an 85.7-percent mark after the 1990 season).

Evans: 26 HRs, 97 RBI

With the retirement of Carl Yastrzemski after the 1983 season, Boston's mantle of leadership fell upon Dwight Evans. An eight-time Gold Glove-winner, the right fielder helped the Red Sox to the American League East Division flag in 1986 by batting .259 with 26 home runs and 97 RBI. In the World Series, Dewey batted .308 with nine RBI.

Dwight Evans

Tim Raines

Don Mattingly, Wally Joyner

Joyner, Don Star at First

Wally Joyner *(right)* blasted out of the starting gate in 1986 to finish right behind Jose Canseco in American League Rookie of the Year voting. Joyner batted .290 with 22 home runs and 100 RBI in his debut season. Many considered Joyner to be the second coming of Don Mattingly *(left)*. In 1986, Mattingly notched a major league and club-high 238 hits. The crackerjack first baseman also spearheaded the majors in doubles (53), total bases (388), and slugging average (.573) that season.

1986

- The Hall of Fame inducts Willie McCovey, Bobby Doerr, and Ernie Lombardi.

- KC's Frank White reclaims status as AL Gold Glove second baseman.

- Angel Bob Boone, at age 38, becomes the oldest to win a Gold Glove when he snags award given to AL catchers.

- Gary Gaetti of Minnesota and Tony Fernandez of Toronto both win their first Gold Gloves—at third base and shortstop, respectively.

- Pittsburgh's Sid Bream sets NL record for first basemen with 166 assists.

- Carlton's ML record skein of 534 consecutive starts without any relief appearances ends on August 5.

- Fernandez sets the ML record for most hits by a shortstop (213).

- Cardinal Willie McGee sets NL record for largest drop in BA by a defending batting champ—97 points.

- Mike Hargrove retires with a .400 career OBP, the first player since 1970 to quit with an OBP that high.

1986

Bo Jackson

Bo Makes His Debut

The Royals were betting that Bo Jackson knew baseball, as they selected the 1985 Heisman Trophy winner in the fourth round of the 1986 free agent draft. Jackson (shown batting for the Memphis Chicks prior to his call-up) played just 53 games in the minors before reporting to the majors. The left fielder ended his 1986 debut with a total of two home runs and nine RBI in 25 games.

Don Sutton

Sutton, 41, Wins 300th

In 1986, at the age of 41, Don Sutton won 15 games. Recording his 300th career triumph on June 18 against the Rangers, the righty became the 19th pitcher to reach the milestone. Sutton made other marks on history that year as well. When he went up against Tom Seaver of the White Sox on June 9, the occasion marked the highest combined victory total—Sutton had 298 triumphs, Seaver had 306—of two opposing hurlers. When he faced Phil Niekro of the Indians on June 28, the event signified the first time two 300-game winners faced off since 1892.

Carter Blasts into Spotlight

After two years of relative anonymity, Joe Carter made his presence known in 1986. That season, he topped the majors with 121 RBI, batted .302, and nailed 29 home runs (including three in one game on August 29). In the succeeding four years, Carter's average fell substantially—yet he still averaged more than 100 RBI per year. A large percentage of his hits were extra-base blows.

Joe Carter

- Gorman Thomas departs from majors with a .225 career BA, lowest ever by an outfielder active ten or more years.

- Cliff Johnson retires with an ML record 20 pinch-hit home runs.

- Greg Gagne of the Twins hits two inside-the-park home runs in a game.

- Pete Incaviglia of Texas fans 185 times to set a new ML rookie record.

- John Cangelosi of the White Sox sets AL rookie record with 50 steals.

- Mitch Williams of the Rangers sets rookie record for pitchers when he appears in 80 games.

- Jim Deshaies of Houston sets ML record by striking out the first eight batters on Sept. 23.

- Don Baylor of Boston sets an AL record when he's hit by 35 pitches.

- Hank Greenberg dies.

- Ted Lyons dies at age 85.

Astros Clinch NL West

Mike Scott & Co. celebrate their berth in the National League Championship Series in 1986. The 6' 2", 210-pound righty hurled a no-hitter against the Giants to snare the league's West Division title for the Astros. Manager Hal Lanier administers the customary dousing of champagne. The mood of the Astros would become somber as they battled the Mets through an extremely tight NLCS before bowing in six games.

Mike Scott, Hal Lanier

Fernando Valenzuela

Fernando Wins 21

Fernando Valenzuela bypassed the 20-game mark for the first time in his career in 1986, as he led the National League in victories with 21. In the All-Star Game, the Dodger lefty pitched three scoreless innings, which included five straight strikeouts. When Tommy Lasorda was asked what Valenzuela signified to him, the Dodger manager replied, "It is good for the Dodgers. It is good for baseball. It is good for Mexico. It is good for our relations with Mexico. And it is very good for Tommy Lasorda."

Rickey Henderson

Rickey Repeats 20/50 Year

In 1986, Rickey Henderson whacked 28 home runs and stole 87 cushions (tops in the American League) to post his second consecutive 20/50 season. Style Dog led the loop with 130 runs scored, collected 74 RBI, and made his sixth All-Star squad in eight seasons. The greatest leadoff hitter in the history of the sport, Henderson holds the all-time record for home runs leading off a game (36).

1986

- Red Ruffing dies.
- On June 28, Indian Phil Niekro faces the Angels' Sutton in the first duel between 300-game winners since 1892.
- On Feb. 28, 11 players are fined and/or suspended for varying lengths of time for cocaine involvement.

- Orioles set ML record when they hit only 13 triples.
- Tim Raines leads NL in batting (.334) and OBP (.415).
- Philly's Von Hayes tops NL in doubles (46) and runs produced (186), and ties Tony Gwynn for NL lead in runs (107).

- Gwynn tops NL in hits (211) and is a strong third in BA (.329).
- New York's Keith Hernandez leads NL in walks (94).
- The Reds' Eric Davis is second in NL with 80 steals and sets ML record for most steals by a player who hits 30 or more home runs.

Mets Go All the Way

The New York Mets (shown prior to World Series action at Fenway Park) were unstoppable in 1986, finishing a whopping 21$^1/_2$ games ahead of the runner-up Phillies. When it came to postseason play, however, the team met up with some stiff competition. The Mets battled the Astros for six games before reigning victorious in the League Championship Series, and the fall classic ran the entire seven games before the Mets could triumph over the Red Sox.

New York Mets Dugout

Keith Hernandez

Hernandez: .310, 83 RBI

The Mets relied heavily on Keith Hernandez in 1986, as he propelled them to the National League pennant by batting .310 with 13 home runs and 83 RBI. His defense was nearly flawless, as the first baseman led the loop in fielding percentage with a .996 average. Hernandez leads all first basemen in lifetime assists (1,662).

Jose Canseco

Canseco Is AL ROTY

Oakland slugger Jose Canseco captured the title of American League Rookie of the Year in 1986 when, despite setting a club season record for strikeouts (175), he smacked 33 home runs while driving in 117 runs. Canseco represented a new breed of ballplayer—a muscleman with speed to match.

- Rickey Henderson leads majors with 130 runs.
- Cleveland's Joe Carter paces ML in RBI (121) and runs produced (200).
- Mike Scott leads ML in innings (275) and Ks (306), and ties teammate Bob Knepper for most shutouts in NL (five).

- Detroit's Jack Morris leads ML with six shutouts, is second in AL in wins with 21.
- Blyleven leads AL in innings pitched (272).
- Cleveland's Tom Candiotti tops AL in CGs (17).

- The Mets win 108 games, leading NL in runs scored (783) and fewest runs allowed (578).
- Mets lead NL in batting (.263) and ERA (3.11).
- Cleveland leads AL in runs (831), but again has poor pitching (4.57 ERA).

TWINS SPARKLE IN HOMER-HAPPY SEASON

Record-breaking performances by novices and veterans alike were the name of the game in 1987. Mark McGwire, Oakland's imposing first baseman, set a rookie record with 49 homers. Yankee first sacker Don Mattingly set one mark and tied another, smacking a single-season record six grandslams and homering in eight consecutive games. And Cincinnati superstar Eric Davis tied a major-league record with three grandslams in May.

Mike Schmidt, the 37-year-old third baseman for the Phillies, notched his 500th career home run. Angel Bob Boone, age 39, caught his major league-record 1,919th game. Darrell Evans of the Tigers became the first 40-year-old to tally 30 homers in a season (he had 34 dingers). Cleveland's Phil Niekro cranked up his 48-year-old knuckleball to combine with brother Joe for 530 career wins, a sibling record.

Nolan Ryan, the 40-year-old Houston pitching phenom, fanned 200 batters for a record 11th year. (Although Ryan topped the National League in strikeouts with 270 and ERA at 2.76, the hard-luck Texan finished with just an 8-16 record.) Andre Dawson, the NL's Most Valuable Player with a .287 average and 137 RBI, belted 49 homers for the Cubs, tying for first in the majors and for 18th place on the all-time single-season list.

St. Louis won 95 games, three better than the Mets, to snare the National League East. Oft-injured Jack Clark nailed 35 home runs with 106 RBI. Rabbit Vince Coleman (.289) swiped a league-best 109 bases, the first major leaguer to record 100 steals in three consecutive seasons. "Wizard of Oz" Ozzie Smith had his finest season at the plate, hitting .303 with 75 RBI. At the other end of the scale, Chicago came in last despite Rick Sutcliffe's league-leading 18 wins.

The Giants heated up after the Fourth of July to finish 6 games ahead of Eric Davis (.293 average, 37 homers, 100 RBI, 50 stolen bases) and the Cincinnati Reds in the NL West. Will "The Thrill" Clark, San Fran's 23-year-old first baseman, hit .308 with 35 homers and 91 RBI. The Padres, who finished dead last in the West, had a bright spot in Tony Gwynn and his major league-leading .370 average.

In the AL East, George Bell almost single-handedly carried the Blue Jays to first place. Although the hard-hitting outfielder seized the MVP Award by blasting .308

with 47 homers and a circuit-topping 134 RBI, Toronto faded. Detroit won the division by a pair of games. Shortstop Alan Trammell finished third in batting with a .343 average, 28 home runs, and 105 RBI. Juan Nieves of third-place Milwaukee had the season's only no-hitter, winning 7-0 over Baltimore on April 15.

Baseball's biggest surprise, however, was the AL West champion Twins. Nearly unbeatable at home, they won just nine road contests after the All-Star Game to finish with 85 victories. Kirby Puckett, the short and stocky outfielder, posted a .332 average, 28 homers, and 99 RBI while southpaw Frank Viola anchored the staff with a 17-10 season.

Minnesota's Tom Brunansky mauled the Tigers in the American League Championship Series, hitting two homers and four doubles and walking four times in the four-games-to-one romp. In the NLCS, St. Louis lost the slugging Clark to injury but managed to hang on in seven games.

The World Series spoke volumes for home cooking. In the deafening Metrodome, Minnesota routed the Cards to take a lead of two games to none; at Busch Stadium, St. Louis swept three. Back home, the Twins feasted on John Tudor in game six, winning 11-5. Viola started game seven and Jeff Reardon finished it, giving Minnesota the franchise's first World Series triumph since the Washington Senators won in 1924.

1987

- Twins win in AL with .525 win pct., lowest ever by AL winner.
- Cards cop their third flag in 1980s.
- In NLCS, Cards beat SF in seven games, shutting out the Giants in games six and seven.
- SF's Jeff Leonard hits .417 and ties LCS record with four homers.

- In ALCS, Twins beat Detroit in five games.
- Twins win first World Series since move to Minnesota in seven games, as both clubs are unable to win on the road.
- Frank Viola is Series MVP with two wins for Twins.

- Tigers win AL East on last day of season after Jays begin final week with seemingly insurmountable lead.
- Andre Dawson of Cubs named NL MVP.
- George Bell of Toronto is AL MVP.
- Roger Clemens repeats as AL Cy Young winner.

Posting his highest winning percentage (.630) thus far in his career, Frank Viola drove the Twins to their World Championship title over the Cardinals in 1987. The southpaw crafted a 17-10 record with a 2.89 ERA during the regular season. After winning game four of the ALCS, Sweet Music went 2-1 in that year's World Series to take MVP honors.

- Steve Bedrosian wins Cy Young in NL, as he saves an ML-leading 40 games.

- Mark McGwire of A's is AL ROTY, as he hits rookie record 49 homers.

- Padre Benito Santiago is NL ROTY after setting new frosh record by hitting safely in 34 straight games.

- Tony Gwynn takes NL bat crown with .370 BA, highest in NL since 1948.

- Wade Boggs wins fourth AL bat crown in 1980s (.363).

- Cardinal Vince Coleman steals 100 or more bases for ML record third straight season.

- Brewer Paul Molitor hits in 39 consecutive games, most in AL since Joe DiMaggio's 56 in 1941.

- Arbiter Thomas Roberts rules owners guilty of collusion after they fail to sign free agents.

- NL wins All-Star Game 2-0 in Oakland in 13 innings.

Andre Dawson

Dawson: 49 HRs, 137 RBI

In 1987, Wrigley Field fans thrilled to the exploits of newly signed free agent Andre Dawson. Dawson, who had requested in spring training that Cub general manager Dallas Green fill in the numbers on a blank contract, hit .287 with circuit-topping totals in home runs (49) and RBI (137). His performance earned him the distinction of being the first player on a last-place team to be voted National League MVP. His salary for the season was $500,000.

George Bell

Bell Pulls Out the Stops

George Bell had a banner year in 1987. Not only was he named American League MVP, he was also christened *Sporting News* Player of the Year. Despite playing for a ballclub which let a pennant slip away in the dying days of the season, the slugging left fielder was recognized for nailing 47 four-baggers, driving in a circuit-topping 134 runs, and batting .308.

McGwire Is AL ROTY

Oakland welcomed the second half of the "Bash Brothers" to the lineup in 1987 in the person of Mark McGwire. Teamed with Jose Canseco to form one of the most potent one-two power combinations in history, the first baseman set a major league rookie record with 49 dingers (besting the old record by 11). Batting .289 and driving in 118 runs in his debut season, McGwire was named American League Rookie of the Year.

Mark McGwire

1987

- Don Mattingly hits six grandslams in season, and also hits at least one homer in eight consecutive games.

- Juan Nieves of Milwaukee no-hits Baltimore on April 15—first no-hitter by Brewers pitcher.

- Brewers tie ML record by opening the season with 13 consecutive wins.

- Angel Bob Boone sets new career record for catchers when he catches in his 1,919th game.

- Milwaukee's Rob Deer sets AL record when he fans 187 times.

- Reggie Jackson retires with ML career record 2,597 Ks.

- Detroit's Darrell Evans sets ML record for players over 40 years old by hitting 34 homers.

- Evans sets AL record for players over age 40 with 99 RBI.

- Cal Ripken Sr. of Orioles is first man to manage two sons in ML—Cal Jr. and Billy.

Ripken Clan Fuels Orioles

The Ripken family loomed large in Baltimore in 1987, as father Cal *(center)* managed the team and sons Billy *(left)* and Cal Jr. started at second base and shortstop, respectively. Ripken the skipper got off course, as the talent-poor Orioles finished in last place in '87 with a 67-95 record. Cal Jr. socked 27 home runs and tallied 98 RBI that season, started his fourth straight All-Star Game, and was forced by ownership to end his consecutive-innings-played streak on September 14. Cal's double-play partner, Billy, gave an especially surprising performance that season, batting .308 after being called up in July.

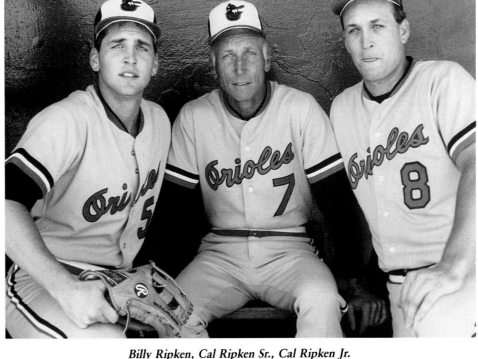

Billy Ripken, Cal Ripken Sr., Cal Ripken Jr.

Molitor Hits a Streak

Despite missing 44 games due to injuries in the first half of the 1987 season, Paul Molitor made headlines that year as he hit in 39 straight games, the seventh-longest hitting streak in history. The third baseman also managed to spearhead the American League in runs scored (114) and doubles (41) while batting a career-high .353 (second in the circuit). Had he played the full season, he may have scored 150 runs.

Paul Molitor

Parrish Joins the Phillies

Signing as a free agent with Philadelphia in 1987, Lance Parrish batted .245 with 17 home runs and 67 RBI that season. The onetime bodyguard to singer Tina Turner had enjoyed better days in the American League. A six-time All-Star, the catcher hit .286 with 24 home runs and 82 RBI in 1980; in 1982, his 32 homers shattered the AL record set by Yogi Berra for home runs by a catcher.

Lance Parrish

- Ripken sons are the first brothers to form a regular keystone combo in ML.

- Cal Ripken's record skein of the most consecutive innings played (8,243) comes to an end.

- Attendance tops 52 million, as the Dodgers, Cards, and Mets each draw more than three million.

- A record 4,458 homers and 19,883 runs are produced in ML during the regular season.

- Every team in the AL hits more than 160 homers.

- The Yankees' payroll tops $18.5 million.

- Four teams in AL East win more games than AL West champ Twins.

- The Hall of Fame inducts Billy Williams, Catfish Hunter, and Ray Dandridge.

- KC rookie Kevin Seitzer hits .323 and ties for AL lead in hits with 207.

Steve Bedrosian

Boggs Wins AL Bat Title

In 1987, Wade Boggs (being·greeted by teammate and designated hitter Jim Rice) led the American League in batting for the third year in a row, posting a .363 average combined with an even 200 hits. A good contact hitter, he batted .390 when he was 0-2 in the count. After six years in the majors, the third baseman had achieved a lifetime batting average of .354. That season, Boggs also socked 24 home runs (three times his previous year's total), tallied a .588 slugging average (third in the loop), and posted a circuit-high on-base percentage (.467).

Wade Boggs

Bedrosian Snares Award

Steve Bedrosian enjoyed a spectacular season in 1987, winning both the Fireman of the Year and the National League Cy Young Awards. The Philadelphia righty reliever wrapped up a year in which he appeared in 65 contests, collected 40 saves, five wins (against only three losses), and a 2.83 ERA.

1987

- NL outfielders Eric Davis, Dawson, and Gwynn, all offensive superstars, also win Gold Gloves in 1987.

- In 154 innings, Cleveland's Ken Schrom has a 6.49 ERA, the worst in the majors in the past 50 years.

- Tim Raines leads majors with 123 runs.

- Gene Mauch parts with the Angels, leaving with the record for the most years as a manager without winning a pennant (26).

- Detroit's Alan Trammell and Lou Whitaker become first keystone combo in ML history to play on the same team as regulars for ten seasons.

- LaMarr Hoyt, the AL Cy Young winner in 1983, is suspended for a full season after three separate drug infractions.

- On August 3, catcher Geno Petralli of Texas sets AL record by committing six passed balls, as he can't handle Charlie Hough's knuckler.

Roger Clemens

Davis: 37 HRs, 100 RBI

Eric Davis joined the list of outfielders inviting comparison to the great Willie Mays as he enjoyed a spectacular season in 1987. Getting off to an early start, he clubbed three home runs in a game played on May 3, 1987. Finishing the season with a .293 average, he totaled 37 home runs, 100 RBI, and 50 stolen bases. He won both his first All-Star selection and Gold Glove Award that year.

Eric Davis

Clemens Wins AL Cy Young

Although his Red Sox made an early departure from the American League pennant race in 1987, Roger Clemens continued to dazzle. Reigning victorious in 20 games (tied for first in the league), he led the loop in winning percentage (.690), complete games (18), and shutouts (seven) that season. His final victory that year was gained on the last afternoon of the season, as the righty pitched a masterful two-hitter against the Brewers at Fenway Park. The Rocket's performance earned him his second consecutive Cy Young Award that season—only the fourth pitcher ever to do so.

Boone Catches a Record

Bob Boone made his mark in 1987 by shattering a major league record for games caught with his 1,919th game; by season's end, his total stood at 1,935. At age 39, he caught 128 games, batted .242, and won his fifth Gold Glove Award that year.

Bob Boone

- On April 9, Phil Niekro and Steve Carlton pitch for Indians—first time since 1891 two 300-game winners have appeared in a game for the same team.

- The Salt Lake Trappers of the Pioneer League break the OB record by winning 29 consecutive games.

- ChiSox send Floyd Bannister and Dave Cochrane to KC for four minor leaguers.

- Phils trade Glenn Wilson and two other players to Seattle for Phil Bradley and a minor leaguer.

- Detroit trades John Smoltz to Atlanta for Doyle Alexander.

- Pittsburgh deals Rick Reuschel to the Giants for Jeff Robinson and Scott Medvin.

- Royals manager Dick Howser dies of a brain tumor.

- Dodgers coach Don McMahon dies of a heart attack after pitching batting practice.

Twins Trump the Cards

Among the sluggers the Cardinal pitching staff had to face in the 1987 World Series were *(left to right)* Twins Tom Brunansky, Kirby Puckett, and Kent Hrbek. Puckett, who finished the regular season batting .332, had the best Series average of the trio, turning in a .357 mark. Brunansky scored five runs and Hrbek tallied one home run and six RBI in the fall classic. The Twins outdid the Cards in runs scored (Minnesota collected 38, St. Louis had 26), and home runs (seven to two).

Tom Brunansky, Kirby Puckett, Kent Hrbek

Trammell: 28 HRs, 105 RBI

For the second time in his career, Alan Trammell put together an MVP season only to be denied the honor. Racking up 109 runs scored and 205 hits, the shortstop led the Tigers to a dramatic final-game clinching of the American League East Division in '87. Enjoying his best season to date and batting cleanup for the first time in his career, he hit .343 (third in the loop) with 28 home runs and 105 RBI. Trammell finished a close second to George Bell in the MVP vote.

Tony Gwynn

Gwynn Racks Up .370 BA

Tony Gwynn donned his second National League batting crown in 1987, as he hit .370 with a loop-high 218 hits. The outfielder's average was the best mark in the senior circuit since Stan Musial batted .376 in 1948. With his average placing 32 points higher than that of the runner-up, he became the 15th player in the history of the major leagues to win the batting title by a 30-point margin. He also placed second with 13 triples, a .450 on-base percentage, and 56 stolen bases. At the end of the '87 season, Gwynn led the Padres in career batting average (.335).

Alan Trammell

1987

- Travis Jackson dies at age 83.

- Dodgers executive Al Campanis is fired after saying that blacks don't have the necessary skills to perform in baseball management positions.

- Orioles pitchers surrender an ML record 226 home runs.

- In a game vs. Baltimore, Toronto hits an ML record ten homers.

- Nelson Doubleday Jr. and his partners buy Mets for $100 million dollars.

- Nolan Ryan tops NL with 2.76 ERA and 270 Ks but has only an 8-16 record.

- Oakland's Dave Stewart and Clemens tie for AL lead in wins with 20.

- Clemens tops ML in win pct. (.690), shutouts (seven), and CGs (18).

- Hough leads ML in innings with 285.

- Mark Langston wins third AL K crown in four years (262).

Kirby Puckett

Hrbek: 34 HRs, 90 RBI

Kent Hrbek

Kent Hrbek enjoyed a solid season while helping the Twins to the World Championship in 1987. He batted .285 with 34 home runs and 90 RBI for the season. In postseason play, he made the last putouts in the game that clinched the American League West Division, in the decisive game five of the League Championship Series, and in game seven of the fall classic. The burly first sacker also whacked a grandslam in game six of the Series (No. 14 in the history of the tournament). As a kid, he lived so close to Minnesota's Metropolitan Stadium (the ballpark of the Twins) that he could see the stadium lights from his bedroom. Some 20 years later, in the Metrodome (the team's new digs), he was pulling in more than $1.5 million as the first baseman for the Twins.

Puckett: .332 BA, 99 RBI

Kirby Puckett was the inspirational leader for the Twins during their Cinderella season of 1987. The diminutive center fielder led the American League that year with 207 hits while batting .332 with 28 home runs and 99 RBI. His outstanding fielding made him a fixture of season highlight films and earned him his second Gold Glove. In a poll of major leaguers, Puckett ranked as one of the top three players his peers would pay to see play.

Mark, Wally: AL's Best

The American League West Division had two of the best young players in baseball in Mark McGwire of Oakland *(foreground)* and Wally Joyner of the Angels. Between them, the two whacked 83 home runs and drove in 235 runs for the '87 season. McGwire hit three home runs against the Indians on June 27 and another two dingers on the 28th, matching the major league record for home runs in consecutive games. Joyner, the MVP for the Angels, established a club record for home runs by a first baseman with 34. He also became the ninth player to post consecutive 100-plus RBI seasons in his debut and sophomore years.

Wally Joyner, Mark McGwire

- Toronto's Tom Henke leads AL in saves with 34.

- Chicago's Rick Sutcliffe paces NL in wins with just 18.

- Reuschel ties with Fernando Valenzuela for most CGs in NL with 12—a new loop low for a leader.

- Three Dodgers pitchers—Orel Hershiser, Bob Welch, and Valenzuela—rank one-two-three in innings, Hershiser leading at 265.

- Dawson paces NL in RBI (137), total bases (353), and homers (49).

- Bell paces AL in RBI (134) and ML in total bases (369).

- McGwire is first rookie since Al Rosen to top AL in homers; he also paces ML in SA (.618).

- Jack Clark of the Cards tops NL in SA (.597), OBP (.461), and walks (136).

- Montreal's Tim Wallach leads majors with 42 doubles.

Off the field, he was Dodger righthander Orel Hershiser. Once he took the mound, he was "Bulldog," leading the National League in shutouts in 1984 (with four), in winning percentage in '85 (.864 for a 19-3 record), and in innings pitched in '87 (265) and '88 (267).

Hershiser's most remarkable feat, however, was "The Streak." At the end of August, the Los Angeles stopper became virtually unhittable, pitching 59 scoreless innings to beat Don Drysdale's record of 58 set in 1968. To no one's surprise, Hershiser was named the winner of the Cy Young Award, racking up a 23-8 season, a 2.26 ERA, 15 complete games, and eight shutouts.

It was a surprise, though, that Los Angeles won the West, 7 games ahead of the talented Reds. Although Cincinnati was good—Danny Jackson led the league with 23 wins, Tom Browning had a perfect game against Los Angeles on September 16, and the team racked up a division-topping 122 home runs—they weren't good enough. Dodger manager Tommy Lasorda coaxed clutch performances from slugger Mike Marshall (20 home runs and 82 RBI), Steve Sax (.277 average with 42 stolen bases), and ex-Tiger Kirk Gibson, the toughest Dodger of them all. A wide receiver in college at Michigan State, Gibson was named the National League's Most Valuable Player—only the third player to

Orel Posts 67 O's In A Row; LA Ousts A's

win the award who didn't bat .300 (he averaged .290), hit 30 home runs (he belted 25), or drive in 100 runs (he totaled 76).

New York right fielder Darryl Strawberry, many opined, was more deserving of the title. The Straw Man led the league with 39 home runs and had 101 RBI, as New York won 100 ball games, 15 better than the second-place Pirates. The quietest left fielder in baseball, Kevin McReynolds let his bat do the talking, hitting .288 with 27 round-trippers and 99 RBI. Minor league sensation Gregg Jefferies joined the club in September to hit a sizzling .321.

The man in the American League that everyone was talking about was circuit MVP Jose Canseco, the first man in baseball history to hit 40 homers and steal 40 bases in a single season. Leading Oakland to its first pennant since 1974, the 6'3", 220-pound slugger terrorized the opposition with his major league-best 42 tape-measure home runs and 124 RBI and his .307 batting average.

In the American League East, Boston was going nowhere fast

until long-standing coach Joe Morgan replaced John McNamara in the middle of July. The Red Sox won 19 of their first 20 contests under Morgan, finishing just 1 game ahead of Sparky Anderson's Tigers. Wade Boggs ignored his off-the-field exploits (a $6 million palimony suit) to lead the league in hitting—with a .366 average—for the fourth consecutive season, topping the majors in three of those years. And a 24-year-old outfielder named Mike Greenwell hit like a young Ted Williams, racking up a .325 average, 22 home runs, and 119 RBI.

The NLCS was a hard-fought battle. The Dodgers and the Mets alternated victories for the first six contests, with Los Angeles clinching the title in a seventh-game shutout courtesy of Hershiser. The A's swept the Red Sox in the ALCS. Canseco homered in the first, second, and fourth matches and had four RBI.

The World Series matched the surprising Dodgers against the mighty A's. Game one had one of the most improbable at-bats in Series history: Trailing 4-3 with one on and two out in the bottom of the ninth, an injured Gibson limped to the plate as a pinch hitter. Gibson nailed a two-run homer over the right-field fence to give Los Angeles a 5-4 win.

The rest of the race belonged to Hershiser, the Series MVP. The Bulldog won games two and five as Los Angeles stunned Oakland four games to one.

1988

- Dodgers win their first NL flag since 1981.

- A's cruise to easy AL flag.

- In NLCS, LA wins in seven games over Mets, who had won the NL East by 15 games.

- A's bury Boston in four games in ALCS.

- Enormous underdogs, the Dodgers win World Series in five games.

- Orel Hershiser wins two CGs in Series and bats a perfect 1.000 (3-for-3).

- Hobbled Dodger Kirk Gibson wins game one with a pinch-hit homer in the bottom of the ninth.

- Mickey Hatcher, a sub for the injured Gibson, leads all World Series players with .368 BA and five RBI.

- Minnesota's Frank Viola wins AL Cy Young.

- Hershiser wins NL Cy Young.

- Gibson named NL MVP.

Orel Hershiser continued his 1988 regular season heroics—23 wins, eight shutouts, 2.26 ERA—into the World Series that fall, as the righty triumphed in a pair of games and tallied a 1.00 ERA in the five-game affair. The Bulldog (shown here in action from the World Series) batted 1.000 (3-for-3) in the fall classic. In the National League Championship Series against the Mets, he sported a 1.09 ERA, set a tournament record for innings pitched ($24^2/3$), and won the game that clinched the pennant.

- Jose Canseco named AL MVP, as he becomes the first to steal 40 bases and hit 40 homers in same season.

- Walt Weiss is third consecutive Oakland A's player to win AL ROTY.

- First night game at Wrigley Field is played on August 6, Mets vs. Cubs.

- Hershiser sets new ML record with 59 consecutive scoreless innings pitched.

- Billy Martin is fired as Yankee manager a record fifth time.

- Twins are first AL team to draw three million in attendance in a season.

- Orioles open season by losing 21 consecutive games to set ML record.

- Padre Tony Gwynn leads NL with .313 BA, lowest in history by NL leader.

- Met Kevin McReynolds sets ML record when he's a perfect 21-for-21 in steal attempts.

Rick Reuschel

Big Mac Has a Whopper of a Year

Kevin McReynolds enjoyed an outstanding season in 1988, as he hit .288 with 27 home runs and 99 RBI. The Mets left fielder set a major league season record for most stolen bases without being caught (21). In that year's National League Championship Series, Big Mac tied the tournament record for most hits in a game (four).

Kevin McReynolds

Reuschel Wins 19

Rick Reuschel received a new lease on his career with the Giants, as he won 19 games in 1988, his first full season with the ballclub. The righty tied for the lead in the National League in both starts (36) and sacrifice hits (19). Big Daddy finished the season with the most career victories (194) among active senior circuit pitchers.

Viola Wins AL Cy Young

Frank Viola won the American League Cy Young Award in 1988 as he compiled a 24-7 record with a 2.64 ERA. The New York native also won the All-Star Game by pitching two scoreless innings. Viola helped the Twins to a 91-71 record that season.

Frank Viola

1988

- Don Mattingly awarded record $1.975 million salary in arbitration.

- AL wins All-Star Game 2-1 in Cincinnati.

- Don Baylor retires after breaking Ron Hunt's modern career record for being hit the most times by pitches.

- Toronto's George Bell is first player in ML history to hit three home runs on Opening Day.

- Tom Browning of Cincinnati hurls a perfect game vs. LA on Sept. 16.

- Toronto's Dave Stieb is denied a no-hitter in two consecutive games by a two-out base hit in the ninth.

- David Cone has a 20-3 record for Mets and tops NL with .870 win pct.

- Only 3,180 homers hit in ML—1,278 fewer than in 1987.

- Darryl Strawberry tops NL with 39 homers and .545 SA.

- Canseco tops majors with 42 homers, 124 RBI, and .569 SA.

Howell Sacked in NLCS

National League President A. Bartlett Giamatti *(right)* inspects the glove of Jay Howell after it was discovered that the Dodger reliever had used pine tar while pitching the eighth inning of game three of the 1988 League Championship Series. Giamatti, after much reflection, decided to suspend Howell for three games. An appeal cut the suspension to two games. Howell didn't resurface until the ninth inning of game three of the World Series. The A's won the contest 2-1.

A. Bartlett Giamatti

Mike Greenwell

Greenwell: 22 HRs, 119 RBI

In his first full season with the Red Sox, Mike Greenwell proved that he was worthy to succeed the great Jim Rice as guardian of The Green Monster. The left fielder batted .325 with 22 home runs and 119 RBI with just 38 strikeouts in 1988. Like Rice, the young slugger was a sometimes brutal fielder who was foiled time and again by the tricky bounces that balls took off the left-field wall in Fenway Park, located 310 feet from home plate.

Kirk Gibson

Gibby Bags NL MVP

The Dodgers snared a pennant in 1988 when they secured the services of Kirk Gibson. The free agent enjoyed a career season, winning the National League MVP Award with a .290 batting average, 25 home runs, and 76 RBI. He then went on to rack up a pair of home runs and six RBI in the League Championship Series. One of his home runs, a 12th-inning dinger, won game four; the other, a three-run round-tripper, won game five.

- Expo Andres Galarraga tops NL in hits (184), doubles (42), and total bases (329).

- Wade Boggs tops AL with .480 OBP, highest in majors since Mickey Mantle's .488 in 1962.

- Boggs leads ML in batting (.366), doubles (45), walks (125), and runs (128).

- Minnesota's Kirby Puckett tops ML in hits (234), runs produced (206), and total bases (358), and has .356 BA.

- Viola leads ML with 24 wins and AL with .774 win pct.

- Every team in NL scores fewer runs in 1988 than in 1987; eight of the 12 teams score more than 100 runs less.

- Cubs have now gone 43 years without a pennant to break old ML record of 42 years held by St. Louis Browns.

- Bob Boone and Carlton Fisk are first ML catchers to still play regularly behind the plate at the age of 40.

- The Hall of Fame inducts Willie Stargell.

Jose Canseco, Mark McGwire, Walt Weiss

Trio Takes A's to Flag

The brash, cocky A's won their first of many American League pennants in 1988 with a nucleus of young stars led by *(left to right)* Jose Canseco, Mark McGwire, and Walt Weiss. They formed a trio of successive American League Rookies of the Year. In '88, Canseco topped the circuit in home runs (42), RBI (124), and slugging average (.569). McGwire gave a solid performance, clubbing 32 four-baggers and driving in 99 runs. Weiss had an encouraging first full year with the A's, hitting .250. All three bombed in the '88 World Series, however. Canseco hit .053, McGwire batted .059, and Weiss hit .063.

Wrigley Field Brings an End to an Era

In 1988, Chicago's Wrigley Field became the last major league ballpark to install lights. Although the issue met with opposition from nostalgic fans as well as residents, Wrigley executives nevertheless forged ahead with the plan. According to the agreement, the Cubs are limited to a maximum of 18 night games a season until the year 2002.

Wrigley Field

1988

- White Sox Jerry Reuss becomes the second pitcher in ML history to win 200 career games without ever having a 20-win season.

- Baltimore's .335 win pct. is franchise's worst since 1939, as the Birds finish last in AL for first time since the move to Baltimore.

- Carl Hubbell dies.

- Harvey Kuenn dies.

- Edd Roush, the last surviving participant of the 1919 World Series, dies at age 94.

- Braves finish last in NL with .338 win pct., the franchise's worst since 1935.

- Minnesota trades Tom Brunansky to the Cards for Tommy Herr.

- The Royals trade Danny Jackson and Argenis Salazar to the Reds for Kurt Stillwell and Ted Power.

- Baseball films *Bull Durham* and *Eight Men Out* are released.

Tony Gwynn

Gwynn Takes NL Bat Title

Despite the fact his batting average dropped a colossal 57 points from the previous season, Tony Gwynn still led the National League in batting in 1988 with a .313 average. Like Wade Boggs, his American League counterpart, the outfielder sacrificed much of his power for average; in 1988, Gwynn hit seven home runs and drove in 70 runs.

Don Mattingly, Darryl Strawberry

Orel Hershiser

Don, Darryl Star in NY

Don Mattingly *(left)* and Darryl Strawberry were the virtuosos of New York in the late 1980s. In 1988, Mattingly batted .311 with 18 home runs and 88 RBI for the Yankees, and Strawberry hit an NL-leading 39 homers with 101 RBI. Despite the pressure on both franchises for a Subway Series, the only time the two stars and their teams would meet that year was in the annual Mayor's Trophy charity game.

Hershiser Is Unhittable

No hurler ever finished a season the way Orel Hershiser wrapped up 1988. First, he pitched five straight shutouts. Then the righty broke Don Drysdale's consecutive-scoreless-innings streak (58 frames) of 1968 with a ten-inning scoreless no-decision against the Padres in his last start of the season. Finally, he stretched his 59-inning streak to 67 in the National League Championship Series against the Mets. Finishing the season with a 23-8 record and a 2.26 ERA, Hershiser received the league's Cy Young Award.

- Doug Jones sets a new Cleveland record when he posts 37 saves.

- Jones sets an ML record when he registers saves in 15 consecutive relief appearances.

- Toronto's Fred McGriff is runner-up in AL in homers (34) and also has second-highest SA in majors (.552).

- Galarraga tops NL with just 184 hits, fewest ever by NL leader on a 162-game schedule.

- Andy Van Slyke of Pittsburgh tops majors in triples (15) and is second in NL in runs produced (176).

- Cincinnati's Kal Daniels has the only .400 OBP in NL—.400 on the nose.

- SF's Will Clark leads NL in RBI (109), runs produced (182), and walks (100).

- Robin Yount, Willie Wilson, and Seattle's Harold Reynolds tie for AL lead in triples with 11.

- Rickey Henderson returns to top of AL in steals with 93.

American League Championship Series

A's Sweep the BoSox

Dave Stewart of the A's strikes out Wade Boggs of the Red Sox with the bases loaded in the second inning of the opening game of the 1988 American League Championship Series. The Red Sox lost the game 2-1, then the Series in four straight games. Over the course of the sweep, Stewart recorded one win, a 1.35 ERA, and 11 strikeouts in 13 1/3 innings; Boggs tallied a .385 average with three RBI.

Dennis Eckersley

Eckersley Saves ALCS

Oakland's Dennis Eckersley saved all four games of the 1988 American League Championship Series against the Red Sox. Coming off a banner year in '88, the righty spearheaded the circuit with a phenomenal 45 saves—just one short of the major league record—and averaged 8.6 Ks a game. Wild in his early years, Eckersley walked just 11 men in 76 innings during the season.

1988

- Vince Coleman once again leads NL in steals but with only 81, his lowest total to this juncture.

- Brett Butler of the Giants leads NL in runs with 109.

- Hershiser and the Reds' Jackson tie for NL lead with 23 wins and 15 CGs.

- Hershiser tops NL in innings with just 267 and also in shutouts with eight.

- Joe Magrane of the Cards has best ERA in ML (2.18).

- Allan Anderson of the Twins leads AL in ERA at 2.45—one point better than Teddy Higuera of Milwaukee.

- Dave Stewart wins 21 games for the A's and leads ML in innings with 276.

- Roger Clemens tops majors in strikeouts (291) and ties Stewart for AL lead in CGs (14).

- Cincinnati's John Franco heads NL with 39 saves.

Kirk Gibson

Reardon Saves 42

Jeff "The Terminator" Reardon saved a career-high 42 games in 1988 (second in the American League). The fireballing righty was the lone reliever to rack up at least 20 saves each season from 1982 through 1988. With a total of 287 saves after 1990, Reardon ranks among the game's all-time leaders in saves.

Jeff Reardon

Dawson: 24 HRs, 79 RBI

Despite a sharp drop-off from his career-year stats in 1987, Andre Dawson enjoyed a solid season in 1988, capturing a Gold Glove Award for outfielding while batting .303 with 24 home runs and 79 RBI. The former Expo was easily the best free agent signing in Cub history.

Andre Dawson

Gibson Wins Game One

A 1990 poll of sportscasters named Kirk Gibson's home run that clinched game one of the 1988 World Series as one of the most dramatic moments in the history of the sport. The injured outfielder could only hobble around the bases after whacking a 3-2 pitch from A's reliever Dennis Eckersley to bag a 5-4 Dodger victory. In his only Series at-bat, he fouled off four pitches before nailing the clincher. It was the perfect finale to Gibson's '88 year (.290 average, 25 round-trippers, and 76 RBI).

- Veteran Dennis Eckersley of the A's blossoms into a relief ace, leading the majors with 45 saves.

- Mark Gubicza wins 20 for the Royals, is second in AL in innings (270) and fourth in ERA (2.70).

- Nolan Ryan again tops NL in Ks (228).

- Cubs lead NL in hitting at just .261.

- The NL hits a composite .248, falling below .250 for first time since 1972.

- Boston avoids the cellar for an AL record 57th straight year—unfortunately, the Sox haven't won a World Series in 70 years.

- Fifth-place Yankees finish only 3½ back of AL East winner Boston, as all but Cleveland and Baltimore stay in race till the final few days.

- The shift in power has switched from the AL East to the AL West; Oakland (104) and Minnesota (91) are the only 90-game winners in the league.

WORLD SERIES SHAKEN BY TRAGIC QUAKE

At 5:04 p.m. on October 17 in San Francisco's Candlestick Park—just a half-hour before game three of the 1989 World Series—fans and players felt a strange vibration. For a few seconds, they didn't know what to make of the tremors, but then they realized the scary reality: Earthquake.

When the quake had ended, Candlestick Park was still intact—there were even plans to go ahead and start the game on time. That was, of course, before the billions of dollars of damage began to unfold. The earthquake measured 7.1 on the Richter Scale, the largest in San Francisco since the 8.3 monster of 1906.

As the city's disaster took its toll, commissioner Fay Vincent postponed game three indefinitely, putting the contest into perspective by calling the World Series "our modest little sporting event."

The Bay Area earthquake was the biggest tragedy in a year filled with dark moments. In August, after months of investigation, Reds manager Pete Rose was banned from baseball for life for allegedly betting on his own team. Commissioner Bart Giamatti, perhaps stressed from the Rose ordeal, died of a heart attack September 1. Baseball stars Wade Boggs and Steve Garvey made scandalous headlines when they were sued by women with whom they had affairs. And in December, Billy Martin was killed in a truck crash.

All the turmoil overshadowed some impressive on-field performances, especially by the game's relief pitchers. Virtually every team had a standout closer, and baseball's relievers totaled an unprecedented 1,079 saves. Among the stellar stoppers were San Diego's Mark Davis (44 saves, 1.85 ERA), Texas' Jeff Russell (38 saves, 1.98 ERA), and Oakland's Dennis Eckersley (33 saves, 1.56 ERA). Davis won the NL's Cy Young Award, while Kansas City starter Bret Saberhagen (23-6, 2.13 ERA) took the AL crown.

In a pitcher's year, San Francisco's Kevin Mitchell posted giant numbers (47 homers, 125 RBI). Mitchell was named NL MVP, while Milwaukee's Robin Yount (.318, 21 homers, 103 RBI) won his second AL MVP prize.

The young Baltimore Orioles were the darling team of 1989. After losing 107 games in '88, the "Baby Birds" hung in the 1989 pennant race until the final weekend, before bowing to Toronto.

The playoffs, though, were dominated by just two men: San Francisco's Will Clark and Oakland's Rickey Henderson. Against Chicago in the NLCS, the sweet-swinging Clark set NL playoff records for batting average (.650), hits (13), extra-base hits (six), total bases (24), and slugging (1.200). Clark cracked a grandslam in game one, and won game five with a two-run, eighth-inning single.

Despite Clark's virtuosity, however, perhaps the best LCS performance ever belonged to Oakland leadoff man Henderson. In a five-game set against Toronto, Henderson won the first contest with a takeout slide, swiped four bases in game two, and powered two home runs in game four. In all, Henderson led the series in runs (eight), on-base percentage (.609), slugging (1.000), home runs (two), RBI (five), total bases (15), and steals (eight, including a tiptoed non-slide into second which infuriated the Blue Jays).

Oakland dominated the first two games of the World Series, outscoring San Francisco 10-1. Ten days passed before game three was played, but it was the same story. The A's clubbed the Giants 13-7 and 9-6, completing the first Series sweep since 1976.

Dave Stewart, who started games one and three, was named MVP, but the award could have gone to Rickey Henderson (.474 average), Dave Henderson (.923 slugging percentage), Carney Lansford (.438 average), or Terry Steinbach (seven RBI).

1989

- A's cop second straight AL flag.
- Giants win first NL pennant since 1962.
- Giants defeat Cubs in five games in NLCS.
- Blue Jays fall to A's in five games in ALCS.

- A's sweep Giants in most one-sided World Series ever.
- Massive earthquake in San Francisco Bay area prior to game three forces ten-day delay of World Series.
- Dave Stewart voted World Series MVP, as he wins two games.

- KC's Bret Saberhagen wins second Cy Young in AL.
- San Diego reliever Mark Davis wins Cy Young in NL.
- SF's Kevin Mitchell named NL MVP, as he tops ML in homers (47), RBI (125), SA (.635), and total bases (345).

A tragic earthquake shook San Francisco's Candlestick Park prior to game three of the World Series. Here, Kevin Mitchell (*left*) and Willie Mays walk off the field together. No one was hurt inside Candlestick, but the quake killed several dozen people in the Bay Area. Commissioner Fay Vincent postponed the Series for ten days.

- Robin Yount wins second AL MVP Award and is the first player to win the honor at two different positions.

- Kirby Puckett tops ML with .339 BA and 215 hits.

- Ranger Ruben Sierra tops AL in SA (.543), RBI (119), triples (14), and total bases (344).

- Nolan Ryan Ks his 5,000th victim, Rickey Henderson.

- Ryan tops ML with 301 Ks and becomes, at age 42, the game's oldest strikeout king ever.

- Cardinal Vince Coleman steals ML record 50 consecutive bases without being caught.

- Pete Rose banned from baseball for gambling activities.

- Commissioner Bart Giamatti dies of heart attack shortly after banning Rose.

- Wade Boggs collects 200 hits for 20th-century record seventh consecutive year.

Puckett Wins AL Bat Title

Kirby Puckett pounded out a .339 average to capture his first American League batting title in 1989 and to become just the second righty in 20 years to seize the crown. The center fielder for the Twins bested the loop with 215 hits while tallying 85 RBI that season. As a testament to his fielding prowess, he captured his fourth Gold Glove Award that year.

Robin Yount

Yount Takes Second MVP

Robin Yount became the first player ever to win an MVP Award at two different positions. He had won one at shortstop for the Brewers in 1982 and—after moving out of the infield due to a serious knee injury—copped another MVP trophy as a center fielder in 1989. In '89, Yount hit .318 with 21 home runs, 103 RBI, 101 runs scored, and a .511 slugging percentage.

Kirby Puckett

1989

- Baltimore's Gregg Olson is AL ROTY after he sets a new AL rookie saves record with 27.

- Chicago's Jerome Walton is NL ROTY.

- AL wins All-Star Game 5-3 at Anaheim—the first time since 1958 that AL has won two games in a row.

- Orioles improve to 87-75, a gain of 32¹/₂ games over their 1988 record.

- Toronto's Tony Fernandez makes just six errors and sets ML FA record for shortstops (.992).

- Network and TV contracts give ML teams $230 million to divvy up.

- Angel Jim Abbott, the first one-handed pitcher since the 1880s, wins 12 games and strikes out 115 batters.

- Boggs and Steve Garvey both make headlines when they're sued by women with whom they've had affairs.

Saberhagen Wins Cy Young

Bret Saberhagen returned to his 1985 pitching form in 1989, as he captured the American League Cy Young Award. The Royals righty put up a circuit-topping 23 wins and 2.16 ERA that season, the lowest mark in the loop since 1978. Known for pitching well in odd years and poorly in even years, Saberhagen fell to 5-9 in 1990.

Bret Saberhagen

Wade Boggs

Mr. Clean Hit by Dirt

Steve Garvey once said: "God has laid out the game plan. I walk around as if a little boy or a little girl was following me and I don't do anything physically or mentally to take away from the ideal they might have for Steve Garvey." His words came back to haunt the former ballplayer in 1989. He was slapped with paternity suits from two different women that year.

Steve Garvey

Boggs Drops to .330 BA

Wade Boggs was dragged through the mud in 1989, as his affair with Margo Adams made scandalous headlines. Boggs was so affected by the ordeal that his season average plummeted to .330, lowering his career average to .352. For the first time in five years, Boggs did not win the AL bat crown. Still, he led the league in runs (113), doubles (51), and on-base percentage (.430).

- Houston's Terry Puhl ends the season with the best career FA of any outfielder in ML history (.993).

- Ken Griffey Sr. and Ken Jr. are first father and son in ML history to both be active in majors at the same time.

- The SkyDome opens on June 5, Milwaukee vs. Toronto.

- Thanks in part to their new home, the Blue Jays set a new AL attendance record.

- Billy Martin dies in a truck crash.

- Mark Davis signs with Royals as a free agent after topping ML with 44 saves for San Diego.

- Saberhagen leads ML with 23 wins and also has ML's top win pct. (.793).

- Tony Gwynn wins NL bat crown (.336).

- Ozzie Smith sets ML record for shortstops when he cops his tenth Gold Glove.

Jim Abbott

Will Thrills with .333 BA

Will Clark proved to be a hitting machine during the 1989 season, as he batted .333, collected 23 home runs and 111 RBI, and spearheaded the National League with 104 runs. Nicknamed "The Thrill," he was the latest in a splendid string of Giant first basemen including Hall of Famers George Kelly, Bill Terry, Johnny Mize, and Willie McCovey. In the 1989 League Championship Series, Clark turned in a towering .650 batting average with a pair of home runs and eight RBI. In that fall's World Series, he was good for a .250 average.

Will Clark

Abbott Wins a Dozen

Jim Abbott inspired America in 1989 as he made his major league debut with the Angels. Born with only his left hand, the former Olympic and University of Michigan star pitcher jumped directly to the big leagues from his college team. Abbott both won and lost 12 games in '89, collecting two shutouts. Despite his handicap, the pitcher was a star quarterback in high school.

1989

- Smith sets an ML record when he tops his league, the NL, for the ninth time in assists by a shortstop.

- The Hall of Fame inducts Johnny Bench, Carl Yastrzemski, Red Schoendienst, and Al Barlick.

- Former Angels relief ace Donnie Moore commits suicide.

- Bill Terry dies.

- *Field of Dreams,* featuring baseball legend Joe Jackson, is one of the top movies of the year.

- Yankees deal Henderson back to the A's for Luis Polonia, Eric Plunk, and Greg Cadaret.

- Minnesota trades ace lefthander Frank Viola to the Mets for Rick Aguilera and four other players, all of whom are pitchers.

- For the fourth straight season, ML teams have 24-man rosters; teams have the option to take on a 25th player but none do so.

Clark Good for 26 HRs

Jack Clark was one of the most enigmatic players of the 1980s. Between 1984 and 1989, he played on four different teams—that is, when he wasn't on the disabled list. In 1989 with San Diego, Clark led the league in walks (132), yet was second in strikeouts (145). He was second in the NL in on-base percentage (.410), yet hit just .242. Nevertheless, Clark remained a reliable power hitter, smacking 26 home runs in '89.

Aging Boone Rolls Along

In 1989, Bob Boone extended his major league record for most games at catcher to 2,183. Boone, who along with Carlton Fisk is the only player to catch regularly past the age of 40, showed no let-up in 1989. At age 42, he caught 131 games and batted .274—20 points higher than his career average. He even stole three bases that season.

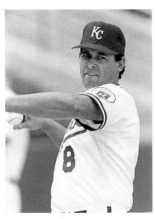

Bob Boone

Jack Clark

Smith Tops in Fielding

Ozzie Smith closed out the decade by winning a record tenth consecutive Gold Glove Award. His fielding virtuosity, acknowledged as being the greatest of any shortstop ever, was rewarded by an annual salary of $2.34 million for three years (beginning in 1987), easily the highest compensation ever paid to a middle infielder at the time. Smith hit .273 and totaled 82 runs scored in 1989.

Ozzie Smith

- Dodgers extend their own ML record by playing their 84th consecutive season without finishing in the cellar.

- Kent Tekulve retires with record for most career relief appearances without ever starting a game (1,050).

- Henderson ties AL record when he tops AL for ninth time in steals.

- Tim Raines has highest career stolen base pct. in ML history (.867).

- Philly's Tommy Herr ends the 1989 season with the best career FA by a second baseman (.988).

- Bob Boone extends his own ML record for most games as a catcher—2,183 through 1989.

- For just the second time since 1959, righthanded batters finish one-two in the AL bat race—Puckett at .339 and Oakland's Carney Lansford at .336.

- Boggs tops ML with 51 doubles and ties for lead in runs (113).

- Boggs tops ML for fifth year in a row in OBP (.430).

Bay Area Is Ravaged

Millions of television viewers who thought they were tuning into the third game of the 1989 World Series instead saw this startling perspective of the Bay Bridge collapse. This dramatic photo was shot from the blimp that was assigned to cover the fall classic action. A day earlier, local fans boasted of the first-ever Bay Area Series. It was a bit of cruel irony that the bridge that linked the two Bay cities had collapsed.

Bay Bridge

Rose Banned for Gambling

In one of the biggest scandals since the Black Sox, Pete Rose was banned from baseball for allegedly gambling on the Reds, the team he managed. Though evidence was not conclusive, many believed Rose actually bet on his team to lose. Rose suffered an even worse fate in 1990 when he was sentenced to prison for tax evasion. Many predicted that Rose's sins would deny him entry to the Hall of Fame. Few seemed to realize that Ty Cobb, a man who committed several brutal assaults, was the first man voted into the Hall.

Pete Rose

1989

- Jeff Russell of Texas paces AL with 38 saves.

- Saberhagen tops ML with just 12 CGs—fewest ever for ML best.

- San Diego's Bruce Hurst and LA's Tim Belcher top NL in CGs with just ten—fewest ever by a loop leader.

- Saberhagen tops ML with 262 innings—fewest ever by ML leader.

- Orel Hershiser also sets new NL record for fewest innings by a leader (257).

- Belcher tops ML with eight shutouts despite working only ten CGs.

- SF's Robby Thompson leads NL with 11 triples.

- Houston's Mike Scott is the only NL hurler to win as many as 20 games.

- Stewart wins 21 games and Mike Moore and Storm Davis win 19 each to give the A's 59 wins from their top three hurlers.

Eckersley Saves the Day—Again

Teammates mob Dennis Eckersley (smiling) after the hurler saved game four of the 1989 World Series. Oakland won the decisive game 9-6. Since the first three games of the Series were blowouts, this was the only one Eckersley had a chance to save. The reliever displayed his skills in the American League Championship Series, though, saving four games against Boston in 1988 and three more against Toronto in '89.

Dennis Eckersley

Rickey Henderson

Henderson Leads A's to Title

The A's picked up Rickey Henderson from the Yankees in June 1989 and he sparked the team to the World Title. Henderson topped the league in runs (113) and walks (126), and led the AL in steals (77) for the ninth time. In the five-game American League Championship Series against Toronto, Henderson was unstoppable. He batted .400 with two homers, seven walks, eight steals, and eight runs.

- Scott Garrelts of the Giants paces NL in ERA at 2.28.

- Comeback Player of the Year Lonnie Smith of Atlanta tops NL in OBP (.415) and is third in batting (.315).

- San Diego's Jack Clark tops NL in walks (132) and has .410 OBP despite hitting only .242.

- Toronto's Fred McGriff tops AL in homers (36).

- Cleveland's Joe Carter trails McGriff by only one homer for AL crown and has 105 RBI, but hits just .243 and has an equally dismal .292 OBP.

- California's Bert Blyleven achieves 3,500 Ks.

- Cardinal Pedro Guerrero and Expo Tim Wallach tie for NL lead in doubles with 42; Guerrero is also second in RBI (117).

- Howard Johnson of the Mets is a member of the 30/30 club for second time in his career, as he swipes 41 bases and bangs 36 homers.

Baseball hadn't fielded a dynasty team since the 'Swingin' A's of the early 1970s. But by 1990, one dynastic club had emerged—and again it was the Oakland Athletics. Oakland, which had made it to the World Series in 1988 and had swept the fall classic in 1989, was storming toward another World Title in '90.

These A's were loaded—especially after picking up former All-Stars Harold Baines and Willie McGee in August. In fact, by the end of the season, Oakland could field a lineup that contained nine one-time All-Stars. The big guns included Rickey Henderson (.325 average, 28 homers, 65 steals), Jose Canseco (37 homers, 101 RBI), and Mark McGwire (39 homers, 108 RBI). The pitching staff was even better, led by Bob Welch (27-6), Dave Stewart (22-11), and Dennis Eckersley (48 saves, 0.61 ERA). Oakland won 103 games without breaking a sweat.

In the National League, another team was making its mark. The Cincinnati Reds won their first game of the season and never looked back, leading the National League West from wire to wire. Despite no standout starters, the Reds boasted a brilliant bullpen duo known as the "Nasty Boys." Randy Myers saved 31 games, while fireballer Rob Dibble whiffed 136 men in 98 innings.

However, before the A's and Reds stepped to the plate in 1990,

RIJO AND THE REDS AMAZE THE A's

baseball's labor negotiators were stealing the headlines. After failing to sign a new collective bargaining agreement, the owners locked the players out of training camp. The dispute wasn't resolved until late March, and the players were given just two-and-a-half weeks to prepare for a delayed Opening Day.

The labor dispute infuriated fans, who considered both owners and players spoiled and greedy. After all, the owners were sitting pretty after signing a fat $1 billion TV contract with CBS. Superstars were now earning $3 million a year, and Canseco signed for five years at $23.5 million.

The '90 season was also the Year of the No-Hitter. A record nine were fired. The most amazing of all came off the fingers of Ranger Nolan Ryan, who threw his sixth career no-hitter. Ryan won his 300th game in 1990 and, at age 43, led the AL in strikeouts with 232. White Sox relief ace Bobby Thigpen also entered the record books, as he notched 57 saves.

Thigpen sparked his young Sox to 94 wins, though they finished 9 games behind Oakland in the AL West. Boston, which was led by Roger Clemens (21-6, 1.93 ERA), edged out Toronto by 2 games in the AL East. While the Tigers finished a distant third in the East, their first baseman, Cecil Fielder, led the majors with 51 homers and 132 RBI.

In the NL East, Pittsburgh beat out a talented Mets team by 4 games. The Pirates were powered by Barry Bonds (.301 average, 33 homers, 114 RBI, and 52 steals) and Bobby Bonilla (32 homers, 120 RBI). The Reds won their division by 5 games.

Oakland broomed Boston in the ALCS, winning 9-1, 4-1, 4-1, and 3-1. Pittsburgh fell in five games to the Reds, who were led by outfielder Paul O'Neil (.471 average).

Most experts predicted Oakland's Big Green Machine to pulverize the Reds in the World Series. But it wasn't to be. Instead, the world saw Cincinnati sweep the A's in the biggest upset since 1969.

Jose Rijo won two of the four games, yielding just one run in both of his starts. The Reds' Billy Hatcher netted seven hits in his first seven at-bats, and hit an all-time record .750 for the Series (9-for-12). Chris Sabo batted .563 and was brilliant defensively at third base. Overall, the Reds outscored the A's 22-8 and won their first World Title since 1976.

1990

- Oakland cops its third straight flag in the AL.
- Cincinnati takes its first NL pennant since 1976.
- A's sweep Boston in ALCS, just like they did in 1988.
- Boston manages just one run in each ALCS game.

- Cincinnati beats Pittsburgh in six games in NLCS, thanks to several outstanding defensive plays in the outfield.
- Reds shock the baseball world by sweeping the mighty A's in the World Series, as Oakland's offensive stars muster just eight runs.

- Reds pitcher Jose Rijo wins two World Series games, yielding one run in two starts; Rijo takes the Series MVP Award.
- Cincinnati's Billy Hatcher hits an all-time Series record .750 (9-for-12), as he collects seven hits in his first seven at-bats.

Mark McGwire finds Jose Rijo unhittable in game one of the 1990 World Series. Rijo, spotting his fastball and slider wherever he wanted it, won both of his Series starts. In 15¹/₃ innings, he yielded just one run and nine hits. The hulking McGwire managed just three harmless singles in the affair.

- Cincinnati's Chris Sabo hits .563 with two homers and five RBI in the Series and is brilliant defensively at third base.

- Spring training doesn't begin until late March, as the owners lock out the players until the two sides reach a collective bargaining agreement.

- Detroit's Cecil Fielder leads the AL in homers (51), RBI (132), slugging (.592), total bases (339), and strikeouts (182).

- Fielder is the first ML player to hit 50 homers since 1977 (George Foster), and the first ALer to do it since 1961 (Roger Maris and Mickey Mantle).

- Rickey Henderson leads the AL in runs (118), stolen bases (65), and OBP (.440).

- Henderson steals his 893rd base, breaking Ty Cobb's American League record.

- George Brett leads the AL in batting (.329) and ties in doubles (45).

Clemens Wins 21 Games

Rocket Roger Clemens appeared headed toward his third American League Cy Young Award in 1990 when arm trouble sidelined him for much of September. The righty still ended up with 21 victories—two of which were back-to-back complete-game shutouts—as he led the Red Sox to their third division crown in five seasons.

Dennis Eckersley

Roger Clemens

Eckersley Saves 48 Games

Dennis Eckersley continued his dominance of American League hitters in 1990, as he saved a career-high 48 games. A master of control, the A's reliever averaged nearly a strikeout for each of his 73¹/₃ innings pitched and allowed just four walks for the entire season. The righty ran out of steam in that fall's World Series, however. He allowed three hits in 1¹/₃ innings and lost game two in the tenth inning.

1990

- Brett becomes the first player in ML history to win BA titles in three different decades.

- Oakland's Bob Welch tops the AL in wins (27) and win pct (.818).

- Welch's 27 wins are the most in ML since 1972 and the most in AL since 1968.

- Roger Clemens goes 21-6 for Boston and leads the AL in ERA (1.93) and shutouts (four).

- Texas' Nolan Ryan, still throwing hard at age 43, leads his loop in Ks (232) for the 11th time.

- Ryan wins his 300th game.

- White Sox Bobby Thigpen breaks the ML save record with 57 saves.

- Dennis Eckersley saves 48 games, posts a 0.61 ERA, and walks four batters in 73¹/₃ innings.

- Ryne Sandberg leads the NL in home runs (40), runs (116), and total bases (344).

Bobby Thigpen

Thigpen Sets Saves Record

No reliever has ever enjoyed the success that Bobby Thigpen did in 1990. The White Sox stopper shattered the major league single-season record by notching 57 saves, obliterating the old mark of 46 saves. The righty won four additional games and compiled a 1.83 ERA. With Thigpen in the pen, the White Sox won 94 games—25 more than in 1989.

Darryl: 37 HRs, 108 RBI

After beginning the year with a protracted contract squabble, Darryl Strawberry had a banner season in 1990. The Met superstar batted .277 with 37 home runs and 108 RBI and nearly carried the Mets to the playoffs. Despite off-field problems and numerous squabbles with teammates and management over the years, he reached 26 homers for the eighth straight year. Strawberry signed a five-year, $20-million contract with the Dodgers after the '90 season.

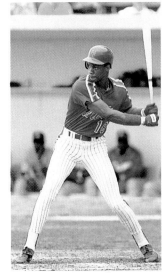

Darryl Strawberry

Canseco: 37 HRs, 101 RBI

Despite his recurring back trouble and extended stays on the disabled list, Jose Canseco signed the most lucrative contract in the history of the game in 1990—$23.5 million over five years. The right fielder proved his worth over and over again that season, as he batted .274 with 37 home runs and 101 RBI to spearhead the A's to 103 victories and the World Series. He fell with the rest of the ballclub in the fall classic, hitting .083 with one home run and two RBI.

Jose Canseco

- Willie McGee, traded from St. Louis to Oakland in August, still wins the NL BA title (.335).

- McGee becomes the first ML player to win a BA title without being in the league at the time he won it.

- Vince Coleman wins his sixth straight steals crown (77).

- Pittsburgh's Doug Drabek leads NL in wins (22) and win pct. (.786).

- On August 17, Carlton Fisk hits his 329th homer as a catcher—a new ML record.

- Pittsburgh's Barry Bonds becomes the first player to hit .300 with 30 homers, 100 RBI, and 50 stolen bases.

- Andre Dawson becomes the second player in ML history to compile 2,000 hits, 300 homers, and 300 steals (Willie Mays was the first).

- Seattle's Ken Griffey Sr. and Ken Griffey Jr. become first father-son duo to play on the same team in the majors.

1990

Cecil Fielder

Lance Parrish

Ryne Sandberg

Fielder of Dreams

In 1990, the Tigers plucked Cecil Fielder, the former Blue Jay first baseman, from Japan as a free agent and Fielder responded with a career season. The 11th player in major league history to smack 50 home runs, he clubbed 51 dingers in '90, including two round-trippers in the last game of the season. Fielder led the American League in RBI (132), slugging (.592), total bases (339), and strikeouts (182) that year.

Parrish Hits 24 HRs

Having been one of the chief victims of the owners' collusion against free agents in 1986, Lance Parrish was granted free agency by the Angels at the end of the 1989 season. The catcher promptly re-signed with the Angels and batted .268 with 24 home runs and 70 RBI in 1990.

Sandberg Hits 40 HRs

In 1990, Ryne Sandberg became the first second baseman since Dave Johnson in 1973 to hit 40 or more home runs. Sandberg hit exactly 40, driving in 100 runs and batting .306 for the Cubs in 1990. The best second sacker in the major leagues since Joe Morgan, Sandberg posted 344 total bases that year—the highest mark in the majors (higher than even Cecil Fielder's 339 total).

1990

- For the 13th straight season, Detroit fields a keystone combo of Alan Trammell and Lou Whitaker.

- Wade Boggs fails to reach 200 hits for the first time in eight seasons.

- After the league signs huge TV contracts, ballclubs spend their excess millions on free agents.

- Player salaries soar, with several players surpassing the $3 million-a-year mark.

- New free agents are tending to pick their new teams based on location; many opt for California-based teams.

- Jose Canseco signs new pact with A's: $23.5 million for five years.

- A's payroll averages over $1 million per man.

- Pete Rose is sent to prison for cheating on his taxes.

- Fay Vincent orders George Steinbrenner to give up controlling interest of Yankees because of alleged gambling activities.

Ken Griffey Jr.

Brett Wins Third Title

George Brett won his third career batting title in 1990 as he batted .329 to lead the American League. Brett, who won batting crowns in 1976 and '80, became the first player to win titles in three different decades. The heroics of their first baseman were the lone bright spot in a dismal season for the Royals, who had spent megabucks for free agents in the off-season.

Griffey: .300 BA, 22 HRs

Ken Griffey Jr. continued to show his great talent in 1990, as he batted .300 with 22 home runs and 80 RBI in his sophomore year. In September, he met up with his father, Ken Sr., who joined the Mariners after being released by the Reds. The Griffeys have the distinction of being the first father-son duo to play in the major leagues at the same time.

George Brett

- On July 17, the Minnesota Twins become the first ML team to make two triple plays in one game.

- Nine no-hitters are thrown during the season—a new ML record.

- California's Mark Langston and Mike Witt no-hit Seattle on April 11.

- Seattle's Randy Johnson no-hits the Tigers on June 2.

- Ryan fires an ML record sixth no-hitter vs. the A's on June 11.

- Oakland's Dave Stewart no-hits Toronto on June 29.

- LA's Fernando Valenzuela no-hits St. Louis on June 29.

- On July 1, Yankee Andy Hawkins no-hits Chicago in a regulation nine-inning game, but loses 4-0.

- On July 12, White Sox Melido Perez no-hits New York in a rain-shortened six-inning game.

- On August 15, Philadelphia's Terry Mulholland no-hits San Francisco.

Sabo: .563 in Series

Cincinnati's Chris Sabo is tagged out at second by Willie Randolph in game two of the 1990 World Series. Though Sabo didn't like the call, he had little else to complain about in the Series. Not only did his team win every game, he also hit .563. In game three, he clubbed two homers and grabbed everything in sight at third base. Sabo's performance undoubtedly enhanced his status as a cult hero. With his crewcut and goggles, he earned the nickname "Spuds" for his resemblance to a certain beer mascot.

World Series

Alan Trammell

Trammell: .304, 89 RBI

Alan Trammell continued to make his case for Hall of Fame consideration in 1990, batting .304 with 14 home runs and 89 RBI while leading the Tigers to a surprise third-place finish. At age 32, the shortstop completed his 14th season in Detroit with no sign of slowing down. Trammell rebounded from an injury-plagued 1989 season, in which he hit a meager .243 with five home runs.

Carlton Fisk

Fisk Sets HR Record

Carlton Fisk rewrote the record books in 1990. He surpassed the career home run mark for catchers previously held by Hall of Famer Johnny Bench, by tallying 18 four-baggers. With a .285 batting average and 65 RBI, Fisk also played an instrumental role in leading a young White Sox team to a 94-victory season and a second-place finish (9 games out) behind the Oakland A's.

1990

- On Sept. 2, Toronto's Dave Stieb no-hits Cleveland.
- The AL wins All-Star Game 2-0 at Wrigley.
- The Hall of Fame inducts Jim Palmer and Joe Morgan.
- Ranger Rafael Palmeiro leads AL in hits with 191.

- Mark McGwire tops AL in walks (110).
- Toronto's Tony Fernandez heads AL in triples (17).
- Stewart leads AL in innings (267) and CGs (11).
- Phillie Lenny Dykstra ties for NL lead in hits with Giant Brett Butler (192).

- Dykstra and Met Dave Magadan tie for the NL lead in OBP (.418).
- SF's Matt Williams leads NL in RBI (122), becoming the third different Giant in three years to do so.
- Bonds tops the NL in SA (.566).
- San Diego's Jack Clark again paces the NL in walks (104).

Nolan Ryan

World Series

Oliver's an Unsung Hero

Little-known catcher Joe Oliver took game two of the World Series with a game-clinching ground-ball single in the bottom of the tenth inning. His hit came off baseball's toughest pitcher, Dennis Eckersley, who yielded only five earned runs during the regular season. In the Series, Oliver batted .333 with three doubles.

Ryan Wins No. 300

Ageless wonder Nolan Ryan, the all-time leader in strikeouts and no-hitters, had a milestone year in 1990. The Ranger righty won his 300th game on August 1, against the Brewers, to become both the 20th pitcher ever (and the third hurler age 43 or older) to reach the mark. On June 11, he pitched his sixth career no-hitter, a major league record. Ryan led the American League with 232 strikeouts while winning 13 games that season.

- New York's Gregg Jefferies leads the NL in doubles with 40.

- Cincinnati's Mariano Duncan tops the league in triples with 11.

- Houston's Danny Darwin leads the NL in ERA at 2.21.

- New York's David Cone tops the NL in Ks with 233.

- The Mets' John Franco leads the loop in saves with 33.

- Despite a mere 91-71 record, the Reds stay in first place every day of the season.

- Cincinnati leads NL in batting (.265) and fewest errors (102), and is second in ERA (3.39).

- Bonds captures the NL MVP Award, while Henderson accepts the AL prize.

- Welch wins the AL Cy Young Award; Drabek nabs the award in the NL.

- Cleveland catcher Sandy Alomar Jr. (.290 average) is named AL ROTY, while Atlanta's David Justice (28 homers) takes the NL honor.

TWINS CHOP BRAVES IN TIGHTEST SERIES EVER

Not since 1890 had a major league team leapfrogged from the cellar to a pennant the following year, but in 1991 two clubs pulled off this astounding feat. The Atlanta Braves vaulted from the worst record in the majors in 1990 to the NL pennant, and the Minnesota Twins scrambled out of the AL West basement to snatch their second AL flag in five years.

Atlanta overcame a 9½-game deficit to beat out LA in the NL West. Bobby Cox's Braves boasted the best starting rotation in the majors, headed by Cy Young Award winner Tom Glavine (20-11, 2.55 ERA) and 21-year-old Steve Avery (18-8). Providing the offense were David Justice, Ron Gant, and free-agent third sacker Terry Pendleton. A dismal .230 hitter in 1990, Pendleton won the 1991 batting title (.319) and also captured the league's MVP Award.

The Twins had two key free-agent acquisitions—DH Chili Davis and Minnesota native Jack Morris. Both, like Pendleton, were coming off sub-par years. In 1991, however, Morris rebounded to win 18 games, and Davis paced the Twins with 29 homers and 93 RBI. When manager Tom Kelly also got 20 wins from Scott Erickson, 42 saves from Rick Aguilera, the usual fine season from Kirby Puckett, and a surprise contribution from Rookie of the Year second sacker Chuck Knoblauch, Minnesota reeled off 16 straight victories and was never caught.

Yet all the accolades in 1991 did not belong to the two flag winners. Julio Franco, with a .341 average, became the first Texas Ranger to win a batting title. Two other Rangers, Ruben Sierra and Rafael Palmeiro, joined Franco to give Texas a trio of 200-hit men. Meanwhile another Ranger, the unstoppable Nolan Ryan, notched his seventh career no-hitter.

Other AL honors went to Tiger Cecil Fielder, a repeat homer and RBI champ; BoSox fireballer Roger Clemens, winner of his third Cy Young Award; and Oriole Cal Ripken, who parlayed one of the greatest offensive seasons ever by an AL shortstop (.323 average, 34 homers, 114 RBI) into his second MVP Award.

In July, two Montreal Expos hurlers, Mark Gardner and Dennis Martinez, no-hit the Dodgers twice in three days. Martinez's no-hitter was a perfect game, though Gardner lost his no-no in the tenth. Cardinal reliever Lee Smith set a new NL saves record with 47, although he could not help his club stall the Pirates, runaway winners in the NL East.

The Pirates' outstanding outfielders—Barry Bonds, Bobby Bonilla, and Andy Van Slyke—fizzled in the NLCS, allowing the Braves to triumph in seven games. Minnesota, in contrast, needed just five frays to dispose of the Toronto Blue Jays, perennial late-season floppers.

The World Series was a true fall classic—perhaps the greatest of all time. The Twins took the first two in Minnesota, winning game two 3-2 on a Scott Leius homer in the eighth. The Braves, inspired by their fans' "Tomahawk Chop," then swept the next three in Atlanta. They won game three 5-4 on a Mark Lemke single in the 12th, then captured game four 3-2 when Lemke tripled and scored in the ninth. Atlanta blew out the Twins 14-5 in the fifth contest.

The Twins, though, got revenge in the Metrodome. In game six, Puckett broke a 3-3 tie with an 11th-inning solo homer. In game seven, Morris and John Smoltz pitched a nail-biting 0-0 gem through nine-and-a-half innings. But in the bottom of the tenth, Minnesota's Gene Larkin singled home Dan Gladden with the Series-winning tally.

Morris's complete-game 1-0 triumph earned him the Series MVP Award. Meanwhile, the Twins had won their second fall classic in five years without winning a single Series game on the road.

1991

- Minnesota wins AL pennant, polishing off Toronto in just five games, after finishing last in its division in 1990.

- The Braves, also a cellar-dweller in '90, cop their first NL flag since moving to Atlanta.

- Braves need the full seven games to wrest NLCS from Pittsburgh, which loses its second LCS in a row when its big hitters—Barry Bonds, Bobby Bonilla, and Andy Van Slyke—again fail in postseason play.

- The Twins bag their second World Championship in five years.

- For the first time since 1962, the World Series goes the full seven games and ends with a 1-0 verdict.

- The 1991 World Series is the first since 1924 to go the ultimate limit— a seven-game, extra-inning clash won by the home team in its last at-bat.

- Jack Morris of the Twins bags Series MVP Award after winning finale 1-0.

- Gene Larkin of the Twins delivers Series-winning hit, a pinch single in the tenth plating Dan Gladden.

Kirby Puckett gets all of a Charlie Leibrandt pitch in the 11th inning of game six of the 1991 World Series. Puckett's solo homer gave the Twins a 4-3 win and knotted the Series at three games apiece. For drama, the blow rivaled Carlton Fisk's overtime shot in the sixth game of the 1975 Series. Puckett hit .319 during the regular season and paced the Twins in both runs and total bases.

- A base-running gaffe by Atlanta's Lonnie Smith costs Braves a run that might have won World Series finale.

- Both Series skippers, Bobby Cox of Atlanta and Tom Kelly of the Twins, are selected Manager of the Year in their respective leagues.

- Atlanta is first ML team since the 1889-90 Louisville Colonels to win a pennant after posting the worst record in its league the previous year.

- Third baseman Terry Pendleton of Atlanta wins NL hitting crown (.319) and also tops the loop in hits (187).

- Hal Morris of the Reds goes 3-for-4 on the season's final day to end up at .318, one point behind Terry Pendleton and short of the bat title.

- San Diego's Tony Gwynn hits .317, with 11 triples and just 19 strikeouts, before an injury idles him for the season.

- Pendleton wins NL MVP Award in the closest MVP vote since 1979. Bonds, 1990's NL MVP, is runner-up.

- Howard Johnson of the Mets paces NL in home runs (38) and RBI (117).

Knoblauch Named ROTY

In 1989, Chuck Knoblauch was a defensive whiz at shortstop for Texas A&M. In 1990, while playing for Double-A Orlando, he made a successful conversion to second base, though he was still considered a long shot to make the Twins in the spring of 1991. Knoblauch not only won the Minnesota keystone slot but achieved every freshman's dream when he won the AL Rookie of the Year Award and a World Championship ring.

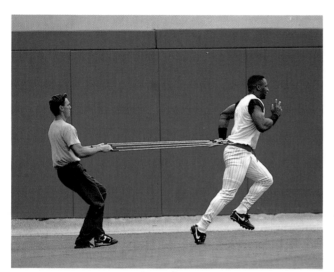

Bo Jackson

Injured Bo Joins Sox

Bo Jackson was released by Kansas City in the spring after he suffered an apparent career-ending hip injury in an NFL playoff game. However, Jackson vowed to return to the majors in '91. Bo, seen here working out after being signed by the White Sox, needed a stint in the minors to regain his playing skills. He fulfilled his prophecy when he joined the White Sox for a few games late in the campaign.

Cal Ripken

Rip Rises to New Heights

Cal Ripken earned the AL MVP Award by posting some of the greatest stats ever by an AL shortstop. He became the only shortstop in history other than Ernie Banks to bat .300 with at least 30 homers and 100 RBI. Ripken played in all of Baltimore's games, keeping him on course to break Lou Gehrig's consecutive-games-played record in 1995.

Chuck Knoblauch

1991

- Johnson has 302 total bases, one behind NL co-leaders, and a .535 SA, .001 point behind leader Will Clark.

- Dodger Brett Butler tops NL in runs (112) and walks (108) and is second in OBP (.401).

- Bonds is second to Butler in walks with 107 but tops NL in OBP with .410.

- A late-season injury hampers Clark in his bid for NL RBI crown; he finishes with 116.

- Padres first baseman Fred McGriff finishes season with a .522 career SA, highest among active players with at least 2,000 at-bats.

- Marquis Grissom of the Expos leads ML with 76 stolen bases.

- Atlanta's Otis Nixon swipes 72 bases to set a new 20th century Braves record but is suspended for the rest of the season after failing a drug test.

- David Cone of the Mets leads all NL pitchers with 241 strikeouts.

- Cone ties NL record when he fans 19 Phillies on the final day of the season.

Fred McGriff

McGriff: ML's Top Slugger

At the end of the 1991 season, San Diego first sacker Fred McGriff's .522 career slugging average led all active players with over 2,000 at-bats. McGriff provided the Padres with 31 homers and 106 RBI in his first year with the team after being acquired in a trade with Toronto. Few sluggers are more consistent or more feared than McGriff.

Harvey: 46 Halo Saves

Bryan Harvey set a new Angels franchise record in 1991 when he logged 46 saves. With Harvey in the bullpen to bail them out of trouble, California's three top starters—Jim Abbott, Mark Langston, and Chuck Finley—had an aggregate 55-27 record. Nevertheless, the Angels finished in the AL West cellar when the team's other hurlers could combine for only a 26-54 mark. Kirk McCaskill went 10-19.

Bryan Harvey

Cecil Fielder

Hefty Fielder Hits a Ton

In 1991, Detroit heavyweight Cecil Fielder became the first AL player since Jimmie Foxx in 1933 to repeat as both the loop's home run and RBI king. Fielder knocked home 133 runs and pounded 44 dingers in 1991. Both figures were major league highs. But to Fielder's disappointment, he once again finished second in MVP voting, this time to the more well-rounded Cal Ripken.

- Dennis Martinez of the Expos pitches a perfect game against the Dodgers on July 28, winning 2-0.

- Two days before Martinez's gem, Mark Gardner of the Expos loses a no-hitter to the Dodgers, 1-0 in ten innings.

- Martinez leads NL with a 2.39 ERA and five shutouts and also ties Tom Glavine of the Braves for NL lead in CGs with nine.

- Glavine wins 20 games for the Braves and bags NL Cy Young Award. The only other NL hurler to win 20 games is John Smiley of Pittsburgh.

- Greg Maddux of the Cubs leads NL in innings pitched with 263.

- Reliever Lee Smith of the Cards sets new NL record with 47 saves.

- The AL save leader is Bryan Harvey with 46, a new Angels record.

- Boston's Roger Clemens paces AL in ERA (2.62), strikeouts (241), innings (271), and shutouts (four) and wins his third Cy Young Award.

Frank Thomas

Big Frank Powers Sox

In his first full major league season, Frank Thomas hit .318, the best mark by a White Sox regular since Chet Lemon hit .318 in 1979. Thomas also paced the American League with a .453 on-base percentage and set a new Sox club record when he drew 138 walks. Thomas banged 32 homers and tallied 109 RBI. He also walked a league-leading 138 times. Big Frank is one of very few players in White Sox history to showcase power, patience, and the talent to hit for a high average.

Montreal's Martinez Perfects LA

Montreal pitcher and National League ERA leader Dennis Martinez hurled a perfect game against the Los Angeles Dodgers on July 28, 1991, winning 2-0. Two days earlier, another Montreal pitcher, Mark Gardner, was less fortunate. Despite tossing a no-hitter through nine innings against those same Dodgers, Gardner lost 1-0 in the tenth frame.

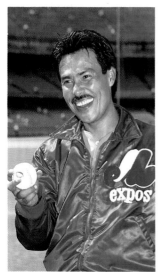

Dennis Martinez

Sierra, Mates Crack 200

In 1991, Ruben Sierra joined with Julio Franco and Rafael Palmeiro to give the Texas Rangers three 200-hit men. The trio also combined with five other Rangers to give the team eight players with at least 15 home runs. Texas topped the majors in runs with 829 and was second only to the Detroit Tigers in homers. Nevertheless, the Rangers were able to finish no better than a distant third in the American League West.

Ruben Sierra

1991

- Clemens ties AL record for the fewest wins (18) by a starting pitcher who copped a Cy Young.

- Dennis Eckersley of the A's notches 43 saves to became first hurler ever to collect more than 160 career wins and 160 career saves.

- Cecil Fielder of Detroit paces AL in both homers (44) and RBI (133).

- Jose Canseco of the A's ties Fielder for AL homer crown and also is second in the loop in RBI (122).

- Julio Franco becomes first member of Rangers franchise to win AL bat crown when he hits .341.

- Rafael Palmeiro, Franco, and Ruben Sierra of the Rangers all collect over 200 hits to tie AL team record.

- Milwaukee's Paul Molitor paces ML in both runs (133) and hits (216) and finishes with a .325 average.

- KC's Danny Tartabull tops AL with a .593 SA, tops by far in ML.

- Frank Thomas of the White Sox tops ML with 138 walks and a .453 OBP. His 138 walks are a new White Sox franchise record.

Knock-Kneed Franco Captures AL Batting Title

Hitting from a unique knock-kneed batting stance with his bat held high behind his ear, the Rangers' Julio Franco hit .341 in 1991 to bag the American League batting crown. Franco was the first member of the Washington-Texas Rangers franchise ever to win the prize; he was also the first right-handed-hitting second sacker since 1954 to be a bat leader. During the last few weeks of the season, Franco's chief pursuer was Milwaukee's Willie Randolph, another righty-hitting second baseman, who finished the season with a .327 average.

Ramon Martinez

Ramon Wins 17 Games for Dodgers

Ramon Martinez slipped from 20 wins in 1990 to 17 in 1991, but he was still the top winner on the best overall mound staff in the majors. In 1991, the Dodgers' 3.06 ERA paced both leagues by nearly a half-run, with Martinez, Tim Belcher, and Mike Morgan doing most of the labor. Los Angeles cemented its ERA title on the final day of the season when five pitchers blanked the Giants 2-0.

Julio Franco

Jeff Bagwell

Bagwell Bags ROTY Prize

First baseman Jeff Bagwell was the crown jewel of the Houston Astros' youth corps in 1991, winning the NL Rookie of the Year Award for his frosh performance. The first player from the Astros franchise to win the ROTY, he had 15 home runs, 82 RBI, 75 walks, a .437 slugging average, and a .387 on-base average, all of which led Houston that year.

- Rickey Henderson tops Lou Brock's record for career thefts, finishing season with 994 stolen bases.

- Henderson also cops his AL-record 11th stolen-base crown, with 58 thefts.

- Cal Ripken wins his second MVP Award, as he extends his consecutive-games-played streak to 1,572.

- Ripken leads AL in total bases with 368, is second in hits with 210, and is also second in doubles with 46. He is first shortstop in AL history to hit .300 with 30 or more homers and 100 or more RBI.

- Cincinnati sets record for the lowest winning percentage (.457) by a defending world champion.

- Replacement umpires are employed on Opening Day—the result of an ML umpires labor dispute.

- The Tigers become third team in AL history to lead loop in homers while finishing last in batting.

- Joe Carter of Toronto becomes first player to collect 100 RBI for three different teams in as many seasons.

Jays' Alomar Flies High

Toronto second baseman Roberto Alomar attempts to complete a double play against the Twins. Alomar, acquired from San Diego prior to the 1991 season, helped the Jays tighten their infield and also gave the club a valuable offensive weapon. In 1991, Alomar hit .295 and stole 53 bases. Meanwhile, keystone mate Manuel Lee set a major league record for the most whiffs by a player without a home run (107).

Roberto Alomar

Twins Soar Over Blue Jays, Take ALCS in Five Games

Twins third sacker Mike Pagliarulo leaps to spear a throw as Toronto's Devon White slides in safely with a stolen base in game four of the ALCS. The Jays exited from postseason play the next day when they lost their third straight game at SkyDome. During the regular season, White hit a surprising .282 with 110 runs and 33 stolen bases.

NLCS

Braves Bump off Bucs

Pittsburgh shortstop Jay Bell bowls through Atlanta third baseman Terry Pendleton in game four of the NLCS. Both Bell and Pendleton were surprising stars throughout 1991. Pendleton hit .319 to win the National League bat crown and MVP Award; and Bell, after struggling at the plate in his first five seasons, paced all NL shortstops with 164 hits. Pittsburgh won game four 3-2 in ten innings but lost the series in seven games, losing the finale 4-0.

ALCS

1991

- The Expos are forced to finish their season on the road after a section of Olympic Stadium collapses.

- The Blue Jays set new AL attendance record when they draw over four million fans to SkyDome.

- Cleveland finishes with baseball's worst record (57-105) and sets a team record for losses.

- For the sixth season in a row, the Blue Jays have a winning record both at home and on the road.

- The Angels (81-81) become first team in ML history to finish in the basement without a losing record.

- The Dodgers post a 3.06 staff ERA, best in the majors.

- The Twins top ML with a .280 BA.

- Rookie Ivan Rodriguez of Texas catches 88 games at age 19—the most since 1949 by a teenage backstopper.

- Rob Deer of Detroit hits just .179, the lowest BA in 105 years by a regular outfielder.

1991

Smith Blunder Kills Braves

Minnesota's Brian Harper tags out Atlanta outfielder Lonnie Smith in game four of the 1991 World Series. Ironically, it was Lonnie's timidity on the basepaths that ultimately cost the Braves the Series. With game seven still scoreless in the eighth inning, Smith hesitated in rounding second base and was unable to score on a long double by Terry Pendleton. The Twins won the unforgettable finale 1-0 in ten innings.

Jack Morris

Morris Wins 1-0 Finale

In 1991, Jack Morris had an 18-12 record but a suspiciously high 3.43 ERA. Skeptics wondered if he was merely reaping the rewards of pitching on a pennant-winner. In postseason action, Morris silenced doubters with a strong showing that culminated in a 1-0, ten-inning, complete-game win in game seven of the World Series. It was the first time in history that a fall classic was capped by a route-going overtime triumph.

World Series

World Series

Braves Take Game Four in 12 Innings

Twins catcher Brian Harper and Atlanta's David Justice await umpire Drew Coble's call in the bottom of the 12th inning in game three of the 1991 World Series. When Coble's decision went Justice's way, it gave Atlanta a thrilling 5-4 victory and kept Minnesota from taking a 3-0 lead in games. The 1991 Series was the first in history to go the seven-game limit and feature three extra-inning clashes. Five of the games were decided by one run, including the last two.

- The A's Mark McGwire hits a mere .201, lowest BA in 103 years by a regular first baseman.

- The Mariners break .500 for first time in franchise history but fire manager Jim Lefebvre anyway.

- Rod Carew, Gaylord Perry, and Fergie Jenkins are voted into the Hall of Fame.

- AL wins All-Star Game 4-2 at Toronto.

- Nolan Ryan throws his ML-record seventh no-hitter on May 1 against Toronto.

- At the end of the '91 season, Ryan has 314 wins, tied for 14th on the all-time career list.

- Bo Jackson is released by the Royals prior to the season after suffering a hip injury while playing pro football.

- Jackson signs with the White Sox and, after a long rehabilitation, returns to action late in the season.

- The Brewers go 40-19 in the last two months to finish at 83-79.

BLUE JAYS TAKE TROPHY NORTH

Prognosticators had their finest hour in 14 years as three of the four defending division champions won again in 1992. Only the Minnesota Twins stumbled, ceding the AL West crown to Oakland. The A's return to the top after a year's absence was all that kept 1992 from being a reprise of 1978, when all four division winners repeated.

If the four pennant races offered no surprises in 1992, the battles for individual honors were for the most part waged by unexpected combatants. In the AL, Rangers outfielder Juan Gonzalez, still short of his 22nd birthday, snared the home run crown with 43 dingers. Edgar Martinez of Seattle emerged to lead the ML with a .343 average, while Texas' Kevin Brown, 9-12 in 1991, shared the AL lead in wins with 21.

Several of the NL's individual champs also caused eyes to blink. Gary Sheffield, a .194 hitter in 1991 with Milwaukee, benefitted so much from a change of scenery after he was dealt to San Diego that he won the NL hitting title with a .330 mark. The senior loop's RBI crown went to an equally stunning overachiever, Phillies catcher Darren Daulton. A career .222 hitter, Daulton crushed NL hurlers for 27 homers and 109 RBI in 1992.

As Daulton, Sheffield, Martinez, and numerous other players burst forth with unforeseen great seasons in 1992, several longtime stalwarts fizzled, costing their teams dearly. Receiv-

ing little offensive help from Cal Ripken, Baltimore was unable to catch Toronto, which often during the season seemed ripe for the taking. Wade Boggs's plummeting batting average, which bottomed out at .259, paralleled Boston's drop through the AL East until the Sox wound up in the division basement. The 1991 NL home run and RBI champ, Howard Johnson, staggered after the Mets moved him to center field, tallying just 43 runs and seven homers. Injuries slowed Darryl Strawberry and Eric Davis, LA's prize offseason pickups, leading to the franchise's first cellar finish since 1905.

Atlanta and Pittsburgh again required seven games to settle NL honors. With the Pirates ahead 2-1 and just one out away from claiming the pennant in the LCS finale, Steel City fans were poised to celebrate their team's first World Series appearance in 13 years. Instead, little-used backup catcher Francisco Cabrera lined a two-run pinch single off reliever Stan Belinda to hand Atlanta a 3-2 triumph.

Cito Gaston's Toronto club needed no last-gasp heroics to dust favored Oakland in the ALCS. Led by second sacker Roberto Alomar, the LCS MVP and the club's leading batsman (.310 average) during the regular season, the Blue Jays, arguably the best ML team for the past decade, at long last proved they could win the big one. After dropping the A's in six games, Toronto used Alomar, Joe Carter (119 RBI), Dave Winfield (108 RBI), and the hot bat of catcher Pat Borders to suppress the Braves likewise in six contests. Despite suffering its second straight Series defeat, Atlanta demonstrated that its 1991 rise from worst to first was no fluke. With repeat 20-game-winner Tom Glavine again the mound linchpin and defending batting champ Terry Pendleton (.311) and Deion Sanders (.304) providing the firepower, Bobby Cox's club topped the ML with 98 victories.

But in the end 1992 belonged to one of the game's steadiest performers for many years, Dave Winfield, who was the active leader in both home runs and RBI that season. Winfield set several season marks for a player over age 40 and then avenged an abysmal showing in the 1981 fall classic, his only previous World Series appearance. It was Winfield's hit that won game six, the uphill 11-inning thriller that made Toronto the first world championship team from outside the United States.

1992

- Atlanta is first NL team since 1977-78 Dodgers to win back-to-back pennants.

- The Pirates win their third consecutive NL East pennant but miss NL flag when they lose game seven of NLCS in bottom of ninth.

- Seldom-used backup catcher Francisco Cabrera's two-out, two-run

pinch single hands Braves 3-2 win in game seven of NLCS.

- Toronto downs Oakland in six games in ALCS.

- Dave Winfield, at age 41, becomes oldest player to hit HR in WS play.

- Winfield's double gives the Blue Jays an electrifying 11-inning triumph in

game six to bring Canada its first world championship.

- Jack Morris pitches for his third different championship team in nine years, but fails to become the first hurler in history to bag a WS triumph with three different teams.

- Toronto catcher Pat Borders grabs the Series MVP prize.

Veteran Blue Jays catcher Pat Borders hit just .242 with 13 homers during the 1992 regular campaign, but he came alive in the postseason. Shown here singling in game three of the World Series, Borders batted .450 with three doubles and a key homer in the fall classic to win Most Valuable Player honors. A fine defensive catcher, Borders also hit .318 in the ALCS to spark the Blue Jays' victory over Oakland.

- Dodgers first sacker Eric Karros bags NL ROTY Award.

- The Padres acquire Gary Sheffield from the Brewers before the season. He rebounds from miserable .194 season with Milwaukee to win NL batting title with .330 mark.

- Sheffield is serious contender for Triple Crown before finishing first in batting, third in homers, and fifth in RBI.

- Barry Bonds wins NL MVP Award after leading majors with .624 SA.

- Unable to meet Bonds's salary demands, Pittsburgh in December helplessly watches him sign a multiyear contract with the Giants worth over $43 million.

- Bonds also tops majors with 127 walks and .456 OBP and leads NL in runs scored with 109.

- Fred McGriff of San Diego tops NL with 35 homers and places third in RBI with 104.

- Phillies catcher Darren Daulton surprises all by leading NL in RBI with 109.

Bud Selig

Selig Gains Top Post

After commissioner Fay Vincent resigned on September 7, 1992, Milwaukee Brewers owner Bud Selig became the game's commissioner pro tem. He oversaw baseball, with the assistance of the executive council. Growing animosity between owners and players, questions about future TV contracts, and disagreements among owners promised as many off-field as on-field headlines in the 1990s.

Brett: 4-For-4, 3,000 Hits

In 1992, Kansas City's George Brett became the 18th player to reach 3,000 career hits. After missing two games with an aching left shoulder, the 39-year-old DH reached the milestone September 30 in Anaheim. Entering that evening's game with 2,996 hits, Brett slashed two singles and a double in his first three at-bats before bouncing a single to right in the seventh against the Angels' Tim Fortugno to conclude his dramatic chase.

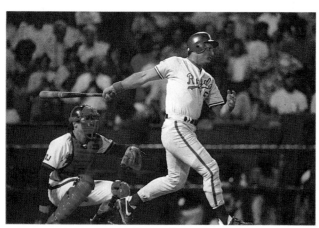

George Brett

Jeff Reardon

Reardon Nails Save Record

On June 15, 1992, at Fenway Park, Jeff Reardon shut down the Yankees to collect the 342nd save of his career. That evening, he passed Rollie Fingers and moved into first place on the all-time career saves list. Reardon collected 20 or more saves for the 11th consecutive season. In August, the veteran stopper was acquired by Atlanta and collected three wins and three saves in 14 games down the stretch for the pennant-winning Braves.

1992

- Daulton also clubs 27 homers and posts .524 SA, after hitting .196 in 1991.

- Andy Van Slyke of Pittsburgh tops NL with 45 doubles and is third in triples with 12.

- Atlanta third sacker Terry Pendleton ties Van Slyke for NL top spot in hits with 199.

- Pendleton, the defending NL batting titlist and MVP winner, hits .311 to pace pennant-winning Braves.

- Carlos Baerga of Cleveland is first second baseman in AL history with .300 average, 200 or more hits, 20 or more homers, and 100 or more RBI.

- Cleveland rookie Kenny Lofton sets AL frosh record with 66 stolen bases.

- Lofton loses AL ROTY to Brewers shortstop Pat Listach, whose 54 thefts also top the old AL rookie record.

- Marquis Grissom of the Expos paces majors with 78 stolen bases.

- Despite turning 38 two months after the season ends, shortstop Ozzie Smith of the Cards swipes 43 bases.

Barry Bonds

Rockies Draft

Rockies Acquire Nied

David Nied goes down in history as the first player chosen in the 1992 Expansion Draft. A 23-year-old righty pitcher from the Atlanta organization, Nied was tabbed by the Colorado Rockies to anchor their starting rotation after his impressive 3-0 showing with the Braves late in the 1992 season. The Rockies also drafted veteran Charlie Hayes, Joe Girardi, and Alex Cole in the first round.

Daulton Dominates

In 1992, 30-year-old Phillies catcher Darren Daulton finally enjoyed the big season many had predicted for him. Frequent injury problems had hampered Daulton in the past, but in 1992 he became the first NL player to win an RBI crown in fewer than 500 at-bats, pacing the league with 109. The first-time All-Star also finished high in the leader boards in home runs, walks, on-base percentage, and slugging percentage.

Darren Daulton

Bonds Bashes Way to MVP

Pittsburgh's Barry Bonds destroyed NL pitching in 1992 as he captured the MVP Award. He clubbed 34 homers, batted .311, swiped 39 bases, and paced the league in on-base percentage, slugging average, walks, and runs scored. He also hit .392 with 11 homers after September 1 to help the Pirates hold off the charging Montreal Expos. Bonds, trying to shake off his poor reputation for clutch performance, hit .261 with a key home run in the NLCS.

- Dennis Eckersley of the A's sweeps AL Cy Young and MVP Awards.

- In his tenth ML season, Van Slyke breaks .300 mark for the first time when his .324 BA is second in NL.

- Edgar Martinez becomes the first Mariner to win batting title when he raps .343.

- Martinez shares ML lead in doubles (46) with White Sox Frank Thomas.

- Chicago's Lance Johnson leads AL with 12 triples.

- Minnesota's Kirby Puckett tops majors with 210 hits.

- Gary Sheffield leads majors with 323 total bases.

- Puckett is AL's total base pace-setter with 313.

- Thomas once again leads AL in OBP with .439.

- Thomas's 122 walks tie Mickey Tettleton of Detroit for AL top spot.

- After winning '92 NL Cy Young Award, free agent Greg Maddux

Yount Nails Hit No. 3,000

Robin Yount, a Brewer since 1974, collected his 3,000th hit in Milwaukee County Stadium September 9. With 47,589 fans screaming encouragement, Yount lined a single to right-center in the seventh inning off Cleveland hurler Jose Mesa. At 36 years and 11 months, Yount was the third-youngest player to reach this historic plateau. The Milwaukee center fielder had also collected his 1,000th and 2,000th hits (in 1980 and 1986, respectively) off Indians' pitching.

Robin Yount

Maddux: 20-11, 2.18

The first Cub hurler to notch a 20-win season since Rick Reuschel in 1977, Chicago's Greg Maddux captured the 1992 NL Cy Young Award with a 20-11 mark. The durable right-hander finished third in the league in strikeouts, placed third in ERA, and led the NL in innings pitched for the second year in a row. Maddux topped 200 frames for the fifth straight season in 1992, winning 87 games in that span.

Greg Maddux

Sheffield Hits .330 to Win Crown

Acquired from Milwaukee for pitcher Ricky Bones just before the start of the 1992 season, 23-year-old Gary Sheffield starred at third base for the San Diego Padres. He won the NL batting title with a .330 mark, clouted 33 homers, drove in 100 runs, and piled up a league-best 323 total bases. He and teammate Fred McGriff (.286 average, 35 homers, 104 RBI) combined to form the league's top 3-4 combination for the third-place Padres.

Gary Sheffield

1992

signs huge multiyear contract with the Braves.

- Detroit's Cecil Fielder becomes second player in history to top ML in RBI three years in a row.

- Juan Gonzalez wins AL homer title with 43 dingers and sets Rangers four-bagger record in the process.

- After suffering the worst year of his career, Wade Boggs is not offered a contract by the Red Sox and signs with the Yankees as a free agent.

- Mark McGwire of the A's recovers from .201 BA in 1991 to finish second in AL in homers with 42.

- Three Twins tally more than 100 runs—Puckett (104), Chuck

Knoblauch (104), and Shane Mack (101).

- Three Tigers—Fielder, Rob Deer, and Mickey Tettleton—crack 32 or more home runs.

- Atlanta hurler Tom Glavine and Maddux tie for NL lead in victories with 20.

Dennis Eckersley

Dennis Eck-cellent Again

A 7-1 record, a 1.91 ERA, and an AL-best 51 saves earned Dennis Eckersley a special double salute—he won both the Cy Young and Most Valuable Player trophies. "Eck" failed to convert only three save opportunities during the regular season. While he enjoyed his sixth straight top season out of the bullpen, he unfortunately blew a critical one in game four of the ALCS as Toronto beat the A's and went to the World Series.

Juan Gonzalez

Gonzalez: 43 HRs at 22

Rangers center fielder Juan Gonzalez won the 1992 AL home run title at age 22. He became the youngest player to lead the junior circuit in four-baggers since Joe DiMaggio turned the trick for the Yankees in 1937. Gonzalez, who hit .260 with 109 RBI, slugged his 43rd homer on the season's final day to break a tie with Oakland's Mark McGwire and capture the crown.

Edgar Martinez

Martinez Puts M's on Map

Seattle third baseman Edgar Martinez became the first Mariner ever to lead the league in a Triple Crown category, batting .343 to pace the loop in 1992. His closest competitor, Kirby Puckett of Minnesota, finished 14 points behind. Martinez, who turned 29 before the season, was named the AL Player of the Month in both July and August. He also tied for the league lead with 46 doubles despite missing his final 19 games due to shoulder surgery.

- John Smoltz of the Braves edges New York's David Cone for NL strikeout crown, 215 to 214.

- Cone paces NL in walks with 82, lowest total ever by a senior loop leader.

- After helping Blue Jays win Series, Cone in December signs with Kansas City as a free agent.

- Greg Maddux paces majors with 268 innings.

- Terry Mulholland of Phils tops NL with 12 complete games.

- Jack McDowell of the White Sox leads AL in complete games with 13.

- Lee Smith of Cards leads NL with 43 saves.

- Eckersley tops majors with 51 saves.

- Seattle's David Fleming is voted AL's best rookie hurler after he bags 17 wins for last-place Mariners.

- Randy Johnson of Mariners tops majors with 241 strikeouts.

- Rollie Fingers and Tom Seaver are inducted into the Hall of Fame.

1992

NLCS

Sid Slides in Safely

With various Pirates, Braves, and 51,975 spellbound fans looking on, Atlanta first baseman Sid Bream slides in just ahead of Pittsburgh catcher Mike LaValliere's tag to score the winning run in game seven of the NLCS. Bream, who hit .261 with ten homers during the regular season, never possessed great running speed. He barely beat left fielder Barry Bonds's throw to score from second, sending Fulton County Stadium into a frenzy.

Roberto Alomar

Gant's Grand Slam Sinks Pirate Ship

Braves left fielder Ron Gant, who belted 17 homers during the 1992 regular season, added a key grand slam in game two of the NLCS to help defeat the Pittsburgh Pirates 13-5. Otis Nixon, Jeff Blauser, and David Justice scored ahead of Gant on the fifth-inning homer, which came against Pirate hurler Bob Walk. Gant's postseason heroics stopped here, however, as he slumped and was benched in favor of Deion Sanders in the World Series.

NLCS

Alomar Takes Eck Deep

With a 6-4, ninth-inning lead in game four of the ALCS and Dennis Eckersley on the mound, the Oakland A's figured they had things well in hand. However, Toronto's Devon White singled to lead off the frame, and Roberto Alomar followed with a game-tying home run to right. The All-Star second sacker celebrates the blast, which helped earn him the ALCS MVP Award. Alomar hit .423 for the Series.

1992

- Hurler Hal Newhouser and umpire Bill McGowan are elected to the Hall of Fame by the Veterans Committee.
- Second sacker Mickey Morandini of Phils performs first unassisted triple play in NL since 1927.
- Dodgers, after setting all-time record by avoiding cellar for 86 consecutive years, plummet to NL basement.
- The Red Sox finish in AL East basement for first time since division play began in 1969.
- Bill Swift of San Francisco leads majors with a 2.08 ERA.
- Jack Morris of Toronto and Kevin Brown of Texas tie for AL lead in wins with 21.
- After seemingly selling the Giants to a Tampa Bay group, owner Bob Lurie is forced to take a lesser offer that will keep team in San Francisco.
- Fay Vincent, under unrelenting pressure, steps down as commissioner.
- Cincinnati owner Marge Schott faces barrage of accusations that she is racist after season closes.

Flag Flap

Flag Mishap Sparks Flap

In 1992, with a Canadian team competing in the fall classic for the first time, an international incident was almost certain to take place. Before the start of the second game of the World Series in Atlanta, the U.S. color guard inadvertently carried an upside-down Canadian flag onto the field. Though no offense was meant by anyone, the error rankled some Canadians, who only found solace in the Jays' 5-4 victory that evening.

Smith Clears the Bases

Lonnie Smith is congratulated by Braves teammates Dave Justice *(left),* Deion Sanders *(right),* and Terry Pendleton *(obscured)* after his grand slam off Jack Morris in the fifth inning of game five of the Series. The homer broke open a close game and gave the Braves a 7-2 win. Smith, playing in his fifth fall classic, hit the first World Series grand slam by a National Leaguer since Ken Boyer's clout in 1964.

World Series

Winfield's Hit Wins Series

Dave Winfield

Blue Jays slugger Dave Winfield points to his ecstatic teammates who are celebrating his 11th-inning double off Atlanta's Charlie Leibrandt in game six of the Series. At age 40, the DH sparked the Blue Jays with 26 homers, 108 RBI, and a .290 average during the regular season, and homered twice against Oakland in the ALCS.

White Gyps Justice

Devon White

In the fourth inning of game three, Toronto center fielder Devon White made a catch many called one of the best in World Series history. The speedy White raced to the wall and made a leaping, over-the-shoulder catch to rob Dave Justice of a two-run double. White then fired the ball back to the infield as the Jays nearly turned a triple play.

- Florida Marlins and Colorado Rockies are accepted as new franchises for 1993 season.

- Braves mound prospect David Nied is first player chosen in Expansion Draft when Rockies select him.

- Baltimore inaugurates its new stadium, Oriole Park at Camden Yards.

- George Brett of Royals and Robin Yount of Brewers both collect their 3,000th hits in 1992.

- Ozzie Smith wins his 14th straight Gold Glove.

- Jeff Reardon breaks Rollie Fingers's record of 341 career saves and finishes campaign with 357 saves.

- Lee Smith moves into second place on all-time list with 355 saves.

- Rickey Henderson becomes first player in ML history to garner 1,000 career stolen bases as he finishes 1992 campaign with 1,042.

- Deion Sanders of Braves becomes first MLer to play in a World Series game and an NFL game in same week.

BLUE JAYS PERCHED ON TOP AGAIN

In the fall of 1992, the Giants franchise seemed headed for the Tampa-St. Petersburg area. Instead, a new group of owners salvaged the club for San Francisco, then hired Dusty Baker to manage it. When the Bay Area team also procured Barry Bonds, the 1992 NL MVP, from the Pirates as a $43 million free agent, Candlestick Park, the Giants' much maligned home, suddenly became a hot ticket.

Behind Bonds's booming bat, the Giants led the NL West defending-champion Atlanta Braves by a wide margin deep into the summer. Meanwhile, the three-time National League East champion Pirates, missing Bonds's long-ball artillery, also lagged far off the pace. The Bucs' thunder was usurped by the Phillies, yet another team to surge to the fore in the 1990s after finishing last the previous year.

In the season's final week the Phils clinched their first division crown since 1983, managing to hold off a furious charge by the Montreal Expos, but the situation in the NL West was still unresolved. After leading the Braves all summer, the Giants were passed in early September.

But then the Giants surged again. On the last Friday morning of the season the two foes were deadlocked at 101-58. But while the Braves played a three-game set at home that weekend against the expansion Colorado Rockies, the Giants' schedule called for a finish in Los Angeles.

The Braves routinely won their first two contests against the hapless Rockies, and the Giants unexpectedly kept pace. If both were victorious again on the last Sunday of the season, the Giants had a huge advantage, having won the right to host the division playoff game, if necessary.

But San Francisco's Cinderella story ended unhappily. The Braves decked the Rockies in their finale, 5-3, to set a new franchise record with 104 wins. Giants players, hearing the final score even before their game started in Dodger Stadium, could not rise to the must-win situation. San Francisco's starter, 21-year-old rookie Salomon Torres, got into deep water early, and Baker's bullpen, exhausted by overuse in the stretch, had no one to bail out Torres. Buoyed by Mike Piazza's two home runs, the Dodgers blasted the Giants' dream, 12-1.

In the AL, Toronto and Chicago had both clinched their respective divisions long before the final Sunday. Chicago whipped home eight games ahead of the Texas Rangers, and Toronto presented Cito Gaston with his third division crown by a seven-game margin over the New York Yankees.

Toronto and Atlanta were prohibitive favorites to meet for the second straight time in the World Series. The Blue Jays did their part, winning the ALCS in six rounds, but the Braves found the road to a return engagement barricaded. After taking a 2-1 lead in games, Atlanta skipper Bobby Cox helplessly watched his vaunted offense spin its wheels against the Phils. Spearheaded by center fielder Lenny Dykstra and pitcher Curt Schilling, the Phils put the Braves away in six games.

The Blue Jays needed just six games to grab their second consecutive World Series. Joe Carter's three-run homer in the bottom of the ninth in game six lifted the Jays to a come-from-behind 8-6 win over Phils closer Mitch "Wild Thing" Williams. Williams also dropped game four, a 15-14 donnybrook that broke the 20th century mark for the most runs in a postseason game.

Paul Molitor, the AL hit leader in 1993, was named the Series MVP, but Dykstra could easily have won the award in a losing cause. Dykstra's dazzling fall showing culminated a brilliant season. His 143 runs in 1993 were the most by any NL player since another Phils outfielder, Chuck Klein, crossed the plate 152 times in 1932.

1993

- Phillies capture their fifth pennant in franchise history—their first since 1983.

- Blue Jays defeat White Sox in six games in ALCS.

- In a bid to win their third straight pennant, Braves instead fall to Phillies in six games in NLCS.

- When the Phillies and Blue Jays tally 29 runs in game four of the 1993 World Series, a new 20th century record is set for the most runs in a postseason game. Mitch Williams is the loser in this 15-14 slugfest.

- Toronto becomes first team since 1977-78 Yankees to win consecutive world championships.

- Blue Jays free-agent acquisition Paul Molitor bags World Series MVP Award.

- Danny Jackson of the Phils becomes the third pitcher in history to start a WS game with three different teams.

- Jack McDowell captures AL Cy Young Award with a 22-10 record. He is AL's sole 20-game winner.

Media members battle to interview Series hero Joe Carter as he is lofted skyward in the SkyDome by his jubilant Toronto teammates. Moments earlier, Carter's last-ditch three-run homer in game six had made the Blue Jays the first club since the 1977-78 Yankees to win two consecutive world championships.

- Free-agent acquisition Greg Maddux leads the Braves and the majors with a 2.36 ERA.

- Maddux also paces NL in innings pitched (267) and CGs (eight) and is third in strikeouts with 197.

- For his stellar work, Maddux earns his second straight Cy Young Award.

- Barry Bonds posts a .677 SA, highest by an NL player since 1948, when Stan Musial slugged .702.

- Bonds, the NL MVP, leads NL in homers (46) and RBI (123).

- Colorado's Andres Galarraga is the first player on a first-year expansion team to win batting title.

- Mike Piazza of the Dodgers breaks records for a rookie catcher with 35 homers, 112 RBI, and .561 SA.

- Randy Myers of the Cubs sets a new NL record with 53 saves.

- Braves become the first 20th century team to blank an opponent for an entire season when they go 13-0 versus Colorado.

Big Hurt Named AL MVP

Frank Thomas reached career highs in home runs (41) and RBI (128) in 1993, sparking the White Sox to their first division title since 1983. After pacing the AL in both walks and on-base percentage the previous two years, Thomas "sank" to 112 walks and a .426 OBP (fourth in AL) in 1993. His unmatched combination of power and patience earned him the AL MVP Award.

Frank Thomas

Johnson is K King

Randy Johnson matured in a big way in 1993. The 6'10" southpaw's .704 winning percentage was second only to Jimmy Key's in the AL. Johnson's 304 strikeouts, however, were in a class by themselves. His continued success caused the Expos to regret all the more the 1989 deal that sent him to the Mariners.

Randy Johnson

Barry Bonds

Bonds: Like Father, Like Son

Barry Bonds accomplished something his famous father, Bobby, never did when he topped 40 homers in 1993, finishing with 43. Bobby's peak mark was 39 in 1973. Barry also set a new Bonds record with 123 RBI in 1993. The elder and younger Bonds hold virtually every father-and-son career slugging record. In 1993, Barry won his third MVP Award in four years and his fourth straight Gold Glove.

1993

- Phils are the third team in three years to win a pennant after finishing in division basement the previous season.

- The A's are the first team since the 1915 Philadelphia Athletics to finish in last place after having the best record in their league the previous year.

- Kenny Lofton breaks his own one-year-old Cleveland record when he swipes 70 bases.

- Lenny Dykstra of the Phils tops NL in hits with 194. His 143 runs are the most by an NL player since 1932.

- Anthony Young's record 27 straight losses break Cliff Curtis's old mark.

- Sparky Anderson becomes first manager since Connie Mack to manage 24 consecutive years in majors.

- Blue Jays John Olerud, Paul Molitor, and Roberto Alomar finish 1-2-3 in AL batting race. Toronto is first team since 1893 Phillies to have its loop's top three hitters.

Maddux Wins NL Cy Young

Not since Catfish Hunter in 1975 has a free-agent hurler had a better year with his new club than free-agent-signee Greg Maddux did with the Braves in 1993. The former Cub treated his new employer to his second consecutive 20-win season. Maddux also led the NL in ERA (2.36), innings (267), and complete games (eight) en route to capturing his second straight Cy Young Award.

Dave Winfield

Winfield: Hit No. 3,000

Dave Winfield accepts accolades at the Metrodome after tapping Oakland's Dennis Eckersley for his 3,000th career hit—a ninth-inning RBI single on September 16. In 1993 Winfield also set a new ML record for the most home runs by a player over age 40 when he ripped 21 four-baggers, giving him 47 dingers since turning 40. Winfield finished the season with 1,786 RBI, the most by any active player.

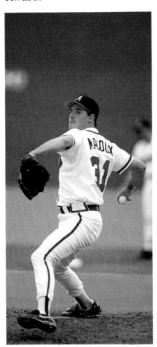

Greg Maddux

Piazza Unanimous ROTY

NL Rookie of the Year Mike Piazza showcases the swing that made him the best-hitting rookie catcher in history in 1993. The Dodger maskman collected 174 hits and 317 total bases, just one short of Yogi Berra's all-time single-season mark by a catcher. Piazza's 317 total bases did tie him, however, with an earlier Dodgers backstopping star, Roy Campanella, for the NL record. Piazza was the 13th Dodger to be named Rookie of the Year.

Mike Piazza

- Dykstra (129), Darren Daulton (117), and John Kruk (111) are first trio of teammates since 1949 to garner 100 walks in a season.

- Reggie Jackson is the only new selection to the Hall of Fame in 1993.

- Molitor leads the majors in hits with 211.

- Carlos Baerga is the first second sacker ever to collect 200 or more hits, 20 or more homers, and 100 or more RBI two seasons in a row.

- Lance Johnson of White Sox tops AL with 14 triples. He is the first player ever to win two three-bagger crowns in seasons in which he failed to hit a single home run.

- John Olerud's 54 doubles are the most in the majors since 1978, when Hal McRae also had 54.

- Florida's Chuck Carr sets a record for the most steals by a player on a first-year expansion team when he tops NL with 58 thefts.

- San Francisco is the first team since 1980 Orioles to fail to win a division

Tim Salmon

Kenny Lofton

Lofton Swipes 70

Kenny Lofton is the reason that someday Eddie Taubensee may become a footnote in the record book for being involved in one of the most one-sided trades in history. Cleveland swapped Taubensee, a career backup catcher, to the Astros in December 1991 for Lofton. In 1993 Lofton had the finest season of any Indians center fielder since Larry Doby as he stole a Tribe-record 70 bases and garnered a .325 average.

Salmon Named AL ROTY

Early in the 1993 season Tim Salmon was over-shadowed by fellow Angels rookie teammate, J.T. Snow. But by the end of the campaign, Snow was ticketed to begin the 1994 season in the minors while Salmon took home the AL Rookie of the Year trophy. Along with his 31 dingers (a new Angels yearling record), Salmon hit .283 with 95 RBI and tied for the American League lead in outfield assists (12).

Randy Myers

Myers's 53 Saves Set New NL Record

Normally a reliever on a team that struggles to break .500 has little to show in the way of individual stats, but in 1993 Cubs bullpenner Randy Myers was a stunning exception. Though Chicago posted just an 84-78 won-lost mark, Myers set a new National League record for saves when he nailed down 53 of the Cubs' 84 victories. The hard-throwing southpaw averaged more than a strikeout per inning with a 3.11 ERA in 1993.

1993

title despite posting 100 or more victories. The Giants' 103 victories are the most by a division or league runner-up since the 162-game schedule was adopted.

- The Expos' 94 wins are one short of the club record of 95, set in 1979.

- Phils top NL in runs (877), while the Giants lead the loop in BA (.276).

- Atlanta posts far and away the lowest staff ERA in majors at 3.14.

- Maddux's mound teammate Tom Glavine ties San Francisco's John Burkett for NL lead in wins (22).

- Seattle's Randy Johnson paces majors with 308 strikeouts, the most by an AL southpaw since 1971, when Mickey Lolich also fanned 308.

- The NL strikeout king is Jose Rijo of Cincinnati, with 227.

- Jeff Montgomery of the Royals and Toronto stopper Duane Ward tie for AL save crown with 45.

- Kevin Appier of the Royals wins American League ERA crown with a 2.56 mark.

Lee Smith

Smith Becomes First to Ring Up 400 Career Saves

By the close of the 1993 season this hurler was headed for the Hall of Fame even though he possessed only a 67-78 career won-lost record. That's because Lee Smith in 1993 also became the first pitcher ever to collect 400 career saves. Smith's milestone save came with the Yankees, who acquired him late in the year for a stretch drive that failed to materialize.

Galarraga Hits .370

The Cardinals saw no reason to retain Andres Galarraga when he hit just .243 in 1992 after tumbling to .219 the year before. But the first sacker regained his old form and more when he joined the expansion Rockies. The nine-year veteran hiked his career average a phenomenal 12 points, from .267 to .279, ripping NL hurlers to the tune of .370 and garnering the senior loop batting crown.

Andres Galarraga

Sammy Sosa

Sosa Joins 30/30 Club

Like Andres Galarraga, Sammy Sosa in 1993 jolted the many pundits who'd given up on him. After collecting just 37 homers in his previous four seasons combined, Sosa hammered 33 round-trippers in 1993, his first full season playing in the friendly confines of Wrigley Field. By combining his 33 dingers with 36 steals, Sosa became the Cubs' first-ever 30/30 performer.

- Jimmy Key, the Yankees' most important off-season free-agent signing, tops AL with a .750 winning percentage.

- Dave Winfield collects his 3,000th career hit off Jose Mesa of the Indians.

- San Diego's Phil Plantier sets an all-time record with 100 RBI on just 111 hits. His .240 BA is one of the lowest ever by a player with 100-plus RBI.

- For the 12th straight season, Jesse Orosco makes at least 45 mound appearances.

- Colorado's Andres Galarraga's .370 BA is the best ever by a first-year expansion player and the highest in the NL since 1987.

- Galarraga's .602 SA sets record for a player on a first-year expansion team.

- Playing half their games in "Mile High" Denver, the Rockies produce the worst ERA in majors (5.41).

- Albert Belle's 129 RBI give Cleveland its second AL RBI leader since 1965.

- Frank Thomas bags AL MVP Award.

Controversy in Chicago: Bo Starts, Bell Benched

George Bell of the White Sox shakes hands with Toronto hurler Dave Stewart prior to game three of the 1993 ALCS at SkyDome. Pointedly avoiding eye contact with his Sox teammate is Bo Jackson. At the beginning of the championship series, Jackson was named the White Sox's starting designated hitter by manager Gene Lamont, bringing howls of protest from Bell, who had served in the role all season. Jackson went 0-for-10 in the series, causing fans as well as pundits to question the wisdom of Lamont's decision.

ALCS

Phils Down Braves in Ten

John Kruk is greeted *(from left to right)* by Phils teammates Wes Chamberlain, Lenny Dykstra, and Darren Daulton as he crosses the plate with the winning run in the tenth inning of the opening game of the 1993 NLCS. After doubling earlier in the inning, Kruk was chased home by sub third sacker Kim Batiste's single to left. An errant throw by Batiste had allowed the Braves to score the tying run in the top of the ninth inning, sending the game into extra innings.

NLCS

Braves Bow Out to Phils

Braves shortstop Jeff Blauser strives to dodge Phillies catcher Darren Daulton's tag in this moment of action from the 1993 NLCS. After plating 14 runs in game two and nine more in game three, Atlanta bats suddenly went dead. The Braves scored just seven runs in the final three contests to bow out 4-2 after holding a 2-1 lead in games.

1993

- Juan Gonzalez of Texas repeats as AL homer champ with 46. He also bags slugging crown with a .632 SA.

- On September 7, Mark Whiten of the Cards clubs four homers and 12 RBI, tying Jim Bottomley's all-time single-game RBI record.

- The Cubs' Sammy Sosa joins 30/30 club with 33 homers and 36 swipes.

- Cal Ripken ties a loop record for shortstops when he leads AL in assists for the seventh time.

- Bo Jackson, playing with an artificial hip after missing all of 1992, hits .232 for the White Sox in 85 games.

- Giants third sacker Matt Williams, after a dismal season in 1992, clouts 38 homers and logs 110 RBI.

- Williams and Barry Bonds rip 84 homers, most by a pair of Giants since the days of Mays and McCovey.

- Bonds wins his second straight NL MVP Award, vindicating the Giants for making him the most expensive free-agent signee to date.

- Tim Salmon of the Angels parlays his 31 homers to win AL ROTY honors.

World Series

Molitor Bags Series MVP Award

Series MVP Paul Molitor pokes yet another of his 12 hits against the Phillies. When the bat of the Blue Jays designated hitter came out of the SkyDome starting gate smoking, Toronto pilot Cito Gaston rearranged his offense, installing Molitor at third base in place of Ed Sprague once the Series moved to Philadelphia for games three through five. Molitor collected 22 total bases to go with his 12 hits for a .917 slugging average.

Williams Blasted in Series

Mitch Williams can't explain to reporters what went wrong. Neither could anyone else, for that matter. Williams bagged 43 saves on a 3.34 ERA during the regular season in 1993 and then continued to shine in the NLCS, racking up two saves and a 1.69 ERA in four outings. His World Series line, however, showed a 20.25 ERA and two losses in three appearances, including the disastrous finale.

Mitch Williams

Carter Celebrates Series Win

Joe Carter jumps for joy as he heads toward home with the run that won the 1993 World Series. Carter's three-run homer off Mitch Williams scored Rickey Henderson and Paul Molitor ahead of him and gave Toronto a come-from-behind 8-6 win. The Series featured a string of high-scoring games sandwiched around Curt Schilling's 2-0 shutout gem in game five that saved the Phils for one more round and set up Carter's heroics.

Joe Carter

- Piazza's overwhelming rookie year brings him NL's top yearling honor.
- The Indians play their final game in Cleveland Stadium, the Tribe's home since 1932.
- For the first time in team history, Cleveland draws over two million fans both at home and on the road.

- The Pirates, in pursuit of their fourth straight division title, instead plummet to 12 games below .500.
- Dodgers shortstop Jose Offerman leads all NL performers in errors with 37.
- Lee Smith becomes the first hurler to collect 400 career saves when he finishes the season with 401.

- Dodgers center fielder Brett Butler leads NL in singles for a record fourth straight season.
- Two Cleveland relievers, Tim Crews and Steve Olin, are killed in a preseason boating accident.
- Gonzalez is the first player since Jim Rice in 1977-78 to win consecutive AL home run crowns.

Jacobs Field

Tribe Gets New Home

Cleveland unveiled beautiful Jacobs Field in 1994. Named after owner Richard Jacobs, the Indians' new home was deliberately designed to look like an old-time park, and for the first time in 40 years the Tribe also had the look of old. A perennial contender prior to the mid-1950s, Cleveland was in the process of making its first serious pennant bid since 1959 when the strike halted the Indians' playoff hopes. Jacobs Field was an integral part of the renaissance the city of Cleveland underwent in the mid-'90s and a contributing factor to renewed fan interest in the Tribe.

Bagwell Bags NL MVP

Jeff Bagwell, whose left wrist was broken by a pitch on August 10, had been having the best year of any major leaguer prior to the strike and his injury. Bagwell had been mustering himself for a drive to become the NL's first Triple Crown winner since Ducky Medwick in 1937. The Astros star had to content himself with the NL RBI title (116) and a .368 batting average, second in the NL.

Jeff Bagwell

Thomas Wins AL MVP

Frank Thomas combined awesome power, a high average, and excellent strike-zone judgement on his way to his second straight AL MVP Award in 1994. He had hoped to collect a World Series championship ring as well. The Sox were locked in a tight three-way race with Cleveland and Kansas City for the top spot in the AL Central at strike time but counted on prevailing with the best pitching staff in the American League.

Frank Thomas

1994

- Ken Griffey Jr. tops AL with 40 homers but has just 90 RBI, the fewest ever by a 40-homer man.

- Griffey's .674 SA sets a new Seattle franchise record.

- Chuck Knoblauch tops majors with 45 doubles and is on course to approach Earl Webb's season doubles record when the strike stops action.

- Lance Johnson of White Sox paces majors with 14 triples.

- Kenny Lofton of Cleveland leads the majors with 60 stolen bases.

- Twins center fielder Kirby Puckett collects 112 RBI to top AL.

- Cleveland's Albert Belle hits .357 with 36 homers and 101 RBI, trailing

Thomas's heroics by a narrow margin.

- Baltimore's Lee Smith heads majors in saves with 33.

- John Hudek of Houston becomes first pitcher ever to be selected for the All-Star Game before he posts his first big-league win, and in fact completes 1994 season still winless.

Paul O'Neill

O'Neill Bats .359 for NY

Thanks to the strike, Yankee Paul O'Neill became the first ALer since Billy Goodman in 1950 to win a batting crown despite playing fewer than 100 games in the field. O'Neill was also the first player since Dale Alexander (1932) to bag an AL bat title with fewer than 400 at-bats. His .359 mark was the best in 40 years by a Yankee.

Cone Captures Cy Young

After leading the majors in total strikeouts from 1990 through 1992, David Cone decided to concentrate on control and rely on his defense in '94. As a result, he took home his first Cy Young Award. Taking command of his once-fiery temper, Cone had streaks of eight straight wins and 29 consecutive scoreless innings in 1994. He averaged seven hits, seven strikeouts, and less than three walks per nine innings. He was untouchable on May 22, when he tossed a one-hit shutout against the Angels.

David Cone

Tony Gwynn

Gwynn's Quest Cut Short

Were it not for the strike in 1994, Tony Gwynn of the Padres might have been the first NLer since 1930 to bat .400. Instead, Gwynn ended the season hitting .394. Matt Williams might also have become the first NLer to hit 60 home runs, and a host of other senior loop records might have toppled as well. Craig Biggio and Larry Walker (44 doubles each) could have challenged Earl Webb's major-league record of 67. Only Hack Wilson's record of 190 RBI remained, as always, beyond assault.

- Jason Bere of the White Sox tops majors with an .857 winning percentage (12-2).

- Yankees lefty Jimmy Key collects the most wins in majors with 17.

- When he finishes third in ERA at 2.94 and second in wins with 16, David Cone of the Royals wins AL Cy Young Award.

- The National League Cy Young Award winner is the Braves' Greg Maddux (16-6, 1.56).

- Seattle's Randy Johnson is the only ML hurler to top 200 Ks with 204.

- Bret Saberhagen of Kansas City allows only 13 bases on balls in 177 innings pitched.

- Andy Benes of the Padres leads NL with 189 Ks despite just six wins.

- Oakland's Steve Ontiveros wins AL ERA crown (2.65).

- Dwight Gooden of the Mets is suspended on June 18, 1994, for violating his drug aftercare program for the second time.

John Valentin

Williams on Pace to Break HR Record

Matt Williams was a heavy favorite before the strike interruption to break the NL single-season home run record of 56. Whether he would also have broken Roger Maris's major league single-season mark we'll never know, as he wound up with 43 dingers on the shortened year. The strike-abbreviated season also contributed to Williams being the first NL player since 1973 to club 40 or more homers with fewer than 100 RBI.

Matt Williams

Mondesi Monstrous in '94

The Dodgers continued their phenomenal streak of producing NL ROTY winners. The latest, out-fielder Raul Mondesi, hit .306 with 16 homers in '93. Mondesi's 42 games and 86 at-bats in 1992 would have excluded him from rookie status at one time. Shoeless Joe Jackson's .408 BA in his first full year, for example, is not considered the rookie record because he had previously played 30 games in the majors.

Raul Mondesi

Valentin Turns Three

When he hit .316 in just his second full big-league season, Boston's John Valentin awakened observers to the fact that he might one day be a treasure. Valentin also displayed good power, finishing second on the Red Sox in slugging average. On July 8, 1994, Valentin became the second player in big-league history to perform an unassisted triple play and hit a home run in the same inning.

1994

- Kevin Mitchell of the Reds, Julio Franco of the White Sox, and Shane Mack of the Twins, all .300 hitters in 1994, opt during the strike to play in Japan in 1995.

- Bob Hamelin of the Royals wins AL Rookie of the Year Award on the strength of his 24 homers and .599 slugging average.

- Boston's John Valentin becomes the second player in big-league history to perform an unassisted triple play and hit a home run in the same inning.

- Damage to Kingdome roof forces M's to finish season on the road.

- Cleveland ties Yankees for highest AL team BA at .290.

- Alan Trammell and Lou Whitaker of the Tigers are keystone partners for the 18th straight year, a big-league record.

- Jim Deshaies of the Twins has a 7.39 ERA, the worst since World War II by an ERA crown qualifier.

- Chicago's Frank Thomas hits 38 homers in 113 games, leads the AL in

Rogers Perfect in Nine

Texas catcher Ivan Rodriguez and first sacker Will Clark hug pitcher Kenny Rogers after Rogers hurled the first perfect game in Rangers history—and only the 14th in baseball history—on July 28, shutting down California at The Ballpark in Arlington. Rogers's perfecto was the highlight of both his and his team's otherwise rocky season. Despite winding up ten games below .500, the Rangers were nonetheless poised for their first postseason appearance when the strike dashed their hopes.

Kenny Rogers

Griffey Sets M's Records

Ken Griffey Jr. seemed destined for a super season in 1994. After collecting 20 home runs in his first 42 games—matching Mickey Mantle's '56 start—he appeared on the cover of *Sports Illustrated* a single-season-record three times. A mid-year slump followed by the strike held down Junior's numbers, but he still set Mariners franchise records for home runs (40) and slugging average (.674).

Ken Griffey Jr.

SA (.729), and collects his second consecutive MVP Award.

- Marvin Freeman of the Rockies goes 10-2 to lead NL with an .833 winning percentage.

- Carlos Baerga is unable to extend his record two-year streak of 20 homers, 200 hits, and 100 RBI by a second sacker because of the strike.

- Raul Mondesi of the Dodgers wins NL ROTY Award when he hits .306.

- Bo Jackson announces his retirement after batting .279 for the Angels.

- On July 18, Kenny Rogers of Texas becomes first AL hurler since 1984 to throw a perfect game, beating the Angels 4-0.

- On June 29, Giants outfielder Darren Lewis's record of 392 consecutive errorless games comes to an end.

- Steve Howe continues his bizarre career by posting a perfect 3-0 record for the Yankees with a 1.60 ERA and a club-leading 15 saves.

- Although he has yet to win more than 16 games in a season, Dennis

Winless Hudek an All-Star

Rookie Astros relief ace John Hudek in 1994 became the first pitcher ever to be selected for an All-Star Game before achieving his first major league win. Hudek finished the 1994 campaign still searching for his initial big-league victory but compiled a club-high 16 saves.

John Hudek

Greg Maddux

Maddux Earns Third Consecutive Cy Young

Atlanta's Greg Maddux became the first hurler ever to win the Cy Young Award three years in a row. Maddux was clearly the best pitcher in either league. There was little need to vote: Maddux led the league in ERA (1.56), complete games (ten), and innings pitched (202) and tied for the lead in wins (16) in the strike-shortened season.

Hamelin Cops AL ROTY

Kansas City fans called him the "Hammer." Bob Hamelin earned that nickname by becoming the team's top slugger as a 1994 rookie and batting .282 with 65 RBI. The burly slugger carried off the AL Rookie of the Year prize on the basis of his 24 homers, but most veteran baseball experts believed Cleveland outfielder Manny Ramirez was by far the most promising junior circuit frosh.

Bob Hamelin

1994

- Martinez of Cleveland wins in double digits for the 16th time in his career.
- Harold Baines homers in double digits for 15th straight season, longest current such streak in ML.
- Ryne Sandberg retires abruptly on June 13, sacrificing his multimillion-dollar salary because he feels he can no longer play at his usual high level.

- Steve Carlton is elected to the Hall of Fame by the BWAA, and the Veterans' Committee selects Leo Durocher and Phil Rizzuto.
- Padres are the only ML team to fail to draw a million, finishing with a 953,857 attendance figure.
- Albert Belle is suspended for three games when a White Sox claim that

he used an illegally corked bat against them is upheld.
- Dennis Eckersley ends season with 482 career wins and saves, most by any pitcher except Cy Young. Eck also continues to be one of the few pitchers with more than 2,000 career strikeouts and fewer than 200 career wins.

1994

Fehr-Well to 1994 Season

Flanked by Tigers slugger Cecil Fielder on his right and Braves lefty ace Tom Glavine on his left, Players Association chieftain Donald Fehr gives the rank and file the latest piece of bad news on the baseball strike. Many observers believed the strike put Fehr in over his head. Even more people believed that, given the mercurial mentality of the owners Fehr was matched against, even Disraeli would have been in over his head.

Donald Fehr

Ryne Sandberg

Sandberg Steps Down

Ryne Sandberg set baseball on its ear when he announced his retirement at a press conference on June 13, claiming he no longer felt he was earning his multimillion-dollar salary. Sandberg stepped down with the highest career fielding average in history by a second baseman as well as 245 career home runs, the most by any National League middle infielder except Joe Morgan since World War II.

Tiger Duo Still Turns Two

On September 9, 1977, Alan Trammell *(left)* and Lou Whitaker *(right)* formed the Tigers keystone combo for the first time. They were still keystone mates in 1994, shattering all records for longevity by a shortstop/second-base teammate duo. Trammell's and Whitaker's endurance mark notwithstanding, the Tigers finished last in the AL East in 1994—albeit with a better record than Texas, the AL West leader when the strike shut down the season.

Alan Trammell, Lou Whitaker

- Tiger Cecil Fielder's string of four straight 100-plus RBI seasons is broken when the strike leaves him ten short.

- A second suspension for substance abuse in June requires Gooden to sit out entire 1995 season.

- Thomas tops majors with a .487 OBP. At the close of the '94, his career OBP is third in history only to Babe Ruth's and Ted Williams's.

- Giants sign free-agent problem child Darryl Strawberry after a torn Achilles tendon kayoes right fielder Willie McGee for season.

- Cubs announcer and Hall of Famer Harry Caray celebrates 50 years in broadcasting.

- Eddie Murray is the only MLer to play 100 or more games in both the 1981 and '94 strike seasons.

- White Sox sign basketball megastar Michael Jordan to a minor-league contract.

- Jordan hits .202 with three homers and 51 RBI in 436 at-bats for the Double-A Birmingham Bulls.

BRAVES PREVAIL IN PLAYOFF FREE-FOR-ALL

With the strike that halted the 1994 campaign still unresolved when spring training opened in 1995, major-league owners laid plans to use replacement players. Alarmed, the striking players finally agreed to return to work without a new labor contract, but the protracted negotiations delayed the start of the season until late April and abbreviated the schedule to 144 games.

Baseball moguls, instead of working to heal the wounds left by the strike, immediately opened new ones when their ill-conceived postseason playoff and TV arrangements were announced. Unlike in every other professional sport, the plan offered no advantages to a team with the best regular-season record. Even more disturbing to fans, games for the four first-round playoff series were played at the same time, with games broadcast only regionally.

Despite these obstacles, the 1995 season proved an aesthetic, if not financial, success, as the two best teams in the majors snaked through the labyrinthine playoff structure to meet in the World Series.

The American League entry, for the first time since 1954, was the Cleveland Indians. Buoyed by Albert Belle's record slugging feats—and ample support from Manny Ramirez, Jim Thome, Carlos Baerga, and Kenny Lofton—the Tribe ripped through the regular season, winning 100 games and topping the AL

Central by a whopping 30 lengths. Their reward was to draw the AL East-champion Boston Red Sox, owners of the AL's second-best record, in the first round of the playoffs. Still, Cleveland breezed to a three-game sweep.

The other AL division playoff paired the wildcard New York Yankees and the Seattle Mariners. The Cinderella Mariners had caught the Angels in the final week, forcing a one-game shootout for the division crown. Strikeout king Randy Johnson won it for the Mariners—and then won game three of the division playoff to avert a Yankees sweep. The Mariners took games four and five as well, winning the finale 6-5 on AL batting champ Edgar Martinez's two-run double in the bottom of the 11th. The victory dubbed Lou Piniella's Mariners "The Refuse to Lose Boys."

Although Seattle won the opener of the ALCS, its bubble then burst when Cleveland's supe-

rior pitchers—Dennis Martinez and Orel Hershiser especially—asserted themselves. The Indians won in six.

The NL playoffs offered little drama. The Reds swept Los Angeles in the opening playoff round, while Atlanta received a fight from wildcard Colorado before prevailing in four games. Like the Indians, the Braves were not given home-field advantage in the LCS despite having the top record in the NL. However, the Braves took only the minimum four contests to squelch Cincinnati in the NLCS.

In the World Series, the Braves opened at Fulton County Stadium, and their raucous home crowd helped spur them to victories in two straight one-run pitchers' battles. Atlanta lost two one-run games in Cleveland but sandwiched them around a 5-2 win in game four behind pitcher Steve Avery. Bobby Cox's crew returned to Georgia up 3-2 in games.

Game six matched Tom Glavine and Dennis Martinez. Elbow trouble sidelined Martinez in the fifth inning, and in the following frame David Justice rifled a drive over the right-field barrier off Tribe reliever Jim Poole. Justice's solo shot held up, as Glavine and closer Mark Wohlers hurled a combined one-hitter. The Braves' crisp 1-0 triumph made them the first team to win a world title representing three different cities—Boston (1914), Milwaukee (1957), and Atlanta.

1995

- The opening of the season is delayed, and the season abbreviated to 144 games, because of the players' strike.

- Cleveland goes 100-44 to win the AL Central by 30 games.

- In the AL East, both first-place Boston and the wildcard Yankees make the playoffs.

- Seattle wins the AL West in a one-game playoff with California after finishing the regular season tied with the Angels.

- In the first year that the best-of-five division playoffs are instituted, the Mariners-Yankees series is the only one to go the full five games.

- Edgar Martinez doubles home the tying and winning runs in the bottom of the 11th to give Seattle a 6-5 comeback victory in the finale of its division playoff with the Yankees.

- Cleveland needs only three games to humble Boston in a division playoff pitting the two teams with the best records in the AL.

David Justice hoists his arms triumphantly after the final out in game six of the 1995 World Series. The Atlanta right fielder's solo homer in the sixth inning represented all the scoring in the postseason finale. The Braves'. victory brought the Georgia capital its first postseason championship in any professional sport after numerous failures.

- Cleveland wins its first AL pennant in 41 years by taking Seattle in six in the ALCS.

- Atlanta (East), Cincinnati (Central), and Los Angeles (West) are the NL's division winners.

- Cincinnati needs only three games to erase LA in the first playoff round.

- Colorado, the NL wildcard qualifier, pushes Atlanta to four games before bowing in the division playoffs.

- Atlanta needs just four games to eliminate Cincinnati in the NLCS.

- The Braves win their first World Championship since moving to Atlanta by topping Cleveland in six games in the World Series.

- Braves pitchers hold Cleveland heavy hitters to a meager .179 BA in the World Series.

- David Justice's solo home run wins the Series finale 1-0 for Tom Glavine.

- Although he loses all the AL slugging crowns to Cleveland's Albert Belle, Boston's Mo Vaughn beats out Belle for the junior circuit MVP Award.

Belle's 50 HRs Fall Short

Albert Belle watches one of the 50 home runs he hit in 1995 leave the yard. Belle, who reached the 50 figure in just 143 games, became Cleveland's first home run king since 1959. However, his churlish behavior outweighed the most awesome slugging stats in the majors, at least in the minds of many AL sports writers. The junior circuit MVP Award went to Boston's Mo Vaughn, who edged Belle in the voting 308 to 300.

Albert Belle

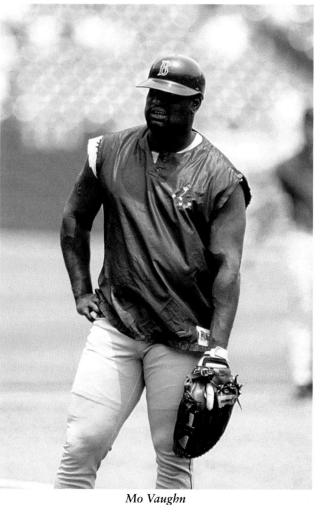

Mo Vaughn

Johnson Wins 18 Out of 20

Only the shortened season kept Randy Johnson from collecting 300 strikeouts in 1995 for the second time in his career. Virtually nothing else impeded the Mariners fireballer as he recorded a 2.48 ERA and a .900 winning percentage (18-2). Johnson, combined with one of the game's most potent offensive attacks, steered Seattle to the AL West crown and a near-pennant.

Randy Johnson

Vaughn Wins MVP Award

Mo Vaughn led all AL first basemen in putouts and double plays in 1995, but who noticed? His 39 homers and 126 RBI were the interior of the cake that earned him the AL MVP Award. The icing was his on-field leadership, which faltered only in the postseason. Vaughn and his BoSox slugging partner Jose Canseco were a combined 0-for-27 against Cleveland in the division playoff.

1995

- Cincinnati shortstop Barry Larkin is selected the NL MVP.

- Maddux wins his record fourth straight NL Cy Young Award.

- Seattle lefty Randy Johnson tops the majors with 294 strikeouts.

- Johnson becomes the first Seattle Mariner to earn a Cy Young Award.

- Johnson's glittering 18-2 record gives him a .900 winning percentage, the best in the AL.

- Maddux surpasses even Johnson, going 19-2 with a .905 winning percentage to top the ML in both wins and win pct.

- Tony Gwynn of San Diego wins his sixth NL batting crown (.368).

- Seattle DH Martinez hits .356 to win his second AL batting crown.

- On Sept. 6, Baltimore's Cal Ripken plays in his 2,131st consecutive major-league game, breaking Lou Gehrig's record.

- The Rockies' 4.97 staff ERA is the highest to date in this century by a team that qualified for the playoffs.

Hideo Nomo

Cal Breaks Lou's Record

The numbers in lights above the Camden Yards scoreboard tell the story. Orioles shortstop Cal Ripken has just broken Lou Gehrig's record by playing in his 2,131st consecutive game. The event was much celebrated throughout North America, and Ripken added to the excitement by homering in the 2,129th, 2,130th, and 2,131st games. Ripken's streak, which reached 2,153 games by the end of the season, was all the more amazing in that it was never, even for a moment, in serious jeopardy of being terminated.

Nomo Wows Fans, Batters

In 1995, American audiences and batters alike saw something completely new in the person of Hideo Nomo. Not only was Nomo the first Japanese-born star to make an impact on the American major-league game, but his unorthodox delivery had hitters everywhere sawing the air. The Dodgers' rookie went 13-6 with a 2.54 ERA and a league-high 236 strikeouts. Interestingly, his numbers in the Japanese Pacific League had been similar, though not quite as good.

Larkin Wins MVP Honors

Shortstops seldom pose with a bat in hand, but Barry Larkin is a rare exception. The Reds star ended his tenth major-league season with a .298 career average, the highest of any NL shortfielder at a comparable point since Arky Vaughn in 1941. Also a stalwart in the field, Larkin easily won senior loop MVP honors.

Barry Larkin

Cal Ripken

- Dodgers pitcher Hideo Nomo wins the NL ROTY Award after pacing the loop in strikeouts—236 in just 191 innings.

- Colorado's Dante Bichette leads the NL in homers (40) and RBI (128) and finishes third in batting.

- Mike Piazza of the Dodgers compiles the highest combined BA and SA figure of any NL catcher in history (.952) when he hits .346 and slugs .606.

- Belle is the first slugger in history to compile both 50 doubles and 50 homers in the same season.

- Belle leads the AL with 50 homers, 126 RBI, a .690 SA, and 377 total bases.

- Martinez and Belle tie for the AL lead in both doubles (52) and runs (121).

- Cleveland center fielder Kenny Lofton tops the majors in triples with 13.

- Lofton bags 54 thefts to win his fourth straight AL steals crown.

- Florida rookie Quilvio Veras leads the majors with 56 stolen bases.

Anderson Hangs Up His Spikes

Sparky Anderson

Boston fans watch Sparky Anderson leave the Fenway Park field for perhaps the last time. Anderson stepped down as Tigers manager after the 1995 season, ending the most lustrous dugout tenure in recent times. His 2,194 career wins (with Cincinnati and Detroit) rank him behind only Connie Mack and John McGraw.

Dante Bichette

Bichette's Numbers Soar

In 1991, at age 27, Dante Bichette hit .238 for Milwaukee in his first season as a full-time regular. Four years later with the Rockies, he made a run at the first NL Triple Crown since 1937 before finishing with two legs of it and a third-place finish in batting. Is Bichette really so vastly improved, or are his stats only another Mile High aberration?

Gwynn Tops .360 Again

In 1995, Tony Gwynn became the first NL player since 1930 to post back-to-back .360-plus seasons. The Padres' hitting wizard copped his second straight bat crown with a .368 mark and also tied for the ML lead in hits with 197. Gwynn eventually became the first player since Stan Musial to achieve both 3,000 hits and a .330-plus career batting average.

Tony Gwynn

1995

- Mike Mussina of Baltimore ties Maddux for the most wins in the majors as he leads the AL with 19 victories.

- Johnson leads the AL with a 2.48 ERA.

- Cleveland tops the ML with a .291 BA and a .479 SA.

- Atlanta's 3.44 ERA is the best in the majors.

- Colorado debuts its new home park, Coors Field, by leading the National League in both BA (.282) and SA (.471).

- The Rockies' 11-9 win over the Mets in 14 innings in their opener at Coors Field is the longest debut game in the 20th century for a new ballpark in both length and time (4:47).

- Maddux tops the majors in both ERA (1.63) and CGs (ten).

- Yankee Jack McDowell tops the AL in CGs with eight.

- Jose Mesa of Cleveland leads all bullpenners with 46 saves.

Jose Mesa

Piazza's the Best Behind the Plate

Over 1,500 amateur players were picked ahead of Mike Piazza in the 1988 free-agent draft. Few are still playing professionally, and none had anywhere near Piazza's career stats at the close of the 1995 season. Piazza finished his third big-league campaign with a .322 lifetime average, the highest of any catcher in big-league history at that juncture in his career. In 1995, he hit .346 with 32 homers.

Mike Piazza

Mesa Slams the Door

A flop as a starter, Jose Mesa emerged as 1995's top bullpen ace after Cleveland turned to him early in the year out of desperation. Upon winning the closer's job by default, Mesa proceeded to rack up an ML-high 46 saves and gain the nickname "Señor Slam."

Biggio Tops NL in Runs

Craig Biggio continued on his unique career course in 1995. The previous year, the Astros second sacker became the first big-leaguer to win a stolen-base crown after having served as a regular catcher for one or more seasons. In 1995, Biggio added an NL runs-scored title to his laurels.

Craig Biggio

- Cubs closer Randy Myers tops the NL with 38 saves.

- Tom Henke of the Cardinals sets a new mark for the most saves by a pitcher in his final season when he retires after bagging 36 saves.

- Mike Schmidt, Richie Ashburn, Leon Day, Vic Willis, and William Hulbert are voted into the Baseball Hall of Fame.

- Ramon Martinez of the Dodgers pitches a no-hitter against Florida on July 14.

- For the second year in a row, White Sox slugger Frank Thomas leads the majors in walks (136).

- Craig Biggio of the Astros leads the majors in runs with 123.

- Eddie Murray becomes the 20th player in ML history to collect 3,000 hits.

- Cleveland goes 54-18 at Jacobs Field to compile the best home win pct. (.750) since 1975 by an ML team.

Mickey Mantle's Funeral

The Mick Passes On

Yankees great Mickey Mantle is laid to his final rest in Dallas. Upon being diagnosed with inoperable liver cancer, Hall of Famer Mantle received a controversial organ transplant. Although the new liver failed to save him because the disease had spread too far, the attempt spurred a groundswell of organ donations throughout the nation.

ALCS

Hershiser Quiets M's in ALCS

Orel Hershiser lets it all out in game five of the ALCS. The ex-Dodgers ace was the surprise of the Cleveland mound staff in 1995. His critical 3-2 win against Seattle in the fifth game helped him become the first performer to win LCS MVP honors in both major leagues.

AL Division Series

Griffey, M's Blast Yanks

Seattle's Ken Griffey Jr. blasts a home run in game one of the 1995 AL Division Series against New York. Griffey, showcasing his talents in the postseason for the first time, unloaded on Yankee pitching, batting .391 with five home runs. His dash from first to home in the bottom of the 11th inning of the finale won the series for Seattle.

1995

- The Indians tie Atlanta for the best road win pct. (.639) in the majors.

- Colorado ties for the best home winning percentage in the NL (.611) despite being outscored by opponents at Coors Field 490 to 485.

- Pitcher Mark Langston wins his fifth consecutive Gold Glove Award with the Angels.

- Catcher Charles Johnson is the first member of the expansion Florida Marlins to win a Gold Glove Award.

- Texas catcher Ivan Rodriguez becomes the youngest four-time Gold Glove winner when he bags his fourth award at age 23.

- Oakland slugger Mark McGwire shatters all records for the most homers in fewer than 350 at-bats when he hammers 39 dingers in just 317 at-bats.

- McGwire leads the major leagues in home run percentage (12.3) while collecting more walks (88) than he does hits (87).

- McGwire's 90 RBI in just 317 at-bats tie George Grantham's 20th-century

Braves Broom the Reds

NL MVP Barry Larkin tries unsuccessfully to elude Atlanta shortstop Rafael Belliard's tag. Larkin was Cincinnati's lone bright spot in the senior loop pennant series. His seven hits represented one-quarter of the Reds' total in their disappointing four-games-and-out tussle with the Braves. Atlanta used eight pitchers in the Series and each was successful, as they yielded a total of just five runs.

World Series

NLCS

Glavine Shuts Down Tribe

The camera catches Tom Glavine in game two of the 1995 World Series. The Braves lefty beat Cleveland 4-3 that night and again polished off the Tribe six nights later, 1-0. Glavine's one-hitter in the Series finale, with relief help from Mark Wohlers, was marred only by Cleveland backup catcher Tony Pena's looping single in the sixth inning. Glavine was named Series MVP.

Cleveland Bats .179 in Series

Braves second sacker Mark Lemke stretches for a throw as Cleveland's Kenny Lofton slides safely into second. The Tribe's star center fielder swiped six sacks against Atlanta in the 1995 World Series but batted only .200. Lofton nevertheless tied for the Cleveland team lead in hits with five as the Indians' vaunted offense was held to just a .179 batting mark.

World Series

season record for the most RBI in fewer than 350 at-bats.

• Lou Whitaker and Alan Trammell of the Tigers play in their 1,915th game together on September 13 to set a new AL record for teammates.

• John Vander Wal of the Rockies sets a new record for the most pinch hits in a season with 28.

• The Rockies are only the second team in big-league history to have four 30-homer men when Dante Bichette, Andres Galarraga, Larry Walker, and Vinny Castilla all rap 30 or more dingers.

• Murray finishes the season with the record for most career games played at first base with 2,412.

• Minnesota posts the highest ERA in the ML at 5.76.

• Dave Winfield retires after 23 seasons and 3,110 hits.

• Sparky Anderson resigns as Detroit's manager, ending his franchise-record streak of nearly 17 years at the Tigers' helm.

NEW YORK RETURNS TO THE TOP OF THE HEAP

The 1996 regular season opened with tragedy and ended in shame. On Opening Day, umpire John McSherry became only the second on-field fatality in major-league history when he succumbed to a heart attack at Cincinnati's Riverfront Stadium. The last week of the season was marred by a clash between Baltimore second baseman Roberto Alomar and umpire John Hirschbeck that culminated when Alomar spit in Hirschbeck's face, triggering a threatened postseason walkout by arbiters in both leagues.

In between those events, fans saw more runs scored than in any season ever. Seattle, Cleveland, Baltimore, Texas, Boston, and Colorado each scored more than 900 runs, a feat not achieved by any team since 1953. Six men hit 47 or more home runs. Oakland's Mark McGwire smashed 52 in just 423 at-bats.

Meanwhile, the Indians posted the best record in the majors for the second year in a row. Their reward was to open the first round of the playoffs on the road at Camden Yards against the wildcard Baltimore Orioles, a team that had blasted an ML-record 257 round-trippers. In the opener, Brady Anderson led off the Orioles' first inning with a home run that put the Indians in a hole from which they never escaped. Cleveland ultimately fell in four games.

AL Central champion Texas likewise succumbed in four games. In their first-ever postseason appearance, the Rangers and their league MVP slugger, Juan Gonzalez, surprised AL East titlist New York by winning the opening game at Yankee Stadium. But Texas's shaky bullpen then allowed Joe Torre's men to squirm off the hook by surrendering leads in each of the next three games, thus setting the stage for a Yankees-Orioles battle in the ALCS.

The two NL division playoff matches were dull in comparison. Central champ St. Louis and East repeat titlist Atlanta both needed just three games to dispatch San Diego and Los Angeles, respectively. Perhaps the two West entries were exhausted from their down-to-the-wire chase, which saw the Padres sweep the final three contests of the season at Dodger Stadium to win the West by a single game.

Fans, moguls, and TV executives were disgruntled that all four division playoffs ended early and afforded far too little drama to erase the bad taste left by the Alomar debacle. The two LCSes seemed destined to follow the same pattern when New York laid the Orioles to rest in just five games and St. Louis streaked to a 3-1 lead with game five slated for Busch Stadium.

But Atlanta then staged the most remarkable five-game run in postseason history. After winning games five (14-0) and six (3-1), the Braves humiliated St. Louis 15-0 in the decisive seventh game. Bobby Cox then took his team into Yankee Stadium and likewise embarrassed the Yankees, winning the first two games of the World Series by a combined 16-1 count.

Given little chance of stopping the Braves' steamroller, Torre got a gutty effort from starter David Cone in a game three victory at Atlanta. In game four, a three-run homer by Jim Leyritz rallied the Yankees from a 6-0 deficit. The Series was suddenly tied at 2-all. In game five, Atlanta's bats were chilled by Andy Pettitte and John Wetteland, and Cecil Fielder's RBI base hit provided all the scoring.

Back in New York for game six, Jimmy Key continued to stymie the Braves' offense, and Wetteland took the hill in the top of the ninth with a 3-1 lead. A last-gasp rally fell a run short when Mark Lemke fouled out to third baseman Charlie Hayes to end the game. Wetteland recorded his fourth Series save and ended the Yankees' longest championship drought since 1903-22.

1996

- New York, Texas, and Cleveland win their AL divisions, while Baltimore makes the playoffs as a wildcard.

- New York defeats Texas in four games in the AL division playoffs.

- In the division playoff against New York, Texas's Juan Gonzalez becomes the first man to homer in each of his first four postseason games.

- Baltimore beats Cleveland in four games in first-round action.

- New York defeats Baltimore in five games in the ALCS.

- Twelve-year-old Jeffrey Maier helps the Yankees win game one of the ALCS when he interferes with a long fly by Yankee Derek Jeter.

- Needing just one win in their final three games of the season to clinch the NL West, the Dodgers fall prey to a San Diego sweep that gives the Pads the crown.

- Atlanta and St. Louis are NL division winners, while the Dodgers make it as a wildcard.

Gleeful New Yorkers flaunt the *Post*'s sports headline as their Yankees end an 18-year title drought. The Bombers' 1996 World Series triumph may have been their most satisfying to date. Even many Big Apple diehards would have been happy just to avoid a sweep after the Yankees dropped the first two games at home.

- For the second year in a row, the Dodgers are humiliated in the NL division playoffs, bowing in three straight games to Atlanta.

- The Cardinals sweep San Diego in three division playoff games.

- Atlanta rallies to win the NLCS after trailing St. Louis three games to one.

- The Yankees defeat Atlanta four games to two in the World Series.

- Atlanta rookie sensation Andruw Jones, age 19, slugs two homers in game one of the World Series.

- Yankees closer John Wetteland becomes the first hurler to bag four saves in a World Series.

- Ken Caminiti of the Padres wins the NL MVP Award.

- Texas slugger Juan Gonzalez edges Alex Rodriguez to win the AL MVP.

- John Smoltz of Atlanta bags the Cy Young Award.

- Blue Jays bulwark Pat Hentgen wins the AL Cy Young Award.

Willie Mays, Bobby Bonds, Andre Dawson, Barry Bonds

Younger Bonds Joins 300 Club

Willie Mays (*left*), Bobby Bonds (*second from left*), and Andre Dawson join Bonds's son Barry (*far right*) in celebrating his 300th career home run in 1996. These four greats are the only players in history to amass both 300 homers and 300 steals in their careers. Barry reached 40 of each in 1996, becoming just the second major-leaguer to turn the trick. Dawson retired after the season.

A-Rod Posts Stunning Statistics

Pictured is Alex Rodriguez as he might have looked when news of the AL MVP vote reached him. A-Rod narrowly missed out on MVP honors, finishing second in voting to Juan Gonzalez by a count of 290 to 287. The Mariners' sophomore star had the greatest offensive season ever by a shortstop: AL-high .358 average, 215 hits, 54 doubles, 36 homers, 141 runs, and 123 RBI. His 15 errors were five fewer than AL Gold Glove winner Omar Vizquel committed.

Alex Rodriguez

Anderson Smacks 50 HRs

Many pundits cited Brady Anderson as absolute proof that the ball was juiced in 1996. The Orioles center fielder began his ninth major-league campaign with just 72 career home runs. He ended it with 122 after being the first leadoff man ever to hammer 50 dingers in a season.

Brady Anderson

1996

- Todd Hollandsworth of the Dodgers is the NL ROTY.

- Derek Jeter is a unanimous winner of the AL ROTY Award.

- San Diego's Tony Gwynn hits .353 to win his seventh NL batting crown, cracking the .350 mark for the sixth time.

- Rodriguez hits .358 to become the first AL shortstop since 1944 to win a batting title.

- Barry Bonds of the Giants is the first in NL history to bag 40 stolen bases and 40 homers in the same season.

- Bonds sets a new NL record when he collects 151 walks.

- The Indians (99-62) compile the best regular-season record in the ML two years in a row.

- Mark McGwire of Oakland becomes the first player in ML history to compile 50 home runs in a season before collecting his 400th at-bat.

- McGwire leads the ML with 52 homers, a .730 SA, and a .467 OBP.

Belle Rings Up 48 HRs and 148 RBI

Moody Albert Belle again rang up MVP numbers in 1996—and again was denied the award. In his final season in Cleveland livery, Belle hit 48 homers and set a new Tribe career home run record with 242. He also became only the second Indian to win back-to-back RBI crowns, as he knocked home 148.

Albert Belle

Andres Galarraga

Galarraga Nets 150 RBI

In 1996, Andres Galarraga set a new season record for the most RBI by an NL first baseman. Galarraga's loop-leading 150 ribbies broke Don Hurst's old mark of 143. It also topped his own personal high by a margin of 44. Galarraga had just 72 RBI in 1991-92 combined, his last two seasons before joining the Rockies in mile-high Denver.

Molitor Cracks No. 3,000

Paul Molitor led the AL with 225 hits in 1996. Molitor celebrated his first year with the Twins by setting a flock of season batting records for 40-year-old performers. Among his amazing numbers were a .341 average, 99 runs, 41 doubles, 113 RBI, and even 18 stolen bases. He also collected his 3,000th career hit after being considered an extreme long shot to achieve that pinnacle ten years earlier. Molitor had just 1,203 hits through 1986 (age 30).

Paul Molitor

Caminiti Claims NL MVP Award

Ken Caminiti spent his first eight years in the majors with Houston, where he never got so much as a single MVP vote. In 1996, just two years after being dealt to San Diego, he was a unanimous choice for the NL's top prize. Facing shoulder surgery, he nevertheless set a new senior loop home run mark for switch-hitters with 40. He batted .326 with 130 RBI and led San Diego to a division crown.

Ken Caminiti

- Colorado's Andres Galarraga leads the NL in homers (47) and RBI (150).

- Ellis Burks of Colorado tallies 142 runs to pace the majors.

- The AL leader in runs scored is Rodriguez with 141.

- Rodriguez leads the AL in runs (141) and sets new all-time shortstop marks for SA (.631), doubles (54), and hits (215).

- Albert Belle of Cleveland paces the AL in RBI with 148.

- Minnesota's Paul Molitor, age 40, tops the AL with 225 hits.

- Molitor becomes the first member of the 3,000-hit club to have a higher career batting average at age 40 than he did at age 30.

- Cleveland's Kenny Lofton tops the AL in steals (75) for the fifth straight season.

- Baltimore's Eddie Murray becomes only the third MLer ever to collect both 500 home runs and 3,000 hits.

Smoltz Bags Cy Young

John Smoltz owned a so-so 90-82 career record after his first eight seasons, all spent with powerhouse Atlanta. His ninth season, 1996, resulted in 24 wins—the most by any NL hurler since Dwight Gooden bagged 24 in 1985. Smoltz was also the Braves' top hurler in the World Series, surrendering just one earned run in two starts against the Yankees. He won game one 12-1 and lost game five 1-0.

John Smoltz

Roger Clemens

Clemens Fans Another 20

BoSox manager Kevin Kennedy (*far left*) and catcher Bill Haselman congratulate Roger Clemens after he becomes only the second hurler in history to fan 20 batters in a nine-inning game on September 18, 1996, against Detroit. Clemens was also the first pitcher to do it, ten years earlier. Despite his 20-K game and loop-leading 257 strikeouts, Clemens was just 10-13 for Boston.

Pettitte Wins 20, Loses Cy

Only a late surge prevented Andy Pettitte from becoming the first AL southpaw since Billy Hoeft in 1956 to win 20 games with an ERA above 4.00. Apparently, sports writers were aware of this dubious distinction when they cast their Cy Young ballots at the end of the regular season. Had the vote waited until postseason action was complete, the Yankees lefty probably would have prevailed after his clutch win in game five of the World Series.

Andy Pettitte

1996

- The Mets' Todd Hundley sets an ML record for homers by a catcher (41).

- The Rangers' Ivan Rodriguez sets a new ML record for the most doubles in a season by a catcher (47).

- Lance Johnson sets a new Mets franchise record as he leads the majors in hits with 227.

- Johnson paces the ML with 21 triples, the most by an NLer since 1949.

- John Wetteland of the Yankees tops the AL with 43 saves.

- The ML leaders in saves are Jeff Brantley of Cincinnati and Todd Worrell of LA with 44 each.

- Cincinnati owner Marge Schott is suspended by her fellow owners for her insensitive racial remarks.

- Umpire John McSherry suffers a fatal heart attack on Opening Day at Cincinnati's Riverfront Stadium.

- Brady Anderson of Baltimore is the first leadoff man in ML history to compile 50 home runs in a season.

Juan Gonzalez

Gonzalez Named AL MVP

Juan Gonzalez, who batted .314 with 47 homers and 144 RBI, was nevertheless a surprising AL MVP choice. After a slump-ridden September, Gonzalez seemingly lost the prize to Seattle's Alex Rodriguez, who set a swarm of season batting records for shortstops. Gonzalez's monster slugging performance in the division playoffs against the Yankees, albeit in a losing cause, made the award more palatable to fans—if no less shocking.

Kevin Brown

Kirby Puckett

Kirby Says Good-Bye to Baseball

Kirby Puckett announces his forced retirement from baseball after learning he has glaucoma. The longtime Twins star finished with over 2,000 hits and a .318 career batting average, second only to fellow former Twin Rod Carew among postexpansion-era players who are now retired.

Brown Posts a 1.89 ERA

In the 1996 NL Cy Young voting, Kevin Brown was picked No. 1 on two ballots and No. 2 on the remaining 26. Some experts claimed that Brown was the majors' most impressive performer in a season when offensive records fell by the truckload. His 17 wins and glossy 1.89 ERA (0.83 better than anyone else) enabled the Florida Marlins to make a late dash at a .500 finish before ending two games under the break-even mark.

- Helped by Anderson, Baltimore rips an ML-record 257 home runs.

- Two other AL teams, Seattle (245) and Oakland (243), also shatter the 1961 Yankees' old ML season mark of 240 home runs.

- Colorado ties the NL record for home runs in a season with 221.

- Baltimore sets a new ML record for the highest team ERA (5.14) by a postseason qualifier.

- Roberto Alomar is almost suspended for the postseason when he spits in the face of umpire John Hirschbeck near the end of the regular season.

- ML umpires threaten not to work postseason games when AL president

- Gene Budig delays acting against Alomar after the spitting incident.

- Smoltz leads the majors with 24 wins.

- The Yankees' Andy Pettitte tops the AL in wins (21).

- Detroit loses a franchise-record 109 games.

Murray Hits 500th Homer

Eddie Murray

Eddie Murray reached his coveted 500th home run in 1996. He had the pleasure of hitting both his first and his 500th career homers in Baltimore livery. In between, he was with three other teams. Murray, who had collected his 3,000th hit in 1995, became only the third player in major-league history (after Willie Mays and Hank Aaron) to reach both magical marks.

AL Division Series

Gonzalez Can't Save Texas

Rangers players hold out their hands to welcome teammate Juan Gonzalez after his homer against the Yankees in game one of their division series. The Rangers won 6-2 at Yankee Stadium, then took an early lead again the following night on another Gonzalez bomb before their bullpen faltered. The same pattern was repeated three games in a row, leading to the Rangers' early exit in their first-ever postseason appearance. As for Gonzalez, he homered in each of the four games, including two dingers in game two. He finished with a .438 batting average and 1.375 slugging mark.

NLCS

Braves Club Cards in NLCS

Cards catcher Tom Pagnozzi helplessly watches Javier Lopez score for the Braves in game six of the National League Championship Series. St. Louis took a stunning three-games-to-one lead over the defending champs, but then Atlanta really poured it on in the last three contests. The Braves won game five 14-0 (on 22 hits), game six 3-1, and game seven 15-0. Lopez wound up the series with 13 hits and a .542 average, while the Braves posted a 1.92 ERA to the Cards' 6.60 mark.

1996

- Detroit batters collect an ML-record 1,268 strikeouts, led by Melvin Nieves with 158.

- Detroit's 6.38 staff ERA sets a new mark for the highest in AL history.

- The Mariners have three players who tally 120 or more runs—Rodriguez (141), Ken Griffey Jr. (125), and Edgar Martinez (121)—as Seattle scores 993 runs, most in the majors since 1950.

- Cleveland leads the majors in batting (.293).

- Smoltz tops all ML hurlers with 276 strikeouts.

- Boston's Roger Clemens leads AL hurlers in Ks with 257.

- Kevin Brown of Florida registers the finest ERA in the majors by far when he finishes at 1.89.

- After rebounding from throat cancer to return to action in September, LA's Brett Butler suffers a season-ending injury within days of his return.

- Hentgen tops the majors in both innings pitched (266) and CGs (ten).

1996

Yanks, Kid Do In O's in ALCS

Cal Ripken looks on as Orioles right fielder Tony Tarasco exhorts umpire Rich Garcia to call fan interference on Derek Jeter's controversial eighth-inning home run in game one of the ALCS. Though replay cameras seemed to show that a 12-year-old spectator, Jeffrey Maier, had scooped a catchable ball out of Tarasco's grasp and into the stands, Garcia's call stood. This allowed New York to tie the game and ultimately win it in extra innings. New York took the series in five games.

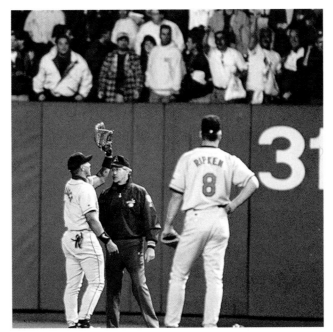
ALCS

Yanks Pile Up Playoff Road Wins

A Yankee win was a familiar sight in the 1996 postseason. Skipper Joe Torre led a victorious charge out of the Yankees dugout 11 times over a three-week period. Just three of the Bombers' victories came at home, though, as Torre's men shattered all such postseason records by winning eight out of eight games on the road, including three in the World Series.

Momentum Shifts in Game Three

Braves rookie Andruw Jones upends Yankees shortstop Derek Jeter at the front end of an attempted double play in game two of the 1996 World Series. Atlanta won the fray 4-0, thereupon taking a seemingly commanding 2-0 lead in games. But Jeter, the AL Rookie of the Year, helped mount a comeback that saw the Yankees sweep the next four games.

World Series

Joe Torre

- Earl Weaver, Ned Hanlon, Jim Bunning, and Bill Foster are elected to the Hall of Fame.

- Twins star Kirby Puckett is forced to retire when he learns he has glaucoma.

- Joe Torre sees his record for the most games as either a player or a manager without making a World Series appearance come to a halt when his Yankees win the AL flag.

- Frank Thomas hits the first-ever regular-season home run in March during the White Sox-Mariners opener at the Kingdome on March 31.

- On August 16, 1996, in Monterrey, Mexico, San Diego beats the Mets 15-10 in the first ML game ever played outside the U.S. or Canada.

- Al Leiter notches the first no-hitter in Florida Marlins' history when he beats Colorado 11-0 on May 11.

- Following a heart attack, Tom Lasorda steps down as Dodgers pilot after 20 years at the helm.

MARLINS BEAT TRIBE IN SERIES THRILLER

Fans of the Florida Marlins didn't have to wait long to celebrate a world championship. The 1993 expansion club squeaked into the playoffs through the wildcard but knocked off three heavily favored teams to sit atop the baseball world—if only for a little while.

The Marlins, headed by veteran manager Jim Leyland, featured just three pitchers in double figures in wins (Kevin Brown at 16-8, Alex Fernandez at 17-12, and Al Leiter at 11-9). But they had quality players at every position, including left fielder Moises Alou (23 homers, 115 runs batted in) and Gold Glove catcher Charles Johnson (19 dingers, 63 RBI).

After earning the wildcard berth, Florida knocked off the Giants in the first round. San Francisco led in each game, but ultimately fell. The underdog Marlins then took the Braves in six to win the NL title, battering Atlanta pitching stars Tom Glavine and John Smoltz. Prior to losing the NLCS, the Braves had easily extinguished NL Central champ Houston.

The biggest individual stories in the NL were Tony Gwynn, who hit .372 in winning his eighth bat crown, and MVP winner Larry Walker, who slugged 49 homers for the Rockies. Only one NL pitcher, Denny Neagle of Atlanta, won 20 games, but the senior circuit's Cy Young winner was Montreal's Pedro Martinez (1.90 ERA, 305 whiffs).

Meanwhile, despite great seasons from AL Cy Young winner Roger Clemens (21-7, 2.05 ERA) and Randy Johnson (20-4), homers flew out of AL ballparks. Mark McGwire rapped 34 homers for Oakland before a July 31 trade to St. Louis, where he added 24 more. Big Mac's 58 homers were the most hit by any player since Roger Maris in 1961. Frank Thomas of the White Sox hit .347 to win the batting title and added 35 homers of his own. Seattle's Ken Griffey, the AL's MVP, knocked 56 four-baggers and drove in 147.

Griffey's heroics helped the Mariners win the AL West, but Seattle was shut down by Baltimore in the first round of playoffs. The Orioles then went on to lose to the Cleveland Indians, who had previously vanquished the wildcard Yankees, in the ALCS.

Cleveland connected for a club-record 220 homers, with Jim Thome (40), David Justice (33), and Matt Williams (32) helping to overcome the Tribe's mediocre starting pitching.

The World Series, though sometimes comically sloppy, was highly entertaining. After splitting the first two games in Miami, the teams moved to Cleveland and were greeted by high winds and freezing rain. Game three, which took more than four hours to play, featured six errors in a 14-11 Marlins win. The Tribe had blown an earlier 7-3 lead and allowed seven runs in the ninth.

The teams then traded victories before returning to much warmer Miami. In game six, Chad Ogea stepped up and pitched Cleveland to a 4-1 win, forcing a final winner-take-all matchup.

Game seven was one of the most thrilling World Series games ever. The Indians held a 2-0 lead before the Marlins scored one on Bobby Bonilla's seventh-inning homer. In the last of the ninth, facing defeat, Florida tallied again on second baseman Craig Counsell's sacrifice fly.

In the home 11th, Counsell reached on Tony Fernandez's error. A walk and an infield out later, he stood on third. Marlins shortstop Edgar Renteria then rapped a single up the middle to score Counsell, end the series, and send 67,204 fans into hysterics.

However, Miami fans' ardor was cooled during the winter. Owner Wayne Huizenga, intending to sell the club, cut costs by trading most of the key players from the series club.

1997

- Florida wins the NL wildcard berth, edging Los Angeles by four games.

- The Marlins plow through playoff opponents San Francisco and Atlanta to advance to the World Series in just their fifth season.

- The Indians win the AL Central by six games, then outlast the Yankees and Orioles to win the pennant.

- The Marlins win a thrilling World Series, sliding by Cleveland 3-2 in an 11-inning game seven on Edgar Renteria's RBI single.

- Sandy Alomar of the Indians bats .367 and knocks in ten runs against Florida in the World Series.

- Marlins righthander Livan Hernandez wins twice in the NLCS and

twice more in the World Series, winning both LCS and Series MVP honors.

- Atlanta wins 19 times in April to set a major-league record for the season's first month.

- Giants improve 22 games and win the NL West.

Florida shortstop Edgar Renteria laces a single up the middle to give the Florida Marlins a 3-2, 11th-inning win over the Cleveland Indians in game seven of the 1997 World Series. Renteria, who batted .290 in the series, knocked in second baseman Craig Counsell with the deciding tally as the Marlins captured the world title in just their fifth year of play.

- Florida's Kevin Brown no-hits the Giants 9-0 at Candlestick Park on June 10.

- In the first-ever combined ten-inning no-hitter, Pittsburgh's Francisco Cordova and Ricardo Rincon blank the Astros 3-0 on July 12.

- In the 50th year since Jackie Robinson broke the color line, baseball announces plans to retire his No. 42 permanently.

- The major leagues institute interleague play. On June 12, the Giants beat Texas 4-3 in the first interleague game.

- Marlins sign outfielder Gary Sheffield to a six-year contract extension worth $61 million.

- Seattle's Ken Griffey Jr. leads the AL with 56 homers, 120 runs scored, and 147 RBI.

- Griffey is the unanimous AL MVP and takes home his fourth Gold Glove.

- Frank Thomas of the White Sox leads the AL with a .347 average and a .461 on-base percentage.

Walker Cops MVP Award

Larry Walker did it all for the Colorado Rockies in 1997. The oft-injured Walker managed to stay healthy and (not coincidentally) enjoyed his finest season. He hit for power (a league-leading 49 homers) and average (.366), drove in 130 runs, stole 33 bases, drew 78 walks, and even threw out 12 baserunners from right field. As his reward, Walker took home the NL's Most Valuable Player trophy.

Larry Walker

Mark McGwire

Big Mac Blasts 58 Homers

A July 31 deal sent Mark McGwire from the Oakland Athletics to the grateful St. Louis Cardinals. McGwire had already hit 34 homers for Oakland and added 24 more in 51 games with the Redbirds, becoming an instant fan favorite in the Mound City. His 58 total homers tied the mark set by Jimmie Foxx in 1932 for the most ever by a righthanded hitter.

Junior: 56 HRs, MVP Award

Seattle's Ken Griffey Jr. batted .304 with 56 home runs and 147 RBI (both of which led the AL) in 1997 to become the 13th man to win unanimous selection as his league's Most Valuable Player. Griffey had the best season of his career, leading the Mariners to the playoffs. Unfortunately for Seattle fans, Seattle lost to Baltimore in the Division Series as Junior was just 2-for-15.

Ken Griffey Jr.

1997

- Colorado's Larry Walker paces the NL in on-base percentage (.452) and slugging percentage (.720).

- Walker wins NL MVP honors and snags his first Gold Glove.

- Tony Gwynn of the Padres wins his eighth National League bat crown, hitting .372.

- Montreal's Mark Grudzielanek hits 54 doubles.

- Indians catcher Sandy Alomar's two-run homer carries the AL to a 3-1 All-Star Game win in Cleveland.

- Knuckleballer Phil Niekro is the only player inducted by the writers into the Baseball Hall of Fame.

- Boston shortstop Nomar Garciaparra is the unanimous choice for AL ROTY.

- Scott Rolen of the Phillies is a unanimous NL ROTY.

- Juan Gonzalez of Texas hits 42 homers despite missing the first month with a thumb injury.

Mike Piazza

Piazza Raps .362, 40 HRs

Cementing his reputation as the top offensive catcher in baseball history, Dodger Mike Piazza rapped 201 hits in 1997 and batted .362. He added 40 homers and 124 RBI. In another season, Piazza might well have piled up the awards. But for the second straight year, he finished second in NL MVP voting—this time behind Larry Walker of the Rockies.

Craig Biggio

Biggio Rings Up 146 Runs

Craig Biggio, Houston's scrappy second baseman, had one of the all-time great run-scoring campaigns in 1997. Crossing the plate 146 times during the club's division-winning season, Biggio scored more runs than any NL player since Hall of Famer Chuck Klein tallied 152 in 1932. How did Biggio do it? Batting .309 with 84 walks, 22 homers, 37 doubles, and 47 steals didn't hurt, and batting ahead of Jeff Bagwell helped too.

Rocket Wins Triple Crown

Just one year after being called "washed up" by some in Boston, Roger Clemens won his fourth AL Cy Young Award—for the Blue Jays. Clemens won the pitching "Triple Crown," leading the AL in strikeouts, wins, and ERA, becoming the first AL hurler to do so since Detroit's Hal Newhouser in 1945. Oddly, Clemens was 21-4 against the junior circuit but 0-3 against NL clubs.

- Labor-relations trailblazer Curt Flood dies at age 59.

- Expo pitcher Pedro Martinez's 13 complete games are the most by an NL pitcher since 1988.

- Martinez cops the NL's Cy Young.

- Barry Bonds of the Giants amasses 40 homers and 145 walks.

- Mark McGwire hits 34 homers for the Athletics—despite being traded to St. Louis on July 31.

- McGwire's 58 homers tie the mark set by Jimmie Foxx for most ever by a righthanded batter.

- Randy Myers of Baltimore blows just one save in 46 chances.

- Roger Clemens of Toronto wins his fourth AL Cy Young.

- Clemens leads the AL in wins, strikeouts, ERA, innings pitched, complete games, and shutouts.

- San Diego's Greg Vaughn signs a $15 million contract, then hits .216 in 120 games.

Martinez Steps It Up

First baseman Tino Martinez of the Yankees, always an outstanding defensive player, enjoyed a breakout 1997 season. Finishing second in the AL with 44 homers and 141 RBI, he set a new major-league record by knocking in 34 runs in April. He led the Yankees in most key offensive categories as the club won the AL wild-card berth.

Tino Martinez

Bonds Piles Up BBs, SBs

The seemingly mechanical superstar, Barry Bonds of San Francisco enjoyed another monster year in 1997, hitting .291 with 145 walks and 40 home runs. He also swiped 37 bases. It was the 33-year-old Bonds's fifth season of 30 homers and 30 steals, matching the mark held by another star Giants outfielder—his father, Bobby Bonds.

Pedro Martinez

Martinez Mows 'Em Down

Young Pedro Martinez of Montreal made a quantum leap in 1997 and became the game's top pitcher. Pacing the NL with a 1.90 ERA and 13 complete games, Martinez fanned 305 hitters and fashioned a 17-8 mark for an Expos team that finished 78-84. The financially strapped Montreal club responded to Pedro's great season by trading him to the Boston Red Sox.

Barry Bonds

1997

- Randy Johnson of the Mariners strikes out 19 batters twice during the season and finishes 20-4 with 291 whiffs.

- Tony Womack of the Pirates steals 32 consecutive bases en route to leading the National League with 60 swipes.

- Yankee Mariano Rivera saves 43 with a 1.88 ERA and is the AL Fireman of the Year.

- Rookie Rey Ordonez of the Mets wins the NL Gold Glove at shortstop.

- The Cardinals and Padres play a three-game series in Honolulu on April 19-20.

- Angels lefthander Chuck Finley wins ten consecutive starts.

- Curt Schilling of the Phillies whiffs 319, most ever by an NL righthander.

- Cincinnati's Jeff Shaw is named NL Fireman of the Year with 42 saves, 38 more than his previous career high.

Davis Back from Illness

When Orioles outfielder Eric Davis was diagnosed in midseason with colon cancer, many thought he would retire. Davis, however, returned to active duty on September 15. He even clouted a home run in the Birds' playoff series loss against Cleveland. After the season, he was presented with the Baseball Writers Association's Tony Conigliaro Award for his courage and determination.

Eric Davis

Neagle Goes 20-5, 2.97

In his first full season for the Atlanta Braves, lefthanded hurler Denny Neagle blossomed into one of the league's most effective pitchers. He set career highs in nearly every category, ending with a 20-5 mark and a fine 2.97 ERA. The 29-year-old, who got his big outs with a devastating change, also tossed 12 scoreless innings in the NLCS before undergoing shoulder surgery days later.

Denny Neagle

Tony Gwynn

Gwynn Wins NL Bat Crown

San Diego's amazing Tony Gwynn enjoyed his greatest season in 1997. Playing on bad knees at age 37, Gwynn led the majors by batting .372, added 49 doubles, and drove in 119 runs. He won his fourth straight batting crown (and eighth overall), rapped 220 hits, and even hit an inside-the-park grand slam against Los Angeles.

- Greg Maddux of Atlanta is 19-4 and leads the NL in winning percentage.

- Andres Galarraga of the Rockies paces the NL in RBI (140) for the second straight season.

- St. Louis hitters strike out 1,191 times, just 12 short of the senior-loop record.

- Brewers reliever Doug Jones walks only nine hitters in 80⅔ innings.

- Sammy Sosa of Chicago homers 36 times but also leads the NL with 174 strikeouts.

- Cincinnati's Deion Sanders steals 56 bases, then retires to concentrate on pro football.

- Thomas and Albert Belle of the White Sox become the second pair of teammates ever to hit 30 homers and bat in 100 runs in a season.

- Just 24-61 at the All-Star break, the Phils win 36 of their last 58.

- Maddux wins his eighth Gold Glove—all consecutive.

Thome Jacks 40 Homers

Jim Thome

When the Cleveland Indians acquired star third baseman Matt Williams from San Francisco, holdover Jim Thome took his glove across the diamond to first base and just kept on hitting. He slugged a career-best 40 homers, drove in 102, and led the AL by drawing 120 walks for the Tribe in 1997. Thome then added two homers in the World Series.

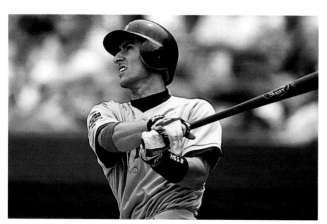

Nomar Garciaparra

A Star Is Born in Beantown

Busting into the majors with one of the greatest rookie seasons in recent memory, Boston shortstop Nomar Garciaparra hit .306 with 44 doubles and 30 homers and paced the AL in at-bats, triples, and hits. An outstanding shortstop with good range and a rocket arm, the former first-round pick won favor both from fans and sports writers, who voted him a unanimous Rookie of the Year.

Fish Beat Braves in NLCS

Pitcher Livan Hernandez and catcher Charles Johnson of the Florida Marlins embrace following the club's 2-1 win over the Atlanta Braves in game five of the NLCS. Hernandez, the eventual series MVP, whiffed a league championship series-record 15 hitters in the victory, which gave Florida a 3-2 lead in games. The Fighting Fish wrapped up their first league championship two nights later in Atlanta.

NLCS

1997

- Bonds's Gold Glove is his seventh.

- Walker's 409 total bases are the most since Stan Musial had 429 in 1948.

- Catcher Charles Johnson of Florida does not commit an error all season.

- Hector Espino, holder of the minor-league home run record with 484, dies in Monterrey, Mexico.

- Catcher Ivan Rodriguez of the Rangers wins his sixth straight Gold Glove.

- Luis Gonzalez of Houston hits in 23 straight games, the longest such streak in the NL during 1997.

- Cubs second sacker Ryne Sandberg retires again, this time for good, at the end of the season.

- Pete Rose Jr., son of the all-time hits leader, makes his big-league debut on Labor Day for the Cincinnati Reds.

- On November 5, the day he is given AL Manager of the Year honors, Davey Johnson quits the Orioles.

- The Los Angeles Dodgers are sold to Rupert Murdoch for approximately $350 million.

Deion Sanders

Ogea's Two Series Wins Fall Short

Righty Chad Ogea of the Indians won two games in the World Series—both victories, ironically, coming in Florida. Ogea (just 8-9 in the regular season) and the Tribe had vanquished the Yankees in a five-game Division Series and the Orioles in a six-game ALCS to reach the fall classic, but once again came away disappointed at Series time.

Chad Ogea

Sanders Returns in Style

After taking the 1996 season off to concentrate exclusively on his football career, Deion Sanders returned to the Cincinnati Reds in 1997. Despite playing just 115 games (still a career high), Sanders finished second in the NL in stolen bases with 56. He batted .273 and led the injury-riddled Reds with 127 hits in what would be his final season as a major-league baseball player.

Counsell Scores Winning Run

Craig Counsell of the Marlins has just scored the winning run in game seven of the 1997 World Series. His teammates, including Gregg Zaun (grabbing Counsell) and Bobby Bonilla (#24), have already begun celebrating. Counsell, a 26-year-old rookie, took over at second base for Florida late in the 1997 season and batted .299 in 51 games to help spark the club's surprising World Championship.

World Series

- The Rockies lead the NL in attendance for the fifth straight season.

- Major-league attendance is 63,168,689, the second-highest total ever.

- Maddux inks a five-year contract extension at $57.5 million, making him the highest-paid player in the game.

- First baseman Eddie Murray retires with 504 homers and 3,255 hits.

- On November 5, the Milwaukee Brewers elect to move from the American League to the National for the 1998 season.

- Baseball holds an expansion draft on November 18 to stock two new clubs: AL's Tampa Bay Devil Rays and NL's Arizona Diamondbacks.

- Within two months of winning the World Series, Florida trades stars Moises Alou, Kevin Brown, Jeff Conine, Robb Nen, and Devon White in an attempt to dump salaries.

The New York Yankees blew the rest of major-league baseball off the map in 1998. The Bombers won 114 regular-season games, dismissed the Rangers and Indians in the playoffs, and swept the NL champion San Diego Padres to win their record 24th World Championship.

But even the Yankees' achievements could not overshadow the feats of sluggers Mark McGwire of the Cardinals and Sammy Sosa of the Cubs.

McGwire, who had smashed 58 long balls in 1997, exploded for an all-time record of 70, obliterating Roger Maris's old mark of 61 by a wide margin. "Big Mac," who also knocked in 147 runs for St. Louis, was hotly pursued in the race by Chicago's Sammy Sosa, the eventual NL MVP who hit 66 home runs of his own.

The race between McGwire and Sosa, which both fans and the media found endlessly fascinating, was the talk of the baseball world all summer. Mac crushed No. 62 on September 8, hugging Maris's children after the dramatic blow. He then blasted five long ones on the final weekend—two in the final game—to reach the magical 70.

While McGwire finished ahead in the home run race, Sosa's Cubs, also fueled by the emergence of rookie strikeout pitcher Kerry Wood, won a dramatic battle for the NL wildcard slot by defeating the San Francisco Giants in a one-game playoff.

MAC BLASTS 70 HOMERS; YANKS WIN 114 GAMES

San Diego rode the strong arms of starter Kevin Brown (18-7) and closer Trevor Hoffman (53 saves) and the power bat of Greg Vaughn—who hit "only" 50 homers and drove in 119—to an unlikely NL West championship. They then defeated favored Houston, who featured a balanced attack and five strong starting pitchers (including Randy Johnson, 10-1 after a midseason trade to the Astros), to advance to the NLCS.

The Atlanta Braves, paced by five 15-game winners on their pitching staff including Cy Young winner Tom Glavine, had the senior circuit's best record at 106-56. After whipping the Cubs in the Division Series, the Braves came up against San Diego—and were beaten in six games. The Braves scored just three runs in their four losses and went home unsatisfied yet again.

Ken Griffey Jr. paced the AL with 56 homers after also connecting for 56 the season before. However, his Mariners finished a poor third. AL West champion Texas featured Juan Gonzalez, who hit .318 with 50 doubles, 45 homers, and 157 RBI to win his second MVP in three seasons.

After losing four of their first five contests, the Yankees then captured 25 of their next 28 games and were 9½ games up in the AL East by late May. The race was never close, but the runner-up Red Sox compiled the league's second-best record on the strength of a good overall effort and the right arm of pitcher Pedro Martinez (19-7, 2.89 ERA). The only reason Martinez didn't win the AL Cy Young was Roger Clemens of Toronto, who picked up his fifth such trophy by pacing the league in wins, ERA, and strikeouts.

In the AL playoffs, the Yankees quickly disposed of the Rangers, while the Red Sox fell in a close series to the Indians. Cleveland, which won the AL Central with power and a fine bullpen, was not as strong as in previous seasons and bowed to New York in a six-game ALCS.

The Yankees seemed to regard each challenge as an opportunity to reaffirm their greatness. DH Chili Davis missed most of the season with injuries, and several other players took turns on the DL as well. Yet the Yankees, led by shortstop Derek Jeter and batting champ Bernie Williams, overcame every obstacle. While San Diego often played well in the Series, the Padres never really had a chance against the Bombers.

1998

- Yankees win 114 regular-season games, setting an all-time AL record and nearing the 1906 Cubs' record of 116.

- Yankees steamroll Rangers in three straight to win their Division Series.

- Red Sox take the AL wildcard berth, but lose to Cleveland in an exciting four-game Division Series.

- Indians challenge Yankees, taking two of first three games in the ALCS, but eventually lose in six games.

- Cubs win NL wildcard berth by beating San Francisco in a one-game playoff.

- Braves beat the Cubs in their NL Division Series, allowing Chicago to score just four runs in three games.

- Padres rip the heavily favored Astros and Braves to advance to the World Series for the first time since 1984.

- Yankees sweep the Padres in four games to win the World Series, the franchise's 24th title.

- Stringbean reliever Mariano Rivera picks up three saves against the Padres in the World Series.

Cardinals first baseman Mark McGwire raps out his 70th and final home run of 1998, one of two he hit in the season's last game. McGwire hit .299, drove in 147 runs, set the single-season homer record, and broke the all-time NL mark with 162 walks. The affable and photogenic "Big Mac," a true-life hero in St. Louis, also did yeoman work in lifting baseball back into the national spotlight.

- Third baseman Scott Brosius of New York bats .471 with two homers to win series MVP honors.

- Padres outfielder Tony Gwynn bats .500 with a homer in a losing effort against the Yankees in the Series.

- Mark McGwire of St. Louis breaks Roger Maris's all-time single-season home run record by slugging 70.

- McGwire breaks the all-time NL record for bases on balls in a season, drawing 162.

- McGwire tops the NL in both on-base percentage (.470) and slugging (.752, highest in ML since 1927).

- David Wells of the Yankees tosses a perfect game against the Twins on May 17, the 13th perfecto in history.

- Atlanta's Tom Glavine is 20-6 with a 2.47 ERA, leading the NL in wins for the fourth time.

- Trevor Hoffman of the Padres notches an ML-leading 53 saves in 54 opportunities.

- Glavine barely edges out Hoffman for NL Cy Young honors.

Selig Named Baseball's Commish

After six years of serving as "acting" commissioner of baseball, Milwaukee Brewers owner Bud Selig ceded day-to-day control of his club to daughter Wendy Selig-Prieb on August 4, 1998, and accepted the commisioner's position permanently. Although Selig had often claimed to not want the job, baseball's Executive Council could agree on no other acceptable candidates.

Bud Selig

Ramirez: 45 HRs, 126 RBI

In 1998, the Indians' attack centered in large part around 26-year-old right fielder Manny Ramirez. He set career highs in homers (45), RBI (126), and runs (108) and finished sixth in AL MVP voting. On June 15-16, Ramirez homered in four consecutive plate appearances to tie a big-league record. He also hit .343 with four homers in the postseason.

Manny Ramirez

Kerry Wood

Wood Strikes Out 20 'Stros

Rookie Cubs hurler Kerry Wood is shown here on May 6, when at age 20 he tied an all-time major-league record by fanning 20 men in a dramatic 2-0 complete-game one-hitter over the visiting Houston Astros. Wood finished his first season 13-6 with 233 strikeouts in just 167 innings. He was chosen the NL's Rookie of the Year.

1998

- Roger Clemens of the Blue Jays wins his second straight pitching Triple Crown, pacing the AL in wins (20), ERA (2.65), and strikeouts (271).

- Clemens is awarded the AL Cy Young for a record-breaking fifth time, this time unanimously.

- Clemens becomes the 11th pitcher to reach 3,000 strikeouts when he whiffs Tampa Bay's Randy Winn on July 5.

- Rick Helling of Texas and David Cone of the Yankees tie Clemens atop the AL list with 20 wins.

- Sammy Sosa cracks 66 home runs and drives in 158 for the Cubs, pacing the NL with 226 runs produced.

- Sosa is voted the NL's MVP.

- Texas outfielder Juan Gonzalez hits .318 with 45 homers and leads the AL with 50 doubles and 157 RBI.

- Gonzalez is AL MVP for the second time in three years.

- Ken Griffey hits 56 home runs and knocks in 146 runs.

David Wells

Harry Caray

Harry Caray Passes On

Legendary 83-year-old Cubs broadcaster Harry Caray, a hero to Chicago fans and a veteran of more than 50 years behind the mike, died on February 18, 1998, due to complications from a stroke. He had called the action for the Cubs since 1981 after jobs with the Chicago White Sox, Oakland A's, and St. Louis Cardinals. The unabashed Cubs rooter was famous for the phrases "holy cow!" and "let's get some runs!"

Wells Tosses Perfect Game

Veteran southpaw David Wells enjoyed a career year in 1998. Shown here celebrating his May 17 perfect game over the Minnesota Twins at Yankee Stadium, Wells was 18-4 with five shutouts for the Yankees. He fanned a career-high 163 and walked only 29 men in 214 innings, ultimately finishing third in AL Cy Young Award voting. In the postseason, he went 4-0.

D'Backs Debut at the BOB

The NL's newest franchise, the Arizona Diamondbacks, played their home games in the new Bank One Ballpark, a $354 million structure that took 28 months to build. The park was the first one in the world to feature a retractable roof, real grass, and air conditioning. More than three and a half million fans filed into the park in 1998 to see a mediocre Arizona club.

Bank One Ballpark

- Cubs righty Kerry Wood strikes out 20 Houston Astros on May 6, tying the all-time one-game mark.
- Wood wins the voting for NL ROTY.
- Ben Grieve of the A's is AL ROTY.
- Only one player, pitcher Don Sutton, is voted into the Hall of Fame by the BBWAA.

- The Hall of Fame's Veterans Committee selects Larry Doby, Lee MacPhail, Bullet Joe Rogan, and George Davis for enshrinement.
- In their first season as an NL club, the Milwaukee Brewers finish 74-88.
- Edgar Martinez's .429 on-base percentage is the AL's best.

- Star reliever Dennis Eckersley retires at age 44 holding the all-time record for games pitched (1,071).
- Three players—Todd Walker of Minnesota, Barry Bonds of San Francisco, and John Olerud of the Mets—each collect nine consecutive hits.

Sammy Sosa

A-Rod: 42 HRs, 46 SBs

At age 23, Seattle's Alex Rodriguez broke the AL record for homers in a season by a shortstop, connecting 42 times. He also swiped 46 sacks to become just the third player in big-league history to reach 40 of each. The well-spoken Rodriguez also made his mark in other ways, leading the league in hits (213), appearing in all 161 Mariners games, and playing Gold Glove-caliber shortstop.

Sosa Slams 66 Homers

Even Sammy Sosa's biggest boosters could never have imagined him enjoying a season like 1998, when he hit 66 home runs, won the NL's MVP trophy, and cemented his position as an international idol. Sosa helped the long-suffering Cubs into the playoffs with his all-around game, leading the NL by scoring 134 runs and driving in 158—the most in the majors in 49 years.

Igor Drives in 157 Runs

Rangers slugger Juan "Igor" Gonzalez tattooed AL pitchers during 1998, batting .318 with 47 homers, leading the league with 50 doubles and 157 RBI, and winning his second MVP Award in three seasons. The 28-year-old Gonzalez couldn't duplicate his outstanding performance in the postseason, however. He was just 1-for-12 as the AL West champion Rangers lost their Division Series to the Yankees.

Juan Gonzalez

Alex Rodriguez

1998

- Cal Ripken ends his games streak at 2,632 on September 20.

- Bud Selig is elected commissioner on July 8.

- Greg Maddux wins his ninth consecutive Gold Glove.

- San Diego's Greg Vaughn hits 50 homers.

- Pittsburgh's Tony Womack sets a record by going 980 plate appearances without hitting into a double play.

- Randy Johnson is 9-10 for Seattle before being traded to Houston, for whom he goes 10-1 with a 1.26 ERA.

- Baltimore's Eric Davis hits in 30 straight games.

- Larry Walker of the Rockies bats .363 to win the NL batting crown, adding 46 doubles and 23 homers.

- Sosa hits 20 home runs in June, an all-time record for one calendar month.

- Sosa homers 12 times against Milwaukee.

Glavine Cops the Cy

Lefty Tom Glavine picked up his second Cy Young Award in 1998, posting a 20-6 record and a fine 2.47 ERA to help the Braves win the NL East once again. Glavine's Cy was the sixth won by Atlanta pitchers during the 1990s, and his 20 wins were his fourth league-leading total. A complete athlete, Glavine also batted .239 with seven RBI in 1998.

Tom Glavine

Cal's Streak Ends at 2,632

Baltimore third baseman Cal Ripken voluntarily ended his consecutive-games streak on September 20, 1998. It was the first time he took a day off from the Orioles since May 29, 1982. His all-time consecutive games played mark, which stands at 2,632, will be a tall order for anyone to match. Even batting just .271 with 14 homers, the legendary Ripken was an All-Star starter again in '98.

Cal Ripken

Greg Vaughn

Vaughn's 50 Go Unnoticed

Launching "just" 50 home runs in the year of Mark McGwire and Sammy Sosa, San Diego left fielder Greg Vaughn was seemingly forgotten by everyone but his Padres teammates and the club's fans, who knew just how critical his big bat was to the Friars' success. Playing his first injury-free season since 1993, Vaughn drove in 119 runs and finished fourth in league MVP voting.

- The AL outlasts the NL 13-8 in the All-Star Game, played at Denver's Coors Field.

- Roberto Alomar of the Orioles is the All-Star MVP, going 3-for-4 with a home run.

- Houston's Craig Biggio is the first player since 1912 to notch 50 doubles and 50 steals in a season.

- Bernie Williams of the Yankees wins the AL batting title with a .339 average.

- Albert Belle of the White Sox, who hits .328 with 49 homers and 152 RBI, is paid $10 million.

- Rickey Henderson of Oakland, age 39, bats just .236 but tops the AL with 118 walks and 66 stolen bases.

- Henderson scores his 2,000th run during the season, becoming just the sixth man ever to do so.

- The Marlins' salary dump continues on May 15 as they send Gary Sheffield, Charles Johnson, Bobby Bonilla, and Jim Eisenreich to the Dodgers for Mike Piazza and Todd Zeile.

Albert Belle

Belle Blasts 49 Homers, 48 Doubles

Playing in relative obscurity for a White Sox club far removed from the pennant race, controversial slugger Albert Belle whacked 99 extra-base hits in 1998, the second-highest total in AL history and just four behind his own record, set in 1995. He hit .328 with 49 homers and 48 doubles for the Sox, then signed as a free agent with Baltimore.

Kevin Brown

Brown Carries Padres to WS

Righthander Kevin Brown helped lift the Padres into the World Series in 1998. With an 18-7 record, 2.38 ERA, and 257 whiffs and only 49 walks in 257 innings, Brown finished third in NL Cy Young balloting. He also fanned 46 men in the playoffs and World Series to set a record for strikeouts in postseason play. Following the season, Brown inked a seven-year, $105 million deal with the Los Angeles Dodgers.

Big Unit Revs It Up in Houston

After spending nine years with the Mariners, dominating lefthander Randy Johnson was dealt to Houston on July 31. Johnson was an amazing 10-1 with a minuscule 1.26 ERA in 11 starts for his new club, tossing shutouts in each of his first four Astrodome starts. In Houston's Division Series loss to San Diego, the "Big Unit" was 0-2 despite allowing just three earned runs in 14 innings.

Randy Johnson

1998

- On May 22, the Marlins deal Piazza to the Mets for three minor-leaguers.

- Chicago loses two broadcasting legends in one year, as both Harry Caray and Jack Brickhouse pass away.

- Curt Schilling of Philadelphia paces the NL in strikeouts for the second straight season, whiffing 300.

- Paul Molitor retires from the Twins with 3,319 hits, which rank eighth on the all-time list.

- Shorn thin of talent by budget-driven trades, the World Champion Marlins fall to 54-108, the worst mark in the game.

- On August 23, Barry Bonds of the Giants becomes the first man ever with 400 homers and 400 stolen bases.

- Montreal's Vladimir Guerrero hits 38 home runs in his first full season.

- Chet "Red" Hoff, the oldest living major-leaguer, dies at age 107.

- The first-year Arizona Diamondbacks finish last in the NL West at 65-97.

NLCS

Scott Brosius

Brosius Slugs Key Homer

Yankees third baseman Scott Brosius exults as he sees his eighth-inning three-run homer clear the fence, giving New York a 5-3 lead in game three of the World Series. (NL President Leonard Coleman, sitting in the front row in a tan jacket, is not quite so thrilled.) Brosius, the eventual Series MVP, batted .471 with two homers and six RBI in the Yankees' four-game sweep of San Diego.

San Diego Topples Atlanta

Atlanta Braves left fielder Ryan Klesko seems to be asking the TV cameraman to supply him with a new ball after Ken Caminiti of the Padres drove one over the left-field fence in the first inning of game five of the NLCS. Despite Caminiti's two-run homer, the Braves won 7-6. However, San Diego whipped the Braves 5-0 in game six to complete a surprising series triumph.

Yanks Erase Pads in Four

New York Yankees shortstop Derek Jeter eludes the slide of San Diego's Greg Vaughn to complete a double play in the decisive game four of the Series. Jeter scored two runs in the 3-0 win, giving the Yankees their 24th World Series trophy. New York's finest have more championships to their credit than any other professional sports franchise.

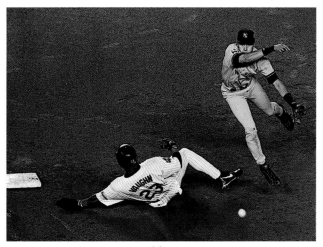

World Series

- Arizona hitters fan 1,239 times to set a new NL record.

- The Indians are the only AL Central club to finish over the .500 mark.

- Angels owner Gene Autry dies on October 2.

- The Tampa Bay Devil Rays, the AL's expansion club, go 63-99.

- Arizona's Dave Dellucci leads the NL with 12 triples despite batting just .260 and stealing only three bases.

- Tom "Flash" Gordon of Boston, a converted starter, paces the AL with 46 saves.

- Former Royals reliever Dan Quisenberry dies of a brain tumor on September 30 at age 45.

- Pitcher Kevin Brown signs a seven-year, $105 million deal with the Los Angeles Dodgers.

- The Rockies fire Don Baylor, the club's manager since its inception, immediately after the season.

- Baseball sets an all-time attendance mark as 70,618,731 fans enter the parks.

YANKEES SWEEP BRAVES FOR 25TH TITLE

The Yankees closed out the 20th century by winning their 25th World Series title, their third in four years. A four-game Series sweep of the Atlanta Braves simply restated the Bombers' domination of America's game.

During the regular season, New York won "just" 98 times, a far cry from their 114 victories of 1998. Considering the circumstances, however, it was a tremendous accomplishment. Manager Joe Torre was diagnosed with prostate cancer, DH Darryl Strawberry was arrested for drug possession, and pitchers Roger Clemens and Andy Pettitte struggled through subpar seasons.

Yet the Yanks marched on. Bernie Williams, Paul O'Neill, Derek Jeter, and Tino Martinez each knocked in more than 100 runs, and closer Mariano Rivera didn't allow a run after July 21. Pitcher Orlando "El Duque" Hernandez, signed after defecting from Cuba, led the staff with 17 wins and shined in October.

The NL champion Braves also dealt with trauma. First baseman Andres Galarraga, diagnosed with cancer, sat out the year, while pitchers Kerry Ligtenberg and John Smoltz and catcher Javier Lopez lost time with serious injuries. However, MVP third baseman Chipper Jones hoisted the offense onto his back (.319, 45 homers, 126 walks), while center fielder Andruw Jones dazzled at bat and in the field.

And when Greg Maddux "slumped" to a 3.57 ERA, and Tom Glavine fell to 14-11 and 4.12, young Kevin Millwood came through with an 18-7 season. The Braves' pitching was the difference in the Division Series, where they beat Houston in four, and in the NLCS, where Atlanta outlasted New York in six tough games.

The Mets, who smashed the ML record for fewest errors (68), featured four offensive stars: catcher Mike Piazza and infielders John Olerud, Edgardo Alfonzo, and Robin Ventura. The veteran pitching carried the Mets to victory over Arizona in the Division Series, but their bats failed against Atlanta in the NLCS.

Home runs were again a big part of the game in 1999, but they didn't always lead to wins. Despite 65 jacks from Mark McGwire, the Cardinals could do no better than fourth in the NL Central, and the Cubs were last despite Sammy Sosa's 63 dingers.

In the AL playoffs, the Yankees breezed past both the Rangers and Red Sox. New York rendered the Rangers' lineup impotent, negating MVP Ivan Rodriguez and sluggers Juan Gonzalez and Rafael Palmeiro (47 home runs).

Boston, the AL's wildcard team, defeated perpetually disappointing Cleveland in their Division Series but was no match for New York in the ALCS. The Red Sox boasted Pedro Martinez (23-4, 2.07) and a deep bullpen, but aside from shortstop Nomar Garciaparra (.357, 42 doubles, 27 homers) lacked the horses to run with the Yanks.

Game one of the World Series saw the Yankees explode for four runs in the eighth en route to a 4-1 victory. Following a 7-2 Yankees win, in which David Cone allowed just one hit over seven innings and Millwood was blown out, New York led the Series 2-0 with the action shifting to the Bronx.

Game three was the Braves' best chance. Up 5-1 after four innings, Atlanta appeared to be back in the series. However, the Yankees' bullpen threw 6⅓ scoreless frames and the offense slowly climbed back into the game, tying it by the eighth. Chad Curtis's tenth-inning blast catapulted the Yankees to a 6-5 win.

The next evening, Roger Clemens won his first World Series ring after yielding just one run in 7⅓ innings. The Yankees prevailed 4-1, leaving no doubts that they were the best team not only of the year, but of the decade and the century as well.

1999

- Mets defeat Cincinnati in a special one-game playoff to become the NL's wildcard team.

- Rangers win the AL West, but they're swept in the Division Series by the Yankees for the second straight year.

- Boston pounds Cleveland 23-7 in game four of their AL Division Series, then wins in five games.

- In losing the ALCS in five games to the Yankees, the Red Sox make ten errors, nearly all of them costly.

- Yankee pitcher Orlando Hernandez, a Cuban refugee, is the ALCS MVP.

- Mets reserve catcher Todd Pratt's tie-breaking, tenth-inning, game-four homer gives New York the Division Series win over Arizona.

- Houston's "Killer Bs"—Jeff Bagwell, Craig Biggio, and Derek Bell—combine to hit just .143 with no RBI in the club's Division Series loss to Atlanta.

- Braves defeat the Mets in six games in the NLCS. Braves catcher Eddie Perez, who raps .500 with two homers in 20 at-bats, is named MVP.

Yankees second baseman Chuck Knoblauch attempts a twin killing against the Braves in the 1999 World Series. The Yanks not only swept the Braves, but they extended their World Series winning streak to 12 games (they'd stretch it to 14 in 2000). It also gave them 18 wins in their last 19 postseason contests.

- Yankees allow just nine runs to Atlanta in their World Series sweep.

- Chad Curtis's two home runs, including a decisive tenth-inning blast, help the Yankees win game three of the Series 6-5.

- Veteran Roger Clemens pitches the Yankees to the Series title with 7⅔ innings of one-run ball in game four.

- New York's Mariano Rivera saves two games, wins another, and is named World Series MVP.

- Atlanta's Chipper Jones is voted NL MVP after hitting .319 with 116 runs, 45 homers, 110 RBI, 126 walks, and 25 steals.

- Ivan Rodriguez of Texas wins his first MVP award. He is the first AL

catcher ever to hit .300 with at least 100 runs and 100 RBI.

- Rodriguez's .332 batting average is the highest by an AL catcher since Bill Dickey batted .332 in 1937. He also steals 25 bases.

- Boston ace Pedro Martinez is a close second in controversial AL MVP balloting.

Jones Powers Way to MVP

A beefed-up Chipper Jones garnered NL MVP honors in 1999. After hitting the weights with a vengeance, and learning to take lefties deep, he powered a career-high 45 home runs. He also walked 126 times, stole 25 bases, and ripped a league-high .417 in clutch situations. His September heroics carried the Braves to the division title.

Chipper Jones

Pudge Earns Top AL Prize

Ivan Rodriguez

Ivan "Pudge" Rodriguez of the Rangers won the 1999 AL MVP Award, beating out Boston pitcher Pedro Martinez in a controversial vote. Rodriguez helped Texas win its third straight AL West title with a .332 average, 35 homers, 113 RBI, and 25 steals. He started his eighth straight All-Star Game and recorded the majors' highest caught-stealing percentage (54.2) of the decade.

Gabriel Perre

Cuba Team Plays in USA

Cuba's Gabriel Perre celebrates near the visitors' dugout in Baltimore's Camden Yards on May 3. That night, the Cuban national team defeated the Orioles 12-6. It was the first time a Cuban team had ever faced a major league club on American soil. Back on March 28, the O's had edged the Cubans 3-2 in an 11-inning contest in Havana, with Fidel Castro watching attentively from the stands.

1999

- Martinez, the Cy Young winner, leads the league with 313 strikeouts, 23 wins, and a 2.07 ERA—1.37 runs lower than any other eligible AL pitcher.

- Randy Johnson of Arizona wins the NL Cy Young with a 17-9 record, 2.48 ERA, 12 complete games, and 364 whiffs.

- Cardinal Mark McGwire's 65 home runs lead the NL for the second straight year. He also wins his first RBI championship with 147.

- On January 12, McGwire's 70th home run ball from 1998 is auctioned off for $2.7 million.

- Sammy Sosa of the Cubs slams 63 homers to finish second to McGwire.

- In March, the Orioles become the first ML team to visit Cuba since 1959. They defeat a team of Cuban amateurs 3-2 in 11 innings.

- On April 4, the Rockies beat the Padres 8-2 in Monterrey, Mexico— the first ML regular-season game ever played outside the United States or Canada.

Fans Mourn Death of DiMaggio

When legend Joe DiMaggio passed away on March 8, 1999, a nation mourned. The Yankee Stadium flag was immediately lowered to half-mast, while everyone from former teammates to President Bill Clinton paid tribute. During his fabled 13-year career, the "Yankee Clipper" captured three MVP trophies and won legions of fans with his stylish play. He became somewhat of a recluse after his retirement.

Fernando Tatis

Tatis Jacks Two Slams in an Inning

Cardinals third sacker Fernando Tatis clubs his second grand slam of the third inning on April 23, 1999, at Los Angeles. Tatis, who ended the '99 campaign with 34 homers and 107 RBI, is the only player ever to hit two grannies in the same inning. His eight RBI in the frame also set a record. Dodgers pitcher Chan Ho Park was in the game long enough to serve up both slams.

Joe DiMaggio Memorial

Flash Saves 54 Games in a Row

Red Sox closer Tom "Flash" Gordon, who led the AL with 46 saves in 1998, pitched in only 21 games in 1999. Before going down with an elbow injury, however, he recorded his 54th save in 54 opportunities, setting a major league record. The achievement didn't receive much fanfare nationwide, but to fellow relievers it was the equivalent of Joe DiMaggio's 56-game hitting streak. Gordon had been a starter for much of his career.

Tom Gordon

- San Diego's Tony Gwynn singles off Montreal's Dan Smith on August 6 for his 3,000th career hit.

- On August 7, Tampa Bay's Wade Boggs collects his 3,000th hit—a home run off Cleveland's Chris Haney.

- On April 23, Fernando Tatis of the Cardinals becomes the first ML player to club two grand slams in one inning, both against the Dodgers' Chan Ho Park.

- In searing heat in New York, Yankee David Cone fires a 5-0 perfect game at the Expos on July 18.

- Cardinals rookie Jose Jimenez no-hits the Diamondbacks on June 25.

- Eric Milton of the Twins, pitching against a reserve-filled Angels lineup, throws a no-hitter on September 11.

- McGwire belts his 500th home run on August 5 against San Diego.

- Kansas City center fielder Carlos Beltran is AL ROTY. Beltran is the first rookie since Fred Lynn in 1975 to both score and bat in 100 runs.

Mac Belts 65 More

After launching 70 home runs in 1998, Mark McGwire swatted 65 more in '99—the second most in major league history. Incredibly, he belted his 500th homer a year after slamming his 400th. He also broke Lou Gehrig's major league record for home runs by a first baseman. At season's end, he and Gehrig were the only first sackers named to the MLB All-Century Team.

Mark McGwire

Ramirez Plates 165

Powering the ball to all fields, Manny Ramirez drove in 165 runs in 1999—the most in the majors in 61 years. Incredibly, he did it in only 147 games. The Cleveland right fielder cracked .333 with 44 home runs—and blasted .386 with runners in scoring position. Top-of-the-order men Kenny Lofton and Roberto Alomar, who were often on base, scored a combined 248 runs in 279 games.

Manny Ramirez

Safeco Field

Mariners Open Pricey Safeco Field

The Mariners' new home, Safeco Field, opened for business on July 15, 1999. Sadly for the local fans, the game went to the visiting Padres 3-2. Safeco featured a retractable roof, considered a necessity in Seattle because of the city's wet weather. The park, friendlier to pitchers than the cozy Kingdome had been, cost $517 million to build—$100 million more than originally estimated. That was just another unpleasant part of a 1999 season in which the Mariners finished a disappointing 79-83.

1999

- Reds reliever Scott Williamson wins NL ROTY honors after going 12-7 with 19 saves and a 2.41 ERA.

- Red Sox shortstop Nomar Garciaparra wins the AL bat crown with a .357 mark and chips in 27 homers.

- Derek Jeter of the Yankees paces the majors with 219 hits.

- Houston's Jeff Bagwell leads the majors in walks (149) and runs (143). He also slams 42 home runs.

- Colorado's Larry Walker fronts the NL in batting average (.379), on-base percentage (.458), and slugging percentage (.710).

- Tony Womack of the Diamondbacks leads the majors with 72 steals.

- In his final season with Seattle, Ken Griffey Jr. hits 48 home runs to lead the AL.

- Indians win the AL Central for the fifth straight season, climbing into first place for good on April 8.

- Clemens sets an AL record by winning 20 straight games (over two seasons).

Hampton Pitches, Hits Way to 22-4

With his 22-4 record and 2.90 ERA, Houston lefty Mike Hampton propelled the Astros to their third straight NL Central crown in 1999. Hampton paced the league in wins, ranked third in ERA, and helped his own cause with great defense and a .311 batting average. He finished second in Cy Young voting to former teammate Randy Johnson.

Mike Hampton

David Cone

Cone Achieves Perfection

Yankees pitcher David Cone is hoisted on his teammates' shoulders after tossing a perfect game on July 18, 1999. Getting extra bite on his slider, Cone threw 68 strikes and only 20 balls. Before the game, ironically, Yogi Berra caught a ceremonial first pitch from Don Larsen. They were the battery that had combined for a perfect game in the 1956 World Series.

Bagwell: 42 Homers, 143 Runs

With his strong, quick hands, Jeff Bagwell hammered 42 home runs in 1999, leading Houston to the NL Central title. His great instincts for the game were reflected in his other numbers. He walked 149 times, third most in league history, and—despite mediocre speed—swiped 30 bags. On base an NL-high 331 times, he ended up scoring 143 runs, another league high. Bagwell became only the seventh member of the 40-homers/30-steals club, and he finished runner-up to Atlanta's Chipper Jones in NL MVP voting.

Jeff Bagwell

- Mets set an ML record by committing just 68 errors.
- Following the All-Star break, the Mariners move to new Safeco Field.
- On June 9, prior to a Dodgers-Rangers game, three-year-old Rex Spjute of Meridian, Idaho, sings the national anthem.
- The Braves' 103 regular-season wins are the most of any team.
- Atlanta wins the NL East by 6½ games despite losing first baseman Andres Galarraga for the season due to cancer.
- Houston moves out of the Astrodome, its home since 1965, following the season's conclusion.
- Astros manager Larry Dierker is sidelined nearly a month after suffering a seizure in the dugout.
- Arizona's NL West title, coming in just its second year of play, is the quickest championship ever for an expansion team.
- Detroit's Tiger Stadium closes down after 88 seasons.

Sammy Sosa

Martinez Breezes to Cy

Pedro Martinez, Boston's overpowering right-hander, collected his second Cy Young Award in 1999. The NL's recipient in 1997, Martinez in '99 led the AL in wins (23), winning percentage (.854), strikeouts (313), and ERA (2.07), almost single-handedly carrying Boston to the playoffs. During the season, he fanned 15 batters twice and 16 once, and he fired a one-hitter in which he struck out 17.

Pedro Martinez

Sammy Slams 60 Again

On September 18, 1999, Cubs slugger Sammy Sosa connected for his 60th homer of the season against Milwaukee's Jason Bere at Wrigley Field. He thus became the first player ever to bash 60 homers twice. But as in 1998, Sammy eventually lost the four-bagger crown to Cardinals star Mark McGwire, who connected for 65.

1999

- Mariano Rivera saves 45 for the Yankees to lead the majors.

- Ugueth Urbina of Montreal saves 41 games, most in the NL.

- On June 5, Boston reliever Tom Gordon blows a save, ending his ML record-setting streak of 54 consecutive saves.

- An injury-riddled Cal Ripken Jr. plays in only 86 games—but hits .340.

- Devil Ray Fred McGriff sets an ML record by homering in 35 different stadiums throughout his career.

- Cleveland rings up 1,009 runs, becoming the first club to clear a grand since Boston in 1950.

- Montreal's Vladimir Guerrero hits .316 with 42 homers and 131 RBI. He also authors a 31-game hit streak.

- The Hall of Fame inducts seven men, including Nolan Ryan, George Brett, Robin Yount, and Orlando Cepeda.

- In Milwaukee, three people are killed during construction of the Brewers' new stadium, Miller Park.

NLCS

Boone's HR Dooms the Red Sox

New York third baseman Aaron Boone crosses home plate with the deciding run in game seven of the 2003 ALCS. Boone's 11th-inning walk-off homer extended the "Curse of the Bambino," as the Red Sox—who appeared to have the game in hand in the eighth inning—once again failed to bring home the bacon. The thrilling Yankees-Red Sox playoff featured three one-run games and several thrilling comebacks.

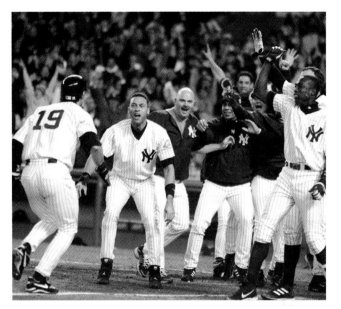

ALCS

Cubs Curse Continues

Cubs fan Steve Bartman (*in cap and black sweatshirt*) picked a bad time to test his fielding skills. Chicago left fielder Moises Alou claimed Bartman interfered with the ball on this play in the eighth inning of game six of the 2003 NLCS. The floodgates immediately opened, as the Marlins plated eight runs to win 8-3. They then beat Kerry Wood in game seven, 9-6, extending the Cubs' World Series drought to 58 years.

World Series

Gonzalez Tallies Winning Run

Marlins shortstop Alex Gonzalez slides home in the fifth inning of game six of the 2003 World Series. The tally, which came on Luis Castillo's single, gave the Marlins a 1-0 lead. Florida added another in the next inning and held on for a 2-0 victory. The Marlins were outscored 21-17, out-homered 6-2, and outhit .261 to .232, but great mound outings by Josh Beckett and Brad Penny propelled Florida to the title.

- Philadelphia's Veterans Stadium and San Diego's Qualcomm Stadium close down after the conclusion of the regular season.

- Baltimore pitcher Steve Bechler dies after a spring training workout on February 17. His death is linked to the performance-enhancing supplement ephedra.

- Cincinnati first baseman Dernell Stenson is murdered in Phoenix on November 5.

- The U.S. national baseball team fails to qualify for the 2004 Olympics in Athens, Greece.

- The BBWAA votes Gary Carter and Eddie Murray into the Hall of Fame.

- A newly configured Hall of Fame Veterans Committee fails to elect a single player.

- Florida's Jack McKeon and Kansas City's Tony Pena are named Manager of the Year in their respective leagues.

- Boston fires manager Grady Little two days after the conclusion of the World Series.

Take That, Babe! Sox Reverse the Curse

Every team wants to end the season on a winning streak—especially if the last game clinches the World Series. The 2004 Boston Red Sox did just that. A rough and tumble aggregation, the Sox shucked the "Curse of the Bambino" and steamrolled to the world championship, winning their last eight games.

After finishing a strong second in the AL East to the Yankees, wildcard Boston wiped out West champ Anaheim in a three-game ALDS. Meanwhile, the Yankees won their ALDS in four games against Minnesota, the Central champions, who despite good starts from Cy Young winner Johan Santana twice blew leads in the late innings. Ruben Sierra delivered a key pinch homer in game four to break the Twins' backs.

While the nation anticipated a classic Red Sox/Yankees ALCS, the first three games were all New York. After taking 10-7 and 3-1 wins at home, the Yankees thoroughly embarrassed Boston, 19-8, in game three. When the Yanks went ahead 4-3 in game four, the Red Sox looked done.

But a ninth-inning rally, sparked by Dave Roberts's clutch stolen base, tied the fourth game, and David Ortiz won the contest with a 12th-inning homer. The next night, Boston again outlasted the Yankees, this time triumphing on Ortiz's 14th-inning single. Red Sox fans, deprived of a world title since Babe Ruth was dealt to the Yankees in 1919, rallied around a new slogan: Keep the Faith.

Back in New York, the Red Sox won game six behind Curt Schilling, who pitched seven strong innings despite a torn ankle tendon. With clear momentum, Boston wiped up New York 10-3 in game seven, completing perhaps the greatest postseason comeback in history. No major-league team had ever won a postseason series after being down three games to none.

Some great performers watched the postseason on TV. Seattle finished last despite Ichiro Suzuki's .372 average and all-time record 262 hits. Barry Bonds took a staggering 232 walks and captured his seventh NL MVP Award, but the Giants finished second. Young arms Santana and Jake Peavy (of the Padres) served notice, while 40-year-old Randy Johnson authored a perfect game. Roger Clemens won his seventh Cy Young Award, this one

for Houston. Teammate Roy Oswalt's 20 wins propelled the Astros, who appeared dead in August before erupting in September. Wildcard Houston then took the Braves in a five-game NLDS.

In the NLCS, St. Louis (which had eliminated NL West champ Los Angeles) found holes in Houston's bullpen and eked out a league championship in seven tough games. Led by offensive bludgeons Albert Pujols, Scott Rolen, and Jim Edmonds, the Cardinals had finished 105-57.

Still high from their ALCS comeback, Boston took game one of the World Series, breaking a 9-9 tie on Mark Bellhorn's eighth-inning homer. After winning game two 6-2 at Fenway, Boston then shut down the Redbirds 4-1 and 3-0 in St. Louis for a convincing four-game sweep. Rolen and Edmonds combined to go 1-for-30. It was almost too simple. The surprising sweep set New England into another frenzy of celebration.

Far from the spotlight, the Montreal Expos ended their tenure in Canada after yet another frustrating season of low attendance and poor performance. Washington, D.C., was scheduled to welcome the club for 2005. One thing Washington *didn't* welcome was baseball's growing steroid scandal. Steroid revelations sullied the reputations of Mark McGwire, Jason Giambi, and Barry Bonds, with no end in sight.

2004

- Houston, left for dead in August, wins 28 of its last 35 games under midseason managerial hire Phil Garner to capture the NL wildcard.
- The Braves, winners of the NL East, fall to Houston in a five-game NLDS.
- The NL Central champion Cardinals dispose of West champ Los Angeles in a four-game NLDS.

- St. Louis wins a thrilling NLCS in seven games.
- Houston outfielder Carlos Beltran clubs four homers in the NLDS and four more in the NLCS.
- Wildcard winner Boston sweeps a three-game ALDS from West champion Anaheim.

- New York defeats pesky Minnesota in four ALDS games.
- Boston falls behind three games to none in the ALCS before staging a shocking comeback, taking four straight from the Yankees.
- The Red Sox finish with eight straight wins, as they sweep St. Louis in four games to win the World Series.

Shaggy-haired Red Sox center fielder Johnny Damon, helmet flying, scores the winning run in Boston's 5-4 triumph over the Yankees in game five of the ALCS. Damon, who came around on David Ortiz's 14th-inning single, typified Boston's never-say-die attitude. Though just 3-for-29 through the first six contests, he belted two homers and drove in six runs in game seven.

- Boston's Manny Ramirez is named World Series MVP after hitting .412 with four RBI.

- Curt Schilling of Boston starts and wins game two of the World Series despite pitching with a torn tendon in his right ankle.

- Boston's David Ortiz drives in 19 runs in the postseason.

- Anaheim's Vladimir Guerrero is named AL MVP.

- Guerrero bats .337 with 39 home runs and tops the AL in runs (124) and total bases (366).

- Twins lefty Johan Santana (20-6) is the AL Cy Young winner, garnering all 28 first-place votes.

- Santana's league-leading 2.61 ERA is more than two runs below the AL's average. He also leads the junior loop with 265 strikeouts.

- Barry Bonds of the Giants wins his seventh NL MVP Award—and fourth in a row.

- Bonds leads the NL in BA (.362), OBP (a record .609), and SA (.812).

Petco Park

Fans and Pitchers Delighted with Petco

San Diego's Petco Park opened to rave reviews in 2004. The ballpark incorporated the city skyline and boasted stucco walls, a palm court, jacaranda trees, and even water walls. Beyond the outfield fence, fans could enjoy a "beach" and a "park." Petco also featured pitcher-friendly dimensions. The Padres hit just .256 with 57 homers at home in 2004, as opposed to .288 with 82 round-trippers on the road.

Steroids Scandal

Steroids Scandal Rocks the Game

Some players may have followed this young fan's suggestion late in the 2004 season, when the game's simmering steroid scandal reached full boil. Revelations of steroid use from former MVPs Jason Giambi, Mark McGwire, and Ken Caminiti (who died on October 10) led to rumors concerning other stars, including Barry Bonds and Gary Sheffield. Commissioner Bud Selig promised action, but some wondered whether the problem would ever be fixed.

2004

- Bonds homers 45 times in only 373 at-bats.

- Bonds belts his 700th career home run on September 17.

- Bonds breaks his own single-season major-league record with an eye-popping 232 walks—120 of which are intentional.

- Bonds breaks the ML career walk record, previously held by Rickey Henderson, on July 4. He finishes the season with 2,302.

- Roger Clemens, coming out of retirement to sign with the Astros, wins his seventh Cy Young Award.

- Clemens, at age 42, finishes 18-4 with a 2.98 ERA and 218 strikeouts.

- Ichiro Suzuki of Seattle sets an all-time major-league record with 262 hits, breaking George Sisler's mark of 257.

- Suzuki's .372 average is the best in the junior circuit since 1980.

- Miguel Tejada, in his first year as Baltimore's shortstop, knocks in 150 runs to pace the major leagues.

Jim Edmonds

Edmonds, Cards Fall Short in WS

Center fielder Jim Edmonds and the St. Louis Cardinals dominated the NL Central during the 2004 season, finishing 105-57. The team's top three sluggers— Edmonds, Scott Rolen, and Albert Pujols—rapped a combined .316 with 122 home runs and 358 RBI. The trio smashed 12 homers in the NLDS and NLCS, but in the World Series they ran out of gas, combining for just one RBI.

Red Sox fans

High-Flying Lowe Wins All Three Clinchers

The 2004 regular season was a struggle for Derek Lowe, who racked up a 5.42 ERA. In October, however, he came up big. With Boston's pitching staff in tatters, Lowe (shown here with catcher Jason Varitek) won all three clinchers. First, he triumphed in game three of the ALDS in relief. Then as a starter, he defeated the Yankees in game seven of the ALCS and wrapped up the World Series in game four.

Derek Lowe

Finally, Red Sox Fans Can Die Happy

"Cursed" since 1918, when Boston last won the World Series, Red Sox fans finally realized their dream in 2004. On October 30, more than three million fans attended a celebratory parade through Boston. Said Red Sox Chairman Tom Werner: "So many people in their 90s have come up to me and said, 'I just want to live long enough to see one championship before I die.' This is for them."

- Philadelphia opens Citizens Bank Park after having played in Veterans Stadium since 1971.

- The Phillies, expected by many to win the NL East, instead finish a disappointing second. Manager Larry Bowa is fired.

- In anticipation of Hurricane Ivan, the Marlins are forced to play two

"home games" vs. the Montreal Expos at Chicago's U.S. Cellular Field on September 13-14.

- A long-suppressed steroids scandal rears its head throughout the season and after the World Series. Several superstar players, including Jason Giambi and Barry Bonds, are implicated.

- Ken Caminiti, the 1996 NL MVP, dies on October 10 of drug-related heart problems.

- Former Reds owner Marge Schott dies on March 2.

- The Montreal Expos, an NL franchise since 1969, play their final game on October 3. The franchise moves to Washington for 2005.

Johnson, Alex, 365, 400, 401, 405, 454
Johnson, Arnold, 284, 324
Johnson, Byron "Ban," 11, 12, 16, 20, 24, 88, 122, 146, 186
Johnson, Charles, 606, 616, 622, 630
Johnson, Cliff, 472, 533
Johnson, Dave, 397, 399, 426, 524
Johnson, Davey, 622
Johnson, Howard, 569, 570, 576
Johnson, Lance, 579, 587, 594, 612
Johnson, Randy, 581, 586, 588, 595, 600, 602, 603, 604, 616, 620, 624, 628, 630, 634, 641, 645, 648, 649, 651, 652, 654, 656, 657, 660, 672, 677
Johnson, Roy, 150, 156, 178
Johnson, Walter, 36, 37, 43, 46–49, 55–57, 60, 61, 68, 73, 79, 80, 84, 86, 90, 95, 104, 110, 111, 115, 116, 124, 146, 177, 194, 196, 240, 504, 505
Johnston, Doc, 86, 88
Jones, Andruw, 609, 615, 670
Jones, Bert, 10
Jones, Bobby, 640
Jones, Chipper, 632–634, 670
Jones, Doug, 621
Jones, Randy, 446, 449
Jones, "Sad Sam," 96, 100, 102, 104
Jones, Todd, 644
Jones, "Toothpick Sam," 291, 301, 312, 314, 318
Joost, Eddie, 210, 214, 250, 277
Jordan, Michael, 599
Joss, Addie, 19, 24, 37, 40, 41, 50, 52, 468
Joyner, Wally, 532, 543
Judge, Joe, 104, 112, 162
Jurges, Billy, 170, 175, 192
Justice, David, 567, 568, 575, 582, 583, 600, 601, 616, 640

K Kaat, Jim, 338, 343, 360, 366–368, 371, 375
Kaline, Al, 284, 290, 293, 294, 304, 314, 328, 335, 350, 376, 378, 384, 387, 419, 432, 435, 474, 483
Kamm, Willie, 97, 98, 121, 150, 162
Karros, Eric, 577
Kauff, Benny, 64, 66, 68, 71, 72, 80, 82, 84, 91
Keane, Johnny, 352, 353, 374
Keeler, Willie, 11, 15, 28, 198, 206, 467
Kekich, Mike, 426, 428
Kell, George, 240, 254, 255, 262, 263, 271, 508
Keller, Charlie, 194, 198, 202, 205, 206, 211, 212, 218, 230, 233
Kelley, Joe, 16, 412
Kelly, George, 92, 95, 104, 108, 126, 428, 517, 556
Kelly, Tom, 569
Keltner, Ken, 206, 248
Kennedy, Adam, 656, 662
Kennedy, Bob, 206, 253, 287
Kennedy, John, 304, 358
Kennedy, Kevin, 612
Kent, Jeff, 640, 641, 643
Kerr, Dickie, 84, 94
Key, Jimmy, 586, 589, 595, 608
Kile, Darryl, 656, 660, 661
Killebrew, Harmon, 293, 314, 317, 322, 336, 338, 344, 348–350, 352, 368, 375, 376, 381, 383, 392, 393, 400, 409, 411, 413, 442, 443, 516
Killian, Ed, 28, 46
Kim, Byung-Hyun, 648, 655
Kindall, Jerry, 362, 364
Kinder, Ellis, 255, 258
Kiner, Ralph, 237–239, 242–245, 248, 249, 255, 257, 260, 263, 266–269, 273, 278, 280, 282, 443, 670
Kingman, Brian, 668
Kingman, Dave, 473, 476, 496, 499, 501
Kirkland, Willie, 311, 325
Kittle, Ron, 504, 506
Klein, Chuck, 134, 135, 140–142, 146, 147, 152, 155, 158, 163, 178, 483, 584, 619
Klem, Bill, 210, 282
Klesko, Ryan, 631
Kluszewski, Ted, 284, 287, 292, 293, 306, 314
Knepper, Bob, 470, 488
Knight, Ray, 492, 496, 528
Knoblauch, Chuck, 568, 570, 580, 594, 595, 633

Koenig, Mark, 116, 122 152
Konstanty, Jim, 260, 261, 265, 288
Koosman, Jerry, 388, 389, 392, 396, 398, 468, 472
Koslo, Dave, 256, 271
Koufax, Sandy, 315, 336, 338, 339, 343–345, 347, 351, 352, 354, 360–363, 367–370, 374, 420
Krause, Harry, 44–46
Kremer, Remy, 120, 127, 143
Kruk, John, 587, 590, 592
Kubek, Tony, 302–304, 323, 327, 342
Kucks, Johnny, 296, 319
Kuenn, Harvey, 279, 281, 301, 313–315, 317, 318, 321, 325, 466, 496, 497, 499, 548
Kuhel, Joe, 158, 192, 232
Kuhn, Bowie, 392, 400, 424, 432, 448, 449, 515
Kurowski, Whitey, 212, 229

L Laabs, Chet, 224, 225
Labine, Clem, 290, 296, 298, 301
Lajoie, Nap, 11, 12, 14, 16, 20, 21, 24, 26–30, 32, 48–51, 54, 62, 65, 186, 196
Lamont, Gene, 590
Lamp, Dennis, 525
Landis, Judge Kenesaw Mountain, 88, 89, 91, 96, 106, 122, 146, 151, 179, 196, 223, 224, 226, 229
Langford, Rick, 459, 485, 488, 495
Langston, Mark, 519, 542, 565, 571, 606
Lanier, Hal, 534
Lanier, Max, 213, 218, 221
Lansford, Carney, 484, 491, 500, 552, 557
Lansing, Mike, 647
Larkin, Barry, 602, 603, 607
Larkin, Gene, 568
Larsen, Don, 290, 297, 299, 304, 320, 336
LaRussa, Tony, 504, 660
Lary, Frank, 296, 301, 316, 320, 328, 335
Lary, Lyn, 148, 165, 180, 186
Lasorda, Tommy, 520, 525, 534, 544, 615
Laudner, Tim, 489, 490
Lavagetto, Cookie, 197, 242
LaValliere, Mike, 582
Lavender, Jimmy, 70, 71
Law, Vern, 320, 325
Lazzeri, Tony, 112, 116, 119, 120, 122, 178, 188
Leach, Tommy, 16, 20, 44
Lee, Bill, 170, 175, 189, 193, 440
Lee, Derrek, 664
Lee, Manuel, 574
Lefebvre, Jim, 360, 364, 366, 575
Lefebvre, Joe, 502
LeFlore, Ron, 434, 454, 467, 476, 486
Leibrandt, Charlie, 569, 583
Leiter, Al, 615, 616, 647
Leius, Scott, 568
Lemke, Mark, 568, 607, 608
Lemon, Bob, 248, 252, 256, 257, 260, 261, 272, 284, 285, 293, 296, 452, 465, 474
Lemon, Chet, 458, 478, 492, 512, 519, 572
Lemon, Jim, 301, 322
Leonard, Dennis, 456, 462, 480, 495
Leonard, Dutch, 59, 64, 67, 68, 72, 74, 82, 122, 199
Levsen, Dutch, 118
Lewis, Buddy, 198
Lewis, Darren, 597
Leyland, Jim, 616
Leyritz, Jim, 608
Ligtenberg, Kerry, 632
Lima, Jose, 647
Lindell, Johnny, 221, 227, 229, 242, 254
Lindstrom, Fred, 104, 106, 109, 130, 151, 452, 493
Listach, Pat, 578
Little, Grady, 664, 671
Litwhiler, Danny, 214, 216, 232
Lofton, Kenny, 578, 586, 588, 592, 594, 600, 603, 607, 611, 663
Lolich, Mickey, 363, 382, 384, 391, 408, 409, 411, 416, 418, 444, 649
Lollar, Sherman, 241, 270, 304, 314, 315
Lombardi, Ernie, 156, 185, 188, 191, 193, 198–200, 205, 214, 461, 532
Lonborg, Jim, 376, 377, 380, 382, 422, 448
Long, Dale, 297, 485
Long, Herman, 26

Lopat, Eddie, 253, 254, 258, 269, 273, 278, 281
Lopes, Davey, 438, 442, 444, 452, 471
Lopez, Al, 247, 272, 299, 460
Lopez, Javier, 614, 632, 670
Loretta, Mark, 678
Loria, Jeffrey, 658
Lowe, Derek, 644, 659, 679
Lowell, Mike, 664
Lowrey, Peanuts, 259, 276, 280
Lucas, Red, 157, 162, 184, 191
Luderus, Fred, 63, 68, 76
Lumley, Harry, 26, 32
Luque, Dolf, 100, 103, 110, 112, 114
Lush, Johnny, 25, 34
Luzinski, Greg, 447, 448, 452, 456, 464, 480, 504
Lyle, Sparky, 421, 423, 448, 457, 462, 468
Lynn, Fred, 440–442, 472, 473, 476, 492, 496
Lyons, Ted, 118, 119, 125, 127, 139, 216, 294, 533

M Mack, Connie, 12, 44, 48, 49, 51, 52, 60, 61, 64, 66, 113, 128, 134, 135, 144, 146, 149, 150, 157, 158, 163, 164, 169, 186, 196, 235, 260, 262, 284, 300, 586, 604
Mack, Earle, 49
Mack, Shane, 580, 596
MacKenzie, Ken, 339
MacPhail, Larry, 193, 210, 220, 239, 242, 247, 307, 468
MacPhail, Lee, 312, 627
Maddox, Garry, 428, 444, 448, 450, 456, 480, 498
Maddux, Greg, 571, 579–580, 581, 585, 587, 595, 598, 601, 602, 604, 621, 623, 628, 632, 669, 676, 678
Madlock, Bill, 428, 435, 441, 445, 451, 460, 491, 505
Magadan, Dave, 566
Magee, Sherry, 48, 63, 66, 67, 82
Maglie, Sal, 236, 260, 262, 266, 267, 272, 284, 296, 298
Maier, Jeffrey, 608, 615
Malone, Pat, 134, 137, 138, 142, 143, 152
Maloney, Jim, 344, 347, 360, 361, 395
Malzone, Frank, 304, 306
Mantle, Mickey, 266, 270–272, 276, 278, 279, 281, 282, 290–293, 295–297, 299, 302, 304, 305, 308–311, 320, 322–324, 326, 328, 329, 333–336, 339, 341, 344, 348, 352, 354, 359, 362, 376, 378, 386, 392, 398, 411, 436, 522, 561, 597, 606
Manush, Heinie, 116, 117, 119, 125, 128, 129, 131, 132, 145, 158, 160, 356, 413
Maranville, Rabbit, 64, 65, 99, 108, 288
Marberry, Firpo, 104, 105, 110, 117, 137, 157, 168
Marichal, Juan, 322, 344, 347, 348, 351, 359, 360, 368, 371, 384, 387, 388, 392, 397, 508
Marion, Marty, 212, 224, 226, 228, 240, 263
Maris, Roger, 320, 322, 324, 328, 329, 331–334, 336, 344, 348, 376, 522, 561, 592, 593, 596, 616, 624, 625
Maroth, Mike, 666, 668
Marquard, Rube, 40, 52, 55, 56, 58–60, 62, 70, 72, 412
Marshall, Mike, 428, 431–433, 436, 438, 439, 479, 520, 544
Marshall, Willard, 244, 245, 259
Martin, Billy, 272, 278, 279, 290, 306, 313, 319, 322, 392, 394, 418, 422, 431, 439, 443, 448, 456, 458, 464, 465, 467, 469, 474, 483, 488, 491, 494, 497, 500, 520, 526, 545, 552, 555
Martin, Pepper, 130, 146, 147, 150, 158, 161, 164, 166
Martinez, Carmelo, 518
Martinez, Dennis, 479, 568, 571, 572, 592, 597–598, 600
Martinez, Edgar, 576, 579, 581, 600, 602, 603, 614, 627, 640, 642, 653
Martinez, Pedro, 616, 619, 620, 624, 632–634, 638, 641, 659, 664, 667, 669
Martinez, Ramon, 573, 605
Martinez, Tino, 620, 632, 648, 655
Matheny, Mike, 663, 670
Mathews, Eddie, 278, 282, 283, 290, 302, 314, 317, 327, 331, 342, 350, 379, 387, 468
Mathewson, Christy, 12, 13, 20, 22, 24, 27–29, 31,

Paciorek, Tom, 495
Padgett, Ernie, 102
Page, Joe, 242, 254, 256, 258
Pagliarulo, Mike, 574
Pagnozzi, Tom, 614
Paige, Satchel, 167, 238, 248, 251, 253, 276, 277, 362, 366, 412, 501
Palmeiro, Rafael, 568, 572, 632, 646, 666, 669
Palmer, Jim, 368, 392, 395, 403, 404, 408, 424, 425, 431, 441, 449, 450, 455, 462, 471, 479, 496, 515, 566
Pappas, Milt, 367, 418, 420
Parent, Freddy, 24, 421
Park, Chan Ho, 650, 653
Parker, Dave, 440, 459, 466, 468, 472, 520, 523
Parker, Wes, 366, 407
Parnell, Mel, 255, 259, 298
Parrish, Lance, 508, 512, 539, 564
Parrott, Mike, 481
Pascual, Camilo, 336, 343, 344, 351, 366
Paskert, Dode, 76
Pasquel, Jorge, 241
Passeau, Claude, 230, 232
Pearson, Albie, 309, 312, 350
Pearson, Monte, 152, 175, 188, 190
Peavy, Jake, 672
Peckinpaugh, Roger, 66, 92, 104, 110, 115, 154
Pelekoudas, Chris, 375
Pena, Alejandro, 519
Pena, Tony, 516, 607, 671
Pendleton, Terry, 568, 569, 574, 576, 578, 583
Pennock, Herb, 100, 104, 128, 131, 152, 156, 166, 253
Penny, Brad, 664, 671
Pepitone, Joe, 365, 397
Perez, Eddie, 632
Perez, Melido, 565
Perez, Tony, 378, 382, 390, 392, 394, 407, 416, 417, 420, 426, 440, 448, 449, 452, 504, 646
Perini, Lou, 241, 278
Perry, Gaylord, 368, 384, 387, 401, 405, 416, 417, 431, 437, 444, 465, 469, 470, 484, 498, 504, 507, 575
Perry, Jim, 320, 349, 400, 401, 403
Pesky, Johnny, 212, 215, 216, 236, 241, 248, 254
Peters, Gary, 344, 348, 355, 368, 375, 380
Peterson, Fritz, 426, 428, 436
Petrocelli, Rico, 395
Pettitte, Andy, 608, 612, 613, 632, 640
Pfeffer, Jeff, 38, 72
Pfiester, Jack, 35, 36, 37
Phillippe, Deacon, 12, 20, 22, 23
Phillips, Damon, 228
Phoebus, Tom, 387, 395
Piazza, Mike, 584, 585, 587, 591, 603, 605, 619, 629, 630, 632, 640, 647
Picciolo, Rob, 477, 525
Pierce, Billy, 290, 294, 302, 310, 336, 342
Pierre, Juan, 652, 664, 670
Piersall, Jimmy, 282, 301, 307
Pierzynski, A.J., 662
Piles, Warren, 298, 306, 418, 476
Piniella, Lou, 392, 397, 520
Pinson, Vada, 316, 327, 328, 334, 335, 347, 350, 382
Pipgras, George, 128, 132, 152
Pipp, Wally, 79, 94, 96, 104, 109, 110, 116
Plank, Eddie, 20, 28, 30, 48, 51, 60, 71, 76, 345
Plantier, Phil, 589
Podres, Johnny, 282, 290, 291, 294, 300, 302, 307, 314, 317, 328, 334, 344
Podsednik, Scott, 676
Pollet, Howie, 218, 236, 240, 254
Porter, Darrell, 477
Posada, Jorge, 668
Potter, Nels, 224, 230
Powell, Boog, 368, 372, 374, 400, 407, 412
Powell, Jack, 16, 19, 27
Powell, Jake, 176, 177, 179, 180
Power, Vic, 282, 311, 312, 348, 356
Pratt, Del, 75
Pratt, Todd, 639
Priddy, Jerry, 265

Prim, Ray, 230
Prior, Mark, 661, 667
Prothro, Doc, 105
Puckett, Kirby, 536, 542, 543, 547, 553, 554, 557, 568, 569, 579, 580, 581, 594, 613, 615, 655
Puhl, Terry, 480, 555
Pujols, Albert, 651, 653, 656, 666, 670, 672, 677, 679
Pulliam, Harry, 17, 20, 40

Q Qualls, Jim, 394, 399
Quilici, Frank, 364
Quinn, Jack, 64, 128, 134, 143, 144, 151
Quisenberry, Dan, 487, 498, 505, 508, 512, 519, 527, 531, 631

R Radatz, Dick, 342, 346, 353
Radbourn, Old Hoss, 198
Radcliff, Rip, 180, 205
Rader, Doug, 405
Raines Jr., Tim, 654
Raines Sr., Tim, 488, 491, 492, 501, 503, 507, 518, 528, 532, 534, 540, 557, 654
Ramirez, Manny, 592, 598, 600, 626, 636, 645, 658, 669, 673, 675
Ramos, Pete, 333
Randolph, Willie, 444, 448, 463, 464, 566, 573
Raschi, Vic, 254, 263, 265, 266, 272, 273, 278, 281
Ray, Johnny, 517
Reardon, Jeff, 492, 527, 536, 551, 578, 583, 589
Reed, Jack, 341
Reese, Pee Wee, 208, 209, 242, 256, 258, 259, 263, 272, 277, 283, 308, 516
Regan, Phil, 375, 391
Reiser, Pete, 206–210, 212, 215, 217, 236, 239, 242, 365, 393
Renteria, Edgar, 616, 617, 670
Repulski, Rip, 286, 300
Rettenmund, Merv, 458
Reulbach, Ed, 28, 32, 41, 43, 76
Reuschel, Paul, 445
Reuschel, Rick, 445, 541, 546, 580
Reuss, Jerry, 483, 485, 487, 488, 548
Reynolds, Allie, 221, 240, 242, 254, 266, 267, 272–274, 276, 278, 281
Reynolds, Craig, 494
Reynolds, Harold, 549
Rhem, Flint, 116
Rhoads, Dusty, 42
Rhodes, Dusty, 284, 287, 289
Rice, Del, 307
Rice, Jim, 440, 442, 457, 462, 464, 466, 469, 470, 472, 479, 504–506, 516, 528, 540, 547, 591
Rice, Sam, 104, 106, 110–112, 114, 116, 120, 143, 144, 162, 348, 437
Richard, J.R., 413, 470, 472, 475, 480–482
Richards, Gene, 460, 485, 494
Richards, Paul, 323, 333
Richardson, Bobby, 309, 323, 326, 328, 332, 336, 340, 342, 343, 355, 364
Richert, Pete, 341, 412
Rickey, Branch, 38, 63, 73, 116, 130, 151, 183, 197, 212, 214, 218, 220, 228, 231, 235, 242, 274, 365, 380
Riddle, Elmer, 206, 209
Righetti, Dave, 468, 489, 504, 507, 531
Rijo, Jose, 517, 560, 561, 588
Rincon, Ricardo, 617
Ripken, Billy, 538, 539
Ripken Jr., Cal, 496, 498, 504, 508, 522, 523, 538, 539, 568, 570, 571, 573, 576, 590, 603, 615, 628, 629, 638, 639, 646, 652–654, 669
Ripken Sr., Cal, 538, 539
Ripple, Jimmy, 200, 203
Risberg, Swede, 76, 80, 82
Ritchey, Claude, 39
Rivera, Mariano, 620, 624, 632, 633, 638, 641, 647, 648, 652, 675, 676
Rivers, Mickey, 439, 444, 448
Rixey, Eppa, 68, 70, 95, 96, 110, 348
Rizzuto, Phil, 209, 212, 217, 218, 220, 223, 254, 258, 260, 264, 277, 598
Roberts, Brian, 675

Roberts, Dave, 672
Roberts, Robin, 260, 264, 272, 273, 275, 278, 279, 284, 286, 290, 291, 295, 301, 452
Robertson, Bob, 408, 414
Robertson, Dave, 72, 76, 79
Robinson, Brooks, 324, 333, 352–354, 358, 368, 370, 399, 400, 404, 412, 437, 443, 461, 471, 508, 517
Robinson, Eddie, 253, 264, 282, 300, 305
Robinson, Floyd, 341
Robinson, Frank, 296, 297, 299, 300, 328, 333, 335, 339, 367–369, 375, 392, 399, 407, 412, 421, 429, 440, 441, 494, 500, 658
Robinson, Jackie, 10, 228, 235, 238, 242, 243, 254–256, 266, 278, 283, 295, 296, 301, 337, 341, 420, 440, 445, 617, 639
Robinson, Wilbert, 107, 234
Rocker, John, 643, 644
Rodgers, Buck, 488
Rodriguez, Alex, 609, 611, 613, 614, 628, 640, 643, 646, 648, 650, 653, 658, 661, 664, 666, 668, 669
Rodriguez, Eddie, 655
Rodriguez, Francisco, 659
Rodriguez, Ivan, 574, 597, 606, 610, 612, 622, 632–634, 664, 675
Roe, Preacher, 247, 254, 268, 282
Rogan, Bullet Joe, 627
Rogers, Keny, 597
Rogers, Steve, 470, 478, 488, 503, 511
Rogovin, Saul, 266, 271
Rojas, Minnie, 383
Rolen, Scott, 618, 656, 670, 672, 679
Rolfe, Red, 152, 194, 196
Rollins, Jimmy, 652
Rommel, Eddie, 96, 97, 116, 128, 134, 155, 247
Root, Charlie, 122, 123, 126, 134, 152, 170, 188
Rosar, Buddy, 238
Rose, Pete, 344, 346–348, 367, 382, 384, 387, 391, 392, 396, 399, 404, 406, 423–425, 427, 429, 430, 433, 440, 442, 447–449, 451, 454, 455, 464, 465, 467, 472, 474, 480, 486, 488, 489, 493, 504, 509, 514, 515, 520, 521, 523, 524, 530, 552, 553, 558, 564
Rose Jr., Pete, 622
Roseboro, Johnny, 351, 360
Rosen, Al, 106, 264, 272, 274, 276, 278, 288, 302
Roth, Braggo, 69, 70
Roush, Edd, 68, 73, 74, 76, 80, 84, 108, 116, 126, 340, 548
Rowe, Schoolboy, 164, 166, 170, 200, 205, 220
Roznovsky, Vic, 374
Rucker, Nap, 42, 43
Rudi, Joe, 422, 423, 431, 432, 436, 439, 449, 492
Rudolph, Dick, 64, 66
Ruelbach, Ed, 33
Ruether, Dutch, 84, 110
Ruffing, Red, 133, 150, 153, 164, 182, 185, 188, 194, 203, 212, 218, 223, 271, 380, 534
Ruiz, Chico, 357
Runnels, Pete, 312, 326, 340
Ruppert, Jake, 65, 67, 132
Rusie, Amos, 460
Russell, Bill, 464, 471
Russell, Jack, 168
Russell, Jeff, 552, 558
Russell, Reb, 60, 63, 72, 78
Ruth, Babe, 7, 19, 58, 64, 66, 68, 69, 71–74, 76, 78, 80, 83–86, 88, 89, 91–93, 96, 98, 100–102, 104, 105, 107, 110, 111, 116, 117, 120–123, 125, 127–129, 131, 132–135, 140–144, 146–148, 152, 156, 158, 161, 164–168, 170–172, 176, 177, 180, 188, 189, 192, 194, 196, 211, 230, 250, 251, 328, 463, 599, 639, 651, 652, 653
Ruthven, Dick, 480
Ryan, Nolan, 412, 419, 424, 426, 427, 430, 432, 435, 437, 438, 441, 451, 454, 455, 457, 461, 462, 473, 479, 482, 488, 490, 504, 505, 520, 522, 536, 542, 551, 553, 560, 562, 565, 567, 568, 575, 638

S Saberhagen, Bret, 520, 521, 527, 552, 555, 558, 595
Sabo, Chris, 560, 561, 566

Drew Sparks Braves to NL East Title

Viewed as a disappointment in St. Louis, outfielder J.D. Drew was dealt to Atlanta prior to 2004 and enjoyed his best season, leading the Braves to the NL East title. Batting .305 with 31 homers and 118 walks, Drew ranked fourth in the league in on-base percentage, adding punch to a formerly sagging Braves lineup. He also avoided serious injury for the first time, playing in a career-best 145 games.

Adrian Beltre

Adrian Belts 48 Big Flys—a 3B Record

Dodgers third sacker Adrian Beltre, in the last year of his contract, exploded into MVP territory in 2004, batting .334 and topping the majors with 48 home runs—tied with Mike Schmidt for the most ever by an ML third baseman in a season. Many of his homers were game-winners, as he almost singlehandedly lifted the Dodgers to the NL West title. Following the season, he signed a five-year, $64-million deal with Seattle.

J.D. Drew

Mariano Rivera

Rivera Racks Up 53 Saves

Those who already felt that the Yankees' Mariano Rivera was the greatest closer in baseball history could point to his career-high 53 saves in 2004, a total that led the majors. Helping New York win an AL-best 101 games, the 34-year-old Rivera again used his trademark cut fastball to shatter bats, allowing just three home runs in 79 innings.

- Tejada wins the Home Run Derby with a record 27 total homers.
- Manny Ramirez tops the AL with 43 homers and a .613 SA.
- Catcher Ivan Rodriguez signs with Detroit and hits .334 with 86 RBI.
- Rodriguez wins his 11th Gold Glove, a record for catchers.
- St. Louis racks up 105 wins, the most in baseball and the highest NL total since 1998.
- The Yankees' 101 wins are the most in the AL.
- Baltimore's Melvin Mora hits .340 with 27 homers and paces the AL with a .419 OBP.
- Brian Roberts of the Orioles hits .273 with just four homers, but he leads the AL with 50 doubles.
- Tampa Bay's Carl Crawford emerges as one of the AL's most exciting players, leading in triples (19) and stolen bases (59).
- Atlanta's Julio Franco, who is at least 45, raps .309 over 125 games.

Guerrero Garners MVP Award

Anaheim right fielder Vladimir Guerrero gives thanks. Escaping the moribund atmosphere of Montreal, Guerrero moved to sunny California in 2004 and led the Angels' charge to the AL West title. Earning the AL MVP Award on the strength of a .337-39-126 performance, the 28-year-old superstar topped the AL in runs (124), total bases (366), and outfield assists (13). He became the first Angels outfielder to start in the All-Star Game since Reggie Jackson in 1984.

Vladimir Guerrero

Miguel Tejada

Tejada Lets 'Em Fly in HR Derby

On July 12, 2004, the Orioles' Miguel Tejada belted a record 27 homers in the Home Run Derby, held in Houston prior to the All-Star Game. Tejada's Derby performance was just part of a stellar campaign in which he played in all 162 games and amassed a league-leading 150 RBI. He also ranked among the AL's top ten in homers, hits, doubles, total bases, and extra-base hits.

Maddux Logs 300th Win

On August 7, 2004, Cubs right-hander Greg Maddux notched his 300th career victory at San Francisco. After the season, he was awarded a Gold Glove—the 14th of his career. Overall, however, 2004 was disappointing for the Hall of Fame-bound 38-year-old. While he finished 16-11, winning at least 15 games for an ML-record 17th consecutive season, Maddux had to watch the playoffs on television. The Cubs, in the catbird seat for the wildcard berth, lost five straight at home in the season's final week.

Greg Maddux

2004

- Schilling leads the junior circuit with 21 wins.

- Mariano Rivera of the Yanks saves 53 games, pacing the AL for the third time.

- Boston trades superstar shortstop Nomar Garciaparra to the Cubs on July 31.

- Rangers reliever Frank Francisco, involved in an argument with a fan, causes injuries when he throws a chair into the stands at Oakland on September 13.

- Oakland shortstop Bobby Crosby (22 homers) is named AL ROTY.

- Pirates outfielder Jason Bay (.282 with 26 homers) is the NL ROTY.

- Dodgers third baseman Adrian Beltre wins his first home run crown (48).

- Brewers outfielder Scott Podsednik hits .244 but leads the majors with 70 stolen bases.

- The Diamondbacks finish 51-111, the worst record for an NL club since 1965.

Bonds: 232 Walks, 700th Home Run

Though Barry Bonds won a record seventh NL MVP Award in 2004, his season was tainted by allegations of illegal steroid use. During the campaign, Bonds belted 45 home runs, including his 700th career four-bagger on September 17. He also took his second batting title (.362) and drew a ridiculous 232 walks, shattering his own major-league record by 34. The steroid furor, however, further diminished the public's tepid regard for the 40-year-old superstar.

Barry Bonds

Santana Rocks! Wins AL Cy Young

In his first year as a regular starter, Minnesota's Johan Santana posted ERAs of 5.40 in April 2004 and 5.79 in May. After that, he was utterly unhittable, not allowing more than two earned runs in 21 of his final 22 starts. He was 5-0 in September, allowing just two runs overall. An easy Cy Young Award winner, the lefty went 20-6 and paced the AL in ERA (2.61) and strikeouts (265).

Ichiro Suzuki

Ichiro Zips by Sisler, Sets New Hits Mark

Seattle's Ichiro Suzuki shakes hands with George Sisler's grandson on October 1, 2004, after collecting his 258th hit of the season, which broke Sisler's major-league record. While Ichiro's Mariners finished last, the charismatic star rapped .372, winning his second bat crown. He also stole 36 bases and won his fourth Gold Glove. His 704 at-bats ranked just one short of the all-time single-season record.

Johan Santana

- The Diamondbacks' Randy Johnson, age 41, paces the majors with 290 strikeouts. His 2.60 ERA ranks second in the NL.

- One of Johnson's 16 wins is a perfect game at Atlanta on May 18.

- Rockies infielder Vinny Castilla tops the NL with 131 RBI.

- Pittsburgh's Craig Wilson is hit by 30 pitches, the majors' highest total since 1998.

- The Indians rout the Yankees 22-0 on August 31.

- Jason Schmidt of the Giants fires two one-hitters en route to an 18-7 season.

- Beltran, dealt to Houston, clubs 23 homers in 90 games for his new team. He also swipes 28 bases without being caught for the Astros.

- Albert Pujols of St. Louis tops the majors with 389 total bases.

- Pujols hits .331 with 51 doubles and 46 homers.

Killer Bs Deadly in October

While the Astros didn't get to the World Series, it certainly wasn't the fault of Lance Berkman or Carlos Beltran. Berkman batted .348 in the playoffs with four homers and 12 RBI. Beltran, meanwhile, blasted .455 with four homers and nine RBI in the NLDS and .417 with four more homers in a losing effort against St. Louis in the NLCS. Beltran also displayed spectacular defense in center field.

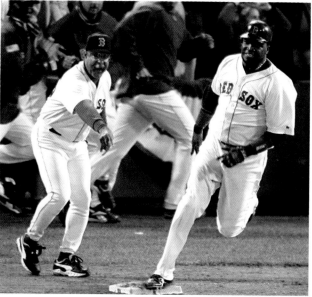

David Ortiz

Lance Berkman, Carlos Beltran

Ortiz Bashes the Big Hits

Red Sox designated hitter David Ortiz, who slugged .301 with 41 homers and 139 RBI in 2004, amassed 19 RBI and cracked three game-winning hits in the '04 postseason. First, he won the clinching game three of the AL Division Series with a walk-off homer against Anaheim. He also ended game four of the ALCS against New York with a post-midnight homer. Here, on the same day, he wins game five with a 14th-inning single.

Schilling Bleeds for Boston

Curt Schilling could have made a fortune on eBay selling his bloody *red sock*. This photo comes from game six of the ALCS, in which—despite suffering from a torn ankle tendon that eventually required surgery—Schilling pitched seven quality innings to earn a 4-2 victory over the rival Yankees. Schilling, who led the AL with 21 wins during the regular season, also won game two of the World Series.

Curt Schilling's bleeding ankle

2004

- Colorado's Todd Helton bats .347 with 49 doubles and 32 homers.

- Cubs righty Greg Maddux wins his 300th career game on August 7 at San Francisco.

- Maddux wins his 14th Gold Glove.

- Thanks to spacious new Petco Park, the Padres hit just 57 homers in 81 home contests. They club 82 big flys on the road.

- Japanese relievers Shingo Takatsu of the White Sox and Akinori Otsuka of the Padres finish among the top three rookies in their respective leagues in ROTY voting.

- Ken Griffey, Jr., swats his 500th home run on June 20.

- The AL wins yet another All-Star Game, blowing out the NL 9-4 at Houston on July 13.

- San Diego's Mark Loretta raps .335 (third in the NL) with 208 hits.

- In position to win the NL wildcard, the Cubs collapse in the final week, losing five straight at home.

Glaus Tops AL with 47 Home Runs

In just his second full big-league season, hulking third baseman Troy Glaus enjoyed his breakout campaign in 2000. At his best swining for the fences, he connected for 47 home runs to pace the American League. Glaus and teammates Garret Anderson, Tim Salmon, and Mo Vaughn were the first AL foursome ever to homer more than 30 times each. Their heroics, however, couldn't get the Angels any higher than third place in the AL West.

Troy Glaus

Ken Griffey Jr.

Junior Goes Home to Cincy

Star center fielder Ken Griffey Jr. takes a mighty rip for the Reds, who acquired him from Seattle in a five-player deal before the 2000 season. Griffey, a Cincy native whose dad coached for the Reds in 2000, hit .271 with 40 homers, 118 RBI, and 94 walks. However, his production fell short of the perhaps inflated expectations of pennant-starved Queen City fanatics.

Jeff Kent

Kent Plates 125, Wins MVP Award

Heretofore a steady but never superstar-quality player, San Francisco second baseman Jeff Kent exploded in 2000, batting a career-best .334 with 41 doubles, 33 homers, and 125 RBI. He was voted National League MVP—beating out teammate Barry Bonds—as the Giants won the NL West. Kent ranked in the top ten among NL hitters in 11 offensive categories, though he didn't lead in any.

---

100 runs, 100 RBI, and 100 extra-base hits.

- Seattle deals Ken Griffey Jr. to Cincinnati in a five-player deal.

- At age 30, Griffey becomes the youngest player ever to hit 400 home runs when he reaches the milestone on April 10 at Colorado.

- The Elian Gonzalez custody battle touches baseball, as several players boycott games on April 25 to protest the government's decision to return Elian to Cuba.

- Kansas City's Johnny Damon leads the AL with 46 steals and 136 runs.

- Atlanta's Tom Glavine paces the majors in wins (21). It is his fifth 20-win season and the fifth time he has led the NL in victories.

- Florida second baseman Luis Castillo steals 62 bases, tops in the NL. He also bats .334.

- Seattle shortstop Alex Rodriguez rips .316 with 41 homers, 132 RBI, and 100 walks.

Comerica Park

Carlos Delgado

Tigers: New Ballpark, Same Old Team

The overcast skies that greeted the Tigers for the first game ever at Comerica Park served as an uncomfortable metaphor for the team's future. Unlike in Baltimore and Cleveland, the new park did not rejuvenate fans or the ballclub as much as management had hoped. After the season, the Tigers pared their payroll to help offset the cost of the stadium.

Delgado Named ML's Top Player

Toronto's Carlos Delgado wreaked havoc on AL pitchers in 2000. The 28-year-old first sacker made a run at the Triple Crown before finishing at .344-41-137. He led the league with 57 doubles and rated second with 123 walks, a .470 on-base percentage, and a .664 slugging percentage. His fellow players voted him Major League Player of the Year.

John Rocker

Rocker Suspended

Braves reliever John Rocker holds a press conference at New York's Shea Stadium on June 29. Prior to the season, Rocker had made negative comments in the national press concerning his disdain for New Yorkers and minorities, drawing fire from some teammates and opponents as well as millions of fans. Major League Baseball suspended him for two weeks.

2000

- Kevin Brown of the Dodgers leads the NL with a 2.58 ERA.

- Atlanta pitcher John Rocker ignites a scandal with his uncomplimentary comments in a national magazine about homosexuals, immigrants, and New Yorkers.

- Years of labor strife with umpires finally results in the dissolution of the

- Major League Umpires Association, which comes after the union miscalculates its bargaining strength.

- AL umpire John Hirschbeck is voted the first president of the World Umpires Association, which promises to work more closely with MLB.

- Florida's Antonio Alfonseca leads the majors with 45 saves.

- Detroit's Todd Jones and Boston's Derek Lowe save 42 games each to pace the AL.

- David Wells of the Blue Jays and Tim Hudson of the A's tie for the AL lead in wins (20).

- Mark McGwire plays only 89 games due to knee injuries, but he still clouts 32 homers for the Cardinals.

Helton: .372, 42 Homers

Colorado first baseman Todd Helton posted incredible numbers in 2000, including a .372 average, 59 doubles, 42 home runs, 147 RBI, 138 runs, and 103 walks. While the thin air of Denver surely contributed to his totals, Helton did bat .353 with 15 homers on the road. He captured the NL's Hank Aaron Award, given to the league's premier slugger.

Johnson Whiffs 347

Arizona's Randy Johnson won his second straight Cy Young Award in 2000 after leading the majors in strikeouts (347) for the third consecutive year. The fire-balling southpaw so dominated lefties that managers routinely stacked their lineups with eight or nine right-handed hitters. Johnson opened the season 14-2 and finished 19-7.

Jason Giambi

Giambi Cops MVP Award

Jason Giambi of the A's won the American League's MVP trophy with a spectacular season that included 43 homers, 137 RBI, and a .333 average. He led the majors in on-base percentage (.474), not to mention grand slams (six). As Oakland struggled to hold on to first place down the stretch, Giambi homered five times in his last seven games, securing the West Division crown. Jason's brother, Jeremy, also played for the A's.

Todd Helton

Randy Johnson

- Tigers open new Comerica Park on April 11.
- A May 16 altercation at Wrigley Field between the Dodgers and several Cubs fans results in fines and suspensions for 16 Dodgers.
- On May 29, Oakland's Randy Velarde turns an unassisted triple play against the Yankees.

- Pittsburgh's Three Rivers Stadium shuts its doors. It had been home to the Pirates since 1970.
- The surprising White Sox roar to the AL Central crown. Chicago takes over first place for good on April 19.
- Milwaukee tears down venerable County Stadium.

- Manny Ramirez, in his last season with Cleveland, paces the AL with a .697 slugging average.
- Houston's new Enron Field yields a barrage of home runs.
- Atlanta first baseman Andres Galarraga returns from a year's absence due to cancer and bats .302 with 28 home runs.

Galarraga Returns from Cancer

Atlanta Braves first baseman Andres Galarraga, who missed the entire 1999 season after undergoing surgery to remove a cancerous tumor from his lower back, assumed his position on the field for the Braves in 2000. The courageous "Big Cat" cracked .302 with 28 four-baggers and 100 RBI at age 39. He also earned a spot on the NL All-Star team.

Kaz Sasaki

Sasaki, 32, Named ROTY

The Mariners have always had an eye out for international talent, and in 2000 they benefitted from the performance of sinkerballing closer Kaz Sasaki. The Japanese-born right-hander made his major league debut with a club-record 37 saves, including 15 in a row at one point. It was enough to earn him the AL Rookie of the Year Award—even though he was 32 years old.

Andres Galarraga

A-Rod Swats 41 Big Flys

At age 25, Alex Rodriguez again had one of the best offensive seasons ever for a shortstop. A-Rod ripped .316 with 34 doubles, 41 homers, 132 RBI, 100 walks, and even 15 steals. He scored 134 runs and played superb defense. Following the season, he inked a ten-year contract with the Rangers for $252 million—a sum that stunned the nation.

Alex Rodriguez

2000

- Toronto slugger Carlos Delgado finishes fourth in the AL in batting average (.344), home runs (41), and RBI (137) and leads with 57 doubles.

- The Hall of Fame elects five men, including Tony Perez, Carlton Fisk, and Sparky Anderson.

- Fred McGriff of Tampa Bay slugs his 400th home run on June 2.

- Rafael Palmeiro of Texas blasts his 400th homer on September 23.

- Minnesota shortstop Cristian Guzman's 20 triples lead the major leagues.

- Frank Thomas of the White Sox enjoys a spectacular comeback season, hitting .328 with 43 homers, 143 RBI, 115 runs, and 112 walks.

- Cal Ripken Jr. of Baltimore collects his 3,000th hit in Minnesota on April 15.

- San Francisco posts baseball's best record (97-65) in its first season at new Pacific Bell Park.

- Jeff Bagwell scores 152 runs for the Astros—most in the majors since 1936.

NLCS

Mets Knock Off Cardinals

Mets pitcher Mike Hampton beats out an infield single in game one of the 2000 NLCS. Hampton tossed seven scoreless frames in a the Mets' 6-2 victory over St. Louis. In game five, he pitched a three-hit shutout to clinch the series. The Cards sorely missed Mark McGwire, who could only pinch hit due to injury and went 0-for-2 in the series.

Sojo's Hit Clinches WS

In game five of the World Series, Luis Sojo came to bat in the ninth inning with the score 2-2. Facing tired Mets starter Al Leiter, Sojo ripped his 142nd pitch for a single to plate the go-ahead run. The Yankees won 4-2 after reliever Mariano Rivera slammed the door in the bottom of the ninth. Derek Jeter called the Mets the toughest opponent in the Yankees' four recent World Series triumphs.

World Series

World Series

Piazza, Clemens Clash in Subway Series

The biggest flap of the 2000 World Series came during game two at Yankee Stadium. In the first inning, Roger Clemens induced a grounder from Mets catcher Mike Piazza, breaking his bat. When a piece of the bat flew toward the mound, an angry Clemens tossed it in Piazza's direction, setting off a bench-clearing incident. The two had history: Earlier in the season, Clemens drilled Piazza in the head with a pitch.

- KC's Mike Sweeney becomes the first AL player to hit .330 with 200 hits and 140 RBI since Al Rosen in 1953.

- Colorado's Mike Lansing hits for the cycle on June 18 against Arizona— and completes the cycle in the fourth inning.

- Rockies catcher Brent Mayne pitches on August 22 and gets the win over Atlanta. He is the first position player to post a win since 1968.

- Jose Lima of Houston serves up 48 home runs, the most ever by an NL pitcher.

- Preston Wilson of Florida, baseball's only 30/30 man, strikes out 187 times, just two whiffs short of the ML record.

- LA's Dave Hansen clubs an ML-record seven pinch-hit home runs during the season.

- On October 1, Detroit's Shane Halter plays all nine positions in one game. He also cracks four hits.

- In December, the Rangers sign free agent Alex Rodriguez to a ten-year, $252 million deal.

Baseball's 2001 campaign, full of surprises early and late, was entertaining throughout.

Some teams that were expected to contend collapsed out of the gate, such as the White Sox, Rangers, and Rockies. Other clubs, namely the Twins, Phillies, and Cubs, surprised early but slumped down the stretch.

Big-ticket free agents, such as Alex Rodriguez of Texas and Mike Hampton of the Rockies, couldn't help their clubs to the top. The year's best "new" player was Seattle speedster Ichiro Suzuki, who after nine brilliant seasons in Japan won AL MVP honors (.350, 242 hits).

However, as the Mariners drove toward the all-time record for wins, and Giants slugger Barry Bonds threatened Mark McGwire's home run mark, baseball was knocked out of the nation's consciousness. The September 11 terrorist attacks brought baseball to a standstill for a week. When the players and fans returned, they were greeted with patriotic touches, including flags on players' caps and jerseys and the singing of "God Bless America" during the seventh-inning stretch.

Bonds eventually knocked 73 apples out of the park, passing McGwire on the season's last weekend. Unfortunately for the superstar slugger, his Giants couldn't reach the postseason. In the end, a familiar cast made the playoffs: Atlanta, Houston, St.

D'Backs Beat Yankees in Drama-Filled World Series

Louis, Arizona, the Yankees, Seattle, Oakland, and Cleveland.

The Mariners, who had captured 116 games, stumbled through their Division Series with Cleveland and died in five to the Yankees in the ALCS. And the Astros, with the best record in the NL, immediately crumbled in their Division Series to the Braves, who in turn fell to the upstart Diamondbacks.

When Arizona and New York met in the World Series, it was more than a simple tradition-against-expansion story; it was a thrilling seven-game set. Arizona, with Cy Young winner Randy Johnson on the hill, blew out Mike Mussina and the Yankees 9-1 in game one. The following night, Curt Schilling handcuffed the visiting Bronx Bombers 4-0.

The clubs journeyed to New York, where a game-three 2-1 win by Roger Clemens put the Yankees on the board. What happened next stunned the nation.

In game four, Schilling pitched seven strong frames for the Diamondbacks, who took a 3-1 eighth-inning lead. However, Arizona closer Byung-Hyun Kim served up a two-out, two-run, ninth-inning homer to Tino Martinez. One inning later, Derek Jeter rocked Kim for a game-winning blast.

The next night, Arizona led 2-0 in the ninth, but again the Yankees struck. Scott Brosius's two-out, two-run homer—again off Kim—tied the game. In the 12th, New York pushed across a run to take the game and establish a 3-2 series lead.

Returning west for game six, the Yankees imploded again, suffering a 15-2 pasting by Arizona. Schilling and Clemens met in game seven. Arizona led 1-0 after six, but the Yankees scored in the seventh and took a 2-1 lead in the eighth on Alfonso Soriano's homer. Johnson, the game-six starter, relieved and shut the Yankees down.

In the last of the ninth, the Diamondbacks rallied. A Mark Grace single and a throwing error by pitcher Mariano Rivera on a bunt attempt put two men on. Tony Womack's double tied the score, and when Luis Gonzalez fisted a bloop over second base, the Diamondbacks won the World Series. Baseball once again assumed its place as a healer of national ills, and the exciting postseason garnered the best TV ratings in years.

2001

- Arizona beats St. Louis in a thrilling Division Series that ends on Tony Womack's bloop single in game five.

- Braves allow only six runs in their NLDS sweep of Houston.

- Yankees shock the A's in their ALDS matchup by becoming the first team to win a postseason series after losing the first two at home.

- Indians take the mighty Mariners to the limit in their Division Series, but they lose game five 3-1 to Jamie Moyer and three relievers.

- Yankees wipe away the Mariners in a surprisingly easy five-game ALCS.

- Diamondbacks down the Braves in five NLCS games. Randy Johnson pitches a shutout in game one.

- In the World Series, Arizona takes a 2-1 lead in games before New York stages two miracle comebacks.

- After Tino Martinez's two-out, ninth-inning homer ties game four of the World Series, Derek Jeter's tenth-inning bomb wins it.

- Scott Brosius's two-out, ninth-inning blast ties game five of the World

Randy Johnson stood tall after Arizona's dramatic game-seven victory in the 2001 World Series. Still throwing gas at age 38, Johnson became the first pitcher since Mickey Lolich in 1968 to go 3-0 in a fall classic. Besides his wins in games two (4-0 shutout) and six (15-2), the Big Unit tossed 1⅓ innings of relief in the finale. He shared the Series MVP Award with teammate Curt Schilling, who posted a 1.69 ERA in three starts.

Series. The Yankees win in the 12th on Alfonso Soriano's RBI single.

- Facing elimination in game six, the Diamondbacks come back to thrash the sloppy Yankees 15-2.

- Down 2-1 in the bottom of the ninth of game seven, Arizona rallies for two runs to shock the Yankees 3-2.

- Johnson and Curt Schilling share Series MVP honors. Johnson wins three games, while Schilling allows only four runs in three starts.

- Diamondbacks win the World Series in just their fourth year of existence, the quickest that any team has won a championship in major league baseball history.

- As a result of the September 11 terrorist attacks, no major league games are played for a week while minor league playoffs are canceled.

- When baseball returns on September 17, "God Bless America" replaces "Take Me Out to the Ballgame" as the seventh-inning sing-along at ballparks everywhere.

Mark Mulder

Clemens Starts Out Year at 20-1

Roger Clemens enjoyed yet another spectacular campaign in 2001, winning his unprecedented sixth Cy Young trophy. Posting a 20-3 record after a 20-1 start, the 39-year-old righty ranked just ninth in the league in ERA but third in strikeouts (213). He also moved into third place on the all-time whiff list with 3,717.

Mulder Goes 21-8, Beats Every Foe

In his first full season as a big-leaguer, southpaw Mark Mulder paced the AL in wins (21) and shutouts (four) in 2001. Mulder's 21-8 record and 3.45 ERA indicated his value to the Athletics, who rebounded from an early slump to reach the playoffs. He not only defeated every AL team that he faced, but he beat each of the four NL West clubs that he pitched against.

Roger Clemens

Ichiro Suzuki

Ichiro Wins Bat Title, MVP

A seven-time batting champion in Japan, Ichiro Suzuki filled the void of free-agent defector Alex Rodriguez in Seattle. With blinding speed and incredible hand-eye coordination, Ichiro led the AL in batting (.350), hits (242), and steals (56). The leadoff man ignited the best offense in baseball and helped Seattle to 116 wins. He was named AL Rookie of the Year as well as league MVP.

2001

- Seattle finishes the regular season with a spectacular 116-46 record. The Mariners' win total sets an AL record and ties the 1906 Cubs for the ML mark.

- With Houston's win over NL Central rival St. Louis on the season's final day, both teams finish with 93-69 records. The Astros earn the division crown thanks to a 9-7 head-to-head record against the Cardinals.

- Barry Bonds of San Francisco belts 73 homers to break Mark McGwire's ML mark.

- Bonds's record-shattering 71st tater comes off the Dodgers' Chan Ho Park on October 5 at PacBell Park.

- Bonds also sets ML records for slugging (.863) and walks (177). His .515 on-base percentage is the highest in a season since 1957.

- Bonds wins his record fourth NL MVP Award.

- Seattle's Ichiro Suzuki becomes the first to win ROTY and MVP honors in the same season since 1975.

Sammy Sosa

Gonzalez Tinkers With Stance, Hits 57 Homers

At age 34, Luis Gonzalez exploded with a 57-homer campaign in 2001. He also knocked in 142 runs for the Diamondbacks and batted .325. Always a solid out-fielder with good line-drive power, Gonzalez made a minor alteration in his batting stance, turning to face the pitcher even more dramatically than he had before. The adjustment gave Gonzalez extra time to see—and crush—pitchers' fastballs.

Albert Pujols

Sosa Slams 64 More, Scores 160

While Sammy Sosa was eclipsed by Barry Bonds's home run prowess in 2001, the Cubs superstar put on a tremendous show of his own. He drove in 160 runs, the most in the majors, and crossed the plate 146 times to lead all of baseball by a wide margin. He clubbed 64 homers, giving him a record 243 over a four-year span. Also disciplined, Sosa batted .328 with 116 walks.

Luis Gonzalez

Rookie Pujols Tees Off

After spending all but 14 at-bats of the 2000 campaign (his first professional season) in Class A, Albert Pujols broke camp with St. Louis in '01 and quickly hit his way into the everyday lineup. He never left it, batting .329 with 47 doubles, 37 homers, and 130 RBI. He also played all over the diamond, starting at least 32 games each at first base and third base and in left field and right field. Pujols was named to the All-Star Game, was the runaway NL Rookie of the Year, and even finished fourth in league Most Valuable Player voting.

- Suzuki captures the AL bat crown with a .350 average and collects 242 hits, the highest total in the major leagues since 1930. The speedy right fielder also paces the majors with 56 stolen bases.

- Roger Clemens of the Yankees finishes with a 20-3 record and earns a record sixth AL Cy Young Award.

- Clemens parlays 16 consecutive victories into a 20-1 start.

- Randy Johnson (21-6) wins his fourth Cy Young Award.

- Johnson paces the bigs in ERA (2.49) and strikeouts (372).

- Rickey Henderson of the Padres scores his 2,246th run on October 4

to break Ty Cobb's major league record.

- Henderson breaks Babe Ruth's walk record of 2,062 on April 24. He also collects his 3,000th hit on the season's final day.

- Sammy Sosa of the Cubs smashes 64 homers and paces the majors with 146 runs and 160 RBI.

Schilling: 22 Wins, 293 Ks

Pitcher Curt Schilling's postseason heroics were well documented in 2001, but he was something special during the regular season as well. Durable, he paced the NL with 35 starts, 256⅔ innings, and six complete games. More importantly, he tied for the league lead with 22 wins. His 2.98 ERA and 293 strikeouts ranked second in the circuit behind teammate Randy Johnson's marks.

Cal Ripken

Cal's Great Ride Comes to an End

On October 6, 2001, Orioles fans waved goodbye to Cal Ripken. Actually, several AL teams threw farewell parties for the veteran infielder, who at one point had played in 2,632 consecutive games. Ripken retired among history's Top 20 in games, at-bats, hits, doubles, total bases, and RBI. Though he hit just .239 in his final season, Ripken did enjoy one last hurrah in the All-Star Game, belting a home run and earning the MVP Award.

Henderson Sets Career Runs Record

San Diego's Rickey Henderson completes a home run trot with a slide into the plate against the Dodgers on October 4, 2001. Fans could forgive the flamboyance considering Rickey had scored his 2,246th run, breaking Ty Cobb's 73-year-old major league record. Back on April 24, the 42-year-old Henderson eclipsed Babe Ruth's career walk record of 2,062. He also cracked his 3,000th career hit on the season's last day.

Curt Schilling

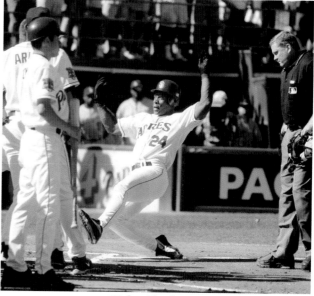

Rickey Henderson

2001

- Colorado's Larry Walker captures his third batting crown in four years with a .350 mark.

- Arizona's Curt Schilling wins 22 games to tie for the NL lead. He finishes second among NL hurlers in ERA (2.98) and strikeouts (293).

- Cardinals ace Matt Morris wins 22 games to tie Schilling for the NL lead.

- Seattle's Freddy Garcia leads the AL in ERA at 3.05.

- Boston's Hideo Nomo paces the AL in strikeouts (220).

- Nomo throws a no-hitter against the Orioles on April 4.

- Oakland lefty Mark Mulder paces the AL in wins with 21.

- Yankees closer Mariano Rivera collects an ML-leading 50 saves.

- Colorado's Juan Pierre ties for the National League lead with 46 stolen bases.

- Rookie shortstop Jimmy Rollins of the Phillies swipes 46 sacks to tie for the NL lead.

Boone's 141 RBI Power M's

Mariners Jay Buhner, Bret Boone, and Edgar Martinez *(left to right)* celebrate Seattle's clinching of the AL West title on September 19, 2001. Boone put together one of the top hitting campaigns ever by a second baseman. He paced the AL with 141 RBI while cracking .331 with 37 homers and 37 doubles. Martinez enjoyed his sixth .300-20-100 season over a seven-year stretch.

Jay Buhner, Bret Boone, Edgar Martinez

Comiskey Park

Baseball Honors America

Fans at Chicago's Comiskey Park honored America and the visiting Yankees on September 18, 2001, the first day of action for American League teams since the September 11 terrorist attacks. Each major league club saluted the heroes and remembered the victims with special pregame ceremonies. At Comiskey, players and firefighters lined the infield for the national anthem and a moment of silence. For the rest of the season, all major league players wore American flag patches, which were sewn on both their jerseys and caps.

BB Breaks Homer Mark, Blasts 73!

Barry Bonds basks in the afterglow of his 71st home run, which he clubbed at home off L.A.'s Chan Ho Park on October 5, 2001. While breaking Mark McGwire's longball record, Bonds posted a .515 on-base percentage and surpassed Babe Ruth's marks for walks and slugging percentage in a season, finishing with 177 and .863. Barry became the first man to win his fourth league MVP Award.

Barry Bonds

- Luis Gonzalez of the Diamondbacks clubs 57 home runs, 26 more than he had previously hit in a season.

- Todd Helton cracks .336 with 49 homers and 146 RBI, but the Rockies still finish last in the NL West.

- St. Louis's Albert Pujols wins the NL ROTY Award and finishes fourth in MVP balloting.

- Pujols rips .329 with 37 homers, 47 doubles, and 130 RBI.

- Suzuki's MVP win over Oakland's Jason Giambi is one of the closest votes ever.

- Giambi leads the AL in doubles (47), walks (129), on-base percentage (.477), and slugging (.660). He places second to Suzuki in batting (.342).

- Texas shortstop Alex Rodriguez leads the AL with 52 home runs (an ML record for a shortstop) and 133 runs scored.

- Seattle second baseman Bret Boone leads the AL in RBI with 141.

- Three icons of the 1980s and 1990s —Tony Gwynn, McGwire, and Cal Ripken—choose to retire.

Arizona Tops Cardinals in NLDS

Arizona's Craig Counsell (in helmet) hugs Danny Bautista *(center)*, who just scored the winning run in game five of the team's 2001 NLDS. With St. Louis and the Diamondbacks tied 1-1 in the bottom of the ninth, Tony Womack cracked a two-out single to send Arizona to the NLCS for the first time. Arizona's Curt Schilling went 2-0 with a 0.50 ERA in the Series, while Cardinals slugger Mark McGwire concluded his career with a 1-for-11 performance.

NLDS

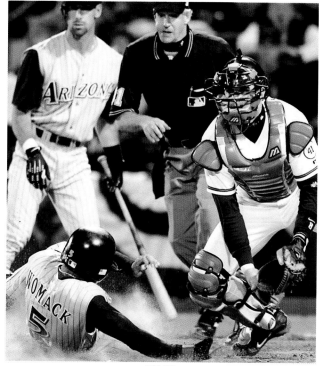

NLCS

D'Backs Breeze in NLCS

Tony Womack scores against Atlanta in game four of the 2001 NLCS, part of an 11-4 Arizona rout. The Braves, who had reached the playoffs for the tenth straight year, went home disappointed for the ninth time, as the Diamondbacks took the Series in five games. Series MVP Craig Counsell rapped .381, while Randy Johnson won games one (2-0) and five (3-2).

ALCS

Yanks Bomb M's in ALCS

Bernie Williams takes Jamie Moyer deep in game three of the 2001 ALCS. The two-run, first-inning shot seemed to doom the Mariners, who had already lost the first two games on their own turf. Seattle rallied to win this affair 14-3, but New York eliminated the 116-game winners in just five games. Williams homered in each of the last three contests.

2001

- Spending most of the year on the disabled list, Gwynn collects only 33 of his 3,141 career hits.

- McGwire leaves the game with 583 home runs, fifth on the all-time list, but hits only .187 with 29 dingers in 2001.

- Ripken retires with 3,184 hits, 14th all-time.

- Florida's A.J. Burnett no-hits the Padres on May 12, walking nine men and plunking another in the process.

- Cardinals rookie Bud Smith no-hits San Diego on September 3.

- L.A.'s Shawn Green clubs 49 homers.

- Juan Gonzalez of the Indians bats in 140 runs.

- Baltimore's Tim Raines Sr. and Tim Raines Jr. appear in the same game on October 3, becoming the second father-son duo ever to do so (Ken Griffey Sr. and Jr.).

- Milwaukee establishes a major league record by striking out 1,399 times. Three Brewers total at least 150 whiffs.

Martinez's HR Stuns the D'Backs

Arizona reliever Byung-Hyun Kim stands shell-shocked after serving up a homer in the bottom of the ninth of game four of the 2001 World Series. In the first ML game ever played on Halloween, Tino Martinez treated New Yorkers with a stunning two-out, two-run homer to tie the game, 3-3. As the game stretched into November, Yankee Derek Jeter climaxed the drama with a walk-off homer in the tenth.

World Series

Gonzo Wins Thrilling Game Seven

Arizona's Luis Gonzalez celebrates his historic game-seven hit with coach Eddie Rodriguez. Victimized by Yankee comebacks in games four and five, the D'Backs turned the tables in the finale. After Alfonso Soriano's homer gave New York a 2-1 lead in the eighth, Tony Womack tied it in the bottom of the ninth with an RBI double. With the bases juiced, Gonzalez blooped a single over second base, scoring Jay Bell for a 3-2 triumph.

World Series

Deja Vu! Brosius HR Rocks Kim

Scott Brosius launches another Yankee miracle homer, this one in game five of the World Series. Helping New Yorkers heal after the September 11 attacks, Brosius cracked a two-out, two-run clout in the bottom of the ninth to tie Arizona, 2-2. D'Backs submariner Byung-Hyun Kim again served up the tying blast. New York won in 12 innings on an Alfonso Soriano RBI single, giving them a 3-2 Series lead.

World Series

- Brewers draw 2,811,041 fans to new Miller Park, which features a retractable dome.

- Pittsburgh's PNC Park also opens, but the Pirates finish at 62-100.

- Colorado's Mike Hampton ties an NL pitcher record by bashing seven home runs. He bats .291 with a .582 slugging percentage.

- Just 38-42 on July 1, the Athletics go 64-18 over their final 82 games and capture the AL wildcard.

- Houston's Lance Berkman cracks .331-34-126 and leads the majors with 55 doubles.

- Lenny Harris of the Mets collects his 151st career pinch hit on October 6 to break Manny Mota's old record.

- Pittsburgh reserve Craig Wilson bombs seven pinch-hit homers to tie the all-time single-season record.

- Dave Winfield and Kirby Puckett are elected to the Hall of Fame.

- Two days after the World Series, MLB Commissioner Bud Selig announces plans to eliminate at least two small-market teams.

The Anaheim Angels and their fans caused plenty of headaches in 2002. With an animated "Rally Monkey" on the scoreboard, and huge crowds banging Japanese-styled Thunder Sticks, opponents at Edison Field were jolted by volume.

But in addition to the show-biz, the Angels had real talent, racking up a 99-63 record. Though lacking a big-name superstar, Anaheim sported outfielder Garret Anderson (.306, 56 doubles, 123 RBI), third baseman Troy Glaus (30 homers), and starter Jarrod Washburn (18-6, 3.15 ERA).

Actually, Anaheim wasn't the top team in the AL West. The Oakland A's, riding MVP shortstop Miguel Tejada (.308-34-131) and a terrific starting rotation, reeled off a 20-game winning streak and took the division by four games. The A's, though, couldn't get past Minnesota in their Division Series. Minnesota, which had won the AL Central by 13½ with strong defense, a balanced attack, and deep pitching, took Oakland in five games.

Minnesota had the honor of facing Anaheim in the ALCS, because the Angels had defeated the AL East champ Yankees in four games. New York second baseman Alfonso Soriano was the year's biggest surprise, exploding for 39 homers, 51 doubles, and 41 steals.

The Angels' World Series opponent was another wildcard

Angels Slay Giants For First-Ever World Title

club, San Francisco. Barry Bonds had one of the greatest years in history, batting .370 with 46 homers and setting single-season ML records for walks (198) and on-base percentage (.582). He clubbed his 600th homer and won his record fifth MVP Award.

San Francisco disposed of NL East champ Atlanta in a five-game Division Series, battering Tom Glavine for 13 earned runs in two starts, then beat St. Louis in a five-game NLCS. The Cardinals had previously dumped the NL West-winning Diamondbacks, whose ace, Randy Johnson, had gone 24-5 with 334 strikeouts to claim his fifth Cy Young.

The Cardinals overcame adversity en route to their NL Central title. Hurler Darryl Kile died unexpectedly in Chicago on June 22, four days after legendary Cards broadcaster Jack Buck passed away. St. Louis used 14 starting pitchers during the year, yet still took the division by 13

games. Scott Rolen and Albert Pujols were offensive spark plugs.

As much fun as 2002 was, the postseason almost didn't happen. The players scheduled a walkout due to the owners' plan to unilaterally impose a salary cap. A work stoppage was barely averted on August 31, when the two sides agreed to a new four-year labor deal.

As the nation settled down for a West Coast World Series, the spotlight fell on Bonds, whose previous postseason performances had been criticized. This time around, after blasting four homers in the first two rounds of the postseason, Bonds unloaded on the Angels for four homers.

Bonds alone couldn't vanquish the scrappy Angels. The Giants drubbed Anaheim 16-4 in game five at PacBell Park to go up 3-2. In game six in Anaheim, San Francisco jumped ahead and led 5-0 in the bottom of the seventh. However, Scott Spiezio's three-run homer cut the lead to 5-3. Then, in the last of the eighth, the amazing Angels rallied for three more on a homer by Darin Erstad and a two-run double by Troy Glaus to pull the game out, 6-5.

With momentum clearly on the Angels' side, game seven was almost anticlimactic. Anderson's three-run double in the third inning broke a 1-1 tie and led to a 4-1 series-clinching win, Anaheim's first world title. It was enough to make anyone go ape, and Angels fans did.

2002

- The wildcard Angels roll over the Yankees in their AL Division Series, scoring 31 runs in the four games.

- Minnesota edges the Athletics in five games to advance to the ALCS.

- Anaheim blows away the Twins in a five-game ALCS, outscoring Minnesota 29-12. Anaheim's Adam Kennedy clubs three homers.

- San Francisco beats the Braves in a five-game NL Division Series. Russ Ortiz goes 2-0 for the Giants and Barry Bonds hits three home runs.

- St. Louis sweeps Arizona in its Division Series, outscoring the Diamondbacks 20-6.

- It takes the Giants just five games to win the NL title from the exhausted

Cardinals. The final three games of the series are one-run affairs.

- Giants, up three games to two in the World Series, lead game six 5-0 in the seventh inning but lose 6-5.

- Angels win game seven of the World Series 4-1, clinching their first world title in their 42-year history.

After their surprising triumph in the 2002 World Series, Anaheim third baseman
Troy Glaus (*left*) and manager Mike Scioscia celebrate at Disneyland. Glaus rapped
.385 with three homers in the fall classic to earn MVP honors, while Scioscia was
the AL Manager of the Year. Scioscia piloted a club that was expected to finish
20 games back in the AL West.

- Shortstop Miguel Tejada of Oakland wins the AL MVP Award after batting .308 with 34 homers and 131 RBI.

- Oakland's Barry Zito wins 23 games to pace the junior circuit and cop the AL Cy Young Award.

- Bonds is the unanimous NL MVP after winning the bat crown (.370),

belting 46 homers, and setting ML records for walks (198) and OBP (.582). He also leads the majors with a .799 slugging percentage.

- Bonds slugs his 600th career homer on August 9.

- Randy Johnson of the Diamondbacks, the unanimous NL Cy Young Award winner, leads the senior circuit

in wins (24), ERA (2.32), and strikeouts (334).

- Toronto third baseman Eric Hinske is voted AL Rookie of the Year after batting .279 with 24 homers.

- Pitcher Jason Jennings of the Rockies, 16-8 in 32 starts, wins NL ROTY honors.

Shawn Green

Green Socks Four HRs— And Six Hits

On May 23 in Milwaukee, Shawn Green of the Dodgers enjoyed one of the greatest days ever for a hitter. Green went 6-for-6 with four homers, a double, and a single off the hapless Brewers in a 16-3 pounding, driving in seven runs. Green became the 14th big-leaguer in history to belt four homers in one contest. Moreover, his 19 total bases set an ML single-game record.

Alfonso Soriano

Eckstein, Anderson Power Halos

Two unheralded players helped spark the 2002 Angels to a team-record 99 wins. All-Star outfielder Garret Anderson (*right*) contributed a .306 average with 123 RBI and a league-leading 56 doubles. Scrappy shortstop David Eckstein (*left*) scored 107 runs and paced the league (for the second straight season) in both hit-by-pitches (27) and sac bunts (14). Eckstein, who clubbed just eight homers, also led the majors with three grand slams.

David Eckstein, Garret Anderson

Soriano's a Smash in New York

Alfonso Soriano made the Yankees' machine run in 2002. The young Dominican enjoyed a spectacular campaign, hitting .300 with 51 doubles, 39 homers (eight of them leading off a game), and 41 stolen bases. This made him the first second baseman ever to reach the 30-homers, 30-steals club. Though Soriano fanned 157 times and drew just 23 walks, he led the AL in both runs (128) and hits (209).

2002

- Major League Baseball takes over the operations of the Expos and names Frank Robinson manager.

- Padres outfielder Mike Darr is killed in a spring training auto accident.

- The Florida organization is gutted during spring training as Montreal owner Jeffrey Loria buys the club and replaces most Marlins employees.

- Yankees second baseman Alfonso Soriano leads the AL in runs (128), hits (209), and steals (41) while batting .300 with 51 doubles, 39 homers, and 102 RBI.

- Alex Rodriguez of Texas paces the AL with 57 homers, 142 RBI, and 389 total bases. He finishes second in MVP voting.

- Manny Ramirez of the Red Sox wins his first batting title, hitting .349 and kicking in 33 homers in 120 games. He also leads the AL with a .450 OBP.

- In his final year with Cleveland, Jim Thome racks up AL bests in slugging (.677) and walks (122) while belting 52 homers.

Jim Thome

Ted Williams

Splendid Splinter Passes On

Ted Williams once said that he wanted people to look at him and say, "There goes the greatest hitter who ever lived." By the time he died at age 83 on July 5, 2002, he had realized his ambition. The "Splendid Splinter," still the last man to hit .400 in a season, was respected by current players as well as his contemporaries. Unlike many old-timers, he kept up with the game he loved.

Vladimir Guerrero

Guerrero Amasses 40 HRs, 39 SBs

Montreal outfielder Vladimir Guerrero, a legitimate MVP candidate stuck with a nearly invisible franchise, led the NL in 2002 with 206 hits and 364 total bases, batting .336 (third best in the league) with 111 RBI. A dazzling blend of speed and power, he stole 40 bases and swatted 39 home runs. He came "that short" of becoming the majors' fourth 40-40 man when his long fly during the season's final game banged off the wall.

Thome Bids Adieu After 52 Homers

In his final year with Cleveland, Jim Thome slugged 52 home runs in 2002, adding to his legacy as the team's all-time longball king. His 334 homers in Tribal garb were nearly 100 more than any other Indians player had ever hit. In 2002, Thome also knocked in 118 runs and paced the AL in both walks (122) and slugging percentage (.677). Following 12 years with Cleveland, he signed with the Phillies for 2003.

- Anaheim wins a team-record 99 games with just three pitchers in double figures in victories and three refugees from independent minor leagues.

- Rookie reliever Francisco Rodriguez of the Angels pitches just six innings in the regular season, then goes 5-1 in the playoffs and World Series.

- The A's win an AL-record 20 games in a row beginning on August 13 and finish with 103 wins.

- Zito, Tim Hudson, and Mark Mulder of the Athletics each finish in the AL's top ten in ERA.

- Despite no household names, the Twins become baseball's darlings, running away with the AL Central.

- Pedro Martinez of the Red Sox goes 20-4 and paces the AL in strikeouts (239) and ERA (2.26).

- Derek Lowe of the Red Sox goes 21-8 with a 2.58 ERA and throws a no-hitter.

- Eddie Guardado of the Twins saves 45 games to lead the AL.

Tony LaRussa

John Smoltz

Smoltz Snuffs Out the Fires

Former starter John Smoltz of the Atlanta Braves (shown shaking hands with catcher Henry Blanco) made a successful conversion to the bullpen after two years of elbow problems. In 2002, his first full season as a closer, Smoltz saved 55 games to establish an NL record. He blew just four save opportunities during the year and fanned 85 men in 80 innings.

Cards Overcome Tragedy

St. Louis manager Tony LaRussa stands in front of the jersey of pitcher Darryl Kile, who died unexpectedly on June 22, 2002. Kile had been one of the Cardinals' top starters as well as a beloved team leader. His jersey hung in the Cardinals dugout for the rest of the season. The club could have been forgiven for crumbling, but instead the Cards came together and captured the NL Central by 13 games.

Hunter Stars in ASG Tie

Torii Hunter's first-inning, over-the-wall catch robs Barry Bonds of a home run in the 2002 All-Star Game, staged in Milwaukee. Ichiro Suzuki watches Hunter's acrobatics. Unfortunately, the lasting memory of the midsummer classic is of the result: a 7-7 tie. Commissioner Bud Selig called the game after 11 innings when both managers claimed that they didn't want to overuse their last pitchers. Few fans were sympathetic.

Torii Hunter

2002

- Baltimore reliever Buddy Groom appears in 70 games for the seventh straight year to set an ML record.

- Scrappy infielder David Eckstein of the Angels is hit by 27 pitches, the most in the major leagues.

- Boston's Nomar Garciaparra returns from a serious wrist injury to hit .310, score 101 runs, drive in 120 runs, and rap out an AL-leading 56 doubles.

- Garret Anderson of the Angels breaks through, tying Garciaparra for the AL lead with 56 doubles and batting .306.

- Mike Cameron of Seattle (May 2) and Shawn Green of the Dodgers (May 23) both homer four times in one game to tie the ML record. Green sets the total bases record with 19.

- Johnson and Curt Schilling of the Diamondbacks are the first teammates to strike out more than 300 men in the same season. Schilling whiffs 316.

- Braves win their record 11th straight division title.

Barry Zito

A-Rod Bops 57 Homers, Wins Gold

While Alex Rodriguez couldn't lift the Rangers into contention by himself in 2002, he certainly did his best. He cemented his reputation as the AL's most dangerous hitter by pacing the league with 57 homers (an ML shortstop record), 142 RBI, and 389 total bases. Rodriguez also led AL shortstops in putouts and double plays and won his first Gold Glove. He finished second to Miguel Tejada in league MVP voting.

Lance Berkman

Berkman Spearheads NL in RBI

Lance Berkman was the Astros' Mr. Everything in 2002. Converting to center field, he shined defensively while wreaking offensive havoc all year. He hit .292 with 42 homers, 107 walks, and an NL-high 128 RBI. He also ranked among the league's top ten in home runs, on-base percentage, total bases, and slugging percentage. Berkman became one of just five switch-hitters ever to bash 40 homers in one season.

Curveballing Zito Cops Cy

Southpaw Barry Zito's 23-5 season in 2002 boosted the Athletics to the AL West title. Besides his league-leading win total, he ranked third in the AL in ERA (2.75) and strikeouts (182). For his efforts, the lefty curveball specialist picked up the AL Cy Young Award. Illustrating how the game had changed over the years, Zito won the Cy Young despite recording just one complete game all season.

Alex Rodriguez

- Former starting ace John Smoltz of the Braves saves 55 games, an NL record.

- Cardinals lose broadcaster Jack Buck on June 18 following a long illness.

- St. Louis Cardinals pitcher Darryl Kile dies suddenly of a heart condition on June 22 in his hotel room in Chicago.

- St. Louis rookie pitcher Jason Simontacchi, an independent league refugee who pitched in Italy in 2000, goes 11-5 for the Cardinals.

- Cubs rookie Mark Prior strikes out 147 hitters in 117 innings, going 6-6, 3.32 in 19 starts.

- Dodgers rookie pitcher Kaz Ishii posts a 14-10 record before his season is ended by a line drive that fractures his skull.

- Brian Giles of the Pirates hits .298 with 38 homers, 103 RBI, and 135 walks.

- The 66-96 Padres suit up 59 players during the season to tie the big-league record.

Miguel Tejada

Tejada's Key Hits Lead to MVP Award

AL MVP Miguel Tejada chipped in plenty of big hits during the Athletics' 20-game winning streak that began on August 13, 2002. On September 1, his second homer of the game—a three-run walk-off shot—gave the A's their 18th consecutive victory. The next day, his ninth-inning single again plated the winning run. Tejada also enjoyed a 24-game hitting streak en route to his .308, 34-homer campaign.

Barry Bonds

BB Sets ML Records for Walks, OBP

Giants left fielder Barry Bonds enjoyed another epic season in 2002. He won his first batting title at .370, shattered his own ML record for walks in a season with 198, and clubbed his 600th career homer on August 9 off Pittsburgh's Kip Wells. Bonds struck out just 47 times and nearly matched the figure with 46 home runs. His .582 on-base percentage also established an all-time single-season mark.

Angels Slide Past Twins in ALCS

Angels pinch-runner Chone Figgins was out on this play in game three of the 2002 ALCS. However, A.J. Pierzynski and the Twins couldn't win the game, losing 2-1, or the series, which they dropped in five games to the surprising Angels. Late Anaheim rallies in games four and five blew open what had been close matches. Angels second baseman Adam Kennedy homered three times in the series and was named ALCS MVP.

ALCS

2002

- Vladimir Guerrero of the Expos hits .336, third best in the NL, and leads the league with 206 hits, 364 total bases, and 14 outfield assists. He also falls a homer short of a 40-40 season.

- Luis Castillo of the Marlins swipes 48 sacks, most in the ML. He also has the game's longest hitting streak at 35 games.

- Houston's Lance Berkman tops the NL with 128 RBI. He also kicks in 42 homers and 107 walks.

- Sammy Sosa of the Cubs wins his second home run championship with 49 and also paces the NL with 122 runs.

- Larry Walker of Colorado hits .338 to finish second in the NL, while

teammate Todd Helton ranks fourth at .329.

- Phillies outfielder Bobby Abreu paces NL hitters with 50 doubles while hitting .308 with 104 walks and 31 steals.

- The All-Star Game is called off after 11 innings with the score tied 7-7. Both teams had run out of pitchers.

Giants Club the Cards in NLCS

Kenny Lofton takes exception to a high, inside pitch from St. Louis pitcher Mike Crudale in game one of the 2002 NLCS. Lofton and San Francisco had little trouble subduing catcher Mike Matheny and the rest of the Cardinals. Giants pitchers allowed just 16 runs in five games, and San Francisco sluggers Barry Bonds, Rich Aurilia, and Benito Santiago drove in a combined 17 runs.

NLCS

Monkey Helps Rally the Angels

A seemingly innocuous idea—flashing a picture of a monkey jumping up and down on the scoreboard at Edison Field at Anaheim—grew into something special in 2002: the Rally Monkey phenomenon. When the Angels were down late in the game and needed a comeback, pictures of the leaping monkey would work fans into a frenzy, giving the Angels a special home-field advantage.

World Series

Spiezio Spanks the Big Hits

Anaheim first baseman Scott Spiezio lashes a two-run triple in game three of the 2002 World Series at San Francisco's PacBell Park, helping his club to a 10-4 thrashing of the Giants. Spiezio, who had stroked .285 with 82 RBI during the regular season, also delivered a huge hit in game six. With the Angels down 5-0 in the seventh, his three-run homer started a comeback that culminated in a 6-5 win.

Rally Monkey

Baseball suffers bad publicity as a result.

• The players and owners avert an imminent work stoppage by agreeing to a contract on August 31, 2002.

• The gap between good and bad teams grows: Three teams win 100 games, while four teams lose 100.

• Former Cardinals and Padres shortstop Ozzie Smith is the only man elected to the Hall of Fame.

• Legendary slugger Ted Williams dies on July 5 at age 83.

• Pitcher Tanyon Sturtze of the Devil Rays leads the AL in all the wrong categories: losses (18), hits (271), earned runs (129), and walks (89).

• Detroit loses its first 11 games and finishes 55-106.

• Tampa Bay also finishes with a 55-106 record.

• San Francisco skipper Dusty Baker resigns following the World Series and later becomes manager of the Cubs.

For many baseball fans, 2003 was an exercise in what might have been. Hopes for a World Series of the historically misbegotten were dashed when the Boston Red Sox and Chicago Cubs lost their World Series bids in heart-breaking fashion.

The surprising Cubs captured the NL Central behind new manager Dusty Baker and a strong starting rotation. Chicago blew by the Atlanta Braves in their NLDS, then went up three games to two in the NLCS on the Florida Marlins (who had previously eliminated the Giants). But down 3-0 in the eighth of game six at Wrigley Field, the Marlins exploded for eight runs and an 8-3 victory. Carrying the momentum into game seven, Florida clinched the NL pennant with a 9-6 win.

The Marlins had snagged the wildcard with a combination of youth and experience. Manager Jack McKeon, age 72, took over a 16-22 squad in May and led it to the game's best record over the last four months. Catcher Ivan Rodriguez was a key contributor, and Ugueth Urbina, acquired in a trade, bolstered the bullpen. But kids provided the Marlins' magic. Their starting rotation was among the youngest in the game, with lefty Dontrelle Willis the NL Rookie of the Year. Speedsters Juan Pierre and Luis Castillo set the table for sluggers Derrek Lee and Mike Lowell.

The AL picture wasn't quite as surprising. The Yankees and

Oh, My Josh! Fish Prevail in Dramatic Postseason

Red Sox finished first and second in the East, then won their Division Series to set up a "dream" ALCS. Down 3-2 in games, the Red Sox beat the Yankees in game six at Yankee Stadium, then led 5-2 in the last of the eighth in game seven. But the Yankees came back and tied the score against Red Sox ace Pedro Martinez, who in retrospect stayed in the game too long (a decision that cost Boston manager Grady Little his job). The nail-biter ended in the last of the 11th when Aaron Boone's homer sent the Yankees to a 6-5 win and another trip to the World Series.

The vaunted Yankees and their legacy, however, held no sway over the young Marlins, who confidently split the first four games of the fall classic. Game five was the turning point. Yankees starter David Wells left after one inning with back spasms. Florida jumped on the Yankees bullpen, then held on for

a 6-4 win. Game six, back at Yankee Stadium, was all Josh Beckett. The oft-injured young Marlins hurler shut out the Bronx Bombers on five hits to give his team its second world title, despite being outscored in the series 21-17.

While salaries continued to rise, and the Red Sox and Yankees dominated the headlines, the good news for fans of "small market" teams was that for the third straight year, an unexpected club won it all. Each world champ prevailed through teamwork and a varied attack rather than relying on one or two big-salaried stars. And the TV ratings for the exciting postseason bore out the value of unexpected participants.

While Barry Bonds of the NL West-champion Giants won his sixth NL MVP Award, most award winners finished far out of the playoff picture. AL MVP Alex Rodriguez's Texas Rangers placed last. AL Rookie of the Year Angel Berroa played for Kansas City, which contended early but slumped, and Cy Young winner Roy Halladay toiled for third-place Toronto. Eric Gagne, who saved 55 straight for the Dodgers, won the NL Cy Young, though his club finished 15 games out. Also out of contention were the Montreal Expos, who played 22 of their "home" games in San Juan, Puerto Rico, as Major League Baseball continued to consider relocating the club.

2003

- Wildcard winner Boston defeats Oakland in a nail-biting five game ALDS.

- New York beats Minnesota easily in a four-game ALDS. The Twins score just three times in the final three games.

- Florida upsets San Francisco to win their NLDS in four games.

- The Cubs upend the favored Braves in a five-game NLDS.

- The Marlins, down three games to one, come back to defeat the Cubs in the NLCS.

- The Yankees win a thrilling seven-game ALCS over the luckless Red Sox, as Aaron Boone ends it with an 11th-inning homer.

- The Marlins capture their second World Series title in their 11-year history, defeating the Yankees in six games.

- The Marlins take the title despite hitting just .232 and being outscored 21-17 by New York.

- Brad Penny wins two games for Florida in the fall classic, and Josh

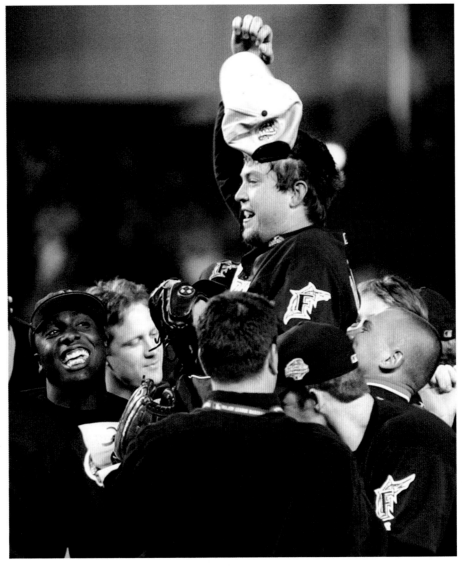

Josh Beckett gets a lift from his teammates after stifling the Yankees in the clinching game six of the 2003 World Series. Beckett, who due to injury was just 9-8 during the regular season, dominated New York in the fall classic, allowing just two runs in 16 innings. While the Yankees' two victories were both 6-1 affairs, the Marlins won four close games and walked away with the trophy.

Beckett throws a five-hit shutout in the clincher.

- Jack McKeon, who takes over the Marlins' helm in May, is at age 72 the oldest manager ever to win a World Series.

- Barry Bonds of the Giants is named NL MVP for the sixth time—and the third year in a row.

- Bonds leads the NL in both SA (.749) and OBP (.529) for the third consecutive season. He logs 148 walks (61 intentional) in 130 games.

- Bonds's father, Bobby Bonds, a former Giants star, dies of cancer on August 23.

- Cubs righty Kerry Wood leads the NL with 266 strikeouts.

- Wood's 21 hit batsmen are the most by a major league pitcher since 1969.

- Atlanta's Russ Ortiz (21-7) is the National League's only 20-game winner.

- San Francisco's Jason Schmidt leads the NL in ERA (2.34) and win pct. (.773).

Detroit Tigers

Tigers Lose AL-Record 119 Games

When this photo was snapped during 2003 spring training, neither Tigers manager Alan Trammell (*left*) nor owner Mike Ilitch knew what misery lay ahead. The Tigers set an AL record for losses (43-119) and had to win five of their last six to avoid tying the 1962 Mets' ML record. Starters Mike Maroth, Jeremy Bonderman, Nate Cornejo, and Adam Bernero were 9-21, 6-19, 6-17, and 1-12, respectively, and the "attack" scored 108 fewer runs than any other AL club. The Tigers also led the league in errors.

Rafael Palmeiro

Hudson, A's Pitch Way to West Title

Once again, Oakland's formidable starting pitching led the A's to the playoffs in 2003. The Big Three of Tim Hudson (*pictured*), Barry Zito, and Mark Mulder helped Oakland lead the league with a 3.63 ERA and clinch the AL West by three games over Seattle. Hudson finished 16-7 while ranking second among AL hurlers with a 2.70 ERA.

Tim Hudson

Palmeiro Joins 500-Homer Club

Texas' Rafael Palmeiro, shown clubbing his 500th career homer against Cleveland's Dave Elder on May 11, 2003, had long been one of the game's most consistent and underrated hitters. Palmeiro clouted at least 38 homers every season from 1995 through 2003, making him the first slugger in ML history to achieve the feat nine straight years.

2003

- Alex Rodriguez of the Rangers becomes the first AL player to win the MVP Award while playing for a last-place club.

- A-Rod tops the AL in homers (47), runs (124), and slugging (.600).

- Dodgers closer Eric Gagne saves 55 games in 55 chances and takes NL Cy Young honors.

- Gagne blows the save in the All-Star Game, allowing Ranger Hank Blalock's game-winning homer.

- Roy Halladay of the Blue Jays wins 15 consecutive decisions en route to a 22-7 record and the AL Cy Young Award.

- Albert Pujols of St. Louis wins the NL batting title, edging Colorado's Todd Helton by one point, .359 to .358.

- Pujols also leads the NL in hits (212), runs (137), doubles (51), and TBs (394). He amasses 43 homers and 124 RBI.

- Preston Wilson of the Rockies paces the NL with 141 RBI.

Clemens: 300 Ws, 4,000 Ks

Yankee Roger Clemens had been chasing 300 wins and 4,000 strikeouts for years, and on June 13, 2003, he achieved both feats in the same game against St. Louis. He ended the season in possession of the American League's all-time strikeout record. Late in the year, Clemens announced plans to retire, but he recanted and later signed with Houston for 2004.

Roger Clemens

Mark Prior

Cubs Pitching a Prior-ity

In his first full ML season, Cubs starter Mark Prior proved to be one of the game's dominant pitchers. Heading a strong rotation that also included Kerry Wood, Carlos Zambrano, and Matt Clement, Prior ranked among the NL's top three in wins (18-6), ERA (2.43), and strikeouts (245). The Cubs' strong hurling led to a surprising NL Central title and an upset of the Braves in the NLDS.

Rookie Willis Sparks Fish

Lefty Dontrelle Willis made just six starts in Double-A before joining the Marlins in May 2003. He proceeded to go 9-1 by July 13 and 14-6 overall, earning the NL Rookie of the Year Award. The Marlins, under 72-year-old skipper Jack McKeon, won a surprise wildcard spot en route to their World Series upset of the Yankees.

Dontrelle Willis

- Philadelphia's Kevin Millwood throws the year's only individual no-hitter, on April 27 against San Francisco.

- Houston first baseman Jeff Bagwell cracks his 400th homer on July 20.

- Jim Thome of the Phillies clubs an NL-high 47 homers but fans a league-high 182 times.

- Switch-hitting Bill Mueller of the Red Sox cops the AL bat crown at .326.

- Mueller clouts grand slams from both sides of the plate at Texas on July 29, becoming the first ML player ever to do so.

- Boston's Pedro Martinez leads the AL in ERA (2.22).

- Oakland's Keith Foulke paces AL relievers with 43 saves.

- Toronto's Vernon Wells leads the AL in hits (215), doubles (49), and total bases (373).

- Yankee Jason Giambi gives fielders a breather by clubbing 41 homers and topping the AL in walks (129), HBPs (21), and strikeouts (140).

Barry Bonds

Delgado Slugs Way to RBI Crown

Toronto first baseman Carlos Delgado led the AL with 145 RBI in 2003, besting second-place Alex Rodriguez by a margin of 27—one of the largest gaps in history. Delgado also finished second in the AL in home runs (42), on-base percentage (.426), and slugging percentage (.593). On September 25, he smashed four homers in one game against the Devil Rays.

Bonds Stars in Bittersweet Season

Barry Bonds couldn't fully enjoy his record sixth NL MVP season in 2003. In addition to smashing .341 with 45 homers, he recorded his 500th career stolen base on June 23, making him the first ever to steal 500 sacks and hit 500 homers. Moreover, the Giants won 100 games and ran away with the NL West. Unfortunately, Bonds's joy was tempered by the loss of his father, former Giants standout Bobby Bonds, who died of cancer on August 23.

Posada Lifts Yanks to 101 Wins

In another year, Yankees catcher Jorge Posada (pictured with manager Joe Torre) could have been voted AL MVP. A fine defensive catcher, Posada in 2003 rapped .281 with 30 homers and a .405 on-base percentage, fifth best in the circuit. Despite lacking a dominant pitcher or hitter, and finishing third in the AL in runs and third in ERA, the Yankees won 101 games, tops in the AL.

Joe Torre and Jorge Posada

Carlos Delgado

2003

- Marlins pitcher Dontrelle Willis wins NL Rookie of the Year honors.

- Royals infielder Angel Berroa is named AL Rookie of the Year.

- Yankees hurler Roger Clemens wins his 300th game and records his 4,000th strikeout in the same game, on June 13 versus St. Louis.

- Clemens ends the season with 4,099 career strikeouts, an AL record.

- Detroit loses 119 games to set an AL record.

- Mike Maroth of the Tigers becomes the first ML pitcher to lose 20 games (9-21) since Oakland's Brian Kingman in 1980.

- In May, The Walt Disney Company sells the Anaheim Angels to West Coast businessman Arturo Moreno for approximately $182 million.

- Boston scores ten runs in the first inning on June 27 before Florida can record an out. The Sox win 25-8.

- Sammy Sosa of the Cubs clubs his 500th homer on April 4.

Red Sox No. 1 in Runs

In 2003, the Red Sox led the major leagues in runs with 961. David Ortiz belted 31 homers, while Manny Ramirez, Nomar Garciaparra, and batting champion Bill Mueller also bashed the cowhide. The pitching was thin, but Pedro Martinez led the league with a 2.22 ERA and finished second (by just one) in strikeouts despite making just 29 starts. Boston earned a wildcard berth with 95 victories.

David Ortiz and Pedro Martinez

A-Rod Named AL MVP

Though his Rangers finished last in the AL West in 2003, Alex Rodriguez earned the AL MVP Award. A-Rod won his third straight home run title (47) and paced the league in runs (124) and slugging percentage (.600). He also captured his second Gold Glove, and on April 2 he became, at 27, the youngest player ever to reach 300 homers. A-Rod finished 2003 with 344 homers as a shortstop, trailing all-time record-holder Cal Ripken by just one.

Roy Halladay

Halladay Cops AL's Cy

Toronto's Roy Halladay did not win a single game in April 2003, but he finished 22-7 thanks to 15 straight victories—a performance that earned him the Cy Young Award. Halladay allowed the most hits in the league (253), but he walked only 32 men in 266 innings. His 3.25 ERA ranked fifth in the AL.

Alex Rodriguez

- Sosa is suspended for seven games after being caught using a corked bat on June 3.

- Rafael Palmeiro of Texas slugs his 500th homer on May 11.

- Greg Maddux of the Braves sets an ML record by winning 15 or more games for the 16th consecutive season.

- Atlanta shortstop Rafael Furcal turns an unassisted triple play on August 10.

- On September 25, Toronto's Carlos Delgado homers in four consecutive at-bats in one game, victimizing the Devil Rays.

- Major League Baseball forces the Montreal Expos to play 22 "home" games in 2003 in San Juan, Puerto Rico.

- Jesse Orosco, age 46, pitches in 65 games but just 34 innings.

- Orosco extends his ML record for games pitched to 1,252.

- Seattle uses just five starting pitchers all year.

Pujols Wears Bat Crown

Third-year man Albert Pujols of the Cardinals continued to scale new heights in 2003. Besides winning the batting title at .359, he clubbed 43 homers and led the NL in runs (137), hits (212), total bases (394), and doubles (51). Pujols, runner-up in MVP voting to Barry Bonds, shared with Ralph Kiner the ML record for most homers (114) by a player in his first three seasons.

Albert Pujols

Braves Slug Way to 101 Victories

The Braves in 2003 won 101 games, the most in the NL, but did so—surprisingly—with great hitting rather than their usual pitching skill. Outfielder Gary Sheffield was the club's offensive star, rapping .330 with 39 homers and 132 RBI, but the attack was balanced. Catcher Javy Lopez, second baseman Marcus Giles, shortstop Rafael Furcal, and out-fielders Andruw Jones and Chipper Jones all helped make Atlanta's offense the league's most productive.

Gary Sheffield

Gagne Saves 55 in 55

Dodgers closer Eric Gagne, celebrating after collecting one of his NL-record-tying 55 saves in 2003, was an easy NL Cy Young winner. Gagne didn't blow a single save chance during the season, and through the end of the campaign had converted an ML-record 63 consecutive save opportunities. Fanning 137 men in just 82 innings in 2003, Gagne successfully completed his transformation from struggling starter to the game's most overpowering late-inning reliever.

Eric Gagne

2003

- On July 25, Colorado's Chin-Hui Tsao becomes the first Taiwanese pitcher in ML history.

- Tampa Bay's Carl Crawford paces the AL in stolen bases (55), but his on-base percentage is just .309.

- The Marlins' Juan Pierre leads the NL in steals (65), and his club's 150 swipes are the most in the game.

- Cubs pitchers set an ML record with 1,404 strikeouts.

- The Braves lead the NL with 907 runs scored.

- Boston paces the AL with 961 runs.

- Four Mariners win Gold Gloves: John Olerud, Bret Boone, Mike Cameron, and Ichiro Suzuki.

- The Cardinals also field four Gold Glovers: Edgar Renteria, Jim Edmonds, Scott Rolen, and Mike Matheny.

- Todd Zeile of the Expos becomes, on September 5, the first player ever to homer for 11 different ML clubs.

- Brad Wilkerson of the Expos hits for the cycle—in order—on June 24.

Sadowski, Bob, 338
Sadowski, Ed, 338
Sadowski, Ted, 338
Sain, Johnny, 241, 248, 249, 260, 271, 278, 281
Sallee, Slim, 84, 86
Salmon, Tim, 588, 590, 643
Samuel, Juan, 518
Sandberg, Ryne, 501, 508, 512–514, 516, 562, 564, 598, 599, 622
Sanders, Deion, 576, 582, 583, 621, 623
Sanders, Ken, 415
Sanford, Jack, 304, 336
Sanguillen, Manny, 403, 419, 472
Santana, Johan, 672, 673, 677
Santiago, Benito, 537, 663
Santiago, Jose, 383
Santo, Ron, 354, 357, 374, 380, 382, 388, 394, 414, 428
Sarni, Bill, 268
Sasaki, Kazuhiro, 641, 646
Sauer, Hank, 259, 272, 273, 284
Sax, Steve, 498, 502, 544
Schacht, Al, 58
Schalk, Ray, 76, 98, 294, 405
Schang, Wally, 74, 80, 110
Scheib, Carl, 223
Schilling, Curt, 584, 591, 620, 630, 648, 649, 652, 654, 660, 672, 673, 676, 678
Schmidt, Bob, 198
Schmidt, Jason, 665, 677
Schmidt, Mike, 433, 443, 445, 448–451, 478, 480, 481, 487–490, 493, 499, 507, 512, 515, 517, 529, 530, 536, 605, 639
Schoendienst, Red, 232, 261, 263, 300, 302, 304, 306, 307, 319, 556
Schott, Marge, 582, 612, 679
Schulte, Frank "Wildfire," 32, 48, 52, 53, 68, 76
Schultz, Barney, 359
Schumacher, Hal, 158, 164, 176
Schupp, Ferdie, 76, 78
Schwall, Don, 328, 330
Scioscia, Mike, 657
Score, Herb, 290, 292, 296, 299, 302, 303, 365
Scott, Everett, 96, 102, 113, 160
Scott, George, 381, 412, 443
Scott, Jack, 96, 127
Scott, Jim, 66, 76
Scott, Mike, 528–530, 534, 535, 558
Scott, Rodney, 487
Seaton, Tom, 61, 63
Seaver, Tom, 376, 377, 392–394 396, 400, 401, 403, 408, 411, 412, 418, 419, 423–425, 427, 429, 441, 444, 446, 452, 455–457, 459, 463, 468, 472, 478, 479, 488, 491, 492, 501, 504, 520, 523, 533, 581
Seerey, Pat, 251
Seitz, Peter, 441
Seitzer, Kevin, 539
Selee, Frank, 24
Selig, Bud, 578, 592, 593, 626, 628, 655, 660, 674
Selkirk, George, 152, 176, 192
Sewell, Joe, 88, 90, 111, 115, 121, 125, 133, 156, 166, 460
Sewell, Rip, 218
Sexton, Jimmy, 502
Seybold, Socks, 16, 19, 39
Seymour, Cy, 28, 31
Shamsky, Art, 373
Shannon, Spike, 35
Shantz, Bobby, 272, 273, 276, 302, 304, 324, 325, 332, 356
Sharman, Ralph, 83
Shaw, Jeff, 620
Sheckard, Jimmy, 12, 32
Sheehan, Tom, 326
Sheffield, Gary, 576, 577, 579, 580, 617, 630, 670, 674
Shepard, Bert, 7, 230, 232, 233
Sherry, Larry, 314, 319
Shibe, Ben, 48
Shires, Art, 138, 145
Shocker, Urban, 92, 95, 96, 122, 127, 132
Shore, Ernie, 64, 68, 72, 76, 78

Shotton, Burt, 60, 242, 254
Sierra, Ruben, 553, 568, 572, 672, 672
Sievers, Roy, 257, 288, 302, 305, 307
Simmons, Al, 109, 110, 112, 128, 134, 137–141, 144–146, 152, 154, 165, 166, 190, 282
Simmons, Curt, 260
Simmons, Ted, 445, 458, 484, 496, 503
Simontacchi, Jason, 661
Singer, Bill, 403, 421, 430
Singleton, Ken, 422, 424, 430, 472
Sisler, George, 58, 70, 71, 76, 83, 84, 88, 89, 91, 95–97, 100, 103, 112, 121, 131, 196, 198, 428, 677
Sizemore, Ted, 392, 397
Skowron, Bill "Moose," 296, 302, 308, 309, 320, 326, 328, 333, 342, 344
Slagle, Jimmy, 36
Slaughter, Enos, 199, 212, 214, 215, 217, 218, 236, 239, 250, 257, 288, 294, 524
Smalley, Roy, 269
Smiley, John, 571
Smith, Bob, 124
Smith, Bud, 654
Smith, Elmer, 88, 114
Smith, Frank, 28, 30, 43, 45, 288
Smith, Hal, 320, 326, 327
Smith, Lee, 511, 514, 568, 571, 581, 583, 589, 591, 594
Smith, Lonnie, 496, 502, 559, 569, 575, 583
Smith, Ozzie, 348, 482, 492, 496, 502, 520, 527, 536, 555, 557, 578, 583, 663
Smith, Reggie, 415, 456, 457
Smith, Sherry, 72
Smith, Tal, 493
Smoltz, John, 568, 581, 609, 612, 613, 614, 616, 632, 660, 661
Snider, Duke, 254, 263, 272, 277, 278, 281, 283, 286, 287, 290, 292, 296, 298, 299, 307, 308, 314, 483
Snodgrass, Fred, 52, 56, 60
Snow, J.T., 588
Sojo, Luis, 640, 647
Soriano, Alfonso, 648, 649, 655, 656, 658
Sosa, Elias, 471
Sosa, Sammy, 589, 590, 621, 624, 626, 628, 629, 632, 634, 638, 640, 642, 651, 662, 668, 669
Sothoron, Al, 87, 95
Soto, Mario, 510, 519
Southworth, Billy, 253
Spahn, Warren, 71, 214, 241, 246, 248, 257, 260, 263, 268, 278, 281, 296, 302–304, 308, 309, 311, 313, 314, 318, 320, 323, 325, 328, 330, 331, 343–346, 351, 428
Spalding, Al, 9, 12, 37, 38, 198
Speaker, Tris, 45, 56, 58, 59, 67, 72, 73, 75, 80, 82, 87, 90, 92, 100, 101, 107, 112, 119, 122, 128, 130, 134, 186, 196
Spence, Stan, 228, 229
Spiezio, Scott, 656, 663
Spujte, Rex, 637
Spooner, Karl, 287, 413
Sprague, Ed, 591
Stahl, Chick, 35, 37
Stallard, Tracy, 328, 331
Stallings, George, 61, 64, 66
Stanky, Eddie, 232, 235, 236, 248, 256, 259, 289
Stanley, Bob, 499, 528
Stargell, Willie, 368, 394, 395, 408, 409, 413, 419, 424, 425, 429, 432, 437, 440, 468, 472–474, 478, 502, 547
Staub, Rusty, 382, 397, 422, 424, 431, 444, 509, 510
Steinbrenner, George, 425, 435, 454, 456, 464, 465, 467, 469, 499, 516, 564, 592
Steinfeldt, Harry, 32, 36
Stengel, Casey, 64, 100, 101, 251, 254, 255, 258, 260, 272, 273, 278, 284, 296, 302, 304, 305, 307–309, 320, 336, 344, 346, 355, 372, 443
Stenson, Dernell, 671
Stephens, Vern, 224, 229, 245, 248, 251, 254, 255, 287
Stephenson, Johnny, 355
Stephenson, Riggs, 117, 134, 152

Stewart, Dave, 488, 542, 550, 552, 558, 560, 565, 566, 590
Stieb, Dave, 503, 519, 546, 566
Stirnweiss, Snuffy, 223, 226, 228, 230, 231, 234, 252
Stone, George, 28, 32
Stone, Steve, 481, 484
Stoneman, Bill, 395, 418
Stottlemyre, Mel, 352, 358, 363, 367, 374
Stovey, George, 10
Stratton, Monty, 193, 259
Strawberry, Darryl, 504, 506, 528, 544, 546, 549, 563, 576, 599, 632
Stuart, Dick, 312, 349
Sturdivant, Tom, 296, 302, 319
Sturtze, Tanyon, 663
Suhr, Gus, 163, 182, 183, 186
Sullivan, Frank, 290, 293, 294
Sutcliffe, Rick, 474, 512, 513, 517, 536, 543
Sutter, Bruce, 459, 472, 473, 477, 482, 495, 514, 531
Sutton, Don, 485, 486, 488, 496, 522, 528, 531, 533, 627
Suzuki, Ichiro, 648, 650, 651, 653, 660, 670, 672, 674, 677
Sweeney, Bill, 59, 65
Sweeney, Mike, 647
Swift, Bill, 582
Swoboda, Ron, 392, 398

T Tabor, Jim, 196, 220
Takatsu, Shingo, 678
Tanana, Frank, 446, 462, 463, 492
Tannehill, Jesse, 12, 22, 26
Tarasco, Tony, 615
Tartabull, Danny, 572
Tartabull, Jose, 383
Tatis, Fernando, 635
Taubensee, Eddie, 588
Taylor, Dummy, 15
Taylor, Jack, 16, 17, 22, 25, 33
Tejada, Miguel, 656, 657, 661, 662, 674–676
Tekulve, Kent, 471, 472, 478, 557
Templeton, Garry, 461, 470, 474, 476, 478, 492, 502
Tenace, Gene, 416, 417, 424, 439, 461
Terry, Bill, 128, 138, 140–142, 146, 147, 150, 153, 156–158, 163, 164, 168, 180, 288, 556
Terry, Ralph, 319, 320, 327, 336, 342, 343
Tesreau, Jeff, 56, 58–60, 62, 80, 83
Tettleton, Mickey, 579, 580
Thevenow, Tommy, 116, 121
Thigpen, Bobby, 560, 562, 563
Thomas, Frank, 308, 319, 572, 579, 586, 589, 592, 594, 596–597, 599, 605, 615, 616, 621, 640, 646
Thomas, Gorman, 475, 499, 509, 533
Thomas, Roy, 15, 18, 35
Thome, Jim, 592, 600, 616, 622, 658, 659, 667
Thompson, Danny, 452, 453
Thompson, Hank, 242
Thompson, Robby, 558
Thompson, Sam, 436
Thompson, Tommy, 58
Thomson, Bobby, 244, 245, 266, 267, 271, 284, 287, 288
Thon, Dickie, 502, 517
Thorpe, Jim, 76, 78
Throneberry, Marv, 309, 320
Thurston, Sloppy, 109
Tiant, Luis, 384, 386, 391, 397, 416, 423, 424, 438, 440, 447, 472
Tinker, Joe, 18, 19, 24, 31, 32, 42, 49, 50, 63, 64, 67
Tipton, Joe, 259, 318
Tobin, Jack, 95
Tobin, Jim, 217, 227
Tolan, Bobby, 392, 407, 448
Toney, Fred, 76, 77
Toporcer, George "Specs," 94, 95, 121
Torchia, Tony, 391
Torre, Joe, 397, 408, 410, 444, 475, 496, 608, 615, 632, 641, 668
Torres, Salomon, 584